The Greenwood
Dictionary of Education

The Greenwood Dictionary of Education

Second Edition

John W. Collins III and
Nancy Patricia O'Brien, Editors

GREENWOOD

AN IMPRINT OF ABC-CLIO, LLC
Santa Barbara, California • Denver, Colorado • Oxford, England

Library of Congress Cataloging-in-Publication Data

The Greenwood dictionary of education / John W. Collins and Nancy Patricia O'Brien, editors. — 2nd ed.
    p. cm.
 Includes index.
 ISBN 978-0-313-37930-7 (hardback) — ISBN 978-0-313-37931-4 (ebook)
 1. Education—Dictionaries. I. Collins, John William, 1948- II. O'Brien, Nancy P.
 LB15.G68 2011
 370.3—dc23

                     2011022915

ISBN: 978-0-313-37930-7
EISBN: 978-0-313-37931-4

15 14 13 12 11   1 2 3 4 5

This book is also available on the World Wide Web as an eBook.
Visit www.abc-clio.com for details.

Greenwood
An Imprint of ABC-CLIO, LLC

ABC-CLIO, LLC
130 Cremona Drive, P.O. Box 1911
Santa Barbara, California 93116-1911

This book is printed on acid-free paper ∞

Manufactured in the United States of America

Contents

Foreword

Specialized dictionaries, such as this one for the field of education, provide context for the terminology used by practitioners, scholars, and theorists. With the publication of the second edition of *The Greenwood Dictionary of Education,* we see expansion of the lexicon as it reflects new areas of interest and emphasis in the field of education. Greater focus on neurosciences in educational behavior, gaming strategies as a learning technique, social networking, distance education, and other areas, supplement the extensive content from the first edition published in 2003. Revisions to terms previously included represent shifts in educational practice and theory.

The *Dictionary* documents the history of education as well as its future trends. As an education historian, I am well aware that the ongoing influences of the past affect current society. A dictionary that encompasses lexicography of past events, as well as the terminology that describes current and future trends, is a critical resource. This second edition provides a timely update with 680 completely new terms that add to the value of the education lexicon along with numerous revisions. The many contributors to the *Dictionary* are from specialized areas within education and reflect the varied aspects of education in its ongoing development. Whether it is significant legislation, social justice concepts, or practical pedagogical practice, the relevant terminology may be found in this updated edition.

In a constantly changing linguistic environment, where technical nouns become verbs, new words continuously emerge, and others become passé, a dictionary that captures contemporary usage in a discipline such as education is a necessity. This second edition of *The Greenwood Dictionary of Education* offers a comprehensive view of education terms and, when compared to its lexical predecessors, a glimpse of how rapidly that terminology changes.

Education impacts everyone. Those who practice in the field, their students, and all who are concerned with education, will find that this new edition of *The Greenwood Dictionary of Education* provides access to language that can inform and empower.

James D. Anderson
University of Illinois at Urbana-Champaign

Preface

The preface to the first edition of *The Greenwood Dictionary of Education* stated, "Not since Carter V. Good's *Dictionary of Education,* last published in 1973, has there been a comprehensive dictionary of education." While there have been specialized dictionaries published since then, this dictionary remains unique in its breadth and scope. Other publications offer a narrow or specialized focus–health education, or British educational terminology, for example. *The Greenwood Dictionary of Education* continues to be the only publication to offer comprehensive coverage in the field.

The focus of the *Dictionary* continues to be on current and evolving terminology specific to the broad field of education. Terms from closely related fields used in the context of education are included. This updated second edition will aid in the contemporary understanding and use of terms as they apply to educational research, practice, and theory. Directed to educators, researchers, scholars, and students, this reference source will also be of value to anyone concerned with education issues. Staff in public, academic, and school libraries will find the *Dictionary* immensely helpful in interpreting the terminology used in education.

This second edition updates and expands the coverage provided in the first edition. Some 850 new terms and complete revisions have been included along with other updates. New categories of coverage such as neuroscience in education have been added, and extensive additions to the areas of educational technology and media, along with measurement, evaluation, and assessment are included. Users of the *Dictionary* will find it extremely valuable to the contemporary understanding and use of more than 3,500 terms as they apply to educational research, practice, and theory.

As we embarked on the ambitious task of producing a second edition of this work, we enlisted the aid of scholars with a wide variety of expertise. Our contributing editors and contributors represent many of the foremost authorities in their field. In addition to the continued support and contributions from first edition authors, over 100 additional contributors participated in this project. The quality of this publication reflects the expertise of the contributors and the care and commitment they gave to this effort.

Following the successful model of the earlier edition, each contributing editor to the second edition had the option of gathering a group of colleagues to develop definitions for terms in their respective areas. Each contributing editor who chose to do so was subsequently responsible for identifying and recruiting contributors to write definitions within specific guidelines. The contributing editors were also responsible for defining the boundaries of their topical areas; selecting words for inclusion; collecting, reviewing, and editing the submissions from their contributors; and submitting the results to the editors-in-chief. The individual contributors, drawn from a vast array of education professionals, were responsible in turn for identifying potential terms for inclusion, writing the definitions, and submitting the results to the contributing editors.

The terms for inclusion in this edition of the *Dictionary* were collected over a three-year period. The editors-in-chief, John Collins, librarian of the Harvard Graduate School of Education, and Nancy O'Brien, head of the Education and Social Science Library, University of Illinois at Urbana-Champaign, consulted widely with colleagues throughout the project on matters relating to the identification of new topical areas for inclusion in the *Dictionary* and in the identification of appropriate individuals to serve as contributing editors.

The editors-in-chief were extensively involved in a continual review of the education literature to seek terms for inclusion. In addition, they also provided each contributing editor with a starter list of words for consideration, sample definitions, and guidelines for inclusion and submission. They also coordinated the work of the *Dictionary,* managed deadlines, and compiled and edited the hundreds of submissions. In consultation with colleagues and scholars from a variety of academic institutions, the editors-in-chief also identified gaps and omissions in the submitted terms. Contributing editors to this second edition were also provided with the terms and definitions appearing in the first edition and asked to update them, as appropriate.

While there was no specific time period defined for inclusion, contemporary usage of terms is emphasized rather than historical. As deemed appropriate, terms from earlier centuries are included, but in general, users are urged to consult one of the older dictionaries when seeking a definition of an educational methodology or technology no longer in use.

Terms from closely related fields used in the context of education are included, but we have tried to avoid terms that focus on specific aspects of information technologies used in education. We expect that readers can find those terms in specialized dictionaries that deal with computers, electronic resources, and other related areas when needed. The focus of the *Dictionary* is on education as it is practiced in the United States. However, given the current global nature of society, the terms are relevant to many aspects of education practiced in other countries.

One of the interesting developments we noted as we worked with our contributing editors to the first edition was the number and variety of resources they consulted as they defined the lexicon of their respective areas in education. We included their list of references in the first edition and have continued that practice here, updating the extensive and helpful list of sources at the end of this volume. Not only are books, journal articles, technical reports, encyclopedias, and dictionaries cited, but many references are to websites that provided background information as definitions were developed. We believe this consultation of a variety of sources reflects the increasing availability of information to anyone seeking education information. The source list is included in the *Dictionary* because it represents a valuable collection of important and influential works. Researchers will find this extensive bibliography useful in tracking the development of language in the field of education.

As editors of this work, we have reviewed every term and definition several times. Our editing has traveled with us as we engaged in professional conferences or trips with our families. We have carried segments of the manuscript across country and across continents. Cyberspace has held a continuous flow of terms as we collaborated with our contributing editors and with one another. We accept the final responsibility for any errors that may appear in this work. Credit for the immense amount of work represented in this new edition, however, is shared among the contributing editors, contributors, and many others who provide invaluable assistance.

We believe that this new edition of *The Greenwood Dictionary of Education* offers a major contribution to the understanding of terminology in the critically important field of education. We hope that the *Dictionary* will be widely consulted and that it will continue to grow and expand in the years to come.

John W. Collins III
Nancy Patricia O'Brien

REFERENCE

Good, C. V. *Dictionary of Education.* 3d ed. New York: McGraw-Hill, 1973.

Acknowledgments

An undertaking of this size would not be possible without the support of many people. As editors, we are extremely grateful for the contributions of our colleagues, students, and families. We thank them for their unwavering patience, encouragement, and, more practically, proofreading and advice. We are indebted to each of the contributing editors and contributors for lending their expertise to this project. The number of contributors to this volume is staggering. For their contributions on a daily basis we acknowledge the research assistance of Harvard students Vanessa Tantillo, Alicia Safier, and Paul Kennedy; and the technological support from colleagues Sheetal Patel, Kenneth Ng, Netta Davis, and Joseph Gabriel. Mark Shelton, head of collection development at Gutman Library, provided considerable expertise on many levels. His contributions were invaluable. Throughout the entire process, beginning with the 1st Edition of this *Dictionary* and through to the completion of this 2nd Edition, Anne Thompson, Senior Development Editor, ABC-CLIO—Greenwood Press, has been a marvelous person to work with. There are many others to thank, and we offer a collective note of appreciation to all who have contributed to this project. We would be remiss, however, if we did not single out the work of Ann S. Flentje, our Harvard colleague, whose keen eye, profound editorial prowess, and tireless efforts toward the completion of this volume have been remarkable. Without her, this volume would not have been possible.

How to Use This Book

All terms, acronyms, and initialisms have been included in one alphabetical arrangement of dictionary entries, in "word-by-word" style. For example, "EFL" follows immediately after "effective schools research" rather than appearing in a separate index or preceding all entries beginning with the letter "e." Since this is a dictionary, there is no index.

Initials identify each contributor after the definition that he or she wrote. A list of those initials, cross-referenced to their full names, appears at the back of the *Dictionary* following the list of contributors and their affiliations.

When multiple meanings of a term are used in the field of education, we have included those in the definition. The meanings are not identified with a separate numeric prefix as they are in general dictionaries. Instead, we have indicated that when used in one educational context the term has a certain meaning, while in another context it has a different connotation.

The Greenwood Dictionary of Education, 2nd Edition, focuses on contemporary terminology used in education. While we have included words and definitions related to the history and foundations of education, terms that have fallen from usage are not included and should be sought in older dictionaries. Although the focus of this dictionary is on education, relevant terms from other disciplines such as psychology and sociology may be included, if they are defined within the context of education.

Other parts of the work include a foreword by the distinguished historian James D. Anderson, and a preface describing the process and background of how the *Dictionary* came into being. The dictionary entries follow this prefatory material. At the end of the *Dictionary* can be found an extensive list of sources used by the contributors and contributing editors as they developed definitions. This list reflects the diversity of subject areas within education. The final components of the *Dictionary* are lists of contributing editors for specialized areas within education, contributors, and an index to the initials of each contributor that provides the full name.

A

AAE/AAVE (See African American English/African American Vernacular English)

AAHE (See American Association for Higher Education)

AASCU (See American Association of State Colleges and Universities)

AAU (See Association of American Universities)

AAUP (See American Association of University Professors)

AAUW (See American Association of University Women)

ABA (See applied behavior analysis)

ABC art (See minimalism)

ABD
Abbreviation for "all but dissertation." Used to indicate the status of a graduate student who has completed all of the requirements for a doctorate in a given discipline except for the completion of his or her dissertation. (jbm)

ABE (See adult basic education)

ability
Capacity to perform a task, as in talk of "high ability" or "low ability." Degree of skill at task performance. Intelligence. There is much disagreement over the question of whether intelligence is unitary or multiple, genetically determined or socially developed, and whether the tests purported to measure it can do so. (jc)

ability grouping
Assigning students to separate classrooms, groups, or activities on the basis of their perceived academic abilities or performance. Grouping can be either homogeneous (students of similar abilities placed together) or heterogeneous (students of mixed abilities placed together). (bba)

ABLE (See Adult Basic Learning Examination)

absolute constant
A constant that always has the same value, such as numbers in arithmetic. (kgh)

absolute knowers
Students for whom there is only one right answer, and who place the teacher as the

sole legitimate source of knowledge and insight. These students see knowledge as something to be received, as well as something to be mastered. (hfs)

absorbent mind

According to Montessori, the absorbent mind of the child "absorbs each experience in a powerful and direct way that, through the process of such absorption, the mind itself is formed" (Roopnarine and Johnson, 2000, 196). Montessori has proposed two stages in the development of the absorbent mind: the unconscious state where impressions or mental constructions are formed based on the young child's uses of the senses and movement; and a more conscious state where the child is able to use memory to compare experiences and problem-solve. (pw, yb)

abstinence-only-until-marriage

An approach to school-based sexuality education that is limited to an "abstinence only" approach to delaying sexual activity, preventing unwanted pregnancies, and reducing sexually transmitted diseases amongst adolescents. These federally funded programs do not provide information on basic topics in human sexuality such as puberty, reproductive anatomy, and sexual health; empirical research consistently demonstrates the ineffectiveness of this approach. A combination of "abstinence only" and comprehensive sexuality education has proven to be the most effective way of reducing harmful adolescent sexual behavior. (jb2)

abstract

Not concrete; that which exists beyond a particular object or example as an idea or quality. A particular poem may be beautiful, but beauty itself is an abstract concept. Abstract painting features the use of lines, colors, and forms to represent attitudes and emotions rather than photograph-like representations of particular objects. Abstract art may appear accidental in its making even when it has been carefully planned and executed. The art of very young children is often likened to abstract art because it aptly represents human qualities and emotions even as it disregards details of pictorial representation. (kpb)

abstract algebra

Sometimes referred to as "modern algebra." A branch of mathematics that studies the underlying algebraic structures, such as groups, rings, fields, modules, and vector spaces. The focus is on investigation and proof of theories behind the development of algebraic rules and procedures. (mlf, rlk)

abstract reasoning

An ability to comprehend and manipulate abstract concepts such as symbols, language, relationships, and the like, that is often associated with human intelligence. (jcp)

abstract singleton

Used in relation to the child's construction of 10 as a unit. Here the child distinguishes between those items that can be counted using the sequence 10, 20, 30, 40 from those to be counted using the standard number-word sequence but does not see one 10 as composed of 10 ones. (amr)

abstract unit

Constructing a number as a set of singletons while maintaining its whole (e.g., thinking of 10 as 10 ones while maintaining its tenness). The number 10 is thus a mathematical entity that can be thought of simultaneously as one thing and 10 things. (dc)

abstract unit items (counting)

Items do not need to be created in order to be counted. The child can take the counting words themselves as objects to be counted. A child at this level will be able to successfully solve tasks like the following: 6 + __ = 8. (amr)

See **also** children's counting schemes.

abuse

Acts of physical, sexual, and/or psychological/emotional harm directed at another person. The perpetrators of abuse toward children frequently include caregivers or parents but may also include other children. Threatened harm is also considered abuse. (vm)

academe

A general term or collective noun for reference to the academic world at large; originally the grove outside of Athens where Plato taught his students. (cf)

academic

Pertaining to college and university events, rituals, and ceremonies. Related to scholarly aspects of education beyond the high school. Ranges from praise to sarcasm: academically sound or merely academic (i.e., pedantic, formalistic, meaningless). (cf)

academic accommodations in higher education

Adjustments or modifications in the academic environment enabling an individual with a disability to experience equal access to academic programs, services, and activities, as mandated in the Vocational Rehabilitation Act of 1973 (Section 504). Reasonable and appropriate accommodations reduce the impact of the functional limitations of an impairment by reducing or eliminating barriers in acquiring information or access to academic programs. Academic accommodations are relevant to specific course or degree requirements and are not applicable to open ended interpretation. (ecb, nl1)

academic achievement

The attainment of knowledge, competencies, and higher-level status, as reflected in grades, degrees, and other forms of certification or public acknowledgment. (cf)

academic advisement

At its most basic level, involves assisting students in designing a course of study that includes taking the required course work for a degree. The definition provided by the professional organization, the National Academic Advising Association (NACADA), however, goes well beyond this by noting that academic advising is a teaching and learning process involving student outcomes that are guided by both the students' goals and the institution's goals. (sn)

See also National Academic Advising Association.

academic affairs

The division of a college or university that administers the educational and research missions of the institution. Academic affairs administrators handle faculty issues, such as recruitment, supervision, and evaluation of academic deans; academic policies and standards; and advising the president concerning tenure, promotion, and leaves. (cf)

academic calendar

The system by which the institution structures its school year. The three common types of calendars are the semester, the quarter, and the trimester. (cf)

academic culture

A general term for the numerous characteristics that permeate college and university campuses, facilities, programs, alumni, faculties, students, and other constituencies; sometimes defined as those features without which a particular institution would not be an institution of higher learning. (cf)

academic freedom

The custom and practice that accords university professors and, to a lesser degree, K–12 teachers the freedom to teach and conduct research without interference of administrators, government officials, or other outside parties. In 1940, the

American Association of University Professors issued its Statement of Principles on Academic Freedom and Tenure, which has served as a guide for school officials and legal interpretations of the purpose and scope of academic freedom in educational institutions. Doctrine that professors and students are free to inquire, to learn, and to teach in a climate of judgmental neutrality; to teach in the absence of political, religious, or social censorship. Derived from the German concepts of *Lernfreiheit* (uncontrolled study) and *Lehrfreiheit* (freedom of teaching). (cf, kl)

academic honesty (See academic integrity)

academic integrity
Academic integrity is academic honesty integrated into all aspects of academic life, including crediting sources used in all forms of publications, research, experiments, assignments, and papers. Academic integrity also encompasses students refraining from cheating on examinations and in all of their classroom assignments. Academic integrity is the standard by which individuals are expected to create their own work and not reproduce or copy the work or ideas of others without giving proper credit. (pw1)

academic language
A variant of language that is particular to school settings and tasks; language often used in textbooks, in lectures, and on tests; a more formal, standardized version of a language, which usually contains longer sentences, uses rarer vocabulary words, and varies across content disciplines. It is also referred to as school language, advanced language proficiency, academic discourse, and school discourse. (cld)

academic rationalist
An individual who believes that the intent of education should be to expose students to the thinking of the "great" minds and books of history. An academic rationalist assumes that there is an identifiable body of legitimate knowledge and that there are people qualified to select material from this body of knowledge to design meaningful curricula. (jqa, jwc)

academic regalia (See regalia)

academy
A term that may refer to a school of philosophy, such as the gymnasium founded by Plato. In the arts and sciences, the term refers to a society or professional community seeking to advance art, science, or literature. In education, the term denotes a legally incorporated institution providing a relatively advanced form of schooling beyond the elementary level. Private academies were particularly common in the 19th-century United States before the growth of public high schools. (kt)

acalculia
A learning disability which may leave an individual capable of understanding general mathematical concepts, but unable to carry out simple calculations. (jcp)
See also dyscalculia.

accelerated learning
A pedagogical method that emphasizes using the whole person (both mind and body) in order to increase a learner's ability to learn more in a shorter period of time. Accelerated learning techniques involve the use of creativity, music, images, and/or color to enhance learning. (chm)

acceleration program
An approach to serving academically gifted students by increasing the pace at which they complete their education through practices such as skipping grade levels. (bba)

access and equity
The right to enter an institution as a participant, to enroll in programs and courses, and to derive benefits and advantages.

Terms are often used together, as in access and equity issues in higher learning. (cf)

accessibility
Access to public and federally funded buildings, transportation, and facilities for individuals with mobility, visual, hearing, and other impairments. (sr)

accommodation
Jean Piaget's "Theory of Cognitive Development" describes the alteration of established schemes in order to incorporate new information as accommodation. Accommodation may involve the changing of existing cognitions to gain an understanding of a new concept. Also, changes, additions, or other alterations to a program, service, curriculum, or environment to meet the unique needs of a person with a disability. (mf, sr)

accountability
The ethical or legal requirement that delegated authority be exercised responsibly. The obligation to give explicit justification to those having the authority to demand or expect an explanation. An extension of responsibility to give evidence that duties have been performed as agreed. A higher order of responsibility; faculty may be responsible for teaching courses but are accountable to deans and department heads. Also, the idea that districts, schools, and teachers should be held responsible for ensuring that students master the specified curriculum at a particular grade level. (cf, bba)

accreditation
The process of receiving and maintaining approval for a unit (school, college, etc.), or program (teacher, counselor, and/or administrative certification, etc.) based on state and/or national standards established by a government or official educational organization, such as a state's educational governing board or NCATE (National Council for Accreditation of Teacher Education). Organizations providing an accredited program must pass periodic reviews by the accreditation agency in order to keep their accredited status. (dek, ep)

accrediting agencies
Private, nonprofit organizations designed for the specific purpose of facilitating the process used by higher education to review colleges, universities, and educational programs for quality assurance and quality improvement. (cf)

acculturation
The process of acquiring a culture different from one's own. Usually occurs when one cultural group adopts the cultural norms of a dominant group and takes place when groups with different cultural backgrounds come into contact. It also can represent the blending of cultures between diverse groups of people. (jqa, jwc)

ACE (See American Council on Education)

achievement rating
A measurement of student achievement on a standardized test to compare individual growth in a subject area against a standard; an evaluation of something accomplished, such as an athletic skill or academic test. (dsm)

achievement test
One of a class of assessment instruments designed to measure an individual's current skill or mastery of a specific academic task. Scores on these tests are strongly influenced by academic exposure and cultural experiences. Unlike intelligence tests, which are designed to help predict future academic performance, achievement tests are designed to assess mastery of materials one has already learned. For example, they may assess mastery in one or more of the following areas: reading, written language, mathematics, and oral expression. Achievement tests seek to determine the degree to which an individual has learned a set of objectives or other goals within

an instructional curriculum. The administration of this type of test will normally take place at the end of an instructional sequence, which can be at the end of an entire course term, or at the end of a particular module within the course. (kc, scmc, bdj, bkl)

ACLS (See American Council of Learned Societies)

acoustic phonetics (See phonetics)

acrasia (See akrasia)

ACT (See Action for Children's Television)

ACT (See American College Testing)

ACTE (See Association for Career and Technical Education)

ACTER (See Association for Career and Technical Education Research)

Action for Children's Television (ACT)
A national grassroots organization started in 1968 by Peggy Charren and a group of volunteer women in Newton, Massachusetts, who were concerned about a lack of quality children's programming on television. Efforts by the group resulted in the 1990 passage of the Children's Television Act. ACT was also concerned with the advertising aimed at children during children's programs. (ms)

action learning
A form of action research that brings small teams of peers together at their workplace to find solutions to problems in real contexts, to try new ways of operating, to assess their progress, and to make necessary adjustments. Any learning through doing. (alm)

action plan
A document used by a school or district to articulate its goals and how it hopes to achieve them. One component of system-wide education improvement initiatives in the Pre-K–12 sector. After data are collected and thoroughly analyzed for weaknesses related to areas such as instruction, a team of school or district leaders develops a plan that typically includes a goal statement, action steps, timeline, resources required, responsible parties, and indicators of success. (mf1)

action research
Action research describes many dissimilar forms of inquiry that include teacher-originated, administration-directed research, as well as collaborative research with university faculty, involving practitioners as change agents in pursuit of the betterment of schools, curriculum, teaching, and learning. The goals of action research are multifold: to improve the knowledge base for educational theory; as a means of personal fulfillment, empowerment, and the professionalization of teaching; and to improve and refine teaching practice specific to a teacher-researcher's context. Research in which the researcher participates in the phenomenon being studied. It is usually undertaken with the intent of changing a specific situation or problem. (ja, las)

active learning
The process of having students engage in some activity that forces them to reflect upon ideas and upon how they are using those ideas. Requiring students to regularly assess their own degree of understanding and skill at handling concepts or problems in a particular discipline. The attainment of knowledge by participating or contributing. The process of keeping students mentally, and often physically, active in their learning through activities that involve them in gathering information, thinking, and problem solving. (dsm, bba)

active learning time (ALT)
The amount of time that students are actively participating in meaningful move-

ment skills related to the goals of instruction. (rf)

active listening

The act of attending to the speech, body language, facial expressions, and implied meanings of a person's communication. Active listening can also be demonstrated through reflecting what one has heard another say by rephrasing or reiterating the statement and confirming the statement's meaning and intent. A microcounseling skill that involves attending to and understanding what a client is saying. Also involves "listening with a third ear," that is, listening to both what he or she is saying and to what he or she really means. Specific types of listening responses include: clarifying statements, paraphrasing what was said, reflecting feeling(s), and summarizing what was said. (kdc, ksp)

active participation

Hands-on, experiential learning. A classroom that values active participation provides children with many types of activities, designed to help children explore, experiment, practice emerging skills, and learn new concepts and skills. (kdc)

active role-play area

An area where children use their experiences and act out what they have experienced within their environment, such as acting out what they see adults do at different times of the day or acting like an animal or a superhero seen on television. The area also may facilitate children's learning to empathize by placing themselves in another person's shoes. The role-playing process helps a child to imagine what it is like to be someone else and how it feels, and to practice using language—verbal and nonverbal—in different ways, or try out and test imaginative ideas. (pw)

activist

An individual who engages in direct political, civil, or social action designed to influence political or social change. (jqa, jwc)

activity center

An activity center is an area where either an individual or a small group can interact with interesting objects laid out for them. Activity centers are provided to promote many aspects of learning at the same time, such as using fine motor skills, movement or large motor skills, auditory discrimination, and language development in comfortable, stimulating settings. (pw)

ACUHO-I (See Association of College and University Housing Officers—International)

ad hoc committees

Appointed for specified purposes and length of service, with expectations that when its mission is accomplished, the committee will no longer exist. (cf)

ad valorem (See tax abatement)

ADA (See Americans with Disabilities Act)

adaptive physical education

Accommodations made to the physical education program to address the unique needs of students with disabilities. (sr)

adaptive technology (See assistive technology)

adaptive testing

The adaptive testing concept refers to tests that shape themselves to the particular level of ability for individual test takers. Rather than have all test takers work through an entire set of test items, an adaptive test will tailor the items or tasks that each person is presented with based on the developing picture of his or her ability on those items. Test takers end up taking only the number of items necessary to identify their level of ability. This is accomplished by presenting items from preestablished difficulty levels and using these to zero in on the level at which the test taker's responses indicate he or she cannot handle anything more difficult. Strictly speaking, any test that "adapts" in real time to an ongoing estimate of student ability is an adaptive test, including such assessments as face-to-face interview testing; however, the term is typically applied to multi-item assessments. (bkl)

See also computer-adaptive testing.

ADD (See Attention Deficit Disorder)

addends
Any of the members of a set of numbers being added. (kva)

addiction
A term with an evolving definition based on recent discoveries of brain mechanisms. In scientific terms, addiction is typically replaced by "substance dependence," which, according to the 2004 *Diagnostic and Statistical Manual of Mental Disorders* (DSM-IV), signifies impaired behavioral control over substance use, presumably caused by dysfunction in the brain's medial forebrain bundle, or pleasure pathway. Tolerance to a drug's action or withdrawal symptoms may or may not accompany addiction. The term is distinct from drug abuse and misuse, which implies willful use, as opposed to addiction, which implies brain chemistry malfunction. (sdc)

See also substance abuse; substance-related disorder.

additive inverse
The number that when added to the original number results in a sum of zero; for example, -3 is the additive inverse of 3 because $3 + \{-3\} = 0$. (ps)

additive reasoning
Involves constructing the relationship between addition and subtraction and developing appropriate strategies for solving problems related to adding and subtracting. (smc)

ADHD (See Attention Deficit Disorder)

adhesive adaptation
The addition rather than subtraction of cultural behaviors, values, and attitudes by immigrants to their preexisting belief systems and relationships. It suggests that new cosmologies and understandings are complexly superimposed upon the old instead of the complete replacement or destruction of previous systems of values, beliefs, and understanding. (hfs)

adjunct faculty
Individuals appointed on a temporary or provisional basis to perform specific academic duties but who do not carry full faculty privileges and responsibilities; the academic credentials of adjunct faculty are often comparable to those of tenured faculty, but the appointments of adjunct faculty may be restricted for reasons such as concurrent appointment with another institution or organization. (cf)

adjustment disorder
A reaction, usually lasting less than six months, that occurs in response to a stressful event or situation (i.e., starting school, a new job, moving, retiring). It is characterized by the development of emotional or behavioral symptoms in response to an identifiable stressor and occurs within three months of the onset of the stressor. Symptoms are considered significant if the distress exceeds what would be expected or if there is significant impairment in social, occupational, or educational functioning. Adjustment disorders may occur with depressed mood, anxiety, disturbance of conduct, or a combination of the three. When symptoms last longer than six months because of either the persistence or severity of the stressor it is referred to as Chronic Adjustment Disorder. (tsw, mgg)

adjustment, occupational
Response of a person to stimuli furnished by a job and its circumstances correlated

with personal values, abilities, and interests. (jm)

adjustment, vocational
The degree to which a person is suited by personality, interests, and training to an occupation. The establishment of a satisfactory, harmonious, or otherwise proper relationship to one's employment, occupation, or profession. An aspect of personal development. (jm)

adlerian therapy
A phenomenological approach to psychotherapy that emphasizes the importance of viewing an individual from his or her subjective worldview or frame of reference. Central to Adlerian therapy is the importance of goal-directed behavior and individual optimal development, balanced with one's need for social responsibility and belonging. (jbb)

administrative development
The organized activities and events that provide learning opportunities for preservice or inservice academic administrators; includes administrative fellowships, internships, attendance at conferences, participation in training seminars/workshops or in other scheduled occasions to observe, study, and review administrative duties and responsibilities. (cf)

administrative leadership
The efforts of academic administrators, in addition to their assigned responsibilities and delegated authority, to improve an institution's performance in pursuit of its specified mission and goals; includes efforts to involve others productively and positively in the achievement of institutional objectives. (cf, npo)

administrative officers
Administrative officers include institution presidents, provosts, and deans, as well as senior professionals working in various offices. Many faculty members do administrative work as well, serving on committees, acting as department chairs, and the like. Some full-time administrative officers are also part-time faculty members, and others may have been professors or instructors before joining the administration. (cf)

administrative professional
A comprehensive job title that encompasses a variety of academic positions wherein professional work is done; typically, tenure requirements are not mandated for those administrative professional positions serving in a managerial or oversight capacity. In most postsecondary educational settings, administrative professional (AP) positions do not include teaching assignments. Sometimes this title is also given to jobs that are more secretarial in scope. (jbm)

administrative theory
An educational term referring to a set of interrelated concepts, assumptions, and generalizations that systematically describes and explains regularities in behavior in educational organizations. It is related to practice in that it forms a frame of reference and guides decision making. (mm)

admissions
The process of admitting or allowing to enter into an institution or program. *Admission* has a more general meaning than *admittance*, which is used only to denote the obtaining of physical access to a place. To gain admittance to a fraternity or sorority is to enter its facilities; to gain admission is to become a member. (cf)

admissions officer
In education, an admissions officer is typically a member of a postsecondary academic staff responsible for admitting students into a postsecondary program. An admissions officer gathers and maintains student admissions data and

reports admissions data to the administrators of the educational organization. An admissions officer also communicates appropriate admissions information to students, parents, and educational professionals, and/or others, as needed, as long as the confidentiality of any student's admissions information is not compromised. (tp)

admissions tests

(As related to entrance exams) Standardized tests, such as the SAT and ACT, are administered, scored, and reported prior to the acceptance and enrollment of applicants to undergraduate education. Tests nationally administered for professional and graduate schools include the MCAT, LSAT, MAT, and GRE. (cf)

adolescence

A period of physical and psychological development beginning at 11 to 13 years of age and extending into the early twenties. Changes in build and body structure are prominent during this period. Initiated by a short period of puberty, it continues for many years after the arrival of sexual maturity. (jw)

adult (See adult learner)

adult basic education (ABE)

Education that serves adults over the age of 16, not currently enrolled in school, and functioning at or below the 12th grade level so they can gain the basic skills necessary to function in family and society. This includes securing needed literacy training and education to become more employable, productive, and responsible citizens by completing instruction in areas that may include English as a Second Language (ESL), General Education Development (GED), and an assortment of basic literacy skills. The area of adult education that focuses on the language, mathematics, and social skills that adults need in order to carry out their everyday life roles. (jpc, dmv, pgg)

adult basic learning examination (ABLE)

A norm-referenced test that measures reading comprehension by asking adults to answer multiple-choice questions about reading passages provided in the test and by completing fill-in-the blank items. The reading passages are similar to K–12 texts. (jpc)

adult development

Changes in consciousness or cognition over the course of the adult lifespan. Different theorists treat these changes, variously, as conscious or unconscious, as by-products of events and activities, or as predictable, sequential progressions in an individual's life course. Stages or levels of cognitive and emotional development that take place after adolescence. These developmental levels describe different ways of knowing and learning. (jpc, chb)

adult education

Organized experiences designed to meet the learning needs of people who are beyond the normal school-leaving age and who are no longer full-time students. (chb)

Adult Education Act (AEA)

The legislation that established adult education as a permanent part of the U.S. Department of Education in 1966. The AEA continued through 1999 when the Workforce Investment Act became law. (jpc)
See also Workforce Investment Act.

Adult Education and Family Literacy Act (AEFLA)

Title II of the Workforce Investment Act of 1998; the act provides for federal funding to be used for adult basic education. In addition, it establishes a comprehensive performance accountability system measuring state performance in several areas: demonstrated improvement in literacy skill levels in reading, writing, and speaking the English language; numeracy; problem-solving; English-language acquisition and other literacy skills; placement, retention, or completion of postsecondary education, training, unsubsidized employment or career advancement; receipt of a high school diploma or equivalent; and other objective, quantifiable measures, as identified by state agencies. (las)

adult education center

A place where adult education takes place. (jpc)

adult educator

Individuals involved in the development, organization, and provision of adult education. The term applies to teachers, tutors, administrators, counselors, and curriculum developers. (jpc)

Adult Language Assessment Scales (A-LAS)

A test that assesses the oral language, reading, writing, and math skills of adults. It assesses skills from the most basic to a level sufficient for entry into employment or academic training. The test questions draw from life situations. The test is used for assessment and placement of students in adult basic education programs. (jpc)

adult learner

An adult who is a participant in an organized adult education program, or any adult who is engaged in learning. In most state and national legislation an adult is someone who is not in K–12 and is 16 or older, but for some states adulthood begins at 18 for educational purposes. (jpc)

adult learning

The engagement of adults in either organized adult education programs or self-directed learning. The learning that an adult does, both in planned educational activities and through unplanned, incidental experiences. (jpc, chb)

adult literacy

The ability of adults to read and write according to a standard set by society, and especially in the learner's social context. Recently the definition of literacy has been expanded to include skills and knowledge as diverse as computer expertise and financial acumen, which increase a person's ability to function as a productive member of society. In the legislation funding adult literacy programs in the United States, the term is defined as the ability of adults to read, write, and speak English, compute and solve problems at levels of proficiency necessary to function on the job and in society, to achieve their goals, and to develop their knowledge and potential. (dmv, jpc)

adult new readers

Adults who left school with very low literacy skills and learned to read well as adults or are presently improving their reading skills. (jpc)

adult numeracy

The ability of adults to solve life problems by using numbers and math information and processes. (jpc)

Adult Performance Level (APL)

A 1971 study by the U.S. Office of Education assessed the performance of adults on literacy tasks and reported the mean scores for each of five levels of education: less than eighth grade, eighth through twelfth grade, high school graduate, some college, and college graduate. (jpc)

adult secondary education (ASE)

Programs that provide adults with an opportunity to acquire a high school diploma, either through taking a test or through passing a set of courses. (jpc)

adult student (See adult learner)

adult vocational education

Education aimed at preparing adults to enter the workforce or advance in their careers. (las)

adult-child ratios

Refers to the maximum number of children allowed in the care of an individual adult in child-care settings. Ratios are usually based on the age of the youngest child in the group, with the youngest groups allowing fewer children to each adult. State regulations or accrediting agency standards determine ratios. (jlj)

advance organizer

Any information (verbal, quantitative, or graphic) that is presented to learners prior to a learning experience with the goal of making the instruction or presentation easier to follow. (mkr)

advanced placement

Academic credits or standing earned prior to matriculation at an educational institution by which a student exempts certain courses or other academic requirements; includes credit-by-examination, acceptable credits earned at another institution, and credits awarded for experiential work. (cf)

advancement

The continued improvement or progress of institutions and individuals. The continuing acquisition and development of resources, programs, services, and activities of colleges and universities. The progression of a student from one grade to another. (cf)

advancement office

Unit of a college or university that engages in external fundraising and the cultivation of donors. Maintaining relations with alumni is frequently part of the work of the advancement office. (sn)

adventure

Adventure refers to intentionally confronting risk, or voluntarily placing oneself in a position that forces exposure to risk while having taken steps to mitigate or manage that risk. For example, going for a hike into inaccessible woods far from

a hospital, after having gained knowledge of navigation, first aid, and having access to survival tools, such as a compass and first aid kit. (bhg, ahs)

adventure education

The term "adventure education" is often used interchangeably with Project Adventure. It is an experiential approach to curriculum that involves games, initiative problems, trust activities, high and low elements of a ropes course, risk-taking, problem solving, and cooperative learning. Activities utilized can be performed indoors or outdoors and often involve challenging people to go beyond their perceived capabilities. Also, to place students within authentic, team-based, immersion events with the intention that they must take individual responsibility for achieving a positive shared experience. (pbc, rf)

advertising

The action of calling attention of others via an announcement in the media (e.g., warning, notification, information). A paid public announcement, especially by printed notice or broadcast, intended to arouse a desire to buy or patronize. In social studies, advertising is studied as a phenomenon related to societal trends and issues. (ewr)

advisee

One who is assigned to or seeks the assistance of an adviser. In a scholastic setting, this relationship is established to gain information and recommendations about personal, curricular, and vocational concerns. (jw)

adviser/advisor

In an educational context, an adviser is an informed person in a given area who provides specific information to another individual or individuals on such things as course selection or future education plans. A member of the faculty who provides information to and guides the activities of a given class is called a class adviser. (gac)

advisor, vocational

A qualified person who assists individuals in choosing an occupation by informing them about occupational preparation, entry, and progression. Someone who aids individuals in making satisfactory adjustments to the work environment. (jm)

advisory committee

In career and technical education, advisory committees are groups of employers and community representatives who advise educators on the design, development, operation, evaluation, and revision of career-technical education programs. (sk)

advocacy

To actively and positively respond to, support, and represent the welfare of young children and/or families by staying and keeping others well-informed and taking action as needed, including phone calls, writing letters, serving on committees, and so on. Advocacy activities might include reporting suspected abuse, seeking social services for children and/or families, and taking action to influence public policies. (db1)

AEA (See Adult Education Act)

AEFLA (See Adult Education and Family Literacy Act)

AERA (See American Educational Research Association)

aesthetic

Having to do with the study of beauty or taste. Also, artistic, having to do with the arts. The appealing or artful aspects of an experience. Having to do with standards for taste or beauty. Cognitivists have embraced the notion of aesthetic knowing as the special mode of cognition, understanding, experience and percipience associated with the arts. (jd)

See also aesthetic education; aesthetic whole; aesthetics.

aesthetic development

The development of perceptive skills with regard to attending to and making sense of visual art. From a cognitive perspective, the ability to discover meaning in and make sense out of artistic creations. Aesthetic development has been studied by cognitive psychologists, notably Michael Parsons and Abigail Housen, with an eye to changes in aesthetic response that may be associated with age and experience. After Piaget, five stages of development have been noted, ranging from the earliest sensual responses to color, form, and personal association to the most advanced understanding of the challenges and vision that the artist embraces. (jd)

aesthetic education

The education of perception, specifically artistic vision that can be applied to every experiential situation. Focusing on literary texts and musical creations as well as on response to works of art, aesthetic education is dedicated to what philosopher Maxine Greene calls an "awakening of the imagination"—an ability to make sense of experience through the lenses of works of art and literature. The Lincoln Center Institute (LCI) in New York, spearheaded by Greene, has launched an aesthetic education program that has been emulated across the country and features summer training of teachers, working closely with professional artists who later make visits to the teachers' classrooms. (jd)

aesthetic knowledge

The understanding of hope as held and felt by students for the possibilities of change inherent in a given situation. Such insight is generated through participatory learning, meaning making, the engagement of imagination, and affective as well as cognitive perception. (hfs)

aesthetic whole

A unified composition, whether in music, visual art, or writing, in which the parts of the whole are integrated seamlessly. The result is twofold: The disruption of any part would render the whole significantly diminished or meaningless; and the whole is greater than the sum of its individual parts. After Langer, aesthetic expressions deliver multiple and challenging meanings determined as surely by the aesthetic properties of the symbols (words, line, tones) as by the meanings they deliver. The construction of an aesthetic whole (see Aristotle and Arnheim) is a triumph of meaning revealing itself to the artist (adult or child) when the work appears "right" or done. (jd)

aesthetics
The study of beauty and value, and of the perception and appreciation (the experience) of beauty and value. The central questions of aesthetics are "What makes something beautiful (or valuable)?" and "What makes us experience something as beautiful (or valuable)?" In the formation of educational policy and curriculum, aesthetics is a central concern, if most often an unrecognized one, since determinations of what belongs in the curriculum are always questions of what is valuable for the student to learn. Traditionally, a branch of philosophy dealing with the nature, creation, and appreciation of beauty, art, and taste. The Greek term *aisthetikos* means "pertaining to sense perception." The special way that we perceive art objects—"the aesthetic experience"—is of interest in education. Philosopher and educator John Dewey argued for aesthetic perception as a way to make sense of daily experience. Following Dewey, educational philosopher Maxine Greene has developed programs fostering such appreciation under the rubric of "aesthetic education." Cognitive psychologists study the modes of response to artistic symbols and have demonstrated stagelike development in aesthetic perception. (jc, kpb)

affectional orientation
(See sexual orientation)

affective
Affective learning stands in contrast to cognitive learning, as it is used to denote those aspects of learning that involve emotions, feelings, and attitudes. (crl)

affective development
The social and emotional dimensions of a child's growth. According to Erikson (1963) stages of psychosocial development, a child's affect grows in concert with his or her physical and cognitive dimensions. (ecr)

affective education
Programs and practices that address and promote positive social and emotional growth in children. A healthy self-concept and prosocial relationships with other children are goals of an affective education program. In affective education, adult interaction with children is responsive to their emotional needs and their expressed feelings. (ecr)

affective neuroscience
Affective neuroscience refers to the neuroscientific study of affective phenomena such as emotions, moods, and feelings, with the goal of mapping out their underlying neuronal and neurochemical basis. (mf2)

affinity group
A group of individuals who share common interests or roles and who interact with one another to provide support, problem-solve, network, and/or share knowledge and expertise. In the context of adult education, affinity groups may be formed to provide learners with the opportunity to have small group discussions, focused on connecting curriculum to their practice, with peers from similar professional environments. (ln)

affirmative action
Enacted September 24, 1965, through Executive Order 11246, Affirmative Action prescribes equal opportunity employment standards for government employment. Affirmative action commits government contracting agencies to nondiscrimination

in the areas of race, color, religion, sex, and national origin, and the law's broad coverage includes protection for workers in the areas of promotion, advancement, transfer, recruitment, and layoff or termination, as well as rates of pay and other forms of compensation. (jqa, jwc)

affirmed female
A person whose biological sex is male or intersex and who has affirmed their gender identity as female. Referred to as a girl, a woman, or an affirmed female. A term more frequently used with gender-variant children and adolescents than adults. The same concepts apply to affirmed males. (jb2)

AFQT (See Armed Forces Qualification Test)

African American English/African American Vernacular English (AAE/AAVE)
Although AAE is the term more common used today, AAVE is still an acceptable term. These acronyms refer to the dialect of English used by many African American English speakers in the United States. AAE/AAVE has a grammar, vocabulary, and pronunciation that vary from Standard English and other English dialects. (jas)

African American language
Sometimes referred to as Black English or Ebonics, African American language is the language typically spoken within the African American community. According to Williams, the term "acknowledges its African cultural roots, identifies its geographical residence, and reflects the linguistic integrity of this effective communication system." (jqa, jwc)

African dance
A multidimensional art form originating in African tribal cultures. The communicative and expressive properties of African dance are bases for the different intersocial and aesthetic activities for rituals, festivities, religious observances, rites of passage, political ceremonies, and professional activities, though tribal cultures differ in language, movements, storytelling, and costuming. African drumming as a means of communication is an essential component to the recreational, aesthetic, and symbolic dance forms. The African slave population in America devised a method of communicative drumming by attaching stones and pebbles to the bottoms of shoes, which has evolved into the art form of tap dancing. (kbc)

Afro-American studies
A field of cultural studies that emerged in the United States during the 1960s, which focuses on the academic, social, and cultural aspects of African American life. Distinguished from Negro history, black history, and African history, Afro-American studies flourished on American college campuses as students demanded a curricular relevance to the needs of black communities. The field encompasses many subject areas and core courses, including: black history, religion, arts, sociology, psychology, politics, and economics. (jqa, jwc)

Afrocentric curriculum
A curriculum that focuses on concepts, issues, arts, and literature from the perspectives of Africans and African Americans. Viewed as an alternative to Eurocentric-based curriculum, Afrocentic curriculum is more inclusive and less exclusionary and provides many students the opportunity to learn from their own cultural perspectives. (jqa, jwc)

Afrocentric education
An approach to education that decenters European history and culture and replaces it with African and African American history and culture as the lens through which education is focused. The premise of Afrocentric education is that the privileged position given to European history and

culture in the school curriculum disadvantages children of African descent by alienating them from their cultural and historical heritage and/or from their education. Philosophy that recognizes the existence of cultural, intellectual, psychological, and emotional bonds and connections within all persons of African ancestry. Teaching and learning requires critical inquiry and reflection on the varied consequences and inherent contradictions of African existence in European-dominated societies, and by extension, the world. It is an orientation that places the examination of the African experience and cosmology centrally as subject in the development of intellect, curriculum, pedagogy, goals, and outcomes. (jc, hfs)

See also multicultural education.

afrocentrism

Afrocentrism is considered a frame of reference in which phenomena are viewed from the perspective of an African person. In education, it is the belief that African cultural heritage should be represented more completely in curricula. Most Afrocentrist work relates closely to the books of Molefi Asante and his contention that black cultural and ethnic identity should be discussed and studied more closely. (jwn)

AFT (See American Federation of Teachers)

after-school care

Extended care for school-age children in the hours between the end of the school day and the time the parents are available to pick them up. Simple activities and assistance with homework are often included. (jlj)

after-school programs

Supervised programs for school children, located in schools or other community resource centers, that extend from the end of the school day until late afternoon or evening. After-school programs serve one

or more of the following purposes: providing child care for children of working parents; providing educational support and enrichment; and promoting youth development. (bba)

age-graded approach

The assignment of students to grade levels solely on the basis of their chronological age. (bba)

ageism

Discrimination, hatred, or prejudice directed against people based on their age. (jqa, jwc)

aggregation

In a sociological context, this term can mean the voluntary clustering of individuals by race. In schools, this type of aggregation can be seen in classroom seating arrangements, cafeteria groupings, and the like. Some sociologists suggest that aggregation can be viewed as a measure for assessing student attitudes toward interracial and intercultural grouping. (jqa, jwc)

agricultural education

One of major program areas in career and technical education, which was established in Georgia in 1734. Teaching of agriculture in public schools can be traced back to elementary schools in Massachusetts in 1858. Programs that prepare students for careers in production, agriculture, horticulture, agricultural mechanics, agribusiness, and emerging agricultural fields. (jb)

AHA Committee of Seven

A group of historians who were appointed by the American Historical Association in 1896 and reported in 1899 about the status of history and civic education in the United States. In their report, they stressed the importance of teaching historical thinking as a preparation for civil government, as well as the necessity for studying civil government from a historical perspective. They also emphasized the teaching of responsible citizenship and the

algorithm 17

capacity for students to deal with political and governmental questions. (jwn)

AI (See artificial intelligence)

AIHEC (See American Indian Higher Education Consortium)

AIM (See American Indian Movement)

AIR (See Association for Institutional Research)

akrasia
A moral educational term used to denote either a lack of self-control or an unwillingness to follow one's ethical conclusions. Akrasia is often used to discuss instances where moral educational approaches are successful in teaching students to know what ought to be done but unsuccessful in teaching students to carry out such actions. Lawrence Kohlberg's approach, for example, is commonly critiqued for teaching students to determine what should be done while concurrently failing to motivate them to do so (see Carr 1996). For instance, schools might be successful in teaching that bullying is inappropriate, and students may be able to state why bullying is "wrong," and yet, some students will still persist in bullying their peers. (dpb)

A-LAS (See Adult Language Assessment Scales)

alcohol education
A proactive approach to dissuade students from drinking and abusing alcohol by instructing them on its negative influence (dsm)

algebra
The study of general methods of understanding patterns, relations, and functions by representing and analyzing them using mathematical symbols called variables. The use of variables allows relationships to be identified and generalized from the specific numbers or constants of arithmetic to larger sets of numbers representing a range of values. (kva)

algebraic expression
Numbers and/or variables, usually with operation signs between them and possibly with symbols of inclusion (e.g., parentheses). The following are examples of algebraic expressions: $2x + 3$, $3(x - 2)$, $x^2 + 2/x - 1$. (rdk)

algebraic insight
The absence of formulas and manipulatives, which encourages independent thinking as well as logical reasoning. Being able to determine when it is and is not appropriate to use another means and change one's thought process to solve a problem. (jmg, ldz)

algebraic irrational numbers (See irrational number)

algebraic reasoning
Thinking in variables. Using the general behavior of numbers, patterns, relations, and functions, to solve problems, evaluate the validity of those solutions, and verify conjectures. (gtm)

algebraic symbols
Symbols used to represent an unknown value or range of values. (kva)

algorithm
A procedure for quickly and efficiently performing a calculation or solving a routine problem. Traditionally, algorithms are developed by more experienced mathematicians and become standard procedures that are taught to students of mathematics. There has been a move in mathematics education in recent years away from teaching standard algorithms, toward encouraging students to develop their own meaningful procedures to use in these situations. (amr)

all aspects of industry

As defined by the School-to-Work Opportunities Act, the phrase "all aspects of industry" refers to all aspects of the industry or industry sector a student is preparing to enter, including planning, management, finances, technical and production skills, the underlying principles of technology, labor and community issues, health and safety issues, and environmental issues related to the industry or industry sector. This term also includes the collection of occupations and careers in an industry, from the most simple to the most advanced. (jb)

allegory

A story, play, poem, or picture is an allegory (or allegorical) when the characters or events represent particular human qualities or ideas, most frequently related to some moral, religious, or political meaning. In this way abstract concepts like virtue, beauty, nature, or truth may be represented by fictional figures (e.g., an innocent child) or an instance (e.g., an act of kindness) standing for a human quality (e.g., virtue). (kpb)

allocated time

The amount of time that is assigned or scheduled for the instruction of specific subjects or content. (bba)

allographic

Writing, as in a signature, made by one person to represent the signature of another (as opposed to autographic in which the signature is original). A performance of a musical composition is allographic. The composer has written the work and the performer interprets it artistically so that it can stand for (though it is not literally the same as) what the composer has written, even though, like the re-created signature, it is now written in the hand (or voice or through the instrument) of the performer. (kpb)

ally

A person who actively helps and supports members of a community other than his or her own. One who openly affirms the rights of GLBTQ people. (jb2)

alphabet

Generally, the complete set of letters or other graphic symbols representing speech sounds used in writing a language or in phonetic transcription. More specifically, it is the sequential arrangement of the letters used to write a given language. Almost every alphabetic language in the world has its own unique alphabet. (smt)

alphabetic principle

A systematic and predictable relationship between written letters and spoken sounds. Successful reading acquisition depends on understanding this relationship. (mmd)

ALT (See active learning time)

alternate day kindergarten

A delivery system for kindergarten in which the five-year-olds attend school alternate weekdays (Tuesday, Thursday, and Friday, or Monday, Wednesday, and Friday) instead of five half-days each week. The longer school day can reduce transition times and save on transportation costs but has not been shown to be educationally superior. (ecr)

alternative assessment

Alternative assessments examine student progress through direct observation of student performance and/or judgment of learning products. The aim is to gather information about how individual students approach "real-life" tasks in a particular domain. When alternative assessments are used, information is often collected from a variety of "authentic" sources, for example, observation/anecdotal notes, student oral reading/presentation, and collections of student work. Evaluative rubrics that spell out criteria for various levels of proficiency often accompany the use of the assessment. Alternative assessments can also be described as authentic assessments or performance assessments. (al, aw)

alternative education
Any variety of education that is apart from the common public school. Most often used to describe schools that are created within the public school system for "at risk" or special populations of students (e.g., gifted/talented or children with special needs), the term is also used to describe private schools as alternatives to the public school, and it includes home schooling. (jc)

alternative education programs
Alternative education programs address the needs of students who have dropped out of school or those who are at risk of dropping out of school. These programs emphasize academic as well as socialization skills. (jt)

alternative route to certification
A path to teacher licensure provided by institutions of higher education as a substitute for a four-year or graduate education program, devised to meet the needs of professionals already holding a bachelor's degree who are interested in entering the teaching profession. An intensive course of study may include courses in content, educational theory, and methods, followed by an internship. (clk)

alternative school movement
A broad term used to describe a wide variety of public and private alternatives to traditional public educational curriculum and methodology. Among the many varieties of alternative schools popular in the United States over the past 30 years are free schools, freedom schools, open schools, survival schools, schools-within-schools, magnet schools, and charter schools. (sw)

alternative teacher certification
The process of acquiring initial teacher licensure that varies from the traditional college-based initial teacher education. According to requirements determined by each state, programs allow individuals who have college degrees in other fields or who have college degrees but have been out of the work force for a time (stay-at-home parents, retirees) to transition into teaching and complete certification requirements while working in a classroom. Components for alternative certification programs may include orientations, training programs, course work, and/or field experiences. (dek, cp)

alternative teacher certification programs
Programs that are now offered in most states to prepare teachers for rapid entry into teaching, primarily in high-needs areas. Generally, colleges or universities permit individuals who already have degrees in a discipline to take an abbreviated program, which involves practice teaching in a school district. Not without controversy, many professional teacher educators have been critics of the programs, and research about their effectiveness has yielded mixed results. (sn)

alternative teacher compensation
Unlike uniform salary schedules that fix compensation to years of service and/or union contract salary tiers, alternative teacher compensation plans are merit-based systems. Performance-based systems reward teachers for changing and improving teaching practices, including expansion of professional skills. Such programs encourage teachers to implement new teaching practices and instructional tools. Outcomes-based systems reward teachers for the performance of their students. Such programs encourage teachers to seek alternative ways of reaching students and also to seek additional support through working directly with administrators or

other professionals to advance student performance. (ms)

American Association for Higher Education (AAHE)

This organization addresses the challenges higher education faces and promotes the changes necessary to ensure its effectiveness in a changing world. AAHE provides individuals and institutions committed to change with the knowledge needed to bring those changes about. Individual members are faculty, administrators, and students from all disciplines, plus policy makers from foundations, business, government, accrediting agencies, and the media. (cf)

American Association of State Colleges and Universities (AASCU)

This Washington-based association consists of more than 400 public colleges and universities and systems across the United States and in Puerto Rico, Guam, and the Virgin Islands. AASCU's programs promote understanding of public higher education's essential role and advocate for public higher education policy issues at the national, state, and campus levels. (cf)

American Association of University Professors (AAUP)

Founded in 1915 by Arthur Lovejoy of Johns Hopkins and John Dewey of Columbia University. Its mission is to advance academic freedom and shared governance; to define fundamental professional values and standards for higher education; and to ensure higher education's contribution to the common good, most clearly articulated in the famous 1940 Statement of Principles on Academic Freedom and Tenure. During the era of McCarthyism the AAUP was called upon to protect faculty members suspected of Communist Party affiliation. It is currently a nonprofit organization that is open to membership by any academic professional. The association continues to publish reports on topics germane to academics and is called upon to investigate infringements on academic freedom. (rih, cf)

American Association of University Women (AAUW)

A national organization founded for the purpose of achieving gender equity in education and fostering societal change. Members are required to hold college degrees from colleges and universities approved by the association. The AAUW was formed in 1921 from a merger between the Association of Collegiate Alumnae (founded in 1881) and the Southern Association of College Women (founded in 1903). Currently, it is an international organization for 150,000 college graduates of both sexes. It funds, evaluates, and disseminates original educational research, monitors voting records of elected officials, supports litigants in sexual harassment cases, and provides educational materials to voters. (pjm)

American College Testing (ACT)

A nationally administered college entrance examination. The multiple choice test covers four areas: English, mathematics, reading, and science. There is an optional writing test. A second major college entrance examination is the SAT Reasoning Test. Some states now administer the ACT to assess the performance of schools and require all high school students to take the ACT, regardless of whether they are college bound. (sn)

American Council of Learned Societies (ACLS)

Founded in 1919 as an umbrella organization to represent U.S. humanities and social sciences interests at the Union Academique Internationale (UAI). The ACLS has developed and administered fellowships, grants-in-aid, and other programs intended to promote social science and humanities research, publications, and conferences. The ACLS is noted for its pioneering work in language teaching materials, especially in the era after passage of the National Defense Education Act (1958). (vmm)

American Council on Education (ACE)

Founded in 1918 and the nation's best-known higher education association. ACE is dedicated to the belief that equal educational opportunity and a strong higher education system are essential cornerstones of a democratic society. Its approximately 1,800 members include accredited, degree-granting colleges and universities from all sectors of higher education. (cf)

American Democracy Project

Sponsored by the American Association of State Colleges and Universities, over 220 public colleges and universities have joined this initiative with the goal of producing graduates who are committed to civic engagement. The ADP sponsors a variety of national and regional meetings and encourages numerous campus initiatives, including voter education and registration, curriculum revision, and a wide variety of projects related to political and civic involvement. (sn)

American Educational Research Association (AERA)

Founded in 1916, the AERA is a professional organization that seeks to support the field of education through scholarly inquiry and research. The AERA is an influential national research society that represents a wide range of disciplines. The association emphasizes scholarly inquiry as well as the use of research to improve education. It publishes several key journals, including the *American Educational Research Journal, Educational Evaluation and Policy Analysis, Journal of Educational and Behavioral Statistics, Review of Educational Research,* and *Review of Research in Education.* (ms, sn)

American Federation of Teachers (AFT)

Founded in 1916, the American Federation of Teachers, an affiliate of the American Federation of Labor, represents over one million teachers, K–12 and higher education support staff and faculty, and health care, state, and municipal employees. The organization represents member interests in collective bargaining, legislative efforts, professional development, and research initiatives. (mm1, jwc)

American G.I. Forum

Founded originally in 1948 by Hector P. Garcia as the American G.I. Forum of Texas, the national American G.I. Forum was created in 1958 as a civil rights organization devoted to securing equal rights for Hispanic Americans. The Forum initially fought to secure G.I. Bill benefits denied to Mexican Americans returning from World War II in Texas, but it has also participated in broader civil rights struggles related to equal educational opportunity (including school desegregation cases), voter registration, and access to health care, as well as those related specifically to the needs of migrant workers and veterans. (vmm)

American Indian Higher Education Consortium (AIHEC)

The AIHEC was founded in 1972 by six tribally controlled community colleges to meet the common challenges of these institutions. Now it is a cooperatively sponsored effort on the part of 32 member institutions in the United States and Canada and serves over 25,000 students from more than 250 tribal nations. The stated mission of the AIHEC is "to nurture, advocate, and protect American Indian history, culture, art and language, and the legal and human rights of American Indian people to their own sense of identity and heritage." (cf)

American Indian Movement (AIM)

Founded in 1968 in response to complaints by Native American residents in Minneapolis, Minnesota, concerning police brutality, AIM was devoted to promoting cultural awareness and political self-determination for Native Americans, including: improved city services, recognition of treaty rights between Native Americans and the U.S. government, and the development of "survival schools" that would teach the Native American culture. Patterned after the Black Panthers and most successful in urban areas, AIM's militancy and violent tactics eventually led to government crackdowns and imprisonment of its leaders. AIM officially disbanded by 1979 but was revived in the early 1990s as the Confederation of Autonomous AIM Chapters. The original "AIM Survival School," now called Heart of the Earth Survival School, continues to provide an educational alternative for Native American children in Minneapolis. (ld)

American Indian Studies

Often referred to as Native American Studies, this interdisciplinary field of study focuses on the cultural, historical, and contemporary aspects of Native Americans. Coinciding with the emergence of other ethnic studies programs in the late 1960s, this field developed in response to the demands of Native American and non-Native American students who wanted to learn more about the history, culture, and social concerns of these people. The field includes visual arts, literature, and music, as well as many other aspects of social sciences, humanities, history, anthropology, and the applied sciences. (jqa, jwc)

American Paidea

Concept developed by Lawrence Cremin to describe the explicit philosophy of the good life intentionally translated into educational practice and philosophy in order to instruct the young, inform men and women beyond their school years, shape public opinion and perceptions, influence and shape politics, and transfer American culture to the world at large. (hfs)

American Sign Language (ASL)

The most widely used of the conventional, grammatical, natural languages of the deaf. Like all manual languages, ASL uses hand configuration, location, and movement, accompanied by cues from facial expression and body position, to express a full range of linguistic meaning. ASL is spoken by over a half million deaf people, mainly in the United States, and has many dialects and varieties. Pidgin versions of ASL are sometimes used therapeutically with certain hearing populations, such as the mentally retarded. (mhi-y)

American Student Union (ASU)

Student collegiate organization formed in 1935 from the merger of the National Student League and the Student League for Industrial Democracy. The ASU had its peak operations in the late 1930s, with an estimated membership of 20,000. It organized one-hour strikes against war and promulgated numerous reforms, including federal aid to education, government youth programs, academic freedom, racial equality, and prolabor advocacy. The signing of the Nazi-Soviet pact in 1939 and anticommunist sentiment led to the collapse of the ASU in 1940–1941. (vmm)

American studies

Examines diverse aspects of social constructions and cultural productions in the Americas, particularly the United States. American studies is a multidisciplinary approach to a diversity of theoretical and methodological analyses of the Americas. Such studies emphasize cultural studies, popular culture, and material culture with regard to a global transitional setting of commodity and cultural exchange. American studies includes knowledge and perspectives from such disciplines as cultural studies, ecology, ethics, government, history, literary criticism, art, politics, sociology, and women's studies. (hrm, ew, jkd)

American Vocational Association (See Association for Career and Technical Education)

Americanization Movement

A term identified with efforts aimed at providing recent immigrants with instruction in the English language and civic education during the early 20th century. Because the size and the "foreign" character of the wave of immigrants coming to America from 1880 to 1920 aroused nativist concerns, Americanization involved mandates for students to assimilate to dominant linguistic, cultural, and political norms. The movement was spurred by the widely accepted concept of the melting pot, the needs of an industrial economy, and the "progressive" concerns of social workers and educators. Stricter immigration laws imposed after World War I made the movement gradually seem unnecessary. (jv)

Americanization programs

A term that was popular in the early part of the 20th century, which describes educational programs for immigrants that provide English and citizenship instruction. (jpc)

Americans with Disabilities Act (ADA)

The Americans with Disabilities Act of 1990 is a broad civil rights law that prohibits discrimination against people with disabilities. As such, it guarantees equal opportunity for individuals with disabilities in the areas of employment, transportation, telecommunications, and access to public places. Schools, both public and private, are mandated to comply with ADA requirements. (acp)

AmeriCorps

A national community service program established in 1993 with the passage of the National Community Service Trust Act. AmeriCorps is an outgrowth of VISTA, the Peace Corps, and other U.S. government service programs. AmeriCorps members number in the thousands and work on programs in the areas of literacy, health education, welfare to work, and a number of other community service initiatives. (jwc)

amygdala

Part of the limbic system, this small structure located deep within the temporal lobe is necessary for both the conscious experience of fear and some of the automatic physical responses associated with fear. The amygdala may also play a role in some positive emotions. (pk1)

analogy

From the Greek *ana logon,* "according to a ratio." Originally a similarity in proportional relationships. A comparison between things based upon observations of a significant similarity between them, while acknowledging that they are otherwise dissimilar. Makers of analogies use them to illustrate or explain complex or unfamiliar ideas. For example, an analogous relationship is often drawn between the aging process and the four seasons (e.g., youth is the spring of one's life, old age the winter). (kpb)

anal stage

The second phase in Freud's theory of psychosocial development is the anal phase, which begins at age two and lasts about one year. During this phase, the young child seeks gratification through either withholding or eliminating feces. During this time the first conflict surfaces between the internal instincts and external demands (from adults). (xss)

See also psychosocial development.

analysis

The process by which one examines a document, event, trend, or other source of data to determine its essential elements or to determine specific factors such as cause, effect, similarity, or difference. Separating the whole into individual parts for comparison in the search for understanding. (jjc, dsm)

analytic writing rubric

A rubric that gives several scores, each one based on a particular component of a student's writing, such as organization or conventions. By assigning separate scores, the instructor gains insight into a writer's proficiency on several individual components of the task. (cld)

analytical philosophy

Although various methods of philosophical analysis have been used since Plato's time, and explicit references to philosophical "analysis" have been common since the 17th century, it was only in the 1960s that the term "analytical philosophy" came into widespread use to refer to the work of Bertrand Russell, G. E. Moore, Ludwig Wittgenstein, Rudolph Carnap, Gilbert Ryle, A. J. Ayer, J. L. Austin, and others. Analytical philosophy is not a "school of thought" united by shared doctrines as much as it is a loosely defined style of investigation employing a variety of logical, linguistic, and epistemological methods, resting in the belief that such methods are useful in solving or dissolving a variety of philosophical problems. (rc)

anchored instruction

Instructional design in which students acquire useful knowledge rather than static factual information through teacher-guided discovery. This model of instruction requires the development and maintenance of an authentic task environment in which the utility of skills and knowledge can be examined as they are acquired, as well as the applicability of both in a given situation or circumstance. (hfs)

andragogy

A term, popularized by Malcolm Knowles in *The Modern Practice of Adult Education,* that describes the science of helping adults learn. It functions under four assumptions: adults are self-directed learners, adults have a reservoir of experience that is a resource for learning, adults are motivated to learn the developmental tasks of their social roles, and adults are looking for learning that serves an immediate need. The term focuses on the needs of the adult learner, as opposed to pedagogy, which is child-centered. Andragogy is now frequently used to refer to learner-centered education for people of any age. (jpc, jsj)

anecdotal notes

A tool used for collecting information as one observes a child's behavior of interest; notes regarding the behavior are jotted down and may include recording frequencies of the behavior over a period of time. The notes may help in identifying patterns regarding the occurrence of the behavior (for example, when, where, and why). (pw)

animation

Bringing to life, animating. In art, the making of an animated cartoon or film in which the illusion of movement is achieved by creating individual frames that capture subtle changes in a drawing over time. Claymation is a version of animation most popular with children in art classes. Instead of drawings, clay figures are adjusted and photographed in frames, capturing their changes over time and giving the illusion of actual motion. (jd)

anime

Anime (pronounced An ee may). Refers to a style of animation developed in Japan primarily featuring bold characters drawn in the style of Japanese comic books (manga). Adult themes, male heroes (e.g., robots, swordsmen), explicit sexuality, and violence are often included. Extremely popular among Japanese teens and young adults, anime is an art movement that has received worldwide attention and is typically included in scholarly study of youth culture. (jd)

Annenberg Rural Challenge

An educational reform movement funded by Walter Annenberg, which aimed at creating a curriculum of place and a set of interstate contacts among 750 participant schools between 1995 and 2000. It lives on strongly in the form of the Rural School and Community Trust, a policy forum, capacity builder, and advocacy group. (lr)

answer keys

Teacher-made or text sheets with answers that serve as tools to aid teachers in assessing student performance on tests. (dsm)

anthropocentrism

The belief that humans are the central and most significant entities on the planet. Recognizable in the Judeo-Christian belief that humanity is created in the likeness of God, but found commonly throughout history. Often seen by environmental theorists as being a key conceptual challenge to be overcome if a more sustainable and equitable world is to be achieved. (sb1)

anthropology

The study of the origins of humans and humanity based on the natural sciences and the humanities and emphasizing cultural and social development. From the Greek, *anthros* meaning the study of humans and *logia* meaning discourse, the term anthropology was first used in 1593. Anthropology includes physical or biological changes and cultural or ethnographical changes, such as the arts and literature, based on the social sciences that provide the tools for scientific inquiry and explanation. In the social studies, anthropology informs the content, processes, and context based on artifacts and evidence gathered by archaeologists associated with the holistic changes experienced by humans over time. (npg)

anthropomorphism

From the Latin *anthropomorphous,* meaning "of human form." The representation of nonhuman beings, whether real or fictitious, in human form. The ascription of human attributes, characteristics, and/or preoccupations to nonhuman beings. In Aesop's fables or the stories of Beatrix Potter, for example, the animals speak to one another in human voices, wear humans' clothes, and have human emotions. Young children often produce anthropomorphic drawings. Their houses or trees will have eyes, arms, and human expression. (kf)

anti-bias curriculum

Planned learning activities that deliberately seek to teach children to value and respect people of all races, cultures, genders, abilities, and ages. A curriculum designed to counter racism, sexism, and other biased and discriminatory aspects of society; to encourage school children to discuss, explore, and be exposed to issues of race, ethnicity, gender, religion, diversity, socioeconomic status, physical ableness, and so on. (jlj, jqa, jwc)

antidepressant

A category of psychotropic medication. Its most common use and intended therapeutic effect is to treat mood disorders, in particular, depression, by acting on neurotransmitters in the brain. The three main types of antidepressants are: monoamine oxidase inhibitors (MAOIs), tricyclic compounds, and selective serotonin re-uptake inhibitors (SSRIs; e.g., Prozac, Zoloft). (mkt)

See also psychotropic.

Antioch Plan

A cooperative work-study plan of education, introduced by Antioch College President Arthur E. Morgan in 1921 as part of a reorganization of the struggling institution. The Antioch Plan is credited with incorporating cooperative education into the liberal arts, departing from the earlier practice of applying the idea to only technical education. The plan calls for students to alternate between course work and employment in an effort to prepare them for leadership roles in the community and in industry, while providing for their development into more well-rounded and complete individuals. (trc)

antioppressive education
A term coined by educator and activist Kevin Kumashiro (2002) in reference to strategies employed by teachers focused on challenging multiple forms of oppression in schools. Antioppressive education is not as concerned with positing a series of strategies and practices, but rather focuses on bringing poststructural conceptual and cultural resources to bear on education discourses and practices with the intent of disrupting systems of oppression functioning unjustly in schools. (bda)

anti-racist education
Used particularly within the United Kingdom and Canada, this term refers to attempts by educators to eliminate racism from schools and society and to help students. Anti-racist education addresses issues in the curriculum as well as in teacher hiring, school policies, and all aspects of school life in which institutional racism may be manifest. (jqa, jwc)

anxiety disorder
A category of mental disorders characterized by excessive or inappropriate anxiety that produces significant distress or impairment in important areas of one's life. Anxiety disorders involve problems with apprehensive anticipation of future danger or misfortune, frequently accompanied by a feeling of dysphoria or somatic symptoms of tension. Among the most common mental disorders found in the general population, anxiety disorders include panic disorder, agoraphobia, specific phobia, social phobia, obsessive-compulsive disorder, posttraumatic stress disorder, acute stress disorder, and generalized anxiety disorder. (bd)

anxiolytic
A category of psychotropic medication. Its most common use and intended therapeutic effect is to prevent or manage anxiety and anxiety-related symptoms. The term anxiolytic may also be used to describe the antianxiety effect of a given treatment. (bd)

See also psychotropic.

aphasia
A neurological disorder leading to language disorders that are not caused by specific sensory problems or broad cognitive impairment. Individuals with aphasia generally display problems with spoken communication, either in those with severely impaired speech (nonfluent) or in highly verbal individuals whose speech contains no meaning (fluent). (jcp)

APL (See Adult Performance Level)

APLU (See Association of Public and Land-Grant Universities)

APPA (See Association of Higher Education Facilities Officers)

appellate courts
Increasingly involved in school matters, an appellate court is a state court that has the power to review the judgment of another tribunal in order to evaluate the decision and administer justice at a higher level. The officials of this court review trial records from a lower court that have resulted in a decision considered adverse by one side. (mm)

applications-based learning
Knowledge associated with academic subject matter used to solve actual problems encountered in the workplace, often through simulations. (db)

applied academics
Courses that emphasize academic subject matter as utilized in real-world circumstances, hands-on learning activities, and problems drawn from the workplace (e.g., applied mathematics, applied biology). (db)

applied arts
Produced primarily for utilitarian purposes, the applied arts include architecture,

ceramics, jewelry, textiles, and musical instruments. A distinction between applied and fine arts came into view during the Industrial Revolution when arts education addressed contemporary needs such as technical drawing and product design. In reaction to industrialization, some American artists expressed a need to replace dying spiritual values with purely aesthetic ones, setting fine art above and apart from the rest of life. Nonetheless, the values of craft and related systems of aesthetics are often defended in a challenge to the distinction between the fine and the applied arts. (kpb)

applied behavior analysis (ABA)

ABA is a behavior modification technique that uses consequences to affect behavior. ABA was derived from B. F. Skinner's work and is based on the principle that rewarded or reinforced behavior will increase, while ignored or punished behaviors will decrease. ABA provides the basis for one popular treatment method for young children with autism, but it can be used with other behavioral issues, such as toilet training. (vm)

apprentice

An individual who, in agreement with an employer and under the supervision of that employer, learns a skilled trade, occupation, or job. In teacher education, a preservice or novice teacher who is learning through participation about authentic practice—the ordinary daily practices of teachers in his or her field—from an experienced teacher. (jm, peb)

See also youth apprentice.

apprentice coordinator (See coordinator, apprentice)

apprentice method

A plan of instruction whereby an inexperienced performer or worker is matched with one or more experienced, well-qualified workers for learning skills and competencies in a vocation, occupation, or profession. (jm)

apprentice teacher

A preservice or novice teacher who is learning to teach through classroom participation with an experienced teacher. Also called resident teacher. (dm2, eb)

apprenticeship

An occupational and educational practice where a person, under a written agreement and the direction of an already skilled employee, learns a skilled or semiskilled trade, occupation, or job, usually requiring two or more years of supervised work experience on the job, supplemented by related classroom instruction. (ea, jm)

See also registered apprenticeship.

apprenticeship, registered (See registered apprenticeship)

apprenticeship education

A form of education where an individual or apprentice signs an agreement with a sponsor to be trained in the sponsor's field of work. It is the sponsor's responsibility to educate the apprentice in a learning environment that is usually hands-on in nature. This form of education was extremely popular in the eighteenth and early nineteenth century United States before the founding of public schools, and often included a responsibility on the part of the employer to provide basic literacy skills. (rih)

apprentice training

An organized system for providing young people with the technical skills and theoretical knowledge needed for competent performance in skilled occupations and related studies. (jm)

approximation

An inexact result or relationship, adequate for the given purpose. All measurements and calculations derived there from are considered approximations rather than exact values, because the tools used for measuring are precise within a certain range of values. Their closeness to the real value is dependent on the precision of the measurement tool. (amr)

aptitude

A natural or acquired ability to be or become proficient in a given area. Aptitude may be measured by the effort or time required by a learner to reach the point of mastery. (jw)

aptitude, vocational (See vocational aptitude)

aptitude test

One of a class of standardized instruments designed to assess an individual's potential performance/achievement in a particular area. Unlike achievement tests, aptitude tests attempt to predict one's future ability to develop skills or to attain information. These tests range from specific (e.g., assessment of clerical skills) to general (e.g., assessment of intelligence). (kc, scmc, bdj)

AR (See augmented reality)

arbitrary constant

A constant that assumes a certain value for a particular problem. (kgh)

archaeology in the social studies

As the study of the human past using the evidence of material culture, both content and methods from archaeology are sometimes included in social studies courses in various ways. Archaeological content extends knowledge of human chronology, technology, migration, inventiveness, and culture formation and complexity beyond that gained from historical records alone. Methods of inquiry and analysis used in archaeology are also helpful in promoting cognitive skills in students at various levels. Because archaeological information and skills are interdisciplinary in nature, an archaeological perspective can serve as an integrating vehicle for various social studies areas, such as history, geography, and economics. (msb)

architecture

From the Latin *archi,* meaning a leading and distinguished sort, and *tecture,* meaning pertaining to construction, architecture is the art and science of designing and constructing buildings, structures, and other environmental features. Like other art forms, architecture is concerned with principles such as design, composition, form, light, color, and patterns. It is distinguished by its fundamental focus on usable space. While painting represents space and sculpture displaces space, architecture encloses space. The study of architecture introduces a critical approach to investigating and understanding the structures in our communities. (npg, kf)

area career center

A specialized public or nonprofit educational institution used exclusively or primarily for the preparation of students seeking employment immediately after high school or to continue at the postsecondary level. (db)

area studies

The interdisciplinary study of culturally coherent geographical regions through the use of a multidisciplinary approach that draws upon literature and scholarship in history, geography, anthropology, sociology, art, and language. The term originally referred to the study of the classical civilizations of the ancient world. This interdisciplinary field focused on the ways in which the Greco-Roman civilizations of the Mediterranean basin were to be understood and analyzed. Since World War II, the term "area studies" has come to include the broader range of geographical regions for examination. (hrm, ew, jkd)

area vocational school

A term currently coming into use for a vocational school at the secondary level that serves joint vocational school districts, set up so that each school district need not have a vocational high school of its own.

May be named in some places "joint vocational school." (jb)

arête

The Greek word most often translated as "virtue," it corresponds more closely to the idea of "excellence of a kind." That is, there is an *arête* for humans (what we call virtue), but also an excellence for horses or even bricks. *Arête* is different for each kind of thing, and each kind of thing has its own *arête,* form of excellence, its own fulfillment of an ideal. In Greek thought, the task of an individual is to develop his or her own personal *arête,* that is, to be virtuous. The educational task is to develop *arête* (virtue) in the student. (jc)

argumentation

In writing, a type of text that sets forth an argument, which is then supported with evidence. This type of writing is important because it is a genre students are often expected to produce using academic discourse. (cld)

arithmetic

The science or art of computing by positive, real numbers. The study of numbers and the properties and operations that can be performed on them. Facts and computational procedures. (dc)

arithmetic progression

A list of numbers in which there is one common difference between any and all consecutive numbers in the list. For example, the list {1, 2, 3} is an arithmetic progression because between 2 and 1 the difference is 1, between 3 and 2 the difference is 1, and thus between all consecutive numbers in the list, there is a single common difference. Additionally, the common difference may be negative or less than one. (dbc)

Armed Forces Qualification Test (AFQT)

A screening test developed by the U.S. military that measures vocabulary, arithmetic, spatial ability, and tool recognition. The test places adults into one of five levels, with one being the highest and five being the lowest. (jpc)

Army Alpha Test

A standardized test given to recruits in World War I, believed to be the first paper and pencil mental tests designed for use on mass groups. This test was used to classify recruits by officer or enlisted ranks and comprised true/false and multiple-choice questions aimed at measuring the person's English, arithmetic, and analytical level of knowledge. The test was revised when the Army realized the majority of recruits were illiterate, and therefore the measurements were incorrect. The Army Alpha tests paved the way for widespread testing in the public schools as part of the 20th-century intelligence testing movement. (rih)

Army Beta Test

The revised version of the Army Alpha Test that tried to identify the best placement for recruits. Unlike the Alpha version of the test, worded questions were limited, because the Beta targeted illiterate and non-English-speaking recruits. Illustrations and diagrams were used to ask and answer questions. (rih)

art

Creations made by human beings that express their individual and shared humanity, tell the stories of their lives, and describe and question their realities. Once thought to include only those products (created in artistic domains such as painting, sculpture, music, and dance) that could be described as beautiful, works of art can be difficult to confront and complex in their structure. In light of the difficulty of determining what is and is not art, philosopher Nelson Goodman suggested rewriting the question of "what is art?" to "when is art?," suggesting that the context and appreciation of an object determined its symbolic and transitory status as art. An activity reserved for and determined by human beings, art is the product of emotion and thought and worthy of continued study throughout our children's education. (jd)

art area

An area where children can express their creativity through the use of many types of materials and media, which may incorporate colors, shapes, sounds, and textures. This area encourages the child to express ideas, perceptions, and impressions of the world around him or her by permitting exploration and experimentation of artistic materials and techniques. Common tools found in the area are scissors, staples, stamps, brushes, awl, hole puncher, sponges, cups, rulers, stencils, eyedropper, ink pads, popsicle sticks, potatoes, paint, easels, and the like, which allow the senses to stimulate a child's creativity. Children can be encouraged to use materials they find interesting, such as leaves, pasta, pictures from magazines, and so on, in their creative expression through art activities. (pw)

art cart

A sign of the marginalization of the arts curriculum, the art cart is the vehicle that art teachers wheel into classrooms for arts activities when no space, studio, or room has been designated for holding art classes. The cart holds paints, crayons, papers, and other supplies to scaffold in-class arts activities, often restricted to table-top art. (jd)

art criticism

Writing that evaluates art, such as the criticism of Clement Greenberg; or any writing on art, such as the historical work of Georgio Vasari. A distinction is often made between art criticism, which is outwardly judgmental and opinionated, and art history, which is ostensibly more neutral and factual. Description and evaluation, however, are arguably mixed in all writing. John Dewey proposed that art criticism should not appraise or judge, and others view criticism as imaginative reenactment of creation or perception. In Discipline Based Art Education (DBAE), art criticism entails describing, interpreting, evaluating, and theorizing about works of art. (lj)

art education

Education in the various forms of art (e.g., music, dance, visual arts, and drama) in American schools dates back to before the turn of the 19th century. Its purposes over time have included the acquisition of skills to advance a developing nation, the expression of emotion in the development of the whole child, and most recently, the recognition of links with cognition that suggest the inclusion of arts in the curriculum to develop habits of learning that have implications across academic subjects. The arts have traditionally been marginalized or relegated to extracurricular activity. Arts advocates struggle today as they have throughout history to find timely rationales for the inclusion of arts learning in our children's education. (jd)

art history

Knowledge or study of the visual arts within a historical framework. Until the 19th century, accounts of art and aesthetics implied that there were traceable patterns of historical development within the visual arts. In the 19th century, a concerted attempt was made to give art history a philosophical basis. At the end of the 20th century, art history in the Western world was characterized by a pluralism of approaches. The field is no longer concerned with creating one comprehensive and universal account of art. Art history generally flourishes in advanced industrial societies, counting as a luxury in less developed nations. (kf)

art integration

Incorporating the arts into the general curriculum. Art integration can range from the simple inclusion of an arts activity (e.g., writing and producing a play about a historical event studied in history class) to full-scale, schoolwide, project-based curricula (e.g., studying heroes across all grade levels and disciplines, including as equal partners art, drama, music, and visual arts). Arts-integrated curricula are most effective when nonarts as well as arts teachers study each others' objectives and practices with an eye to developing balanced, arts-integrated curricula. (jd)

art museum
A building where art objects of interest and/or value are collected, conserved, exhibited, and interpreted. The word "museum" derives from the Greek, meaning "abode of the muses." While some argue that art museums are educational instruments by virtue of the systematic organization and presentation of their collections, others insist that it is the educational programs that they offer (which grew widely in the 20th century) for school children and adults that give them an educational perspective. Unlike history, science, or children's museums that are clearly dedicated to educational objectives, the priorities and usefulness of the art museum to general education is a subject of debate. (kpb)

art specialist
An individual responsible for in-school art education (typically in visual arts) in K–12. Often professionally certified, the art specialist either works in a designated art room in a particular district school or, more frequently, delivers arts education to a variety of schools during any given week, rotating through grade levels and classrooms. Art specialists have been phased out of many schools in this country in which budget cuts have provoked a reliance on art taught by classroom teachers or by visiting artists, or even the elimination of in-school art education. In areas in which art education is being reinstated (e.g., New York City), the need for art specialists is growing, and issues of appropriate training abound. (kpb)

art therapy
A human-service profession that employs the artistic process in many different art forms for therapeutic purposes. The activity of painting may be used to assess and treat developmental, medical, educational, social, or psychological problems. Artwork created as art therapy is considered reflective of the artist's abilities, concerns, conflicts, personality, and interests. Art and music therapy are large and growing fields, separate from, but not exclusive of, notions of healing and the arts. While healing and the arts value and practice art in a therapeutic sense, art therapy utilizes art making in the actual assessment of and treatment for problems recognized in the human development and psychological fields. (km)

articulated credit
Credit for courses taken at the secondary level that counts toward a postsecondary degree or certificate. Credit awarded once the student has enrolled at the postsecondary level and demonstrated mastery through assessment, more advanced course-taking, or other demonstration of competence. (db)

articulated curriculum (See curriculum, articulated)

articulation, horizontal
Continuity existing among the various parts of a curriculum at a particular level so that, taken together, the parts have some degree of unity and coherence at a specific level. (db)

articulation, program (See program articulation)

articulation, vertical
Continuity and interrelation between a lower-level grade or institution and higher levels to enhance the interrelation of successive levels of the educational system to facilitate the continuous, economical, and efficient progression of learners (e.g., 2 + 2, 2 + 2 + 2). (db)

articulation agreement

A formal agreement between educational institutions, typically secondary schools and community and technical colleges or between community and technical colleges and four-year colleges and universities, ensuring a sequential and coherent progression of skills and knowledge from the secondary to the postsecondary level. A formal agreement designating how college-level credits are awarded for student mastery of secondary-school courses and course content. (db)

articulatory phonetics

A term that relates to how the articulators of the vocal tract make speech sounds. The study of these processes allows for categorization and classification of the features of speech sounds. For example, it is possible to categorize sounds as either vowels or consonants according to the way in which they are produced. Vowels can be differentiated from one another by the portion of the tongue used in articulation, the tongue position, and the degree of lip rounding. Consonants are differentiated from one another by voice, place, and manner of articulation. Understanding of how speech sounds are produced can give educators insights into children's speech sound errors, as well as errors in decoding and spelling. (rcr)

See also phonetics.

artifact

Any object made or modified by human beings for use in a particular culture. Examples of artifacts include automobiles as well as stone tools. Artifacts can serve as primary sources for learning about human activity, belief systems, and lifestyles in different time periods and cultures. (dv, msb)

artificial intelligence (AI)

An attempt to emulate the capabilities, if not the underlying processes, of the human mind using computer software, hardware, or both. Artificial Intelligence researchers contribute to a better understanding of how to educate and how to learn through the construction of architectures and algorithms that reflect human information-processing techniques. The successes and failures of these systems often provide empirical data that inform our understanding of how physical entities can be "intelligent." (eh)

artist

An individual who regularly creates artistic objects (e.g., paintings, sculptures, musical scores), performs (e.g., dance, music, theater), or writes (e.g., poetry, literature). Young children are often regarded as natural artists, creating and performing with enthusiasm and ease. As a possible result of society's ambivalence toward artists or of schools' limited attention to the arts, most students graduate as self-declared nonartists. Nonetheless, artists historically have provided positive role models demonstrating civic responsibility through initiatives such as educational public art or the creation of arts centers that open doors for disenfranchised youth. (jd)

artist-in-residence

A professional artist who works in or with artistic or educational environments for a sustained length of time. In an artistic environment (e.g., museum, artists' colony, community art center), the artist-in-residence is often given funding, workspace, and support to create new artworks and may be required to educate or involve the public in his or her artistic processes. In a school, the artist-in-residence works with groups of students on specific art projects (e.g., a theater specialist might do drama workshops with groups of students and work with students to create an original play at the culmination of the residency). (em)

artistic

Behavior that is of or like an artist (a maker of art). Having to do with the making and the ability to make art. While artistic behavior might be thought of as relevant to any art making (painting, clay-making, photography, etc.), it is mostly reserved for the description of art making thought to be at, or as if it were at, a professional level. Similarly, children who demonstrate perceived talents in art are said to be "artistic" and thought to be imbued with a special variety of talents. Remembering that the modernist movement in art included the replication of artistic techniques used by very young children, we may think of all children as coming to school with artistic gifts. (jd)

See also art; artistic process.

artistic domains

The domains of art are delineated according to the various sets of symbols out of which artists craft meaning. Accordingly, visual arts, drama, poetry, and music may be considered different artistic domains because of the different symbols (image, action, word, and notes, respectively) each offers to the artist to employ. (jd)

artistic process

The process that artists employ to create works of art. The artistic process is often characterized as being integrative of thought, feeling, and skill; flexible, marked by an appreciation of mistakes as generative; and considerate of the views of maker and perceiver. Csikszentmihalyi has studied the intense and transformative quality of the artistic process as representative of what he calls "flow." Educators have emulated aspects of the artistic process, such as ongoing reflection, process-based assessment, and dedicated attention to process over product in framing pedagogical strategies such as the portfolio-based assessment. (jd)

See also portfolio assessment.

arts, extracurricular

The most usual of scenarios for arts learning in our schools, in this model, the arts are viewed as extras and are reserved for spaces outside of the daily curriculum, like the after-school play or poetry club. Extracurricular arts programs are often a challenge for students and teachers to balance: Late rehearsals five nights a week may take a toll on student performance in school. When schools do not provide an arts extras situation, parents often find them for themselves in the piano teacher who comes to the house, the city children's theater, or the community art center. (jd)

arts cultura curriculum

A curriculum in which the arts are seen as connecting the individual child's culture (worldview) to the cultures of immediate communities (including neighborhood, families, school), to the cultures of nations and race, and to culture itself as humankind. Based on such a cycle, the essentiality of arts education emerges as a way to provide the tools for and facilitate meaning making and communication within and across all cultural perspectives. Accordingly, the arts cultura curriculum features the study of artistic products and processes associated with each and all perspectives embodied in this interconnected paradigm. (jd)

arts education

The broadest descriptor for training in the art forms taught in schools. The term "art education" is generally associated with the visual arts (including drawing, painting, sculpture, photography etc.); music education with music theory and performance (singing or playing an instrument); dance education with venues such as ballet, modern, and tap; and drama education, with role play, improvisation, and theater production. But the term "arts education" refers to all art forms and their relative inclusion (dance is least frequently taught) in the curriculum. (jd)

arts integration

Through arts integration, teachers and students approach a single topic (e.g., heroism or capitalism) through a number of interrelating lenses, some of them mainstream (like history or math) and others arts-based (like visual arts or music). Notably in this venue, the arts are on equal academic footing with other subjects, and arts specialists, artists, and nonarts teachers collectively employ learning methods that are usually associated with the arts. Examples include improvising dramatic scenes from history in the study of the Civil War, comparing the intervals in African drumming with mathematical ratios in the study of structural relationships, or comparing the composition of a painting with that of a poem in the consideration of balance in science. (jd)

ARTS PROPEL

An arts-curricular approach developed at Harvard Project Zero in the early 1980s, which builds on the activities of the professional artist in various artistic domains. PROPEL focuses on three aspects of the artist's process: production (the making of art, at the center of activity); perception (the attention to details/response to the work); and reflection (thinking about the activity in terms of works that have been made by other artists). Students maintain processfolios that document their artistic process over time rather than store examples of their best work. Tested in the Pittsburgh Public Schools, PROPEL is often contrasted with Discipline-Based Art Education (DBAE) as a cognitive approach that features *making* at the center of arts study. (jd)

arts-based curriculum

In which the arts are featured both as core subjects and as entry points into all aspects of the curriculum. The arts in this paradigm are seen as a basis for learning, a model for learning, and a way into learning. In this framework, students study the arts in their own right and learn other subjects through the window of the arts. For example, the composition of a painting can serve as a way into balance in writing or symmetry in science. For examples of arts-based curricula, see the Bernstein Institute and A schools. (jd)

arts-expanded curriculum

In an arts-expanded curriculum, the arts are employed as vehicles for extending school-based education beyond school walls into the larger community. In an arts-expanded curriculum, student learning includes regular trips to the art museum (a place that when visited by schools at all is rarely visited more than once a year), or the local community art center, or concerts in the setting of the concert hall. Arts-expansion models focus on the familiarization of students with behaviors in and the resources of cultural institutions. (jd)

arts-included curriculum

Curriculum in which the arts are included in the standard roster of courses offered. In an arts-inclusion school, for example, all of the children might have, along with spelling, Latin, math, English, and social studies, classes in visual art, music, theater, and dance. In an arts-included curriculum, the arts are taught alongside of and considered on an equal par with what are more traditionally regarded as important, core, or basic subjects. Examples of arts-included curricula can be found in arts magnet or pilot schools and independent schools dedicated to the inclusion of art in the general curriculum. (jd)

arts-infused curriculum

Curriculum in which the arts are infused into the general curriculum, brought in almost as a handmaiden to other subjects. Music of a period may be played on a CD in the history class; students may be asked to create felt collage maps in geography or tribal masks in social studies. Arts-infused curricular activities include the case of the visiting artist—the poet coming into English class, the folk-singer in history, or the group Shakespeare and Company performing for the whole school. In arts-infused curricula, the arts enter the scene from outside in and enrich whatever is going on. (jd)

arts-professional curriculum
Curriculum in which the arts are taught with an eye to serious training and preparation for adult careers in the arts. Even in arts-based or arts magnet schools, careers in the arts are not always viewed as viable outcomes for student learning. Arts learning is more often thought of as a means to something else—even if it is knowledge of a vocabulary that will enable students to participate as literate appreciators of dance, music, and visual arts. Most often the students who seek arts-professional curricula have recognized talent or a belief in the benefits of professional training. (jd)

ASE (See adult secondary education)

ASHE (See Association for the Study of Higher Education)

ASL (See American Sign Language)

ASPIRA
A national association devoted to the education and leadership development of Puerto Rican and other Latino youth. ASPIRA ("aspire") was founded in 1961 by Antonia Pantoja and a group of Puerto Rican educators in New York City as a means to combat low educational attainment among Puerto Rican youth. In 2000, ASPIRA had offices in six states and Puerto Rico. Youth Leadership Development (YDL) programs carried out in the school-based ASPIRA clubs form the core of the organization. Students learn the ASPIRA process of "awareness, analysis, and action," through participation in leadership training, cultural enrichment activities, and community action projects. (vmm)

aspiration, career or occupational
A goal-directed attitude that involves conception of the self in relation to a particular level of the occupational prestige hierarchy or career progression. (jm)

assertive discipline
Developed by Lee Canter in the 1970s, assertive discipline is an approach to classroom management that emphasizes the right of teachers to insist on appropriate and responsible behavior from students. In assertive discipline, teachers develop a discipline plan consisting of clearly stated rules for behavior, disciplinary consequences for rule violation, and positive reinforcement for appropriate behavior. (ba)

assessment
Any method used to better understand the current knowledge that a student possesses. Assessment may affect decisions about grades, advancement, placement, instructional needs, and curriculum. Information gathered may include social, educational, and psychological observations used to identify an individual's strengths and weaknesses. The methods and procedures used in gathering and interpreting information about students, institutions, and programs for purposes of evaluation, appraisal, accreditation. (dsm, sr, cf)

assessment center
An organization or organizational unit that uses multiple evaluation techniques (exercises, simulations, discussions, interviews, etc.) to assess an individual's behaviors; typically used prior to making a hiring or promotion decision, to identify people who possess qualities or competencies related to successful job performance. At a college or university, a unit that tests students prior to their placement in courses or programs. (chb)

assessment of prior learning
A process for recognizing and assigning academic value to learning that adults have achieved through formal education or through informal, nonacademic experiences. Among the methods of assessment

are examinations and reviews of portfolios that document an individual's learning. (chb)

assigned responsibilities

Duties and activities that are required for effective performance in a particular job classification; one-half of an old maxim that responsibilities can be assigned to others, but they cannot be delegated. (cf)

See also delegated authority.

assignment

The act of prescribing mental or physical tasks to a group or to an individual. The given duties or work to be completed by a student or a class. (jw)

assimilation

Jean Piaget's "Theory of Cognitive Development" describes the process of encoding new information into cognitive structures as assimilation. A child's reference to an unfamiliar animal as "dog" is an instance of incorporating something new into an existing category. In this instance, the child has generalized in terms of his or her existing schemes. (mf)

See also cognitive development.

assistantship

The opportunity for an enrolled student to work on a college campus or other related site, usually in the area of the student's study. The work can be teaching, research, or administrative. An assistantship usually involves a stipend, and a discount or waiver of tuition. (cf)

assistive technology (AT)

The use of devices and/or methods to increase the mobility, communication, access to education, and overall independence of people with disabilities by compensating for functional limitations. Assistive technology can range from sophisticated high-tech computer software and hardware to low-tech devices such as ergonomic can openers or TV remote controls.

In education, low- or high-technology approaches for enabling students with disabilities to access or demonstrate their understanding of the general curriculum. For instance, to facilitate reading challenges, a low-tech approach, such as using a piece of cardboard to help track the text on the page, or a high-tech approach, like a text-to-speech tool, may be employed. (nl1, ecb, kg1)

Association for Career and Technical Education (ACTE)

Founded in 1926 as the American Vocational Association, ACTE is a national education association dedicated to the advancement of education that prepares youth and adults for successful careers. (ea)

Association for Career and Technical Education Research (ACTER)

Organized in 1966, as the American Vocational Education Research Association, ACTER is a professional association for scholars and others with research interests in the relationship between education and work. The purposes of the organization are to stimulate and foster research and development activities related to career and technical education, stimulate the development of training programs designed to prepare persons for responsibilities in research in career and technical education, and to disseminate research findings. (ch, sa)

Association for Institutional Research (AIR)

This international association is dedicated to professional growth of all who participate in decision making related to higher education via management research, policy analysis, and planning. Its members work in many different postsecondary areas (finance, academic affairs, instruction, student services, and institutional development) and in various offices at the international, state, system, or campus levels. (cf)

Association for the Study of Higher Education (ASHE)

A scholarly society, ASHE is dedicated to higher education as a field of study. The Association promotes collaboration among its members and others engaged in the study of higher education through research, conferences, and publications. (cf)

Association of American Universities (AAU)

The AAU was founded in 1900 by 14 universities offering the PhD degree. Today AAU consists of 60 American universities and two Canadian universities with approximately half being public and half private institutions. The association serves its members in two major ways: (a) it assists them in developing national policy positions on issues that relate to higher education; and (b) it provides them with a forum for discussing a broad range of other institutional issues. (cf)

Association of College and University Housing Officers–International (ACUHO-I)

Founded in 1951, ACUHO-I is an international higher education association dedicated to representing and serving students and staff members involved in student housing environments in the academy. (cf)

Association of Higher Education Facilities Officers (APPA)

Founded in 1914, APPA (acronym for Association of Physical Plant Administrators, its former name) is an international higher education association dedicated to maintaining, protecting, and promoting the quality of educational facilities, including buildings and infrastructure, in the academy. (cf)

Association of Physical Plant Administrators (See Association of Higher Education Facilities Officers)

Association of Public and Land-grant Universities (APLU)

Founded in 1887, the association adopted the name National Association of State Universities and Land-Grant Colleges (NASULGC) in 1963 with the merger of the National Association of State Universities and the American Association of Land-Grant Colleges and State Universities. APLU is the nation's oldest higher education association. It is a voluntary association of public universities, land-grant institutions, and public university systems, and APLU campuses are located in all 50 states, the U.S. territories and the District of Columbia. As of May 2011 the association's membership stood at 221 institutions, including 76 land-grant universities (of which 18 are the historically black public institutions created by the Second Morrill Act of 1890) and 27 public higher education systems. In 1994, 33 tribal colleges became land-grant institutions and are represented through membership of the American Indian Higher Education Consortium (AIHEC). In March 2009 the name changed to the Association of Public and Land-Grant Universities to increase recognition of the association's core values and identity. (cf, npo)

associative play

Associative play occurs when children are involved in a similar activity, usually near each other, but where the children are free to pursue their own individual interests. A child may imitate the behaviors of the other child, exchange information, or trade materials during this type of play. The children may build upon each other's ideas or contributions, but interdependency is not required during the play activity. This type of play can commonly be seen with preschoolers. (yb)

associative property (addition)

The property stating that when finding the sum of three or more numbers, any two numbers may be added in any order to obtain the correct sum. The grouping of the sums has no effect on the final answer; for example, $1 + (2 + 3) = (1 + 2) + 3$. (ps)

associative property (multiplication)
The property stating that when finding the product of three or more numbers, any two numbers may be multiplied in any order to obtain the correct product. The grouping of the products has no effect on the final answer; example, $1 \times (2 \times 3) = (1 \times 2) \times 3$. (ps)

assumption
A presumed belief or supposition applied to a person, group of persons, place, and/or thing without concrete evidence of proof or accuracy. An assumption may be a statement based on hypothesis, theory, conjecture, or guess that is taken for granted or accepted without scientific analysis. (npg)

astronomy
The branch of science that studies the universe both as a whole and as individual, interrelated parts. Includes topics such as the relative positions of celestial bodies, energy and matter distribution, history, composition, exploration, and evolution of the universe and its parts. (tw)

asynchronous discussion
Typically, an online discussion where the participants do not have to be present at the same time. For example, participants in an asynchronous discussion can offer comments, read previous posts by others, and continue the discussion over time. (mid)

asynchronous learning
A learning process in which interactions between instructors and students occur with a time delay so students can self-pace their own learning process. For example, threaded discussions and wikis enable asynchronous interactions during online learning. (hh)
  See also synchronous learning.

at risk
A term used to describe children who have, or could have, problems with their development that might affect their ability to learn. (sr)

ataxia
Lack of muscle coordination, appearance of being clumsy, literally "lack of order." Particularly associated with cerebral palsy, individuals with ataxia may have difficulty with standing, walking, and other physical activities. (sr)

atelier
A room in which an artist or designer works. The studio in which a developing artist apprentices with a veteran artist, as did many great artists in the 19th century in France. The "atelier" model for art education involves this paradigm, in which young artists work to assist, learn from, and be mentored by veteran artists. Tim Rollins and his Art and Knowledge Workshop KOS (Kids of Survival) in the Bronx, New York, is a well-known example of atelier-style learning. (jd)

athletic training
The care, prevention, and rehabilitation of athletic injuries. (rf)

athletics
Organized efforts to engage students in physical activity to foster learning about teamwork, sportsmanship, and competition; competitive sports/activities involving an individual or group of people, incorporating the physical skills of individuals. (dsm)

at-risk children
Children susceptible to the adverse effects of physical, genetic, physiological, environmental, or developmental conditions are said to be "at risk." Examples of environmental conditions that could place children at risk include low income of families, lack of health care services, and caregiving that is neglectful or abusive. (mc2)

at-risk student
A student who shows greater disposition for dropping out of an educational program or institution before completion than a typical student. (db)

attachment style (See attachment theory)

attachment theory
A psychological theory proposed originally by John Bowlby, which attempts to explain the human tendency to develop strong bonds with important others. A basic premise of attachment theory is that humans have a genetic predisposition to exhibit various behaviors that keep them in close proximity to important others. How important others typically respond to proximity-seeking behaviors will establish a basis from which an individual evaluates and responds to subsequent interpersonal interactions. A related term is attachment style, which represents an attempt to categorize common patterns of interpersonal interaction. (kc, scmc, bdj)

attendance
The act of being present. The people or number of people present. (jw)

attending behavior
A microcounseling skill used to encourage, or in some instances discourage, talking. Involves orienting oneself physically toward a client and communicating, both verbally ("ummhmm," "please tell me more") and nonverbally (affirming head nods, open body posture), interest in what a client is saying and/or not saying. Skillful use of attending behaviors allows a counselor, or therapist, to identify and interpret a client's intended/unintended message(s) more easily. The appropriateness of these behaviors is, however, culturally determined. (ksp)

attending skills
Skills that involve the pragmatics of listening, turn-taking, topic maintenance, and retelling for understanding, all of which are part of communication skills. (pw)

attention
Attention is the cognitive process of selectively concentrating on, and biasing processing toward, a subset of information from among the general pool of information available for processing at any point in time. This general pool of information includes both information currently delivered through sensory channels, such as the auditory, visual, and tactile, as well as information already present in memory. Attention is a limited capacity process, meaning that only a limited number of blocks of information can be attended to at any point in time. Processing a larger number of blocks will have to be done in a serial fashion. Importantly, attention also has to be understood as a bidirectional process, with both a bottom-up and a top-down component. The bottom-up component is present, for example, when we hear our name being mentioned in a nearby conversation even though we were at the time engaged in a different conversation ourselves, with the perceptual process driving what is being attended to in a reflexive manner. In contrast, the top-down component is present, for example, when we force ourselves to study algebra on a nice summer day with all of our siblings having fun playing out in the garden in front of the house, regulating in a voluntary manner what is being attended to. (mf2)

Attention Deficit Disorder (ADD)
Difficulty in focusing on information and sustaining attention. May be combined with hyperactivity (ADHD), characterized by overactive behavior and impulsivity. (sr)

attention span
The span or time spent on attending to a task, whether the task is listening to a story being told, making a product, or conversing with a peer. Children that have

short attention spans usually have a problem with inappropriate behavior as well as a lack of listening skills. Increasing attention span to task helps children accomplish tasks and build self-esteem, deterring them from inappropriate behavior. (pw)

attitudes

Attitudes exist in a person's mind as abstractions and cannot be quantified. These beliefs represent a disposition toward people, behaviors, or things. Actions can be observed that are made based on these beliefs. Law binds some of these, and some are bound by society (family and friends). Values shape an individual's attitudes toward actions, people, and things. Attitudes also direct a person's aspirations and ambitions. (kf1)

audience

Individuals that perceive, respond to, and/or judge works of art from the perspective of those that fill the seats in an auditorium, taking in a play or dance performance; a reader of a book of poetry; or visitor to an art museum. The audience completes the cycle from creation to appreciation. Through the sense they make of what they see, hear, or read, audiences contribute new meaning and assign place and value to works of art. (jd)

audiobook

Also called books on tape or books on CD. Audiobooks are recordings of people reading books. The books are read aloud by a live reader and recorded for playback. Many people enjoy audiobooks, but they are also used as an accommodation for students who are vision-impaired or have dyslexia. The verbal presentation of written material gives these students access to grade-appropriate text. (ab1)

See also Recording for the Blind and Dyslexic.

audition

A short performance given by a performing artist (e.g., actor, musician, or dancer) to show his or her ability and suitability for a particular venue (e.g., play, film, or show). Often called the "try out," auditions are used in schools to determine the cast (lead roles and other parts) of dramatic and musical productions. Auditions are often required of students applying to performing arts-based schools and to community art centers. (kbc)

auditory discrimination

The ability to recognize the likenesses and differences in sounds. Specifically, for speech sounds, the ability to tell differences in phonemes, stress, or intonation patterns. Usually, an auditory discrimination test presents pairs of words that are different only in one phoneme (e.g., *pat-bat*) and asks the listener to determine the likeness or difference of the pairs. Auditory discrimination is often tested in the context of second/foreign-language learning, in the therapeutic setting for treating language acquisition problems, or for the diagnosis of comprehensive reading abilities. (h-jk)

auditory phonetics (See phonetics)

augmented reality

Also known as "AR," augmented reality is an emerging technology that overlays the real world, whether site-specific or unspecific, with virtual information. It is most currently being used in education to create simulations that use location-aware handheld computers. Students physically work through interdisciplinary simulations in the real world, using collaborative learning and problem-solving skills. As GPS-tracked locations are approached, new virtual information appears in a variety of multimedia formats that allow users to retrieve content, analyze data, and collaborate in order to progress to the next stage of the simulation. (kd)

Ausubelian program

An approach to preschool curriculum and instruction that balances child-directed and teacher-directed instruction. In this approach, the teacher takes the lead to teach and model, using "zones of proximal development," or windows of opportunity, to relay important concepts. This program supports "subsumption" learning or "advanced organizing lessons," in which children are first taught themes or superconcepts and then gradually learn the more detailed aspects of the lesson, often referred to as "hierarchical classification." (kdc)

authentic assessment

A form of assessment that offers an alternative to standardized tests. It helps measure how effectively students apply knowledge to the real world. Authentic assessments come in many forms (e.g., work samples, teacher report forms, and observation notes), but all are connected to the real world. An assessment that is designed to closely mirror the teaching and learning process, resulting in greater instructional fidelity for the tests. (aw, peb)

authentic instruction

Activities that help establish relationships between school-based learning and work-based learning as described in the School to Work Opportunities Act of 1994. Activities may include encouraging business involvement, evaluating program outcomes, providing technical assistance to teachers, and matching students with work-based learning opportunities. (sa, kg)

See also School-to-Career System.

authenticity

The experience of authenticity relates to one's sense of agency or meaningful engagement in the world. What is authentic is understood by the individual to be genuinely one's own or inherently true. As such, an authentic education seeks to promote a similarly self-affirming yet socially sanctioned engagement in the world. Notions of authenticity in education have changed over time and vary across cultures. A robust pursuit of authenticity in education considers the construction of particular notions of truth while seeking to address change, complexity, local needs, and unprescribed results. (ak, asf)

authoring tool

A software application designed for use by a noncomputer expert to create computer programs. It allows an instructor to generate specific e-learning courses by arranging various types of teaching materials containing text, graphics, and/or charts via a series of templates. Authoring tools are designed to be used by individuals without substantial programming knowledge or skills. (hh)

authoritarian discipline

A method of shaping a child's behavior characterized by strict control, absolute rules, and respect for tradition. The adult requires compliance to preestablished, nonnegotiable standards and values and rewards the child's obedience. (ecr)

authoritative discipline

A method of shaping a child's behavior characterized by flexible control, rational demands, and warmth shown to the child. The adult is receptive to the child's attempts at self-control and negotiates with the child to reach solutions that are reasonable to both child and adult. (ecr)

authority

The right, power, or ability to give orders and make decisions, or the power to exercise control or influence over others. One's authority may also refer to a source of expert information or opinion. (ce)

autism

A developmental disability that is a neurological disorder affecting an individual's ability to communicate, social interaction, and behavior. Other characteristics often associated with autism include engagement in repetitive activities, resistance to environmental change or changes in daily routines, and unusual responses to sensory experiences. The term Pervasive Developmental Disorder is also used to describe many of the same characteristics. (sr)

auto education
Within a Montessori classroom, auto education promotes self-education as driven by the child's own inner desire to learn. The teacher is present as a guide and an observer, rather than the child's main source of information, as in a traditional classroom. (nrs)

autographic
Written in one's hand, as in an autograph that is signed directly by an individual. The recordings of a musical performance would be classed as autographic because they are mechanically reproduced with no artistic interpretation on the part of the reproducer that might alter the original details as would happen with photographs, prints, and cast sculpture. (kpb)

automaticity
Quick, accurate identification of single words such that reading is effortless. Automaticity of reading occurs when the reader moves beyond conscious and strenuous efforts to decode words. Automaticity is one of the best predictors of comprehension. Automaticity differs from fluency in that fluency involves automaticity as well as prosody. (rcr)

autonomy
Synonymous with a feeling of independence, it is the ability to accomplish a task unassisted or to take care of oneself. Feelings of independence and autonomy fostered in young children help in the development of confidence and initiative. The state of being independent or self-governing. At the level of the individual: not under the control of another. At the aggregate level of the teaching profession: self-governing. (kdc, jc)

AVERA (See Association for Career and Technical Education)

average class size
The sum of all students regularly in a teacher's class divided by the actual number of regular teachers in those specific classes: For example, if four second grade rooms have 14, 16, 18, and 18 (n = 66) students, the average grade two class size is 16.5 (or 16) students. (cma)

axial age
Term originated by the philosopher Karl Jaspers in *On the Origin and Goal of History,* to describe a paradigmatic shift in human thinking that occurred between 800 and 200 B.C.E.—most prominently with reference to the mystical turn in Hinduism, the prophetic turn in Judaism, and the origins of Buddhism, Confucianism, and Greek philosophy. According to Jaspers, these loosely connected movements of the "axial" period formed the beginnings of a great global, multicultural movement for the cultivation of personal wisdom, which can now serve as the template for mindful global education in a mindlessly globalized world. Also called "The Great Leap of Being" by philosopher Eric Voeglin in *The New Science of Politics.* (bn)

axial symmetry (See symmetry—line/rotational)

axiology
The branch of philosophy that deals with questions of value, both aesthetic and ethical. (jc)

B

baby talk (See child-directed speech)

baccalaureate degree (See degree, bachelor's)

bachelor's degree (See degree, bachelor's)

back-to-basics
An educational reform movement begun in the 1950s focused on traditional academic disciplines. Begun by Robert Bestor as a reaction to both progressive educational efforts that emphasize personal growth and development and vocational-technical education, which focuses on work-related skills. The back-to-basics movement advocates that all students should be required to master the same academic disciplines, "the basics," with differences in individual ability being accommodated through the pace of coverage rather than the content of the curriculum. Rooted in perennialism. (jc)

See also essentialism; perennialism; progressivism.

Bakke case (See *Regents of the University of California v. Bakke,* 438 U.S. 265 [1978])

balance
A condition in artistic and musical compositions in which the articulation of the artistic statement is coherently constructed, with parts making sense in terms of one another such that clarity in comprehension is achieved on the part of the viewer or listener. (jd)

See also aesthetic whole; composition; unity.

balanced calendar schools (See year-round schools)

balanced literacy
Balanced literacy programs are characterized by instruction in reading skills, such as phonics knowledge, as well as experiences with authentic literature. Balanced literacy came about after the Reading Wars (1980s–1990s), during which teachers and researchers debated the merits of literacy programs that focused either on skills development (phonics) or on experiences with authentic literature (whole language). Proponents of the balanced literacy approach believe that children benefit from both types of instruction. (jas)

balanced scorecard
A strategic planning and management system used in public, private, and

not-for-profit organizations. This performance measurement framework adds strategic nonfinancial measures to traditional financial metrics to create a more "balanced" view of organizational performance. Developed by Drs. Robert Kaplan and David Norton, the balanced scorecard methodology enables organizations to better align their activities to their vision and goals, improve communication, and monitor performance against strategic priorities. (jz)

ballet
A classical Western dance form originating in Europe in the 15th century, ballet is characterized by grace and precision of movement and by elaborate formal gestures, steps, and poses combining dance, music, scenery, and costumes to tell stories or to create a particular mood. A musical composition written for this dance form is also called a "ballet," as is the group or company that performs the dance. Well-known ballets from the 19th century include *The Nutcracker, Swan Lake,* and *Giselle.* (kbc)

band
A group of musicians playing woodwind, brass, and percussion instruments (rarely including string instruments); an ensemble of any one type of instrument (e.g., a brass band, wind band, marimba band). Marching or parade bands perform while in motion; dance bands (including rock and jazz) provide backgrounds for social dancing. Jazz bands (e.g., swing, "big" bands, or jazz orchestras) are usually smaller in size than concert bands, and the brass section is most often reduced to trumpets and trombones, woodwinds to clarinets and saxophones, and, instead of percussion, there is a rhythm section of piano, bass (electric or acoustic) and drum set. Rock bands minimally include a lead guitar, rhythm or bass guitar, and drums. (jbl)

Bank Street College
Since its beginning in 1916, Bank Street College of Education has been a leader in education, a pioneer in improving the quality of classroom education, and an advocate for children and families. Through its independent graduate school of education, a model school for children, a family center, a division of continuing education, and a publications and media group, Bank Street conducts research and creates programs that meet the emerging needs of children, youth, families, and educators. (bjl)

Bank Street curriculum
A curricular approach often referred to as a "developmental-interaction" approach. Based on the belief that cognitive learning cannot be separated from interpersonal activity, social studies is the core of this curriculum, and students and teachers focus on relationships between people and their environment. Children are encouraged and allowed to develop their own sense of self, while teachers use overarching themes to guide the development of lessons. Democratic living and beliefs are emphasized. (kdc)

Bankhead-Jones Act
An act of Congress originally passed June 29, 1935, providing funds for agricultural research during the Great Depression. Its stated purpose included "to promote a sound and prosperous agriculture and rural life as indispensable to the maintenance of maximum employment and national prosperity." Money and land were donated for further development of cooperative agricultural extension work, and the more complete endowment and support of land-grant colleges. Research relating to improvement in the quality of, production of, distribution of, and markets for agricultural products was the intended result of this legislation. Land-grant universities were the direct beneficiaries. (bsb)

banking education
A process of formulaic schooling identified by Paulo Freire, whereby a teacher, or

expert, actively deposits information and skill sets into the minds of docile students who are themselves devoid of any useful inherent knowledge. As such, the flow of knowledge is unidirectional from teacher to student. In this model, an overemphasis on memorization inhibits the development of a critical sense of consciousness. The concept symbolizes oppressive relations and power dynamics present both in schooling and in the other structures and institutions of a society. (hfs)

bar graph
A graph that displays data through the use of equally proportional rectangular figures called bars. The height of these bars indicates the amount of each set of data. (kr)

administration at a likely performance level, rather than at the most basic questions. (jcp)

basal ganglia
This set of structures located deep within the brain is highly interconnected with many parts of the cerebral cortex and is a link between the cortex and the thalamus. Their best understood function is in control of movement and muscle tone, but they have additionally been linked to executive function, response selection, procedural learning, and mood disorders. (pk1)

base ten number system
The most commonly used number system, where the powers of 10 determine the

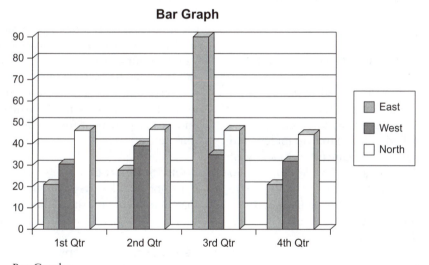

Bar Graph

barrier
A physical or architectural obstruction that impedes or limits access of people with disabilities. (sr)

basal
In cognitive and academic assessments, which generally begin with easier questions and become increasingly harder, a continuous series of items answered correctly so it is assumed all earlier items have been mastered. This permits beginning test

place value in the positional representation of a specific number. For example, 3024 means $3 \times 10^3 + 0 \times 10^2 + 2 \times 10^1 + 4 \times 10^0$. (kva)

base-10 blocks
Also known as Dienes blocks. One of the most commonly used materials for representing place value. They consist of small unit cubes (representing 1), a stack of 10 unit cubes fixed together (representing 10), a 10-by-10 array of cubes fixed

together (representing 100), and a large cube made using 10-by-10-by-10 small cubes (representing 1,000). (amr)

basic competencies

Possession of required or adequate skills, knowledge, and capacity in a particular subject. These skills and knowledge accumulate from one grade to the next, providing for later learning and achievement. Basic competencies are first learned in a step-by-step manner and later integrated into structured complex knowledge. (ce)

Basic Educational Opportunity Grants (See Pell Grant)

Basic English Skills Test (BEST)

A test that assesses both oral language and literacy skills of adults. The test is focused on survival and preemployment skills. (jpc)

Basic Interpersonal Communicative Skills (BICS)

A term (originally coined by James Cummins) for the context-bound, simple language used in everyday interactions. This framework, developed to help understand the language development and facility of English learners, is said to develop in two to three years, in contrast with Cognitive Academic Language Proficiency. (cld)

See also Cognitive Academic Language Proficiency.

basic skills

Basic skills are the fundamental abilities that lay the foundation for the application of knowledge. They are a form of knowledge that includes the activities necessary for functioning and progressing on a daily basis at work and in society in general. Basic educational skills typically include speaking, spelling, reading, writing, and computational abilities. Some consider these to be the essential school subjects. Social skills are taught by peer groups and are necessary for social acceptance, the nature of these skills being dependent upon

the cultural context of the particular group and upon its age level. Study habits, attention training, and other specific tasks that assist in the development of independence and self-esteem may also be emphasized. In addition to reading, writing, and arithmetic, educators and employers include multiple cognition, interpersonal abilities, and employability skills. (mm, kg)

basic skills education

Organized learning opportunities, primarily in literacy and numeracy, provided to adults who are functionally illiterate, who did not complete high school, or whose first language is not English. (chb)

See also compensatory education; remedial instruction.

basic skills tests

Examinations frequently given in technical or specialized courses to assure that student are adequately prepared for advanced course work in their respective academic fields; more recently, basic skills is a term used for tests focusing on reading and writing as essential learning tools, and as a requirement for teacher certification. (cf, sn)

behavior disorder

Behavior that deviates from the norm and that interferes with the ability to learn or function in a given environment. (sr)

behavior management

Behavior intervention that focuses on preventive management of identified undesired behaviors. This approach seeks to anticipate the undesired behaviors and institute preventive measures, with a focus on reinforcing good behaviors rather than punishing poor behaviors. The practice of manipulating environmental stimuli to direct children's behavior toward a chosen goal. Different theories of how children are socialized (behaviorist, constructivist, ecological, sociocultural) lead to different methods of behavior management. (sr, ecr)

behavior modification

The use of various intervention strategies stemming directly from theories of operant and classical conditioning for the purpose of changing behavior. Examples of operant conditioning techniques include positive reinforcement, negative reinforcement, and punishment. Classical conditioning is used to explain how behaviors are learned based on association. Pairing is one of the main techniques used from this theory. Behavior modification approaches can be used to increase desired behavior, decrease unwanted behavior, or make behavior contingent on specific circumstances. This is a psychological method for treating maladjustment and for changing observable behavior patterns. Applied behavior analysis is used to develop educational techniques to be tailored to each individual's requirements. Behavior modification is a systematic approach that causes a change in response patterns of an individual. (fa, dsm)

behavior therapy

A diverse group of therapeutic techniques that have their origin in behavioral learning theories. Behavior therapists emphasize the identification and modification of environmental antecedents and consequences of behavior. The basic premise of this approach is that behaviors are learned. Therefore, they can also be unlearned and relearned. Examples of commonly used behavior therapy techniques include progressive muscle relaxation, exposure and response prevention, thought stopping, pleasant event scheduling, and systematic desensitization. These techniques largely ignore internal cognitive processes, emotions, and underlying causes of disorders. Theoretically, when behaviors change to be more adaptive, thoughts and feelings also change. Behavior therapy is present-focused, problem-specific, and time-limited. (fa)

behavioral blame

Conceptualizes attributions of success and failure to issues of the effort of the individual (i.e., what one has done). Effort characteristics exist within the purview of individual control and development as alterable and mutable achievement attributes. (hfs)

behavioral genetics

Behavioral genetics is a field of study that tries to understand how the interaction of genes and environment influence human behavior. Researchers seek this understanding both for basic science purposes and in the hopes of using the knowledge to inform treatments and interventions. Research methods include twin studies, adoption studies, and animal studies. (sd1)

behavioral medicine

A subspecialty of medical science that integrates social science theory and research with the traditional medical model. It is an interdisciplinary subspecialty that views the etiology and/or treatment of medical disorders as needing to incorporate and consider the three-way interaction between biological, psychological, and social influences. (kc, scmc, bdj)

behaviorism

A research program that seeks to understand human behavior as predictable response to stimuli (Pavlov, Watson). A scientific-materialist view of humanity that excludes feelings and mental states as real things, defining them as the individual's disposition to behave in certain ways (Ryle, Skinner). Behaviorism has a strong influence in modern education, being the theoretical foundation for many common school practices, including teaching a specific and clearly defined sequence of objectives (Bloom), carefully sequenced curricula, and control of student behavior through "classroom management" or "behavior management" programs with strict positive and negative reinforcement schedules. (jc)

belief

The psychological, philosophical, and/or spiritual condition in which one's affective or emotional foundations are established based on a premise that may or may not be accurate. Beliefs usually are manifested as dispositions or outlooks visible in one's words, actions, and interactions, such as faith, conviction, principles, and confidence. A belief differs from knowledge, as a belief does not extend from concrete evidence or proof. (npg)

benchmark

A benchmark in mathematics is a known point or idea. For example, when considering 35 percent of a number, one might first find "benchmarks" such as 25 percent and 10 percent in order to compute 35 percent. Other examples of benchmarks occur in measurement, such as suggesting that a meter is approximately the height of a doorknob or a centimeter is approximately the width of a small paper clip. If one has developed meaningful benchmarks in mathematics, these benchmarks may be helpful in estimating and solving more complicated tasks. (sdt)

Berea College v. Commonwealth of Kentucky, 211 U.S. 45 (1908)

In October 1904, Berea College was convicted of violating a law prohibiting "any person, corporation, or association of persons to maintain or operate any college, school, or institution where persons of the white and Negro races are both received as pupils for instruction." Upheld by the Kentucky Court of Appeals, the case went to the U.S. Supreme Court on the basis that such a prohibition restricted the rights of individuals to fully exercise their rights under the 14th Amendment. The Supreme Court upheld the lower courts, saying that states can impose limits on corporations within their boundaries. (mb)

BEST (See Basic English Skills Test)

best practice

An activity or procedure that has produced outstanding results in one situation and could be adapted to improve effectiveness, efficiency, ecology, and/or innovativeness in another situation. In professional settings, a method, technique, or process that is recognized for successfully achieving a desired result or outcome. (cma, ln, rbp)

bias

The tendency or preference toward a particular belief or action. Bias is demonstrated through one's support of or favoritism advocating a specific person, group of persons, place(s), thing(s), and/or belief(s); or through one's opposition to and resistance against promotion of a specific person, group of persons, place(s), thing(s), and/or belief(s). Biases can be cultural, ethnic, racial, gender, political, religious, economic, geographic, personal, and professional, resulting in prejudice, preconception, and partiality. In testing, bias is systematic and persistent alteration of test results due to factors other than the construct(s) being assessed; social or cultural (typically) negative perception of a test's results as being differentially fair to a particular group of test takers. (npg, fd)

See also Differential Item Functioning.

bibliographic databases

Databases that contain indexed listings of information sources: books, articles, and other media. When such databases are searched, the retrieved records indicate where the information can be found. For example, a record for a book might include a library location or call number, whereas a record for an article might include a journal title, volume, issue, and page number. Students utilize bibliographic databases in the form of library catalogs and indexes to literature. Bibliographic databases may also include links to other databases that contain the full text of the material cited. (ac)

bibliotherapy

The use of written texts, such as self-help books, client manuals, fictional novels, children's storybooks, and factual accounts, to educate and to assist individuals of all ages striving for personal/therapeutic change. More recently, the Internet has been used as an adjunct treatment of this kind, because a considerable amount of educational material is now available electronically. (fa)

BICS (See Basic Interpersonal Communicative Skills)

bicultural education
Education in which two cultures, inclusive of language, norms, customs, and images, are studied simultaneously without the privileging of one over the other or regarding one as a subset of the other. Bicultural education honors the parallel multiple consciousnesses needed to actively participate and negotiate two cultural, often competing or contradictory, worlds. Bicultural education gives credence to the difficulties of navigating both worlds simultaneously, consequently making explicit the various codes of cultural capital. (lev)

biculturalism
The state of being and interacting in two cultures at once, where the languages, ways of thinking, values, customs, norms, and capital are continuously navigated, analyzed, and experienced. Critics suggest that biculturalism sets up artificial binaries between cultures and provides a limited recognition of multiple cultures. Biculturalism may also include dual language proficiency or at least readability/communication. (lev)

big books
Children's books that have been enlarged so they can be seen by all of the children in the group as they are held in front of the teacher or in the teacher's lap. (jlj)

bilingual/bicultural education
Instruction that incorporates, and is sensitive to, cultural norms held by primary and second language learners. (jqa, jwc)

bilingual education
An approach in which students are taught for part of the day in English and part of the day in their native language. (bba)

bilingual vocational education
Vocational education and English-language instruction to persons with limited English proficiency to prepare these persons for jobs in recognized (including new and emerging) occupations. (jb)

bilingualism
The ability to speak or understand a second language other than one's native language. However, the ability to read and write a second language may or may not be associated with bilingualism. The ability to speak two languages with equal, or nearly equal levels of fluency. (mc, jtr)

biliteracy
The ability to read and write in more than one language. (mc)

binary operation
A process applied to pairs of elements to produce a single element. For example, multiplication and division are binary operations. (kva)

biological sex
Refers to chromosomal, hormonal, and anatomical characteristics that determine what sex category a person falls into. In many cultures, though not all, there are two primary sex categories—female and male. However, scientific data and research demonstrate that biological sex is far more varied than two discreet categories. In order to organize human relations, social order, and cultural power structures, sex categories are simplified into male, female, and sometimes intersex. The terms *sex* and *gender* are often erroneously used interchangeably. (jb2)

biology
The branch of science that studies life, life processes, and living things, including

their classification, structure, function, distribution, growth, origin, and evolution. Subdivisions include botany and zoology. (tw)

biomechanics
Application of mechanical principles to the study of human movement. (rf)

biphobia (See homophobia)

bisexual
Refers to individuals who are attracted emotionally and/or sexually to both women and men. A person who self-identifies as bisexual may or may not be attracted equally to both sexes, and the overall degree of attraction may vary over time. She or he may also not necessarily be involved sexually with both men and women. Some people who have been involved sexually with both men and women may not self-identify as bisexual. (ti)

bisexuality
A type of sexual orientation that consists of being attracted romantically, sexually, and emotionally to males and females. Depending on the person, her/his attraction may be stronger to women or to men, or they may be approximately equal. Because of bias against bisexuality as a legitimate sexual orientation, there is a lack of research that would provide data for estimating the percentage of the population that is bisexual. (jb2)
See also heterosexuality; homosexuality.

Black English (See African American language)

blend
To combine the sounds that are represented by the graphemes in order to pronounce a word. Blending can be achieved either by single letters (e.g., b-l-e-n-d) or by onsets and rimes (e.g., bl-end). Blends are a string of consonant letters that are joined at the beginning or end of a syllable with minimal change in their sounds. The combined letters are restricted in their location and sequence. An example: str- as in "street" in the syllable-initial position; -ts as in "bats" in the syllable-final position. The term *consonant cluster* is also used to refer to blend. Blends are similar to compound words in that they are formed by combining two or more words; however, blends tend to be produced through the close association of two words and are created by joining parts of them. For instance, usually the first part of the first word is joined to the last part of the second word (e.g., smoke + fog = smog). Compound words combine whole parts of other words (e.g., blackboard, highchair). Most blends are nouns (e.g., brunch, camcorder, infomercial, motel, telethon); however, there are examples of verbs (e.g., electrocute, gues(s)timate), and adjectives (e.g., bodacious = bold + audacious) as well. A significant number of blends were created in the 20th century when the need for new words to cover various topics in culture, politics, and science was dramatically increased. (h-jk)
See also digraph; portmanteau word.

blended courses
Courses that are a combination of online and face-to-face instruction. The requirements and ratio of face-to-face instruction versus online instruction will vary depending upon the subject matter of the course and the instructional methodology of the professor. Some courses will require a specific number of face-to-face class sessions, while the content of other courses may determine the mix of face-to-face and online instruction. Typically, a majority of the course will be taught through online means to reduce seat time. Also called hybrid courses. (pw1)

blind (See visual impairment)

block play
Play in which children gain hands-on experience in basic math concepts, such as

geometric shapes and spatial relations, by building with and manipulating blocks. (jlj)

block scheduling
A school scheduling procedure that provides large blocks of time (for example, four 90-minute periods a day) for teachers or teams of teachers to arrange instruction. With block scheduling, teachers can more effectively individualize instruction to meet the various needs and abilities of students. Restructuring of the typical school day (usually six or seven classes of approximately 50 minutes each) in which courses are scheduled for two or more continuous periods or days in order to give them more uninterrupted time for project work, laboratory instruction, work-based learning, and other similar activities. Block scheduling has been shown to facilitate academic and vocational integration. (bba, jm)

blocking
Also called "staging," is the physical movement of actors on a stage in a scene, or the process by which actors and director physically put a scene on the stage,— that is, decide where actors will move at particular moments. Blocking decisions are purposeful, often made to enhance the meaning and emphasize the dramatic action of the scene. Relevant to blocking: *upstage* is the back and *downstage* is the front (closest to the audience) of the stage; *stage right* and *stage left* are the sides of the stage from the perspective of the actor facing the audience. (em)

blocks
Children's building toys that come in various geometric shapes. Blocks are hard or soft and may be made of wood, cardboard, styrofoam, plastic, or foam covered with vinyl or fabric. (jlj)

blog
Blog is an abbreviation of the word weblog. Blogs are in essence freeform online diaries, which the authors update on an ongoing basis. A blog's author (a.k.a., blogger) can limit access to specific groups or allow access by the general public. The subject matter for a blog is unrestricted and endlessly varied. Many blogs allow readers to post comments or contribute to discussions. Blogs are typically updated daily, monthly, or anywhere in between. "Blog" may also be used as a verb, as in "The teacher blogged about the class field trip." (ab1, mid)

Bloom's taxonomy
A classification developed by Benjamin Bloom that categorizes questions commonly occurring in educational settings by their level of abstraction. The six categories are: knowledge, comprehension, application, analysis, synthesis, evaluation. (peb)

BMI (See body mass index)

board of education
Boards of education exist and function at the state and local levels. They comprise either a publicly elected or appointed body of representatives that influence, propose, adopt, and support educational policy within their jurisdiction. The board of education is the primary policy-making body for educational issues at the local level but may or may not be at the state level, where it may be supplanted by the individual state legislatures or by some other state educational agency. (tm)

Board of Regents
The governing board of an institution or a statewide system of public institutions; the authority that selects and evaluates the president and provides for the financial welfare and general operating policies of the institution or unit. The terms *regent* and *trustee* are generally considered interchangeable; there is no appreciable difference in duties or areas of authority. (cf)

Board of Trustees

The governing board of an institution or of an educational unit; the authority that selects and evaluates the president and provides for the financial welfare and general operating policies of the institution or unit. The term *trustee* is the word most commonly used for a member of a governing board. (cf)

bodily-kinesthetic intelligence

One of Howard Gardner's (1983) multiple intelligences, the aptitude and ability to control one's body with expertise and elegance and the predisposition to use bodily and tactile sensations to learn efficiently. A child with bodily-kinesthetic intelligence learns by moving his body and by manipulating objects in his environment. Young children are notoriously bodily-kinesthetic in their orientation to learning. Examples of expert performance in this domain are a tennis champion, a ballerina, and a glassblower. (ecr)

body mass index (BMI)

BMI provides an indication of the appropriateness of a student's weight relative to height. The mathematical formula to calculate BMI is a person's body weight in kilograms divided by the square of the height in meters. Some states require that schools report students' BMI to parents and to the state department of education to maintain records of childhood obesity. (kpr)

BOLD response (See functional Magnetic Resonance Imaging)

bonding

A process in which two people become emotionally available and responsive to one another. Bonding can include time spent together, shared activities, holding, talking, or listening. (kdc)

bookmobile

A wheeled vehicle, generally a large van, that serves as a traveling library, usually following a regular circuit. Such vehicles extend the ability of libraries to reach out to underserved clients in areas that are remote from established libraries, especially in rural areas. (lr)

border pedagogy

An educational process that calls all forms of subordination into question. As such it aims to replace the authority of memorization and recitation with student-directed reflection, inquiry, and knowledge development through their own histories, collective memories, and perspective. Simultaneously, the aim is to challenge and critically examine the ways in which knowledge and power are legitimated and constructed. The emphasis is on engaging students and teachers in the process of decentering Western ideologies, codes, and cultural, social, and academic knowledge by developing a multiplicity of perspectives, voices, histories, identities, and subjectivities. (hfs)

border studies

A focus of study centered on the United States–Mexican border, encompassing various issues relating to migration, economics, cultural influences, and politics affecting the United States and Mexico. (jqa, jwc)

botany

The branch of biology that studies plants. (tw)

bottom-up cognition (See top-down vs. bottom-up cognition)

bottom-up model

The bottom-up model is a decision-making model intending to involve all educational stakeholders in the fundamental decision-making processes of an educational organization. These educational stakeholders include students, parents, community members, business representatives, and school administration. In a bottom-up model all decisions, policies, systems, and mechanisms are supposed to be developed, approved, and implemented in a participatory manner that creates a sense of ownership and involvement among all stakeholders in the success of the educational process. The bottom-up model is often contrasted to the top-down model, which is based on supervisory management, and in which all decisions, policies, systems, and operating mechanisms are produced by a management group that does not involve all stakeholders but claims to represent their interests. (tm)

bound morpheme (See morphology)

brain development
Development of the brain is due to genetic and epigenetic (one stage building upon another) influences. Formation of brain regions is timed with more primitive and caudal parts (brain stem) formed before more complex and evolved structures (cerebral cortex). Brain growth varies by region, and growing regions are most vulnerable to teratogens (a virus, drug, radiation, etc.). Brain development occurs before birth and continues throughout the life span. (vm)

brain-based learning
The utilization of current knowledge on how the brain functions and how knowledge is acquired by the brain to design instruction. As brain development changes, teaching methods also change. Brain-based learning employs real world problems and experiential feedback; understanding that each brain learns in a different way; understanding of the big picture; and utilization of positive emotions for reinforcement. (ms)

brainstorming
A technique for quickly generating large lists of ideas, problems, or issues from a group. Individuals are encouraged to contribute any suggestion, no matter how remote or unconventional; all ideas are recorded. Individual suggestions are reviewed and evaluated only after the brainstorming is completed. (jsj)

brick and mortar
A descriptive phrase used to distinguish colleges and universities with on-campus buildings and facilities from universities, colleges, or schools providing comparable instruction via mail, television, radio, or computer networks. (cf)

bridge programs
Programs designed to facilitate transition from adult basic education programs to postsecondary educational institutions. Through participation in transition programs, learners build academic literacy skills and acquire strategies for success in college and vocational training. (las)

bridging ten strategy (See thinking strategies)

brief therapy
Although psychotherapy that lasts 15 sessions or less is usually considered to be "brief therapy," some systems of therapy define brief as less than 6 sessions. Most typically, the overriding goal of brief therapy is reducing behavioral or emotional symptoms rather than providing insight into underlying causes of problems. It usually focuses on well-defined treatment goals, as opposed to broad change, and on a client's cognitions and overt behaviors. (tsw, mgg)

Broca's area
An area in the frontal lobe known to be important in speech production is called Broca's area. First discovered by Pierre-Paul Broca in the 1800s through his case study of a patient with damage to the area who had profound difficulties producing speech, but in whom speech perception nevertheless seemed largely unaffected. (pk1)
    See also Wernicke's area.

Brown Berets

Founded in East Los Angeles in 1967, the Brown Berets were a paramilitary group associated with the Mexican American (or Chicano) civil rights movement. Patterned after the Black Panthers, the Brown Berets lent their support to efforts aimed at ending discrimination against Mexican Americans in education, employment, and the free exercise of civil rights. As part of the broader Civil Rights Movement, the Brown Berets actively supported efforts to reform K–12 schools and to introduce ethnic studies into the college curriculum. (sw)

Brown v. Board of Education of Topeka, Kansas, 347 U.S. 483 (1954)

U.S. Supreme Court case in which Oliver Brown and other African American parents charged that racially segregated public schools violated the 14th Amendment, which guaranteed equal protection under the law. The Kansas Board of Education argued that their public schools were racially separate but equal in all measurable aspects, such as physical facilities and funding. Supreme Court judges ruled in favor of Brown, calling racially segregated schools "inherently unequal" and illegal. It also ruled that segregation deprived minority children of equal educational opportunity by creating feelings of inferiority, thus negatively affecting the motivation to learn. Often referred to as *Brown I,* the Supreme Court in its 1955 *Brown II* case (349 U.S. 294) ordered that segregated schools begin to be dismantled. (snr)

Buberian philosophy

The philosophy of Martin Buber (1876–1965), a Jewish existentialist philosopher and theologian born in Austria, is best known for his philosophy of dialogue expounded in such works as *I and Thou, Between Man and Man,* and *The Knowledge of Man.* He played a significant role in advocating a binational solution to the Arab–Jewish conflict in Palestine. His work on developing a philosophical anthropology of humankind, on education, on religion, and on Zionism managed to cross disciplines and boundaries such that it has influenced a number of fields, from education to religion, from psychology to political science. Major philosophical themes in his work include the dialogical relation and its contribution to personhood; existential presence; the relationship between humans and God (as well as the nature of God); evil and its presence in the world; the contributions of Hasidism to the modern world; the significance of meeting the other the willingness to embrace uncertainty and the concomitant transcendence of the many either–ors present today in a dialogical "sphere of between." Major educational themes in his work include dialogue as a fundamental means and end of education; education as a process of meaning making, confirmation, and inclusion; the unique and asymmetrical dialogical relationship between the teacher and student; the need to situate education on an existentially "real and primal" ground in the present realities of students and teachers; and that education can help us develop a "living relationship to the world" (Buber, 1947; Buber, 1957). His work has influenced educational thinkers such as Carol Gilligan, Nel Noddings, and Nicholas Burbules in considering moral development, the ethic of care, and the capacities of dialogue. (cs)

budget

A budget can be defined as a plan for the financial operation of the educational needs of the school. This plan includes an estimate of proposed expenditures for a given period of time (generally referred to as the fiscal year) and a proposed means of financing those expenditures, and it is the expression of educational hopes and aspirations relating to the school. During the fiscal year, three budgets are managed at once—the preparation of next year's budget, administering and monitoring the current budget, and preparing the financial report for the past budget. Some approaches taken in budgeting have been: Planning Programming Budgeting and Evaluation Systems, Zero-Based Budgeting, Site-Based Budgeting, Strategic Planning, and Total Quality Management. (jr)

built environment

Everything that is and has been humanly created, arranged, or maintained (e.g., cities, homes, parks, bridges, and the spaces that connect these structures). The built environment possesses a dual role: to fulfill human purposes and to provide a context for human actions and endeavors. The built environment is artificially constructed and consists of tangible artifacts (e.g., buildings, roads, automobiles) in order to manipulate and modify the natural environment for human purposes. (hrm, ew, jkd)

bullying

Behavior that repeatedly and over time intentionally inflicts physical and/or psychological injury on another individual. School-based bullying intervention programs and policies often ignore or underemphasize the emotional violence of chronic bullying. (jb2)

See also harassment.

Bureau of Refugees, Freedmen, and Abandoned Lands

A federal agency created by Congress on March 3, 1865, to respond to the social and economic dislocations caused by the American Civil War. It had authority over war refugees, emancipated slaves, and Confederate States property and other lands abandoned after the war. The bureau provided emergency rations, negotiated labor contracts, acted as a court of law if local courts failed to deal equitably with newly freed African Americans, and assisted in establishing schools. It curtailed most activity in 1870 and ceased to exist in 1872. Popularly known as the Freedmen's Bureau. (rb)

bureaucratic roles

Bureaucratic roles are defined by sets of expectations, which are combined into positions and offices in the organization. In schools, the positions of principal, teacher, and student are critical, and each is defined in terms of a set of expectations. Bureaucratic expectations specify the appropriate behavior for a specific role or position. A teacher, for instance, has the obligation to plan learning experiences for students and has the duty to engage students in a pedagogically effective manner. (jt)

bureaucratic structure

In education, the structure that the formal organization specifically establishes to achieve explicit goals and carry out administrative tasks. Structural properties such as rules, regulations, hierarchy, and division of labor are consciously designed to attain those goals effectively. Bureaucracy employs authority through means to achieve rational decision making and maximize efficiency. (ks)

burlesque

Characterized primarily by exaggeration, caricature, parody, satire, and mockery, a style of drama or literature that ridicules people and subjects by portraying their opposites: for example, trivializing "serious" subjects, treating trivial matters with exaggerated mock importance, turning "intellectuals" into ignorant buffoons, and portraying those whom society sees as knowing little as geniuses. In comparison with satire, which is thought to have a "meaner" edge, burlesque seems more playful and good-hearted. Commonly also refers to variety-type shows with stripteases, magic acts, slapstick comedy, "dirty" jokes, and songs, dances, and skits filled with sexual humor and innuendo. (em)

business and information technology education

A combination of business and information technology for students in preparation for an occupation in this field. Students receive intensive and cooperative instruction and actual work experience. (jb)

business education

Major program educational area in career and technical education designed to provide students with instruction and preparation for managerial, computer, and office occupations. It includes the knowledge and understanding of the principles, skills, and applications needed to be successful in the world of business. Students receive intensive and cooperative instruction and actual work experience. (ea)

buzz group

A small subgroup of learners in a class, formed at the request of the teacher or facilitator, who discuss a topic briefly among themselves before returning to a full-group conversation. Adult educators commonly invite students to get together in buzz groups in order to stimulate spontaneous conversation on a topic. A teaching technique in which students are put into small groups to discuss a question or issue and then all groups share what they have learned with each other. (chb, jpc)

C

CAGS (See Certificate of Advanced Study)

CAI (See computer-assisted instruction)

CAL (See characteristics of adults as learners)

calculus
The field of mathematics developed during the last half of the 17th century by Leibniz and Newton, whose central idea is the concept of limit. Differential calculus is the branch dealing with the rate at which a function changes, and integral calculus deals with finding areas on the Cartesian plane. (gtm)

CALDEF (See Cuban American Legal Defense and Education Act)

calibration
Calibration refers to a procedure that attempts to maximize precision of scoring and minimize bias introduced by a scoring system. When this scoring system consists of human raters, calibration typically compares ratings of scoring samples with an expert or benchmark score in order to ensure that ratings are consistent within raters, and consistent between raters, or that individual raters are not too severe or too lenient. (js2)

California Master Plan
The comprehensive and often controversial plan created in 1960 to reorganize the higher education system of California. The plan created a tiered system of higher education consisting of community colleges, state universities, and research universities. The plan included uniform admission standards, increased state funding of community colleges, free tuition for Californians, student financial aid, a full-year calendar, and the creation of new campuses. This model plan was studied and partly adopted by several other state systems of higher education and brought international acclaim to its architect, Clark Kerr. (ks2)

call and response
A way of singing, found especially in church music, in which the leader sings a line (the call) and the audience answers with another. In African American drumming, the call and response can be between two drummers. In some community art centers that focus on African American cultures, the call and response form of making music (through drumming, singing, and dancing as in tapping a call and response)

is thought to be an excellent vehicle for increasing the concentration and engagement of the young student of the arts. (jd)

calligraphy

The art of fine or beautiful handwriting. Usually cursive, although sometimes angular, produced chiefly by brush, ink, ink-stone, and paper ("the four treasures of the study" in China) or specially designed pens. Regarded as a form of artistic expression in many parts of the world, calligraphy is most widely practiced in the Islamic culture and in cultures using Chinese or Chinese-influenced writing, including China, Japan, and Korea. It is appreciated on the basis of the calligrapher's skill, imagination, and ability to give "spirit" to his or her strokes. Islamic calligraphy aims to exercise a religious effect upon its viewer's mind, and Chinese calligraphy requires each stroke to carry the energy of a living thing. (yjl)

CALP (See Cognitive Academic Language Proficiency)

CAM (See certificate of advanced mastery)

camera obscura

A camera-like device whereby an image is projected through a darkened chamber and lens onto an exterior surface. This method is used in the transfer of designs and drawings for paintings. Today, camera obscura exists for the most part in children's museums and science classrooms, and it serves as a tool for learning about light, perspective, and projection. In the 17th, 18th, and 19th centuries, however, camera obscura was used to a large extent as part of the process of making many Realist paintings. (km)

campus

The landscape upon which are located the buildings and facilities of an institution used for instruction, research, and/or service. (cf)

campus planning

A process involving the preparation and implementation of guidelines, often including maps, to support and promote the orderly physical growth and development of an institution. Also describes the title of the department responsible for these activities. (cf)

canon

In art and literature, the group of unquestionably great or greatest artists and works (masterpieces). Originally referred to the saints who were canonized by the Roman Catholic Church. The idea of a canon of artists and works of art is particularly Western and male and exclusive of many unrecognized historical voices in the art world, including those of women, nonwhite, and non-Western artists. Postmodernism is challenging the very idea of a canon. With the idea of what counts as art and literature expanding (including photography, performance art, video, craft, and design) and previously unrecognized artists coming to light, the plausibility or usefulness of an agreed-upon list of most important works is being dismantled by artists, art historians, writers, and contemporary critics. (jd)

capacity building coaches

Individuals who provide professional development through a collaborative process to achieve the goal of increased student achievement. (mlp1, rbp)

capital

One of the four basic categories of resources, or factors of production, including manufactured (or previously produced) resources, used to manufacture or produce other things. Common examples of capital are factories, buildings, trucks, tools, machinery, and equipment used by businesses in their productive pursuits. The primary role of capital in the economy is to improve the productivity of labor as it transforms the natural resources of land into wants-and-needs-satisfying goods. (mkg)

capital renewal

In the context of facilities, including buildings and infrastructure, refers to all construction projects necessary to remedy existing deferred maintenance and to prevent future deferred maintenance by adequately funding reinvestment in facilities. (cf)

See also deferred maintenance.

capitalism

Economic and social systems within a free enterprise in which production is privately controlled, goods and services (labor) are exchanged in a free market, and profits are both invested in new technologies and distributed among the investors. Capitalism is considered entrepreneurialism promoting industrialism, consumerism, and commercialism. (npg)

capstone course

In technical education, a course taken at the end of a program of study that requires students to demonstrate their accumulated knowledge in solving real-world problems through the application of knowledge from academic and career-technical education courses. (db)

cardinal number

A number used to denote the numeric value of a set of objects. Another term used in elementary mathematics is "counting number." The cardinality or "count" of a set indicates the number of objects in the set. (amr)

Cardinal Principles of Secondary Education (1918)

Influential report of the National Education Association's Commission on the Reorganization of Secondary Education that was critical to the establishment of the comprehensive high school model in the United States. Best known for its articulation of seven "main objectives of education" intended to lend coherence to the subject-centered curriculum. The seven "cardinal principles" were health, command of fundamental processes, worthy home membership, vocation, citizenship, worthy use of leisure, and ethical character. (wgw)

care, ethic of (See ethic of care)

career

The sequence of occupations and other life roles that combine to express one's commitment to work in his or her total pattern of self-development. The series of remunerated and nonremunerated positions occupied by a person from adolescence through retirement, of which occupation is only one. Includes work-related roles such as those of student, employee, and pensioner, together with complementary avocational, familial, and civic roles. (kg, ea)

career academy

School-within-a-school operated by a small group of teachers from different disciplines who provide course work and work experiences arranged according to a career theme. Students gain the necessary skills for entry into the workforce and progression into postsecondary education, and often curriculum is designed with business partners. (db)

career and employability skills

A set of skills that are integrated into career and technical education courses to help students prepare for the transition to work and advanced education; includes career exploration, resumes, interviewing, teamwork, and so on; also called "workplace basics" or "SCANS (Secretary's Commission on Achieving Necessary Skills) skills" (based on the government reports from the early 1990s). (rz)

career and technical course (See course, career-technical or vocational)

career and technical education

Organized educational programs that teach students knowledge and skills for career pathways in high schools, trade schools, career centers, and community or technical colleges. Programs provide a series of courses that develop competencies for targeted careers and/or prepare students for additional educational experiences. (nk)

career and technical education center
A school at the secondary level specializing in the instruction of career and technical occupational areas: agricultural education, business education, family and consumer sciences education, health occupations, marketing education, technology education, and trade and industrial education. It is typically designed to serve more than one school or school district and may be called a vocational school or center. (ea)

career and technical education concentrators
Students who take three or more credits in a particular career or occupational area, compared to an "explorer," who may take one or two credits. (rz)

Career and Technical Education Research
A refereed journal that publishes articles that examine research and research-related topics in vocational/career and technical education, career development, human resource development, career issues in the schools (grades K–12), postsecondary education, adult and lifelong learning, and workforce education. (ea)

career and technical high school (See high school, specialized)

career and technical student organizations (CTSOs)
A group of students within a school who have a common career interest who meet regularly, organize activities, and serve as an integral part of the students' learning climate, in combination with classroom instruction. CTSOs serve as a medium to

allow the students to gain important practice at applying leadership skills. (db)

career and technical subject
Any school subject designed to develop specific skills, knowledge, and information that enable the learner to prepare for or to be more efficient in his or her chosen trade or occupation. (jm, sa)

career and technical teacher education
Programs that prepare individuals to teach occupational skills in high schools, trade schools, community colleges, agricultural and technical colleges, adult continuing education programs, armed forces training, and industry. (jb, sa)

career awareness
Activities intended to make students aware of careers and/or occupations in the workforce. Some activities may include field trips and classroom speakers, curriculum redesign, and other planned and integrated activities. (ea, kg)

career choice
A decision-making process in which an individual chooses a skill or a vocation to be pursued as a career. The end result of vocational planning. (jm, ea)

career clusters
Core of courses focused on skills and knowledge common to several related occupations. Career clusters are intended to provide students with choices and stronger foundations in a specialized career or profession. (jb)

career coordinator (See coordinator, career)

career counseling
Guidance by a trained, competent counselor or mental health professional of individuals or groups aimed at facilitating career exploration and promoting/optimizing occupational potential and

satisfaction. Such guidance includes, but is not limited to, assessment and test interpretation feedback; intake of personal and career history; investigation of career aspirations and expectations; formal consideration of personal and career-related interests, abilities, and values; and the identification of current resources and data trends. Also, a process that provides students with personal and professional information that can be used to assist them in making educational and occupational decisions. (mm, ao, ea)

See also career guidance.

career decision making
Method for understanding, analyzing, and appreciating a variety of careers or career options through exploration, guidance, and planning. It utilizes reasoning-centered processes, including mental and/or graphic depictions of career decision-making steps involved in goal-setting and goal-attaining career development. (lrm)

career development
A lifelong process through which an individual develops and identifies with an area of the working world. Involves the results of an individual's education and career-related choices, along with one's aptitudes, interests, beliefs, and self-concept. (kg)

career development theory
Theory that attempts to describe the factors that motivate career behaviors or understand the structural characteristics and career attitudes desired for employment. (kg)

career education
An educational concept born in the 1970s addressing the relationship between traditional educational programs and occupational aspects of society. Career education is a comprehensive approach to education to prepare learners to be productive citizens. Infused with existing educational curricula and intended for learners of all ages, these programs may help develop an understanding of the nature of careers or a specific career, as well as teach the skills needed for success in any career or in a specific career. (ch, jpc)

career education program
All the academic and career-related courses organized to fulfill the same general objectives and conducted along similar lines. (db)

career exploration
Investigative activities or inquiries undertaken inside and outside the classroom to search out information about a future occupational or professional interest or goal. (jm)

career goal (See goal, career)

career guidance
The process by which persons are assisted in selection of a career and of adequate career and technical training or retraining that is realistic in light of actual or anticipated opportunities for gainful employment and situated in each case to the counselee's interests, needs, and ability to benefit from such training. (jm)

See also career counseling, occupational guidance.

career high school (See high school, specialized)

career indecision
Difficulties in deciding on a career goal. These difficulties typically involve the inability to choose a career goal or the unwillingness to choose a career goal. They can, however, also involve experiencing uncertainty regarding a previously expressed, or chosen, career goal. (sc)

career interest inventory
An assessment tool that measures an individual's vocational interests. Specifically, an individual's likes and dislikes of a variety of activities, objects, and types of people are compared with the likes and

dislikes of individuals who are performing in, and satisfied with, specific occupations and career fields. Occupations and career fields are displayed graphically on a profile. Low, moderate, and high vocational interest levels are identified for each occupation and career field. The Strong Interest Inventory (SII), the Campbell Interest and Skills Survey (CISS), and the Kuder Occupational Interest Survey (KOIS) are representative examples of career interest inventories. (sc)

career ladder
A career ladder system establishes multi-levels of teaching positions; provides opportunities to teachers for continued professional advancement; requires improved teaching skill for advancement to a higher level; and has other components such as additional higher-level instructional responsibilities and demonstration of pupil academic progress. Some career ladder programs use a performance-based compensation system. A career ladder system provides teachers with opportunities for professional career advancement based primarily on improved or advanced teaching skills, evidence of pupil academic progress, and higher-level instructional responsibilities. (klb)

career maturity
The degree to which an individual is ready to make a career choice. According to Donald Super, career maturity is a developmental process within the career exploration stage, one of the five primary stages of career development. During this stage, an individual typically experiences the following: orientation to the role of work in one's life; crystallization, the process of developing preferences for a particular occupation or career field; specification, the process of becoming certain and comfortable with a career choice; and implementation, the process of becoming qualified and actually obtaining a career of one's choice. (sc)

career passport
A state-issued, school-validated document indicating a student has met state and/or national competency standards in an occupation. Passport receivers are encouraged to complete industry-issued credentials, certificates, or licenses and incorporate them in the passport. (jb)

career pathway
A planned sequence of articulated academic and career and technical courses that creates an educational program beginning at the secondary level and ultimately leading to a certificate, licensure, and/or postsecondary degree. It is a collaborative educational program supported by secondary and postsecondary educational institutions, business and industry, employers, and community. (ea)

career planning
The development of a plan by a student, with the assistance of counselors and teachers, of well-considered steps in progressing toward entry into a specific job, occupation, or profession. The process of selecting an occupation, securing a job, advancing in that job, and, if necessary, changing jobs. The process involves finding a match between an individual's talents, skills, interests, personality, and values, and a particular career. (db, jtr)

career-technical course (See course, career-technical or Vocational)

career-technical education laboratory
A facility specifically designed, equipped, and used for instruction in some vocation or occupational area. (ea, jb)

caregiver
A person or persons who provide for the everyday physical, intellectual, social, and emotional needs of a child. A caregiver can be a parent, a day care teacher, a grandparent, a sibling, or anyone who is responsible for the care and well-being of a child. A caregiver will feed, clothe, and

manage diapering/toileting, in addition to providing a safe, nurturing, and responsive environment. A caregiver is responsible for meeting the needs of the child across all of the developmental domains. (kdc)

Carl D. Perkins Vocational and Applied Technology Education Act Amendments of 1990 and 1998

Federal legislation passed in 1990 and again in 1998 reauthorizing the Carl D. Perkins Act of 1984. The legislation is intended to improve vocational and technical education programs by promoting high academic standards and the integration of academic and vocational or career-technical education in order to make the United States more competitive in the world economy. (jb)

Carl Perkins Vocational Education Act of 1985

U.S. legislation that designated federal funds to provide vocational-technical education programs and services to youth and adults to prepare them for employment in occupations that do not require a bachelor's or advanced degree. (las)

Carnegie Classification System

Identifies categories of colleges and universities. In 1970, the Carnegie Commission on Higher Education (now the Carnegie Foundation for the Advancement of Teaching) developed a system of classifying universities and colleges that has been widely used by researchers who are studying higher education. The early focus was on the types of degrees conferred, but the 2005 revision consists of a matrix of six different classifications that apply to all institutions. A new edition is planned for 2010. (sn)

Carnegie Foundation for the Advancement of Teaching (CFAT)

A private foundation originally endowed by Andrew Carnegie to provide retirement funds for college faculty, CFAT now serves as an independent policy center and conducts research and policy studies in education. From 1967 to 1993, CFAT funded the Carnegie Commission on Higher Education, and its historic series of reports on Higher Education. (cf)

Carnegie unit

Created by the Carnegie Foundation in the early 1900s and applying to the secondary education environment only, the unit is a standardized measure of the amount of in-class time a student spends with an instructor of a specific discipline over the course of a year. Numerically, the unit represents roughly 130 contact hours per class. (ms)

cartoon

A drawing, often detailed, that is made as a design for a painting of the same size to be executed in fresco or oil, or for a work in tapestry, mosaic, or stained glass. In painting, the cartoon is transferred to the canvas or wall, where it becomes the underdrawing. A cartoon is also any full-page illustration in a paper or periodical, including comics that are humorous, or political drawings. In television and cinematography, a cartoon is any animated sequence of these drawings on film. Pre-adolescent and adolescent children often draw cartoons or comics as a way to tell the stories of their lives and/or to explore the visual language of the media. (lj)

CAS (See Certificate of Advanced Study)

CAS (See Computer Algebra System)

CASAS (See Comprehensive Adult Student Assessment System)

case (See case method)

case conceptualization

A process of considering and summarizing a client's situation from a specific theoretical perspective. The intent of a case conceptualization is to consider all relevant information related to the diagnosis, prognosis, and treatment planning of a client in order to promote the best possible therapeutic outcomes, in part by developing a consistent and comprehensive treatment approach. (kc, scmc, bdj)

case method
An inductive approach to learning, in which learners read a detailed accounting of a situation, institution, event, decision, or problem (a "case") and then discuss it as a group under the guidance of a facilitator or instructor. The goal is to increase the learners' skills of analysis and problem-solving, and/or to deepen their understanding of some field of practice. (chb)

case study method (See case method)

case study research
A type of inquiry within qualitative research. A case is a single entity or a defined system and may be an individual, an event, a process, or an organization. The researcher describes and analyzes the case holistically and in-depth, with particular attention to the context of the case. The researcher usually seeks multiple perspectives on the phenomenon and uses diverse data collection methods and sources. (mas)

CAST (See Center for Applied Special Technology)

caste-like minorities (See involuntary minorities)

categorical data
Data that are grouped according to some common feature or quality. One of the easiest ways to summarize categorical data is through the use of a pie chart. (kr)

categorical funding
Funding given by governmental or other bodies to schools, districts, or states to pay for specific programs designed to serve particular groups of students or particular student needs. (peb)

catharsis
An emotional outpouring that is linked to a need to release unconscious conflicts that are strongly felt but usually repressed. It is both an outer expression of affect or emotion and the inner awareness and acceptance of affect or emotion. Expressing emotion in this way is purported to lead to an increased awareness and acceptance of unwanted or repressed emotions and to greater self-awareness, understanding, and responsibility for one's feelings and behavior, although there is no scientific basis for these supposed positive effects of catharsis. (tsw, mgg)

CBI (See computer-based instruction)

CBO (See community-based organization)

CBT (See cognitive-behavior therapy)

CBT (See computer-based training)

CBTE (See competency-based teacher education)

CCC (See Civilian Conservation Corps)

CDA (See Child Development Associate)

CDE (See Civil Defense Education)

CDF (See Children's Defense Fund)

CD-ROM
Stands for Compact Disk Read Only Memory. A CD-ROM is an optical device for storing computer data. One CD-ROM can hold 680 megabytes of data, which is equivalent to 485 floppy disks. Because of this large storage capacity and the fact that CD-ROMs can be used on

different types of computers (i.e., both PC and Macintosh machines), many educational software programs come on CD-ROMs. In addition, recordable (CD-R) and rewriteable (CD-RW) CDs are useful for storing files that may be too large for a floppy disk, such as multimedia presentations. (kg1)

CDS (See child-directed speech)

CEEB (See College Entrance Examination Board, College Board)

ceiling
In cognitive and academic assessments, which generally begin with easier questions and become increasingly harder, a continuous series of items the subject answers incorrectly. It is assumed all items beyond this point would be too difficult for the respondent, so test administration is stopped. (jcp)

Center for Applied Special Technology (CAST)
A nonprofit research-based organization started in 1984 by a group of hospital-based educational researchers and clinicians. The organization focuses on innovative uses of technology to improve learning for all students, with an emphasis on those with disabilities. Research, service, and development efforts are guided by their concept of employing flexible digital materials called Universal Design for Learning. CAST is recognized for having developed Bobby, a web accessibility tool. (ms)

centers (See learning centers)

central nervous system (See nervous system)

ceramics
From the Greek *keramikos*, "of pottery," and, in spite of certain technical differences, used interchangeably with the term "pottery" as the making of objects out of clay to be glazed and fired. (kf)
See also pottery.

cerebellum
In Latin, cerebellum means "little brain." This structure below and behind the cerebral cortex is primarily known for its functions of fine-tuning and coordinating movements and in motor learning; however, it also contributes to some cognitive functions and is interconnected with the cerebral cortex. (pk1)

cerebral cortex
Thin but convoluted outer layer of the brain, site of processing that underlies all cognitive processes and especially higher cognition (e.g., language, thought, memory, etc.). It can be divided into four lobes and two roughly symmetrical hemispheres. The cortex is a part of the brain that developed relatively late in evolutionary history, and human cortices are more convoluted than those of most other species. The cerebral cortex is also known for its distinctive six-layer structure. (pk1)

cerebral palsy
A condition caused by injury to the parts of the brain that control the ability to use muscles, characterized by disordered movement and posture, delayed motor development, and atypical motoric findings on neurological examination. There are three main types of cerebral palsy: spastic, characterized by too much muscle tone or tightness; athetoid, characterized by uncontrolled body movements and low muscle tone; and mixed, a combination of both, with some high- and some low-tone muscles. (sr)

Certificate of Advanced Mastery (CAM)
Initially associated with educational reform in the state of Oregon, a certificate associated with various career pathways offered during the last two years of high school, providing students with a college-preparatory endorsement or a career or vocational-technical education endorsement, or both. (db)

Certificate of Advanced Study (CAS)

A post-master's continuing education advanced studies program for professional practitioners who wish to update skills, augment knowledge, or develop a specialization. Such programs are primarily self-determined and designed in consultation with an advisor. (ms)

Certificate of Initial Mastery (CIM)

Initially associated with educational reform in the state of Oregon, a certificate demonstrating that students have met the core academic subjects required of secondary schools, typically by grade 10 or age 16. (db)

certificate program

A sequence of courses in a given field or topic, leading to the award of a certificate upon successful completion of the sequence. A certificate program is a shorter, more focused course of study than a full degree program. (chb)

certification

Certification is the approval by a regulatory board or agency that has established standards or criteria, which must be met. State or federal mandates regulate most of these agencies or boards. Certification may be obtained through undergraduate work, post-baccalaureate work, or examination. Many mandates require professional development to update or renew the certification. In education, certification is an official license to teach. Certification takes several forms, such as emergency, initial, or standard, and often requires passing a test and taking specified courses, often as part of a teacher education program. Certification is usually determined separately by each state. (jr, peb)

CES (See Cooperative Extension Service)

CETA (See Comprehensive Employment and Training Act)

CEU (See continuing education unit)

CFAT (See Carnegie Foundation for the Advancement of Teaching)

chain of response model

A theory, put forward by Patricia Cross in *Adults as Learners,* that suggests that an adult's motivation to participate in education is the result of a series of steps. Those steps are self-evaluation of self-confidence to undertake the education, overcoming any negative attitudes about education, and understanding the importance of the goal and the rewards that may follow goal attainment. (jpc)

challenge (See confrontation)

challenge by choice

An adventure education term allowing participants to choose or say no to an activity, knowing that the opportunity for another attempt is always available. (rf)

chancellor

The title of the highest-ranking official in a unit of a university system or in the entire system; used alternately with president, depending upon established precedence in a particular system (i.e., in some university systems, presidents are the titular heads of the separate universities and report to the chancellors of the university system; in other systems, chancellors are heads of institutions and presidents are in charge of the overall system). (cf)

change

An alteration of the focus, emphasis, structures, systems, beliefs, expectations, or mechanisms within the social or educational structure that is characterized by one set of value systems, rules of behavior, or cultural symbols being replaced by another. Change is a result of reflecting, rethinking, or restructuring a system and may result from political, ideological, economic, technological, or demographic influences. Change can be isolated or systemic in an educational entity. In mathematical terms, a difference, such as in shape, size, or location. Change is expressed as motion and is quantified by using terms such as speed, acceleration, or distance traveled, and these terms are expressed as a ratio of the number representing the distance covered divided by the number representing the quantity of time. To move from one state of being or phase to another. In a school setting this process can involve changes in such areas as policy, personnel, or curriculum. Change may be a planned occurrence or a natural occurrence. (tm, kgh, jtr)

change agent
Someone who helps produce or who instigates changes in the status quo. (peb)

character
The sum of a person's vices, virtues, and dispositions to act that makes each person unique. Understanding good character is the central concern of virtue ethics. One of the debates about education today is the extent to which it does and should develop a certain sort of character, or whether the state, in the form of education, should be neutral on issues of character. Debates about the hidden curriculum often are over the extent to which the content of the hidden curriculum shapes character, and in what ways it should do so. The "character education" movement is directed at developing a set of "civic virtues" deemed necessary for civic life. (jc)

See also ethics; moral development; moral education; virtue ethics.

character education
An approach to education that focuses on developing students' character and supporting their moral reasoning and development. (bba)

characteristics of adults as learners (CAL)
A model, developed by Patricia Cross, that describes what is known about adults as learners. It consists of two types of variables: personal characteristics (physiological or aging and sociocultural life phases and psychological or development stages), and situational characteristics (variables unique to adult participants, such as full- versus part-time learning or mandatory versus voluntary participation). (las)

characterological blame
Conceptualizes explanations of achievement associated with self-perceptions concerning unchanging personal and innate attributes and characteristics (i.e., what one is like). These ability characteristics exist outside of the purview of individual control or development as unchanging and stable attributes. (hfs)

charity schools (See pauper schools)

charter schools
Autonomous public schools operating under a contract that has been negotiated between the organizers, who create and operate the school, and a sponsor, who oversees the terms of the contract. Charter schools pursue a set of objectives approved by the chartering agency, which is typically an arm of state government. (bba)

chat
An Internet-based utility that enables individuals to engage in a typed conversation. In a chat room, multiple people from remote locations can simultaneously communicate via typing. For example, students can discuss course concepts in real-time by connecting to an online chat from computers at home or school. (kg1)

CHAT (See CHILDES)

Chautauqua (See Chautauqua Movement)

Chautauqua Institute
A not-for-profit, 750-acre educational center beside Chautauqua Lake in southwestern New York State. Founded in 1874

as a two-week summer institute for Sunday school teachers, its scope was broadened to include academic subjects, music, art, and physical education. (js)

Chautauqua Movement
In 1874, John H. Vincent and Lewis Miller devised an adult education program in connection with a bible summer camp on the shores of Lake Chautauqua in western New York. The idea turned into a widespread adult education movement inaugurated in 1878 as the Chautauqua Literary and Scientific Circle, which included correspondence courses, reading circles, and university extensions. In the early 1900s mobile Chautauquas traveled around the country with speakers and exhibits. By the 1930s the onset of commercial radio, movies, and automobiles contributed to its decline as an active movement of the Progressive Era. (rih)

See also Chautauqua Institute.

CHEA (See Council for Higher Education Accreditation)

checklist
A generic term referring to a list of children's behaviors, teacher competencies, activities, or other items to accomplish, to create, or to maintain a quality service program. It is an easy and quick method to use in determining the effectiveness and needs of children, teachers, or programs. (pw)

checks and balances
A governmental system in which the powers of the legislative, judicial, and executive branches overlap so that each branch can check the actions of the others. The concept of checks and balances is commonly taught in government and U.S. history courses. (cb)

CHEMA (See Council of Higher Education Management Associations)

chemistry
The branch of science that studies matter, how matter interacts and is transformed, and the energy changes that result from these interactions and transformations. Includes topics such as the composition, structure, and properties of matter, and the different ways that matter can combine or react. (tw)

chiaroscuro
From the Italian chiaro (light) and scuro (dark). An effect in painting, drawing, and print making in which areas of light and shadow are emphasized so that objects and figures may appear to have more depth, volume, and weight. For example, when painting a muscled arm, the muscles themselves would be painted with light colors so that they appear to stand out, and the spaces between muscles would be painted with darker colors. Teen artists often explore chiaroscuro (calling it "shading") after comic book artists who feature muscular contour in their drawings. Examples of chiaroscuro abound in paintings by Leonardo da Vinci and engravings by Albrecht Durer. (ap)

Chicano/Chicana studies
A term relating to research and curriculum focused on Mexican Americans in the United States. One of a variety of ethnic studies programs developed in the 1960s and 1970s in response to cultural demands for inclusive and relevant curriculum, particularly at the college and university level. (jqa, jwc)

chief academic officer
A title that designates the principle administrator who has the responsibility and accountability for the entire academic program in a school, school system, or institution of higher education. Formerly such persons were called "associate" or "assistant" superintendents of curriculum and instruction in the elementary or secondary system; they are often called

provost or vice president or vice chancellor for academic affairs in higher education. The change in terminology parallels the use of business and military nomenclature in education, a trend that has a long history in educational leadership. (fwe)

child abuse

An act, or failure to act, by a person responsible for a child's welfare (e.g., parent, caretaker, teacher, employee of residential facility) or by a person who is in a position of power over a child, which results in death, serious physical or emotional harm, sexual abuse or exploitation, or the imminent risk or threat of such serious harm to a child. Major types of child abuse include physical abuse, neglect, sexual abuse, and emotional or psychological abuse. Laws regarding child abuse are determined by the civil and criminal codes of each state. (llf, emm)

child art

The art of children has been of interest to adults since before its praise by the French philosopher Rousseau. The playful and powerful art of children has been emulated by modernist artists like Klée and Miro, studied by cognitive psychologists like Gardner and Winner, and celebrated for its inherent embodiment of human expression by scholars such as Arnheim and Kellogg. Despite the similarities, many prefer to distinguish children's work from that of trained professionals, by calling the work "child art." (jd)

child care (or childcare)

Care that is provided outside of the child's immediate family/home environment. Care may be given during the day or night hours in centers, individual homes, or religious facilities. (jlj)

child care license

A state-issued license indicating that a facility or home has met government/state operation requirements and is authorized to operate. The license states the maximum number of children allowed, the age ranges of children allowed, whether day and/or night care may be provided, and whether or not transportation may be provided. After initial issuance, the facility or home is subject to repeated, unannounced inspections to ensure continued compliance. (jlj)

child development

The stages of maturation from infancy to adulthood. The maturation process is typically sequential and involves physiological, psychological, cognitive, behavioral, and social development. There are many theories of child development that focus on differing aspects. For example, Urie Bronfenbrenner's ecological model of child development considers that the environment (setting, family and other relationships, the larger community, and the individual's physiological and psychological self) contains key influences. Other theorists such as Freud focused on the personality, while some such as Erik Erikson emphasized the role of society. (npo)

Child Development Associate (CDA)

A credential awarded by the Council for Early Childhood Professional Recognition, an organization that advocates for and provides specific training for child care professionals within center-based, home-based, and home visiting programs. The CDA is designed to assess skills of child care providers who manage a program in the home and to assess their abilities to meet the needs of infants, toddlers, and preschoolers. The program of study takes approximately one year to complete, and the CDA is evaluated through a written exam, a verbal interview, and a portfolio. Community or technical colleges may offer curricula supporting study for the CDA credential. (kdc, npo)

Child Find
A process used by school systems to locate, identify, and assess/evaluate children to determine if the child is eligible to receive therapeutic or special education services through the early intervention or public school system. A service directed by each state for identifying and diagnosing unserved children with disabilities, with an emphasis on children ages birth to six years. (kms, sr)

Child Language Data Exchange System (See CHILDES)

Child Study Movement
Created by G. Stanley Hall in the late 1890s, the movement was designed to research children's knowledge bases. Research methodology included student observations and the recording, reflection, and study of these observations. This allowed parents and teachers to more effectively gear teaching methods and materials to the child's level. This movement was a grassroots effort that swept across the nation and became international through the creation of organizations with a membership supporting and promoting these studies. The National Education Association devoted much effort to this movement, though it gained greater recognition through John Dewey's closely related child-centered education platform. (rih)

child-centered curriculum
Developmental or educational activities and interactions that are based on children's interests and the choices they make about learning activities. (mc1)

child-directed activity (See child-directed play)

child-directed play
Children's interactions with materials, play objects, or other persons that reflect the flow of an individual youngster's exploration, interest, curiosity, and invention. (mc1)

child-directed speech (CDS)
Also called motherese, and colloquially, baby talk. A specialized speech register used in some cultures by caregivers with very young children. For example, in many Westernized cultures, CDS is characterized by short simplified utterances, special lexical items, and prosodic features such as exaggerated intonation patterns, exaggerated stress, and higher and more variable pitch than in adult speech. Research suggests that CDS supports children's acquisition of key language features and conversational routines. (jrk)

CHILDES (Child Language Data Exchange System)
A computerized system for the study, analysis, and exchange of child language data (MacWhinney and Snow, 1995). The system has three interrelated components: CHAT (Codes for the Human Analysis of Talk), conventions for the transcription and coding of language; CLAN (Codes for Language Analysis), a package of language analysis programs integrated with CHAT; and a database of child language corpora representing a variety of languages and interactive settings. (jrk)

child-initiated activity (See child-initiated play)

child-initiated play
Instructional or supportive activities facilitated, sustained, or provided by caregivers but that initially reflect observed children's engagements. (mc1)

children's counting schemes
Counting schemes used by children are of four types: perceptual unit items, motor unit items, verbal unit items, and abstract unit items. For a description of each, see under individual listings. (amr)

Children's Defense Fund (CDF)
A private, nonprofit organization founded in 1973 and funded through foundations, corporation grants, and private donations.

The CDF mission statement is "leave no child behind," and the organization advocates for the rights of children through its divisions: Healthy Start, Head Start, Fair Start, Safe Start, and Moral Start. CDF promotes quality, comprehensive health services; affordable, safe child care; and the economic security of families. It educates the public about those children who are victims of abuse, neglect, and domestic violence through public service announcements. CDF has a partnership with the religious community and does not receive money from the U.S. government. (kdc)

children's folk
Since the 1970s, there has been an effort on the part of many folk singers to bring to children quality folk music, through visiting artist appearances in schools, television shows, recordings, and the like. While there are countless folk songs that seem to be particularly well suited to the sort of stories young children are reading in school (e.g., "Frog Went a Courtin,'" "Old Dan Tucker," etc.), the term "children's folk" refers to any folk music presented with care and at a high level of quality for young children. (jd)
See also folk art/music.

Children's Television Act (CTA)
Passed by Congress in 1990, the Children's Television Act legislates an increase in the quality and quantity of television programs aimed at children. The act requires broadcast television stations to develop core programming for children of an educational and informational nature. In support of the act, the Federal Communications Commission (FCC) passed rules that defined what constituted a core program for children, that set a minimum number of hours a week of core programs, and that required that advanced information be made available about the programs to be aired. The act also restricted the amount of advertising allowed during children's programming. (ms)

children's theater
A genre of theater comprising dramatic performances intended for children as audience members, in which either children (often along with adults) or just adults are the performers. Often consists of the dramatization of children's stories, but also includes many original works that span the dramatic range from light and comedic to serious and thought-provoking. Most institutional children's theaters both perform works and provide active educational opportunities—through classes in acting, movement, and improvisation—for children. (em)

choice
In early childhood education, choice is providing children with options from which they may freely choose. These options could be varied or similar, but their presence empowers the learner to express personal interests and needs. (mc1)

choice, vocational (See career choice)

choir
From the Latin *chorus*. Historically used to denote a church vocal ensemble, but currently used to identify both secular and sacred singing groups. Many popular professional singers got their start singing in their church choirs. May also be used to specify instrument-exclusive groups (e.g., flute choir, cello choir) or any organized arts performance ensemble (e.g., dance choir). (jbl)
See also chorus.

choral
As a noun, any hymn tune sung by a chorus or choir or church congregation; as an adjective, having to do with vocal ensemble/chorus music or performance (e.g., the composer specialized in choral music). To be distinguished from chorale, which is specifically a German Protestant (Lutheran) hymn tune that is usually harmonized in four parts vocally (soprano, alto, tenor, bass) or composed for and played

by the organ, as epitomized by the organ chorales of J. S. Bach. (jbl)

choreography

Derived from the Greek *choreia* (dancing) and *graphe* (writing), choreography refers to the arrangement of steps, actions, and movements within a dance piece, and the formal notation of such movements. The "choreographer" is the person who creates the dances for a performance. In a school musical theater production, the choreographer works with the stage director, who is responsible for the entire production. Since so few schools have sequential dance programs, choreography is rarely taught in schools. In community centers, however, choreography is often presented as a skill that may be learned and exercised by advanced dancers. (em)

chorus

Originally referred to an organized band of singers and dancers in the religious collective body of vocalists in drama and music who perform in a group as opposed to those who perform singly. It can also refer to the repeated refrains in vocal music or poetry (e.g., the chorus of the song). Chorus, or the generally extracurricular gathering of groups of songsters at American schools, is a popular school arts activity. (yjl)

See also choir.

chronological age

The actual age of an individual calculated from the date of birth. (sr)

CIM (See certificate of initial mastery)

circle graph

A graph that shows how various categories of a set of data account for certain proportions of the whole. Circle graphs are many times referred to as pie graphs or pie charts. (kr)

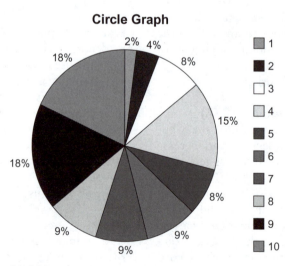

Circle Graph

2% 4% 8% 18% 18% 15% 8% 9% 9% 9%

1
2
3
4
5
6
7
8
9
10

Circle Graph

festivals (such as the choir of a church), or in ancient Greek dramatic performances that explain or comment upon the course of events between "acts." In its modern use, a chorus refers to the

citation analysis

Involves analyzing how many times journal articles or authors have been referenced in other scholarly work. ISI Web of Science and SCOPUS are currently the most well-known sources of citation analysis, but Google Scholar offers similar information. Several library vendors can also provide citation analysis information, but their information is restricted to information provided by their own journals and publications. There has been criticism about the limitations of citation analysis and complaints about the misuse of the results. More recently, there have been questions about its validity given the growth of open access and web publishing. (sn)

Citizen Schools

A nonprofit organization started in 1995 in Boston that conducts after-school programs that are focused on middle school students in partnership with middle schools. Students are given the opportunity to engage in apprenticeship programs under the direction of local community and business leaders who work with the students on real world projects. Students also receive additional extended academic support that is coordinated with the school and the family to increase academic success. Citizen schools can be found in other cities across the United States, including Brooklyn, Houston, and Oakland, California. (ms)

Citizen Schools (historical)

A set of schools developed in the Sea Islands of South Carolina and Georgia during the 1940s and 1950s, established by African Americans such as Esau Jenkins and Septima Clark, in order to provide an education to underserved and undereducated adult African Americans. The schools were established to prepare African American adults for the numerous literacy tests utilized to deny them the vote. Often because of the service provided, the schools were operated clandestinely in the back rooms of businesses. The schools used any material on hand, such as newspapers or hymnals, to teach reading and writing skills. (hfs)

citizenship

The philosophy, words, and actions associated with belonging to and supporting a particular community, such as an organization, town, city, state, or country. Citizenship entails the roles, rights, and responsibilities associated with care, betterment, and promotion of an organization or area through shared governance, economic stability, recreational participation, and public service. (npg)

citizenship education

A type of education offered to immigrants, designed to make them aware of their rights and responsibilities as citizens in a democracy, and to develop an understanding of the importance of being active citizens. Included in this education are the social health traits of honesty; respect for others; kindness; cooperation; respect for home, school, community, and environments; and generosity. In the United States, citizenship education may include preparation for the national citizenship test. (las, knl)

civic education

Education for citizenship. In a democratic polity, civic education includes both history and other course content intended to foster feelings of patriotism and the civic virtues necessary for life as a citizen participating in civic life. American policy makers developed and have supported the common school because of a belief in the importance of civic education; the common school movement was historically charged with civic education as its primary responsibility. (jc)

See also education; vocational education.

civics

The branch of political science that focuses on rights and duties of citizens, and civic affairs. It involves participatory skills as well as knowledge about government and society. Knowledge of civics can help increase understandings about citizenship and society. A form of education aimed at making learners aware of their rights and responsibilities as citizens and building their capacity to exercise them effectively and responsibly. (knl, las)

civil case

A case referring to private or personal rights. Legal advocacy applied to individual cases, such as cases to protect the rights of individuals with disabilities. (sr)

Civil Defense Education (CDE)

At its most basic level, Civil Defense Education is a system of education that imparts various survival tactics in the event of natural or manmade disasters. The most common feature of CDE as practiced in most American schools includes fire and severe weather drills. During the Cold War, CDE took on a different dimension because of the presence of the nuclear threat. "Duck and Cover" drills were routine features of CDE at the height of the Cold War, as schoolchildren across the country were taught how to protect themselves in the event of a nuclear attack. (ah)

Civil Rights Act of 1964

A Congressional act that greatly expanded civil rights protections under U.S. law. This landmark legislation banned racial segregation in schools, employment, residential housing, and public facilities. It was made enforceable with the addition of Title VI, which states that federal funds cannot be used to finance programs or activities where there is "discrimination on the grounds of race, color, or national origin." As federal legislation, it overruled the existing Jim Crow laws, that is, state and local laws enacted in many parts of the United States that essentially mandated segregation in public facilities, including schools. For schools across the United States, the Civil Rights Act of 1964 had the effect of speeding up the desegregation process initiated by the 1954 *Brown v. Board of Education* Supreme Court decision. School districts that refused to integrate not only risked losing government funding but also faced possible legal action, since Title IV of the Act specifically authorized the U.S. attorney general to initiate lawsuits against school districts that continued their patterns of racial discrimination. (acp)

See also *Brown v. Board of Education of Topeka, Kansas*; desegregation.

Civil Rights Movement

Popularly thought of as the political and social movement occurring in the 1960s in the attempt to end discrimination and provide equal rights for African Americans. Now thought of as encompassing women's rights, gay rights, and the rights of all Americans to be free from discrimination. (jqa, jwc)

civil union

A legally recognized union similar to marriage, established to provide same-sex couples with certain rights, benefits, and responsibilities. Such rights are granted by the State and do not include the benefits accorded to a federal civil marriage. (jb2)

See also domestic partnership.

Civilian Conservation Corps (CCC)

The Civilian Conservation Corps, or Emergency Conservation Work (ECW) Act, was enacted as part of the New Deal in 1933. The Act was to ease widespread unemployment while improving the nation's forests. More than three million men enrolled in the Corps. Each CCC camp had an educational component that included reading, writing, arithmetic, and vocational training in areas such as carpentry and forestry. Some camps offered advanced academic courses. Teaching more than 35,000 men to read and write was a significant accomplishment of the CCC. The CCC remained in existence until June of 1942. (lh)

CLAN (See CHILDES)

class
A group, all members of which possess at least one common characteristic. A group of students scheduled to report regularly at a particular time to a particular teacher. The students pursuing a particular subject, frequently at different levels within a school, such as a French-language class in a high school. All students in an educational institution who entered at the same time and graduate together. Class can also be used to denote characteristics relative to socioeconomic status. (gac)

class action
In education, the term is usually applied to a lawsuit brought by one or more persons on behalf of all persons similarly situated as to complaint and remedy sought. Examples might include a group of parents or students bringing suit against a school district due to injury caused by asbestos or lead paint in a school building, or regarding the use of standardized test scores for the purpose of student promotion or retention. (mm)

class adviser (See adviser/advisor)

class (grade) average
A measure of the middle position on a scale of evaluation, the central tendency. Typically the mean is calculated when determining the average for a group of students on a given assessment or group of tasks. Class average can be used to track the direction and degree of individual student deviations from the group mean or for assigning marks. (jw)

class size
The number of students who meet on a regular basis with one particular teacher. Many school districts have established specific teacher–student ratios based on grade level or subject area. (jtr)

classical test theory (CTT)
(See item analysis)

classification
The process of assigning an event, trend, or other data to a category or other generalized description based on similarities to other events, trends, or comparable data. (jjc)

classism
Discrimination based on social class. Typically manifest as discrimination against poor, underprivileged, and/or working-class people. (jqa, jwc)

classroom library
A collection of books and other reading materials located in a classroom and intended for the use of students in the classroom. Classroom libraries may be located in a designated area of the room or on movable carts, and they may consist of either permanent or variable collections of materials. (bba)

classroom management
A teacher's methods for establishing and maintaining an environment in which teaching and learning can occur, including techniques for preventing and handling student misbehavior. (bba)

classroom performance systems
(See clicker technology)

classroom walk-through
A structured or semistructured procedure for observing teachers in classrooms, usually for a very brief period time and offering highly focused comments on very limited criteria. There are several different philosophies of conducting walk-throughs. Some simply use standard evaluative criteria for teachers loaded into an iPod and later downloaded by the principal. Others are much more interested in using the data for self-improvement and promoting critical reflection. (fwe)

class-size reduction (CSR)
Includes the processes to achieve class sizes smaller than the ones presently in

place, such as changing the class size from 25 to 16 or so. One needs accurate pre and post data to support the change process. (cma)

clause
A group of at least two words that contains a subject and predicate; simple sentences are single clauses, while more complex sentences contain multiple clauses. (cld)

CLEP (See College Level Examination Program)

Clery Act (See Student Right-to-Know and Campus Security Act)

click art (See clip art)

clicker technology
A technology used in classrooms that allows students to respond individually using handheld remote devices (clickers) to questions posed by the instructor and projected onto a large screen. Using software specifically designed to work with the clickers, the instructor will project questions onto a screen, students will respond to the questions individually using the clickers, and the responses are electronically recorded. Responses are typically displayed immediately to the entire class, but students may be required to log in, and their individual responses are then recorded and graded. Instructors may use clicker technology to ask questions, review materials, conduct class surveys, or give quizzes. Clickers, also called immediate response devices, are utilized to actively engage students in learning and to provide immediate assessment of students' comprehension of material. Clicker technology is referred to by many names, including interactive audience response systems, classroom performance systems (CPS), student response systems, and personal response systems. (pw1)

client-centered therapy
This nondirective therapy, developed by Carl Rogers and sometimes referred to as Rogerian Therapy, is designed to create an environment in which the client feels accepted and is able to find solutions to his or her own problems. To create this environment, the therapist demonstrates unconditional positive regard (i.e., not evaluating, judging, or criticizing) for the client, is genuine, and demonstrates empathy. In turn, the client is able to see him- or herself more realistically and clearly, which leads to conflict resolution, a reorganization of thoughts and feelings, and a change in behavior. (tsw)

clinic, vocational (See vocational clinic)

clinical experiences
In teacher education, activities or observations accomplished by preservice teachers in Pre-K–12 schools or other authentic sites, usually before student teaching and as a condition to completing a teacher certification program. (peb)

clinical practitioner
Within the area of education, an education professional currently employed in the field who works with or is observed by a preservice or student teacher. (peb)

clinical supervision
Supervision by teachers, professors, or other education personnel of persons receiving clinical experiences in an educational setting. (peb)

clinical training
Work-based learning that is required to accrue knowledge and skills in occupations leading to semiprofessional or professional degrees, licensure, or certification. (db)

clip art
Commercially or publicly available, public domain graphics for inserting into

presentations, posters, and other documents. Clip art is available for a wide range of themes, such as science, geography, and holidays. Teachers or students can use clip art to more effectively convey their message by using graphics in combination with text or to simply enhance the appearance of their computer-generated materials. (kg1)

closed campus
A school policy that requires students, once on school property, to remain on site until the end of the school day. Students must receive permission of school officials to leave school property. (jw)

closed questions
Questions for which there is only one acceptable answer or interpretation. (bba)

closed skill
A motor skill that is performed in an environment that is fixed and does not change. (rf)

close-ended question
A specific type of question that allows a counselor, or therapist, to influence the quantity and quality of a client's response. Typically requires/encourages a short, one- or two-word answer. "Was that hurtful?" is an example of a close-ended question. If used appropriately, these types of questions can help a counselor collect relevant information and/or clarify any misunderstandings. They can be particularly helpful with clients that are tangential and/or who have a tendency to dominate a therapy session. (ksp)

cloze procedure
A testing procedure, typically considered an integrative measure of language proficiency. The term is adopted from "closure" in Gestalt psychology, which refers to the human tendency to complete an incomplete picture or text to construct a whole. A cloze test requires the reader to fill in the gaps in the text. In the standard cloze procedure, the words are omitted at a regular interval (e.g., every fifth word), and the reader is expected to provide exact words to fill in the blanks. Because of the challenging nature of the test, even for a proficient, adult, native speaker, and the strict scoring criteria, some alternative versions of cloze procedures have been introduced. One of them is a modified cloze test, in which blanks are not created at an arbitrary, fixed interval, but at selective places in the text. This technique may be used to assess proficiency in specific grammatical categories. Another version is a multiple-choice cloze test, in which multiple choices are provided for each blank. The other type of cloze tests includes those in which synonyms as well as exact replacements are accepted for correct answers. This technique may, however, suffer from lower reliability. Cloze procedures are widely recognized and often used for teaching and testing of reading comprehension and second language acquisition. Despite the efficiency and reliability of cloze procedures, many have questioned their validity as a tool for measuring global comprehension of text rather than subskills such as syntax, vocabulary, and/or comprehension of text at a local/sentential level. (h-jk)

clumsiness (See motor skill disorder)

cluster grouping
A strategy for serving identified "gifted" students in a mixed-ability classroom by scheduling several (generally five to eight) to the same teacher rather than distributing advanced learners across several classrooms. The location of a small group of exceptionally capable students in a single classroom with a teacher prepared to provide appropriate instruction is intended to provide greater impetus and ease in curriculum differentiation. (bda)

CMI (See computer-managed instruction)

coaching

The actions taken by more experienced peers or adults who guide and support children engaged in a particular learning experience or a sequence of similar experiences. The guidance and support scaffold successive approximations of the competence or conceptualization desired. (mc1)

co-curricular activities

Noncredit academic endeavors conducted by student organizations outside of classroom efforts that promote in-class learning (e.g., language clubs, student publications, moot court, mock trial organizations, etc.). (cf)

coda

Within a syllable the elements (usually consonants) that follow the nucleus (e.g., [nts] is the coda in the last syllable in comments). (smt)

code of conduct

Any set of rules or standards set forth by the governing board of an institution designed to balance the rights and needs of the individual with the responsibility of the individual to meet the needs of the institution. The purpose of a code of conduct is to set forth the standards of conduct expected of members of a community in order to protect the community and to maintain order and stability. Ideally, a code of conduct is not an exhaustive list of punishable misconduct but rather standards to guide individual choices. A code of conduct may or may not include disciplinary consequences for violations, but failure to follow the code of conduct is understood to imply possible removal from the community. Most schools utilize some type of student code of conduct. Some schools, for example, are specific about dress codes while others are not. A school's code of conduct reflects the morals of the community in which it resides. One school may prohibit body piercing and tattoos, while another school may allow them, depending upon the standards of the individual school's community. (dm)

See also ethical principles and codes of conduct.

codes

This term generally refers to a set of laws or principles that stipulate conduct, as in the NEA code, state and local codes of ethics, or a school district's student code of conduct. Because codes are documents that are written for the purpose of guiding behavior, they are necessarily normative or moral in nature. Most address moral or ethical issues. This term may also refer to standards required by government and state regulations, as in building and safety codes that must be followed by the school's building and maintenance department. Another use of the term may refer to codes as formulas for transcription of information, as in the budget codes that are used in budget reporting to identify types of funds and functions of expenditures. (jr)

codes for language analysis (See CHILDES)

codes for the human analysis of talk (See CHILDES)

code-switching

Process by which participants within a conversation, who are fluent in multiple languages, switch between different languages during the course of the conversation. Code-switching may occur formally in order to enhance an ethnic or sociocultural difference, or informally within a multicultural community. (ms)

coding

The process of classifying and sorting research data, resulting in an organizational system to manage the data and facilitate analysis. The researcher reviews the observation notes or interview transcripts to identify important or recurring concepts, ideas, or themes in the data. The researcher marks the relevant data and labels them with descriptive names or categories. The data within each category are then gathered together for further study. (mas)

coed (See coeducation)

coeducation
Instruction of both males and females in the same institution and usually in the same classroom. In America, until the early 19th century, sexes were generally separated when feasible. The distance between schools, rural populace, and the democratizing influences of early republicanhood contributed to the admission of girls to primary and then grammar and secondary schools with boys. In general it was not until after the Civil War that women were admitted to state universities with men. Young women who attended formerly all-male institutions were often called "coeds." (vmm)

cognition
A broad term used to distinguish the abstract, reasoning components of mind/brain from other psychological functions such as affect/emotion, sensation, conditioned learning, and the like. "Cognitive" often precedes the names of certain disciplines. For example, cognitive psychology, cognitive science, cognitive development, or cognitive neuroscience all seek to understand the "thinking" processes of mind/brain through their respective methods and lenses. Research on cognition often encompasses the diverse fields of psychology, linguistics, anthropology, philosophy, and computer science. (dh)

cognitive
Term used to describe the process people use in perceiving, reasoning, understanding, and judging their environment, and the information they receive. A cognitive disability refers to difficulty in learning. (sr)

Cognitive Academic Language Proficiency (CALP)
A term, first used by James Cummins, for the more complex, decontextualized language expected in school assignments and academic settings. This framework, developed to help understand the language development and facility of language learners, is said to take much longer than Basic Interpersonal Communicative Skills (BICS) to develop, often as much as 7 to 10 years in comparison to 2 to 3 years with BICS. (cld)

cognitive apprenticeship
An apprenticeship designed to explicitly teach students the processes used in complex tasks, incorporating factual and conceptual knowledge with problem solving. In teacher education, the experienced practicing teacher models appropriate practice, advises, and scaffolds new knowledge in an authentic context, while gradually reducing the level of support provided to the apprentice. The apprentice learns both from the experienced teacher and from other novices. (kmt, nfd, peb)

cognitive approach to art education
In the 1940s art education was viewed as a means for children to express emotions and develop as "whole" people. This non-academic approach is thought to have kept art education in the margins of general education. With the advent of the electronic computer in the 1950s and a consequent cognitive revolution in thought, art education has been reconfigured by psychologists, educators, and advocates as the education of cognition, of important thinking skills like critical thinking and interpretation and habits of learning appropriate to serious thought. This new approach has advanced the status of art education and spawned movements such as DBAE and Arts PROPEL. (jd)

See also Discipline-Based Art Education; Arts PROPEL.

cognitive-behavior therapy (CBT)

A form of psychotherapy based on the idea that emotional and behavioral reactions are learned and caused by one's thoughts. Therefore, modifying thoughts can change the way one feels and behaves. Rational emotive behavior therapy, rational behavior therapy, and dialectic behavior therapy are popular CBT approaches. Most CBT therapies are time-limited, structured and directive, and assume that a collaborative, trusting therapeutic relationship is necessary but not sufficient for therapeutic change to occur. CBT therapists are active in session, often teaching their clients how to think differently by employing both cognitive and behavioral techniques, such as cognitive restructuring, disputing irrational beliefs, modeling, practice, and assigning homework. (sdc)

cognitive development

Cognition refers to mental processes such as thinking, reasoning, and other abstract abilities and behaviors. Cognitive development is the process an individual goes through to acquire these complex intellectual abilities. Piagetian theories of cognitive development are reflected in stages of sensory-motor, preoperational, concrete operational, and formal operational development. While not all educators agree with these stages, they have had a strong effect on classroom practices. (npo)

See also concrete operational development; formal operational development; preoperational development; sensory-motor development.

cognitive disability (See cognitive)

cognitive disorder

A category of mental disorders characterized by disturbances in consciousness (e.g., delirium) and/or memory impairment (e.g., dementia, amnesia). Associated symptoms often involve disruption in abstract mental activities, such as attention, concentration, judgment and insight, visuospatial abilities, symbol representation, complex rule use, and problem solving. (kab)

cognitive dissonance

A tension experienced in the mind when holding or observing two seemingly contradictory ideas, usually opposing beliefs or understandings of a certain reality, both of which appear equally valid. (sh)

See also dissonance.

cognitive measurement

The practice of evaluating cognitive capacity and abilities through quantitative methodologies. Cognition can also be assessed qualitatively by using a variety of pedagogies through which students can exhibit the understanding of their relationship to knowledge, its intellectualization, and its embodiment, such as portfolios, critical research or topic papers, role plays/skits, multimedia projects, websites, service learning opportunities, and other relevant projects. Cognition is more than the ability to intellectually recollect or apply information; it is the comprehensive understanding of knowledge production through all sorts of interactions in daily living. Such assessments are usually in the form of standardized, norm-referenced tests. These tests are often used as predictors of academic success. (jtr, lev)

cognitive neuroscience

A subdiscipline of neuroscience that studies the neural correlates (e.g., neurotransmitters, brain structures) of cognitive functions (e.g., perception, memory)—or how cognitive functions are produced by the brain. Cognitive neuroscience draws from fields such as cognitive science, psychology, neuroscience, and linguistics. Its approach includes behavioral/experimental paradigms, as well as computational/modeling techniques. Methods include, but are not limited to, neuroimaging, electrophysiology, brain lesion studies, and single and multicell recordings in nonhuman animals. (jok)

cognitive reframe
A therapeutic technique wherein a client's irrational, maladaptive, or negative thoughts are identified and challenged. The client is encouraged to restructure, or "reframe," these thoughts into rational, adaptive, and/ or positive thoughts. (sc)

Cognitively Guided Instruction (CGI)
A philosophy of teaching early mathematics based on research done at the University of Wisconsin-Madison since the 1980s. CGI teachers give children mathematical problems to solve using their own strategies and invented algorithms, then use children's responses to plan and prepare subsequent problem-solving lessons. As an approach to teacher development it focuses on helping teachers become reflective practitioners. (ey)

cohort
A group of people who start and progress through a degree program together. The cohort is meant to provide students with a sense of cohesiveness and identity with the program and with their classmates. Any group of people that persists over time. In teacher education programs, a group of students deliberately placed together to travel through the duration of the course of study and to share common preservice experiences, such as academic and methods classes and field placements in classrooms. (jwg, reb)

Coleman Report (See *Equality of Educational Opportunity*)

colic
Discomfort that often occurs in children between birth and four months of age. This discomfort is often attributed to stomach or gas pains, but the term is also applied to "fussy" children as an explanation for their behavior. Infants with colic seemingly cry constantly, causing stress to themselves and their caregivers. Colicky infants will sometimes curl or arch, seeming to be in pain. Some common remedies include infant massage, changing formula or diet of the nursing mother, holding, rocking, or walking the infant, or taking the child for a ride in a car. Pediatricians should be consulted for advice. (kdc)

collaborative betterment
Process of collaboration in which initiative and efforts are developed and controlled by large institutions such as schools and universities and include advisory community-based representation. Such leadership is thought to limit individual long-term ownership, agency, and self-determination in the community. (hfs)

collaborative empowerment
A process of collaboration in which initiatives and efforts begin in communities and later move to engage and include larger institutions such as schools and universities in those efforts. Such leadership is thought to produce long-term ownership, agency, and self-determination in the community. (hfs)

collaborative group strategies
Small groups of students pursue academic objectives through a cooperative effort. Group activities may include discussing information, problem solving, planning, decision making, and questioning. A group product or presentation often results from this collaboration. Collaborative group work has been shown to enhance attitudes toward school and toward peers. (mje, jah)

collaborative inquiry
An interactive process of mutual exploration of ideas and evidence. Collaborative inquiry provides an opportunity for group creativity and the development of shared meanings and enhances a group's capacity to think and act in a coordinated way. (jsj)

collaborative learning
A method of teaching and learning in which students work together to explore

a significant question or create a meaningful project. Collaborative learning is the umbrella term encompassing many forms of learning, from small group projects to the more specific form of group work called cooperative learning. A group of students discussing a lecture, or students from different schools working together over the Internet on a shared assignment, are both examples of collaborative learning. Collaborative learning has its origins in higher education. (cf)

See also cooperative learning.

collaborative model

In teacher education, a design in which the program is planned, managed, or run through the participation of different entities. These organizations may include various schools, districts, departments in a university, and other stakeholders in the educational process. (peb)

collage

The gluing of paper, fabrics, and natural or manufactured materials onto a flat surface, frequently also embellished with marks in pencil, pen, or paint. The technique of juxtaposing or overlapping elements in an artistic composition, with possible application (as layered complex constructions) in language arts, music, dance, or theater. "Collage" evolved out of "papiers colleés," glued pieces of colored paper that were widely used in the 19th century. The technique became central to modern art after Picasso and Braque created Cubist paintings incorporating a wide variety of materials, including newspaper clippings, pieces of wood and glass, and straw cane. (lj)

collected multiunits

Based on collections of objects (e.g., a 10-unit is made by conceptually collecting 10 single-unit items; a thousand-unit by a collection of 1,000 single-unit items). (amr)

See also sequence multiunits.

collection

Many items brought together as a set; or an experientially bounded plurality. (dc)

College Board (CEEB)

Founded in 1900, this nonprofit membership's association is composed of more than 3,800 schools, colleges, universities, and other educational organizations. Each year the College Board serves over three million students and their parents, 22,000 high schools, and 3,500 colleges through major programs and services in college admission, guidance, assessment, financial aid, enrollment, and teaching and learning. (cf)

College Entrance Examination Board (CEEB) (See College Board)

College Level Examination Program (CLEP)

The College Board's credit-by-examination program, which enables persons to prove college-level achievement in 34 different subject areas and receive up to two years of college credit. Many institutions grant credit for CLEP, but each sets its own policies. CLEP is designed to measure knowledge gained through previous course work, independent study, cultural pursuits, travel, special interests, military service, and professional development. It is frequently associated with the military and is free of charge to qualifying U.S. military personnel. (sn)

college preparation

A program of courses or a curriculum at the secondary level designed for students who wish to enroll at institutions of higher learning following graduation. (jw)

college tech prep

Technical preparation (tech prep) programs providing academic career preparation and vocational-technical courses of study that ensure students are prepared to transition from the secondary to the postsecondary level ready to pursue college-level studies. (db)

See also technical preparation.

college transition (See bridge programs)

collegiality

Collegiality describes the sense of community and shared responsibility in a college or university, or in specific departments and programs. Aspects of collegiality include sharing information about teaching strategies and research projects, joining other members of the university or college community to attend university or community events, and working together in team teaching or coauthored research. Members of an academic community, including faculty, graduate students, undergraduate students, administrators, and other college or university workers, benefit from a sense of intellectual community. Collegiality among individuals opens up communication and makes this community possible. (cf)

Collegiate Anti-Militarism League

A pacifist college organization founded in 1915 that fought against America's entry into World War I and promoted a negotiated peace and a world society free of militarism. Its members included the 1946 Nobel Peace Prize recipient and Wellesley College social economist Emily Greene Balch. (aja)

colonialism

The policy of a sovereign state having a colonial territory abroad. Significant waves of European colonialism occurred from the 16th to the 19th century throughout the Americas, Southern Asia, Australasia/ Oceania, and Africa. While forms of colonialism continued into the 20th century through American, European, Japanese, and Russian rule, decolonization (colonies regaining sovereignty) has also occurred. (vkh)

See also colonization; decolonization; postcolonialism.

colonization

The process of a colonial power taking control of a formerly independent group of people (e.g., British Empire colonizing South Asia). Common practices include the subordination and victimization of a colony's peoples by the ruling colonizer and the exploitation of environmental and natural resources. The process of colonization often includes forcing the colonizer's cultural, social, and political structures, and most significantly, the colonizer's theories, practices, and values of education on the colonized people (e.g., boarding/residential schools for Native American children). (vkh)

See also colonialism; decolonization; postcolonialism.

color theory

Color has three properties: hue or tint (e.g., red); intensity (e.g., bright or dull red); and value, the lightness or darkness of a color. The color wheel describes the relationships between colors and is laid out so that any two primary colors (red, yellow, blue) are separated by the secondary colors (orange, violet, green). Primary colors are basic and cannot be mixed from other elements. One can mix two primaries to get a secondary color. Color has value, and these values can be divided into shades (relative darkness of color) and tints (relative lightness of color). (kpb)

color-blind

The point of view that race and ethnicity should not matter. Advocates of a color-blind classroom, for example, take the approach that the most equitable way to treat students is as if race is irrelevant. In contrast, the multicultural education approach encourages teachers to acknowledge difference in the classroom and to actively engage students in discussions around race and ethnicity. (acp)

comedy

A form of entertainment (e.g., film, play, or book) that is intentionally amusing in its depiction of characters and/or description of action. What all genres, periods, and styles of comedy share is a desire to make the spectator or reader laugh. Characters of humble origins and plots with happy endings framed the basic structure of comedy in classical Greek theater. Later the structure expanded to include "low comedy," akin to burlesque or "slapstick," which uses visuals, gags, and physical blows as comic devices, and "high comedy" like satire, which uses wordplay, allusions, and witty situations for comic staging. (kbc)

comic books

Comic books are magazine-like story-books in which the narrative unfolds through sequential panels of visual images enhanced by story lines and dialogue (contained in bubbles). Featured characters range from superheroes like Superman and Wonder Woman to teen romancers like Archie and Katy Keene, to Disney cartoon characters for younger readers. Classic Illustrated comics presented famous books like *Huckleberry Finn* and *Les Miserables* in condensed comic book form. Beyond the themes, the artwork of comic books has captured the imagination of preadolescent and adolescent artists, who learn about form and style from emulating the work of comic book illustrators. The visual narratives these youthful artists create (in which they explore personal issues) have been of interest to arts researchers like Brent and Marjorie Wilson. Reading expert Jeanne Chall considered the compiling, cherishing, and trading of comic books as an opportunity for all children to experience the joy of compiling a library. As visual culture finds its way into classrooms, comic books—previously dismissed as pop culture—are becoming more acceptable vehicles for teaching and learning. (jd)

coming out (of the closet)

To be "in the closet" is to hide one's sexual and/or gender identity. To "come out" is to publicly declare one's identity. Due to issues of bias and safety, some GLBT (gay, lesbian, bisexual, trans) people are "out" in certain situations but "closeted" in others. Coming out can be difficult because reactions vary from total acceptance and support to disapproval, rejection, and violence. Research indicates that sexual minority youth are coming out at younger ages (i.e., middle school) than in the past. (jb2)

commercialization of education

An increasingly close relationship between commercial interests and education that is often connected to decreased public funding for education, increased pressure from commercial forces, and the growing prevalence of neoliberalism in society. Commercialization can take the form of corporate-sponsored curriculum; field trips and activities; school-business partnerships; advertising in the classroom, hallways, and textbooks; and the renaming of school spaces. The Commercialism in Education Research Unit (CERU) at Arizona State University publishes annual reports on various forms of commercialism in schools, and Alex Molnar (2005) has written about this dynamic in his book *School Commercialism*. (tn)

See also consumerism; neoliberalism; school choice.

Committee of Ten on Secondary School Studies

Refers to the 1893 recommendations of a subcommittee of the National Education Association to standardize secondary school programs and college entrance requirements. The Committee of Ten included Charles W. Eliot, chair of the committee and president of Harvard, and nine educators. The curriculum recommendations were traditional (including Latin, Greek, English, mathematics, physics, history, civil government, and political economy, for example) but also included a place for modern laboratory sciences and foreign languages. Emphasis on the college-bound student was evident in the proposed curriculum, but members insisted the high school would become the "people's college" and should thus prepare students thoroughly for life. (ks2)

Committee on Education Beyond the High School

Appointed by President Dwight D. Eisenhower in 1956, this committee assessed the impact of post–World War II demographic and economic changes on American higher education. According to the committee, educational institutions were "ill-prepared" to meet the challenges created by the recent rise in birth rates and the growing demands for trained college graduates in the workplace. The committee's proposals, published in 1957, focused on teacher recruitment, which it referred to as the nation's "top priority," as well as recommendations concerning student financial aid, equal educational opportunity, institutional funding, and the role of the federal government in higher education. (ag)

commodification

Process by which the logic of materialism and capitalism dominate culture and identity to the extent that individuals and items are simply reducible to their market value. In such a process, people are schooled into being uncritical, unreflective consumers of a marketplace, rather than educated toward freedom and thoughtfulness. (hfs)

common school

Most effectively advocated by Horace Mann in America in the 1830s and 1840s, the common school is based on the ideas that democratic citizenship requires a certain set of civic virtues, including a sense of responsibility and loyalty to country and community, and that it is the job of schools to instill them. Democracy requires social mobility to prevent hereditary classes, and the role of the common school is to identify and reward talented youth regardless of the social class of their parents. (jc)

Common School Movement

Refers to the surge of activities in the mid-19th century (1830–1860) United States on behalf of the creation of tax-supported public schools that would bring all citizens together, hence the word *common*. Predominantly a phenomenon found in the northern and western states, the movement involved notable reformers such as Horace Mann, Henry Barnard, and Catharine Beecher, as well as the work of educational associations and private citizens. The successful crusade resulted in longer school years, more teacher training, the creation of offices of state superintendents of education, and most importantly, taxation to support schools. Common schools are typically considered the forerunners of the modern public school system. (vmm)

common sense

Judgment or intuition made by ordinary people situated within a culture and a history. This is a socially shaped meaning. A set of ideas originating in Aristotle and the biblical Proverbs and developed in the 18th century in England and Scotland (Thomas Reid) and then in America (C. S. Pierce, G. E. Moore) as "common sense realism": reality is and continues to be what our experience tells us it is; carefully examined conclusions of common sense bring with them an obligation to act according to the conclusions; the need to review critically the widespread beliefs of a culture because our naive common sense can also be deceived. A late 20th-century view called "pragmatic" or "internal" realism (Hilary Putnam, Alvin Plantinga), informed by linguistic analysis, phenomenology, and pragmatism, that emphasizes the value of understanding common experience. (sc)

communalism

Belief system or orientation that emphasizes social interdependence rather than object-oriented independence as a core value. (hfs)

communication

The exchange of ideas, including hearing or receiving information, speaking or sending information, and use of language, written, oral, and symbolic. Primarily the transmission of something abstract or otherwise intangible as an outcome of a certain set of causal conditions. Familiar examples of shared matters in communication are theories, beliefs, information, feelings, and entertainment. The instruments of communication typically include speech, writing, flags, icons, gestures, or some other system of signs. Those who participate in communication are often known as communicants and may transmit, receive, or alternate transmitting and receiving. Secondarily, communication may refer, as in the case of a letter, to a physical matter bearing a message. The term also may refer to a field of scholarly study, a field of business, or the transmission of disease. (rdh, sr)

See also dialogue; intersubjectivity; rhetoric.

communication disorder

An inability to understand, hear, or use speech and language to communicate effectively with others. This may include a delayed or disordered development of language comprehension and/or expression, or the impairment of the use of a spoken, written, or communicated system that affects adversely an individual's ability to communicate. (jbb)

communicative action

A type of discussion, described by Jürgen Habermas in *Theory of Communicative Action,* in which people reach a common understanding through dialogue that takes place under a set of specific rules. (jpc)

communicative competence

The ability to convey meaning effectively using linguistic means. Communicative competence entails knowledge that can be classified broadly as: knowledge of the lexicon and structure of a language, so that meaning is communicated as intended; and sociocultural knowledge that governs language use (e.g., paralinguistics, proxemics, kinesics, tone of voice, forms of address) so that meaning is communicated appropriately. The ability, described by Jürgen Habermas in *Theory of Communicative Action* (1984), that all people possess to engage in communicative action. This communication is not dependent on educational attainment. (jrk, jpc)

See also pragmatics.

communicative learning

An education process that seeks the co-construction of meaning through interpersonal interaction, a critical assessment of assumptions that support contested beliefs and values, and critical dialogue that results in a dialectically derived, tentative best judgment and rationale upon which to act. (hfs)

communitarian

A philosophy or belief system that places priority on the community or on social values. The central claim is that meaning in individual life and individual liberty are possible only within a strong and vital interdependent community. Government policies and individual choices should be responsive to the development and maintenance of supporting social values. (hfs)

communitarianism

The view, as against liberalism, that argues that the proper unit for analysis in social and political theory is not the individual, but the member. Emphasizes the importance of communal standards and membership, responsibilities to each other as an equal consideration with the rights of each member, and the ties of affection and loyalty. Emphasizes the importance of what is held in common as against what is individual belief. Emphasizes both the set of beliefs and practices that are seen to be held in common across all communities, and the beliefs and practices that set one community apart from another. (jc)

See also individualism; liberalism.

communities of practice

A general term referring to groups or associations of professionals or specialists actively engaged in the practice of particular skills or activities. Certain uses of the term imply that practitioners are the "final judges" of innovative methods and techniques; other uses refer to a diverse group of individuals engaged in work over a significant period of time during which they solve problems and learn collectively. (cf)

community

A group of individuals sharing an environment, endeavor, ideal, identity, and/or experience. Communities involve conditions that include but are not limited to purposes, locations, beliefs, intentions, resources, and so on. Communities promote unity, cooperation, similarity, and convergence of time, space, and energy. Communities include physical and social organizations such as neighborhoods, villages, towns, cities, states, and countries. (npg)

community art center

A location (often a renovated church, school, or storefront) at which arts education is provided by artists beyond the parameters (though often in conjunction with) school art programs. Featuring adult as well as children's educational programming, urban art centers are often thought to be "safe havens" at which youth who have been placed at risk can find arenas for success and the development of life skills. (jd)

community college

An institution that is accredited to award the Associate in Arts (AA) or the Associate in Science (AS) as the highest degrees. Some community college programs are terminal, but many community college graduates transfer to four-year colleges and universities. (cf)

community education

Adult education programs designed to meet the needs of communities rather than individuals and that have community input into their design. (jpc)

See also community-based education.

community learning center

A place that houses a program designed to serve the residents of a community by offering educational, job training, and job placement services. (las)

community schools

The idea or concept of community schools derives from the community education philosophy that a community school should serve persons of all ages and that learning is a lifelong process. All aspects of the community are recognized as sources in the education of people. Community schools provide opportunities for members of the community to plan together and use all available human and physical resources to develop their full potential. The curriculum and activities evolve from the basic wants and needs of the people served. Community education programs provide opportunities for people to pursue academic, social, physical, recreational, cultural, health, and vocational education programs. (ks)

community-based art education

Any form of art education that is negotiated beyond school walls in geographical neighborhoods or in and of communities more broadly defined. Emerged in the United States at the turn of the 20th century when immigrant populations coming into the United States sought the acquisition of arts-based skills at local settlement houses. Note as examples famous art centers like Karamou House in Cleveland or the Louis Abrams Art Center at the Henry Street Settlement in New York City. Beyond the notion of centers that had a resurgence in the 1960s (when art education was diminishing in schools), community-based art education includes any of the many individual or group efforts of artists either of or moving into the community, sharing their skills with interested adults and children. (jd)

See also community art center.

community-based education
Education delivered outside the structure of traditional educational institutions, in the community, focusing on local issues and concerns. Such education may be sponsored by social service agencies, governmental and nongovernmental bodies, and private and public organizations. It frequently has a radical or social-action agenda that questions accepted social structures. Also called popular education (especially in Latin America) or community education. (chb)

See also service learning.

community-based instruction
Delivering education and instruction in the community setting, in addition to, or rather than, in a school-based setting. (sr)

community-based organization (CBO)
Private, nonprofit organization that addresses the needs of a community or part of a community and often provides job training services or other adult education programs. (kg)

Community-Control Movement
Efforts during the 1970s in the United States to grant power to parents and community members over and above the power provided by parent-teacher associations, parent school councils, or other types of partnerships. Teacher selection and retention, the selection of curricular and instructional materials, as well as budget development and resultant decision

making were some of the central concerns of these efforts. (hfs)

commutative justice (See justice)

commutative property (addition)
The property stating that two numbers may be added in any order to obtain the correct sum $(1 + 2 = 2 + 1)$. (ps)

commutative property (multiplication)
The property stating that two numbers may be multiplied in any order to obtain the correct product $(1 \times 2 = 2 \times 1)$. (ps)

comorbidity
Refers to the presence of two or more illnesses in the same person, occurring either simultaneously or sequentially. The illnesses can be psychiatric, medical, or drug-use disorders. Comorbidity does not imply that one illness is the cause of the other, even if one occurs first. Common examples of comorbidity include alcoholism and depression, obesity and heart disease, and attention-deficit disorder and learning disability. (sdc)

compact
In education, contractual agreements among various community leaders in initiating and sustaining local educational reform, making all parties accountable. Those whose interests are represented are often community decision makers, school superintendents, college presidents, parents, unions, and others. (jb)

comparative adult education
Field of study that focuses on organized learning activities for adults and may include international or within-country comparisons. (las)

comparative analysis
The processing of examining two or more entities and articulating the pluses and minuses of each. The goal of comparative analysis is to summarize strengths and weakness without making a judgment

that one entity is absolutely better than another. (jtr)

comparative testing
This type of assessment makes judgment of one student's performance compared to that of another student, or group of students. It may also compare a student's performance to a defined standard. (jtr)

compare problems
Addition and subtraction problems that involve comparisons between two different sets (e.g., Susan has 7 fish and Miguel has 9 fish. How many more fish has Miguel than Susan?). (amr)

compassion
The feeling of sorrow or concern for the unfortunate condition or circumstances of a person or a group. Compassion may or may not include the resonating emotion of sympathy and empathy (e.g., feeling what the sufferer feels). If it does, it is secondary to the feelings of sorrow or concern. (sv)

See also empathy; sympathy.

compensation strategy (See thinking strategies)

compensatory education
Educational programs that provide adults with an opportunity to acquire basic skills or a high school credential. This opportunity compensates for the educational deficit caused by poor schooling or the environmental barriers to success in school that exists in poor communities. (jpc)

compensatory methodology
The process of developing instructional objectives that circumvent areas of weakness or disability and focus on areas of strength. (sr)

competence/proficiency learning
Learning, as seen in the development or mastery of complex skills (e.g., athletic skills, interpersonal competence in dealing with others, driving an automobile in traffic are skills or competencies we observe every day). (cf)

competencies, occupational
Those concepts, skills, and attitudes essential to a broad occupational grouping. Those competencies with common usefulness to a family of occupations. (jm)

competencies, specific job
Concepts, skills, and attitudes that are highly specialized and related directly to a single job classification and a student's educational program of study. (jm)

competency
An ability, knowledge set, or expertise essential for adequate performance of a given task. For teachers, this means demonstrating subject matter and/or pedagogical competency through state standardized tests for certification. Such competencies are the basis for competency-based education and competency-based teacher education. (dek, cp, peb)

competency-based
Term used to describe educational programs or assessment tests that are focused on specific skill outcomes. Emphasis is placed on acquisition and demonstration of knowledge, skills, and behaviors important for carrying out particular activities, tasks, or jobs. (jpc, las)

competency-based admissions
A method of basing admissions to a higher institution of learning on a student's attainment of an expanded base of competencies, rather than the traditional utilization of grade point average and SAT/ACT scores for determining admissions eligibility. (tp)

competency-based assessment
Assessment of knowledge, skills, and abilities a person applies in an occupational setting. Portable standard of a person's ability to perform a specific task. (jb)

competency-based education

Education in which the curriculum is derived from analysis of desirable practical skills, roles, or competencies, and that certifies student progress on the basis of demonstrated performance of those skills, roles, or competencies. (chb)

competency-based instruction

An approach to teaching and learning in which standards for skills, knowledge, and attitudes are identified in advance for successful completion of a course. A method of instruction in which students are evaluated based on their mastery of required competencies for established performance standards. (jb)

competency-based teacher education (CBTE)

A movement of the late 1960s to conceptualize teachers' roles and functions in terms of specific proficiencies in their areas of knowledge and skills. This movement was an attempt to scientifically validate a knowledge base for teaching and teacher education that would enable a more technically precise means for certifying teachers based on demonstration of discrete, context-free observable behaviors. Central to CBTE were teacher educators who could evaluate preservice teachers on their competency progress and assign additional prescribed training material as necessary until mastery was achieved. Unable to overcome the difficulties inherent in creating a common knowledge base for teaching that relied on discrete skill sets, CBTE faded out as a popular movement by the late 1970s. (sld, ddr)

competitive market

In education, a term referring to people choosing the school and type of education that they think best meet their educational needs. Proponents believe that these forces produce better educational services than do monopolized responses, and that they unleash strong incentives for school reform. It is reasoned that parents and students will opt for the public or private schools they think are more efficient and effective. If not satisfied with the outcomes, they can walk away and send clear signals to educators about the level of school performance. (mm)

composite unit

Constructing a number as the number itself or as separate entities (e.g., thinking of six as one unit of six or as six units of one). (dc)

composition

The arrangement of parts (e.g., words, musical phrases, or elements of design) to form an artistic whole. The ensuing harmony or cohesion of an artistic piece is dependent upon the composition or relationship of its parts. Unity and balance are often thought to be objectives of artistic composition. The composition can also refer to the work itself. In visual arts, music, or writing, a composition refers to the entire artistic piece. Young children have an innate sense of balance of composition that is thought, with development, to dissipate as preoccupation with separate parts obscures a sense of the whole. (km)

comprehension

The ability of an individual to perceive, process, and understand information. The ability to move from one level of abstraction to another. This term is frequently associated with reading. The reconstruction of the intended meaning of a written or oral communication, accurately understanding what is written or said. The construction of the meaning of a written or oral communication through a holistic and reciprocal interchange of ideas in which it is assumed that the recipient and the producer of the message share a common background knowledge and experience, and the interchange is happening within a particular communicative context. The meaning of an utterance or a sentence cannot be derived from simply summing the meanings of individual words, but the recipient has to consider the total meaning of all the components as a whole. (jtr, smt)

comprehension strategies

Comprehension strategies include skills such as making connections (text-to-text; text-to-self; text-to-world), making predictions, asking questions (of the text and of oneself as a reader), visualizing what is happening in the text, making inferences, determining the importance of what one reads, and synthesizing information. Comprehension strategy instruction may be used in a guided reading or reader's workshop approach. (jas)

Comprehensive Adult Student Assessment System (CASAS)

A norm-referenced test that measures reading comprehension by asking adults to answer multiple-choice questions about reading passages provided in the test and by completing fill-in-the-blank items. The reading passages are focused on life tasks. The system comprises over 100 standardized assessments and supporting materials and is based on 300 competencies deemed useful for adults in workplace and societal contexts. Tests cover reading, math, and listening. All tests are scaled to a single proficiency scale and allow instructors to construct individual or class proficiency profiles. Scoring scales range from adults with special learning needs to advanced adult secondary levels. A separate series of reading and listening tests is available for testing English language proficiency. (las)

Comprehensive Employment and Training Act (CETA)

U.S. federal legislation, enacted in 1973, that provides funds to create jobs and training for the unemployed. It was replaced by the Job Training Partnership Act in 1983. (las)

comprehensive examinations

As increasing numbers graduate annually from undergraduate programs, proficiency and general knowledge may be examined to assure that graduates maintain standards established by previous generations of students. Whether administered at transition from lower division to upper division or as "exit exams" for transferring or graduate students, written exams continue to serve as a gate-keeping function in many institutions and statewide systems. (cf)

comprehensive high school

As opposed to a specialized high school with a program designed for a specific interest or occupation, the comprehensive high school is a secondary school that has both general education courses and specialized areas of study in its program. Course areas would include general education, college preparation, and vocational education. (jw)

comprehensive school guidance program

The purpose of the school counseling program is to provide and support the delivery of specific skills and information in a proactive, preventive manner to ensure that all students have the opportunity to achieve school success. It focuses on the academic achievement, personal/social growth, and career development of children from pre-kindergarten through 12th grade. It targets what the children should know, understand, and be able to do within these domains in order to develop into contributing members of society. It also serves to provide intervention and referral services for those students who are experiencing difficulties that interfere with their academic achievement or personal success. The school counselor serves as the program leader and collaborates with other pupil services personnel, as well as other school staff, in the delivery of such services. (tsw)

comprehensive sexuality education

Sexuality education programs that start in kindergarten and continue through 12th grade that include age-appropriate, medically accurate information on a broad set of topics related to sexuality, including human development, relationships, decision-making, abstinence, contraception, and disease prevention. One of the few school-based approaches to sexuality education that provides students with opportunities for developing skills as well as learning information. (jb2)

See also abstinence-only-until-marriage.

compression

One of researcher Alan Tom's principles of good teacher education, compression refers to programs that are both short in length and intense in involvement, and that accurately model and involve students in actual teaching from the beginning. (peb)

compromise

The act of negotiation, concession, conciliation, cooperation, and collaboration to reach a mutual settlement, arrangement, bargain, or agreement. The word *compromise* entails both positive connotations (where both sides gain or win) and negative connotations (where both sides concede or lose). (npg)

compulsory attendance (See compulsory schooling)

compulsory schooling

A state or national mandate that requires children of specific ages to attend and be educated either in a public or private school or through other approved means. The compulsory period, defined by the starting and ending age of the student, varies from state to state. (ms)

computation

Using the mathematical operations of addition, subtraction, multiplication, and division to solve problems and interpret data. Computation may be done mentally, using paper and pencil algorithms, or with calculators and computers. The act of using a series of arithmetical, algebraic, or other operations to achieve a result to a problem. (jtr, gtm)

computational fluency

A quality that allows a person to effortlessly and rapidly use operations to resolve a problem; having and using efficient and accurate methods for computing; being able to make smart choices about which tools to use and when. The person having this quality has mastered the operations and the use of these operations. (gtm)

Computer Algebra System (CAS)

A computer software program that manipulates equations, graphs, and algebraic expressions. Symbolic manipulation is capable through this system, by allowing the user to input data and see a solved example in order to grasp the solution sequence. (jmg)

computer-adaptive testing

The process of assessing learning or mastery by continually adjusting the difficulty level of questions based on user responses. A computer-adaptive testing system is typically based on a complex algorithm and relies on a collection of leveled questions. The system responds to each answer that is selected by a user to reflect the user's mastery of a concept. If a user answers a question incorrectly, the system presents a question considered to be "easier." In contrast, if a student enters a correct answer, the system presents a question considered to be "more difficult." The system thus "adapts" to reflect the user's performance level. The computer-administered version of the Graduate Record Examination (GRE) is an example of computer-adaptive testing. In K–12 education, programs like SuccessMaker® provide adaptive instruction and assessment in reading and mathematics. (sm)

See also item analysis.

computer-aided instruction

A method of presenting information or content through the use of the computer for the purpose of teaching, learning, or training. Computer-aided instruction is often labeled by the pedagogy upon which it is designed. For instance, many of the first educational software products presented a tightly controlled sequence of instruction, practice, and assessment—commonly associated with behaviorist learning theory. However, more recent technological and pedagogical models incorporate multimedia, open-ended interaction, simulations, and complex problem-solving interactions (e.g., virtual biology labs)—commonly associated with constructivist learning theory. The continuum of instructional methodologies ranges from low interactivity to high interactivity. (sm)

computer-assisted instruction (CAI)

The use of computers to present lessons, pose questions, assess student responses, manage information about student performance, and adjust the sequence and difficulty of the lesson to correspond to the student's current level of understanding. A program of instruction presented by means of a computer or system of computers. It often includes skill and drill practice, tutorials, and simulated activities used to supplement teacher-directed instruction. (bba, jtr)

computer-assisted learning

Interactive procedure by which a learner can read, evaluate, and respond to educational material through the use of a computer terminal; the substantive content may be a database, a computer program, or direct human communication via computer. (cf)

computer-assisted testing

Any delivery of tests that makes use of computers can be termed computer-assisted testing. The forms of this assisted delivery can vary from merely providing the stimulus or prompt material, with the test takers responding in a traditional pencil and paper fashion, to having the test takers record their responses on the computer as well. Advantages of computer-assisted testing include being able to provide rich and authentic visual and auditory material in the test items, as well as having the potential to efficiently record individual performances in spoken or written mode. (bkl)

See also computer-adaptive testing.

computer-based instruction (CBI)

Refers to virtually any kind of computer use in educational settings, including drill and practice, tutorials, simulations, instructional management, supplementary exercises, programming, database development, writing using word processors, and other applications. This term may refer either to stand-alone computer learning activities or to computer activities that reinforce material introduced and taught by teachers. (cf)

computer-based training (CBT)

Any training that uses the computer as the central instructional delivery device. Computer-based training can range from simple drill and practice to sophisticated simulations. (chb)

computer-managed instruction (CMI)

The use of a computer system to test students, monitor their progress, store and manage student records, and plan and prescribe instructional materials. (bba)

concept analysis

The process of studying the nature of a construct or logically formed idea. Putting related parts together forms a concept, whereas concept analysis carefully scrutinizes the essential features of the concept in order to gain a more thorough understanding of the relationship between those features. (ce)

concept map

A method of organizing ideas to enable learners to grasp and link abstract concepts in a concrete way; a diagram or other schematic device for organizing meanings and ideas about a particular concept or proposition. A type of graphic organizer showing concepts and their interrelationships. A key word is written in the center, related words are written in categories around the key word, and the categories are labeled. (chm, bba)

concept of word

The ability to track and identify individual printed words in familiar text. A precursor to achieving a concept of word is in using the beginning sound and the empty space between words to recognize word boundaries. (mmd)

conceptual framework

Within teacher education, a conceptual framework is the organizing principles around teacher education programs at a given institution that build a common vision. The vision then guides the development of all curriculum and instruction, including field experiences. (rtc)

conceptual learning

The comprehension of concepts and principles that provide an organized structure for a field of knowledge; often referred to as verbal or symbolic learning, with mastery of related information, topics, and issues in general, technical, or specialized knowledge. (cf)

conceptual mathematics knowledge

A student who possesses conceptual mathematics knowledge understands the meaning and underlying principles of mathematical concepts. These students are able to solve problems in a nonalgorithmic way. They can apply these concepts in new and different ways without specific instruction. Students with conceptual mathematics knowledge are less susceptible to nonsensical errors that occur when students only know how to use the procedure. For example: a student is able to work backwards and find a series of

numbers that have an average, or mean, of 2. (mlf, rlk)

See also procedural mathematics knowledge.

concrete experiences

Activities that provide a child engagement with real, three-dimensional, hands-on materials, which stimulate a full spectrum of sensory learning as a child tastes, hears, sees, smells, and touches in a real-life context. This parallels the cognitive development of a young child as he or she transitions through the sensorimotor (birth to two years) and preoperational (two to seven years) phases identified by Piaget. (db1)

concrete materials

Physical materials that may be used in mathematics classrooms to assist students in learning mathematics. These materials may be commercial materials, such as pattern blocks, tangrams, centimeter cubes, or dot paper, or they may be noncommercial materials, such as buttons, bottle caps, straws, or egg cartons. (sdt)

concrete operational development

This third stage of cognitive development according to Jean Piaget occurs from ages 7 to 12. During this period the child is able to implement logical analysis of situations, and to consider others and their feelings, but is still unable to perform complex, abstract reasoning. (npo)

concurrent enrollment

Secondary school students enrolled in a college and a high school course simultaneously, for college credit, with a principal's and parental approval, are said to be concurrently enrolled. Concurrent students usually pay the costs associated with the college course. Typically the class load of such a student is not to exceed two college credit courses per semester. Should a student exhibit exceptional academic abilities, however, and be capable of college-level work, based upon such factors as grade-point average, ACT or SAT scores, and/or other assessment indicators, higher institution authorities may grant exceptions to the two-college-credit limit. Concurrent students must maintain a "B" average in their high school courses, be making progress toward high school graduation, and make a "C" or better in the college course. (tp)

conduct codes

Institutional policy that outlines what is acceptable student behavior so that students can self-monitor their own activities and behaviors and be good citizens within their educational community. Codes of conduct frequently emphasize character traits such as honesty, integrity, fairness, and respect, as the basis for the rules that are outlined in the code. The rules of the code address student personal and academic behavior, as well as the penalties and practices associated with breaking the policy. (ms)

conduct disorder (CD)

Conduct disorder consists of a repetitive and persistent pattern of behaviors in which the basic rights of others or major age-appropriate norms or rules of society are violated. CD is one of the most prevalent childhood disorders and is characterized by obvious, aggressive, disruptive behavior or antisocial acts such as stealing, lying, and fire setting. This disorder may include both overt and covert acts. Those with this disorder have great difficulty following rules and behaving in a socially acceptable way. The primary features of conduct disorders are often associated with behaviors such as early onset of drug and alcohol use, low self-esteem, school problems, suicidal behavior, and low academic achievement. Typically there would have to be evidence of three or more of these types of behaviors in the past 12 months, with at least one in the past 6 months. The earlier conduct disorders are identified and treated, the better the chance for success. (tsw)

Conferences for Education in the South

A series of educational conferences begun in 1898 in Capon Springs, West Virginia, with the intention of uniting northern businessmen and philanthropists with southern white educational reformers behind the cause of educational improvement in the South for both races. The conferences met annually in the South at various locations from 1901 to 1914. Two influential organizations of the southern education movement evolved from these conferences, the General Education Board and the Southern Education Board. (vmm)

confidentiality

Refers to the "keeping secret" of certain types of knowledge or information. The term is applied most typically to knowledge or information shared in a relationship where a mutual and legitimate expectation of trust exists between a professional (e.g., psychologist, counselor, attorney, etc.) and his or her client. For many professionals, confidentiality is legitimized through ethical codes of conduct and through legal statutes. (dd)

confirmatory bias

The tendency to attend to and seek out information that supports previously held hypotheses and beliefs. Information that refutes these hypotheses and beliefs is typically ignored and/or disregarded altogether. (ktc)

conflict resolution

The reduction of tension or confusion in institutional purposes, policies, programs, services, activities, and interpersonal working relations; the resolving of conflicts of interests among staff members, colleagues, and campus constituencies; includes many administrative, technical, legal, and political problems that must be considered in cooperation with institutional (and other) constituencies. Colleges and universities may offer conflict resolution services for students and faculty, and some now offer degree programs in conflict resolution. (cf, sn, bba)

conflict theory (See critical theory)

confrontation

A counseling technique that involves pointing out noticeable discrepancies between a client's spoken words, expressed feelings, and/or observed behaviors. This technique is useful for increasing a client's self-awareness and for helping him or her to rationally reassess information that may be personally unpalatable, previously avoided, unknown, or unacknowledged, in part so that he or she may become more congruent. (bmm)

congruence

A relationship between two (or more) objects in which the component parts of one object are equal in measure to the corresponding component parts of the second object. The term "equality" is used to denote sameness in number or quantity. The term "congruent" is used to denote sameness in size and shape. (cmdv)

conjecture

A mathematical statement that has neither been proved nor disproved; an educated guess or hypothesis; a judgment made on inconclusive or incomplete evidence; guesswork; an inference on slight evidence; a hypothesis that has been formed by speculation. (wja)

connecting activities

Activities that help establish relationships between school-based learning and work-based learning, as described in the School to Work Opportunities Act of 1994. Activities may include encouraging business involvement, evaluating program outcomes, providing technical assistance to teachers, and matching students with work-based learning opportunities. (kg)

See also School-to-Career System.

connectives

Words or phrases used to connect other words, phrases, or ideas. Connectives often denote relationships such as sequence (first, last), contrast (therefore, consequently), or addition (likewise, in addition). Connectives are important elements for success in writing academic language. (cld)

conscience

The term *conscience* designates two modes of moral cognition, most clearly apparent in the terms *valuing* and *evaluating* and in their cognates *prizing* and *appraising*; the capacity to make judgments of right and wrong in the moral domain. The first or direct conscience designates a habitual way of valuing and is the result of nurture and prior experiences. The technical name is *syntêresis*. The second or reflex conscience involves a reflective judgment, the application of principles to some thing or event. Its technical name is *syneidêsis*. (ig)

conscientization

A term introduced by Paulo Freire in *Pedagogy of the Oppressed* (1970) to represent the consciousness raising that takes place when adults are involved in a process of praxis, which involves critically discussing an issue, acting on that discussion, and then reflecting on that action before moving to act again. In this process, adults can move from magical consciousness (the belief that unseen forces are making the decisions that affect a person's life) to naive consciousness (the belief that powerful people are making those decisions) and, finally, to critical consciousness (the belief that a person can participate in the decisions that affect his or her life). (jpc)

consensus

The act of reaching agreement, accord, harmony, compromise, and/or consent related to a particular issue. Consensus involves an outcome that everyone can accept. Consensus building involves planning, development, and appraising institutional purposes, policies, programs, services, and standards that serve all constituencies with conflicting values, perceptions, and expectations; includes motivational, inspirational, political, and economic efforts contingent upon leadership in establishing purpose, setting goals, developing programs, and assessing institutional effectiveness. (npg, cf)

consensus building

Planning, developing, and appraising institutional purposes, policies, programs, services, and standards that serve constituencies with conflicting values, perceptions, and expectations; includes motivational, inspirational efforts—and administrative leadership in defining purpose, setting goals, developing programs, and assessing institutional effectiveness. (cf)

consequentialism

A theory of morality holding that the rightness of an act is solely a function of the consequences of the act. Consequentialist theories differ about which consequences are valued. Under one theory, a right act is one that produces at least the same proportion of good over bad as any available alternative act. Under another theory, a right act is one that honors more rights than any available alternative act. Consequentialist theories also differ about which people should be considered: ethical egotism determines the rightness of an act based on the consequences for the actor alone; utilitarianism determines the rightness of an act based on the consequences for all people. (mhs)

See also deontological ethics; hedonism; utilitarianism.

conservation

The preservation of the relationship between two quantities. For example, if two quantities are equal and a number of operations are performed on the quantities, but the quantities remain equal, then there has been conservation. Piaget's clinical interviews with children highlighted the importance of the development of conservation with respect to number and space. (smc)

conservation education

A part of science and social studies education frequently integrated with other topics to develop an understanding of the relationship among individuals, groups, society, natural resources, and the use of these resources. Topics studied include the management and preservation of natural resources as well as the use and development of the resources. Economic and environmental concerns both short and long term are also included. A knowledgeable citizen with a responsible, respectful attitude toward natural resources is one main goal. Resources studied could include soil, water, forests, wildlife, energy use, and production. (tw)

conservatism

The word *conservative* derives from the title "conservator," first used in the European Middle Ages to refer to a person who enforced the law. As an ideology, conservatism emerged within the modern period. The British statesman Edmund Burke is generally recognized as the leading figure, in particular because of his essay "Reflections on the Revolution in France" (1790). Although throughout its history conservatives have embraced a wide range of beliefs, they have generally tended to believe in a transcendent moral order, express skepticism toward radical change, and value tradition and piecemeal reform. In terms of education, conservatives typically call for more professional accountability and a return to basic literacy and numeracy skills as the key educational outcome. (td)

consonant

A speech sound that is produced with a narrow or complete closure in the vocal tract. An alphabet letter that stands to represent these sounds. (smt)

consonant cluster (See blend)

consortium
A group of institutions or educational units that have a contractual arrangement to accomplish a shared, common goal. In education, a group of educational entities and sometimes other groups such as employers and community-based organizations that provide services and share information for the advancement of students. Groups may share financial, material, or human resources within and across educational sectors. (cf, kg)

constant
A quantity represented by a number, letter, or other symbol whose value does not change or is considered fixed within a given context, such as in an expression, equation, or sequence of mathematical operations; a variable that represents exactly one value. (kgh)

constituencies
The various but distinct partisans in an institution's different functions and activities: faculties, students, alumni, staffs, administrators, donors, sponsors, benefactors; groups with a clearly recognized vested interest in the institution's effectiveness. (cf)

construct
In assessment the construct is the theoretically or pedagogically defined skill or trait (or set of skills or traits) that the test seeks to measure. However, the construct is ineffable and eventually unobservable. Much effort in testing is spent on written and/or statistical determination or definition of the construct, and its true nature is a never-ending goal of test development and analysis. (fd)
See also validity.

construct irrelevant variance
Construct irrelevant variance occurs when test scores are affected by factors that are not relevant to what the test measures. It is one of the threats to test validity, and it makes difficult the interpretation of test scores. An example of construct irrelevant variance is the effects of computer skills on examinees' performance on a subject test when they are not part of test construct. (hl)
See also validity.

constructive thinking
Thinking that is individual and social, is creative and critical, that involves doubting and believing, that relies on the use of reason, emotions, intuition, and imagination and involves the ability to communicate and relate to/with others. The thinking human beings use to construct knowledge. (bt-b, js)

constructivism
A theory of learning that maintains that learning is a process of constructing meaning, rather than receiving knowledge. There are several strands of constructivism; they all affirm that knowledge is the meaning that people make out of their experience, and people construct meaning as they interact with the world. A view that students actively construct meaning and knowledge based on their prior knowledge, previous experiences, and perspectives. A constructivist approach to instruction asserts that in order for students to gain deep understanding, they must actively come to know (or construct) concepts for themselves. The teacher is seen not as a dispenser of knowledge, but a facilitator and coexplorer in inquiry, problem solving, and collaboration. Single, correct answers are deemphasized. Greater internalization of knowledge is the aim. Constructivism recognizes the social nature of learning and emphasizes the need for active participation by the learner. (js, bba, reb, bt-b)

constructivist paradigm
Epistemology that underlies qualitative research. The idea that human beings actively construct their knowledge and

do not simply absorb or reproduce reality. In other words, an individual creates "the truth as I see it." Because of this, a major goal of qualitative research is to understand an individual's perspective on reality; that is, to see the world from the other's point of view. In addition, since multiple perspectives on reality exist, it is important to understand how the context influences the formation of different perspectives and to portray the interplay of these different perspectives in the social world. Also known as the interpretive paradigm of qualitative research. (mas)

constructivist teaching experiment
In the interactions between the teacher-researcher and the students that take place during a constructivist teaching experiment, the teacher-researcher focuses on learning the students' mathematical thinking and the changes that take place in that thinking as the teaching experiment progresses. A key part of the teaching experiment is the teacher-researcher's creation of learning situations in a systematic manner, as well as the teacher-researcher's testing of conjectures concerning the mathematics learning of the student-participants. The researcher's analysis of the participants' demonstrated thinking results in the creation by the researcher of models of the students' thinking as that thinking develops. (smts)

consultancy exercise
A practitioner presents her/his problem of practice to a small group of peers; the group follows a multistage protocol to clarify and analyze the problem and then interpret and discuss it without further input from the presenter. The process is designed for the presenter to gain fresh insight into the problem and to formulate possible steps toward addressing the problem. (mf1)

consultation
Consultation is an indirect service delivery model whereby a professional (consultant) with expertise in a particular area assists someone (consultee) with a work-related problem they are experiencing. Consultation does not focus on ameliorating the personal issues or problems of a consultee, although there may be a decrease in subjective stress as the problem diminishes. Despite there being numerous models of consultation, the ones with the most empirical support for use in schools are Direct Behavioral Consultation, Behavioral Consultation, and Conjoint Behavioral Consultation. (tsw)

consumer education
Learning activities that are designed to build awareness and skills related to the rights and responsibilities of consumers. The goals of a consumer education program can be to help people save money, buy products and services that are safer or of a higher quality, and make purchasing decisions consistent with another goal, such as preserving the environment. (las)

consumer protection
Protection of the interests of consumers, achieved via laws or regulations governing the manufacturing or use of a product or service. (ewr)

consumer science education (See family and consumer Sciences education)

consumerism
An approach to schooling that emphasizes market logic and business interests over critical investigation and questioning. Consumption is the driving feature of consumerism, thus making the purpose of school to "get" information in the same way that one "gets" merchandise in stores. Shoppers rarely question what exists on shelves (including their placement, advertising, and sales gimmicks). Similarly, students rarely critique what exists in their schools (including the curriculum, the purpose of schooling, tracking, etc.). Consumerism reinforces schools as

training sites both for future workers and for future economic profit in the private sector. (drb)

contemporary art

The style and ideology of art and/or music produced in current times. According to art historical texts, contemporary art refers to visual art created after 1970. This distinction is in contrast with modern art, which usually refers to art created during the period dating from roughly the 1860s through the 1970s. Contemporary art is no longer subject to the strident constraints of a universal definition of art, as the end of the 20th century has produced an expanded definition of art. Some contemporary art aims to be a vital social force that extends beyond the art world into the broader culture. Similarly, contemporary music breaks the paradigms and constraints of the traditional conservatory model to speak across culture and class. (kf)

contemporary dance (See modern dance)

content analysis

Any form of organized and codified analysis of test items or tasks to determine what the tests measure. It may involve inductive reverse engineering of the intention of the test developers or item writers if those people are not part of the content analysis team. Content analysis is contrasted with statistical analysis. (fd)

content area

The subject matter or topics covered by a given teacher, department, or course. European History and Astronomy are both examples of content areas. (jw)

content knowledge (See subject matter [content] knowledge)

content standards

Written descriptions of what teachers are supposed to teach and what students are expected to learn within particular disciplines or subject matter areas. (bba)

content standards in physical education (See NASPE content standards in physical education)

contest mobility

Process or system whereby elite status and attendant power is a prize in an open and fair competition and is attained by individual effort, ability, and merit. Although rules govern the competition, varied avenues and strategies exist for individual success. (hfs)

context

A set of circumstances, events, or facts in which an event occurs. Context may also include the physical, social, perceptual, or emotional environment in which an event takes place. Context helps determine interpretation by giving meaning to situational events or circumstances. An additional meaning of context may be explained as clues that indicate the meaning of a word from surrounding words, phrases, or sentences. In education, any of the diverse and multiple environments, either physical or educational, that form the basis of or intersect with the work of teachers and teaching. The physical, emotional, social, economic, and other aspects of the social-psychological environment of students. Studies of the role of these factors in education began in the 1940s but have greatly accelerated since the 1980s. This is most clearly seen in the qualitative studies attending to the effects of context on the experience of schooling. (ce, reb, sc)

contextual knowers

Students for whom uncertainty around absolute correct and incorrect information, knowledge, and perspective remain, yet who also continue to hold some knowledge claims superior to others. These students emphasize thinking through alternative ideas and the integration of information for specific contextual application. (hfs)

contextual teaching and learning

Instruction that is problem-based, self-regulatory, offered in multiple settings and contexts, sensitive to learners' diverse learning styles and preferences, facilitative of teams and interdependent group structures, and supportive of authentic assessment and multiple methods of assessing student achievement. (ss)

contextualized learning

Learning that is focused on a context that is meaningful to the learner, such as a work task, parenting, or local politics. (jpc)

contingency workforce

Part-time or temporary workforce utilized to supplement a permanent workforce. (jb)

continuing education

Education beyond the traditional period of formal education. Organized instruction for part-time students. The term has also been used synonymously with adult education; evening and weekend programs offered to adults; continuing professional education; extension; university outreach and public service programming; lifelong education; and nontraditional study. Educational programs that take place after formal education has been completed, usually focused on improving skills and knowledge for specific occupations or professions. These programs sometimes provide evidence of successful completion, which participants can use to justify an improvement in salary or job classification. (chb, jpc)

continuing education unit (CEU)

A nondegree credit awarded by an educational institution or organization in recognition of participation in seminars and workshops, typically focused on professional development topics. The CEU is used by many organizations to document a member's participation in continuing professional education activities and may be used to determine salary increases or to meet certification requirements. Typically, 10 hours of formal continuing education is awarded one CEU. (chm, jpc)

continuing professional education (CPE)

As a subset of continuing or adult education, continuing professional education refers to instructional programs and courses intended to keep professionals current in their practice or discipline. Such courses provide opportunities to acquire, reinforce, or improve professional skills or knowledge, and are often mandated by registration and certification requirements. Any educational program designed to enhance the knowledge, skills, or career development of adults in professional careers (medicine, law, architecture, accounting, etc.). Providers of CPE include institutions of higher education, employers, professional associations, and independent consultants. (cf, alm)

continuous progress

An instructional approach in which students progress through a hierarchically organized curriculum, such as mathematics or reading, at their own pace. (bba)

continuous quantities

Quantities that result from measuring length, area, volume, temperature, mass, or time. Such measurements are approximations rather than an exact numeric value. (amr)

See also approximation; discrete quantities.

contour

From the Latin *contornare*, meaning to round off or to turn around. The contour is the outline and other visible edges of a mass, figure, or object. In drawing, contour lines are used to represent subject matter, giving a three-dimensional quality, which shows thickness as well as height and width of the described forms. In music, contours describe the structure of the piece, as in the contours of a melody. (kf)

contract (See learning contract)

contract training
Education and training programs offered primarily by community and technical colleges but sometimes also secondary schools and universities that are targeted toward enhancing the skills and knowledge of incumbent workers. (db)

contrived collegiality
When administrators or leaders are asked to slacken control because of increasing perceptions that others can function independently and successfully, they may instead ease into pseudo-facilitative leadership. This attempt to mandate collaboration while retaining hierarchical methods is a contrived collegiality. (reb)

controversial issues
Topics or matters accompanied by multiple perspectives or viewpoints that influence or are influenced by the individuals, actions, and outcomes associated with them. Controversial issues should be examined by considering the questions and the range of outcomes from all agendas including the pro, con, and neutral positions. Almost all topics in the social studies are controversial issues, as social studies is the study of humans and humanity over time. (npg)

convergent questions (See closed questions; recitation)

convergent thinking
J.P. Guilford characterized thinking that is rigid, stereotyped, and conventional as "convergent thinking." It was used to describe routine thinking and is contrasted with divergent thinking. (vm)

conversion (higher education)
A term in higher education administration that represents the critical decision-making time for students and their families from the point of admission to the point of enrollment at a college or university. Those that convert or yield represent the entering class of new students each year. Colleges and universities use this rate to identify the number of applicants and admits needed to meet goals. (kku)

conversion (mathematics)
Having the flexibility to represent the same problem or solution in multiple ways, in which the meaning does not change, only the model used. (jmg, ldz)
    See also representation.

co-op coordinator (See coordinator, career)

cooperating teacher
A classroom teacher who is recruited by a teacher preparation department to host a preservice teacher in the field. The classroom teacher takes on multiple duties as role model, mentor, counselor, guide, sponsor teacher, friend, defender, confidant, and evaluator. (reb)

cooperative course (See course, cooperative)

cooperative education
An instructional method that operates under the supervision of a school and employer, requiring structured and alternating in-school learning with employment or internship activities. Learning experiences are planned and supervised cooperatively by a school and employer, and each contributes to the student's career development. Education constructed so that work periods and school attendance alternate by half-days, weeks, or other appropriate time frames. (jb, ea)

Cooperative Extension Service (CES)
An organization providing educational programs and information to residents of a state on various topics such as

homemaking, agriculture, youth development, the environment, and public policy. It is based at land-grant universities and is funded at federal, state, and local levels, with offices in most counties of each state. The CES was created when President Woodrow Wilson signed the Smith-Lever Act in 1914. (js)

cooperative inquiry
Self-directed group inquiry grounded in an experience-based epistemology that focuses on the lived experience of the participants, ideally centered on a fostering of trust, vulnerability, and sense of community. Through cycles of action and reflection, participants examine their own lived experiences and resultant perspectives, assumptions, insights, and understandings. (hfs)

cooperative learning
A specific kind of collaborative learning. In cooperative learning, students work together in small groups on a structured activity. They are individually accountable for their work, and the work of the group as a whole is also assessed. Cooperative groups work face-to-face and learn to work as a team. Cooperative learning has its origins in K–12 education. However, recent theorists have begun to focus on the similarities between collaborative learning and cooperative learning, and the terms have begun to be used interchangeably. Cooperative learning stresses collaboration, student leadership, and self-direction. Students in cooperative learning groups share both individual and group responsibility for their learning and are partially rewarded for both group and individual success. Cooperative learning is noncompetitive, active learning that takes place within heterogeneous groups of children of diverse age, abilities, and cultural backgrounds. Key elements include positive interdependence, team formation, individual accountability, social skill development, interpersonal and small group skills, and group processing. (cf, ba, pw, reb)

cooperative learning groups
Groups specifically constructed by teachers to encourage interdependent work. The group may involve group processes, group social skills, and interaction, and also include individual accountability for work performed. There are three types of cooperative learning groups: formal—where the group is created as part of the classroom instruction to promote working cooperatively and may stay together over multiple classes; informal—where the group is formed spontaneously during a class to facilitate learning; and base—where the group remains together for a year or more and the members work together to ensure each other's academic success as well as to complete group tasks and projects. (ms)

cooperative occupational training
A plan that correlates actual work experience in the community with classroom instruction under the supervision of a coordinator or teacher-coordinator who is occupationally qualified. (jm)

cooperative play
Cooperative play occurs when two or more children are engaged in some type of social play, where the children assume different roles working on common goals. A leader may emerge; the leader may direct the orientation of play and assign roles to peers. The complexity of the play varies and may last for quite a while. This type of play is commonly seen in kindergarten and beyond. (yb)

cooperative program
An organizational pattern of instruction that involves regularly scheduled part-time employment, giving students an opportunity to apply classroom learning in practice. Enables students to develop occupational competencies through

training on jobs related to their career interests. (db)

cooperative student
A student who participates in a career and technical education program or class coordinating school instruction with part-time employment in an industry or business pursuing career goals. The student usually receives school credit and pay for work. (jb, ea)

coordinate colleges
Separate women's institutions that are partners to previously established male colleges or universities. Often created out of resistance to coeducation, coordinate colleges share some combination of faculty, finances, facilities, or governance with the original school. Commonly founded before the 20th century, and most frequently in the East and Midwest, many coordinate colleges have since merged or forged more equitable bonds with their partner schools. (le)

coordinate geometry
A branch of mathematics invented by Reneé Descartes whereby a plane is divided into upper and lower portions by the horizontal axis and into right and left portions by the vertical axis (this plane is known as the Cartesian coordinate plane, the coordinate plane, or the x-y plane). Many areas of mathematics, notably analytic geometry and calculus, use coordinate geometry extensively in the solutions of many mathematical problems. (dbc)

coordinate graph
A graph that is formed using two number lines. These number lines contain both positive and negative numbers. They become the x-axis, which is displayed horizontally, and the y-axis, which is displayed vertically. When put together, these axes form a coordinate system. Coordinates are the pairs of numbers formed when one number from the x-axis and one number from the y-axis coincide. Examples of a coordinate are demonstrated in the figure. The dot indicates the ordered pair (2,1). (kr)

Coordinate Graph

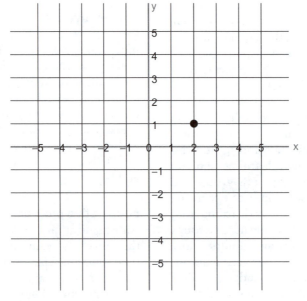

Coordinate Graph

coordinated curriculum

A coordinated curriculum in vocational education synthesizes educational course work in such a way that instructors in varying disciplines can teach related topics simultaneously, using occupational themes as the organizing principle for integrating academic units, occupational concepts, and experiences. (ch)

coordinating boards

Officially authorized for limited responsibilities in such matters as budgeting and finance. Lacking the governance authority of governing boards, they receive, consider, and recommend or disapprove proposed budgets, programs, services, and activities for one or more institutions. (cf)

coordinator, apprentice

A person, usually a school employee, who is charged with maintaining close contact with industry and the work of employed apprentices for the purpose of securing proper apprentice placement and training arrangements and assisting learners to link school-based and work-based learning. (jb)

coordinator, career

A person employed by a school (usually a career and technical education teacher) who is responsible for administering the school program, identifying and securing student employment, establishing work-based training arrangements and agreements, facilitating student evaluations, resolving issues that arise between the school and on-the-job activities, and connecting school and work-based learning. (ea)

coping skills

Strategies involving adaptive behaviors and self-regulation of emotional states that allow an individual to assign meaning, make decisions, solve problems, and/or achieve identified/specified goals. Strategies can fall within several domains, including cognitive (e.g., self-talk), emotional (e.g., expressing feelings, social support), physical (e.g., exercise, nutrition, sleep), and spiritual (e.g., meditation, praying). (llf, emm)

core abilities

Transferable skills common across career clusters essential to an individual's success and lifelong learning, including critical thinking skills, effective learning, good community skills, and cooperative work habits. (jb)

core competencies

In career education, core transferable skills common across career clusters. (jb)

core curriculum

Generally refers to common academic content or common graduation requirements in a differentiated educational system or in a system that allows for elective coursework. During the mid-20th century, the term was also used to describe a problem-based, interdisciplinary secondary school course often planned collaboratively by teachers and students. The discipline or subject matter components of the curriculum that are considered to be essential for students' education. Traditionally, these include reading, language arts, mathematics, science, and social studies. (wgw, bba)

core membership groups (See tight-knit groups)

corporate planning models

Systematic and technical methods adapted for use in business, industry, and finance; includes PPBS (planning programming budgeting systems), MBO (Management by Objectives), ZBB (zero-based budgeting), and other technically sophisticated methods. (cf)

corporate university

A training center or department that provides a broad range of educational programs for the employees of a corporation.

A corporate university is meant to ensure that training and education are aligned with corporate strategic objectives for organizational change, growth, and development. Some corporate universities also provide educational programs for the corporation's suppliers and/or customers; some have a campus-like facility. (mkr)

correctional education

An organized program of vocational and academic learning activities designed to prepare adult offenders in the criminal justice system for lives as responsible community members. Education programs that take place in prisons and jails or involve people who have been convicted of crimes and are under some form of restriction outside of a correctional facility. (chb, jpc)

correlation

Correlation is a statistical term referring to the association between two variables. Its value ranges from −1 to 1, representing the linear relationship between the variables. A positive correlation indicates that the two variables are moving in the same direction (i.e., one variable increases as the other variable increases), while a negative correlation indicates that the two variables are moving in opposite direction (i.e., one variable increases as the other variable decreases). Zero correlation indicates no association between the two variables. (hl)

correspondence course

Courses that are taught through texts, assignments, and tests that are mailed to the student. The student then mails back the answers to tests or the results of instructional assignments, which are then graded. Feedback on assignments and tests is provided to the student through the mail. (jpc)

correspondence study

A form of study in which the learner and the instructor have no face-to-face contact and exchange syllabi, text, examinations, and so on, through the mail. (chb)

cortex (See cerebral cortex)

cortisol

A hormone released by the adrenal gland. Cortisol is the end product of the hypothalamic-pituitary-adrenal (HPA) axis and is widely studied in children, in part because it can be studied through collection of saliva (a noninvasive procedure that is easier than the required blood draws necessary for studying other extracts). Looking at patterns of cortisol levels over time can provide a glimpse into an individual's stress responses. Too much or too little cortisol can be harmful; the body keeps cortisol levels within an optimal range. (sd1)

cosmopolitan education

Education aimed at fostering global citizenship and concern. Cosmopolitanism is a key philosophical component to programs of global education. For further exploration see Martha Nussbaum's 1997 work *Cultivating Humanity*. (dpb)

cosmopolitanism

Often situated in contrast to nationalism or patriotism. This is a sociological and moral position that rests upon the idea that all humanity holds membership in a shared community. As a result, there are norms and values that are consistent and applicable the world over. Cosmopolitan can be translated from Greek to mean "citizen of the world." (sb1)

cost effectiveness

Cost effectiveness is realized when the lowest-cost option is utilized, while achieving the greatest benefit/gain. Cost effectiveness, for example, is reflected when bulk purchases are made (which usually result in significantly reduced costs) and then utilized or applied to such an extent that they produce a maximum benefit/gain for the user(s). Employing comparative cost analyses to determine least cost, yet greatest output or outcome, is suggestive of a cost-effective approach. (tp)

costume

The outfit worn by a performer in theater or dance pieces, communicating important information about a character and/or about the production (e.g., social class of the character or time period of the piece). Costume design decisions may be guided by content, available budget, and/or style concerns of the director and designer, and can play a larger or smaller role in the visual look of a production—ranging from the prominent and even outlandish to the minimal or nondescript. Costuming in school plays provides an opportunity for students interested in design or sewing to contribute to the academic production and/or for parents to get involved. (em)

Council for Higher Education Accreditation (CHEA)

Established in 1997, CHEA is a private, nonprofit organization that coordinates accreditation activities for over 3,000 colleges and universities in the United States. CHEA does not accredit individual institutions, but it serves to improve and coordinate the work of national and regional accreditation bodies such as the Southern Association of Colleges and Schools, and the National Council for Accreditation of Teacher Education. CHEA is the most recent in a line of private coordinating agencies for accreditation, including the Commission on Recognition of Postsecondary Accreditation (1993–1997), the Council on Postsecondary Accreditation (1974–1993), and the National Commission on Accreditation (1949–1974). (sw)

Council of Higher Education Management Associations (CHEMA)

Started in 1968, CHEMA is made up of a group of 3,000 degree-granting colleges and universities. It is primarily an advocacy organization, which provides a national voice for self-regulation and for voluntary accreditation and quality assurance to the U.S. Congress and U.S. Department of Education. (sn)

counseling

An interpersonal process that occurs in the context of a helping relationship. In counseling, a counselor helps a client to adapt optimally to developmental transitions and/or to significant stressors. The types of transitions or stressors most typically addressed in counseling may include grief processes; educational or vocational decision making; adjustment to illness, disability, or other life crisis; adaptation to social or cultural oppression; and spiritual development. Professionally recognized counselors may represent any one of a wide variety of disciplines, including school guidance, social work, psychology, psychiatry, and clergy. (jih)

counseling, preemployment

Assistance given to students by counselors, involving administration of career-related assessments and transmittal of information about occupations and occupational fields. Practice includes teaching strategic methods for locating the type of work desired, and occupational ethics. (jb, ea)

counseling psychology

The branch of psychology that focuses on life transitions and adaptation to potentially significant stressors in the context of comparatively "normal" human growth and development. Client strengths are emphasized. Areas of research and mental health services addressed by counseling psychologists may include, among others, prevention, vocational and educational development, decision making, rehabilitation, issues related to individual and cultural diversity, and economic and social issues. (jih)

counselor

A trained, license-sanctioned professional who practices counseling. The professional may practice in a broad array of specialty areas, including vocational counseling, mental health counseling, and rehabilitation counseling. (dd)

See also counseling; counseling psychology.

counselor, placement
A counselor who is assigned special responsibilities for assisting students to find jobs. (jm)

counselor education
An educational program designed to enable an individual to develop the requisite awareness, knowledge, and skills necessary to practice counseling. (dd)

See also counseling.

counterpoint
The artistic technique of counterpoint is achieved when the sense of dialogue (point, counterpoint) is achieved through elements in a work of art. In music, two or more melodic lines may be introduced in parallel structure in such a way that the listener hears a harmonic relationship (dialogue) even while experiencing the linear individuality of the two melodies (voices). In writing, a composition that similarly introduces parallel lines (e.g., two stories that weave together even as they move quite separately)—that meet and verge and in the verging contrast add clarity to each other. In visual art, the use of contrasting formal elements that, by virtue of their dialectic with one another, make strong individual impressions. (jd)

countertransference
As with transference, clinicians bring a set of expectations, beliefs, and feelings toward their clients. Countertransference reactions may take the form of negative or positive feelings that, when not fully understood and properly channeled, can significantly interfere with the client–therapist relationship. These unconscious or unspoken reactions to clients by their therapists can include, among other behaviors, responding in a positive, idealizing, or even eroticized manner, as well as seeing their clients as unlikable, untreatable, or simply bad. (rnp)

counting (See rational counting, rote counting)

counting number (See cardinal number)

Country Life Commission
Created in 1907 by President Theodore Roosevelt to study rural problems, its 1909 report recommended that farmers become more efficient producers and marketers and that rural schools and churches be strengthened. Schools would be consolidated where possible and their curricula would be broadened. (lr)

Country Life Movement
A broad reform group made up of educators, businesspeople, religious leaders, social scientists, and agricultural scientists who lamented the decline of rural America in the face of urban and industrial expansion. Its efforts were reinforced by Theodore Roosevelt's creation of a Country Life Commission, but the movement, being largely an urban one, died out after World War I. (lr)

couples counseling
Couples counseling generally falls into one of two domains: helping couples improve interactional, intimacy, or communication patterns; and/or assisting one or both parties with individual problems such as depression, anxiety, or other mental health problems that are interfering with their functioning as a couple. Couples counseling is typically short-term and focuses on specific problem resolution. (tsw)

course, career-technical or vocational
A course consisting of instruction in an occupational or career-technical subject, preparing students for competent service in a nonprofessional or semiprofessional occupation requiring less than a

baccalaureate degree. The term is sometimes used to distinguish such a course from academic or liberal arts courses (such as English literature, mathematics, music appreciation) and professional courses (such as medicine, education, engineering, law). (jb)

course, cooperative

A course or program of study designed to form a basis of related academic and career-technical knowledge to supplement the work experiences of students working on a part-time basis. (jm)

course, short

A course in which instruction is scheduled for a period considerably shorter than a regular semester, quarter, term, or session. Typically an abbreviation of a standard course, a presentation of very recent research, a brief review of a broad area of practical knowledge, a refresher course. (cf)

course, survey

A course designed to give a general view of an area of study. (cf)

course credit (See credit)

course management software

Computer software designed for instructors to provide online content and instruction to their students. Course management software may be used as a supplement to face-to-face instruction or may be utilized to teach online courses. Components include chat rooms, e-mail capabilities, testing options, discussion lists, and grading functionality. Common course management software programs are Blackboard, Moodle, Desire2Learn, and WebCT. Also called learning management systems, course management systems, and e-learning systems. (pw1)

course management systems

Software that is used to deliver, track, and manage educational courses taken by students over the Internet, which contains tools for student and faculty communication and collaboration, for developing and organizing course content, and for creating assignments and assessments within online and hybrid courses. (pgg)

course portfolio

An organized collection of materials that summarize teaching and management in a particular course. For many people, a course portfolio includes all of the materials used to teach a course, a list of "what worked" and "what didn't work," and a reflective statement. Suggested documents for a course portfolio are: course syllabus, problem sets, exams, laboratory exercises, samples of student work, midterm assessment, student evaluations of the course, peer evaluations (formal or informal), and a reflective statement. (cf)

See also teaching portfolio.

course requirements

What students must do to pass the course is usually stipulated in the college catalog and in the instructor's initial lectures; what the instructor expects students to learn becomes more evident as the course continues. (cf)

courseware

A suite of functions, usually web-based, used together for instruction in an online environment. Core elements of courseware packages are asynchronous threaded discussion, web pages for presentation of course content, and e-mail functions. Courseware may also include synchronous discussion ("chat"), synchronous collaboration tools, shared student workspace, upload functions for submitting assignments, or other tools to meet specific instructional needs. For online courses, courseware is the primary instructional environment. Courseware can also be used as an adjunct to face-to-face instruction. (ac)

See also hybrid course.

covert/overt behaviors

Covert behaviors are concealed or covered. Overt behaviors are explicit or open. Cross-cultural interactions are accompanied by issues of power and control that are manifested through covert and overt behaviors to fulfill various agendas and personal intentions. Former acts of overt prejudice, such as racism and sexism, now are conducted through covert yet equally harmful acts of hate and bigotry. (npg)

CPE (See continuing professional education)

craft

The planning, making, or executing of handmade goods or works of art. Craft refers to manual dexterity and artistic skill (e.g., the carpenter's craft) and can be associated with ingenuity or guile. Historically, craft has been separated from the loftier realms of aesthetics and fine arts. The arts and crafts movement, influenced by William Morris and John Ruskin in 19th-century England, reacted against industrialization and called for a return to handicraft in the decorative and applied arts. Today, arts and crafts (e.g., weaving, carving, printmaking) are taught in schools, camps, and other institutions as a form of art, recreation, or therapy. (lj)

Creative Commons License

A form of copyright that allows authors to donate their work to the public domain or to grant specific freedoms or partial rights of their choice, such as to allow others to share or remix the work. One can also specify under what circumstances the work may be used, for example, only for noncommercial work or only if the new work is also granted the same license. This license is in addition to fair use regulations that are already within the realms of regular copyright. Creative Commons licensing gives teachers greater access to materials as well as more freedom in how materials are used without having to go through the process of contacting and getting permissions from individual authors. This can be especially beneficial when a teacher or student creates multimedia presentations on particular topics and wants to use others' videos, pictures, or podcasts as part of the presentation. (kd)

creative discovery area

An area that is open-ended, housing diverse implements, materials, and media. The area facilitates children to create, discover, and experience new ways of doing things by molding, changing, constructing, and observing outcomes. This area allows construction of things by using different materials such as sand, water, and clay; inspection of interesting items such as insect and rock collections through microscopes and magnifying glasses; and use and discovery of other items that are developmentally appropriate for the age and interests of individual children and groups. (pw)

creative expression

Those actions that reflect the highest levels of thinking about a particular concept, topic, or event. Creativity is the energetic blending of two or more concepts, topics, or events that were heretofore disconnected in the mind of the child. (mc1)

creative thinking

The analytic, synthetic, and evaluative thinking that leads to creative expression. (mc1)

creativity

The ability or power to create with originality, innovation, self-expression, and imagination. Creativity is thought to involve the breaking of boundaries and to be the basis for the artistic process, driving the synthesis of raw materials into a finished product. Creativity, an ideal of the modernist avant-garde, is viewed as having systematic steps of problem setting and solving, commonly referred to as the "creative process." Educational psychologists like Csikszentmihalyi and Gardner regard creativity as the work of veteran thinkers who fashion products that transform domains and are recognized as doing so across generations. But very young children have a natural sense of creativity that is reflected in their work across artistic media. (kf)

credit

Acknowledgement or certification that a student has completed a specific course of study. Also called course credit. Traditionally, secondary students in the United States are required to acquire a predetermined number of credits in defined curricular areas before proceeding to the next grade level or receiving a diploma. Credits are the unit of measure or value for specific courses and are frequently expressed as credit hours. (jw)

credit, dual

Academic or career-technical courses offered at the high school level that provide for college credit. (db)

credit hour

The unit by which an institution may measure its course work. The number of credit hours assigned to a course is usually defined by the number of hours per week in class and the number of weeks in the session. (cf)

credit-by-examination

Procedure by which a student not formally enrolled in a course may be awarded academic credit for a course by passing an oral, written, or manipulative test. (cf)

Creole

A language, which started as a pidgin language, adopted by a community as its native tongue and learned by children as their first language (e.g., Haitian Creole, based on French; Krio, spoken in Sierra Leone and based on English; Cape Verdian Creole, based on Portuguese). (smt)

crisis counseling

A brief form of counseling used with individuals who are experiencing an extreme reaction to life's events. Crisis counseling is often sought when an individual finds him- or herself unable to cope with a stressful event. It typically involves creating realistic, wellness-enhancing, short-term goals for individuals in regard to their immediate presenting crisis. The primary goal of crisis counseling is to assist an individual in developing effective coping methods in order to regain an effective, or at least baseline, level of functioning. (ay)

criterion referencing

This is both a form of test development and of score usage. Results from criterion-referenced tests are interpreted as the test taker's ability to perform a task or set of tasks (sometimes called a "domain"). Typically criterion-referenced results are not interpreted as rank in a group of peers. (fd)

See also norm referencing.

critical consciousness

The ability to understand the political and social forces that are acting to support and constrain a person's options in life. A person with critical consciousness has the ability to take action to address those constraints. (jpc)

critical ethnography

A method of research and analysis that typically relies on fine-grained, long-term observation and interviewing to expose the way that power relations in schools perpetuate inequalities and injustices. This research approach is typically informed by critical theory; committed to the establishment of equality and social justice through an analysis of how domination operates; and enacted through a constantly reflexive, often collaborative approach to the practice of gathering data and generating knowledge. This method of research and analysis has become very important in educational studies since the 1980s. (baul)

critical friends

Members of a collaborative group that meet regularly and are dedicated to observing each others' practice, examining student and adult work, and providing feedback in order to improve student achievement and teacher practice. Commonly referred to as "Critical Friends Groups" or "CFGs" and associated with the National School Reform Faculty. (mrs, aa)

critical incident

Any significant experience in the workplace that can be examined by human resource developers to inform the design of training programs. Interviews are held with knowledgeable people in the organization to uncover situations that illustrate both positive and negative behaviors on the job. (dmv)

See also critical incident technique.

critical incident technique

An approach to teaching that makes use of short cases that highlight a critical incident as a basis for analysis, discussion, and learning. An assessment method used in human resource development to determine an organization's performance gaps by reflecting on certain experiences in the workplace. Analysis of behaviors involved in an incident can uncover training, educational, and employee development needs. (dmv)

See also critical incident.

critical listening

Thorough listening to a presentation with the intent to analyze what is being heard, not to argue with it. (jw)

critical literacy

Literacy that is taught in such a way that students use their literacy skills to critically reflect on the political and social forces that affect their lives so that they

can take action to overcome the barriers those forces have put in place. (jpc)

critical pedagogy

An approach to teaching and learning that encourages the learner to reflect critically on issues of power and oppression in his or her society and on what might be done to change the current situation. Critical pedagogy helps learners to develop their own sense of identity and power as an important component of their learning experience. An approach to teaching that builds critical consciousness by helping students analyze their lives and identify the political and social forces that are acting upon them, so that they can take action to overcome the barriers those forces have put in place. (chm, jpc)

See also transformative pedagogy.

critical period

A time period particularly early in development in which specific experiences or key developments must take place. A time of unique sensitivity of an organism to a specific stimulus. If the time period is missed, then either normal development will not or is less likely to occur, or the key development will not or is less likely to occur. It is thought that a critical period has a fixed length in time and does not reoccur. In human behavior, language development, mother/infant attachment, and visual perception have been studied for critical periods, not always with success. Similar to a sensitive period as a portion of time in which environmental input is needed for the neural system to develop optimally. (vm, dh)

critical poststructuralism

Concept that commits itself to removing all external claims of objectivity, validity, and authority from texts. Each text must be evaluated on its own terms and by its own claims. In this way, language and speech do not mirror experience; they create experience as transformational representations of multiple, situational, fluid, and developing understandings of given experiences. The removal and rejection of validity instead centers values, attitudes, perspectives, and beliefs as governors of science. (hfs)

critical race theory

Critical race theory (CRT), born in response to the failures of traditional civil rights litigation to produce lasting and meaningful racial reform, and rooted in 1970s legal scholarship, offers an analytical tool for understanding how white supremacy and racism continue to influence social, political, and economic inequity in American society. The core principles of CRT are grounded in three key publications: *Words That Wound: Critical Race Theory, Assaultive Speech, and the First Amendment* (Matsuda, Lawrence, Delgado, & Crenshaw, 1993), *Critical Race Theory: The Key Writings That Formed the Movement* (Crenshaw et al., 1995), and *Critical Race Theory: The Cutting Edge* (Delgado, 1995). These important works offer scholars outside the law community a theoretical framework from which seemingly race-neutral structures in education—knowledge, truth, merit, objectivity, classroom activities and dynamics, curriculum, instructional policies and practices, testing, and "good education"—can be critiqued. Writers in the CRT tradition include such scholars as Derrick Bell, David Carbado, Kimberlé Crenshaw, Richard Delgado, Gloria Ladson-Billings, Charles Lawrence, Laurence Parker, Daniel Solórzano, and Tara Yosso, who contest traditional scholarly forms and genres by presenting metaphorical tales, chronicles, and "counter" narratives generated from multiple historical, sociological, and personal sources to dramatize and give voice to the experiences of peoples of color from the perspectives of writers of color. (dns)

critical relativism

A concept developed by Alain Locke, which recognizes that while values are relative and particular to cultures, they remain subject to objective critique, inquiry, and analysis. The objectivity is grounded in the functionality of values and attitudes in the cultures in which they emerge, function, and develop. While their development and adaptations are neither generalizable nor universal, contextual and cultural values can be investigated and qualified. (hfs)

critical subjectivity

A process of reflection that, when incongruence among ways of knowing or perceiving is detected, the awareness of such requires returning to the experience of the felt encounter for further inquiry and analysis. (hfs)

critical theory

An analytical process that analyzes and challenges the assumptions and values that underlie the way a society functions. It rejects the view that one can use a positivist or value-neutral approach to the analysis of social phenomena, especially when dealing with issues of oppression and power. Understanding and critiquing human action and social life through an analysis of culture and ideology and how they form human consciousness. Critical theory inverts Karl Marx's social theory of base structure (the material basis for social life) and superstructure (culture and consciousness), arguing that superstructure is not, as Marx had it, merely epiphenomenal to base structure but has an independent influence over social life and can affect changes in material life. Critical theory focuses upon how culture, ideology, and social institutions (such as the media, the arts, and schools) maintain individuals and groups in states of unconscious unfreedom and injustice within a society that privileges the ruling group through tacit consensus of the ruled and unprivileged. Some central concepts are domination, culture, ideology, hegemony, and resistance. Central figures in critical theory are Theodor Adorno, Walter

Benjamin, Max Horkheimer, Herbert Marcuse, and Jürgen Habermas. Critical theory has been adapted to educational thinking by, among others, Henry Giroux, Peter McLaren, and Michael Apple. (chm, db-j)

See also culture; hegemony; ideology; resistance.

critical thinking
The ability to use higher-level thinking processes to search for meaning in an action or event. Benjamin S. Bloom (1956) and his colleagues defined the "higher levels" of thinking to be application, analysis, synthesis, and evaluation. Children are often seen using critical thinking skills in their self-selected play activities, and teachers who develop project-based curricula appeal to these higher-level cognitive processes. The kind of thinking we use to question, doubt, compare and contrast, and make judgments. We use critical thinking to make assessments about the evidence we gather, the sources we find, and the assumptions we make, in order to help us decide what to believe and do. We use critical thinking to critique ideas and determine which ones to accept and which ones to reject. Critical thinking is associated with rationality, reasonableness, reflective thinking, and the scientific inquiry process. (ecr, bt-t)

See also constructive thinking; creative thinking; indoctrination; logic; reason; thinking.

critique
French, from the Greek kritik (tekhn), art of criticism. The practice of discussing a work (e.g., of art or literature) critically, focusing on strengths, weaknesses, and the extent to which the work conforms to or deviates from a set of disciplinary traditions and expectations. Recently associated with "critical" as negative judgment, critique (or the "crit" as it is often called in art school when student work is critiqued by instructors and peers) can positively

affirm and redirect works in progress. The self-critique of youth in community art centers has been a source of interest to educational researchers. Students working collaboratively and independently on a shared artistic project seem to find ways to support one another even as they reflect critically on what needs to be done to make their work better. (jd)

cross validation
In statistics, cross validation refers to a process of examining whether the results from one data set are generalized to a different data set and ensuring that the original result is not due to capitalization on chance stemming from sampling errors. In education, cross validation research is often carried out to gather validity evidence. (hl)

cross-cultural competence (See cultural competence)

cross-cultural counseling
Counseling provided to a person who is from a culture that is different from that of the counselor. Effective cross-cultural counseling involves, among other skills, cultural sensitivity and responsiveness, a belief in multiculturalism, and an acknowledgement of the sociocultural context of a client's life. (llf, emm)

cross-cultural literacy
The development of both a clear understanding and knowledge of one's own values, perceptions, and beliefs, as well as an openness to engage in a process of learning about the values, perceptions, knowledge, and beliefs of others. (hfs)

cross-cultural studies
Examines cultural phenomena from the positions of several different cultures. By examining phenomena from different cultural points of view, a more fundamental understanding of human experiences can be constructed. (hrm, ew, jkd)

cross-curricular integration

A cross-curricular educational approach integrating information, knowledge, principles, and values of more than one academic discipline. (ch)

cross-dressing

Wearing clothing most often associated (in one's culture and historical timeframe) with people of a different gender. Cross-dressers usually self-identify with their biological sex but sometimes wear clothing, jewelry, and so on of the opposite gender to fulfill identity-related and emotional needs. (jb2)

CRT (See critical race theory)

CTA (See Children's Television Act)

CTSOs (See career and technical student organizations)

CTT—(classical test theory) (See item analysis)

Cuban American Legal Defense and Education Act (CALDEF), 1980

A nonprofit national organization established to assist Cuban Americans and modeled after the Mexican American Legal Defense and Education Fund. The organization's main function is to ensure fair treatment and opportunities for Cuban Americans and to educate the American populace about the plight and culture of Hispanic Americans. (rih)

cued speech

A manual method of communication for the deaf and hard of hearing that relies upon phonemes and speech sounds found in spoken language. This system of communication uses eight hand-shapes that are placed in four areas around the face. These hand-shapes and locations are used in conjunction with spoken language to assist in lip-reading. (jas)

cultural acquisition (See cultural transmission and acquisition)

cultural anthropology (See ethnography)

cultural appropriateness

The alignment of a teaching practice with the expectations and practices of a cultural group. According to Bredekamp and Copple (1997), Eurocentric educational beliefs and customs, characterized by high levels of independence and competition, can create an instructional mismatch for children who are raised in more interdependent and collaborative cultures, such as African American and Native American families. (ecr)

cultural awareness

The knowledge required to understand the values, behaviors, language, and customs of one's own or another culture(s). (srs)

cultural capital

A concept articulated by French sociologist Pierre Bourdieu, cultural capital is made up of cultural and linguistic knowledge, skills, and dispositions transmitted from one generation to another. Bourdieu's premise is that schools, while presenting a veneer of fairness and equality, implicitly value the cultural capital of the dominant classes, and students who possess these most valued forms of cultural capital are able to translate these resources into academic success and credentials (institutionalized cultural capital). These credentials are subsequently convertible into economic capital in the labor market, tacitly maintaining the social status of middle-class and affluent students, and impeding students who are lacking in the cultural capital of the dominant classes. (adj)

See also politics of knowledge.

cultural competence

The ability to interact effectively and comfortably with all people with cultural characteristics both like and unlike one-self. Cultural competence comprises four components: self-awareness; knowledge of and information about cultures locally to globally; skills and practices to interact cross-culturally; and dispositions and attitudes toward cultural similarities and differences. Developing cultural competence fosters the ability to understand, communicate with, and interact successfully with all individuals like and unlike oneself culturally. Sometimes referred to as multicultural literacy. (npg, acp)

See also multicultural literacy.

cultural context

The totality of socially transmitted behavior patterns, arts, beliefs, institutions, and all other products of human work and thought. Cultural context is therefore that which relates to a specific culture. Cultural context varies widely among and between demographic groups and geographic locations. Cultural context differs among ethnic groups, gender groups, income groups, and so forth. Members of these types of groups view similar events quite differently depending on their own cultural foundation. (jfb)

cultural context of education

Education, as a teaching-studenting process, always takes place within a context, and that context is cultural, specifying such things as language, traditions, beliefs, standards of beauty, and forms of technology. Education is always specific to a certain time and place, and it is affected by many factors, such as the value and importance placed on that which is being learned, as well as the interest and attention of the students and teachers. Culture gives meaning to this educational moment, shapes how we make sense of the learning that is, or isn't, taking place, and specifies what the content of the learning should be. (bt, b)

See also Afrocentric education; ethnicity; multicultural education.

cultural deprivation theory

A theory popularized in education in the 1960s that attempted to explain why low-income students, particularly low-income students from minority groups, did not perform as well as their white, middle-class peers in the classroom. The idea was that low-income children were raised in "inferior" home environments that did not adequately prepare them for learning. The promoters of cultural deprivation theory often advocated for educational programming targeted at students deemed "culturally deprived" to improve academic achievement and suggested changes to the curriculum to address these disparities. Gradually, as members of "culturally deprived" groups protested that this approach stereotyped minorities and those living in poverty, the theory fell out of favor in education. (acp)

See also culturally deprived.

cultural discontinuity theory

A theory based on the assumption that minority students are placed at a disadvantage in schools where the majority culture is significantly different from the culture of the minority. (jqa, jwc)

cultural diversity

A term relating to the many cultural, social, ethnic, racial, religious, and otherwise different backgrounds of individuals and groups. (jqa, jwc)

cultural enrichment

To strive to project a culture in ways that portray that specific culture to be richer and more meaningful than previously considered. Cultural enrichment is often played out in schools by focusing on the artistic, scientific, and academic contributions of a particular culture. Examples would be highlighting these elements of the Native American culture, European American culture, Hispanic American culture, and so forth. Cultural enrichment may also be gender-specific, as in recognizing the contributions of females in a male-dominated society. (jfb)

cultural imperialism

Process by which powerful countries, religions, ethnicities, and cultural groups maintain and exercise control over the identity, understandings, perspectives, and interpretations of the less powerful. This is accomplished through the radiation and imposition of extrinsic ideas, morals, attitudes, and belief systems that present particular visions of the world that benefit the powerful and legitimize their status, typically via the mass media. (hfs)

cultural literacy

The late 20th-century expression of essentialism popularized by E. D. Hirsch. Hirsch argues that one is made literate as one acquires a given body of knowledge shared within the culture, the "tradition." The view is that acquisition of this knowledge happens in the family for many children, but for immigrants and the poor, schools are the places where this happens, which is necessary for social mobility to be a possibility. Having a core, literate knowledge of the culture (i.e., the significant traditions, ideas, values, people, places, events, language, literature, habits, attitudes, history, etc.) of a given society that is requisite for competent functioning (Hirsch et al. 1987) and informed participation (Freire and Macedo, 1987) in that society. (jc, ml)

See also essentialism.

cultural production

A theoretical term that emphasizes the process by which people actively produce knowledge and meaning through a dynamic educational process. In anthropological studies, the term points to how, in the process of "acquiring" elements of cultural knowledge "transmitted" through education, individuals can modify, extend, or contest the knowledge, while producing and adding new knowledge to the common stock. Another use of the term is in relation to theories of social and cultural reproduction, which became popular in the 1970s and 1980s. Such theories suggested that schools serve to reproduce social inequalities through the cultural realm, by privileging certain kinds of cultural styles and knowledge over others, and thereby assigning children from different class and ethnic backgrounds to differential fates. Against these rather deterministic theories, some authors (e.g., Willis, 1977) emphasized the agency of students to respond to the school and shape their own destiny through a process of cultural production. (baul)

cultural proficiency (See cultural competence)

cultural relativism

A doctrine first articulated in the work of Franz Boas, and later taken up by many of his most important students (including Margaret Mead, Ruth Benedict, and Melville Herskovits), cultural relativism is a perspective for explaining and understanding culture and cultural practices. It holds that each culture and its cultural practices should be understood in context, that is, in terms of the institutions, ideas, values, and practices that comprise the whole of the culture. It further maintains that cultures and cultural practices should not be judged through the values and standards of another culture. The essence of the doctrine of cultural relativism is that in order to make sense of culture and cultural practices, it is essential to consider the context in which they actually occur. In contrast to common interpretations of "relativism" and "moral relativism," cultural relativism does not hold that judgments about other cultures or their practices should never or can never be made. Rather, it maintains that the clearest and most accurate assessments and understandings can occur only when culture and cultural practices are interpreted in context. Cultural relativism is one of the core concepts of the discipline of cultural anthropology. (jde)

cultural responsiveness

Awareness, knowledge, and appreciation of different cultures. It includes sensitivity and receptivity to the sociocultural context of others' lives, and the willingness to connect genuinely and collaboratively with others regarding both cultural differences and similarities. Awareness of and attention to individuals' perceptions of individual, cultural, and institutional prejudice are also considered to be important elements of cultural responsiveness. (llf, emm)

cultural sensitivity

A state of awareness heightened by physical, emotional, or spiritual stimuli in social interaction. (srs)

cultural studies

The study of culture from a sociological rather than an aesthetic viewpoint, drawing on the social sciences, for example, politics and semiotics, rather than traditional forms of literary, artistic, or musical criticism; a wide-ranging educational course, generally at the college level, covering all aspects of culture, the arts, sciences, and social sciences. (mkg)

cultural styles

The behaviors, ways, and methods in which we all function are developed in relation to ethnicity, socioeconomic status, race, gender, sexual orientation, and so on. Cultural styles affect the way individuals learn. (jqa, jwc)

cultural transmission

Something transmitted or passed on relating to the arts, interests, and manners that a group of people favors; denoting or derived from, or distinctive of the ways of living by a group of people. (mkg)

cultural transmission and acquisition

Cultural transmission refers to the inculcation of basic cultural knowledge across the generations in a given society. Emphasis is placed on how adult generations educate the young through transmitting core values, dispositions, and skills. Early anthropological work, grounded in theories of structural-functionalism, focused on cultural transmission in order to understand how societies conserved essential features of their cultural and technological repertoires. More recently, anthropologists have emphasized the process of cultural acquisition, examining how relative novices acquire the basic cultural knowledge of a society, bringing their own distinctive interests and traits to the process. Studies of cultural transmission tend to focus on how adults "teach" the young; studies of cultural acquisition focus on how the young "learn" from adults or peers. (baul)

cultural-cognitive tools

Cultural-cognitive tools are patterns and modalities of language and thought that have emerged as a result of cultural-historical processes, which as a result of interiorization come to be individually held as cognitive tools. In the Socio-Cultural Theory of Lev Vygotsky, human beings are considered to be tool-making, which is to say that as a species we have a special relationship to our varied environments via culturally developed mediating artifacts, the most significant of which is language. Tools, once fully adopted into the psychological processes of individuals through interiorization, result in substantively divergent modalities of thought from those which characteristically existed beforehand. Cognitive tools are innumerable in principle, but the body of theory known as imaginative education foregrounds tools such as narrative, binaries, metaphor, humor, imagery, rhythm, and theoretic thinking, to name a few. (tw1)

See also imaginative education; interiorization; socio-cultural theory.

culturally and linguistically diverse (CLD)

In the United States, this term is used to describe students for whom English is a second language. Sometimes written as "linguistically and culturally diverse learner" (LCDL). (acp)

See also language minority.

culturally deprived

A concept related to cultural deprivation theory that emerged in the 1950s, but was in highest usage in the 1960s to describe individuals from low-income families. It was most commonly used to refer to low-income students from minority groups. In a typical account of the concept, Bloom wrote in 1954 that certain groups remained culturally deprived because the root of the problem may be "traced to their experiences in homes which do not transmit the cultural patterns necessary for the types of learning characteristic of the schools, and the larger society." The term promoted stereotyping of minorities and carried with it an assumption that culturally deprived students were not capable of achieving the levels of success of white students. Due to these connotations, the terms "culturally deprived," or "culturally disadvantaged," have gradually fallen out of use in education. (acp)

See also cultural deprivation theory.

culturally disadvantaged (See culturally deprived)

culturally encapsulated counselor

Counselors who remain within a protective "capsule" of their own experiences, perspectives, and realities; assume everyone's perspectives are (or should be) the same as their own; and believe that their world (i.e., culture, subculture) will remain static and is the only reality. Cultural encapsulation can interfere with the counseling process, in part, by disregarding or perhaps even embracing one's cultural biases, engaging in stereotypic thinking, and engaging in exclusionary behaviors. It can also interfere with ethical decision making in counseling. (llf, emm)

culturally relevant pedagogy

A curriculum perspective that includes a shared view of a classroom community whose curriculum is sensitive to all students, raising the question of cultural relevance, and considering the cultural mismatch that often exists between the students, the teacher, and the curriculum. (mkg)

culturally responsive classroom management

The creation of a learning environment characterized by care and respect for students' cultural diversity. Culturally responsive classroom management requires that teachers have knowledge of their own culture and implicit cultural biases and assumptions as well as knowledge of the cultural backgrounds of the students, and the ways that the broader sociopolitical context impacts students and their families. In addition, the teacher must have the skills necessary to create a warm, responsive, and respectful classroom community, and to establish and maintain high expectations for both classroom behavior and academic performance. Finally, the teacher must demonstrate the attributes of a "warm demander," who is able to firmly and explicitly enforce expectations while maintaining positive relationships with students. (sld, ddr)

culturally responsive pedagogy

Instructional approach that recognizes the importance of affirming and building upon students' cultural assets in all aspects of curriculum and instruction. Culturally responsive pedagogy intends to foster a culturally supported, learner-centered context where all students' cultural strengths are valued and used. Culturally responsive classrooms therefore include a broad array of cultural and linguistic practices and values. Culturally responsive pedagogy includes three dimensions: the institutional dimension of school system policies and values, the personal dimension of teachers' cognitive and emotional processes, and the instructional dimension of content, activities, materials, and strategies being utilized in the classroom. Effective culturally responsive pedagogy depends on teacher knowledge of his or her identity and its intersection with that of the students. (sld, ddr)

culturally responsive teaching

Development of curriculum and instructional practices that show awareness of the multicultural backgrounds of students and work to integrate culturally familiar language, stories, events, and activities in order to illustrate ideas and concepts. Culturally responsive teaching bridges the gap between that which is familiar in a student's real world and that which is taught in the classroom. (ms)

culture

The term "culture" has a long and illustrious history. It harks back to the Latin verb for cultivation, or the tending of crops and animals. We see its first English use in the 15th century, whence it quickly developed associations with European notions of progress and evolution in civilization. For hundreds of years, to have culture was to "cultivate" the higher qualities of civilization, to practice or appreciate the arts or sciences, to develop a refined language. Yet by the late 18th century, the German Romantic poets and philosophers were already giving culture a new cast. Anthropologists picked up and developed this sense of culture as the lifeways that every human group develops as part of its historical adaptation. In modern anthropological usage, culture typically refers to the symbolic meanings expressed through language, gesture, dress, and so forth, by which the members of a given society communicate with and understand themselves, each other, and the world around them. Within this definition, social scientists have emphasized different aspects or qualities of culture as: publicly observable symbols (Geertz, 1973), shared knowledge (Spradley and McCurdy, 1997), or cognitive models (Holland and Quinn, 1987). Sociologist Charles Lemert (1995, p. 174) calls culture the "code of practical instructions whereby members are given permission to talk meaningfully about some things while ignoring others." Many social scientists now agree that culture is a form of practice informed by symbolic knowledge stored in the brain; that is, culture is what people do in everyday life, informed by implicit and shared knowledge (Chaiklin and Lave, 1996; Holland et al., 1998). Given the varieties of overlapping cultural membership in complex modern societies, educators and educational researchers attempt to understand how educational processes take place within and between different cultural frameworks. (baul)

culture circle

An instructional technique, developed by Paulo Freire for adult literacy programs, in which students describe, discuss, and analyze a "generative theme," which is usually represented by a picture and a word, that describes an important issue in the lives of the students. (jpc)

culture context

May be defined as the totality of socially transmitted behavior patterns, arts, beliefs, institutions, and all other products of human work and thought. Cultural context is therefore that which relates to a specific culture. Cultural context varies widely among and between demographic groups and geographic locations. Cultural context differs between ethnic groups, gender groups, income groups, and so forth. Members of these types of groups view similar events quite differently, dependent upon their own cultural foundation. (jfb)

culture fair

The lack of cultural bias in language and construction of evaluation instruments, texts, or expectations of behavior. Such models may emphasize nonverbal problems and questions that are common to all children regardless of their racial, social, or cultural background. The purpose of culture fair evaluation is to identify and measure an individual's intelligence by filtering out both verbal and cultural influences. Culture fair tests allow for an improved analysis and prediction of individuals' potentialities. (hrm, ew, jkd)

culture fair tests
Those tests that are designed so as to eliminate or reduce cultural bias in the context of the test. The test is constructed so that the culture of the test author or the test taker does not play a part in the final results of the test. For example, the test content does not make the assumption that all students should be familiar with a particular phrase or illustration when, in fact, much of the language used and the illustrations used may be culturally biased. In reality, no test can be made totally culture fair, but it is important to strive toward that end. (jfb)

culture of contentment
Concept used by John Kenneth Galbraith to describe the attitudes and values of the 87 percent of Americans who do not live in poverty. Absent poverty-based suffering in their own lives, they cannot be easily persuaded or moved to act on the behalf, or in the interests of, the poor, absent a catastrophe such as war, riot, or a severe depression. (hfs)

culture shock
The feelings of disorientation, anxiety, disjunction, isolation, loneliness, and despair that regularly accompany ethnographers (and travelers) when visiting or living in (studying) cultures not their own. Some ethnographers report that for them culture shock occurs when they return to their own culture after an extended period of time away. (jde)

culture-bound syndrome
Maladaptive pattern(s) of behaviors or symptoms that are endemic to a specific social or cultural group. Indigenously considered to be "illnesses." Examples of these types of syndromes, as listed in DSM-IV, include: Amok, Ghost Sickness, and Locura. (js)

cum laude
Latin phrase meaning "with praise," used as a designation for a college or university honor graduate. (cf)

cumulative files (See cumulative record)

cumulative record
A depository of information and documents about individual students, beginning when they start kindergarten and continuing until they leave school or graduate. Cumulative records contain a variety of information, such as personal data, home and family information, school attendance records, standardized test scores, end-of-year academic grades, teachers' anecdotal comments, and other miscellaneous information. (bba)

curriculum
Definitions of curriculum are as numerous as there are philosophers of education. Ralph Tyler's curriculum model brings the needs of the child, the society, and the academic disciplines together in an attempt to formulate the general objectives teachers are to teach and students are to learn. J. Allen Queen, a futurist, views curriculum as society's requirement of the formal educational process to prepare the next generations for adaptability, acceptance, diversity, and survival in an unknown world. Curriculum may also be viewed as a collection of ongoing formal and informal processes and experiences that prepare students to achieve and adapt to personal and societal needs. The courses of study offered at an educational institution represent the overt, intentional curriculum, what we make public and announce we are teaching in school. The overt or explicit curriculum is what

we place in our course catalogues and on our course syllabi. There is also a hidden curriculum, what we teach that we do not make public and many times are not even conscious we are teaching, yet the teaching still goes on. Curriculum in its broadest sense stands for what we teach. (jfb, bt-b)

See also explicit curriculum; hidden curriculum; null curriculum; operationalized curriculum.

curriculum, articulated
A continuous curriculum in which a coordinated effort between elementary school, high school, and college curricula has been forged to reduce unnecessary repetition and bring about a sustained educational progression. (ea, db)

curriculum, experienced (See experienced curriculum)

curriculum, explicit (See explicit curriculum)

curriculum, hidden (See hidden curriculum)

curriculum, integrated academic and career-technical
Secondary and postsecondary curriculum that encourages closer ties between or more extensive fusion of the academic disciplines and career-technical subject matter. Can be associated with courses that are predominantly academic or career-technical, or may refer to entirely new hybrid courses combining academic and career-technical education. (db)

curriculum, null (See null curriculum)

curriculum, operationalized (See operationalized curriculum)

curriculum alignment
Refers to the practice of matching curriculum content with test content. Originally called "curriculum overlap" when it

was discovered that test scores were better when the test objectives "overlapped" specific or parallel curriculum content. Alignment is a specific problem in the United States because of a long history of the decentralization of curriculum development, the lack of a national curriculum or exam as in other countries in the world, and the creation of standardized tests that measure no specific curriculum. (fwe)

curriculum articulation
The organization of classroom instruction, cocurricular activities, and other interdependent and interrelated services of the educational system to facilitate the continuous sequential and efficient educational progression of students from grade to grade, from school to school, or from level to level. Enables students to make smooth transitions from one level to the next. (db, ea)

curriculum auditing
A form of a management audit in which the curriculum, as represented in work documents such as curriculum guides, pacing charts, and scope and sequence specifications, are analyzed as to depth and specificity for effective classroom delivery and aligned with existing accountability measures such as local, state, or national testing programs. Originally called an EPA (educational performance audit) by Leon Lessinger in 1970, the audit has been utilized in hundreds of U.S. school systems since then. (fwe)

curriculum compacting
A strategy for serving advanced learners in a mixed-ability classroom by eliminating the repetition of work once a concept is mastered. After defining the intended goals and outcomes of a given instructional unit, candidates for curriculum compacting are assessed to determine the extent of the material they already know or might master quickly. Advanced and highly motivated students are then provided opportunities to accelerate their

pace through the material and upon demonstrating mastery are provided opportunities to engage in related curricular enrichment building on the mastered concepts. (bda)

curriculum content

Curriculum content is directly related to the required outcomes educators want the students to achieve. Thus, curriculum content reflects the commonly understood mission of the school and the educational philosophy that drives that mission. Curriculum content responds to the needs of the society, the culture, the educational system, the program divisions, and the specific school's instructional model. Curriculum content reflects the needs of the students in the cognitive, psychomotor, and affective domains. (jfb)

curriculum development

Begins with an assessment of the educational outcome desired. Curriculum development continues by determining the skills to be mastered in order to achieve the desired outcome. It is sequential in nature and builds on the continuum of skills previously mastered and skills yet to be introduced, developed, and eventually mastered. By first establishing the goal, curriculum planners may develop a sequence of objectives that lead to the attainment of the final goal or objective. (jfb)

curriculum enrichment

Expanding upon a predetermined course of study or set of content guides to meet the needs, experiences, or interests of an individual or group of learners. Enrichment may extend to a differentiation of entire content areas to accommodate exceptional learners within a heterogeneous group. (jw)

curriculum evaluation

Curriculum is in a perpetual state of evaluation. Curriculum planning and delivery decisions are made on the desired educational outcome. The effectiveness of curriculum is commonly measured on the success of students whose knowledge is tested when the curriculum is aligned with specific learning outcomes and the testing instrument used to measure that outcome. Curriculum evaluation is both formative and summative. When it becomes evident that the curriculum does not have the content necessary for teachers to teach the required objectives, the curriculum is abandoned and a new curriculum is put in its place. The new curriculum becomes subject to the same perpetual evaluation process. (jfb)

curriculum gatekeepers

Coined by Kurt Lewin (1943), the term "gatekeepers" refers to those who must approve of a proposed change before it can be successfully implemented. Curriculum gatekeepers are often viewed as those choosing traditional methods and materials rather than innovative ones. (ks)

curriculum guides

Handbooks used by teachers and curriculum leaders as a map for the systematic delivery of specific knowledge leading to a specific student outcome. Curriculum guides may be prepared by publishers to aid the classroom teacher in the appropriate sequencing and pacing of the educational material being presented. They may also be prepared by local school districts as a tool for guiding teachers through a unique set of learning objectives peculiar to that district, as in local area history, character education, sex education, and so forth. (jfb)

curriculum mapping

A process by which teachers create a visual representation of curriculum as it is delivered, rather than as it is planned. Using a template with predetermined categories and format, instructors "map" their curriculum and then share and examine each other's curricula for gaps, overlaps, redundancies, and new learning, creating a coherent, consistent curriculum within and across schools with the goal to align to standards and be responsive to student data and other school initiatives. (mf1)

curriculum of place

A curriculum of place is one in which teachers draw on their community as a curricular resource at the same time that they produce curriculum that strengthens the community. They use their place as a lever to get at subject matter meaningfully by examining its histories, traditions, resource bases, challenges, and sources of human capital. (lr)

See also pedagogy of place.

curriculum standards

A set of written guidelines established at the national, state, and/or local level of government defining what school-aged students will be taught, how they will be taught, and how student achievement will be evaluated in each recognized content area. Curriculum standards specify what students should know at the elementary, middle, and high school levels. (mkg)

curriculum studies

A disciplinary field of study focusing on curriculum thinking, conceptualizing, analyzing, and living. It closely examines current curriculum structure and orientations, as well as rethinking the nature of curriculum construction for an increasingly meaningful experience. Curriculum studies connect learning and pedagogy to issues of politics, identity, power, and place; therefore, the theorization and planning of curriculum needs to engage, not neglect, these issues. (lev)

curriculum vitae (c.v.)

The academic counterpart to a résumé in the business world, it details all professional accomplishments achieved by a given individual, including degrees awarded, courses taught, presentations given, papers published, grants awarded, and all other similar achievements.

Literally translated from the Latin, it means "course of life." (jbm)

curriculum web

Also called curriculum webbing, this is a method of visualizing and planning curriculum used to guide the planning of classroom activities so that they relate to each other and usually to an important, central theme. Webbing is useful because a planner can list best practices—such as addressing the cognitive, physical, and affective domains—on the spokes of the web and then proceed to brainstorm activities that meet the needs of the group as well as of the individual children. (ecr)

curriculum-based assessment

A type of assessment that uses existing classroom curriculum to determine whether students have mastered a skill. In this type of assessment, children will be asked to use materials that they have been exposed to in the classroom to demonstrate mastery of a particular skill or set of skills. (jas)

customer relationship management (CRM)

A computer-based relationship management system used by colleges and universities, as well as corporations, to better understand student (customer) needs and behaviors. The data collected helps leaders in colleges and universities exceed consumer expectations while increasing the number of applicants, admits, and enrolled students. (kku)

customized training (See contract training)

cut score

A cut score (variously referred to as a cut-off score, passing score, or qualifying score) is a score that defines a boundary between two levels of performance, understanding, competence, expertise, or accomplishment. For example, a cut score on a credentialing test defines the boundary between failing and passing. One cut score on a fourth-grade reading test may differentiate between students performing at the Basic or Proficient levels and another, higher cut score, may differentiate between students performing at the Proficient or Advanced levels. A cut score or set of cut scores is determined through a process referred to as standard setting. (rjt)

See also standard setting.

CVC words

Words that consist of the combination of a consonant–vowel–consonant, such as *cap* and *pin*. The vowel between the consonants is a short vowel. (yu)

CVCe words

Words that consist of the combination of a consonant–vowel–consonant, followed by e. The vowel in between the consonants becomes a long vowel. Examples include *cape* and *pine*. (yu)

cyberarts

A wide spectrum of media arts, often interactive, and including electronic and digital technology as well as experimental methods of programming and engineering. This category of art openly exploits new media, and its subjects include technology itself, as well as concerns that are central to art and humanity. The web is, unsurprisingly, the primary repository and source of information for cyberart. Increasingly, however, these arts are being exhibited in museums. In addition, many community technology centers, schools, and youth organizations are designing art technology programs. (lj)

cyberbullying

When one or a group of children or teens employ the Internet and online social networks, mobile phones, or other digital technologies to threaten, shame, humiliate, taunt, tease, harass, or target another child or teen or group of children or teens. Cyberbullying frequently occurs over an extended period of time, and multiple technologies may be employed. The muscle of cyberbullies does not come from any physical advantage over their victims, but from their skills using digital technology, such as impersonating another person online in order to spread rumors. School staff can also be victimized, for example, as students have used the Internet to spread false or embarrassing information about teachers. (jh, ms)

cyberculture

Unique practices and customs formulated, developed, and followed by Internet users for communication, entertainment, education, business, and other forms of social functioning in cyberspace. The modern cyberculture includes specific values (e.g., concepts of open structure), specific behaviors (e.g., acceptable online behaviors), specific language use (e.g., emoticons, idiosyncratic expressions), and specific communities (e.g., online user groups, online virtual community). The different components of cyberculture can be observed in various Internet applications, such as e-mail, websites, instant messaging, blogs, social network sites, and online games. Educators and students need to be aware of the existence of cyberculture and advocate positive online practices among Internet users. (ys)

cyberspace

A virtual universe of computers, programs, and data. Increasingly, education programs and instruction employ virtual means. (mid)

D

daily living skills
Skills needed to independently accomplish the tasks of daily living, such as dressing, bathing, eating, communicating, and moving about. (sr)

DAISY (See Digital Accessible Information System)

Dalcroze Method
One of the four primary methods of teaching music to young children (along with Kodaly, Suzuki, and Orff). Dalcroze (after the Swiss musician and music educator Emile Jaques-Dalcroze) features three components: eurhythmics, in which children move around listening/responding to music; solfege, in which learning relies on musical scales and melodies sung as "do re mi"; and improvisation, or impromptu creation of music, mostly on the piano. (jd)

dame school
A small private elementary school for young children run by a woman, hence the term "dame." Found in both England and colonial America, they existed until the 19th century, when they were replaced by public schools. Dame schools were typically held in the teacher's home and taught basic skills of reading, writing, and arithmetic in addition to knitting and sewing. (ck)

dance
One of the performing arts, in which movement of the body—improvisational or carefully scripted, often accompanied by music—is the central component. Dance encompasses a wide range of styles and forms, from the classical ballet to more recent creations such as tap, jazz, and modern dance. Styles are characterized and differentiated by variations in posture, rhythm, types of movement, degrees of freedom and restrictiveness in movement, focus on distinct parts of the body through movement, and accompanying music. Of all of the artistic disciplines, dance is the least frequently taught in American schools. (em)

dance education
As a field, dance education is usually reserved for the training of professional dancers, often beyond school walls in ballet or modern dance companies and community art centers. Historically and currently, dance is taught less frequently than any other art form in schools. Reasons range from the regard of dance as being nonverbal and therefore not academic, to the shortage

of specialists in dance or teachers who can teach dance along with their other academic duties. (jd)

dance notation

Recorded directions for the movement of dancers in a choreographed dance. Recordings of floor pattern and footwork from the 17th century showed dance as a series of static positions, rather than a constantly changing flow of movement. The pictures were drawn from the audience's perspective, meaning that dancers would have to reverse everything they read. Labanotation, a system for recording and analyzing human movement, was first published by Rudolf Laban in 1928. A single symbol on a staff indicates the direction of the movement, the part of the body involved, the level of the movement, and the length of time required. Technology is offering new formats for dance notation. (kpb)

dance studio

A large open space required for dance classes and rehearsal, allowing for extension and traveling of movements and step combinations. The facilities of a dance studio should include a barre, a horizontal wooden rail either attached to a wall or as a moveable apparatus, that dancers use to support themselves while doing exercises; a long mirror to check correct positioning and steps; and a dance floor that is smooth and firm for support yet is pliable, not like concrete, to prevent injury from jumps and repetition. One of the reasons given for the lack of dance taught in American public schools is the cost and lack of availability of studio space. (kbc)

Dartmouth College Case

Officially titled *The Trustees of Dartmouth College v. Woodward*, 17 U.S. 518 (1819), the 1819 Supreme Court case concerning the 1816 New Hampshire law that placed Dartmouth College (a private school) under state control. Daniel Webster, arguing for Dartmouth College, won the case, in which Chief Justice John Marshall's majority opinion decided that the contract clause to the Constitution protected private corporation charters. The case is considered the "magna carta" of private colleges and universities to be free from state control, even if the state has chartered their establishment. (ks)

data

The collection of symbols used to represent facts and ideas. Data are processed to produce information usable to human beings. In the context of computing, data refers to the symbols that a computer uses to represent facts and ideas that are processed into information. The processing may include categorizing and counting. Data on computers are organized into databases to make the data more accessible and thereby more useful to humans. In schools, students are expected to acquire data from original sources, a textbook, a lecture, or an electronic database, or to search on their own as part of a research project. (igb)

data analysis

Data are facts or numbers that describe something. To analyze data means to make a judgment, synopsis, or conclusion based on the given data. Many times data are organized in a table or graph. (kr)

data display

The organized and graphic representation of data in the form of maps, matrices, charts, and flow diagrams, produced as a part of qualitative data analysis. Data displays allow the researcher to organize and summarize large amounts of raw data in a way that facilitates further analysis. (rws)

data driven decision making

A process of making decisions based on the analysis of data that has been purposefully and systematically collected. Education professionals use this process to make choices about policies, programs, and individual students, as well as to measure the outcomes of those choices. (sds)

data reduction
The process in qualitative analysis of organizing, clarifying, and metamorphosing raw data from field notes, interview transcripts, and archival sources. It is accomplished through various analytic procedures including coding the data, creating categories of coded data, identifying themes within the data, writing memos about the data, creating data displays, and summarizing the data. (rws)

day care center
A facility that provides group care for children outside of a home environment. (jlj)

day nursery
A child-care model, and movement, established in the United States in the 1830s. The purpose of this movement was not the education of young children; rather it served to meet the needs of poor immigrant mothers. This program emphasized custodial care characterized by inflexible routines, strict hygiene, and overcrowding. (jlj)

DBAE (See discipline-based art education)

DCN (See developmental cognitive neuroscience)

deafness
A profound hearing loss that impairs an individual's ability to process linguistic information through hearing, with or without amplification. (sr)

dean
An academic administrative appointment responsible for the operations of a college at the university setting or a division in the college setting, a dean typically reports to a provost. Deans generally are expected to have terminal degrees in a given field and significant experience and expertise within the areas they oversee. Some deans retain faculty status. (jbm)

debate
The formal rule-driven process of argumentation that leads one to accept or deny a particular point of view. (jfb)

DEC (See Division of Early Childhood)

decentralized school management (See site-based management)

decision making
As an administrative function, includes identifying and constructing alternatives by selecting or choosing appropriate lines of administrative action; ranges from routine administrative decisions to major policy decisions requiring formulation and development of administrative procedures, criteria, evaluation, and professional judgment. Decision making typically includes the gathering of relevant information to create a hypothesis, which is then tested for the purpose of making a final conclusion or judgment. Decision making also involves goal setting and the consideration of alternative ways to achieve the goals. The choice of which alternative course of action is to be pursued is considered to be part of the decision-making process, as well. This "rational" model of decision making is often contrasted with "nonrational" models, such as the so-called "Garbage Can Theory" of decision making. In social studies education, decision making is a curricular component, which, in contrast to the traditional approach, emphasizes the development of critical thinking skills as an integral part of the curriculum. This idea reflects a major goal of social studies as stated by the National Council for the Social Studies: "to help young people to develop the ability to make informed and reasoned decisions for the public good" (NCSS Curriculum Standards, 1994). As such it constitutes a perennial issue for

reform within the social studies. (cf, tp, ks1)

decode
To extract the intended meanings of words through a trial-and-error or a schematic analytic process of: recognizing graphic or spoken symbols or signals; matching these symbols or signals with familiar phonemic, syntactic, and semantic components of speech that they represent; and combining these components into words that bear appropriate meanings. To translate an unfamiliar code of symbols or signals into a familiar one. (ml)

decoding
The act of interpreting verbal input, either auditory or visual, as meaningful information. In reading, this involves viewing letters as representative of phonemes and, in a sense, translating the symbols on the paper into a mental representation of the word. (jcp)

decolonization
The process of a former colony regaining sovereignty. Waves of decolonization occurred throughout the 19th century in Central and South America, and throughout the 20th century in Africa and South Asia. After decolonization, colonial influences commonly remain between the colonizing state and the former colony through various institutions (i.e., educational, political, and socioeconomic). (vkh)

See also colonialism; colonization; postcolonialism.

decomposition method (See number decomposition/recomposition)

deconstruction
Term used to describe a method of critical analysis whereby conventional philosophies, ideas, theories, and foundations, and so on are revisited and critically re-examined, piece by piece, in light of contemporary beliefs, understandings, and political and social contexts. Popularized in the 1960s and 1970s by French philosopher Jacques Derrida, deconstruction has, as a basis, the work of many 20th-century philosophers, including Nietzsche and Heidegger, and is basic to the tenets of critical and feminist theory. (jqa, jwc)

deculturalization
A term, put forward by Joel Spring in *Deculturalization and the Struggle for Equality: A Brief History of the Education of the Dominated Cultures in the U.S.* (2004) as a synonym for cultural genocide, that refers to the institutional and individual processes that systematically disrupt, devalue, displace, and destroy one's cultural identity in order to supplant it with the cultural values of another. Although not limited to schooling, deculturalization has played a significant role in the history of education in the United States, where students have been forced to embrace Anglo-centric curriculum, ideals, and language as the dominant or only culture. By combining this process with notions of republicanism and democracy, the marginalization of other cultural values is legitimized, and prejudice, racism, and religious intolerance become entangled with systems and standards of Americanism. (tmod)

deduction (See deductive reasoning)

deductive reasoning
The process of concluding that something must be true because it is a special case of a general principle that is known to be true. Propositions must be deduced from propositions already proved. Deductive reasoning is logically valid and is the fundamental method in which mathematical facts are shown to be true. (kr)

defense mechanism
A specific psychological process that operates outside of conscious awareness. Defense mechanisms attempt to resolve intrapsychic (i.e., between major internal parts of the self) and extrapsychic (i.e.,

between a consciously recognized aspect of oneself and some demand of the external environment) conflicts. These defensive operations occur within the province of the ego and are employed to avoid psychic pain, tension, and discomfort, and to avert or allay anxiety through the resolution of emotional conflicts. A number of ego-based defense mechanisms have been identified. Among the more familiar of these are denial, repression, projection, displacement, rationalization, reaction formation, isolation, intellectualization, identification, and sublimation. (rnp)

deferred imitation

A child's duplication and use of an action, or use of verbal or nonverbal communication, at a later time or place after having observed it. A child who combs her own hair two weeks later after watching the mother comb her own hair is an example. (at)

deferred maintenance

For facilities, including buildings and infrastructure, refers to an identifiable backlog of major maintenance projects that are beyond the scope of routine preventive maintenance programs, are unfunded in current operating budgets, and are thus deferred to a future budget cycle. (cf)

See also capital renewal.

deficiency or deficit model

An approach to adult education that assumes a norm for adults and then assesses the skill and knowledge deficits of potential adult education students. In this model, adults with low literacy skills are perceived as being fragile and afflicted with deficits requiring treatment, rehabilitation, and remediation in order to fit into mainstream society. The model stems from a clash between the dominant middle-class culture and subcultures among low-literate poor populations. (las)

deficit theories

Theories that postulate that some children are inferior to others and at a disadvantage due to the influence of biological, cultural, or socioeconomic differences. Deficit theories are generally regarded as attempts by the majority to demean and belittle the differences in cultural experiences of minorities. (jqa, jwc)

degree, associate

An academic degree awarded upon completion of two years of undergraduate education; usually identified in terms of the recipient's area of concentration, such as an associate technical degree; increasingly used as a replacement of two-years certificates awarded by technical/vocational schools. (cf)

degree, bachelor's

Any academic degree, earned or honorary, carrying the title of "bachelor"; as in BA (Bachelor of Arts), and BS (Bachelor of Science). In liberal arts and sciences, the degree is customarily granted upon completion of a course of study normally requiring four academic years of college work. (cf)

degree, doctor's

Any academic degree carrying the title of "doctor"; as in PhD (Doctor of Philosophy), MD (Doctor of Medicine), LLD (Doctor of Laws—honorary), and the like. The highest academic degree in a given discipline or profession, based generally on three or more years of graduate work. The two principal academic doctor's degrees are the PhD (applicable to any of the fields of knowledge recognized by four-year institutions) and the EdD (restricted to Education). For the PhD degree, the dissertation must reflect some original research, usually with theoretical and/or rational implications. For the doctorate in applied or professional fields (notably the EdD), the dissertation-study is frequently more practically oriented: toward technique, toward an improvement in economy, toward the collection and interpretation of statistics, and so on. (cf)

degree, honorary

A distinction bestowed in recognition of outstanding achievement or merit. (cf)

degree, master's

Awarded for completion of one or two years of graduate education. The master's degree is intermediate to baccalaureate and doctoral degrees in a widely recognized academic discipline. Traditionally conferred as master of arts degrees in the humanities or as master of sciences degrees in scientific or technological fields. A master's degree is conventionally required for first appointments of college faculty members who teach undergraduate courses. (cf)

degree, professional

A degree signifying the completion of an academic curriculum pertaining to a professional field; for example JD, MD. (cf)

degree, specialist

A degree intermediate between the advanced professional (usually the master's) degree and the doctorate. Used principally in the field of education. (cf)

delegated authority

General and specific duties, decisions, and activities that are vested in positions accountable to a higher level of official control; the other half of the maxim that authority may be delegated to others, but responsibilities must be assigned. (cf)

See also assigned responsibilities.

Delgado v. Bastrop Independent School District, 388 W.D. Texas (1948)

Lawsuit filed by the League of United Latin American Citizens (LULAC) on behalf of Minerva Delgado and other Mexican American parents whose children were placed in separate "Mexican" schools. The plaintiffs charged that segregating Mexican children from other white races without specific state law was, among other things, depriving children of equal facilities, services, and educational instruction. Judge Ben H. Rice of the U.S. District Court, Western District of Texas, agreed, and the practice was ordered eliminated by 1949. The court permitted separate classes on the school campus for first graders who needed language enrichment. (vmm)

deliberation

The process of reflecting thoughtfully and carefully in consideration of particular topics and issues. Deliberation involves mindful, unhurried contemplation about people, places, ideas, and/or events that gives each participant voice, choice, and ownership in the process, which is kind, respectful, and fair. (npg)

Delphi method

A process of group decision making, priority setting, or forecasting, using multiple iterations of written questionnaires and responses. Typically a group of people with expertise in a given area are asked to respond individually to a set of questions; in a second iteration, each respondent learns the distribution of all the responses to the previous set of questions and is given an opportunity to change or explain his or her original answers. The process continues until sufficient consensus is reached. The method has been used to achieve consensus on educational needs. (chb)

democracy

From the Greek word for "rule by the people." A contested term, basic to American political life and education. The most naive, and perhaps most common, understanding is that it is rule by majority. A more complex understanding adds to this that certain rights are protected against the will of the majority, most directly in the Bill of Rights. More complex still is that view articulated by John Dewey, that democracy is a mode of associated living, not just a political form. On this view, democracy is committed to the common pursuit of the common good, rather than individual pursuit of individual good.

Though the form of the U.S. government is usually referred to as a democracy, it is in reality a republic; that is, government is representative, not direct. (jc)

See also radical democracy.

democracy, radical (See radical democracy)

democratic citizenship
Membership in a country with government in which the people hold the ruling power either directly or through elected representatives; a country, state, or the like, with such government; the principle of equality of rights, opportunity, and so on, or the practice of this principle. (mkg)

democratic classroom
A democratic classroom treats students as equal members of a community and allows students to share political equality with their teachers. This community is flexible and adaptive to the needs of its individuals and assures that all members are able to establish shared interests, and have the chance to contribute equally to the decisions and development of the classroom community. Teachers and students are on equal terms in a democratic classroom and share in the decision-making process regarding classroom rules and curriculum, for example. A. S. Neill's Summerhill and some Montessori classrooms offer models of democratic classrooms. (bt-b)

See also democracy; democratic education.

democratic education
An educational system in which all students are valued, and through which the principles of democracy are furthered through critical thinking, access to information, and ideas, providing credible divergent views, and encouraging active participation in public life. (mkg)

democratic tradition
A body of long-established customs or beliefs characterized by free and equal participation by all in government or in the decision-making process of an organization or group. (mkg)

demographics
Characteristics and statistics of the human population, or part of it; especially pertaining to its size, growth, density, distribution, and statistics regarding birth, disease, and death. (mkg)

denouement
A French term meaning an untying (of knots) or an undoing, the part of a performance or work of literature (including dramatic literature) in which the tensions, conflicts, and complexities of plot are clarified and brought to resolution. Often this is the climax of the work, to which point the plot builds, and after which point the work comes to a close. In the creation, teaching, and performance of literary and dramatic works, the denouement serves as an important focal point and guide. (em)

deontological ethics
Deontological ethics refers to ethical theories that emphasize duty and obligation and stress the primacy of the rightness of an action itself rather than the goodness following from an action. Deontological ethics generally considers an act intrinsically right or wrong, and so a moral imperative exists regardless of the consequences of the act. Historically, the moral philosophy of Immanuel Kant (1724–1804) is deontological, and he uses the concept of the moral imperative (his "categorical imperative") to argue that one must always act in a way that is consistent with everyone acting that way. (psc)

See also ethic of care; hedonism.

department
The basic organizational unit in an institution of higher learning, responsible for the academic functions in a field of study. (cf)

depression

In educational psychology, a category of mental disorders characterized by a constellation of symptoms, such as feelings of dysphoria (low mood), lack of motivation, low energy, isolation or social impairment, loss of enjoyment in activities, appetite change, and sleep disturbance. Depression in its more serious/severe forms is associated with suicide attempts. In children, irritability and acting-out behavior may be the most obvious symptoms of depression. The term is also used commonly, though incorrectly, to describe an individual's mood state (e.g., "I feel depressed"). However, "despondent" would, in that case, be a more appropriate descriptor. In economics, an extended period—a decade or so—of restructuring and institutional change in an economy, often marked by declining or stagnant growth in which unemployment tends to be higher and inflation lower than in a regular recession. A depression usually lasts in the range of 10 years, often encompassing two or three separate shorter-run business cycles. The most noted depression in the U.S. economy was the Great Depression of the 1930s. (fa, mkg)

derivation

A morphological process that forms a word with a meaning and/or category distinct from that of its base through the addition of an affix (e.g., the formation of the adjective *understand-able* from the verb *understand*; the change of the meaning of the verb *activate* to the opposite meaning of the verb *deactivate*). (smt)

derivational morpheme

Affixes added to base morphemes to form new words that change the meaning but may or may not change the syntactic category of the new word (e.g., the noun *beauty* changes to the adjective *beautiful*, the verb *to sing* changes to the noun *sing-er*). (smt)

derivative

In mathematics, derivative gives the slope of a graph of a function at a particular point on that function. The derivative is the rate of change of the function at a point on the function. If one has a function describing the displacement of an object with respect to time, for example, taking the derivative of that function at a particular instant would give the rate of change of the displacement at that instant. In other words, the derivative of the displacement function at an instant is the rate of change of displacement, or velocity. (smc)

derive

Forming a connection between an idea and its root of origin in order to see the relationship between the two. Applying a simplified and reduced expression to the original form to see the orientation and reasoning behind the mathematical concept; this allows for a connection to be made between the original and the simplified expression. (jmg, ldz)

derived fact and known fact procedures

Calculating procedures where the numbers in the problem are redistributed to become numbers whose sum or difference is already known; for example, a child might solve 6 + 7 by thinking of 6 + 6 = 12 (a known fact) and adding one more to 12 to obtain the answer to 6 + 7 (thinking of 7 as 6 and one more). (amr)

See also thinking strategies.

deschooling

Ivan Illich coined this term in his *Deschooling Society,* when he argued a neo-Marxist view describing schools as institutions of society that are used to oppress people and limit their capabilities. Schools, through their overt as well as covert curricula, teach children to function in society in certain ways, and not others. Deschooling is unlearning what schools have taught us, so that people are free to live consciously and function in a variety of ways. Deschooling draws our awareness to the acculturation that goes on in schools and insists on addressing the political and ethical questions that schooling raises. (bt-b)

desegregation

The act of eliminating separation by common characteristics. Desegregation in education is generally referred to as the elimination of the separation of opportunity by racial/ethnic background. The desegregation movement in education brought majority and minority students together in a single school setting for the purpose of providing equal educational opportunity for all students regardless of ethnic origin. The placement and inclusion of all students, staff, and faculty in public schools regardless of their race with the goal of ensuring racial balance in schools. Desegregation was placed into law in 1954 as a result of the U.S. Supreme Court rulings *Brown v. Board of Education* and the subsequent *Brown II* case of 1955 eliminating racial segregation in public schools. *Brown* overturned the principles in *Plessy v. Ferguson* (1896) which had stated that facilities for different races were permissible under the constitution if "separate but equal." (jfb, sr2)

design

The act of making plans for the creation of something (a building, stage set, arrangement of a room, city) or the plan itself. A design can also be a pattern, for example, the geometric shapes on a t-shirt or piece of pottery. In any art form the plan for the work, the sketch in visual art or the invention in music, the articulation of an imagined objective. The field of design, often associated with interior design, clothing, or graphic design, is often thought to be on a more practical, less aesthetic, level than fine arts—but all works of art involve the element of design, and planning is an important ingredient in the act of creation. Some cognitivists, information processors, are interested in children's drawings insofar as they reflect the child's ability to plan ahead, to design before doing. (jd)

See also aesthetic; fine arts; graphic design.

deskilling

Process by which the division of labor and technological development leads to a reduction of the scope of an individual's work and education to one, or a few, specialized tasks. As a result, both knowledge and skills are disjointed and fragmented. (hfs)

desktop computer

A computer designed to be stationary. The monitor, keyboard, and central processing unit are usually three separate components. Desktop computers are typically found on tables or desks in fixed locations such as computer labs or classrooms. (kg1)

See also laptop computer.

desktop publishing

Using computer tools to produce published materials. Desktop publishing tools allow digital text and images to be easily manipulated, arranged, and printed. For example, newsletters, documents, posters, greeting cards, and textbooks can all be assembled using desktop publishing software. This method of publishing has all but replaced the manual assembly and layout of publications. In an educational environment, students can engage in desktop publishing to publish a class or school newspaper or to create multimedia materials that demonstrate their knowledge of a subject. Teachers and administrators may use desktop publishing to produce materials for sharing information with faculty, parents, or students. (tll)

detention

Refers to the temporary isolation of a person or persons from their peer group. Detention in an educational setting normally means that a student or group of students may be separated from their peer group in an area of relative isolation for a specific period of time. Detention may manifest itself as not allowing a student to eat lunch in the lunchroom, or placing that student in an area of relative obscurity sometimes known as "time-out." Detention is never permanent and is usually used in a school setting as a time for students to regain control of themselves before rejoining their classmates. (jfb)

determinism

Claims that freedom is an illusion, that science establishes that every mental state or action necessarily has some physical correlate. If, for example, beliefs are caused even in part by something physical, and if the physical operates according to fixed scientific laws, these laws in effect determine or at least shape what can be believed. In response to this line of thought, many philosophers have insisted that freedom does not require the absence of physical causes, but only self-instigation, or the lack of external coercion or constraint. (an)

See also freedom; volition.

development

Development and learning are intertwined. Plato maintained that people develop by learning the forms of knowledge that best approximate the truth about reality. Rousseau, however, asserted that people develop less by learning and more by following their natural tendencies to grow. Piaget proposed that children progress through distinct stages of development, in an invariant, normative sequence. Critics doubt whether such sequences are identical in all contexts, and whether any stage theory can ever be complete. Furthermore, they argue that to call any structure superior is to judge less complex structures as less valuable or inferior. (rt)

See also advancement; child development.

development, moral (See moral development)

development education

Education aimed at increasing awareness of the situation of poor people in the Third World and support for foreign aid. (las)

developmental academic advising

Developmental academic advising is an innovative form of teaching that helps students become involved in their own academic decisions and future plans. The role of the academic adviser shifts as students and conditions in universities change over time. Instilling students with a sense of commitment to their future plans and responsibility for their decisions is the cornerstone of the academic adviser's work. (cf)

See also academic advisement.

developmental appropriateness

Phrase coined by the National Association for the Education of Young Children (Schickedanz, 1986; Bredekamp and Copple, 1997) to describe curriculum and practices that meet a child's developmental, cultural, and individual needs. A child's developmental needs are determined by age and stage of development; for example, a toddler is just learning to walk and talk and needs an environment that supports his or her ability to practice walking and talking. A child's cultural needs are largely determined by his or her family of origin—its structure, its traditions, and its geographic location. A child's individual needs are linked to his or her temperament and personality. (ecr)

developmental cognitive neuroscience (DCN)

A subdiscipline of neuroscience that bridges cognitive neuroscience and human development. Like cognitive neuroscience, DCN studies the neural correlates (e.g., neurotransmitters, brain structures) of cognitive functions (e.g., perception, memory). DCN also takes a developmental approach by studying how these neural systems change over time. Methods include, but are not limited to: neuroimaging, electrophysiology, brain lesion studies, and computational modeling. (jok)

developmental curriculum
Curriculum that matches the level of development of the student(s). (sr)

developmental delay
A typical neurodevelopment characterized by failure to achieve age-appropriate expectations. A delay in the steps or stages of typical growth and development before the age of 18 years. Refers to the extent a child is functioning below expected developmental levels or range in areas such as communication, social, self-help, and physical skills, or to children who are functioning below the established developmental norms for an identified age group. In some states, the term is an acceptable diagnostic term for providing early intervention or early childhood special education services; however, different states may adopt different criteria for what is considered below expected developmental levels or norms. (sr, at)

developmental disability
A term used to describe a range of disabilities affecting brain development or brain injury, which began before birth, at birth, or before the age of 22. This term refers to a severe and chronic disability that limits three or more areas of major life activity, including self-care, language, learning, mobility, self-direction, capacity for independent living, and economic self-sufficiency. (sr)

developmental education
Programs in community colleges that help prepare students who do not have sufficient academic skills to be successful in regular academic courses. (jpc)

developmental kinesiology
The study of how movement skills develop across the life span. (rf)

developmental milestones
Behaviors that represent universal, species-typical accomplishments and that are usually linked to chronological age. Behaviors such as age of rolling over, sitting up, walking, talking, toilet training, menstruation, and growth spurts are examples of behaviors that mark milestones in development. (vm)

developmental motor coordination disorders (See motor skill disorder)

developmental-interaction approach
An early childhood curricular approach, made popular by the Bank Street College of Education, in which thematic studies are provided for young children primarily through learning centers and informal group work. Materials in the learning centers are multidimensional and inspire different tasks for different young children, depending on their developmental age and stage. (ecr)

developmentalist approach
A teaching philosophy that places an emphasis upon the capacity of teachers to apply their knowledge of current student understanding of content, student developmental readiness, and student interest in their practice (instructional decisions, pedagogy, curricula, etc.). (hfs)

developmentally appropriate practice
Educational concepts and practices that match the child's age and stage of development as well as his or her individual and cultural attributes (Schickedanz, 1986; Bredekamp and Copple, 1997). Practices are developmentally appropriate if they appeal to the children's natural abilities and interests and promote their physical, cognitive, social, and emotional growth. Practices that demean young children or disrespect their individual or

cultural understandings are inappropriate and harmful to their development. (ecr)

developmentally sequenced activities

A hierarchy of learning activities or skills, ordered in terms of a typical child's acquisition or demonstration of them. Because many different activities can proceed from a single material, knowing the developmental sequence of use of the materials can assist in planning for and playing with a child productively. For example, with a set of nesting cups, an infant might mouth the cups, a toddler might separate the stack of cups, a two-year-old might stack the cups in a tower, and a three-year-old might nest the cups. To teach an infant to nest the cups, or to teach a three-year-old to mouth the cups, would be to deliver instruction out of developmental sequence. (ecr)

Deweyan

Of or relating to the philosophies of John Dewey. Dewey is considered to be the most significant education thinker of the 20th century. His philosophical writings continue to influence formal and informal education today. Dewey's philosophy of education focuses on pragmatics, interaction, reflection, experience, community, and democracy. (jwc)

diagnosis

The identification of a disease, disorder, syndrome, or condition, usually based on established, predetermined criteria. A diagnosis has multiple purposes. It helps to define a disorder, suggest prognosis, guide treatment, indicate comorbid conditions, and facilitate communication among professionals. In the mental health field, criteria published in the *Diagnostic and Statistical Manual of Mental Disorders,* Fourth Edition (DSM-IV) are the most widely used for diagnostic purposes. The World Health Organization also publishes diagnostic criteria for a wide range of disorders in their series of International Classification of Disease (ICD) manuals. (kc, scmc, bdj)

Diagnostic and Statistical Manual of Mental Disorders, Fourth Edition, Text Revision (DSM-IV-TR)

The diagnostic manual used to classify and code specific psychiatric and psychological disorders. While the diagnostic criteria published in the DSM-IV-TR is identical to the criteria found in the DSM-IV (APA, 1994), the text revision updates sections related to Associated Features and Disorders; Specific Cultural, Age, and Gender Features; Prevalence; Course; Familial Pattern; and Differential Diagnosis sections of the text in order to incorporate the findings from recent research. (kc, scmc, bdj)

diagnostic teaching

Use of observation and instruction to determine learning ability when formal diagnostic methods are ineffective or incomplete. (sr)

dialect

Dialect is a language variant that is distinct from other variants of the same language; typically the differences are in features such as grammar, phonology, or vocabulary. Dialect is often used by a group of people who share commonalities geographically, historically, ethnically, or politically. (cld)

dialectic

In its simplest and oldest form this refers to the process of coming to common understanding by means of conversation or debate. There have been some attempts to give the term stricter meaning by Plato (question and response), Kant (resolution of antinomies by balancing thesis and antithesis), Hegel (philosophical progress will be made as thesis and antithesis resolve into synthesis, a higher unity), and Marx (resolution of all issues of life and knowledge via dialectical method but within a strict historical materialism).

These four philosophers, using similar methods of investigation, came to radically different conclusions about reality and ethics. Today the term is used in the United States to refer to a method of interaction, showing opposite ideas or tendencies and seeking resolution through dialogue. (sc)

dialectical inquiry
A process by which two possible approaches are compared and contrasted with each another, from which a third possibility emerges as a synthesis of the original ideas. Generally the initial ideas are explored by independent parties, followed by a dialogue between the two parties, often with a mediator of some kind, to understand strengths and weaknesses of the particular ideas and develop a shared understanding of an optimal third approach. (sh)

dialogic reading
A specific interactive method of reading books to young children. This also serves as a shared picture book reading intervention for preschoolers. In dialogic reading, adults help children take an active role during book reading sessions. Adults trained in this method ask open-ended questions and expect more from children's participation over multiple book reading sessions until eventually the child is the teller of the story. This method of book reading is associated with children's vocabulary development. (jdc)

dialogical education
An approach to learning, introduced by Paulo Freire, in which teachers engage learners in discussion to understand their perceptions and experiences. Learners become teachers, and teachers and learners grow together through the learning process. (las)

dialogue
There are many conceptions of dialogue. Socratic dialogue is a dialectical form of posing questions and responses to develop rational thinking. Dialogue is often considered as a form of conversation between two or more people. However, many in the field of communication wish to distinguish dialogue from other forms of verbal interaction, such as informal conversation, debate, or discussion, even though they point out dialogue may contain elements of each of these. David Bohm (1996), for example, focuses on the Greek roots of the word, arguing that dialogue represents a flow of meaning between people characterized by careful listening, suspending assumptions, and the intention to develop coherent understandings collectively as peers. For Hans-Georg Gadamer (2004), dialogue is a hermeneutical, conversational means devoted to developing understanding, which includes openness, acceptance of the other, and the attempts to "get inside the other" in developing understanding; here, knowledge unfolds as participants move to a "fusion of horizons" in understanding. A number of philosophers characterize dialogue primarily as a verbal form of communication distinguished by certain orienting assumptions or "rules." Thus, for Jürgen Habermas (1979 and 1984), dialogue is a teleological form of communicative action based in reasoned argument aimed at developing consensus. For a number of other philosophers, however, dialogue is a fundamentally ontological orientation to relationality: for Emmanuel Levinas (1969) the responsive "face-to-face" meeting with the unknowable Other; for Martin Buber (1947 and 2000) the "I-Thou" relationship, characterized by responsiveness, awareness, confirmation, and inclusion of the other; for Mikhail Bakhtin (1981) as the "addressivity" of one to another that establishes the self. From these ontological perspectives, dialogue is not so much a means to an end as it represents an end itself; further, dialogue is not confined to verbal expression but includes all the ways one can address and respond to others and the world with one's whole life, even if the

dialogue is expressed primarily through conversation. From postmodern perspectives, dialogue includes responsiveness to context. For Paulo Freire (1970/2006), dialogue is the encounter between people, "mediated by the world in order to name the world." (cs)

See also communication; Socratic method.

diaspora

The geographic dispersion of a people with a common origin and heritage. (jqa, jwc)

Dienes blocks (See base-10 blocks)

DIF (See Differential Item Functioning)

Differential Item Functioning (DIF)

Refers to a psychometric difference in how a test item functions for two groups of test takers, after those groups have been matched with respect to ability or attribute that the item is purported to measure. DIF analyses determine whether an item performed differently for one group of test takers (focal group) is relative to the way it is performed for another (reference group). There can be several focal/reference pairs of groups in a DIF analysis. The term "DIF" is gradually replacing "item bias," because "DIF" refers to the fact that items can display varying statistical characteristics with different groups of test takers. "Bias" can render an unnecessarily misleading or even pejorative flavor to analysis of test results. DIF (and "bias" before it) has been widely applied in the study of cultural differences on test performance. With the increasing public concern about cultural differences and test performance, measurement specialists have developed several methods for investigating DIF: the delta-plot method, the Mantel-Haenszel statistic, and combinations of item response theory with logistic regression. (sp)

differentiated instruction

Refers to a series of strategies implemented in mixed-ability classrooms in order to accommodate student variance by offering appropriate intellectual challenges. Generally advocated by educators of gifted students, differentiated instruction challenges the presumption that any group of students at the same grade level are essentially alike. Instead, differentiated instruction requires that teachers account for a variety of instructional needs and levels of previous knowledge in curriculum design and delivery. In classrooms and schools that practice differentiated instruction, students may be placed in flexible groups to work on particular skills; they may also be placed in different guided reading groups depending on their reading levels. Differentiated instruction has been shown to have positive effects for many students in mixed-ability classrooms. (bda, jas)

differentiated staffing

Refers to the separation of the generic role of the classroom teacher into smaller components and creating different roles, some lower and some higher than that of the traditional delineation. The first such differentiation occurred when teacher's aides were brought into the classroom to assume some of the more menial tasks normally assigned to the teacher. Later, after the idea of creating a career ladder for classroom teachers was espoused by Dwight Allen of Stanford University, career ladders were tried in over 30 states, notably in Tennessee under the direction of Governor Lamar Alexander. Allen insisted that for a true differentiated staff to materialize there had to be at least three differentiated and distinct teaching levels, each with separate salary schedule; the maximum salary for the top level had to be at least double that of the bottom level; and all levels had to retain significant teaching responsibilities. (fwe)

Diffusion Tensor Imaging (DTI)

A type of MRI method based on water diffusion. DTI allows for the visualization of neural pathways, including direction and connectivity. The principle application of DTI is in the tracking of neural fibers and their connections. In medicine, DTI may be used in the assessment of neural pathways in development, pathology, and degeneration. (mt)

Digital Accessible Information System (DAISY)

A globally recognized technical standard to facilitate the creation of accessible multimedia content. In current practice, these documents are audio-only digital textbooks (Digital Talking Books) that may be voiced with text-to-speech, or a combination of synchronized human voice audio and digital text. Originally, the standard was created to help people who have a print reading disability, but it also has broad applications for improved access mainstream text. (jg1)

digital divide

The gap created by inequities in access to technology and the information it provides. In today's world, information, power, and wealth are inextricably linked. Although use of technology helps to level the playing field among users, poverty, race, and level of education limit access to the extent that some segments of the population are losing ground in their ability to fully participate educationally, politically, and culturally. (igb)

digital portfolio

An electronic collection of student work that may be stored on a central file server or copied onto a CD-ROM. Like traditional portfolios, digital portfolios can be used to assess students' growth over time and provide evidence of their diverse abilities. A digital portfolio can include static digital documents, audio recordings, and movies. Paper-based products, such as worksheets and 2-D student artwork can be scanned to include in the portfolio, and 3-D pieces can be included as digital photographs or movies, while oral presentations or other performances can be stored as audio files or movies. (kg1)

See also portfolio.

digital repositories (See institutional repositories)

diglossia

A word, first used by Ferguson, to mean the use of two languages, or language varieties, within the same community. (gd-b)

digraph

A new sound created by combining two letters: *gh* (e.g., enou*gh*), *ph* (e.g., *ph*one), *sh* (e.g., friend*sh*ip), and *th* (e.g., tru*th*). (h-jk)

direct and inverse word problems

Direct word problems are ones that can be solved using the operation suggested by the semantics of the problem, say multiplication. However, there are problems that can more easily be solved by the inverse of the operation suggested by the problem statement; that is, multiplication is suggested by the semantics, but the problem is more easily solved by using a division strategy. Research indicates that, in situations not related to a person's everyday life experiences, direct word problems are more easily solved than inverse word problems. (cmdv)

direct code

Early literacy instruction that highlights formal teaching of written language conventions, letter-sound correspondences, and spelling. (jrk)

See also indirect code; phonics.

direct democracy (See participatory democracy)

direct instruction

A group of effective teacher behaviors having the goal of systematic teaching of content in small steps, pausing to check for student understanding, and aiming for successful student participation. Six steps have been identified: daily review; presenting new material; graded practice; independent practice; weekly/monthly review; and feedback/corrections. This technique is most appropriate for teaching well-structured explicit material such as reading decoding skills, mathematics procedures, grammatical rules, and science and social studies facts. A teacher-centered instructional approach in which the teacher's role is to disseminate information in the most direct way possible, usually with explanations, demonstrations, guided practice, provision of feedback and correctives, opportunity for independent practice, and regular reviews. (reb, bba)

Direct Instructional System for Teaching Arithmetic and Reading (DISTAR)

Instruction that breaks learning down into its smallest steps; provides direct instruction in phonics and emphasizes basic skills in isolation. (bjl)

direct proof

A method of proving propositions by directly applying axioms, definitions, and previously proven propositions in hopes of leaving no doubt that a conclusion is true. (wja)

director of career and technical education

At the local level, this position is the secondary school administrator appointed to supervise the total career or vocational-technical education program in a school or school district. At the state level, this title refers to the state official directly in charge of the state program of career or vocational-technical education, especially in connection with educational programs subsidized by federal funds under the authority of the U.S. Department of Education, Office of Vocational and Adult Education. (db, jb)

director of career or technical guidance and placement

The school, college, or university administrator who heads and coordinates programs that assist students in choosing, preparing for, entering upon, and progressing in an occupation. (jm)

disability

A physical, cognitive, psychological, or sensory impairment that affects one's ability to develop, achieve, and/or function normally. Disability can occur as a result of injury or illness or can be congenital. (sr)

disability studies

A field of study focusing on issues affecting people with disabilities. Contemporary application of disability studies examines the capabilities of people and their efforts to accomplish and achieve to the best of their ability. (jqa, jwc)

discipline

A system of positive guidance, affirmation, and redirection that encourages the child to regulate his or her own behavior, minimizing the occurrence of culturally unacceptable or harmful activities. In the classroom environment, the control the teacher has over students' behavior. A subject of study, such as mathematics or history. Often conceived of as "classroom management" from a behaviorist point of view, discipline is conceived of by John Dewey as the ability to control one's own actions in pursuit of one's own goals. (kdc, jc)

discipline-based art education (DBAE)

Pioneered by the Getty Education Institute for the Arts in 1983, DBAE was the largest and most heavily funded arts educational initiative of the 20th century. A pedagogical approach designed to educate children in the thoughtful appreciation of art, DBAE provides a framework for curriculum design based on the disciplinary foundations of art making, art criticism, art history, and aesthetics. Throughout the 1980s, the Getty supported implementation of DBAE in numerous American schools as well as related research carried out by educational researchers such as Eliot Eisner, Ralph Smith, and Brent Wilson. Critics of the approach decry its lack of emphasis on artistic production. (kf)

See also Arts PROPEL.

discourse

An extended, formal, written or spoken exchange of presentations on a subject (e.g., a learned discourse on literacy). The content and modes of communication, thought, and behavior that are familiar to and indicative of a specific social group. The next unit of linguistic analysis longer than a sentence. An extended conversation. (ml)

discourse communities

Groups of people who collectively provide the cognitive tools—ideas, theories, and concepts—that individuals appropriate as their own through their personal efforts to make sense of experiences through dialogue and exposure to new ideas and perspectives. In such groups, the learning is not unidirectional. Groups also change through the ideas, ways of thinking, understandings, analysis, and reflection new members bring to the discussion. (hfs)

discovery learning

An instructional approach that encourages students to learn through their own exploration, experience, and inquiry. Learning typically proceeds from identification of a problem, through development, and testing of hypotheses, to drawing a conclusion. (bba)

discrepancy model

Demonstration of a significant difference between ability and achievement. For example, the discrepancy between IQ and educational achievement. (sr)

discrete mathematics

A branch of mathematics that deals with determining, for any given problem, whether there is a solution or not. If so, how many solutions are possible? If more than one solution exists, what is the best solution? Given the importance of discrete mathematics in today's business and industry and because it can easily be included in other "strands" of mathematics, recent curriculum documents advocate increased attention to discrete mathematics throughout pre-K to grade 12 curriculums. (dbc)

discrete quantities

Objects that can be counted to find "how many" result in exact numeric values or discrete quantities. (amr)

See also continuous quantities.

discrimination

Individual critical analysis to make distinctions or discernment. Treatment or consideration based on class or category rather than individual merit; partiality or prejudice (e.g., racial discrimination and sexual discrimination). Many forms of discrimination exist, such as attitudinal, structural, and cultural. (kf1)

discursive symbols

Symbols (for example, numbers and words), that can be strung together in rational order and have in themselves (by virtue of their own construction) no physical resemblance to the subject to which they refer. Contrasted with nondiscursive or presentational symbols (like line or gesture) that embody meaning in the form they present (e.g., a sad painting), discursive symbols rather arbitrarily stand for the object of their representation (e.g., the symbol "5"). Discursive symbols achieve a level of precision that nondiscursive symbols could never achieve. Some researchers argue that schools need to embrace the complexity of nondiscursive systems even as they introduce children to the clarity of discursive systems. (kpb)

discussion

An instructional strategy involving the encouragement of student talk in order to promote critical, or higher-order, thinking. (bba)

discussion forum

An online discussion group in which users, usually with common interests, can exchange open messages. Discussion forums that are issue-based are often used to gauge opinion or solicit ideas. Position statements, links to topic-related websites, and other background information may be presented to encourage discussion and provide grounding in the topic. Policy-based forums that are organized around themes/issues that relate directly to a draft policy follow a similar format. Participants may be encouraged to submit alternative ideas and suggestions, but the format implies that what is being sought is the extent to which participants agree with the proposals, and why. (mid)

discussion group

Individuals who convene to exchange ideas on a topic of shared interest. The group may interact in a face-to-face setting or by utilizing Internet technology. These groups are often formed in adult education environments to complement classroom instruction, allowing participants to translate theory to practical application, apply frames to specific issues, and gain multiple perspectives on a topic. (ln)

discussion method

A learning format in which participants in a class or other small group exchange ideas face-to-face on a topic of shared interest. Discussion method is popular in adult education, because it is highly participatory; it lends itself to problem solving, concept exploration, and attitude change; and it allows participants to become resources for each other's learning. (chb)

disequilibrium (See equilibration)

disorienting dilemma

Such dilemmas arise when unconscious assumptions about the world become at odds with experience through an individual triggering event, or series of triggering events. They may manifest when an individual becomes aware of dissonance between espoused and practiced values or when familiar coping strategies cease to be effective. (hfs)

disposition

A property distinguishable from a so-called categorical property by its relationship to certain subjunctive or counterfactual conditional statements. Fragility, for example, is a dispositional property or disposition because it amounts to the fact that (subject to certain qualifications) a fragile thing, although intact, would shatter were it struck. Squareness, by contrast, is a categorical property that is not conceptually related to any such conditional proposition. The concept of a disposition gained currency in educational philosophy in the 1960s through the influence of Gilbert Ryle, whose logical behaviorism rested in an analysis of mental attributes as behavioral dispositions. (rc)

disruptive innovation (See disruptive technology)

disruptive technology

A term used to describe a change that improves a product or service in ways that an existing market does not expect, often because the change is cheaper, simpler, smaller, or more convenient to use. This new, unanticipated use "disrupts" or challenges more traditional applications of established products in existing markets, thereby representing a significant competitive threat to market leaders. Originally coined by Clayton M. Christensen in 1995, the term has since been applied to the introduction of innovations in many fields, including education. Also called disruptive innovation. (jz)

dissertation

Graduate students pursuing their doctoral degrees complete their programs with a dissertation. After some years of coursework and comprehensive and specialized exams, graduate students conduct research for a dissertation. For the student to graduate, a committee of professors, chosen by the student, signs the dissertation. In many PhD programs, a graduate student undergoes a dissertation defense, presenting the finished work to a committee and answering questions about the research and argument. Some graduate students hope to publish their dissertations as books. (cf)

dissociative disorder

A category of mental disorders characterized by a state of disrupted consciousness, identity, or perception. These disorders typically occur as a defense against traumatic experience and are characterized by a notable lack of a unitary sense of identity. The defense, which compartmentalizes inconsistent and often conflictual representations of the self, serves as a protective mechanism against overwhelming thoughts, feelings, and behavior at the time of trauma, while simultaneously interfering with the necessary "working through" that would provide a balanced sense of perspective. Dissociative disorders include: dissociative amnesia, dissociative fugue, dissociative identity disorder, and depersonalization disorder. (rnp)

dissonance

Encountering two or more contradictory ideas at one time in one's self, among various individuals, or institutionalized in society. Cognitive dissonance occurs when an individual recognizes or perceives influences of two or more forces that may be equal or close to equal in presence and power, resulting in conflict and discomfort. (npg)

distance education

Any instruction characterized by the separation of teacher and learner(s) in space and/ or time; especially, instruction that makes use of technology to facilitate learning at a distance. A planned teaching/learning experience that uses a wide spectrum of technologies to reach learners located remotely from the instructor and is designed to encourage learner interaction and certification of learning. Distance education is defined, for the purposes of accreditation review, as a formal educational process in which the majority of the instruction occurs when student and instructor are not in the same place. Instruction may be synchronous or asynchronous. Distance education may employ correspondence study, or audio, video, or computer technologies. (jsj, cf)

distance learning

The type of learning that takes place in distance education programs or other situations in which teacher and learner have no face-to-face contact. Refers to the reception of instruction at a distance, increasingly by means of technology such as television via satellite transmission, e-mail, and the Internet. Students and community members in small or isolated localities have benefited the most from such arrangements. (jpc, lr)

distance teaching

Refers to the provision of instruction at a distance using technology (television via satellite transmission, e-mail, the Internet) as an increasing means of delivery. Distance teaching has been a particular benefit in rural areas by augmenting the course offerings of small and isolated school districts. (lr)

DISTAR (See Direct Instructional System for Teaching Arithmetic and Reading)

distributed education
An approach to education and training that is intended to be learner-centered, enabling both synchronous and asynchronous interaction through the integration of pedagogically appropriate technologies. Distributed education is conducted when there is separation of place and/or time between instructor and learner, among learners, and/or between learners and learning resources. (cf)
    See also distance education.

distributive justice (See justice)

distributive property
The property stating that when given some factor to be multiplied by a sum or a difference, the factor may be multiplied by each term in the sum or difference first and that result may be added or subtracted last, or the sum or difference may found first and this result may be multiplied by the factor last. For example, $2(3 + 4) = 2 \times 3 + 2 \times 4 = 6 + 8 = 14$ or $2(3 + 4) = 2(7) = 14$. (ps)

divergent questions (See open-ended question)

divergent thinking
J. P. Guilford saw creative thinking as reflected in fluid, flexible, original, and elaborate thinking, which he called "divergent thinking." It was contrasted with convergent thinking. Examples of divergent thinking are reflected in responses and work products where information is changed so that new, unusual aspects are included. Divergent thinking might result in poor performance on tests on which standard, conventional thinking is the norm. (vm)

diversity
When applied to a population can refer to group or individual differences. In reference to group differences, diversity applied to school populations focuses most often on the categorization of students according to race, ethnicity, gender, economic status, color, national origin, sexual orientation, and religion. Multicultural educators attempt to address the educational inequities associated most often with racial and ethnic diversity. In heterogeneous classrooms, diversity refers to a variety of individual differences and can include ability, talent, interests, learning style, intelligence, achievement, background, experiences, and preferences. (igb)

Division of Early Childhood (DEC)
The early childhood branch of the Council for Exceptional Children, which advocates for individuals who work with or on behalf of children with special needs, birth through age eight, and their families. Founded in 1973, the Division is a nonprofit agency that promotes policies and practices that support families and enhance the optimal development of children with nontypical developmental needs. (ecr)

docent
From the Latin *doci,* meaning to teach. A teacher or lecturer at a university who is not necessarily a regular faculty member (often a graduate student). A lecturer or tour guide in a museum, historic home, art gallery, cathedral, or other cultural or educational institution. In art museums, docents are often volunteers trained by museum educators to provide tours for museum visitors. Docents often have backgrounds or interest in art history that are cultivated and exercised through their contributions. (kf)

doctorate
A word referring to such advanced degrees as the PhD or EdD, rather than to first-professional degrees in the medical fields (MD, DDS, etc.), or the JD in law. (cf)

doctor's degree (See degree, doctor's)

document literacy
Defined in the national adult literacy survey as the knowledge and skills required to locate and use information contained in materials that include job applications, payroll forms, transportation schedules, maps, tables, and graphs. (jpc)

documentary
Generally referring to a genre of film, the documentary uses exclusively factual material, real people (not actors or fictional characters), and historical records to tell a story, study a social condition, explore a political issue or movement, or investigate historical events. The documentary form continually evolves and expands, encompassing everything from newsreels to educational films to contemporary creative and artistic variations on the form. While built on a foundation of fact, documentaries are not meant to be devoid of perspective and are in fact often guided by specific ideological concerns. Many youth film centers encourage young people to create documentaries of their lives and neighborhoods. (em)

Dolch Words
The Dolch Word List, which was developed by Edward W. Dolch in 1936 and first published in 1948, is a list of the most commonly occurring words in children's books. The list is divided by grade level from preprimer to third grade and contains a total of 315 words: 95 common nouns and an additional 220 pronouns, verbs, conjunctions, prepositions, and adjectives. The Dolch words are generally considered to be words that children should know instantly by sight, as the majority of the words can't be sounded out (decoded) using phonics (e.g., *blue*). However, there are words on the list that can be decoded using basic phonics rules (e.g., *it*). Teachers often ask students to practice reading and spelling the Dolch words in class and at home to improve their ability to recognize these words quickly when they encounter them in text. (rcr)
See also sight word.

domestic partnership
A legally recognized, state-sanctioned union between two adults in a romantic relationship defined as different from traditional marriage. Domestic partnerships and civil unions convey some of the same rights and responsibilities as marriage, but many have restrictions and limitations on certain rights, and none are universally recognized at the federal level. In some states, domestic partnerships are only recognized for same-sex couples. (jb2)
See also civil union.

doubles plus one strategy (See thinking strategies)

Down Syndrome
A common and readily identifiable chromosomal condition associated with mental retardation. It is caused by a chromosomal abnormality that results in an extra, or 47th, chromosome. (sr)

drafting
Sometimes referred to as mechanical drawing, drafting refers to the process of systematic drawing (with specific tools such as a compass, ruler, and size scales) that represents and sets the stage for further work on mechanical and architectural structures. But drafting is a process of planning for any artistic product. Drafted drawings can act as references for larger paintings; drafts of stories set the stage for the revisions of final work. Nonetheless, the drafting of professional draftspersons is visual dimensional work usually associated with architecture and engineering. Many students acquire the skills of drafting in technical drawing classes offered in secondary schools. (ap)
See also editing.

drama

One of the performing arts, the central focus of which is storytelling through the depiction of people, characters, and situations. Can encompass elements of all of the other arts, including music, movement, and visual imagery, though the central building block is often (but not always) spoken words. Also can be used to describe plays (as opposed to musical theater) or serious plays (as opposed to comedy). Some people make a distinction between drama and theater, defining theater as performance (of dramatic works) and drama as a participatory endeavor (as in education). (em)

See also drama-in-education/theater-in-education; theater.

drama-in-education/theater-in-education

An emerging field in which drama is used for the purpose of teaching and learning. Can include: in-class work in various subjects through dramatization, improvisation, process drama; extracurricular learning and performance activities, such as participation in a school play or drama work in a peer counseling/mediation/leadership group; and learning through watching theatrical performances. Some people distinguish between drama-in-education as educational process, in which students and teachers are engaged together in role playing and discovery, and theater-in-education as observation, in which students watch performances as audience members, though this semantic distinction is less prevalent than it once was. (em)

dramatization

Process or act of putting a story, situation, picture, or idea into a form for theatrical presentation or exploration—that is, using characters, spoken words, and/or created (or re-created) situations. A technique prevalent in classrooms where teachers use drama, in which students and teachers explore social issues, works of literature, academic dilemmas, decision making, conflict situations, or theatrical works by taking on roles and acting, either improvising or using prewritten dialogue and action. (em)

dramaturgy

The art of writing plays and the craft of creating balanced dramatic compositions. Dramaturgy has come to involve the creation of a bridge between the page and the stage—the realization of a play script as a theatrical production. Dramaturgs oversee aspects of theatrical production that ensure a faithfulness to the intentions of the playwright and to the interpretive needs of the audience. The dramaturg is often involved in selecting and preparing scripts for production. With regard to art education, dramaturgs may establish relationships with local educators, consider ways to use theater to enrich curriculum, prepare study guides and relevant educational program materials, and design and lead pre- and postperformance educational experiences. (kc)

drawing

The activity of representing objects and/or ideas through lines delineated on a surface. Drawing, as a preparatory step or final articulation, is essential to painting, architecture, sculpture, calligraphy, and geometry. Often done in pen, pencil, crayon, chalk, charcoal, or other media emphasizing form over color. Artists such as Leonardo da Vinci, Michelangelo, Dürer, Klee, Picasso, and Matisse are famous for their drawing. Young children's drawing comprises much of their art making, as well as the attention of researchers like Arnheim, Piaget, Lowenfeld, and Kellogg, who see drawing as imprinted with levels or stages of understanding, from preschool scribbling to the cartoon-like illustrated narratives of preadolescents. (ap)

dress code

A requirement of a school or school district that students should follow specified guidelines for dress when they are in school. (bba)

drop-in program
An adult education center with an open entry and exit policy, so that students can come at any time that they are able to learn in a class, with a tutor, or by using self-learning resources. (jpc)

dropout
An individual who has withdrawn from the school program prior to graduation or completion of an equivalent degree program. The label is applied regardless of whether the individual leaves the school program while school is in session or whether he or she is beyond the age of compulsory attendance. The term is not applied to students who are dropped from attendance because of a transfer to another academic institution. (jw)

dropout prevention
Programs intended to deter students from withdrawing from school prior to graduation or completion of an equivalent degree. (jw)

DSM-IV-TR (See *Diagnostic and Statistical Manual of Mental Disorders,* Fourth Edition, Text Revision)

DTI (See Diffusion Tensor Imaging)

dual credit (See credit, dual)

dual enrollment
An arrangement for the regular attendance of a pupil at two schools concurrently, with both schools sharing the direction and control of the student's studies. For example, a student may take some courses at a public school and others at a community college or attend a public secondary school part-time and an area career and technical school part-time. Dual enrollment may or may not generate credit in both institutions. (db)

dual relationship
Refers to a situation that occurs when an individual plays two or more roles, or serves in a dual capacity, for another person. In some instances, dual relationships may be benign in nature, such as in a relationship that exists between a faculty member and a student, in which the faculty member serves simultaneously as a course instructor and a program adviser. In other instances, they may be potentially harmful, such as in a professional serving simultaneously as a therapist and business partner of a client. The latter type of dual relationship is prohibited explicitly by ethical principles and codes of conduct. (dd)

dualism
A view that divides a whole into two opposing parts. For example, gender is divided into male and female, or life between human and nonhuman. Often, there is an imbalance in which the first component (i.e., male and human) is given greater value and dominance over the second component (i.e., female and nonhuman). Other common dualisms include culture/nature, mind/body, rational/emotional, and good/evil. There are several theoretical positions critical of hierarchal dualisms (e.g., ecocentrism, ecofeminism, ecojustice, feminism, postcolonialism, postmodernism). (vkh)

dual-language learner/ELL
A person who is learning two languages simultaneously. The dual-language learner may be equally proficient in both languages or more proficient in one language than the other. This term typically refers to students who are learning English primarily at school at the same time as they are learning another language at home. (jdc)

due process
Action taken to protect a person's rights. Due process is used in education settings to refer to actions taken to assure a students' rights to special education services

under the Individuals with Disabilities Education Act. (sr)

duration

A behavior observational technique in which the measure of how long a specific behavior lasts is taken. For the technique to be effective, the target behavior must be clearly defined, especially the initiating and ending behaviors. The observer records the duration of the targeted behavior every time it occurs, usually during routines in which the behavior is expected and within a set length of time each time. (xss, yb)

duty to warn/protect

This legal and ethical obligation refers to the requirement for mental health professionals to warn those who may potentially be harmed by the actions of their client/patient. Legal precedence for duty to warn/protect was established by *Tarasoff v. Board of Regents*. (tsw)

dyscalculia

A developmental learning disability resulting in an inability to develop math concepts and skills. (jcp)

See also acalculia.

dyscoordination disorders (See motor skill disorder)

dyslexia

A learning disability characterized by average to above-average intelligence coupled with a marked difficulty in learning to read and spell, despite adequate opportunity. Although dyslexic children's mechanical, arithmetic, music, and foreign language skills are sometimes impaired, these abilities are much less severely affected than phonological awareness and processing, which involve discriminating, assigning meaning to, decoding, and remembering language sounds. By way of strengths, dyslexic children often show strong talent in visual-spatial and nonverbal problem-solving skills and can be very creative, innovative thinkers. Often unfairly accused of laziness, dyslexics can have difficulty concentrating, remembering, managing their time, and organizing their thoughts or belongings. Developmental dyslexia affects approximately 15 percent of Americans and is probably a family of neuropsychological disorders involving sequencing of information (such as historical dates) and sounds. (mhi-y)

dystopian

The opposite of utopian. Conditions that are horrible and bring out the worst in people instead of the best. (jrw)

E

each one teach one

An approach to teaching literacy to adults developed by Frank Laubach in Third World countries. In this approach, each literate adult teaches an illiterate adult to read. That newly literate adult then teaches another person to read and so on. (jpc)

EAP (See employee assistance program)

early childhood

The period of childhood from birth through age eight, including the years of infancy, toddlerhood, preschool, and primary school years (Schickedanz, 1986; Bredekamp and Copple, 1997). During this time, important and template-establishing growth takes place. Healthy development during this period is crucial to physical health, emotional balance, and cognitive maturity in later life. (ecr)

early childhood education

Planned instruction of children from birth to five years. Activities are geared to interest and challenge, but not frustrate young children as they build on past experiences and learning. The curriculum provides children with opportunities to discover new information about themselves and the world around them, as well as practice, experiment, and test skills useful for everyday functioning and survival. (jlj)

Early Childhood Environment Rating Scale (ECERS)

A nationally recognized and well-respected standardized instrument for the evaluation of preschool classrooms and centers developed by Thelma Harms, Richard M. Clifford, and Debby Cryer in 1980 and revised in 1998. The instrument contains 43 different items to comprehensively evaluate the early childhood classroom using a likert-type scale. Terms such as "Inadequate," "Minimal," "Good," and "Excellent" are identified along the scale, with examples provided under each term for each item. (kdc)

Early Head Start

One of the newer initiatives of the federal Head Start program, EHS serves pregnant mothers and children from birth through age three. In addition to the basic Head Start programs of nutrition, infant-toddler early intervention and education, medical assistance, and parenting support, EHS also includes services for specialized needs such as teen parenting, family literacy, occupational skills development, and substance abuse treatment. (ecr)

early intervention

May refer to a system, process, or delivery of services to children, ages zero to three, who are diagnosed with an established risk condition or experiencing developmental delay in one or more developmental domains as determined by a developmental evaluation. Each state sets the criteria for what constitutes developmental delay. Once eligible for the services, early intervention addresses priorities and needs of families as well as in the care of the children. (kms, yb)

eating disorder

A category of mental disorders characterized by serious disturbance in eating behaviors. Examples include: anorexia nervosa (marked by stringent restriction of food intake and refusal to maintain minimally normal body weight), bulimia nervosa (characterized by repeated eating binges, followed by compensatory behaviors such as vomiting, laxative abuse, and/or excessive exercising), and pica (consuming nonfood items). (mkt)

Ebonics (See African American language)

ECERS (See Early Childhood Environment Rating Scale)

eclecticism

Broadly, the common practice of using relevant aspects from a variety of theories of behavior and behavior change. In psychological terms, eclecticism refers to the application of techniques and strategies drawn from a wide range of theoretical orientations, rather than from a single, unified theory. (rem)

ecocentrism

Ecocentrism begins from a position that all of nature has intrinsic value, rather than the human-centered worldview of anthropocentrism. It is a response to the dominance of male-centered individuality, competition, and hierarchy, which are typically valued within anthropocentrism. With ecocentrism's focus on the centrality of nature, key concepts include wholism, interdependence, and interconnection. Ecocentric thoughts can be found in the works of Rachel Carson (1907–1964), Aldo Leopold (1887–1948), Arne Naess (1912–2009), and Val Plumwood (1939–2008). For further exploration, an ecocentric declaration can be found in *A Manifesto for Earth* (2004) by Mosquin and Rowe. (vkh)

See also anthropocentrism; ecofeminism; ecojustice; land ethic; worldview.

ecofeminism

A theoretical position, coupled with practical implications, that combines feminist, social justice, and ecological thought. Ecofeminism is critical of hierarchal dualism such as culture/nature, male/female, mind/body, and rational/emotional, in which the first mode is given greater value and control over the second. As a way to establish a more just world, ecofeminism supports more holistic positions (e.g., ecocentrism, multicentrism). French feminist Françoise d'Eaubonne is credited with first using the term in 1974. Scholars in this area include Carolyn Merchant, Jim Cheney, Karen Warren, Susan Griffin, Val Plumwood, and Vandana Shiva. A wide sampling of ecofeminist thought can be found in two collections edited by Karen Warren (1996, 1997). Historically significant events from the 1970s include the Chipko movement, the Green Belt movement, and Love Canal. (vkh)

See also dualism; ecocentrism.

ecojustice

A combination of the words ecological and justice. This is a conceptualizing of what justice becomes if rights (to flourish, to reproduce, to exist independent of the demands of humans) are offered to the nonhuman world. Often rests on the assumption that social justice, the rights of all humans, are linked directly with care of and for the environment. Involves a sense of moral rightness in reconnecting the human and natural world and in involving the whole community in decision making for the express purpose of protecting and revitalizing cultures and ecosystems. For an interesting example of ecojustice in practice see the Earth Charter approved by UNESCO in Paris in 2000. (sb1, cm2)

See also justice; ecofeminism.

ecology
The study of the relationships among and between living organisms and their environments. From the Greek word *ecol* meaning house and the word *logia* for discourse, ecology is the study of the environment through the natural sciences of biology and chemistry, in tandem with the applied sciences of conservation and management. Social aspects of ecology focus on human interactions with the environment that affect geographic and sociopolitical issues of interest to the social studies. (cm2, npg, sb1)

Economic Opportunity Act of 1964
U.S. federal legislation that provided the first substantial federal funding for adult literacy. The act provided for assistance to the poor and educationally disadvantaged and established the Job Corps. (las)

economics
The scientific study of financial and money matters focused on production, distribution, consumption, and commercialism of goods and services balancing the means and the ends of a society. Economics applies to all aspects of the social sciences: geography, history, and political science through business, government, education, safety, family, health, and law. Economics addresses both the behaviors of agents involved in the system through microeconomics and the entire system through macroeconomics. (npg)

eco-pedagogy
Eco-pedagogy or Earth pedagogy is a pedagogical movement or curriculum approach that promotes learning as a democratic project for everyday life. It is based on the philosophical teachings of Paulo Freire, Fritjof Capra, Leonardo Boff, Sebastiao Salgado, Boaventura de Sousa Santos, Milton Santos, Francisco Gutierrez, and Cruz Prado. Eco-pedagogy implies redirecting curricula to incorporate values and principles defended by the Earth Charter, a planetary code of ethics and call to action. It not only has meaning as an alternative global project concerned with nature preservation (natural ecology) and the human impact on the natural environment (social ecology), it is a sustainable development pedagogy that demands making changes to economic, social, and cultural structures. As a sustainable pedagogy, eco-pedagogy utilizes strategies, guidelines, and means based on the "reading the world" methodology of Paulo Freire. It is a pedagogy centered on life that is inclusive of people, cultures, respect for identity, and diversity. Eco-pedagogy understands the human being in evolution as an "incomplete, unfinished, and non-conclusive" entity in continuous development, interacting with others and the world. Eco-pedagogy compels educators to welcome students; their welcome and care are the basis for sustainable education. (dns)

ECS (See Education Commission of the States)

ECW (See Civilian Conservation Corps)

editing
To assemble, prepare, modify, or condense written material, including the work of another or others, for publication or public presentation. An editor is someone with organizational, managerial, and policy-making responsibility for a publication or for aspects of the work of a publishing house. As relates to various artistic domains (dance, music, theater, and visual arts), editing means to alter, adapt,

or refine, and it is as actively pursued by artists in self-reflection as by directors in critical review. The arts in education offer students authentic opportunities to critique their own work and that of others with an eye to effective editing. (kpb)

ed-jobber (See jobber)

education
A broadly inclusive term referring to a process of fostering cognitive, physical, social, emotional, or moral growth and development in individuals or groups. It is goal directed, implies a values system, and may proceed informally or formally, as in schooling. Formal education typically aims for some balance between individual needs and societal needs. In the United States, the differential emphasis placed on individual needs and social needs is exemplified in the historical conflict between traditional education and progressive, or open, education. (prg)

See also civic education; moral education.

education, Afrocentric (See Afrocentric education)

education, traditional (See traditional education)

education, vocational (See vocational education)

Education Amendments of 1972 (Public Law 92-318)
Passed by the 92nd Congress in order to amend the Higher Education Act of 1965, the Vocational Educational Act of 1963, the General Education Provisions Act, the Elementary and Secondary Education Act of 1965, and related acts. The law established the Education Division in the U.S. Department of Health, Education, and Welfare, the National Institute of Education (NIE), and a bureau-level Office of Indian Education. The many councils and bureaus created under these amendments

were created to strengthen links between states and strengthen occupational education. Furthermore, the law prohibits sex discrimination in admission to vocational, professional, and graduate schools, and public institutions of undergraduate higher education. (wg)

Education Commission of the States (ECS)
This nonprofit commission was created in 1966 by interstate compact to facilitate cooperation between leaders in education and government. The Commission includes 48 states, American Samoa, Puerto Rico, and the Virgin Islands. Each state appoints seven members, usually including the governor and two state legislators, to serve as an advisory organization, help draft legislation on higher education, and aid its members in communicating with the federal government. (cf)

Education for All
A program that began as part of the United Nations Education, Scientific, and Cultural Organization (UNESCO)'s middle-term plan (1984–1989), which specified targets for early childhood, primary and secondary school, and adult education. Each UNESCO member country was to enact legislation that defined specific goals and provided resources to meet those goals. International development organizations agreed to help fund these plans. (las)

Education for All Handicapped Children Act of 1975 (Public Law 94–142)
Signed into law on November 29, 1975, it requires states to provide a "free appropriate public education" in the least restrictive environment to handicapped children. The law includes parent or guardian participation with educators in the development of an annual Individualized Education Program, or IEP. Procedural safeguards for handicapped children include provisions for

an independent educational evaluation of the child, written prior notice of changes in the identification, evaluation, or educational placement, and procedures for filing complaints, hearings, and judicial matters. Several revisions to the act have been passed, including the 1990 amendment renaming the law as IDEA or Individuals with Disabilities Education Act, which includes P.L. 99–457, which had extended related services and eligibility to infants and toddlers with developmental delays or disabilities and their families. (wg, at, ckc)

education for liberation
An approach to education in which learning is viewed as freeing learners from the constraints of their social and economic class. (las)

education theories
Theories of education offer coherent explanations and rationales upon which to base educational practice. A robust theory of education will address the aims of education, instructional methods and materials, curriculum, the nature of the learner, the role of the teacher, and the sociocultural context of education. Theories of education tend to be rooted in historical, social, and political contexts, as well as theories of learning and philosophical schools of thought. As a consequence, a variety of notions concerning goals, methods, content, and assessment exist. (prg)

education to careers
Alternative terms applied to school-to-work educational programs designed to enhance student transition from school to work or college as authorized under the federal School to Work Opportunities Act of 1994. (db)
See also school-to-work.

educational administration
A process that is charged with developing, identifying, categorizing, and allocating formal and informal interests and energies within a school-based environment. Educational administrative theory has tended to focus on open systems theory. Such theory purports that schools have unique problems and issues, but the basis for many of the interactions within the organization is based on organizational theory common to many social groups. Some view educational administration as an activity separate and apart from policy development. Recent writings have tended to examine the integration of policy development and educational administration. (ly)

educational choice
A program whereby families may determine where their children go to school. Implies that factors other than geographic location may influence where children attend school. (jqa, jwc)

educational dance
An approach to dance that utilizes Laban's Movement Framework and affords students the opportunity to express their ideas through movement. Students are provided experiences that allow them to learn "how to dance" using their natural ways, in contrast to traditional dance where students perform set dance steps. (rf)
See also Laban's Movement Framework.

educational equality
A sought-after ideal in which all children, regardless of their racial, ethnic, or socioeconomic background, receive the same high-quality education. Can be described as equal educational opportunity for all. Most of the current debate on the issues relating to educational equality focuses on the differences between and within school systems and identifies wide disparities in school facilities, student achievement, and financial support. (jwc)

educational equity (See educational equality)

educational facilities

All of the properties and equipment owned and maintained by a school district or campus for the purposes of meeting the instructional needs of students. The properties include all developed and nondeveloped real estate holdings. This is generally assumed to include all school buildings, classrooms, offices, athletic centers, computer networks, buses, and maintenance facilities that are necessary to ensure continued operation of the school system. Facilities can also include all equipment and materials used by the school to continue instructional operations. This can include books, furniture, instructional supplies, general maintenance equipment, and food service supplies and equipment. Current research exists to establish the connection between school facilities and student outcomes. The size of the campus, physical structure and layout of the building, and access issues are all points of study by educational facilities managers. (ly)

educational gymnastics

An approach to gymnastics that utilizes Laban's Movement Framework for curriculum. It allows for a variety of end products within the framework, focusing on broad skill areas such as balancing, rolling, jumping and landing, and weight transfer. Educational gymnastics emphasizes skilled performance within each individual's capacity, in contrast to "Olympic Gymnastics," which focuses on accuracy and perfection of specific skills. (rf)

educational leadership

Most theorists note a difference between educational leadership and managerial leadership, and most also note a difference between leadership in education and in the business world. A common theme involves implementing change. At the elementary and secondary levels, the goal of the leader ultimately relates to improving student achievement. In higher education, although student success is of key importance, leadership goals may vary greatly depending upon the type of institution and its mission. (sn)

educational management

A term often associated with the day-to-day organizational functions in an educational setting. These are often depicted as the structures, roles, and communications networks in a school. The focus of educational management has been directed at the operations of budgets, staffing, and facilities of a school or district. (ly)

educational personnel

A global term representing all employees involved in the educational system. This grouping would include administrative personnel, faculty, aides and office secretarial staff, maintenance, and transportation and cafeteria workers. (tm)

Educational Resources Information Center (ERIC)

Sponsored by the Institute of Education Sciences under the U.S. Department of Education, ERIC is an online digital library consisting of over 1.3 million bibliographic records dealing with the field of education and educational research, developed to be publicly available and easily searchable. In an attempt to be comprehensive, ERIC includes journal literature, books, reports, papers, policy documents, and other education-related materials, such as gray literature (conference proceedings, unpublished reports, etc.), produced by the U.S. Department of Education, other federal, state and local agencies, scholarly, professional, and policy organizations and associations, academic presses, and individuals. Much of the historic material indexed in ERIC is now available in full-text electronic format because of efforts by ERIC to digitize the microfiche version of the many ERIC documents. (ms)

educational stakeholder

An educational stakeholder is any person or organization that is involved with, participates in, or is affected by the educational process. In a given community an educational stakeholder could be a parent, business leader, community member, school board member or regent, student, or any member of the school district, college/university, or public or private educational agency. (tm)

educational technology
The study and ethical practice of facilitating learning and improving performance by using and managing appropriate technological processes and resources, such as software, digital devices, and various Internet learning applications and activities. (pgg)

Educational Testing Service (ETS)
The world's largest private educational testing and measurement organization, ETS is also a national leader in educational research. As a nonprofit company, ETS is dedicated to serving the needs of individuals, institutions, educational agencies, and governmental bodies in 181 countries. ETS develops and administers annually more than 11 million tests worldwide. (cf)

educationally disadvantaged
A label given to a group of students that are underserved in the educational institution in which that group is located. The term underserved is usually measured by student achievement scores, with the educationally disadvantaged group scoring significantly lower than the norm or lower than other subgroups within the population of students at that educational institution. (mds)

edutainment (See entertainment)

EEG
Electroencephalography (EEG) and Event-Related Potential (ERP) measurement are functional neuroimaging techniques that record the electrical activity on the scalp caused by brain activity. Multiple electrodes are placed on the scalp, and activity is recorded over a relatively short period of time (e.g., 20 minutes), while the subject remains in a resting state or performs a particular cognitive task or series of tasks. EEG is particularly useful for imaging the time course of brain activity related to a particular task. EEG is also noninvasive, relatively inexpensive, and easy to transport compared to other functional imaging tools, and unlike fMRI or PET it is a direct measurement of brain activity. The limitations of EEG include its poor spatial resolution (it is difficult to determine exactly where in the brain the activity is occurring) and the fact that recording is limited to the surface of the brain. EEG is a useful tool both in neuroscience research and in the diagnosis of certain brain diseases such as epilepsy. (mt)

EFF (See equipped for the future)

effect size
Effect size measures the strength of the relationship between two variables after taking into account variability in data and scale differences between studies. There are two major uses of effect size in educational research. One use is to indicate whether statistically significant differences are meaningful in practice. Effect size is also popularly used in meta-analysis because it allows comparisons of results from studies with different sample sizes and scales. Standardized mean difference, correlations, and odds-ratio difference are common types of effect size. (hl)

effective schools research
A term in education that describes research efforts of scholars and policy makers to determine the distinctive characteristics of schools with high levels of student learning and staff commitment. It is generally agreed that effective schools research has yielded five factors common to all effective schools: strong leadership by the principal, especially in instructional matters;

high expectations by teachers for student achievement; an emphasis on basic skills; an orderly environment; and frequent, systematic evaluation of students. (ly)

EFL (See English as a foreign language)

egocentrism
Egocentrism is a narrow, self-centered form of thinking, characteristic of children in Jean Piaget's preoperational stage of cognitive development. Egocentric children have the false idea that others share similar thoughts regarding concepts, beliefs, and experiences. (mf)

ego-dystonic
A clinical descriptor applied to signs, symptoms, or experiences that an individual finds uncomfortable or unacceptable. Symptoms of particular mental disorders, such as obsessions in certain individuals diagnosed with obsessive-compulsive disorder, are often considered ego-dystonic. (bd)

ego-syntonic
A clinical descriptor applied to signs, symptoms, or experiences that an individual finds acceptable and consistent with his or her personality. Symptoms of particular mental disorders, such as delusions in certain individuals diagnosed with schizophrenia, are often considered ego-syntonic. (bd)

Eight-Year Study
A landmark study (1932–1940) of the effectiveness of progressive education in the secondary school, this cooperative effort between the Progressive Education Association and 30 public and private high schools explored alternatives to the conventional college-preparatory curriculum. Participating schools pioneered ideas such as integrated core curriculum, multiple forms of assessment, and teacher workshops. A follow-up study of graduates showed that alumni of participating schools out-performed their college classmates on a variety of measures, including academic achievement. Despite the fact that the study suggested that there might be a variety of curricular approaches appropriate for college preparation, the official report of the study, released only months after the United States entered World War II, has been largely ignored. (wgw)

Elderhostel
A nonprofit organization designed to serve the educational needs of older adults through short-term, residential, noncredit programs, typically offered at college or university campuses. Programs are both recreational and academic. Elderhostel began in New Hampshire in 1975 and grew to include locations throughout the United States and abroad. (js)

e-learning
A learning system that uses electronic media (e.g., cable TV, the Internet, or palm-held computers) for human learning. Historically, the first learning system can be called S-learning, using speech as its primary medium to promote learning. Its prominence was gradually replaced by P-learning, the second learning system, which uses paper as its primary learning medium. However, e-learning became a pervasive and important learning phenomenon in the 1990s. It has various forms (e.g., virtual learning, online learning, distance learning, and web-based learning) and involves various components (e.g., e-book, e-library, e-test, and e-classroom). (zy)

elective
A course in the choosing of which a student has a degree of freedom, as opposed to a required course. Students might choose to take an elective to pursue a personal interest, to strengthen knowledge in an area, or to develop a broader frame of knowledge. In some cases, elective courses are ungraded, and some are

offered to nonuniversity students as well. Outside of the core curriculum or requirements for a student's major, electives are important in helping a student to develop a variety of interests and areas of broad knowledge. (cf)

Electroencephalography (See EEG)

electronic discussion list
An asynchronous online discussion for one-to-many communication. A message may be posted to the list by one person, then received or viewed by all members of the group. Listservs accomplish this via an e-mail mechanism; threaded discussions accomplish this within a web environment. Electronic discussion lists in either format may be used as a class discussion mechanism for online education. (ac)

See also courseware; threaded discussion.

electronic portfolio
A digital collection of student work that may be stored on a central file server and most typically presented in a web-based format. Electronic portfolios are purposeful collections of student work in multiple formats (e.g., text-based, visual, audio, multimedia) and reflections on that work. They can be used for both assessment and presentation purposes. They may be constructed developmentally to reflect growth over time or showcase a student's best work. Electronic portfolios represent a form of authentic assessment and may be used both formatively and summatively. (lp, ar)

Elementary and Secondary Education Act (ESEA)
One of the seminal measures passed as part of President Lyndon B. Johnson's "War on Poverty," ESEA was enacted as Public Law 89-10 on April 11, 1965, and authorized grants for elementary and secondary school programs for children of low-income families; handicapped children; adult basic education; school library resources, textbooks, and other materials for school children; supplementary educational centers and services; and strengthening state departments of education. ESEA continues to support these core programs, as well as programs in areas such as basic skills instruction, drug education, bilingual education, special education, Native American education, and educational programs for the homeless and for immigrant populations. (wg)

elementary school
A school that is planned and organized for children in grades K–6, or some combination of those grades. (bba)

elision
The process of omitting sound(s), syllables, or whole words in speech. Elision is generally a later developing phonological awareness skill (between three and four years of age), which involves isolating syllables and individual or groups of speech sounds within a word in order to delete them and produce the word without the given component (e.g., pan without the /p/ is an). In speech, elision can be deliberate or unintentional. Unstressed syllables are most likely to be elided (e.g., "peas 'n' carrots" for "peas and carrots"). (rcr)

ELL (See English-language learner)

e-mail
Stands for electronic mail. An e-mail is a digital letter or note that one individual sends to another via the Internet. In addition, digital files, such as documents or photographs, can be sent via e-mail. E-mail is a quick form of asynchronous distance communication. In educational settings, it can be used for communication between administrators and faculty, educators and students, or educators and parents. (kg1)

See also key pal.

emancipatory education

Education designed to help learners to examine critically the assumptions and values underlying their society, especially the power structures that shape their lives and their current place in society. The principle of emancipatory education is that understanding the working of society will lead to social action and transformation of the democratic process. (chm)

embodied pedagogy

An embodied pedagogy is a holistic approach to teaching and learning in which educational discourse and practice encompasses the rational, the emotional, and the physical, thus seeing the entire body as a site of meaning-making. To include an embodied pedagogy means including the language of the body in our educational endeavors and connecting to things bodily in our teaching and, therefore, to the wholeness of being human. Bodies are respected as important sources of information and knowledge. To teach from an embodied place means acknowledging the students' bodies in the learning process, recognizing that bodies both enact and carry meaning, as well as teaching ideas through the body. Embodied cognition is intertwined with the experiences of everyday life. An embodied pedagogy enables us to connect to what we know and feel in, through, and about our bodies as well as the bodies, and thus lives, of others. (as)

Emergency Conservation Work (See Civilian Conservation Corps)

emergent curriculum

Activity plans that follow the interests of the young children in a particular learning group. Caregivers have curricular goals in mind but do not present them in a predetermined sequence. Instead, they observe children's work closely, act as facilitators for the child's own work, and present supports and challenges to advance the child's initiated activities. (ecr)

emergent design

A central characteristic of qualitative research. The plans for implementing a qualitative research study are tentative and cannot be rigidly designed in advance. Once engaged in the field, the researcher adjusts the procedures in order to be responsive to the topic, participants, and setting. That is, the design emerges as the study progresses. (mas)

emergent literacy

A stage of literacy development in which the young child shows understanding of the processes of reading and writing but does not yet show precise skill in encoding or decoding print. During this period a child might identify signs, call out letters, scribble, draw pictures, retell stories, or write his or her name while actively working out the meanings of literacy symbols. The behaviors, skills, and knowledge developed by young children before they learn to read that support their later reading development. The term reflects the belief that literacy is a "developmental continuum" and that young children's literacy development is not "reading readiness" but true literacy. (jdc, ecr)

emergent perspective

Within the mathematics classroom, this theory describes cognitive development as the intertwining of social norms and opportunities for learning. The learning environments are considered rich in the sense that: the tasks on which students work are open ended and aimed at solving problems; the activities required by the tasks have multiple phases, consisting of group collaboration on problem solving, reporting, and reflection in a classroom setting; and the tools used are multirepresentational. (pmts)

emic(s)

The understandings and perceptions of cultural reality held by members of a culture. Emic includes descriptions, analyses, and judgments of culture (beliefs, behavior, customs, values, etc.) that are consistent with what members of a social group or society hold to be culturally meaningful and valid. An emic perspective emphasizes the categories, thought processes, and beliefs of natives, that is, it is a perspective on cultural phenomena that is generated from the point of view of natives (even though it might be recorded by an outsider). Emic constructions of reality are epistemological, not ontological, in nature. The ultimate arbiters and judges of emic constructions are native informants. The emic/etic distinction, analogous to the terms phonemic and phonetic, originates in the work of linguist Kenneth Pike. In the social sciences, anthropologist Marvin Harris has emphasized the significance of this distinction to theorizing culture. Emic is synonymous with "culture specific." (jde, amm)

See also etic(s).

emotional abuse
An act, or failure to act, by a person responsible for a child's welfare (e.g., parent, caretaker, teacher, employee of residential facility) or by a person who is in a position of power over a child and who has caused or could cause serious behavioral, cognitive, emotional, or psychological harm to a child. Examples of such abuse include habitual blaming, rejecting, shaming, intimidation, or ridiculing of a child; extreme or bizarre forms of punishment; persistent lack of concern for a child's welfare; or exposing a child to domestic violence. Emotional abuse is generally present when other forms of abuse have been identified (e.g., sexual abuse, physical abuse). (llf, emm)

emotional disturbance
A condition exhibiting one or more of the following characteristics over a long period of time and to a marked degree: an inability to learn that cannot be explained by intellectual, sensory, or health factors; an inability to build or maintain satisfactory interpersonal relationships with peers and teachers; inappropriate types of behavior or feelings under normal circumstances; a general pervasive mood of unhappiness or depression; a tendency to develop physical symptoms or fears associated with personal or school problems. (sr)

emotional intelligence
A theory of intelligence related to social intelligence. Emotional intelligence refers to an individual's ability to cultivate positive interpersonal relationships and monitor personal emotions. Individuals possessing a high degree of emotional intelligence are capable of using emotions to inform their thoughts and actions. In schooling, emotions are perceived as a basis for learning, thinking, and socialization. (crl)

emotions
Our emotions are what we use to select what interests us about our qualitative experiences. Emotions are intentional feelings, as opposed to physical sensations such as hunger or pain. The term "affect" can also be used to describe emotions. Philosophers have tended to focus on emotions in terms of the "feel," as behaviors, as concepts, and as evaluative judgments. Each of these approaches tends to reinforce the mind/body split Western philosophy has historically embraced. Feminists describe emotions as collaborative constructions greatly influenced by our contexts as historically situated, uniquely embodied, social beings, in contrast to more traditional conceptions of emotions as private, individualistic, natural, and universal. (bt-b)

emotivism
Suggests that all judgments of moral value are more or less complex expressions or descriptions of emotion. Thus, "X is good" (according to the emotivist) means something like "Bravo, X!" or "I like X." In more complex versions of moral emotivism, "X is good" might mean "the community as a whole likes X." Against

moral realism (the thesis that moral qualities like "good" or "right" are just as real and as independent of moral opinion as qualities such as "two feet long" or "rectangular"), the emotivist insists that these simply refer to various subjective states of sentient beings, that without human minds there would be no good or bad at all. (an)

See also intellectualism.

empathy

The ability to share another person's way of thinking or feeling. The action of understanding, being aware of, sensitive to, or vicariously experiencing the feelings, thoughts, and experiences of another in the past or present without having those feelings, thoughts, and experiences explicitly communicated in an objective manner. The power of projecting one's personality into (and so comprehending) the object of contemplation. The root of empathy is pathos, meaning "suffering." Em refers to "in" or "within"; and so empathy literally means "with-in-suffering." As with sympathy, an empathizer experiences a resonating emotional response to another person's suffering. The empathizer feels what the sufferer feels. (ewr, sv)

See also compassion; intersubjectivity; sympathy.

empiricism

Any view that bases the justification for our knowledge on experience gained by our five senses. The view finds its contemporary roots in the work of John Locke (1632–1704). Most philosophers accept some form of empiricism; thus the view is one of degrees. At the extreme, all knowledge is restricted to an agent's immediate experience. Moderate varieties of empiricism attempt to restrict the thesis to certain spheres of knowledge, allowing problematic cases—like propositions of mathematics—to be explained, roughly, by reducing them to tautologies. An attack on the analytic/synthetic

distinction in the 1960s by the logician W.V.O. Quine (1908–2000) was thought to shatter all hopes of defending a moderate form of empiricism; however, his argument presupposes things about language that modern linguistics rejects—a point recently made by the philosopher Paul Boghossian. (grw)

See also foundationalism; idealism; positivism; realism.

employability skills

Refers to attitudes, values, and behaviors that are associated with successful employment, such as work ethic and behavior, expectations of the workplace, and relationships with others in the workplace. (db)

See also Secretary's Commission on Achieving Necessary Skills (SCANS).

employee assistance program (EAP)

A service sponsored by a company or organization designed to help employees, and often their dependents, find assistance for personal problems that may affect job performance. EAPs typically include benefits such as free counseling and health promotion seminars. Counseling is usually provided by licensed mental health professionals, involving private, confidential services geared toward resolving problems within a limited number of sessions. In some cases, EAPs assist the employee in finding an appropriate referral. Suitable problems for EAPs include, among others, legal/financial concerns, workplace adjustment issues, stress-related problems, and substance abuse. (sdc)

employment survey

An investigation of the personnel requirements of local business and industrial establishments, often made by public schools or government agencies in connection with the development, organization, and maintenance of career and technical courses and programs. (db)

See also occupational survey; vocational education survey.

empowerment

A term used in education to describe the process by which administrators share power, teaching others to use it in beneficial ways to make decisions affecting them and their work. Power may be shared with parents, teachers, and/or support staff members through site-based decision-making committees, curriculum committees, or other special interest groups who share a common interest or goal. (mm)

empty number line

A horizontal line without unit markings used by children to solve addition and subtraction problems with multidigit numbers. Example: 47 + 16 = ? Start mark at 47, jumps by 10 to 57, jumps 3 ones to 60, jumps remaining 3 ones to arrive at answer 63. (ey)

enculturation

The process of cultural transmission, whereby already existing culture, accumulated knowledge, cultural behaviors, values, and beliefs are handed down and learned from one generation to another. Almost synonymous with the concept of socialization, enculturation is significant in the process of cultural maintenance and continuity, but it cannot account for the creation, development, or evolution of new components of culture. (jde)

endowed chair

A college teacher or administrator whose salary or pay is at least partially funded by an endowment, foundation, or other source of specially designated monies in an honorific recognition of the professor's achievements, is considered to hold an endowed chair. (cf)

endowments

A fund-raising mechanism used by schools and higher education to offset increasing costs by establishing a method to receive funds from alumni, other donors, and philanthropic agencies to be used for a specific educational purpose, such as funding student scholarships. Funds are invested with a portion of the interest used to pay for designated programs or projects. (pgg)

engaged learning (See active learning)

engagement

State of being in which students are invested in their education. It is constructed in two parts, an emotional component (identification) and a behavioral component (participation). Identification refers to students' internalized feelings of belonging in school and that school is an important aspect of their identity and experience. Participation refers to the extent to which students participate with some regularity in academic and social school-based activities. Within higher education, engagement is the active extension of public service activities with the intent of ameliorating societal problems and improving the quality of life of citizens. It is related to other terms such as investment, involvement, outreach, and community services that benefit from institutional resources and capabilities. (hfs, cf)

See also student engagement.

Engel v. Vitale, 370 U.S. 421 (1962)

The Supreme Court case brought by parents of students who were subjected to a prayer at the beginning of each school day in Union Free School District of New York. This prayer was recommended by the State Board of Regents and read by the school principal. The Court decided this practice was in direct violation of the Establishment Clause of the Fourteenth Amendment, even when students were not compelled to join the prayer. (dwm)

engineering

Application of scientific knowledge and the study of science, including properties of matter and sources of energy, to practical use such as planning, developing, designing, or building things like machines, structures, electrical applications, or manufacturing processes. (tw)

engineering education
Teaching methods used for engineering. Teaching method that allows students to put scientific knowledge to a practical use, problem solving to design and build some type of project. Frequently collaborative in nature. (tw)

English as a foreign language (EFL)
An area of instruction in which English is taught to people who speak other languages. The term generally applies to instruction that takes place outside of an English-speaking country. (las)

English as a second language (ESL)
An area of instruction in which English is taught to people who speak another language. The term generally applies to instruction that takes place within an English-speaking country and often includes instruction in practical, "survival" English, as well as language appropriate for academic and workplace contexts. (jpc)

English for speakers of other languages (ESOL)
This term replaces ESL with a more accurate description of educational programs that teach English to people who speak at least one other language. (jpc)

English for special purposes (ESP)
Area of English language teaching that emphasizes job-related language, knowledge, and skills. (las)

English Language Proficiency Survey
A U.S. Department of Education study that tested adults over the age of 20 in 1982 and found that 13 percent of the population was illiterate. (jpc)

English learner
People acquiring English in a formal setting, such as an elementary school. In the United States, the term English language learner is used by government agencies and researchers and is seen in teacher education materials. The term English learner is one word shorter than the term English language learner and conveys the same meaning. Use of the term is found in research and some literacy education materials. English learner avoids the confusion created by the term ESL (i.e., English as a second language), regarding which number language it is for the student. (mmd)

English Only (See Official English)

English Plus (See Official English)

English-Language learner (ELL)
An individual who participates in some type of instruction to develop a proficiency in English. (las)

Enlightenment
A period of time, the end of the Middle Ages and the beginning of modernity, in which a large number of influential people came to believe (and to act on the belief) that methods of the new sciences could be applied to all areas of inquiry in order to free the human race from ignorance and impotence. Characterized by a reliance on experience and reason as the means to truth, and a rejection of tradition and authority. A state of personal recognition that is central to human fulfillment or flourishing. Thus, the Buddha is said to have gained true freedom and self-realization (i.e., enlightenment). Less spectacularly, one might become enlightened about another's state of mind or what is occurring on Wall Street. (an)
See also modernism.

enrichment
Additional materials or programs not part of the standard curriculum. (sr)

enrichment activity
Projects or games used in an educational setting to enhance understanding of an idea, concept, or behavior. (srs)

enrollment, dual (See dual enrollment)

ensemble
A group of individuals or parts that work together to produce an aesthetic or pleasing whole, from a performance piece to an arrangement of furniture. In the arts, ensemble performers are musicians, singers, dancers, or actors engaged as a group in a presentation or performance, as for example of music. A work of art or performance, by virtue of its being constructed by a group, may be called an ensemble piece. (jbl)
See also band; choir; orchestra.

entertainment
Art performed or produced for the purpose of an audience's amusement or pleasure. Art-as-entertainment is often associated with light, superficial, or commercial work, contrasting such work with art that provokes or educates. Entertainment is also associated with art that is viewed or observed, rather than art that is experienced or created (e.g., fine art), causing controversy within the field of arts education over the purposes and uses of art. In education, edutainment—teaching through forms of entertainment, such as computer games or television shows— has become popular though controversial in recent years. (em)

entrance examinations
Many institutions require further testing upon enrollment for academic placement, advising, and counseling; entrance examinations thus are used for more specific purposes than admissions tests and may be developed for institutional use only. (cf)

enumeration
Within the context of social policy, when a law enumerates categories it usually identifies types of individuals or things that need to be protected. Safe Schools bills are designed to address the needs of students who experience bullying and harassment. The bill typically identifies the types of behavior that students should be protected from, and the types of students who should be protected. Students from schools with enumerated policies report far less harassment overall than students from schools with general policies. Enumerated policies that include sexual orientation and gender identity as protected categories provide greater safety for students than those that do not. (jb2)

environmental education
A blending of various sciences and social studies topics that affect ecosystems, environmental education is the study of the circumstances and conditions by which an organism is surrounded, how the surroundings affect the organism, and how the organism affects the surroundings. The study may include the causes and effects of changes to the system, whether natural, like climate or competition, or manmade, such as population, pollution, energy, development and use, and urbanization, and the associated impacts. Subdivisions may include forestry, wildlife biology, fisheries game management, and water studies. (tw)

environmental print
Print and other graphic symbols found in daily life, such as on food packages (cereal, milk) and traffic signs. Children often start to recognize letters and words from these objects. (yu)

environmental risk
Risks from the environment that affect the well-being and development of individuals. Such risks for children can cover a broad range, including family structure, prenatal events, airborne and waterborne contaminants, diet, and even the economy of the country in which the child lives. (jb)

environmental studies (See environmental education)

epilepsy

A physical condition that occurs when there is sudden, brief disruption in the normal functioning of the brain. Epilepsy is characterized by seizures. (sr)

epistemologies, standpoint (See standpoint epistemologies)

epistemology

Philosophers historically defined epistemology as the branch of philosophy that develops theories concerning what counts as knowledge, with "knowledge" defined as that which is absolutely true. Epistemologists look at questions about the justification of people's beliefs and concern themselves with the normative status of knowledge claims. They attempt to verify claims that are made, and to prove the validity of arguments. Epistemologists attempt to establish the criteria and standards necessary to prove validity and truth. Epistemologists are concerned with what warrants the knowledge claims we make; therefore, they ask normative questions such as what counts as good evidence, not causal questions concerning how beliefs are developed. The branch of philosophy that studies questions of knowledge and truth, especially questions of justification around the questions of what is true, what we can know, and how we can know whether we in fact know it. (bt-b, jc)

See also standpoint epistemologies.

equal additions

A method of subtraction taught in U.S. schools until the mid-1900s, when it was superseded by the decomposition method. Equal additions method involves adding 10 to the units digit in the minuend and compensating by adding 10 to the 10's digit in the subtrahend to keep the difference the same. It is still used in other school systems internationally. (amr)

equal education (See educational equality)

equality

A statement or equation that has the same value or is identical to another; an equivalence relationship where congruence is preserved, namely a relationship between mathematical objects that is reflexive, symmetric, and transitive. The condition of having equal dignity, rank, or privileges with others. The fact of being on an equal footing with each member of a group, class, or society (or between members of different groups). In persons: fairness, impartiality, equity. In things: due proportion, proportionateness. The state of being equal; the idea that all individuals should be treated the same. In education, often connected to the idea of opportunity, to the idea that schools should serve the function of giving all students the same chances for success in life. (vdf, ewr, jc)

See also equity.

Equality of Educational Opportunity (1966)

Also known as the "Coleman Report," after its principal author. The Civil Rights Act of 1964 required the Commissioner of Education "to conduct a survey ... concerning the lack of availability of equal educational opportunities." Authors James S. Coleman and Ernest Q. Campbell found that traditional measures such as per-student-expenditure and student-to-teacher ratios did little to explain the academic performance of students. The main finding was that the student's family background (including parent socioeconomic status) was the best predictor of academic performance. The implications of the report's main finding stirred debate over the value of compensatory educational programs for several decades and continues to exert an influence on public policy. (dwm)

equating

In testing, the act of matching one assessment to another. Many types of equating are possible: across test versions, across test administrations, and across test scales (such as expressing a test result as a "grade equivalent"). (fd)

equation
A statement indicating that two algebraic expressions are equal. (rdk)

equilibration
The model used in Piaget's theory to describe the process of equilibrium that governs cognitive development. Information about the child's environment is assimilated by the child and becomes accommodated into cognitive structures. The end result of assimilation and accommodation is equilibrium. Disequilibrium occurs when the cognitive structures are unable to accommodate assimilated information. (vm)

equipped for the future (EFF)
A standards movement in adult education established by the National Institute for Literacy, which defines what adults need to know and be able to do in their roles as workers, family members, and citizens. (jpc)

equity
The state or condition of being fair, the idea that all individuals should be treated according to their needs and merits. In education, often connected to the idea that students' needs and abilities should be taken into account in devising educational programming. The term refers to the fairness of education and whether or not all participating stake-holders—males, females, and various population groups—receive the same benefits. (jc, jr)
See also equality.

equivalence
A key concept associated with fractions; the assigning of various names to the same fractional quantity (e.g., 2/4 and 1/2 are equivalent fractions). (ps)

equivalency
A system of providing credentials to people educated outside of school who have acquired and can demonstrate specific knowledge and skills equivalent to those acquired in the formal school system. The General Educational Development (GED) is the most well-known such credential in the United States, intended to be equivalent to completion of secondary education. (cas)

equivalent forms of equations
Having the exact same set of solutions; for example, $2x = 10$ and $x - 1 = 4$ are equivalent equations because the solution set for both equations is the same, 5. (ps)

ergonomic performance aids
Workplace designs that are meant to enhance performance by considering simultaneously the physical and psychological characteristics of workers. Often designed to ease the stress of human–technology interaction, including issues of safety and fatigue; areas of concern include illumination, temperature, noise, vibration, speech recognition, and space arrangements. (mkr)

ergonomics (See human factors engineering)

ERIC (See Educational Resources Information Center)

ERP (See EEG)

error analysis
Finding the underlying problem or error in a student's mathematical computations. Some purposes of error analysis are to identify the patterns of errors or mistakes that students make in their work and to understand why they make them so teachers can provide instruction to correct the errors. (mlf, rlk)

eschatology
An area of theological and philosophical thought concerned with the end of history, or the ultimate destiny of creation, often characterized by themes of hope,

judgment, apocalypse, and redemption. Eschatologies may be generally described as falling into one of three major categories: realized, futuristic, or proleptic. Realized eschatologies emphasize future hope that comes into being in the present moment. Futuristic eschatologies delay hope until after death, with a focus on afterlife and final reckoning. Proleptic eschatologies emphasize an experience of clarity regarding what has been, what is, and what is unfolding. Theories of what is to come, expressions of both fear and hope, can hold tremendous influence over the ways in which educators conceptualize the schooling project, particularly in regards to issues of peace, justice, and reconciliation. One's functional theology or philosophy regarding hope (or lack thereof) for the future shapes convictions and presuppositions about the exercise of power and the potential for transformation through education. (bda)

ESEA (See Elementary and Secondary Education Act)

ESL (See English as a second language)

ESOL (See English for speakers of other languages)

ESP (See English for special purposes)

essentialism

An educational theory that holds, against Progressivism, that the fundamental purpose of education (and function of schools) is to transmit a core of common knowledge and skills that all students should learn. This set of knowledge and skills is practical and related to the skill needs of the particular society (in this regard essentialism differs from perennialism's belief in the permanence of educational value). Education is also about the development of character and good habits. Schools should not dilute their effect by teaching material unrelated to either practical skill or good character. The belief that males and females differ in basic and essential ways according to nature. (jc)

See also cultural literacy; perennialism; progressivism; traditional education; vocational education.

established risk condition

Refers to disabilities, illnesses, or conditions that compromise optimal development of young children. Each individual state's early intervention system is required to provide free and appropriate services to children with established risk conditions, but what qualifies as established risk conditions is determined by the state's legislature. (kms, yb)

estimation (number)

An approximate calculation; a useful, important skill for determining the reasonableness of an answer, particularly with the increased use of calculators for computation purposes. (amr)

See also rounding.

ethic of care

Inspired by feminist scholars such as Carol Gilligan and Nel Noddings, care ethics is shaped by a relational approach to ethics, rather than a principled, rule-governed approach. If ethics insists that moral judgments must be universalizable, then caring is a moral orientation rather than an ethic, for it insists that we can only decide what is good and right within the context of the individual situation. Caring is founded in relationality, and the very act of human caring. Caring involves receptivity, a feeling with the other, and responsiveness to the other, the one cared for, prior to passing any judgment on what is the right or good thing to do. (bt-b)

See also deontological ethics; ethic of responsibility; ethics; virtue ethics.

ethic of responsibility

Carol Gilligan (1982) and Nel Noddings (1984) promoted a feminist ethic based on a Heideggerian assumption that *Sorge* or care is a prerequisite to reasonableness. Erikson claimed that caring about what happens in and to the world was a necessary prerequisite of any ethical or serious inquiry. Kantian ethics focuses too much on logical justification, utilitarian ethics too much on consequences, to accommodate the situated ethic of responsibility, which requires an empathic and careful response to others. An ethic of responsibility is more often expressed through deeds and personal stories than by logical principle or hedonistic calculus. (fh)

See also deontological ethics; ethic of care; ethics; virtue ethics.

ethical principles and codes of conduct

An organized body of guidelines and rules that govern the practice of a professional discipline or activity, such as counseling, psychology, or medicine. They most often serve as a profession's primary source for determining acceptable/unacceptable practice and behavior. They sometimes contain aspirational principles, while also containing codes of conduct that are more prescriptive and legally enforceable. (dd)

ethics

The study of how one ought to live; the study of right and wrong action, how one should act in particular situations; the study of reasons for actions being right or wrong; what is the basis for ethical judgment? The major modern divisions today are between consequentialist ethical systems that judge actions by their consequences, deontological ethical systems that judge actions by their accordance with moral laws, and feminist ethical systems that judge actions by their effects on our interpersonal relationships. (jc)

See also deontological ethics; ethic of care; ethic of responsibility; moral education; virtue ethics.

ethics, virtue (See virtue ethics)

ethnic awareness

The recognition of cultural and racial identity in individuals or groups. The ability to discern the ethnic origins of people through visual cues and other indicators is a sign of ethnic awareness. (jqa)

ethnic group

Individuals who share customs, traditions, and other cultural linkages due to their heritage and communal experiences. Members of ethnic groups have common bonds relating to social, religious, political, and economic interests and often identify with each other in many aspects of their daily life, including language, recreation, and family life. (jqa, jwc)

ethnic identity

Maintaining cultural, familial, and traditional values and recognizing and celebrating individual heritage. (jqa, jwc)

ethnic identity theory

A social theory that postulates that individuals develop their own sense of ethnic identity at different stages and that these stages are identifiable. The theory relates to the individual process of attributing personal significance and meaning to being part of an ethnic group. (jqa, jwc)

ethnic studies

The study and examination of race, tradition, custom, and language of a distinct cultural group. Ethnic studies examine the context of historically underrepresented ethnic groups to develop an appreciation and understanding of ethnically diverse subcultures in the larger society's culture. Typically, college or university courses of study that focus on the sociological, scientific, and humanistic aspects of ethnicity. (jbo, jqa, jwc)

ethnicity

A socially constructed category, based on identification of a person within a particular social group. The social group can be formed based on many factors, including religious beliefs, a common language, history, and geographic location, and even common physical appearances. A person's ethnicity is usually associated with her or his parents' ancestry. Ethnicity refers to a person's social connections with others who share much in common. (bt-b)

See also culture; multiculturalism; pluralism; race.

ethnocentrism

Placing one's ethnic group at the center of thought; the belief that one's ethnic group is the central group in society; sometimes used to indicate a belief in the superiority of one's ethnic group over all others. Sometimes terms denoting race, nationality, or region are used instead of ethnicity (e.g., Eurocentric or Afrocentric). (jn)

See also multiculturalism; pluralism.

ethnography

Though recently equated with qualitative research, ethnography is more appropriately defined as the description and analysis of the culture of a definable human group or setting. Thus one may conduct an ethnographic study of a particular group of at-risk teenagers or of the culture of a particular classroom. Ethnography originally referred to the long-term study of small homogeneous groups by anthropologists and sociologists. The primary methods employed are participant observation and formal and informal interviewing, directed at uncovering the "native's point of view." Ethnography requires a holistic approach and a focus on cultural processes and may include the analysis of written and/or photographic records. (rws)

ethnology

The area of scientific and humanistic inquiry that studies, compares, and analyzes cultures (ethnicities) and culture (social relations, organization, and structures). Often thought of by anthropologists as the theorizing and historical side of ethnography, together ethnology and

ethnography make up the subdiscipline called cultural anthropology. (jde)

ethnomathematics

The concept that considers the ways in which different modes of thought or culture may lead to different forms of mathematics, such as culturally different ways of counting, ordering, sorting, measuring, inferring, classifying, and modeling. In this way, the abandonment of notions of generality, which often cover for Eurocentric particularities, can lead to the acquisition of an anthropological awareness of the ways in which different cultures can produce mathematics. Can also be considered mathematical knowledge expressed in the language code of a given sociocultural group. Different cultural expression of mathematical ideas, manifested in written or nonwritten form, oral or nonoral form. An everyday mathematics that allows individuals to function effectively in the world and, contrasted with academic mathematics, which is taught in schools, allows for elite management of a society's ideas, insights, and knowledge sets. Architects, engineers, accountants, and children have distinct ways of reasoning, of measuring, of coding, and of classifying; each accordingly has developed their own ethnomathematics. A conceptual category that has emerged from the dialectical discourse between mathematics, education, politics, and culture. It includes and examines the interconnectedness of mathematics with all other disciplines, recognizing that while mathematical ideas are expressed in all cultures, those ideas vary as they are expressed in the context of each culture. (hfs, slr)

See also Eurocentrism.

etic(s)

Understandings and perceptions of cultural reality that are formulated independently of the members of a culture. Etic includes descriptions, analyses, and judgments of culture that are produced from the point of view and conceptualizations of outsiders (often social scientists). An etic perspective emphasizes the categories, analytical thought processes, descriptions, and models considered meaningful to outside observers (even when done by natives trained in such outside schemata). Etic constructions of reality are epistemological, not ontological, in nature. The ultimate arbiters and judges of etic constructions are social scientists guided by "scientific" standards. (jde)

See also emic(s).

ETS (See Educational Testing Service)

euclidean space
N-dimensional space exhibiting zero curvature; based on the four undefined terms and five axioms proposed by Euclid. It uses the Pythagorean distance metric, and, as a three-dimensional space, it functionally models the world around us. (ey)

eudaimonia
In classical Greek, "happiness." The word *eudaimonia* derives etymologically from *eu* (good) and *daimon* (god, demigod), and thus suggests a state of blessedness; literally, having a good god within one. The gods were thought to be supremely happy, and philosophers in the Socratic tradition held that human beings are happiest when they devote their lives to the exercise of the most divine element in themselves, namely their intellect, in accordance with the highest virtue, namely sophia or contemplative wisdom. (rc)

eurhythmics
Used on its own for introducing children to music or as a methodological tool in a particular approach to music education. Eurhythmics involves a physical response to what one hears, engaging the child in active improvisation as she encounters live or recorded music. Developed by Swiss musician and music educator Emile Jaques-Dalcroze, Eurhythmics has been included in many versions of music education and was frequently employed in early childhood classrooms of the Progressive era. (jd)

Eurocentric curriculum
A curriculum that emphasizes European literature and history to the exclusion of other cultural representations. Based on the assumption that most of the world's greatest scientific, cultural, and artistic developments have occurred in Europe. Proponents of this curriculum are often referred to as Western traditionalists. (jqa, jwc)

Eurocentrism
A perspective that reflects historical dominance in development and achievement from a European and Western position and excludes contributions from non-European cultures to world civilization. This perspective biases European historical development and deprecates the contributions of non-European cultures to world civilization. (jbo)

evaluation
The systematic investigation into the process or outcomes of the implementation of a particular educational program, also synonymous with "program evaluation": such investigations answer calls for accountability, assist in decision making, aid program development and planning, and serve research. Current approaches to evaluation (in this programmatic sense) stress a comprehensive, naturalistic methodology that goes beyond sole reliance on quantitative analysis. Testing or measurement: evaluation is often used synonymously to refer to all forms of general student testing. In early childhood education, an identification procedure utilized to determine the current status of a child in each of the developmental areas: communication, social/emotional, adaptive, and physical. In some of the professional literature *evaluation* is used interchangeably with *assessment*. (sd, xss)

See also program review.

evaluation assessment
Screening to determine individual characteristics and current level of functioning. (sr)

Even Start program
A subsection of Title I of the ESEA, added in 1988, to assist children and adults from low-income families to achieve the revised and more challenging state content standards and student performance standards of Goals 2000. Even Start provides adult literacy training, along with childhood education, to provide for a family learning experience. It was designed to break intergenerational cycles of poverty and illiteracy by funding family literacy programs that provide early childhood education, adult literacy, and parenting education. (ecr, las)

Event-Related Potential (See EEG)

Everson v. Board of Education, Irving Township, 330 U.S. 1 (1947)
A U.S. Supreme Court case challenging a New Jersey law permitting use of public money to bus students to school, including schools run by the Catholic Church. In a 5–4 decision, with the majority employing a "child-benefit theory," the Court ruled that the law did not violate the First Amendment "wall of separation" between church and state. The case generated hostility toward Catholics for their use of public funds and complicated ongoing congressional efforts toward federal aid to education. (le)

evolution
A biological theory explaining the development and variation of species throughout geologic history. Although Charles Darwin (1809–1882) is typically associated with evolution, the idea of life evolving over time can be traced to Greek thought. Darwin proposed *natural selection* as the process through which evolutionary change occurred. Natural selection is a process of adaptation through interaction with the environment and the passing of inherited traits. Darwin's contemporary Alfred Russel Wallace (1823–1913) is also credited for independently developing a similar theory. In 1858, Darwin and Wallace coauthored *On the Tendency of Species to Form Varieties,* and *On the Perpetuation of Varieties and Species by Natural Selection.* At present, evolutionary theories are demonstrated through genetic processes. (vkh)
See also Scopes Monkey Trial.

examination
Exercises used to assess knowledge or skills. Often a formal set of questions intended to test given information, although the term may include any process of testing ability or achievement. (jw)

examination, final
The primary way of assigning course grades in most undergraduate courses; in large institutions end-of-course exams may be constructed for departmental use across classes, and systemwide exams may be used by multicampus institutions. (cf)

examination, final oral
An examination given to a candidate for a graduate degree, usually a doctor's degree, held under the auspices of the student's committee. The candidate must defend his or her thesis and otherwise satisfy the committee that he or she has met all requirements for a doctoral degree. (cf)

examination, placement
An examination given to decide placement, with or without college-level credit. It is usually taken by prospective college students prior to their first enrollment in college. (cf)

examination, preliminary
An examination given to determine the student's eligibility for candidacy for a degree; eligibility traditionally consists of written and oral examinations. (cf)

examining-and-grading policies

The stated or implied procedures followed in testing academic achievement in course work and the assignment of numerical or alphabetical grades to convey the student's accomplishment of course requirements; often issued in the form of guidelines or suggestions. (cf)

exceptional

A term used to describe students who are considerably different in their learning or behavioral styles from their peers. They may be intellectually gifted or have cognitive, physical, or emotional limitations. Exceptional students may have unique needs that require special educational interventions. (jqa, jwc)

exchange programs

Agreements made between schools, colleges, or universities to allow students from one institution to attend another for a limited time while still eligible to earn academic credit from the home institution. Exchange programs are also available to teachers and faculty to undertake research, study and/or teaching in another setting in order to improve skills and exchange ideas and practices. Exchange programs are established under formal agreements by organizations and governments, and those involving institutions outside of the United States in cooperation with U.S. institutions are subject to government regulations. (jw)

executive education

Professional development institutes for managers and leaders in their fields, not usually resulting in an academic degree. Often refers to programs for business executives, but may also refer to programs for leaders and managers in other fields (including government and education). (ln)

See also institute.

executive function

Executive functions are a loosely defined collection of processes involved in regulating cognition and are particularly necessary for activities such as planning, decision making, abstract thinking, and rule acquisition. They include the focusing on important information, the suppression of irrelevant information, and the temporary binding of relevant information. Executive functions are studied by neuroscientists and psychologists. In neuroscience, executive functions historically were closely associated with activity in the frontal lobes in general and the prefrontal cortex in particular, but in recent years this conceptualization is increasingly being replaced by a systems view of wider cortical distribution. Conceptually, executive functions are closely related to certain aspects of attention, such as selective attention, as well as certain aspects of memory, such as working memory. (mf2)

exercise physiology

Also called exercise science, this is the study of the physiological responses of the body due to exercise. (rf)

exercise science (See exercise physiology)

existential intelligence

Described by Howard Gardner in his Theory of Multiple Intelligences as the ability of some individuals to focus philosophical thought on issues relating to life, death, and other existential realities. (jwc)

existentialism

Celebrates the uniqueness of the individual in opposition to universal conceptions of humankind. It originated as existential thought in the work of Søren Kierkegaard (1813–1855) and Friedrich Nietzsche (1844–1900). Later formulations were developed by Martin Heidegger (1889–1976), Karl Jaspers (1883–1969), Jean-Paul Sartre (1905–1980), Simone de Beauvoir (1908–1986), and Albert Camus (1913–1960). Existentialism identifies personal concerns and values as the determinants of ethical action, rather than human nature and the application of abstract principles to ethical dilemmas. Recognition of responsibility for one's actions causes angst (dread and anxiety), which, according to existentialism, is the motivation for living with authentic recognition of one's freedom. (lkk)

exosystem
In an ecological model of child development (Bronfenbrenner, 1979), a community system that exists outside of the family ("exo," outside of) but which, because of its pervasiveness, has a major impact on the child's socialization. Typical exosystems include school boards, city councils, and churches. (ecr)

expanded notation
Refers to the writing of numbers such that the numeric value of each digit is highlighted; for example, $327 = 3 \times 100 + 2 \times 10 + 7 \times 1$. During the new math movement, emphasis was placed on writing numbers in expanded form under the assumption that this would lead to increased understanding of computational procedures. (amr)

expanding communities
A curriculum design in which children learn about various aspects of life in the context of ever-widening realms of experience, usually geographic realms. Sometimes called "expanding horizons," or "expanding environments," the curriculum approach was popularized by Paul R. Hanna through several elementary social studies textbook series published from the 1930s through the 1970s. Though widely criticized, expanding communities remains the pervasive design for elementary social studies textbooks and curriculum frameworks. (jrs)

expanding environments (See expanding communities)

expanding horizons (See expanding communities)

expansive character education
First proposed by Mclaughin and Halstead (1999), this term refers to forms of character education often associated with virtue ethics and progressive pedagogical approaches. Expansive character education is, for example, associated with a focus on students' deliberative capacities. Prominent proponents include David Carr (1991) and Eamon Callan (1997). (dpb)

See also nonexpansive character education.

experienced curriculum
The course of study experienced by those taught: including the explicit curriculum, the operationalized curriculum, the hidden curriculum, and the null curriculum; what is learned, what meaning is made from what is learned, and how the experiences are sewn together to construct a scheme of the world and the individual's place in it. This curriculum differs from all the others in that the learner may accept, reject, and/or modify these other curricula and emerge with a learning quite different from the meanings of these other curricula. Thus, these other curricula do not, necessarily, mandate what the learner ultimately knows, learns, or believes. (db-j)

See also explicit curriculum; hidden curriculum; null curriculum; operationalized curriculum.

experience-dependent neuronal development
The nervous system requires information from the environment to develop the structures needed for healthy and adaptive behavior. These neuronal structures are modified and refined over time as the individual continues to experience the environment. Experience dependence enables the nervous system to react skillfully to familiar situations (through refinement), while retaining the flexibility to change in the face of new surroundings (through modification). (dh)

experiential education

Experiential education stems from a constructivist philosophy, in which humans create knowledge based on their life experiences. The impact of learning from an experience is dependent on the level of meaningfulness to the learner. It is characterized by differences in (a) relevancy to the learner, (b) emotional reaction to the experience, (c) physical activity involved in the experience, (d) interaction with others, and (e) level of critical thinking skills used. Experiential education is most commonly thought of as learning experiences that elicit higher levels of these characteristics. Four types of formal learning situations are frequently termed experiential: vocational education, service-learning, outdoor education (including adventure, challenge, and environmental education), and less commonly, specifically designed classroom activities. Prominent philosophers in this area include Herbert Spencer, John Dewey, and David Kolb. (sls)

experiential learning

Any learning process in which experience (especially as distinguished from didactic transmission of information) plays a key role. In adult education, this can be learning that takes place outside of the classroom (internships, community-based activities); informal learning (from hobbies, volunteer activities, travel, etc.); or simulations, games, outdoor activities, and the like. Cyclical model of learning, in which learners reflect on experiences to gain new knowledge and insight. Gained knowledge and insights are then tested and modified and then applied to different situations. (jb, ea, alm)

experiential therapy

This term actually refers to a broad range of therapies derived from both existential and humanistic psychology. The process by which change occurs involves the therapist actively experiencing what the client is undergoing with respect to the client's thoughts and feelings so that he or she may help the client integrate past experiences and subjective phenomena into a more realistic and healthy self-concept in the present. (tsw)

Experimental Schools Program

Established in 1970 by the U.S. Office of Education under the provisions of the Cooperative Research Act of 1954, this was a six-year project aimed at testing the hypothesis that lasting educational improvement is best facilitated by a comprehensive approach to educational change. The ESP provided federal support to 18 urban and rural school districts across the country that aimed to model systemic approaches to educational reform for schools serving low-income students, including flagship programs in Berkeley, California, Franklin Pierce (WA) School District, and Minneapolis, Minnesota. (sw)

experimental theater

Theater that breaks accepted conventions of form, content, or stage techniques. While there is a wide range of theater forms that could be categorized as experimental, the common thread through most experimental—or avant-garde—theater is its contrast to, and reaction against, theatrical naturalism and realism. For example, an experimental theater piece might utilize unconventional forms of expression or abstract modes of action, creating work that is impossible to view from a purely logical or rational perspective. (em)

expert system

A computer program that simulates intelligent problem-solving behavior in a given area of expertise. The computer program (the "expert") asks the user for information about a problem, matches that information to a database containing rules to guide the decision process, arrives at a decision, and reports the solution to the user. (chb)

explicit curriculum

Also known as "formal curriculum." A written plan of educational action for any kind of learning community (children, adults, mixed) and found in many venues (classrooms, schools, school districts, and private organizations, e.g., Sunday schools, YMCAs and YWCAs, and Outward Bound programs). Three examples of the explicit curriculum include: (1) district curriculum guides (the most typical explicit curriculum), which usually focuses on content and performance standards for particular grade levels, (2) university or college syllabi, which typically contain lists of materials (e.g., books and readings), content, calendars of events, and assignments, and (3) non-school program guides (e.g., Outward Bound), which typically include general statements of the knowledge and skills intent of the program along with course experiences. (db-j)

See also experienced curriculum; hidden curriculum; null curriculum; operationalized curriculum.

exploratory career education

An educational program, usually in middle or junior high school, providing general introductory instruction about technologies for career exploratory and guidance purposes rather than preparation for a specific occupation. It is intended to lay a foundation for future career choices. The first phase of a work-based learning program designed to offer students opportunities to evaluate their abilities as workers and to become familiar with job requirements. (sa, db)

exponential notation

The method of representing the repeated multiplication of a number or expression. A shorter way of writing an expression times itself a specific number of times. The number that is repeatedly multiplied is called the base, and the amount of times it is multiplied is called the exponent. (gtm)

expression/expressivity

The manifestation and/or representation of inner experience or emotion. Expression in the arts—performing, visual, or literary—is achieved through resources such as gesture, facial configuration, shape and direction of lines and forms, and usage of metaphors and other descriptive language. Leo Tolstoy described the artistic experience as one in which artists pour their emotions into their work to be re-experienced by their audience. Cognitivists like Nelson Goodman see expression as an aesthetic achievement mastered by artists and recognized by viewers without any necessary exchange of felt emotion. Nonetheless, young children's artistic performances are thought to be highly expressive apart from any consideration of their respective mastery of artistic skills. (jd)

expressionism

An artistic movement in the late 19th and early 20th centuries in which works of art and literature focused more on the symbolic, often unconventional representation of inner feeling than on imitative techniques. Works of visual art fall within the category of expressionism if they seek to evoke an emotion rather than an objective representation of the subject. The artist can abstract or distort the formal qualities of the work to create, for example, discomfort in the viewer. Examples of expressionism can be found in paintings such as *The Starry Night* by Vincent van Gogh and *The Scream* by Edvard Munch. (ap)

expulsion

The most severe form of discipline doled out by a school system, in which a student is permanently removed from a school and is no longer allowed to attend or participate in any school- or district-sponsored classes or activities. Such discipline is the result of a single significant illegal or dangerous action on the part of the student, such as possession of a loaded firearm or the assault of a teacher or staff person, or when there is a history of significant misconduct that threatens the education, safety, or well-being of other students, teachers, or staff. (ms)

extended day kindergarten
Educational program for five-year-olds that lasts longer than the traditional half-day. Extended day kindergarten can last a full school day (equal to the school day of older elementary children) or longer, including a full day of care for children who require it. (ecr)

extension agent
An employee either of a county government or a land grant university whose job it is to demonstrate innovative agricultural methods to willing farmers. Extension programs have been integral parts of land grant universities since passage of the Smith-Lever Act in 1914. One who designs and delivers services and programs through the Cooperative Extension Service. A teacher within an extension education program. (lr, chb, jpc)

extension education
The engagement function of a land-grant university that provides community-based career exploration and development in informal educational settings through the 4-H Youth Development Program. Also, adult education focused on the needs of farmers and rural populations. In the United States, this education is provided by local cooperative extension services that help farmers learn from agricultural research. Education offered by the Cooperative Extension Service; university-based continuing education. (jpc, chb)

extensive quantities
Numbers that arise through the act of counting or measuring. (amr)
    See also intensive quantities.

external degree program
A college-level program designed to reduce or eliminate barriers of time or place for adult learners; in some instances, such a program awards degrees based on assessment of learners' competence or ability to perform rather than on their having completed a sequence of formal course work. (chb)

external locus of control
Refers to the belief that events and reinforcers in life are controlled by external factors such as the behavior of others, chance, or fate. In the extreme, an external locus of control may be accompanied by a sense of powerlessness, resignation, or lack of responsibility for one's life. Locus of control can be conceptualized on a continuum from external to internal. (tsw, mgg)

external representations (See representation)

externships
A work-based learning experience where students shadow one or more people in specific occupations to gain understanding of typical work responsibilities and to connect information learned in the classroom to specific occupations. (jb, ea)

extracurricular activities
Student organization pursuits that may be social, athletic, or avocational (e.g., sororities, basketball teams, chess clubs, etc). (cf)

extranet
Similar to the Internet in that it uses the same technology, but the accessibility is limited. An extranet links an organization's own intranet to its business partners' intranets and provides secure access to the shared part of a business's information or operations. (hh)
    See also Internet; intranet.

extrinsic reward
Extrinsic rewards refer to any experience, tangible or intangible, that comes from an external source in the child's environment

and that has the power of increasing the behavior's occurrence. For the extrinsic reward to be effective, it needs to be provided immediately after the occurrence of the behavior so the child will be able to make the connection between his or her behavior and the reward received. For example, smiling by the mother may be an extrinsic reward for a young child who is seeking her attention. The child who repeats making funny faces in order to see the smile in the mother's face is likely to have been extrinsically rewarded by the mother's smile. (xss, yb)

extroversion

A broad personality trait that describes the amount and the intensity of social interaction, activity level, and need for external stimulation. Extroverted individuals are often outgoing, sociable, enthusiastic, and active; they do not particularly enjoy being alone or inactive. These individuals are most comfortable in social situations and being surrounded by people. (tsw)

See also extroversion-introversion.

extroversion-introversion

One of the "Big Five" personality elements studied by Eysenck and Jung; refers to the relative degree to which a person is outgoing and interactive with other people and their preferences for solitary or group situations. Individuals do not fall strictly into one category, although one direction usually dominates. (tsw)

F

face-to-face education

A form of instruction that occurs when the teacher and learner are both physically present in the same location at the same time. The primary advantages of face-to-face education are its ability to create greater familiarity and immediacy in the teaching/learning process and foster more supportive professional networks that can serve as important sources of future learning and ongoing professional development. A disadvantage can be the expense associated with bringing individual learners together in a common location, particularly when less-costly, technology-enabled alternatives may be available. (jz)

face-to-face testing

Tests given (often one-on-one) where the examinee and examiner can see one another are generally called "face-to-face." Such tests can replace or supplement paper-and-pencil or computer-delivered group testing. Face-to-face testing is common when the skills cannot be rendered in written form (e.g., musical performances), when the test taker is not able to respond in written form (e.g., due to a disability), or when the test task itself requires response in oral form (e.g., when testing spoken proficiency in a foreign language). Face-to-face testing allows a combination

of skills in a rich and productive manner but suffers disadvantages in strain on personnel time and consequently on resources. (kh1)

facilitative communication

For individuals with severe communicative disabilities, a system in which an aide assists by physically helping an individual stabilize or move his or her arm to type on or point to a communication device, although the content of the output is assumed to be uninfluenced by the aide's presence. (jcp)

facilitator

Someone who provides support to a learner or group of learners in their process of discovering information or finding solutions to a problem rather than simply providing information or answers. A teacher or trainer who provides opportunities to learn rather than direct instruction. Facilitation is often aimed at fostering adults' capacity for self-direction. (alm, jpc, las)

facilities audit

A comprehensive evaluation of facilities, including buildings and infrastructure, used to identify and prioritize deferred maintenance repair and rehabilitation projects, which are beyond the scope of routine preventive maintenance programs. Results are often expressed as a ratio of accumulated deferred maintenance costs to current facilities replacement value. (cf)

fact

A verifiable occurrence or existence, which can include an event, statistic, name, date, place, and so on. Facts can serve as a basis of theory or ideas and can suggest conclusions and new hypotheses for further study. In schools, factual learning lends itself to memorization and often serves as the core of lessons. Teachers are encouraged to link facts by means of themes or questions that help make the facts more memorable and applicable. (igb)

factitious disorder

A category of mental disorders in which an individual intentionally produces or feigns physiological or psychological signs and symptoms. This may, for example, involve fabricating health complaints, exaggerating preexisting medical conditions, or inflicting injuries on oneself. Individuals with factitious disorders are motivated by a need to assume the sick role, rather than by a desire to benefit from any secondary gains or external reinforcers (as would be the case with "malingering"). (ktc)

See also malingering.

factor analysis

Factor analysis is a statistical procedure that is often used to reduce the number of observed variables to a much smaller number of variables (factors) based on a classical test theory (CTT) approach. Observed variables are assumed to have underlying latent variables called factors. Factor analysis is often used to identify observed variables that are measuring similar constructs and improve the interpretability of the observed variables. There are two types of factor analysis used in practice: exploratory factor analysis and confirmatory factor analysis. Exploratory factor analysis is a data-driven process in which

a researcher allows data to reveal its underlying factors. Confirmatory factor analysis typically starts with a hypothetical structure that defines the relationships among the observed variables. (gl)

factors

Two or more numbers or polynomials that are multiplied together. Each of these is called a factor of the product. (rdk)

faculty

Those responsible for the administration of and instruction in a given school, college, or university. The instructors of an academic institution. (jw)

faculty development

A general term for programs and activities organized to improve the teaching effectiveness and professional responsibilities of college and university faculty members; includes on-campus programs and services as well as statewide and regional efforts. Faculty development activities may take the form of instructional development, professional development, and organizational development. (cf)

FAFSA (Free Application for Federal Student Aid)

The form that students (both undergraduate and graduate) must fill out each year in order to apply for federal aid, including grants, scholarships, student loans, and work-study programs. (sn)

family

A traditional nuclear family consists of a mother, a father, and any offspring, while a traditional extended family expands to include grandparents, aunts, uncles, and cousins. The definition of "family" is changing, however, to include various other structures, such as single-parent homes, custodial grandparents, same-sex couples and their children, blended families, and stepfamilies. Families are integral to the health and well-being of their children and should be included in decision-making processes and all aspects of their children's care. (kdc)

family and consumer sciences education

Educational programs focusing on empowering individuals and families across the life span to successfully manage the challenges of living and working in a diverse, global environment. The mission of family and consumer sciences education is to prepare students for family life, work life, and careers in family and consumer sciences through teaching nutrition and food preparation, parenting and child development, resource and time management, consumer education, housing and home furnishing, personal clothing management, human relationships, and family development. (jb, ch)

family day care

Care for small groups of children in the caregiver's own home. Children learn in mixed-age groups, in an environment that more closely simulates being cared for within a family than in a large-group, center-based setting. (jlj)

Family Day Care Rating Scale (FDCRS)

A standardized instrument for the evaluation of in-home child care settings developed by Thelma Harms and Richard Clifford in 1989. The form utilizes 32 items to comprehensively evaluate the care provided to children in the homes of the nonparental caregivers. (kdc)

Family Educational Rights and Privacy Act (FERPA)

A federal law that gives parents the right to access their children's education records, the right to seek to have the records amended, and the right to have some control over the disclosure of personally identifiable information. When a student turns 18 years old, or enters a postsecondary institution at any age, the rights under FERPA transfer from the parents to the student. In higher education, clarification regarding compliance issues has been necessary, and communications with parents who discover that they do not have automatic access to the records of their offspring have been needed. The FERPA statute is found at 20 U.S.C. § 1232g, and the FERPA regulations are found at 34 CFR Part 99. The law also prevents a school from disclosing a student's educational record without prior written consent, except in cases of appropriate administrative needs such as school transfer, accreditation, financial aid, health and safety, legal requirement, audit, and institutional analysis. A school's right to disclose directory information may be blocked upon request of the parent or eligible student. This law applies to schools that receive federal funds through the U.S. Department of Education. (ms, sn)

family literacy

An educational program in which the literacy needs of both parents and their children are addressed. Family literacy includes programs in which parents and children learn together, and those where they learn separately but parents are given instruction in how to support their children's learning. (jpc)

family therapy

A type of psychotherapy that focuses on the larger family unit. The overriding goal of therapy is to improve the interactional and behavioral patterns of the large family unit and/or subgroups of the unit. The term family therapy refers to the process and not a specific form of therapy, as there are many forms of family therapy, including Behavioral Family Therapy, Structural Family Therapy, and Object Relations Family Therapy, to name a few. (tsw)

fantasy play

Imaginative, freely determined activities, with some to no foundation in reality. Because these activities are not restricted by any parameters of reality, children are free to explore and be inventive without externally enforced limitations or guidelines, also implying without risk of failure. (db1)

farm residents

People who live and work on farms. Farm residents comprise a decreasing proportion of the rural population, given demographic factors such as the growth of corporate farming and the net inflow of nonfarm people to rural America in the 1990s. (lr)

Farrington v. Tokushige, 273 U.S. 284 (1927)

A decision of the U.S. Supreme Court that upheld a Ninth Circuit Court decision affirming the constitutional right of parents to send their children to Japanese language schools. Beginning in 1920, the Hawaii territorial legislature had enacted laws designed to abolish privately owned Japanese language schools, which enrolled over 20,000 students. The schools filed suit, and the case eventually reached the Ninth Circuit Court. Basing its decision on Supreme Court precedents *Meyer v. Nebraska, Bartels v. Iowa,* and *Pierce v. Society of Sisters,* the Court declared that parents had the right to direct the education of their children free of prohibitive restrictions. (eht)

FDCRS (See Family Day Care Rating Scale)

federal education policy

Federal education policy is set forth by the U.S. Department of Education as a plan or course of action intended to influence and determine decisions, actions, and other matters of public education. Federal education policy regulates many areas, notably financial aid to students of higher education, special education regulations, civil rights laws, and student assessment testing. Individual states have the option to follow federal education policy but risk losing federal funding if they decide not to abide by it. (dm)

Federal Equal Access Act

Passed by Congress in 1984, the Equal Access Act guarantees that no secondary school that receives federal financial assistance shall be allowed to discriminate against or deny the gathering or organization of students based on religious, political, philosophical, or content reasons if the school also allows a limited open forum to other student groups. The act indicates that the gatherings must be student-initiated and voluntary, without sponsorship by the school or government, may not interfere with the workings of the school, and may not be conducted, controlled, or regularly attended by non-school persons. Schools do retain the right to ensure order and discipline and the safety of students and faculty. (ms)

Federal Indian Boarding Schools

Introduced in the late 1870s by the U.S. Bureau of Indian Affairs, boarding schools were favored over reservation day schools, because boarding schools were thought to be more effective at separating Indian children from tribal ways of life. The curriculum consisted of a mixture of English and other academic subjects, vocational (farm or household) work, and religious or moral instruction. Native Americans objected to the schools' strong assimilationist goals. By the early 1900s the boarding schools fell into disfavor, and the 1928 Meriam Report influenced the Bureau to emphasize day schools. (klj)

feeding skills

Skills associated with eating and drinking, such as sucking, chewing, and swallowing, and ability in using utensils to obtain nourishment. (kms)

Feinberg Law

Law passed in 1949 in New York stating that any person who was an employee of the New York public school system and a member of an organization that promoted or advocated the overthrow of the U.S. government by unlawful means would be disqualified and removed from their employment. This Cold War era law was upheld in 1952 in *Adler v. Board of Education,* 342 U.S. 485, but later reversed in 1967 in *Keyishian v. Board of Regents,* 385 U.S. 589. (ks2)

fellow
The holder of a fellowship; a member of a learned literary or scientific society; in some universities, a member or trustee of the corporation. (cf)

fellowship
A nontaxable gift of money to support inquiry on the part of students in their field of interest and to provide for their educational expenses and for some or all of their living expenses. (cf)

fellowship, research
A fellowship that requires that a portion of the fellow's time be spent in research. It differs from a research assistantship in that the research is done not for remuneration but as a part of his or her educational program; therefore the income is not taxable. (cf)

fellowship, teaching
A fellowship that requires that a certain percentage of the fellow's time be spent in teaching. It differs from a teaching assistantship in that the teaching is done not for remuneration but as a part of his or her educational program and is therefore not taxable. (cf)

female-to-male (See transsexual)

feminism
There are many different feminist perspectives, but for all the variety that exists there are still some basic concerns all feminists share. These are concerns for the well-being and equal treatment of women and girls, and a valuation of the study of women and girls as an important, worthwhile research topic. Feminists view gender as a socially constructed category in need of continual critique. They argue that men in patriarchal societies have historically described themselves in contrast to women and have placed women in an inferior, secondary, "other" role, as the second sex (Simone de Beauvoir). (bt-b)

feminist pedagogy
A framework for teaching and learning that rejects the assumption of a universal, objective reality as perpetuated by socially privileged groups (e.g., straight white men). Feminist pedagogy emphasizes collaborative and self-critical analyses of the interaction of subjective experiences. (smh, wpa)

feminist theory
A critical theory relating to the unique aspects of women in society. Generally applied to issues of the oppression of women, feminist theorists examine the relationships between gender, politics, empowerment, employment, sex, race, class, and every other aspect affecting women in society with the intent of promoting equality and social justice. (jqa, jwc)

feminist therapy
A theoretical orientation that emphasizes recognition of the societal, cultural, and political contexts of individuals' lives and the effect these contexts have on the issues that bring people into counseling. It includes awareness of individual and societal biases related to race, class, gender, and sexual orientation. Foundational aspects of this orientation include, but are not limited to, challenging the harmful effects of oppression and privilege, establishing an equal power base within the therapeutic relationship, encouraging sociopolitical activism to bring about societal change, and emphasizing the client's capacity for self-healing and self-nurturing. (llf, emm)

FERPA (See Family Educational Rights and Privacy Act)

field-based teacher education

Teacher preparation programs characterized by extensive field experiences in school settings organized to foster a close connection between theories of teaching and practices of teaching. Field-based teacher education is largely a response to education reports of the 1990s, such as those by the Holmes Group and the National Network of Educational Renewal, which advocated substantial changes in teacher education to better prepare educators for effective teaching. In field-based teacher education, field placements support preservice teacher learning through expert coaching by a mentor teacher who offers modeling, coplanning, frequent feedback, and repeated opportunities to practice and reflect. (sld, ddr)

fieldnotes

Broadly conceived, fieldnotes are the written record produced by qualitative researchers doing fieldwork. Fieldnotes consist of researchers' observations of, personal reactions to, reflections on, and preliminary theorizing about, the people, behavior, and context they are studying. Fieldnotes usually include the rough notes recorded during the observation or interview, and the more comprehensive account constructed with the aid of the rough notes after the researcher has left the scene. Fieldnotes are sometimes categorized into descriptive notes, personal notes, and theoretical notes. (rws)

field trip

School-directed time outside of the classroom setting, typically off-campus, when students utilize resources found beyond the school or study a subject in its functional or natural setting. These trips are typically undertaken for educational purposes (to museums, laboratories, etc.) but may be for entertainment purposes as well. (jw)

fieldwork

Refers to research done by qualitative practitioners who travel to the "real-world" settings they wish to study. Though fieldwork originally referred to ethnographic studies conducted by anthropologists, it is now more broadly applied to any studies conducted in naturalistic settings that employ participant observation and contextual interviewing. (rws)

final exam (See examination, final)

final oral examination (See examination, final oral)

financial aid

Financial aid represents a monetary resource for eligible students to gain an education who otherwise would be unable to do so. Financial aid resources assist students who do not have the financial means to meet the full cost of attendance at an educational institution. Types of financial aid can be scholarships and/ or grants, which students do not have to repay, or loans, which students do have to repay. Financial aid programs administered by the U.S. Department of Education typically provide 70 percent of all postsecondary student financial assistance (over $40 billion a year). The most common types of financial aid are Federal Pell Grants (grants that students do not have to repay), subsidized or unsubsidized Federal Stafford Loans (loans that students have to repay), Federal Plus (Parent) Loans (loans that parents have to repay), Campus-Based Supplemental Educational Opportunity Grants (grants that students do not have to repay), Federal Work-Study (federal monies students can earn through work-study jobs that do not have to be repaid), and/or Perkins Loans (low-interest loans that students must repay). (tp)

fine arts

From the French beaux-arts. Fine art is regarded as that which has stood the test of time and epitomizes artistic achievement, as opposed to low art, often regarded as "mass" or "popular" culture. High art consists of the meticulous expression in fine materials of refined or noble sentiment, appreciation of the former depending on such things as intelligence, social standing, educated taste, and a willingness to be challenged. The fine arts include drawing, painting, sculpture, and fine printmaking. Providing an aesthetic experience is the primary purpose of the fine arts. (kpb)

fine motor skills

Movements that utilize the small muscles of the body, usually the hands and/or fingers, for performance. (rf)

finger play

Hand movement routines typically associated with rhythm and/or rhyme, which support fine motor development, a sense of rhythm, and the cognitive task of ordering narrative events in the context of having fun. (db1)

finite

Numerically understood as a fixed amount of objects that can be ascribed a specific whole number. Generally understood as a quality of things that have boundary or limited capacity. (gtm)

fiscal year

A period of one year, not necessarily corresponding with the school year or calendar year, for which the financial program is set up, and at the end of which financial accounts are closed and reports made, usually July 1 to June 30. (cf)

fishbowl

A teaching or training technique in which a small group of participants sit in the middle of a larger group and discuss a question or issue while members of the larger group listen. Under rules agreed to in advance, participants in the larger group can change places with those in the small group. At the end of the fishbowl exercise, the whole group analyzes the discussion. (jpc)

fitness test

Assessment used to obtain a measure of one's level of fitness. Test items may include the following: muscular strength, flexibility, endurance, aerobic capacity, and body composition. (rf)

FITNESSGRAM®

A comprehensive, criterion referenced (compare scores to a health standard, not to other children) fitness test battery for children and adolescents, often used in school physical education. The items on the test are designed to test cardiorespiratory fitness, muscular strength, muscular endurance, flexibility, and body composition. (kpr)

flannelboard

Instructional equipment often used in early childhood group instruction, designed as a flat surface covered with a felted fabric to give it a "gripping" quality that allows a teacher to display images mounted on a similar felted fabric by adding and removing them as desired. This is useful in allowing children to re-create the sequence of events such as those in a story, or for focusing on a number or letter. (db1)

flexible grouping

A strategy for differentiating instruction that accounts for variability in learning outcomes and asynchronicity in academic skill or development. Posited as an alternative to "tracking" or more static ability grouping models, in which students are scheduled according to performance against standardized measures for the entire duration of an academic term, flexible grouping acknowledges that some students may excel in some components of a course of study but not in others. Thus, through arranging instructional grouping in a variety of shifting patterns (whole group, small group, pairs, individual, etc.), teachers are better able to provide appropriate and respectful challenge to all students. (bda)

flexible scheduling

The scheduling of instruction and activities that may vary from day to day, in contrast to the traditional fixed schedule that does not vary from day to day. (bba)

Flexner Report

The official title of this 1910 report is *Medical Education in the United States and Canada*, but it is often referred to by its author's last name, Abraham Flexner (1866–1959). The report is one of the first published surveys of North American medical schools. It was prepared for and published by the Carnegie Foundation for the Advancement of Teaching. It ranked medical schools (and hospitals) into three categories, ranging from best to worst, with a letter grade of an A, B, or C. The Flexner Report is considered a catalyst in the reform of North American medical education, serving as an instrument in institutional standardization. (cm!)

flow

The intense level of engagement experienced by individuals deeply engaged in such pleasurable activities as art making. Coined in the late 20th century by the psychologist Mihaly Csikszentmihalyi, flow has become a familiar term among psychologists and educators in the arts. It is described as optimal experience in which self-consciousness, worry, and any feelings of inadequacy disappear. Children engaged in pretend play exhibit flow in their apparent disregard for anything around them, even as they meet the expectations of their fluid and rule-bound systems of pretense. Flow can also be observed in sports, rituals, pageantry, and children's games. (jd)

fluency

Fluency is a quality of skillful speaking and reading. In reading, fluency is demonstrated through reading texts with appropriate speed, accuracy, and prosody (or expression). (jdc)

fMRI (See functional Magnetic Resonance Imaging)

focus group

A group interview on a particular topic, led by a trained moderator. The group typically consists of 5 to 12 people who have an interest in or experience with the topic; the goal of the focus group is to provide useful insights on the topic. (mkr)

fold culture

The result of blending a variety of cultures into new patterns. (jrw)

folk art/music

Art or music created by ordinary people, often without the benefits or constraints of formalized or institutional art training. Folk art may involve craft processes (e.g., quilting) and is closely tied to the artistic traditions of the local (often homogeneous) community in which it is produced. Much of American folk painting is distinguished by repetitive designs, flat depictions of space and objects, and bold forms and colors (noted as primitivism). Folk music, similarly tied to regional traditions, is often performed on traditional regional instruments. Historical narratives told in accessible language and set to clearly punctuated tunes make folk music popular in music classrooms. (ap)

folk high schools

Nonformal adult schools, founded in Denmark in the mid-1800s as a community education effort, now offering full-time residential study in several northern European countries. These schools are usually publicly funded and offer a varied curriculum, ranging from civic education to vocational training and college preparation. (dmv)

folk school

A term used in the United States to identify a nonformal residential school offering civic and cultural education to adults. Two well-known examples are the Highlander Center in Tennessee and the John

C. Campbell Folk School in North Carolina. Unlike the European model, these schools are not publicly funded. (dmv)

See also folk high schools.

folksonomy

A type of classification system in which the general population classifies content (pictures, videos, blogs, wikis, social bookmarks, etc.) by collaboratively creating and managing tags, which are much like subject keywords from a library's card catalog. Rather than a formal classification system, such as the Dewey Decimal system, creators and users of content create a social classification system based on their perception of the world around them. While folksonomy is often applied to content in general, it can also be used specifically to help organize one's own content. For example, teachers may tag social bookmarks for online lesson plans according to the units they teach. (kd)

folkways

Traditional behaviors and ways of life within a culture that are passed on. This could include practice, custom, or belief shared by the members of a group as part of their common culture. According to William Graham Sumner, the folkways of a social system are a set of norms governing commonly accepted practices, customs, and habits that make up the fabric of everyday life. (kf1)

follow-up, completer

In career education, an organized plan for ascertaining the employment and educational status of graduates from career and technical programs in order to establish the relationship between employment and the career and technical education and training received. (db)

form

The elements of construction of a work of art (e.g., color, shape, arrangement of shapes into composition, medium of construction), as well as the act of making or forming a work of art out of its medium. Insofar as art is a language, the forms employed in an art form are its vocabulary. The philosopher Gombrich talks of artists developing and learning a vocabulary of forms. Children do the same in their drawing, deciding, often by copying from one another, that a particular schema (e.g., a thick brown vertical line with a green ball on top of it) is a satisfactory form. Form has to do with the elements employed, not the meaning conveyed, when artists, for example, face the challenge of representing three-dimensional reality in two-dimensional space. (jd)

formal analysis

Critical writing on a work of art that attends to its form (rather than content or context), including qualities such as line, color, and texture, that cause an initial response. Strictly concerned with the work itself, it assumes no prior knowledge of the artist, art history, or stylistic counterparts. "Formal" here refers to physical form, not aspects of correctness (as in "formal—grammatically correct—language"). While formal analysis is specific to the visual arts, similar modes of inquiry—attending to details of form—are seen in other areas of interest to educators (e.g., literary criticism, linguistics, archaeology, mathematics). (lj)

formal operational development

Jean Piaget's fourth stage of cognitive development occurs from approximately age 12 to adulthood. The formal operational stage includes the ability to use abstract, complex reasoning, understand symbolism in an adult context, and gain theoretical understanding. These lifelong abilities include deductive and inductive reasoning. (npo)

formal properties

The aspects of a work that reflect decisions of the artist regarding medium, space, scale, color, line, shadow, rhythm, tune, timber, tone, and so on. In typical usage, the formal properties of a painting or a piece of music are the design features that are directly observable by the senses and distinguished from the subject matter. For most art traditions, however, this separation between form and meaning is merely semantic. The formal properties of a work often comprise its style and contribute to its content. (lj)

formal standard English (See Standard American English)

formative assessment
Assessments that are administered before teaching a topic or skill to determine students' abilities or prior knowledge. Use of formative assessment allows teachers to target lessons to the areas in which students need to improve, and focus less on areas in which they have already demonstrated mastery. It is typically used in classrooms prior to end-of-course assessments. (jas, js2)

formative evaluation
The systematic gathering and analysis of information used to advise and improve the conceptualization, design, production, and/or implementation of a wide array of products and programs. Formative evaluation takes place before a product or program has been finalized and is premised upon the considerations, patterns of usage, reactions, and comments of intended learners, viewers, listeners, and/or end-users. The purpose of the evaluation is to inform pending decisions specific to the project in order to increase the likelihood that desired outcomes will be reached. (ieh)

formula
An equation containing more than one variable that is used to model a physical situation or express the relationship between two or more quantities. For example, $A = 1/2bh$ is the formula that relates the area of a triangle, A, to the length of its base, b, and its height, h. A formula may be evaluated by replacing all the variables, except one, with known values and then solving the equation for the remaining variable. In the example of the area of a triangle, b and h could be replaced with given values and the area computed, or any two variables could be replaced to give the value of the third. (rdk)

for-profit schools
Educational institutions that are run by private, profit-seeking companies or organizations and operate as businesses, receiving tuition and fees from students who enroll. (pgg)
  See also proprietary schools.

found object/found space
A found object is an item, either synthetic or existing in nature, that is taken and used as a piece of art or as part of an art project; literally an object, not intended for artistic purposes, found and used as art. A found space is a physical space, not intended for performances, used for theater, dance, or performance art; street corners, parks, train platforms, or hillsides are all examples of found spaces when used for performances. Using found objects and found spaces in arts classes challenges students creatively while requiring very little in terms of budgetary resources. (em)

foundation (educational finance)
A term in educational finance that refers to the financing of education through a partnership between the local district and the state as an attempt to achieve some degree of equality of educational opportunity for children in public schools. Through the years, it has served as an attempt to provide a specified minimum, or foundation, educational program within the states that have utilized this financial procedure. (jr)

foundationalism
A view in the theory of knowledge that asserts that all true or reasonable propositions

are either known for certain, known through direct and indubitable connection with the facts, or derived in equally indubitable steps from such foundations. Knowledge is said to be "built" like a perfect building, in which a perfect foundation assures us that the floors above are perfectly reliable. Foundationalism has floundered, since most philosophers have come to believe that no beliefs can be directly and inherently tied to the world but are mediated through the senses and culture. (an)

See also empiricism; idealism; realism.

foundations
The term usually refers to institutions through which private wealth is contributed and distributed for public purpose. Some of the best-known foundations in the United States include the Carnegie, Rockefeller, Lilly, Ford, and Sloan Foundations. In the 1980s and 1990s the number of grant-making foundations increased significantly. Most notable were those developed by financier George Soros and Microsoft founder Bill Gates. Foundation giving doubled between 1990 and 1998 to $19.5 billion. In 1997, the largest recipients of grant dollars were education, health, and human services. (jr)

fourth wall
In theater, the imaginary separation between the onstage world of the characters and the world of the audience, a device used by actors to create an enclosed reality onstage. A key concept in the development of theatrical realism and naturalistic theater, it originated from the notion that on a traditional stage, in addition to the two sides of the stage and the back wall, a fourth wall existed at the front of the stage visible only to the characters onstage—the audience watched the play through this invisible wall. Breaking the fourth wall implies talking to the audience. (em)

four-year institutions
Four-year institutions include universities, liberal arts colleges, and independently organized graduate or professional schools. In addition to work of a type normally creditable toward a bachelor's or higher degree, four-year institutions may also offer other types of instruction (e.g., courses in general education and adult education, short courses, occupational curriculums leading to an associate degree, etc.). (cf)

four-year liberal arts colleges
A classification for 200 or more colleges that have enhanced their status as traditional and prestigious four-year institutions; they are publicly recognized for their excellence in the liberal arts, leaving graduate and professional education to research/graduate universities. (cf)

fraction
The division of two numbers A and B (A/B where B does not equal zero); an expression that indicates the quotient of this division. Fractions can be interpreted from several perspectives: part-whole (area model), measure, set, ratio, and division. (wja)

frame of reference
The structure of assumptions within which perceptions are analyzed and interpreted. As a result of so doing, experience is created. In one dimension, frames are the meaning perspectives that serve as sociolinguistic, ethical, psychological, or epistemic filters or codes to shape, delimit, and distort experience. The second dimension of a frame of reference is a meaning scheme composed of the specific beliefs, feelings, judgments, intuitions, and attitudes that accompany and shape specific interpretation and understanding. More fully developed frames of reference are more inclusive, differentiating, more integrative of an individual's experience and perspective, and more open to alternative perspectives. (hfs)

free appropriate public education
Special education and related services that are provided at public expense, meet the

standards of the state educational agency, and are provided in conformity with the individualized education program. (sr)

free choice

Learning experiences that allow children autonomy or the independence to select either the activity itself or materials and direction to be taken within the context of a particular activity. (db1)

free drawing

Like free writing, free drawing is the activity of drawing anything the student wishes. An alternative to drawing sessions in which the teacher or researcher assigns a drawing task (e.g., draw family scenes, or landscapes), free drawing activities are determined entirely by the intentions and inventions of the child or other artist. (jd)

free morpheme (See morphology)

free schools (See pauper schools)

Free Speech Movement (FSM)

A movement that characterized the rebellious youth counterculture of the 1960s, the Free Speech Movement originated on the campus of the University of California in Berkeley, California, during the fall of 1964. Starting as a localized movement staged by five students protesting the banning of the distribution of political literature on that campus, the movement quickly spread to college campuses in other parts of the country. The events on the Berkeley campus in 1964 are considered the first major student revolt of the 1960s. (ah)

freedom

Liberty of action. There are two types of freedom. Negative freedom is the absence of coercion or interference from other people; the quality or state of being able to act without hindrance or restraint. Positive freedom consists in the power of self-determination, being in charge of the fulfillment of one's aspirations. Within the context of Western liberal political theory (e.g., Locke, Rousseau, Hobbes, Mill), freedom is typically understood as action free from external constraints. Yet critics of Western liberalism (e.g., Gandhi) insisted that freedom has an internal as well as an external component. A free action must not only be caused by the agents themselves. It must be caused by a self that is internally well regulated. For example, a person motivated improperly by fear or love of money cannot act freely, no matter what the external political context. (ewr, an)

See also determinism; volition.

Freedom Schools

A set of schools established in the summer of 1964 by the Student Nonviolent Coordinating Committee (SNCC) in the state of Mississippi. The schools were staffed by college students and other volunteers as a part of the civil rights strategy of the organization. The literacy and numeracy of the students was developed using curricula and pedagogy designed to be culturally appropriate and developmental. (hfs)

See also Freedom Summer.

Freedom Summer

Term for the summer of 1964, when black and white Civil Rights volunteers, many of whom were college students on summer break, traveled to Mississippi to help African Americans secure their right to vote. Another component of Freedom Summer involved the establishment of 41 "Freedom Schools" created to protest the segregated and unequal education black Mississippians received in their schools. Freedom Summer experienced a number of violent incidents, including the Ku Klux Klan murder of three civil rights workers and the fire-bombing of many black churches. (rih)

Freirian

Educational processes that follow the philosophy and practice outlined by Paulo

Freire, a Brazilian educator who began his work with adult literacy programs. Freirian education is inherently political in nature and supports an instructional approach that encourages students to reflect on their history and the forces that affect their lives, use those reflections as a basis for action, and then reflect on the results of that action. (jpc)

frequency count
A behavior-tracking observational technique in which the number of times a behavior occurs in a period of time is measured. (xss)

fresco
A method of painting with water-based pigments on freshly spread lime plaster, either dry (fresco secco) or wet (true fresco). In the latter method, the colors dry and set with the plaster to become a permanent part of the wall. Fresco painting is widely used in murals as it presents a classical style and is durable and long lasting. Michelangelo's paintings in the Sistine Chapel are the most famous of all frescoes. The technique was briefly revived by artists of interest to educators, such as Diego Rivera and other Mexican muralists in the first half of the 20th century. (kpb)

freshman seminar
Freshman seminars are small classes, usually taught by a professor or graduate student, that encourage freshmen to work on discussion, writing, and analytical skills soon after they arrive on campus. The seminars attempt to provide all students with important skills for academic and social college challenges. Many colleges and universities now require freshman seminars for all first-year students. In some cases, a student might place out of this requirement because of an Advanced Placement exam, but often the seminar is key in helping all freshmen develop communication and learning skills for the following years of college and beyond. (cf)

Froebelian kindergarten
An early childhood program developed by Friedrich Wilhelm Froebel (1782–1852), in which teachers and parents tend the "garden of children," acting as facilitators of healthy conditions for growth. Instruction occurs through carefully-designed "gifts," "occupations," songs, and games, which were attractive play opportunities for the child. During play, Froebel believed, children unfold their inner, spiritual lives and unique capabilities, much as a flower naturally opens to the sun, giving the adult a chance to observe the child's qualities and growth. (ecr)

frontal lobe (See lobes of the brain)

frustration reading level
The grade level at which the student can no longer read the words or comprehend the message in a passage, even with a great deal of support. Although there is some variation in criteria, widely accepted standards are: less than 90 percent accuracy in word recognition and 50 percent comprehension. (aw)

See also independent reading level; informal reading inventory; instructional reading level.

FSM (See Free Speech Movement)

Fulbright Act
Federal legislation aimed at providing support for educational exchange programs between the United States and foreign countries. Named for Senator J. William Fulbright, the Fulbright Act was signed by President Truman in 1946. The purpose of the legislation was to create an understanding between the United States and other countries by providing grants for scholars to advance their research and provide for the exchange of students and teachers. Originally enacted as an amendment to the Surplus Property Act of 1944, the Fulbright program was expanded with the passage of the Smith-Mundt Act of 1948 and the Fulbright-Hays Act of 1961

(also known as the Mutual Educational and Cultural Exchange Act). (rih)

Fulbright Program

Funded by the U.S. government, awards grants annually for the international educational exchange of scholars, and for educators, graduate students, and professionals to teach, study, and conduct research abroad. (sn)

full-scale IQ

IQ stands for Intelligence Quotient. A number derived from a weighted average of the verbal and performance IQ scores of the Wechsler Scales of Intelligence. When the difference between the verbal IQ and the performance IQ is great, the full-scale IQ is difficult to interpret and may not be valid. The full-scale IQ is perceived to be a numerical measurement of a person's "overall intelligence," which is a psychological construct and can therefore never be proven. (aw)

full-service schools

Institutions that propose to unify the delivery of social and family services in a single school facility. The interagency connections inherent in these institutions facilitate family preservation and education via a focus on family needs, as well as the needs of individual family members. Schools that make available to students and their families a broad range of human support services, such as immunizations, nutrition counseling, medical and dental screening, employment and housing assistance, and legal and immigration advice. (hfs, bba)

full-text databases

Databases that contain not only citation information, but also the complete text of the items cited. When the database is searched, retrieved records contain or link to the entire text of the document. Some full-text databases include replicas of printed pages, complete with images and pagination. Others include the text, but not accompanying images, and do not preserve the layout of the print version. Some full-text databases contain material not available in print format; many knowledge bases have no print parallel. Researchers find full-text databases to be convenient, especially for work with journal articles. Such databases may contain articles from thousands of publications. Some full-text databases focus on a particular subject, while others are general or news oriented. (ac)

full-time student equivalent (FTSE)

An enrollment unit that is often used by states to allocate funds to schools and is usually determined on a specific date after the first day of classes, commonly by dividing total student credit units of course registration by 15 weeks, for example, for the fall or spring semester. (pgg)

function

A rule that relates an independent variable with a dependant variable. The independent variable is chosen from a list of possible variables and is used to determine the dependant variable based on a rule. For the rule to constitute a function, there must be a unique outcome (dependant variable) for each input (independent variable). Often, functions are denoted as such: $f(x) = y$, whereby the rule is given by $f(x)$ and the independent variable is x and the dependant variable is y. (dbc)

functional assessment

Systematic observation of an individual's behavior and/or ability to perform specific activities and tasks to measure capability and develop a plan for training or for predicting success in related activities. (sr)

functional curriculum

Materials designed to teach skills of daily living, for example, use of money or use of public transportation. (sr)

functional grammar

A system of grammar chiefly concerned with how components function semantically, syntactically, and pragmatically. (cld)

functional limitations
The specific impact on one's ability to perform a range of tasks, simple or complex, due to the severity of symptoms attributable to a medical condition, learning disability, or psychiatric issue diagnosed by a clinician. (ecb, nl1)

functional literacy
A minimal, or survival level, of literacy for one to meet basic personal and social needs, such as writing one's name or reading signs. People who are functionally illiterate experience difficulty in using reading and writing skills for purposes and activities in their daily lives. The level of reading and writing ability necessary to function competently within a particular social context. The literacy needed to engage effectively in all those activities in which literacy is normally assumed in an individual's culture or group. (h-jk, chb, jpc)

functional Magnetic Resonance Imaging (fMRI)
(fMRI) is a special type of MRI that allows the visualization of brain activity in addition to brain structure. fMRI indirectly measures changes in blood flow related to brain activity using the BOLD (Blood Oxygen Level Dependent) response, and it is used primarily in human brain mapping research. fMRI is currently a dominant tool in neuroscience research due to its many advantages: it is noninvasive, it has good spatial resolution, and it can record signals from the entire brain (including deep structures). It also has limitations, however: the BOLD response is an indirect measure of brain activity, fMRI has poor temporal resolution compared to some other methods such as EEG, and the machine is very loud and does not allow for any movement. Most importantly, the interpretation of fMRI results tends to be quite difficult because it is a correlational tool only. On its own, fMRI cannot conclusively determine whether activity in a particular brain area is caused by a certain mental function. (mt)

functional neuroimaging (See neuroimaging)

funding
Funding is a means of obtaining financial resources for a specified or clearly articulated purpose. Funds from state general revenue and from levies on the assessed value of property are the means by which most schools obtain funding. In addition, funding for some schools may come from other sources: the interest on property or other assets, rental on facilities, the profits on enterprising operations, fundraising, grants, or foundations. (jr)

fundraising
Fundraising attempts are generally short-term efforts to obtain monetary supplements for schools, universities, and other institutions in order to support a wide range of student activities. Private and parochial schools may rely heavily upon fundraising, since they lack the state funds that public schools are able to obtain. Charter schools may rely on fundraising to some extent, since they are unable to subsist solely on the basic state funds allotted them. Fundraising activities may include, but are not limited to, ad hoc events, alumni association fundraising work, school-business partnerships, and direct mailing request for contributions. Other more long-term methods of fundraising may be the establishment of development funds or writing grant proposals. The responsibility of fundraising varies due to differences in size and needs. (jr)
See also advancement.

further education
Education that takes place after leaving school and outside the formal higher education system. This can include basic skills courses, vocational or professional

education, or a general liberal arts education. (jpc)

further education college
In the United Kingdom, a public postsecondary institution offering a broad range of academic and especially vocational education to students over the age of 16. Further education colleges do not offer higher-level or degree-granting courses. Most students are over the age of 19, enrolled on a part-time basis. (chb)

fused curriculum
The blending of several specific subjects into one overlapping course of study. A unification of several courses with connected content drawn from each. (jw)

fuzzy theory
Making an approximate reasoning rather than a precise one. Traditional mathematics taught in schools is procedural; fuzzy theory allows for students to develop their own means to a solution of a problem. It requires a sense of flexibility in working with an underdeveloped problem that may have no exact answer. It allows a student to not only determine the answer but understand the structure and concepts of the problem, encouraging them to decide what the proper solution is. (ldz)

G

Gary Plan

School plan developed by Superintendent William Wirt in Gary, Indiana, that relied upon the reforms of John Dewey in creating a more diversified "work-study-play" school. In the Gary Plan, later termed the Platoon School Plan, students were organized into two efficient platoons that switched facilities halfway through the day. The schools included gymnasiums, workshops, a playground, and an auditorium as well as classrooms for instruction. Although 202 cities had adopted similar models by 1929, the Gary Plan did not survive after the Depression. (dwm)

gatekeepers (See curriculum gatekeepers)

gay

An identity label used to signify a person who is attracted emotionally and/or sexually to members of the same sex. This term is typically used to refer to men, and the term "lesbian" is typically used to refer to women. The term "homosexual" is disliked by people who self-identify as gay or lesbian, in part because it overemphasizes the sexual aspect of sexual/affectional orientation and disregards the multifaceted nature of it. (ti)

Gay, Lesbian, and Straight Education Network (GLSEN)

The Gay, Lesbian, and Straight Education Network was founded in 1990 by Kevin Jennings, a secondary school history teacher, and it became a national educational advocacy organization in 1995. GLSEN's mission is to assure that people of all sexual orientations and all gender identities are valued and safe in the K–12 setting. GLSEN provides educators with policy and curricular resources, conducts research on school climate and school safety related to GLBT issues, and assists in starting and supporting Gay-Straight Alliances. (jb2)

Gay, Lesbian and Straight Education Network (history)

Founded in 1990, the Gay and Lesbian Independent School Teachers Network (GLSTN) originated as a group of 70 volunteer gay and lesbian educators with a mission to advocate for the safety, support, and educational needs of LGBTQ students and staff in the schools. Through the promotion of educational environments in which LGBTQ student issues could be openly recognized, GLSTN provided space that enabled LGBTQ youth to utilize their voice through the establishment of Gay-Straight Alliances in schools. In an effort to create a more inclusive space and expand membership in the struggle for creating safe schools for all, regardless of sexual orientation or gender identity or expression, GLSTN became the Gay, Lesbian, and Straight Network (GLSEN). Members of GLSEN work to concurrently inform schools and the general public about the harmful effects of heterosexism and homophobia in a diverse society, as well as advocate for school settings in which all members of the educational community are respected, honored, and heard. (wpa, smh)

Gay, Lesbian, Bisexual Studies

A focus of study, found predominantly in higher education, that emerged in the 1970s, along with many other new disciplines (black studies, feminist studies, ethnic studies, etc.). Gay, lesbian, and bisexual (GLB) studies have developed firm footing in the academy and include a strong body of literature and research studies. GLB studies programs have typically been dedicated to the study of political, historical, cultural, and psychological contexts in which gender identities and sexualities are expressed. This area of academic inquiry, which now often includes transgender identity, currently exists at many colleges and universities and is designated by a variety of names: e.g., Queer Studies, Study of Sexualities, Gender Studies. (jb2, jqa)

See also queer studies, LGBT studies.

gay family

Also called GLBT family, these terms are used to describe families with one or more lesbian, gay, bisexual, or transgender parents. It does not mean that all members of the family are GLBT. (jb2)

Gay Rights Movement

The Stonewall Riots in Greenwich Village in New York City in 1969, where patrons of a gay bar resisted arrest, is seen as the symbolic beginning of the modern Gay Rights Movement. Efforts to combat discrimination against gays and lesbians predate Stonewall and laid the groundwork for significant advances in the 1970s, such as the first Gay Pride parade in New York in 1970, and the American Psychological Association's decision to declassify homosexuality as a mental disorder in 1973. Contemporary efforts to fight anti-gay discrimination are spread out among a variety of GLBTQ social justice organizations (e.g., Human Rights Campaign, Gay Lesbian Straight Educators Network, Gay Lesbian Advocates and Defenders) and can no longer be defined as a single movement. (jb2)

Gay-Straight Alliance (GSA)

Gay-Straight Alliances are student clubs that work to improve school climate for all students, regardless of sexual orientation or gender identity/expression. GSAs function like other extracurricular clubs (i.e., have advisors, hold regular meetings, host events); however there have been legal battles in school districts across the United States due to parental, religious, and political opposition to GSAs. Most legal rulings are determined by the 1984 Federal Equal Access Act, which was initially created to protect students' rights to form religious clubs. Under this Act, students have the right to form GSAs. Research indicates that the presence of a GSA improves the school climate for GLBTQ students. (jb2)

See also Gay, Lesbian, and Straight Education Network.

GE (See grade equivalent)

GEB (See General Education Board)

GED (See General Educational Development Tests)

Gemeinschaft/Gesellschaft

In *Gemeinschaft und Gesellschaft* (1887), German sociologist Ferdinand Tonnies contrasts the forms of human association that emerge from the organic bonds of community (Gemeinschaft) with the looser, more instrumental ties of society (Gesellschaft). While Gemeinschaft relationships are older than Gesellschaft relationships, the two forms of association coexist, complementing and undercutting one another in ways that pose a challenge to educators. In Gemeinschaft (community), people rely on the mutual and tacit understandings that grow out of a shared context, common experiences, and a unity of purpose. In Gesellschaft (society), relationships tend to take the form of transactions, individuals have to work harder to sustain connections, and relationships disintegrate once the parties are no longer useful to one another. For many children, formal schooling, especially public schooling, is a process of moving from Gemeinschaft experience to an introduction to Gesellschaft values. Other children experience more continuity between the culture of schools and that of the home. The educational challenge is twofold. On the one hand, many students quickly learn that the tacit understandings of home and community do not necessarily carry over into the world of schooling. They also learn that school culture has its own set of tacit understandings that they will have to learn to navigate. Unless educators help these children come to terms with the differences between the culture of home and that of school, schooling will be a bewildering and potentially alienating experience for them. On the other hand, public schools need to find ways to strengthen the sense of Gemeinschaft within the school. In many ways, public school communities will be closer to Gesellschaft than to Gemeinschaft. While some educational philosophers might rightly mourn the ensuing lack of a strong sense of ethical normation in schools, others might point to the opportunity for schools to explore the differences between Gemeinschaft and Gesellschaft in ways that better prepare children to cross the threshold from spaces of mutual understanding and acceptance to the more

tenuous spaces in which we are frequently misunderstood. (nl)

gender
"A complex set of characteristics and behaviors prescribed for a particular sex by society and learned through the socialization experience" (Ruth, 1995). Whereas sex is a biological classification and is usually described in terms of female and male, gender is socially constructed and is usually described in terms of masculinity and femininity. (ti)

gender bias
Prejudicial attitudes toward people because of their sex, including the conscious or unconscious expression of these attitudes in writing, speaking, and so on. Gender bias may be experienced in different contexts. In education, for example, it may include differential expectations for academic achievement of boys and girls, greater encouragement for participation from male than female students, limited availability of mentors for women graduate students, and evaluation of faculty based on gender-stereotypic standards. (ti)

gender expression
Gender expression refers to external characteristics and behaviors that are socially defined as either masculine or feminine, such as dress, grooming, mannerisms, speech patterns, and social interactions. Social or cultural norms regarding gender vary widely; characteristics that may be described as masculine, feminine, or neutral in one culture may not be categorized similarly in another. Children whose gender expression does not conform to cultural expectations of gender based on biological sex are referred to as gender variant or gender nonconforming. (jb2)

gender identity
Gender identity refers to one's internal sense and experience of being male, female, something in between, or something

other. Gender identity may or may not conform to societal expectations of gender based on biological sex. Gender identity development begins at birth, with a deepening and solidification of that identity, which may emerge between ages two and four and again in early adolescence. This identification may remain stable over time or may change. (jb2)

gender issues

Aspects of fundamental personal and social sexual identity comprising biological, psychological, and cultural constructions about individuals and groups (such as males, females, and gay and lesbian people). These basic human aspects are often a criterion for social stratification and different political treatment, as well as a favored symbol for expressing essential values and beliefs. Concerns often address such questions as the biology of human reproduction, sex roles in the family and society, the psychology of gender identity, and images of men, women, bisexuals, gays, and lesbians in literature and art. (hrm, ew, jkd)

gender neutral language

Also called gender inclusive and nonsexist language. The use of vocabulary that eliminates reference to females or males in the context of meaning in spoken and written communications. Gender neutral language lacks vocabulary that promotes male-centered, masculine-dominating, patriarchal society in order to better educate and ensure equity for all people in all situations. (npg)

gender nonconforming (See gender variant)

gender queer

A term increasingly used to describe people who reject rigid, "normative" social constructs of gender identity (i.e., female or male) and sexual identity (i.e. gay, straight, or bisexual). These people identify with more fluid and inclusive expressions of those aspects of human identity. Not typically used with preadolescent children. (jb2)

See also queer.

gender roles

The set of roles, behaviors, and expectations assigned to males and females by society and cultures. For example, traditional gender roles in the United States delineated men as providing for the family economically by working outside of the home and women as attending to domestic tasks, including child rearing. In contemporary society there is greater acceptance of females performing traditionally male roles than males performing female roles. Many present-day religious and cultural groups are based on traditional gender role expectations. (jb2)

gender studies

The study of gender as a socially constructed category that varies in different historical and cultural settings. Gender studies makes the categories of male/female explicit, as well as assumptions of sexual orientation such as the description of heterosexuality as the norm, and homosexuality as what is deviant. (bt-b)

gender variant

A term used to describe children whose behavior, interests, and gender expression fall outside of cultural norms and expectations based on biological sex. For example, a girl who consistently prefers activities typically associated with boys (e.g., playing traditionally male sports, rough and tumble play) or a boy who consistently prefers activities associated with girls (dressing up, playing with dolls) is called gender variant. Not applied to children who temporarily explore these activities. A more appropriate term for gender nonconforming children than transgender. Most gender variant children do not evolve into transgender or transsexual adult identities. Also referred to as gender nonconforming. (jb2)

gendered harassment

Any harassing behavior (verbal, physical, psychological) that is in response to those who do not conform to heterosexual gender norms. Types include (hetero) sexual harassment, homophobic harassment, and harassment for gender nonconformity. Research indicates that teachers are less likely to intervene on gendered harassment than other types of bullying and harassment in schools. (jb2)

gender-role socialization

The process by which individuals learn the characteristics and behaviors considered by their culture to be most appropriate/acceptable for their sex. Sources of gender-role socialization include, among others, family, peers, schools, and religious institutions. Differential socialization based on gender may occur through interaction with children (e.g., being more gentle with girls than with boys), overt messages about gender-appropriate behavior (e.g., "boys don't cry"), expectations for academic achievement, peer sanctions for gender-inappropriate behavior (e.g., teasing, social isolation), teachers' differential responses to girls and boys, and role modeling. (ti)

general education

Those areas of learning that are deemed to be the common experience of all educated persons. (cf)

General Education Board (GEB)

Philanthropic organization created by John D. Rockefeller in 1902 and chartered by Congress in 1903 to aid education in the United States "without distinction of race, sex or creed." The GEB was part of the broader southern education movement of the early 20th century, which, in conjunction with the Southern Education Board, raised money and promoted public education in the southern states. GEB funds were also utilized in the southwestern states to aid education for Mexican Americans and for all levels of education including colleges and universities. After 1940 programs other than those in the South were closed. The last appropriation was made in 1964. (vmm)

general education programs

Programs comprising core courses that are intended to provide undergraduate students with a broad, common foundation of study. Programs vary in their focus and are primarily institution-specific, but most attempt to address questions about what students need to know and what constitutes an educated person. Interdisciplinary in nature, most emphasize elements of critical thinking and ethical reasoning. Harvard's general education program is among the most well-known. (sn)

General Educational Development Tests (GED)

A set of five tests that assess writing skills, reading skills, math skills, social studies knowledge, and science knowledge. Successful performance on the tests leads to a high school equivalency certificate, which is commonly referred to as a GED. In order to qualify for the GED, candidates must achieve a minimum score on each test, in addition to a minimum average across the tests. While a national minimum score requirement is set by the American Council on Education, states are free to require higher scores for receipt of the credential. Measures the individual's general education as developed by military service, employment, or other nonschool experiences; uses of the GED have been highly successful in demonstrating abilities and accomplishments of adult learners and others who did not complete high school; also used by colleges in credit-by-examination for World War II and Korean War veterans. (jpc, cf)

generalizability theory (G-theory)

An approach to test analysis that seeks to decompose the variance in test scores. G-theory is used to study the various aspects of testing (e.g., items, persons, raters) that might cause scores to differ. (sp)

generalizable patterns

Ideas that overlap between different mathematical topics, allowing connections to be formed relating one concept to another. They are grouped according to their relevance. (jmg, ldz)

generalizations

Relationships between two or more concepts expressed as declarative statements or summarizing statements with wide applicability. Examples of generalizations often found in social studies include the idea that peoples of the world are interdependent and that people live in a world of constant change. (mje, jah)

generational teaching

Teaching methods that incorporate recognition of the characteristics of the generation to which the student has been assigned or identified. For example, the Millennial generation (Generation Y) has been characterized as using and being more comfortable with technology, social networking, and gaming. It is also viewed as being more socially tolerant than some previous generations. Awareness of these characteristics can help the instructor focus on technologies and techniques that will engage this generation of students. Since each generation has its own characteristics, generational teaching uses the techniques most appropriate to a particular generation. (npo)

generative themes

The words that students learn to read in Freirian literacy programs. They describe important issues related to social problems in students' lives and serve as a means through which students learn to critically examine their lives and society while acquiring literacy skills. (jpc)

See also Freirian.

genetics

A branch of biology that studies how characteristics and qualities are passed from generation to generation. The study could include heredity, genes, variation, and DNA studies, and how these traits may change over time. (tw)

genital phase

The fifth phase in Freud's theory of psychosocial development, the genital phase begins at age 12, around puberty. Individuals become more interested in the opposite gender, according to the theory. (xss)

genius

Native intellectual power, associated with the arts, and denoting a capacity for originality and imagination. Derived in the 18th century, from French *génie* and German *genie*, and from associations with classical *genius* (an attendant spirit associated with the family and carrying potential for good and evil) as well as the Arabic *jinn* (a spirit of blue flame said to interfere in human affairs). As a result, while genius denotes natural aptitude or mental prowess, it also carries overtones of supernatural inspiration. A distinction is often made between genius and talent, the latter considered a more accessible and less spontaneous phenomenon. (lj)

genre

Category for classifying literary and other artistic works, usually by form, technique, or content. Historically, literary genres are comedy, tragedy, and epic. Today they include novel, essay, short story, television play, and motion picture, and prototypical genres such as children's fairy tales and mysteries. The concept of genre has more recently included the social uses of language or "speech genres," such as everyday social exchanges, lectures, sermons, eulogies, formal invitations, letters of recommendation, and scientific reports. Language styles (e.g., formal versus informal), appropriate speech acts, and discourse may be involved in each of these genres. (mc)

genuineness

One of the three attitudes that Carl Rogers believed should be conveyed by a therapist in order for the clients to freely express themselves without having to worry about what the therapist thinks of them. Genuineness is the willingness to relate to clients without hiding behind a professional front. (tsw)

geography

The study of land, features, inhabitants, and phenomena in the context of both direct and indirect impacts upon humans and humanity at any time. Geography includes physical geography—the study of the land, human/cultural geography—the study of the people, and environmental geography—the study of the interactions between the physical and human/cultural factors as changes over time. (npg)

geometric progression

A list of numbers in which there is one common ratio between any and all consecutive numbers in the list. For example, the list {100, 50, 25} is a geometric progression because between 50 and 100 the ratio is 1/2, between 25 and 50 the ratio is 1/2, and thus between all consecutive numbers in the list, there is a single common ratio. Additionally, the common ratio can be negative or greater than one. (dbc)

geometric properties

Measurable attributes of two- and three-dimensional geometric figures, surfaces, and solids. Geometric properties can be local or global and are not affected by transformation, such as scaling and rotating. Examples include congruence, similarity, parallelism, perpendicularity, symmetry, and convexity. (ey)

geometry

From the Greek word *geometria,* meaning "to measure the earth." The mathematical field that describes and manipulates shape, size, pattern, and position. Euclidean (or plane) geometry is named after Euclid (365–300 B.C.E.), who wrote a 13-volume text named *Elements.* This geometry has been joined by non-Euclidean geometries such as spherical geometry, hyperbolic geometry, torus geometry, and taxicab geometry. (ey)

gerontology

A multidisciplinary field of inquiry that addresses issues related to human aging. Disciplines within this field of study include biology, psychology, sociology, history, philosophy, humanities, and the social sciences. Human life is studied specifically through the changes that have occurred when an individual has lived for a relatively long period of time, in terms of human life experience. (hrm, ew, jkd)

Gesellschaft (See Gemeinschaft/ Gesellschaft)

gestalt

German, meaning shape or form. A physical, psychological, or symbolic arrangement of parts so unified as a whole that its properties could not be derived from a simple summation of its parts. Induced from observations of visual perception, the theory's overriding theme is that stimulation is perceived in configurational terms. Patterns take precedence over separate elements and have properties that are not inherent in the elements themselves, often captured by the phrase: "The whole is more than the sum of its parts." A good configuration exhibits simplicity, stability, regularity, symmetry, continuity, and unity. Young children's drawings of human beings are thought to have the gestalt of humanness even though they lack particular identifiable human features. (kpb)

gestalt therapy

A form of psychotherapy that stresses awareness and integration, or interrelatedness, of cognitions, behaviors, and emotions. Gestalt therapy is a holistic approach that emphasizes the importance of viewing an individual within his or her environmental context, as well as alerting an individual to his or her present dominant needs and how to achieve psychological equilibrium. (jbb)

gesture drawing

A quick drawing done usually in seconds or at most a couple of minutes, intended to capture the movement, essence, or gesture of the model or scene being drawn, rather than the details of its form. As an encompassing, often scribble-like first drawing, gesture drawings can be used to explore what aspects of the object of representation bear special attention (perhaps in a more developed work) and what issues of composition should be taken into consideration. Quick gesture drawings often loosen art students up and require that they think beyond the schemas they may have developed for representation. Though often an activity of advanced art students, gesture drawing also provides a useful educational experience for very young students of art. (tkb)

G.I. Bill

In response to the difficulties faced by veterans after World War II, Congress passed the "G.I. Bill of Rights" in 1944 to prepare for the returning G.I.s. This bill guaranteed unemployment insurance for one year, as well as guaranteed loans for building a home or starting a business. American higher education was greatly changed by another aspect of the Bill, which provided coverage of tuition for veterans at the nation's colleges and universities and dramatically increased university enrollment. (cf)

See also Serviceman's Readjustment Act of 1944 (Public Law 78-346).

gifted and talented students
(See gifted students)

gifted education

Consists of strategies, programs, and theories developed and implemented to serve the academic needs of the "gifted student." As a field of study, gifted education emerged alongside the rise in IQ testing in the early 20th century and received widespread attention and support following the Soviet Union's launching of Sputnik, the passage of the *National Defense Education Act,* and the accompanying emphasis on identifying and serving advanced learners to compete in the Cold War political environment (Flemming, 1960). The concept and implementation of gifted education faces several challenges, perhaps most significantly a failure to develop a consensus on the definition of gifted student, its presumed subject. Questions continue to emerge as to whether "giftedness" refers to potential or performance, achievement or ability, and how any of these concepts can be measured or predicted. Further critiques of gifted education point to flaws in identification processes that privilege students based more on economic and cultural background than academic potential, resulting in elitist programs. Advocates of gifted education, however, argue that some students are more motivated, better prepared, and intellectually advanced in relation to the larger student population, and thus alternative learning opportunities to meet their needs are both just and appropriate. A variety of service models with varying degrees of flexibility and rigidity around which students are served reflect a wide range of assumptions and values in the field. (bda)

gifted students

Students who possess outstanding abilities or potential in the areas of general intellectual capacity, specific academic aptitude, leadership ability, creative thinking, visual or performing arts, and psychomotor ability. (bba)

gifts

In the Froebelian kindergarten, gifts are objects, such as wooden balls and wooden cubes of different size and color, that adults share with the children in order that they might experience and learn color, shape, size, counting, comparison, contrast, and other concepts. Teachers present the gifts to the child with instructions and the child follows the teacher's lead in using the materials. (ecr)

See also Froebelian kindergarten.

GLB\TQ

An acronym used for Gay, Lesbian, Bisexual, Transgender, and Questioning. The Q can also stand for Queer. (jb2)

global education

This field of study emphasizes the interdependence of human beings rather than their differences in a worldwide context. Complex issues facing humanity, such as environmental concerns, natural resources, population, migration, health, and so on are addressed in a global context rather than within regional or national boundaries. Global education encompasses areas such as international studies, which is more comparative in nature. (jqa, npo)

GLSEN (See Gay, Lesbian, and Straight Education Network)

goal, career

The occupation for which the pupil or student is seeking to qualify by means of training. (jb)

goal setting

Goal setting is the term commonly given to the process of identifying specific goals that should be accomplished in a certain time frame through the implementation of strategies to aid in achieving the goals; goals are generally set in response to opportunities or problems. Instructional goals are usually focused on what learners should be able to do when they complete the accompanying or specified instruction. (bs)

Goals 2000: Educate America Act (1994)

Law signed by President William Jefferson Clinton as Public Law 103-227. The act provided funds for a variety of K–12 educational programs and established a set of eight educational goals to be achieved by the year 2000 (e.g., "By the year 2000, the high school graduation rate will increase to at least 90 percent"). The act provided support for state and local efforts aimed at establishing goals and standards for academic achievement. Several amendments to the act were incorporated into the Omnibus Consolidated Rescissions and Appropriations Act of 1996, and the act was allowed to expire in 2001. (krk)

going to the balcony

A metaphor, developed by Ronald Heifetz and Martin Linsky, that emphasizes the practice of removing oneself, mentally and emotionally, from an activity to adopt a third-party perspective (as though looking down on a dance floor from a balcony) to gain a more objective understanding of one's actions and impact, as well as possible solutions to problems that are hard to see when close at hand. (sh)

Gong Lum v. Rice, 275 U.S. 78 (1927)

A 1927 Supreme Court decision that upheld the right of states to maintain "separate but equal" educational facilities for white and minority students. Gong Lum, a Chinese American, challenged the classification of his daughter as "colored" and her placement in a Bolivar County, Mississippi, black school, which was located much farther away than the white school in his district. The Court held that the rights of children of Chinese ancestry are not infringed by denying them the right to attend schools established for whites. (gs)

Good, The

Described in Book VI of Plato's (ca. 429–347 B.C.E.) *Republic* as the unknown intelligible source of truth and being (505a-509d). Knowledge of The Good, which is acquired by completing the ideal educational program described in *Republic VII,* is essential to the completion of the philosophical character. Once wholly educated, philosophers will recognize their obligation to rule the polis and educate others. Philosophers must rule because their knowledge of The Good allows them to understand how to make use of the polis's resources in the most beneficial and just way, and they are the only ones who would rule out of a sense of obligation without regard for personal gain. (dl)

See also Right, The.

governance
The procedures followed in proposing, recommending, approving, and referring changes in institutional policies and practices to the appropriate level of authority for consideration and referral to the next (higher) authority; includes faculty promotion, tenure decisions, and salary increases, as well as initial appointments of administrative and professional staffs, the admission of students, the transfer of faculty and students to other academic units, and numerous other decisions that are relatively routine; involves various standing committees as well as different ad hoc committees; often referred to as shared governance when administrative staff work well with faculty committees. (cf)

governing board
An officially authorized body given overall responsibility for the control and management of one or more institutions; also given the authority to appoint administrators and professional staffs to manage and implement board policies. (cf)

governor's school
State-supported residential educational honors programs that give gifted and talented students an opportunity to expand their education in the arts, sciences, and humanities as well as provide opportunities in creativity and leadership. Most governors' schools occur as summer residential programs that may stretch from one to six weeks, although some governor's schools may stretch the entire academic year. Today's governor's schools are modeled after the first, which appeared in North Carolina in 1963. (ms)

GPA (See grade point average)

grade equivalent (GE)
A measure of skills and knowledge applied to adults that is assumed to be equivalent to that of a child who has completed a specific K–12 grade. (jpc)

grade inflation
A trend toward students receiving higher grades, usually with the implication that higher grades are being given for the same quantity and quality of work that previously would have received lower grades. Claims of grade inflation are not new and are not without controversy, but recent concerns have prompted several prominent universities to take steps to prevent it. (sn)

grade point average (GPA)
A measure of scholastic performance over a set of courses obtained by dividing the sum of the grades points earned by the total number of hours of course work attempted in the set for which GPA is assigned. (cf)

grade school (See elementary school)

graded school
A school in which students are classified according to grade level or progress. Materials of instruction are organized according to level of difficulty and students progress from one grade level to the next each year. One-room schools could have a grading system within their classroom walls, but in modern times teachers and students at different classroom levels and chronological age are generally separated into different classrooms. (dwm)

grade-level chair
A teacher with leadership responsibilities for all teachers assigned to a given grade level; typically, only larger elementary schools have grade-level chairs. (bba)

grading
The act of evaluating and recording the achievement level of a student. Using a quantifiable symbol to indicate a student's level of accomplishment or proficiency on a given task or course. (jw)

graduate assistant
Work position contingent upon enrollment as a postbaccalaureate student; may help a professor or administrator by performing research or office work. Usually associated with an offset in tuition. (cf, sn)

Graduate Record Examination (GRE)
Tests developed and administered nationally by Educational Testing Services for the selective admission of students to graduate programs at masters and doctoral programs; comparable to the SAT in the emphasis placed on verbal reasoning and reading comprehension. (cf)

graduate seminar
An organized series of meetings in which participants observe, study, reflect, and report on their learning experiences as related to future performance; involves at least three crucial components: advance preparation, active participation or engagement, and systematic follow-through. (cf)

graduate student
Though the term "graduate student" refers to any student who is pursuing a degree beyond the bachelor of arts or sciences, the phrase usually describes a master's or PhD student. Most graduate students finish their degrees with a thesis or dissertation approved by a committee. Some teach as part of their graduate training and to help pay for their education. Many graduate students receive fellowships, scholarships, and stipends from the university. (cf)

graduation
The stage of academic progression in which students receive formal recognition from a college or university; includes the conferral of a degree, for having completed a program of study. (cf)

graffiti
From the Italian *graffito,* an inscribed design. Graffiti consists of letters, slogans, names, or pictures inscribed in public places (e.g., on building walls), usually without permission. Indeed, the word traditionally refers to illegal markings on walls or sidewalks. As a style of art, graffiti is often associated with urban culture, hip-hop artists, and the visual expression of a need to be heard. Famous artists like Keith Herring have celebrated on canvas (and on walls) the colorful and often geometric shapes that, like the outlined spray-painted bubble letters, have become the trademark of graffiti. (ap)

grammar
In broader linguistic terms, the mental system of rules and categories that allows humans to form and interpret the words and sentences of their language. It traditionally incorporates morphology, syntax, and phonology. More specifically in education, grammar comprises the rules for speaking and writing, and a person's oral and/or written language is judged as good or bad according to its conformity to these rules. (smt)

grammar school
Term initially used for a school that emphasized the teaching of Latin grammar. Grammar schools were the first formal schools in England and were adopted in the American colonies. They began to disappear in the 19th century as secondary education became more widely available.

Today the term is used informally to refer to an elementary school. (ck)

grants

Grants are awards of financial assistance, including cooperative agreements, in the form of money, or property in lieu of money. Grants may be from local education agencies, state educational agencies, or from federal government entities, such as Title I or grants for compensatory education. Grants may also be from partnerships, foundations, or corporations. Grants are usually given voluntarily, typically without expectation of tangible compensation. However, most grants require certain guidelines for those applying. Normally a proposal is submitted, which specifies the scope of work or line of inquiry, performance, targets, time frame, purpose, and amount of the request. This work may contain the history of the organization and projections of future programs. It is not unusual for those granting funds to request a projected budget from the prospective recipients. Certain criteria and time frames may need to be adhered to for the recipients of the grant to continue to receive the funds. However, many grants are given on a single-year basis, with the request of a financial report and/or some type of evaluation at the end of the year. For those grants that may continue beyond one year, it is not uncommon to request audited financial statements, copies of IRS forms, and annual reports. (jr)

graph

A type of diagram used to represent data. There are several different types of graphs, such as bar, circle, coordinate, scatter plot, line, and stem-and-leaf. (kr)

graph theory

The study of graphs that contain points and lines connecting those points, creating vertices and edges. Within this graph every edge has two end points, which may or may not connect to another edge. It is not used in the study of statistical representation. Example: the famous Seven Bridges of Konigsberg problem can be explored using graph theory. (ldz)

grapheme

A written or printed representation of a phoneme. For example, in the word *shoe*, the grapheme *sh* represents the phoneme /(/ and *oe* for /u:/. In English, a grapheme may be a single letter or a group of letters. It includes all the ways that a phoneme could be written or printed. (smt)

See also phoneme.

graphic design

The process of arranging typography, images, and visual elements with design principles and specifications for paper, ink colors, and printing processes that, when combined, convey visual information. Graphic design is commonly used for commercial purposes—for such things as packaging, advertisements, signage, books, and magazines. Individuals who create this type of artwork, either as a vocation or an avocation, are referred to as graphic designers. Graphic design is an apt vehicle for school arts programs as it helps students construct and critique the graphic presentation of public messages such as those found on posters and other print media. (kf)

graphic novel

While a graphic novel may just appear to be a grandiose comic book, thicker and produced on higher quality paper, many readers claim that the differences are more substantive. Graphic novels generally are complete stories or collections of stories, while comic books usually center on one episode in a series. As readers of graphic novels are assumed to be more mature and sophisticated, the themes tend to be more adult and the illustrations more explicit. The writing in graphic novels is often quite excellent. Art Spiegelman's holocaust autobiography, *Maus, A Survivor's Tale* (1991), has won prizes and been included in school curricula. The writing in comic books however, is largely underrated. As it is with graphic novels, many comics contain rich descriptors, sophisticated ideas, and high-level vocabulary. (jd)

graphic organizer (See advance organizer)

graphic symbolization
From a cognitive perspective, the representation through graphic marks on paper of ideas, things, and events. Psychological researchers have long believed that children's drawing or graphic symbolization holds the key to understanding both cognitive and/or emotional development. They focus on the mental structures and the subsequent thinking processes revealed in children's early depictions, or on the healthy or damaged psyche of the child, as revealed in the projected symbols of the drawings. Drawings are seen as important vehicles for constructing knowledge and as a reflection of the natural, biological processes of mental development. (kpb)

gray matter
Gray matter is tissue in the center of the spinal cord and the thin outer layer of the cerebral hemispheres of the brain called the cerebral cortex. It consists of closely packed neuronal cell bodies, neuropil (a dense network of dendrites and both unmyelinated axons and myelinated axons), glial cells, and capillaries. The cerebral cortex has folded bulges called gyri that create deep furrows called sulci. The folds in the brain increase surface area, thereby increasing the amount of gray matter and the quantity of information that can be processed. Encompassing about two-thirds of the brain mass, it is the most highly developed part of the human brain. Gray matter routes sensory and motor stimulus in interneurons of the central nervous system to activate muscle control and sensory perceptions such as seeing and hearing, memory, emotions, and

speech. Gray matter differs in color from white matter mainly from the whiteness of myelin. (ns)

GRE (See Graduate Record Examination)

Great Books Program
A methodology rooted in the belief that the curriculum best suited to deliver a quality education is one based on the literary classics. Robert Maynard Hutchins, former president of the University of Chicago, and philosopher Mortimer Adler are usually given credit for its establishment between the two World Wars. Other sources credit Columbia University's John Erskine with its initial establishment on that campus in the 1920s. More broadly, the "Great Books Curriculum" and "Great Books Concept" were also seen as a way to interest adults in classic books through reading and discussing the literature. It was a grassroots movement for continuing education outside classroom settings. (rih)

Greek chorus
Functioning often as the voice of society and variously as narrator, commentator, interpreter, sympathizer, and critic, the chorus played a central role in Greek theater. The Greek word for actor is *hypokrites*, meaning answerer; the actor's function originally was to answer the chorus. In the theaters in ancient Greece, the chorus sang, danced, and spoke from the orchestra (meaning dancing place), the circular area on ground level in front of the audience. (em)

Greek organization
A collegiate organization whose name uses the Greek alphabet and whose members are selected on certain criteria, whether scholastic or social. The oldest Greek organization in America is the scholastic honor society Phi Beta Kappa, founded in 1776. Social Greek organizations were founded in the 1800s, as an outgrowth

of literary debating societies with Greek names. (cf)

Green v. New Kent County Board, 391 U.S. 430 (1968)

This U.S. Supreme Court case examined whether a "freedom-of-choice" plan that allowed students to choose their own public schools represented compliance with *Brown v. Board of Education.* Green alleged the New Kent County, Virginia,, school board's educational plan was divisive, ineffective, and supported the state's efforts to circumvent federal regulation to integrate schools. In effect, the Court held that the board's plan was unacceptable and firmly stated that the onus was on the board (not the public) to integrate the schools by providing a realistic, expedient, effective, and measurable plan to do so. (cm!)

Greyston Conference

A conference held at Teachers College, Columbia University, in 1971, cosponsored by the National Council of Teachers of Mathematics and viewed by some mathematics education scholars as signaling the beginning of an era calling into question the dominance of quantitative research and its accompanying Piagetian research epistemology in mathematics education research. The conference provided what some view as the first public forum for beginning a dialogue between the established Piagetian cognitive psychological approach and the emerging constructivist approach to mathematics education research. (smts)

grief counseling

A therapeutic approach used when a client experiences a significant loss, such as the death of a close family member or pet; may be time-limited and focus on one of many stage models of the grieving process. (cag)

Griffin v. School Board of Prince Edward County, 377 U.S. 218 (1964)

The Supreme Court case that ordered Prince Edward County, Virginia, to reopen its public schools for both white and black children because the children were being denied "their constitutional rights to an education." The County Board of Supervisors suspended all public education in 1959 rather than integrate its schools, as was required following the conclusion of *Brown v. Board of Education.* This display of "massive resistance" to desegregation made Prince Edward County the only county in the nation to close its public schools entirely for an extended period to avoid desegregation. (ks2)

gross motor activities

Activities that require the use of large muscle groups in the developing child. Large muscle groups include the muscles of head control, trunk movement, the arms, and legs. Such activities include rolling, sitting, walking, running, standing, and hopping. As children develop their gross motor skills, they also develop their fine motor skills. Gross motor skills continue to develop as muscles grow and strength and balance improve. (jb)

group counseling

A form of group work that, in its truest form, is interpersonal and process focused. Counseling groups are either facilitated or cofacilitated by trained professionals. Therapeutic gains are derived largely from interactions among the group members. A number of curative factors have been identified as contributing to the benefits of this treatment modality. The factors vary, but many researchers and clinicians identify universality, provision of hope, interpersonal learning, modeling, altruism, working through conflicts that developed in the primary family group, development of social skills, catharsis, group cohesion, imparting information, and existential factors as common elements that lead to positive outcomes. Group counseling can be preventative, growth engendering, or remedial. (fa)

group dynamics

The forces and processes of interaction operating within a relatively small human group. These interactions are addressed in terms of dealing with individuals, other groups, institutions, and organizations, as well as the basis for the development of these relationships. (jrw, npo)

group size

A cluster of children identified by the number of members, used to identify how many children for whom a particular learning event is deemed appropriate. Example categories include: *small group,* which might indicate anywhere from three children to one-third or half of an entire class; and *whole or large group,* which implies all the children in the class, as opposed to individual instruction. (db1)

groupware

Computer software that facilitates collaboration by automating group processes such as information organization and sharing. Groupware products often provide an integrated user interface that allows access to membership, document archives, asynchronous discussion forums, and synchronous chat. This software resides on a network from which group members can access the information remotely. Groupware can be used by teams of educators or students working on a group project. (tll)

growth, occupational (See occupational growth)

G-theory (See generalizability theory)

Guey Heung Lee v. Johnson, 404 U.S. 1215 (1971)

The Supreme Court Case initiated by Chinese Americans who were petitioning the High Court to stop a Federal District Court's order to reassign pupils of Chinese ancestry in San Francisco public schools in an effort to integrate. Although Chinese Americans sought to maintain community control over their schools, citing the unique bilingual and cultural education these schools provided their children, the Court denied their petition and forced them to comply with integration orders. (dwm)

GUI (graphical user interface) (See user interface)

guidance

The supportive actions taken by more experienced peers or adults to assist the development of socially acceptable emotional or other appropriate responses to events. (mc1)

guidance, career (See career guidance)

guidance, occupational (See occupational guidance)

guidance, vocational (See vocational guidance)

guidance counseling

Term applied to counseling activities in an educational setting for students, kindergarten through high school. These activities may involve providing academic development (attitudes and study skills to improve learning), career development (planning, goal setting, and college preparation/application), and personal/social development (self-concept, emotions, interpersonal relationship skills, behavior management). Counselors help students achieve success in work, family, and school situations. (tsw)

guided practice

A form of assisted performance in which students practice a new skill or strategy while the teacher provides close monitoring, immediate feedback, and assistance as needed. (bba)

guided reading

Reading instruction with a small group of children characterized by children reading books on their "instructional" level, that is, books that require some scaffolding from the teacher to support student comprehension. In this model, the teacher introduces the text, explicitly teaches vocabulary and comprehension skills to use during reading, holds conferences with each student as he or she reads independently, and finishes the lesson with a word study or other type of extension activity. For guided reading groups, children are selected by reading ability or by the need to develop a particular skill in reading. (jas)

guidelines

A term used in education to describe a framework or set of statements used to help determine a course of action. They are less stipulative than codes. For example, school districts use guidelines for curricula in order to help educators carry out the district education plan for students. (mm)

guilt/shame

Self-referential affects. Guilt is a self-judgment that one has acted wrongly. This connection to actions is what differentiates guilt from shame, which attaches to identity. This is a difficult distinction to sustain, as one's actions do, at some point, become defining. Another way to differentiate guilt from shame is that guilt damages one's relations with another and requires one's expiating or compensating for the wrong done, or forgiveness of the one wronged. Shame, on the other hand, is the judgment that one fails to live up to one's own ideals and requires reform rather than expiation. Both affects have the potential to become pathologies, when guilt comes from inappropriate judgments of one's actions, or when shame is the result of unrealistic ideals or self-image. One of the tasks of education is to help children develop an appropriate and healthy sense of self-evaluation. (jc)

See also conscience.

H

habilitation
Training and specialized services to enhance an individual's functioning ability. (sr)

habits of mind
The practices and steps a person takes to make a decision, solve a problem, or carry out another activity requiring a thoughtful approach, generally including steps like forming questions, gathering data, reflecting on observable information, discussing alternatives with others, determining a course of action, and initiating a particular activity. (sh)

Hampton-Tuskegee Model of Education
A type of industrial education curriculum implemented at many African American institutions during the late 19th and early 20th centuries. Booker T. Washington, an alumnus of Hampton Institute, founded Tuskegee Institute in 1881. Endorsing industrial training for blacks (versus a classical-liberal curriculum), the Model was codified through a series of Conferences for Education in the South. The Model was ideologically and financially supported by northern white philanthropists and strongly opposed by African American intellectual W.E.B. Du Bois. The Hampton-Tuskegee model was also adapted for use in missionary schools overseas and for Native Americans and Mexican Americans. (jrb)

handheld computer
A computing device small enough to be held in one hand and operated with the other. Some types utilize a small keyboard and are referred to as palmtop computers. Others use a stylus to input on a touch-sensitive screen and are called personal digital assistants (PDAs). Handhelds may accept accessories such as digital cameras, global positioning devices, cell phone connections, or environmental instruments and probes. These accessories make handhelds useful for students or researchers gathering data directly from the environment. (ac)

handicapism
This term refers to discriminatory behaviors and attitudes against people with disabilities. Since handicap is an outdated term with negative overtones, handicapism reinforces the bias against individuals with disabilities. Current usage prefers the phrase "people with disabilities," since the emphasis is on people rather than the disability. (jqa, npo)

hands-on curriculum/activities

A cornerstone of the constructivist approach, hands-on curriculum and activities are those in which students touch, move, and experiment with materials in the classroom. As they manipulate objects, children think about the objects' properties and relationships. After several such experiences, children develop "theories" about how things work that can be tested with further manipulation. Children's work with hands-on materials can be assessed and recorded as the children are working, and this data can be analyzed to realize the child's learning progress. (yb)

hands-on learning

Learning by doing, or learning in which students are actively engaged in an activity or process. (bba)

harassment

Biased behaviors that have a negative impact on a specific target, which can be an individual or a subgroup of people, and on the environment. Safe Schools initiatives focus on ending all bullying and violence, especially antigay harassment and other bias-based discrimination. Antigay harassment affects all youth perceived to be gay or lesbian, regardless of actual sexual orientation. This perception is typically based on an individual's gender expression. (jb2)

See also bullying; gendered harassment.

harmony

A combination of elements (in visual art, color and form; in music, notes and chords) in which the separate parts are perceived (either through vision or hearing) as working well together and being pleasing to the eye or ear. Consonance and appealing dissonance seem to be the features of parallel structures (e.g., musical passages/pitches or colors) working together harmoniously. Harmonic analysis is the study of the structure and interaction of chords within a musical work. (jbl)

Hatch Act

Signed into law in March 1887, the act established experimental stations for agriculture throughout the country in connection with land grant universities. These stations were federally funded for research into different farming techniques that would assist in the various types of land found throughout the country and improvements that would be beneficial to crops and farm animals. Often said to have bridged the 1862 Morrill Act, which set up land grant universities, and the 1914 Smith-Lever Act, which put researchers directly into the farm fields. (rih)

hate crime

A crime based on bias related to religion, race, gender, sexual orientation, or nationality. Law enforcement statistics for 2008 indicate that anti-GLBT hate crimes have increased more than any other category. Congress passed a hate crimes bill in 2009 that extends protection to GLB people but was perceived as controversial by some GLBTQ advocates because the bill does not include gender identity as a protected category. (jb2)

hate group

Organized groups that harass, demean, or otherwise target for negative purposes categories of people based on their ethnicity, race, or sexual orientation are called hate groups. Although this is not an official term, it is commonly used. In the United States, such groups range from the White Aryan Resistance, a white supremacist group, to the Nation of Islam, a Black Muslim separatist group. (jqa, npo)

HBCUs (See Historically Black Colleges and Universities)

Head Start

First authorized in 1964 by the federal Economic Opportunity Act, now governed by the U.S. Department of Health and Human Services, Administration for Children and Families, Head Start is the largest federally funded program for assisting young children and their families. As part of President Johnson's "War on Poverty," Head Start was designed to help disadvantaged three- and four-year-olds prepare for school by stimulating their cognitive, social, and psychological development, providing health and nutrition programs, and requiring parental involvement. Head Start benefits children with both typical and special needs, providing a "head start" to children in poverty by supplying developmentally appropriate and culturally sensitive educational, medical, and social services to young children and their families. (ecr, ks2)

Head Start providers

The federal Head Start program operates through a system of grants to state and local public and private agencies, called "providers." All grantees and delegate agencies must affirm and adhere to a set of program performance standards that include definitions, timelines, and guidelines for their operation. (ecr)

health literacy

A recent term that refers to the relationship between health and literacy skills but sometimes is used to mean the knowledge and skills needed to successfully use the modern health care system. (jpc)

health occupations education

One of the major program areas in career and technical education, which challenges students to integrate mathematical, natural, and social science concepts through classroom, laboratory, and clinical experiences while preparing for careers in the health care industry. (jb)

health psychology

A subspecialty within the field of psychology devoted to understanding the effect of psychological variables in the prevention, development, maintenance, and recovery of mental/physical conditions among individuals and communities. Coming from a strength-based perspective, health psychology focuses mostly on how to maintain and promote mental/physical health, as opposed to focusing on how to treat and remediate deficits. (kc, scmc, bdj)

health-related fitness

The optimal functioning of the body free of the risk factors involving life-threatening diseases. Aspects of health-related fitness include cardiorespiratory fitness, muscular strength, muscular endurance, flexibility, and body composition. (rf, kpr)

hearing impairment

A disability, whether permanent or fluctuating, that adversely affects a person's ability to receive spoken messages or sounds. (sr)

HEAs (See higher education associations)

hedonism

A thesis in value theory (axiology). From the Greek *hedone* (pleasure), holds that pleasure is the only thing valuable in itself, and that all other goods (e.g., health, wealth, knowledge, virtue) are valuable only to the extent that they lead to the experience of pleasure. Important hedonists, including Epicurus (341–270 B.C.E.) and John Stuart Mill (1806–1873), have held that not all pleasures are equally valuable; pleasures typically associated with the exercise of the intellect are more valuable than those typically associated with bodily experience. (dl)

See also consequentialism; deontological ethics.

hegemonic masculinity

Based on the sociological theory of a variety of masculinities. Hegemonic masculinity is at the top of a gender-based hierarchy. Other types of masculinity and femininity are viewed as inferior. This theory has been criticized for defining masculinity in terms of biological categories of male and female. (jb2)

hegemony

Antonio Gramsci's description of how one group or class dominates others. Two avenues are available: physical, violent control through force (police, prisons), or control through shaping consciousness (hegemony). Consciousness is manipulated, primarily through schools and the media, so that the interests, dispositions, and ways of life of the ruling group are seen to represent the best way to live, and those in power seem deserving of power. The ruling group may incorporate (adopt for different ends) challenges to the status quo or domesticate (remove the dangerous elements and retain the remainder) the challenge, in either case retaining its power and privilege. Other possible responses include ignoring the challenge or marginalizing (portraying it is an idiosyncratic lifestyle) a challenge that does not pose a serious threat yet cannot be incorporated or domesticated. Used only as a means of last resort, force reveals the naked power of the ruling group. (db-j)

See also critical theory; reproduction theory.

HEGIS (See Higher Education General Information Survey)

helicopter parents

A recently coined term used to describe the contemporary parent-child relationship of the current generation of college students. Helicopter parents "hover" obsessively around their child and are ready to provide assistance and guidance and to intervene on their child's behalf on a moment's notice. The child in turn relies heavily upon their parents for advice, information, assistance, and guidance. With the advent of fast and inexpensive communication technology (e.g., cell phones and text messaging), helicopter parents are able to keep in constant contact with their offspring. Helicopter parents may contact professors directly with questions about assignments, tests, and grades and may contact the college or university on

issues ranging from housing to internships. (pw1)

Herbartian Movement

A late 19th-century curriculum movement led by the American followers of German philosopher Johann Friedrich Herbart, widely considered the father of the scientific study of education. The movement promoted a type of liberal-humanist curriculum primarily based on history and literature. It held that teaching and learning occurred in five formal stages: preparation, presentation, association, generalization, and application. The theoretical basis of this curriculum reflected the belief that education should seek to link new experiences with old ones. (dwm)

HERI (See Higher Education Research Institute)

hermeneutics

Hermeneutics was originally the art of interpretation and included rules of interpretation for uncovering the truth in the Bible, the laws, and the classics. Since Schleiermacher, hermeneutics has been more concerned with the philosophical reflection on the conditions of understanding than on the development of a methodology, and the field of hermeneutics has expanded in the sense that not only texts have to be interpreted, but all kinds of human affairs. Hermeneutics is, therefore, not only of interest for the text-based sciences, but also for the social sciences. A process of analysis that holds that texts are understood only through the interpretation of lived experience. Absent a process of interpretation, the significance of textual meanings is neither understandable nor evident. (jb1, hfs)

heterogeneity

A mixture of individuals in a group in which each person has different characteristics. In education, students are often placed in heterogeneous groups based on ability, interests, achievement, gender, race, or ethnicity. These mixed groups are encouraged in order to develop positive intergroup relationships and to reflect the more global makeup of society. (jqa, srs)

heterogeneous grouping
A pattern of grouping students for instruction that does not separate students into groups based on their measured intelligence, school achievement, or physical attributes. (bba)

heteronormative
A term first used in 1991 by Michael Warner, a social critic, to describe pervasive and often implicit "norms" of heterosexuality that have a broad influence on social institutions, scientific and social theory, educational practice, and so on. The concept of heteronormativity is used by some to make explicit the assumptions upon which culturally dominant heterosexuality are based; make explicit the exclusivity of heterosexual norms; and demonstrate why deviations from heterosexual norms are subject to social and legal sanctions. The term is considered controversial by some because it includes criticism of those who disapprove of nonheterosexual behavior. (jb2)

heterosexism
A term analogous to sexism and racism that describes an ideological system that denies, denigrates, and stigmatizes any nonheterosexual form of behavior, identity, relationship, or community. Heterosexism permeates societal customs, social and educational institutions, and legal statutes. Not synonymous with homophobia. (jb2)

heterosexuality
A type of sexual orientation that consists of being attracted romantically, sexually, and emotionally to members of the opposite biological sex. Research indicates that heterosexuality is the majority sexual orientation (95%) for the human population. (jb2)

heuristics
A method of individual problem solving. The method includes systematic analysis and evaluation of a task or problem, the problem-solving process, and the progress toward a solution that is discovered by the student himself or herself. Problem-solving strategies that can be applied in a variety of nonroutine problem-solving situations. Examples of heuristics include "guess and check," where the student tries numbers randomly to see which will solve the problem, or "draw a picture," where the student incorporates the information from the problem in some diagrammatic form to aid in finding a solution. (clk, amr)

hidden curriculum
Lessons we teach in schools not explicitly stated in the curriculum. For example, calling on boys more often than girls teaches the relative importance of boys and girls. The selection of content in literature and social studies classes is the most obvious way the hidden curriculum reflects and teaches subtly and powerfully the way "the world is" and what matters in it. The centrality in texts of white males, the relative invisibility of women and people of color, and the near-complete absence of gays and lesbians teach about place within society. The rightness of capitalism, the value of individuality and competition, and concepts of "fair play" are among the things taught by the hidden curriculum. Its hiddenness, often even from the teacher, makes it difficult to analyze and confront its content. (bt-b)

See also curriculum; explicit curriculum; null curriculum; operationalized curriculum.

high arts (See fine arts)

high school (See senior high school)

high school, specialized
A secondary school of which the educational program is designed especially for

learners studying related occupations or vocations associated with a specific career area or various career areas. Specific vocations or fields of specialized interest include, for example, an agricultural high school or a commercial high school. (db)

High School: A Report on Secondary Education in America (1983)

Report by Ernest Boyer of the excellence movement in the 1980s, which questioned the ability of the American education system to prepare students to face rising global economic competition. The report echoed the concerns about maintaining technological superiority over the Soviet Union raised during the 1950s and 1960s. *High School. . . .* shares prominence with Mortimer Adler's 1982 *The Paideia Proposal: An Educational Manifesto,* and 1983's *A Nation at Risk,* prepared by the National Commission on Excellence in Education, which spurred the nation to begin a series of educational reforms. (dwm)

high school equivalency

A certificate or diploma that provides the same certification as a high school diploma but that was earned outside of regular high school. (jpc)

High Schools that Work

A school improvement effort organized by the Southern Regional Education Board that emphasizes the mastery of rigorous academic and career and technical education studies; requires a motivating and supportive environment, and the collaboration of school leaders, teachers, parents, and the community. Schools that have implemented the program generally show improvement in graduation rates and postsecondary attendance. (rz)

Higher Education Act of 1965 (Public Law 89-329)

Passed by Congress on November 8, 1965, it provided grants for university community service programs, college library assistance, library training and research, strengthening developing institutions, teacher training programs, undergraduate instruction equipment, and student assistance through educational opportunity grants. The law established ensured student loans, extended and amended the College Work-Study Program, amended the National Defense Education Act of 1958 (NDEA), created the National Teacher Corps Program, provided for graduate teacher training fellowships, and amended the Higher Education Facilities Act of 1963. (wg)

higher education associations (HEAs)

Voluntary private organizations formed to represent individuals or institutions having a common interest in one of the wide variety of issues affecting higher education. These groups provide information and expertise to their members through publications, education and training programs, and other networking formats. They often engage in lobbying activities, develop professional guidelines, and furnish advice and services that individuals or institutions are unable to provide for themselves. (cf)

Higher Education General Information Survey (HEGIS)

Started in 1966, the HEGIS was instituted by the U.S. Department of Education to compile data concerning higher education institutions. As a result, financial accounting and reporting methods in the academy attained the uniformity needed to produce revenue and expenditure categories consistent with appropriate accounting procedures. Replaced by the Integrated Postsecondary Education Data System (IPEDS). (cf)

higher education law

The branch of legal studies and practice involving postsecondary education institutions and their students, faculty, and staff members. Studied and reported separately from school law, which covers primary and secondary education. (cf)

Higher Education Opportunity Act

Passed by Congress in 2008, the Higher Education Opportunity Act reauthorizes the Higher Education Act of 1965 with programmatic and legal changes. The law includes the following:

- Additional student aid provisions such as improvements in the financial aid process, and additional resources for veterans.
- Requirements for greater college cost disclosure and reporting, including the development of a net cost and a multiyear tuition calculator by the Department of Education.
- Requirements for code of ethics and greater transparency of policies by lenders and institutions involved in student lending.
- Requirements for greater accreditation transparency and sets accreditor/institution relationship guidelines
- Requirements for greater disclosure and reporting of fire and campus safety, protection of student speech, missing person notifications, textbook cost containment, peer-to-peer file-sharing policies and ramifications, and transfer of credit policies.
- Improvements of teacher professional development through the development of quantifiable goals of teacher programs and reporting of licensure and certification pass rates.
- Requests for new studies including uses of public college and university endowments. (ms)

Higher Education Research Institute (HERI)

Housed at the University of California, Los Angeles, HERI publishes numerous research reports related to higher education, including *The American Freshman* and the *American College Teacher.* (sn)

Higher Learning Commission (HLC)

One of six regional institutional accrediting associations acknowledged by the Council on Higher Education Accreditation. HLC accredits colleges and universities in 19 states. Prior to November 2000, accreditation in the North Central region was coordinated by the North Central Association Commission on Institutions of Higher Education. (cf)

higher-order questions

Questions that promote complex and abstract thinking—deeper mental processing than is required in simple recall or factual questions (lower-order questions). (bba)

Highlander Center for Research and Education

Established in 1932 by Myles Horton in the mountains of east Tennessee as the Highlander Folk School, the Highlander Center brings adults together to learn strategies for solving community problems, especially the problems of poverty, bigotry, and economic injustice in Appalachia and the South. (js)

Highlander Folk School

A training and education institution in Tennessee, founded by Myles Horton, that trains civil rights workers and community activists. The school employs a problem-oriented approach in which learners' needs help determine curriculum and their experiences help derive solutions. Teachers and learners engage in a mutual learning process. (las)

High/Scope curriculum

An approach to learning and assessment built on a routine in which children are individually assisted by an adult to help create intentionality for their actions in a "plan-do-review sequence." First children plan what they choose to be involved with, followed by the actual engagement with materials and activities as they follow the plan. Finally children and adults reconnect to review and reflect on what transpired during the engagement period. (db1)

high-stakes standards

High-stakes standards are created by policy makers with the intent to improve education by raising the bar of achievement. High stakes require that students pass a standardized exam before they can be promoted or graduate. States are now mandating more rigorous academic standards and instituting strict assessment in order to guarantee that students are meeting those standards. Critics argue, however, that standards are so-called high stakes, because they often bring consequences for educators and students. School-wide average scores are used to judge schools, high scores can bring praise or financial benefits, and low scores can bring sanctions and embarrassment. Critics also argue that curriculum and instruction can be distorted if high test scores, rather than learning itself, become the goal of all classroom instruction. (cl)

high-stakes testing

An approach to gathering information through testing programs on student and school performance at the state and/or local level. In high-stakes testing, test results are directly correlated with individual student achievement and school accountability. Important decisions, such as school finance and student grade promotion, are made based on test results. (clk)

high-tech, high-wage, high-demand occupations

The jobs that are typically targeted by career and technical education programs, which require some postsecondary technical training and for which there is a labor demand; sometimes are new and emerging occupations. (rz)

hi-low books

Hi-low books are designed by publishers to be of low readability levels, but of high interest to the young adult and adult readership for which the majority of these books are designed. They are also known as "high interest/low readability books" and "high-low books." (rcr)

hip-hop

Of or pertaining to contemporary urban youth culture, including art forms developed by African American and Latino youth, such as rap music (used interchangeably/thought of as synonymous with hip-hop), break-dancing, and graffiti art. This genre is identified as originating in the 1970s by New York City teens ("subculture" "hip-hop generation") but has been adopted/developed by youth and commercial professional artists throughout the United States across lines of geographical location and socioeconomic status. Hip-hop is associated with giving new form and venue for traditionally underheard voices in society. (jd)

See also graffiti; rap/rap music; voice.

Hispanic Americans

This term refers to Americans who share a culture, heritage, and language that originated in Spain but may have descended through Portugal or Latin America. At times the term "Latinos" is used alternatively. The largest groups of Hispanics in the United States are Mexican Americans (Chicanos), Puerto Ricans, and Cubans. (jqa)

Hispanic-Serving Institution (HSI)

Federal legislative definition for an accredited and degree-granting public or private nonprofit institution of higher education with at least 25 percent or more total undergraduate Hispanic full-time equivalent student enrollment. The federal government identified HSIs in Title V of the Higher Education Act of 1965, as amended. To qualify for Title V funds, HSIs must also have low educational and general expenditures, and 50 percent of the Hispanic students from lower-income households. (vmm)

histogram

A bar chart or bar graph that shows how the data are distributed throughout each interval. (kr)

historical empathy

Empathy directed toward a historical figure as a result of inquiry into or study of the past. (ewr)

Historically Black Colleges and Universities (HBCUs)

The set of public and private postsecondary institutions established prior to 1954 whose primary mission has been the education of African Americans. In 1965, the U.S. Congress passed the institutional aid program named "Strengthening Historically Black Colleges and Universities" (20 USC 1060). As of 1996, HBCUs numbered 103 and enrolled almost 16 percent of all black students in college. Comprising a diverse set of four-year colleges, research universities, and single-sex and coeducational schools mostly in the American South, HBCUs today no longer enroll only African Americans, but share a mission to serve disadvantaged, college-bound students of all races. (dwm)

historiography

The study and writing of history, or the study of historical writing. Also refers to the history and study of various interpretations historians have assigned to methods and theories of historical investigations. The study of history dates back to Ancient Greece. Centuries of historical writing have resulted in numerous schools of thought in the analysis and evaluation of events and people. During the 20th century, the introduction of quantitative methodology has contributed to new schools of thought, including social history, which has greatly expanded the historiography of many fields. (cm!)

history

The study of the past and present from multiple perspectives and the influences on the immediate and long-range future. The study of history involves all written documents and, when possible, first-hand accounts as evidence to supplement stories that have been passed through the generations. Understanding history helps us to function in the present and prepare for the future by investigating events and narratives objectively to reveal cause and effect in the holistic totality of the human experience. (npg)

history of education

The historical study of the educational enterprise, broadly defined. Historians of education examine the history of students, teachers, institutions, administrators, curriculum, reform, and other aspects of the educational experience. In recent years historians have examined more closely the link between class, race, gender, ethnicity, and educational opportunity. These endeavors, in part, are carried out to promote an appreciation of the value of the historical perspective in the formation of educational policy. A relatively new field, the History of Education Society was founded in 1960 (as the successor to the History of Education Section of the National Society of College Teachers of Education) and is affiliated with the International Standing Conference for the History of Education. (vmm)

HLC (See Higher Learning Commission)

holistic

In a holistic system, individual elements are both self-regulating and interdependent, in that they are determined by their relation to all other elements of that system and cannot exist apart from it. A holistic therapeutic approach involves an examination of the intrapersonal, interpersonal, and systemic factors in an individual's life, as well as of spiritual or transpersonal dimensions. (jbb)

holistic writing rubric

A rubric that takes a variety of criteria into account but gives each writing piece one composite score based on all of the factors combined to give a gestalt view of the writer's proficiency. (cld)

Holmes Group

A consortium of the leading institutions of higher education with professional education programs, which developed out of work in the early 1980s by education deans and their concern over the quality, standards, and accreditation of teacher education programs. The consortium, named after the dean of the Harvard Graduate School of Education, Henry Holmes, sought to reform teacher education by improving the interactivity of the education programs with the institutions where they were located. The consortium also sought to reform the teaching profession. To achieve these reforms, the consortium focused on the education of teachers, the schools where they taught, the relationship of those schools to education programs, the establishment of professional standards for entry into teaching, and understanding the knowledge, skills, and commitments of teachers. In 1996, the consortium merged with seven national education associations to form the Holmes Partnership. (ms)

Holmes Partnership (See Holmes Group)

home economics education

Major program area in career and technical education that prepares students for the workforce and for home life through teaching nutrition and food preparation, parenting and child development, resource and time management, consumer education, housing and home furnishings, personal clothing management, and human relationships and family development. (jb)

home groups (See tight-knit groups)

home page

A Web page serving as the entry point or initial access page for a Web site. If a Web site contains more than one Web page, hyperlinks from the home page connect visitors to the additional Web pages. In an educational setting, school districts, schools, teachers, or students may all have home pages for presenting content on the Web. (kg1)

See also hyperlink; web page; website.

home visits

An appointment between parent or caregiver and professional that occurs in the home of the child. Home visits can consist of a variety of activities including parent education, breast-feeding advice, midwifery, health care, services for children with special needs, and counseling. The social service needs of the family are also often addressed as part of home visits. Home visits are offered in several types of programs, including those offered by the Health Department, Head Start, and parent education programs. (kdc)

home-based early intervention

Early intervention services that are provided in the homes of eligible children, including service coordination (or case management), evaluations, assessments, treatment planning, and ongoing developmental intervention, education, or therapy. (kms)

home-based services

An alternative to office-based care, programs are increasingly offering service provision in the homes of families. Nursing care, parent education, therapy for children with special needs, and counseling can be delivered by home visitors within the privacy and comfort of the family home. Professionals have an opportunity to observe a child in his or her natural environment and provide tips and activities that can be easily performed in the home or daycare. (kdc)

homeroom

A classroom to which a group of students reports every day. At the secondary level, reporting may occur less frequently and is done primarily for administrative purposes, such as course selection, advising, and schoolwide activities. (jw)

home-school relations

The relationship between the teacher/ school and the parents/family. Positive and collaborative relationships between parents and teachers are one of the strongest predictors of academic success. However, some families with a history of poor relationships to schools and teachers can subvert their children's school progress. Because parents are so influential in a child's early years, schools and teachers should find ways to include parents in learning about early stimulation, child guidance, literacy, nutrition, and other topics as appropriate to the age of the child and the needs of the parent. (ecr)

homework

Work assigned by a teacher for students to complete outside of the classroom. Homework typically involves either practice or reinforcement of concepts and skills learned in the classroom or preparation for upcoming instruction. (bba)

homogeneous grouping

A pattern of grouping students for instruction that separates students into groups based on their measured intelligence, school achievement, or physical attributes. (bba)

homonegativism (See homophobia)

homophobia

An aversion to, and prejudice against, people who self-identify as gay, lesbian, or bisexual; the traits that characterize them; and their sexual practices, lifestyles, and beliefs. Homophobia may be expressed in terms of personal beliefs, discriminatory acts, and institutional or cultural norms. Other terms used to refer to such prejudice are "homonegativism" and "heterosexism." Such prejudice directed specifically toward bisexual individuals is known as "biphobia" or "monosexism." In classic psychological terms, homophobia is an irrational fear of homosexuality, first used by psychologist George Weinberg in the late 1960s to describe heterosexuals' panic at being near homosexuals. Currently it is used to describe a range of bias or dislike of GBLTQ people, or the behaviors associated with them. Homophobia is often inaccurately used interchangeably with heterosexism. An individual whose virulent prejudice could lead to violence against a GLBTQ person is appropriately described as homophobic. More accurate terms to describe the typical range of bias include straight privilege, heterosexism, antigay bias, and antigay harassment. (jb2, ti)

homosexual

A clinical term, offensive to some, for individuals who are attracted physically, emotionally, and/or spiritually to members of their own biological sex. Preferred terms for common usage are lesbian and gay. (jb2)

See also gay.

homosexuality

A type of sexual orientation that consists of being attracted romantically, sexually, and emotionally to members of the same biological sex. Homosexual behavior and attractions have been described in various cultures, nations, and species throughout the world, and in a wide variety of historical periods. Current research suggests that, depending on how the term is defined, roughly six percent of men and four percent of women have this type of sexual orientation. (jb2)

honor code

A proscribed standard of conduct accepted and enforced by members of an academic community through the agreement to uphold tenets of honesty and civility. (cf)

honorary degree (See degree, honorary)

honorary organizations
Groups whose members are selected because of their achievements in academic or service endeavors; may include students, staff, or faculty members, and alumni and may be local, national, or international in scope. (cf)

honors course
A course designed for students who are gifted or unusually interested in a specific topic that explores the content to a deeper extent and requires work that exceeds the requirements of a standard course in the same subject area. Honors courses typically limit enrollment to students who meet predetermined criteria. (jw)

HOPE
Helping Outstanding Pupils Educationally, Georgia's scholarship program that provides qualified students with financial assistance for degree, diploma, and certificate programs at eligible Georgia public and private colleges and public technical colleges. Since the HOPE Program began thousands of Georgians have received financial assistance through the program, which is funded by the Georgia Lottery for Education. (cf)

Hopwood v. State of Texas, 78 F. 3rd 932, 5th Cir. (1996)
A case brought in 1992 to the U.S. Court of Appeals in which the white plaintiff (Cheryl Hopwood) alleged she was the victim of reverse discrimination in the admissions process for the University of Texas Law School. The 5th Circuit Court decided in 1996 that the practice of using race or national origin as a factor in the admissions decision was illegal. The U.S. Supreme Court declined to hear an appeal from the State of Texas. (dwm)

horizontal articulation (See articulation, horizontal)

horizontal staffing
A practice of staffing teacher education programs with professors teaching a single course in their area of expertise, with little synthesis among the different aspects of the curriculum. This is opposite to vertical staffing, in which faculty members teach multiple courses within a teacher education program. The goal of vertical staffing is to provide a more integrated educational experience for preservice teachers. (clk)

hornbook
An early primer used by European and American children from the 16th to the 18th centuries. Hornbooks were usually small (averaging 2.5 inches by 5 inches), made of wood, and shaped like a paddle. A lesson printed on parchment paper and protected by a thin layer of transparent horn was attached to the paddle and typically included the alphabet, vowels, and the Lord's Prayer. Hornbooks were considered innovative because they allowed children to handle the text they were learning to read for the first time. (jlw)

hostage theory of education
Belief or conviction in the earliest years of desegregation efforts that the mere presence of white children (hostages) in a public school or classroom would shield African American children from inadequate funding and educational opportunities simply because any decrease in resources would negatively affect white children as well. (hfs)

HRD (See human resource development)

HSI (See Hispanic-Serving Institution)

Hull House
University settlement founded by Jane Addams and Ellen Greta Starr in Chicago in 1889 as part of an educational and social outreach movement. In such houses, men

and women from universities went to live and work among the poor in large cities to assist and educate them. (las)

human capital theory

A theory that defines education as a highly profitable investment. It focuses on the individual's earning potential and affirms that a society can foster growth and development by fostering individuals' skill levels. (jwg)

human factors engineering

The study of the interaction between humans and machines. Human factors engineers focus on designing products that increase an individual's productivity while reducing fatigue and discomfort. Products can be as seemingly simple as a child's toy or as complicated as an airplane cockpit. When focusing on computer user interface design, this discipline is referred to as Human Computer Interaction (HCI) or Interaction Design. Also known as ergonomics. (tll)

See also user interface.

human growth and development

Formerly sex education. In education, a course to increase the understanding and knowledge of the structure, functions, and behavioral aspects of human development and sexual reproduction. Topics might include discussions about conception, the development of the embryo and fetus, sexually transmitted diseases, contraception, and the body changes experienced by the students as they grow. Frequently includes the topics of alcohol, tobacco, and other drugs to increase student awareness and knowledge about how these substances affect the body and its growth and development. (tw)

human performance technology

An engineering or systems approach to improving human performance, involving the analysis of gaps in performance in the workplace and the design of empirically validated interventions to close the gaps. It may be applied to individuals, small groups, or large organizations. (chb)

human resource development (HRD)

A collection of training, education, and development activities designed to promote optimal performance across corporations, educational institutions, government agencies, health-care organizations, the military, nonprofit organizations, and community-based groups by increasing the knowledge, skills, and abilities of human resources. Drawing from its roots in vocational education, HRD focuses on lifelong and lifewide learning, beginning at the secondary level. The purpose is to integrate individual and organizational goals and to enhance workforce effectiveness. (alm, jb, sa)

human rights

The fundamental rights and freedoms guaranteed to all humans; the recognition of inherent dignity ensuring equal and inalienable rights to all people as the foundation of freedom and peace. Human rights include civil and political rights of life, liberty, freedom of expression, and equality before the law. Economic, social, and cultural rights include the right to food, work, and an education. (npg, ahs)

humanism

An intellectual orientation emphasizing the perspective, interests, and powers of human beings. Cicero claims Socrates was "the first to call philosophy down from the heavens and set her in the cities of men." "Humanism" is most often associated with an intellectual movement that originated in Italy in the 14th century and spread throughout Europe over the next two centuries. Renaissance humanists advocated an educational program devoted to the study of the humanities based on Greek and Latin classics. "Humanism" acquired its association with atheism in the 19th century as Darwin's work amplified the tension between science and religion. (mbm)

humanistic/existential therapy

A general term that refers to any number of therapeutic approaches that seek to foster the personal growth and potential of the client in an indirect manner by focusing on the present, accepting responsibility for one's behavior, and accepting the validity of one's own feelings and subjective experiences. The therapist does not give advice or encourage clients to make certain choices, but rather seeks to help the client develop self-understanding. (tsw)

humanities

Humanities describes the disciplines that focus on literature, history, philosophy, classical studies, and religion. Most departments in the humanities teach writing, communications, and critical thinking skills. In a liberal arts college or university, undergraduates are usually required to fulfill a humanities requirement before graduation. (cf)

hundred languages of children

A descriptive phrase used by the Reggio Emilia, Italy, constructivists for the many graphic and symbolic ways that young children can express what they know. Also the name of an exhibit of examples of the Reggio curricular projects, original products of young children, photographs, and transcripts of children's conversations about their work. In the Reggio approach, teachers collect and use this data to reflect on the children's understandings, to assess their own support, and to make plans for potential future activities. (ecr)

hurried child syndrome

A condition in which children who are pressured to adopt adult roles, mannerisms, and appearances develop stress responses such as avoidance, depression, and teenage pregnancy. According to Elkind (1988), parents, schools, and the media participate in rushing children to give up the innocence of childhood in order to pretend sophistication in societal and academic skills. (ecr)

hybrid course

A course that is taught using both traditional face-to-face and online instruction. Some course components, lectures, and demonstrations, for example, might be accomplished in a traditional manner, while other components, such as class discussion or group project work, might be mediated by a courseware product. Hybrid course structures allow the instructor to choose media based on effectiveness and allow students to interact both face-to-face and online. A hybrid course allows faculty to design course activities according to the strengths of the particular medium. For example, a dynamic lecturer may choose to make face-to-face presentations and leverage the diversity of web-based resources to extend content. Another instructor may record presentations for online delivery and use class time for facilitated activities. (ac, lp, ar)

See also blended courses; courseware; threaded discussion.

hyperactive

A label used to describe individuals who are more active and have shorter attention spans than the typical person. (sr)

hyperlexia

Hyperlexia, a term first introduced in the 1960s, is used to describe students whose word identification skills are considerably higher than their reading comprehension skills and general cognitive functioning. Though it was once thought that individuals with hyperlexia recognized words by visually memorizing them, researchers now think that those with hyperlexia are not relying solely on visual memory, but are also using decoding and symbol mapping skills. The question of whether hyperlexia is a superability or a disability is a subject of debate, as is the question of whether hyperlexia can be subsumed under other disabilities such as specific language impairment or pervasive developmental disorder. In fact, many children who are characterized as hyperlexic have also been diagnosed with pervasive developmental disorder or a specific language impairment. Many children with hyperlexia have difficulty understanding verbal language and may exhibit challenges with social interaction; however, other children also considered to be hyperlexic do not share these characteristics. (rcr)

hyperlink

A connected reference from one digital document to another. Also known as a link. When users follow a hyperlink, they access the referenced source. Hyperlinks provide a mechanism for researchers to locate additional information on their topic. For example, on the World Wide Web, web pages often contain links to additional sites that contain information about the same topic. In a full-text database, citations contain links to complete articles. (kg1)

hyphenated Americans

A popular term used to describe individuals having two different ethnicities and/ or races. This is a political form of naming that can be viewed as acknowledging and respecting one's heritage, or conversely as labeling individuals as having a stronger commitment to the first part of the hyphenated name, such as European, Asian, or Jamaican than to the fact that one is American (e.g., Croatian-American). (srs)

hypothesis

An explanation for a phenomenon that is posited in such a way that it can be tested using either qualitative or quantitative data to demonstrate its validity. (jjc)

I

ice-breaker
A training technique used to start a training session or program. This technique can take many forms but always provides a way for participants to "break the ice" and get to know each other. (jpc)

icon
From the Greek *eikon,* to resemble. An icon is distinguished as a symbol by virtue of its resemblance to that which it represents or signifies. For example, images of Christ or the Virgin Mary painted on wood are icons representing these religious figures. Indeed, in art history, the word icon generally refers to images of sacred personages in the Byzantine and Greek Orthodox traditions that were worshipped for themselves, as if they were that which they represented. Iconology is the study of icons. Onomatopoeia is an example of a verbal icon, in that the words resemble what they represent. (jd)
   See also symbol.

iconography
From the Greek *eikonographia,* sketch, description. The study of subject matter and symbolism in the visual arts, especially with reference to visual dictionaries (techniques of representation). The study of representative art in general. More broadly, the art of representation by pictures or images, which may or may not have a symbolic as well as an apparent or superficial meaning. (jd)
   See also icon.

ICP (See individual career plan)

IDEA (See Individuals with Disabilities Education Act)

idealism
Rejects the metaphysical claims of realism, that is, that there exists a world independent of our language and subjectivity and that this world can in principle be accurately and objectively understood and described. Idealism counters that realists have failed in explaining how the gap, postulated by realism, between minds and language on the one hand, and facts on the other, could be bridged. The idealist suggests that the world is in some sense simply mind or "Mind." Plato spoke of the material world as a shadow or illusion of a world of forms (e.g., "Beauty," "Triangularity," or "The Good"); Berkeley as well as Emerson insisted that one Mind, operating through each individual mind,

produces the entire environment nonphilosophers take to be reality. (an)

See also empiricism; foundationalism; naturalism; realism.

identity

The sense of self that develops from childhood to adulthood. The development of identity takes place as the child gradually differentiates from the immediate family and participates in society. As an individual's identity develops so do their occupational roles, sexual preferences, ideological commitments, personal values, and a variety of other personal mannerisms. Identity is often considered the essential element of the personality. (crl)

See also integrity; self.

ideological hegemony

A situation in which a particular dominant ideology, set of beliefs, values, or mores is pervasively reflected throughout a society in all principal social, political, and economic institutions and thereby permeates the cultural ideas and social relationships of that society. (hfs)

ideology

Any system of beliefs, ways of thinking, and social constructs that inform an individual's outlook on the world. Political, economic, and social activities and decisions are bound to various ideologies, as they are derived from particular views of human nature, economic relationships, social values, morality, and ethics. Ideology may serve to justify the subordination of one group over another. All educators have an "ideology" as their pedagogical practice, and educational beliefs are founded upon personal views of society, economics, politics, and morality. (crl)

IEP (See Individualized Education Program)

IFSP (See Individual Family Service Plan)

IGI (See individualized group instruction)

illiteracy

Usually refers to a lack of the basic skills of reading but sometimes used to describe a weak ability to use reading, writing, and math in daily life. (jpc)

illiterate

Usually describes a person who has no literacy skills, which is rare in countries that have compulsory education, but is sometimes used to describe people whose literacy skills are extremely low. (jpc)

illocutionary force

The effect of what has been done/said on the hearer. For example, if Person A asks Person B, *Are you too warm?*, Person B may interpret the utterance as an indication that Person A is indeed hot and is requesting Person B to do something about it. (smt)

illustration

From the Latin *illustrare,* to illuminate or make clear. An illustration is a visual artistic work created to accompany another work, usually a piece of literature. An illustration usually explains, expands on, or accompanies a story told orally or through writing. Types of illustrations range from medieval illuminated manuscripts to comic books. Illustrating a story that a student has written is a common way to combine the study of art making and writing exercises. Too often, children cease to illustrate their stories when they master the art of writing with visual detail. Careful introduction to the process should include instruction on the messages that images convey that cannot be translated into words. (ap)

image

The representation or likeness (most frequently visual) either in physical space (e.g., a sculpture or drawing) or in the mind's eye, usually of an object, person, or place. An image can also be a symbol or abstract embodiment of the object, person, or place. A student in a visual arts class can have a mental image of a project that he or she then tries to represent in physical media. When a likeness is strong, one may say, for example, "Oh that boy is the image of his father!" (ap)

imaginary companion

A fictional character invented by a child (usually between the ages of two and four), which is used as a playmate or someone to interact with. Imaginary friends can provide a child with someone to confide in, as well as someone who can provide comfort for the child who may be experiencing distress. (at)

imaginary friend (See imaginary companion)

imagination

The power of the mind to create images, ideas, and invented worlds that never existed, no longer exist, or are not immediately present. Imagination, powerful though little understood, is the foundation of the work of the artist as well as of arts education, preceding and driving creation. Some educators attribute the acquisition of the ability to imagine things as if they were otherwise, to imagine possibilities, as one of the most empowering aspects of effective art education. According to Maxine Greene, imagination is what makes empathy possible, for it is what helps us understand alternative realities. Imagination helps us open up spaces and make room to appreciate each other. It helps us cultivate multiple ways of seeing and stirs us to wide-awakeness. Imagination helps us create new orders as it helps us bring parts that seem to be severed together, as it helps us see patterns where there appeared to be none. Imagination is a cognitive capacity that explores alternatives and transforms our intuition into plans of action. It is a tool we use to help us see the world anew. (em, bt-b)

imaginative education

Imaginative education is a theory of linguistic and intellectual development posited by Kieran Egan that seeks to connect students' emotions, imaginations, and intellects in learning. Originally premised in the work of Vygotsky's Socio-Cultural Theory, imaginative education focuses on the main cultural-cognitive tools that connect students' imaginations with knowledge components of local curricula so as to increase the flexibility, creativity, and energy of thinking. Imaginative education stresses a developmental sequence of five kinds of understanding—the somatic, mythic, romantic, philosophic, and ironic—through which human beings engage with the world as they master language and grow intellectually. Aligned to each mode of understanding are particular cultural-cognitive tools that support the unified development of emotion, imagination, and intellect in relation to a student's current level of linguistic competency: the somatic as prelinguistic, mythical as oral, romantic as literate, philosophic as theoretical, and ironic as reflexive. The end result, for those who arrive there, is the "sophisticated ironist," a liberated and abundant consciousness possessing the ability to interact with the world using varied means of understanding. (tw1)

See also cultural-cognitive tools; sociocultural theory.

IMDL (See Internet-Mediated Distance Learning)

imitation

Mimicry or modeling after something else. The social learning theory purports that much learning occurs through observing and then imitating or modeling behaviors of others, gaining from both the context and the actual behavior itself. (db)

immediacy

A means of direct, "here-and-now" therapeutic communication in which a counselor comments on an issue, event, or observation/impression at the very moment it occurs. Immediacy, if used and timed appropriately, is useful for increasing a client's self-understanding and, in general, for improving interpersonal skills/sensitivity. (bmm)

immediate response devices (See clicker technology)

immersion education

Students are involved in a subject to the exclusion of nearly everything else during immersion education. In the case of language arts, the student is provided intensive language exposure from the earliest age. When learning a second language, the student is taught and given instruction only in the second language rather than the native language. (jqa, npo)

immigrant education

Educational programs that teach language, customs, and citizenship requirements to immigrants. Pertains to the ways educators should take into account the unique circumstances or experiences of immigrant students, including the new social, political, and economic factors that shape their social identities (Noguera, 2006). Since 1965, changes in the U.S. economy have caused a wave of immigrants to enter the United States, bringing with them new immigrant children, particularly refugees and those of Latino/Hispanic descent (Portes, 1996). In educational discourse, immigrant education is often described as English education for those students whose primary language is not English. However, immigrant students face significant circumstances in acclimating to U.S.-based education, including English language acquisition, culture shock, a lack of family support, identity development, assimilation, and acculturation. Educators should work to be aware of the unique circumstances for immigrant students and strive to preserve their home culture and identity while they

learn how to function in a new culture. (sb1, jpc)

See also acculturation; assimilation.

immigrant minorities (See voluntary minorities)

immigrants

Individuals or groups that settle in a foreign country. Education has played a large role in socializing immigrant populations to the United States. Being integrated into the social norms, language, and values of the United States occurs through classroom interactions and instruction. Current educational practices also recognize and respect the diversity brought by immigrant populations. (jqa, npo)

immunity to change

A phenomenon that prevents individuals and organizations from making changes to which they are strongly and sincerely committed. Developed by Robert Kegan and Lisa Laskow Lahey, this dynamic involves the sophisticated interplay of conscious and espoused commitments to change with other "hidden" and equally compelling psychological forces committed to maintaining the status quo. (jz)

impact factor

Measures the frequency with which the average article in a journal has been cited in a particular year or period. The Institute for Scientific Information (ISI) defines the journal impact factor as the ratio of articles published to articles cited during a rolling two-year window. ISI calculates these numbers from its citation indexes and publishes the data annually in *Journal Citation Reports*. (sn)

implicit curriculum (See hidden curriculum)

improvisation

To invent, compose, or perform something without preparation, extemporaneously.

For example, to play or sing music without rehearsal, especially by inventing variations on a melody or creating new melodies in accordance with a set progression of chords. Improvisation in jazz involves two or more musicians listening carefully to each other's contributions to create together new music or new variations on a given piece. To make do with available materials or circumstance. For example, to do paper sculpture when clay is suddenly unavailable or to change the subject of a drawing when an accidental line appears. In theatrical improvisation, actors react to the challenge of a designated situation and improvise a scene of action. This gamelike activity is called "improv." (kbc)

impulse-control disorder
A category of mental disorders characterized by intense impulses or urges to act in some way that can cause harm to an individual or to others. There is usually some feeling of excitement or tension that builds until the behavior is engaged in, at which time there may be a sense of relief or gratification. These behaviors are repeated despite (real or potential) negative consequences. Although there are many behaviors and disorders that could fall into this category, such as alcohol abuse and exhibitionism (flashing or exposing oneself), these two are found under substance use disorders and sexual disorders, respectively. Impulse-control disorders are separated into this category largely because they are not classified under any other type of mental disorder. Examples of these disorders include intermittent explosive disorder (recurrent aggressive outbursts), kleptomania (impulsive stealing), pyromania (fire setting), pathological gambling (compulsive or maladaptive gambling), and trichotillomania (hair pulling). (fa)

in-basket exercise
A simulation used to assess an individual's approach to or performance of management tasks. The individual is presented with a variety of written documents (memoranda, reports, letters, etc.), such as might be found in the in-basket on a manager's desk, and is asked to decide to how to handle or respond to each document. (chb)

incidental learning
Unintentional learning that occurs through life's activities and experiences. (las)

inclusion
The practice of ensuring that all students with disabilities participate with other students in all aspects of school, to the maximum extent appropriate. Support services are brought to the student in the regular education classroom, rather than taking the student to the support services. (bba)

inclusive
Refers to a setting or activity in which individuals with all levels of ability are accepted and included with accommodations and adaptations or assistance as needed. (sr)

inclusive classroom
A regular education classroom in which instruction is adapted (e.g., curriculum content, materials, activities, instruction delivery) to provide education to children who, under the federal Individuals with Disabilities Education Act of 1997, require special education services. The classroom arrangements are also modified in any possible and reasonable ways to support learning needs of the children. (xss, yb)

incremental budgeting
The process of basing budgetary entries on budgets from the previous year. The term usually refers to annual increases that are an acceptable percentage increase in salaries and operating funds. In a zero-based budget, each activity to be funded

must be justified every time a new budget is prepared. (cf)

independent practice
A classroom activity in which students practice newly learned content, skills, or strategies on their own, with no direct teacher assistance available. (bba)

independent reading level
The grade level at which a student can read a great percentage of the words in a passage and can comprehend most or all of the message contained in the passage or book without external support. Although there is some variation in criteria, widely accepted standards are: 99 percent accuracy in word recognition and 90 percent (or better) comprehension. (aw)

See also frustration reading level; informal reading inventory; instructional reading level.

independent school
Independent schools are a category of private schools serving elite clientele. They are not supported by taxes as public schools are, but rather from sources other than public monies. They are characterized in three primary ways: they are primarily supported by tuition, charitable contributions, and endowment income; they are governed by a board of trustees and administrators based on the mission and philosophy of the school; and they are subject to strict procedures for accreditation if they wish to have that status. Other features independent schools may offer are smaller class sizes, personal attention, increased higher-level or critical thinking, emphasis on responsibility and values, and opportunity to participate in many activities. (bs)

independent study
A program of study with topics or problems chosen by the student with the approval of the department concerned and with the supervision of an instructor; primarily designed for students who will not attend classes but seek periodic advice and assignments from instructors. (cf)

Indian Reorganization Act (1934)
Also known as the Wheeler-Howard Act, represented a dramatic shift in federal government policy regarding Native Americans from a philosophy of assimilation to a policy intending to restore Native lands and culture. Initiated by Bureau of Indian Affairs Commissioner John Collier (1933–1945), the act ended the devastating policies of allotment and off-reservation boarding schools, created bilingual teaching materials, expanded teacher training for Native and non-Native American teachers, improved the Indian health care system, and allowed for limited tribal self-government and the control of tribal funds, among other reforms. (klj)

Indian Self-Determination and Education Assistance Act (Public Law 93-638)
Passed by Congress on January 4, 1975, provided for increased participation of Native Americans in the establishment and conduct of their education programs and services. Title II, known as the Indian Education Assistance Act, provides for the education of Indians in public schools and school construction in districts on or adjacent to Indian reservations that are responsible for the education of Indian children. The law encourages local Indian school control, American Indian preferences and opportunities for training and employment, and preferences in the award of subcontracts and subgrants to Indian organizations and Indian-owned economic enterprises. (wg)

indicator
A measurable outcome used as evidence that an abstract standard or goal has been met. An indicator measures progress. Measurable indicators provide a basis for collecting valid and reliable evidence. (clk, eh1, eb)

indigenous knowledge

Sets of accumulated information, understandings, history, values, customs, and beliefs shared in a given locale or within a given community. It is most typically associated with colonial, postcolonial, and postmodern analyses of knowledge production. However, the term applies as well to analyses that seek to avoid recentering Western epistemologies by focusing instead on the centrality and validity of these understandings in the cosmology and worldview of specific communities. (hfs)

indigenous peoples

Often referred to in the United States as Native Americans or American Indians. They are indigenous because their settlement preceded that of European Americans in most cases. Indigenous peoples tend to live in rural communities. When members of organized tribal structures, they retain a significant degree of sovereignty. (lr)

indirect code

Early literacy instruction in which meaningful reading and writing activities, rather than explicit teaching of written language conventions and letter-sound correspondences, are highlighted. (jrk)

See also direct code; whole language approach/instruction.

indirect proof

A method of proving a proposition by assuming the hypothesis to be false and then proceeding by the use of axioms, definitions, and previously proven propositions, in hopes of the assumption leading to a contradiction and therefore proving the original proposition true. (wja)

individual career plan (ICP)

Planned program of courses designed for each student and developed prior to entering the ninth grade. Enables students to focus on specified course work and establish appropriate goals. ICPs are based on assessments of the student's interests and achievements and are updated each year throughout high school. (jb, ea)

Individual Family Service Plan (IFSP)

A plan developed by a team that includes parents, service providers, and anyone else that the parents or family want to be involved in the delivery of early intervention services. The IFSP states parents' priorities, resources, and concerns for their child; goals are written, along with activities and strategies to meet those goals. Every six months, the IFSP is reviewed and amended, as necessary. Parents or families may, at any time, also amend the IFSP. (kms, yb)

individualism

A descriptive term used particularly in the social sciences and philosophy. The common idea is the priority of the individual over the larger society. In economics, for example, this means that each individual should make economic decisions based on enlightened self-interest, which would argue for laissez-faire economic policies. The philosophical ramifications would be that from an ethical viewpoint the consequences of an action for the individual will have priority over consequences for the common good. The implications of this discussion for education are enormous. John Dewey maintained that the goals of education should include the betterment of the individual and the common good. Communitarians (e.g., Bellah and Palmer) continue to blend individual and social objectives together. (wl)

See also communitarianism; liberalism; person.

individuality

The unique identity of a person determined by cultural, social, economic, and political factors. (jjc)

individualized behavior plan

Plans created to target and modify a single behavior of an individual student. The plan includes a written understanding of the bad behavior, a clear description of the good behavior, steps the student can take to employ the good behavior, and a list of the behavior supports indicating both rewards for the good behavior and penalties for bad behavior. (ms)

Individualized Education Program (IEP)

A written education plan for a preschool or school-aged child with disabilities, developed by a team of professionals, the child's parents, and in some cases the child him/herself. A legally binding document aimed at developing an instructional plan that addresses a student's specific learning challenges. Also called individualized educational plan. (sr, aw)

individualized group instruction (IGI)

An adult basic education classroom model, commonly found in GED preparation classes, in which a group of learners, meeting at a specific time, work independently on assigned workbooks or worksheets with a teacher available to help them as needed. IGI is differentiated from "tutoring" in that the learners are not sitting with a teacher one-on-one for the whole time, although one-on-one interactions occur as the learners need help. (cas)

individualized instruction

Adapting a curriculum so that an individual child's developmental or educational needs may be met. (kms, yb)

Individuals with Disabilities Education Act (IDEA)

Originally the Education for All Handicapped Children Act of 1975. The name IDEA came with the 1990 amendment. It is a statute that provides federal funding in the form of grants to states from the Department of Education and confers substantive and procedural rights to individuals eligible for services under IDEA. (sr)

indoctrination

Indoctrination is characterized as any teaching that fails to respect the potential and actual rationality and autonomy of the learner. Indoctrination, it is said, uses "nonrational methods of instruction" (e.g., hypnosis, subliminal suggestion, authority, tradition), or operates upon subject matters immune to rational explanation or adjudication (e.g., astrology). It either intends and/or results in damage to the student's capacity for freedom or reason. The interesting question today is whether religious, moral, and political education are more than indoctrination. (an)

See also critical thinking; reason.

induction (See inductive reasoning)

induction programs

Programs at the local and state levels, generally lasting one or two years, that are designed to provide sustained training and support for new teachers transitioning from the university to the classroom. Elements of these programs may include online or face-to-face seminars, orientations, and/or workshops, opportunities to observe other teachers in action, mentor teachers, networking, and formative assessments. The goals of teacher induction are to improve teacher effectiveness and promote teacher retention. (dek, cp, clk)

inductive reasoning

Reasoning that involves exact or specific examples leading to broad examples, a chain of evidence that begins with an observation and then combines it with the strength of previous observations in order to arrive at a conclusion. Unlike deductive reasoning, inductive reasoning is not designed to produce mathematical certainty. (kr)

industrial education

Term that generally refers to a form of education focusing on the development of manual skills, typically applied to late 19th- and early 20th-century occupations. Historically reserved for post-Reconstruction-era African Americans, Native Americans, and other minority students, industrial education was seen as the acceptable form of education for these populations. Booker T. Washington, founder of the Tuskegee Institute, is the American educator most closely associated with this kind of education. (cm!)

See also trade and industrial education; vocational education.

inequality
In mathematics, a statement that one expression is less than (or greater than) another. (amr)

inert knowledge
Commonly understood to be information possessed by individuals but not used. First defined by A. N. Whitehead in 1929, inert knowledge is information known and understood, but not in ways that make it applicable to effective problem solving. An example of inert knowledge may be seen when a student memorizes a list of facts for an examination and promptly forgets them after the exam. (jwc)

infant
A child from birth to one year of age. (jlj)

infant schools
Robert Owen, the utopian reformer, established the first infant school in New Lanark, Scotland, in 1816. The infant school movement spread throughout England to assist in the educational care of needy children aged 18 months to 6 years of age. The infant school idea spread to the rapidly industrializing United States of the 1820s and was a charitable movement associated with Sunday schools and pauper schools. The movement declined by the late 1830s but was the forerunner of the kindergarten movement. (hbv)

Infant/Toddler Environment Rating Scale (ITERS)
Adapted from the Early Childhood Environment Rating Scale, a standardized instrument for the evaluation of infant and toddler care developed by Thelma Harms, Richard M. Clifford, and Debby Cryer in 1990. The form addresses 35 different items to comprehensively evaluate the infant/toddler classroom using the terms "Inadequate," "Minimal," "Good," and "Excellent." Examples are provided for each term for each item. (kdc)

inferences
Making inferences is deducing or concluding from information known or assumed; the result is probable but not certain. In research, inferences must be strongly supported by analysis of data. Students in schools in the United States are tested on their ability to infer meaning from written material, to understand what is hinted in addition to what is directly stated. Late 20th-century cognition studies suggest that increased domain knowledge improves the ability to draw appropriate inferences. (igb)

infinite
Becoming large beyond any fixed number; greater than any number; boundless; endless; not finite; not countable. A set is countable if it can be put into one-to-one correspondence with the positive integers or if the set is finite. $\{1, 3, 5, 7, 9\}$ is a countable set because it is finite. $\{1, 3, 5, 7, 9, \ldots\}$ is countable because it can be placed into one-to-one correspondence with the positive integers. The interval $(0, 1)$ is not countable. (kgh)

inflectional morpheme
Grammatical morphemes that can appear only in words attached to other morphemes, and are added to complete words according to rules of syntax (e.g., past tense on regular verbs: *to play–play-ed*; plural on nouns: *a song–song-s*). (smt)

See also morpheme.

influence

A sense of mattering, or making a difference to a group, and of the group mattering to its members. Influence is bi-directional. (cma)

informal education

Learning that takes place outside of structured learning experiences. (jpc)

informal reading inventory (IRI)

An individually administered assessment tool designed to help determine a student's skills, strategies, strengths, and weaknesses in reading. An IRI can be compiled by the teacher using materials from the classroom, or it can be one of a number of commercially available kits. The inventory includes graded word lists, graded passages, and comprehension questions, which can be used to determine a student's independent, instructional, or frustration level in reading. (aw)

informal standard english (See Standard American English)

information technology

The branch of technology devoted to the study and application of data and the processing thereof; that is, the automatic acquisition, storage, manipulation, management, movement, control, display, switching, interchange, transmission, or reception of data, and the development and use of the hardware, software, firmware, and procedures associated with this processing. (cf)

informed consent

A procedure whereby a client or person gives their voluntary agreement to participate in therapy or research. Most typically this involves a written form that includes the purpose of therapy/research project, procedures, risks, benefits, alternatives, costs, and confidentiality. Clients or research participants should be aware that they are able to withdraw from therapy/research at any time. Any consequences for refusing or revoking consent must also be discussed. (tsw)

infusion

The process of combining one element to another element to produce a new product and to give it new life. In teaching and learning, infusion involves the natural, holistic, and authentic combination of combining cultural competency to all areas of the curriculum, instruction, and assessment. Its purpose is to teach all learners with honor and respect rather than introducing items pertaining to cultural competency through isolation, tokenism, and skepticism. (npg)

initial teaching alphabet (ITA)

Developed in the 1960s for use as a simplified system to help children to learn to read and write more easily, the alphabet consists of 44 letters and symbols representing sounds in the English language. This combination of letters and symbols provides a partially phonetic approach to reading. The intent is to introduce reading through the ITA system, and then move toward use of the standard English alphabet in spelling, writing, and reading. Mostly used during the 1960s, the system continues to be of interest as a way to simplify teaching English, especially to dyslexic readers. (npo)

inner discipline

In the Montessori classroom, the child develops inner (or self) discipline through her/his exposure to modeled behavior by teachers, and experience through the freedom of choice in activities. (nrs)

innovation

In education, innovation is a new way of teaching or learning that varies from a traditional approach and is typically in response to a need for improved student achievement. Examples of strategies that have been considered to be innovative are:

ability grouping, clustering, block scheduling, project-based learning, reading instruction through a whole language approach, and nongraded schools. (bs)

innumeracy

An inability to deal with and be comfortable with the ideas of numbers, mathematics, and chance; marked by the inability to think and express one's own thoughts quantitatively; not possessing skill with numbers or mathematics. (wja)

inorganic chemistry

The branch of chemistry that studies the compounds other than the organic compounds. (tw)

See also organic chemistry.

inquiry

A systematic, intentional study of one's own teaching practice. Similar terms include action research and teacher research. Inquiry is typically viewed as a cycle, in which teachers pose a "wondering," read relevant literature and create a plan for investigation, collect and analyze data from their practice, make changes in their practice based on findings, and then develop new wonderings to study. (mrs, aa)

inquiry teaching

A form of instruction in which teachers provide students with information, experiences, or problems that serve as the focus for the students' research activities. The students generate hypotheses or tentative solutions, gather relevant data, and evaluate the data to arrive at a conclusion. (bba)

inquiry-oriented teacher education

A general approach to preparing teachers that provides instruction and field experiences that emphasize raising questions about existing educational practices and testing ways to improve upon the status quo. (rtc)

in-service teacher education

Teacher education or professional development educational experiences that take place after initial licensure is granted. The intent is to further develop teachers' professional knowledge and skills in order to enhance and increase student achievement. (clk, mrs, aa)

in-service training

Refers to one-time or short-term training, usually a specific workshop or large-group session to present information or a basic skill, easily learned, usually delivered primarily via one-way communication. The training may include job-embedded elements, but typically there is no follow-up. (cma)

insight

Awareness, recognition, and understanding clearly one's own attitudes, beliefs, and behaviors. Involves the ability to introspect; to look inward dispassionately and accurately; to see, and perhaps voice truths about, oneself; and to acknowledge one's own motives and experiences. Insight may also involve self-reflecting on contingencies that influence/shape one's behavior, and appreciating the effect one's learning history has on current behaviors. (dho)

instant message (See chat)

institute

Within an institution of higher learning, an institute is an agency established for the purpose of research, study, and instruction in a particular field of work. Often responsible for the collection, analysis, and presentation of institutional data upon which informed administrative and faculty decisions can be based. An institute's primary concern is practical research for the solution of institutional problems through the accumulation and analysis of data. In executive education settings, an institute is an intensive, condensed, and comprehensive program adhering to the principles of adult learning. Made up of a cohesive set of learning experiences and offered to a cohort of individuals from common professional settings, it draws on the experiences of learners as well as presenters. Such a program may be of varying lengths (from days to several weeks) and consist of a variety of events (including, but not limited to, interactive classroom sessions, facilitated small group discussion, and peer-to-peer learning opportunities) focused on meeting specific learning objectives. (cf, ln)

See also executive education.

Institute of Education Sciences
Established with the signing of the Education Sciences Reform Act of 2002, this institute replaces the Office of Educational Research and Improvement within the U.S. Department of Education. The institute includes the National Center for Education Research, the National Center for Education Statistics, and the National Center for Evaluation and Regional Assistance. (jwc)

institutional discrimination
Unfair practices and attitudes that are rooted in a society and affect its overall policies toward and treatment of certain classes. Organizational discrimination is similar in that at the organizational level, discriminatory practices are reinforced by long-established practices, rules, and policies. (jqa, npo)

institutional heterosexism
Institutions, including schools and colleges, employ institutional heterosexism through ideologies, policies, and patterns of bias that discriminate against nonheterosexual people. (jb2)

institutional history
Examination of the foundations, growth, and development of a college, university, or university system. Its subject matter includes all facets of institutional development, such as administration, architecture, student body, athletics, and so on. (cf)

institutional memory
The collectivity of an institution's wisdom, wit, and experience, as reflected in its accumulation of stories, folklore, jokes, images, and symbols pertaining to its past; often the memories or memoirs of older staff members noted for the factual information they retain and their storytelling ability. (cf)

institutional performance
A concept of effectiveness in achieving explicit goals or objectives (as viewed from an institutional perspective); can be applied to particular institutions of higher education—or to the sociocultural institutions of higher education as a whole; involves the use of multiple measures or indicators. (cf)

institutional racism
Institutions, including schools and colleges, employ institutional racism through regularized policies and practices that treat one class of people unfairly and negatively. Not only race, but gender, ethnicity, and other factors are included in institutional racism. Institutional racism can have a broader impact than individual racism since it is reinforced by an organization with some recognized standing. (jqa, npo)

institutional repositories
Digital collection of materials produced at a college or university. Materials in the repository may include dissertations, theses, preprints, scholarly articles, student newspapers, archival collections, university records, data sets, and other materials produced by or related to the institution. The repository functions to collect, digitize, organize, archive, and provide open access to the materials. Digital repositories are often managed by the university

library with cooperation from the university archives and the university computer center. (pw1)

institutional research
The collection, analysis, and presentation of institutional data upon which informed administrative and faculty decisions can be based. Its primary concern is practical research for the solution of institutional problems through the accumulation and analysis of data. (cf)

institutional self-study
An essential component of regional accreditation; an extended process in which institutions study their internal programs, services, and activities by using standards as established by regional accrediting associations; uses various indices, measures, and criteria. (cf)

instruction
The guided exercises, lessons, and materials used to teach a subject. The formal act of imparting knowledge or developing skills: teaching. (jw)

instructional core
The relationship between the teacher and the student, in the presence of content, that determines instructional practices. The concept anchors the practice of instructional rounds or other system-wide instructional improvement processes. The concept is rooted in Hawkins's (2002) theory of the interdependent "I" (the teacher), "thou" (the student), and "it" (the content). (mf1)

instructional design
The systematic process of translating general principles of learning and instruction into plans for instructional materials and learning. Instructional design is also a field that prescribes specific instructional actions to achieve desired instructional outcomes; the process decides the best methods of instruction for enacting desired changes in knowledge and skills for a specific course content and learner population. (cf)

instructional development
The implementation of instructional design plans by analysis of the setting and learner needs, by devising of a set of specifications for an effective, efficient, and relevant learner environment; the creation of learner and management materials, and evaluation of the results of the development both formatively and summatively. (cf)

instructional leadership
The practice of understanding and improving interactions between teachers, students, and academic content, to foster more effective teaching and deeper learning by students. Instructional leadership may be undertaken at multiple levels within educational systems and involves the setting of educational goals and the active pursuit of those goals by multiple constituents in a learning community. (sh)

instructional materials
Items used to assist in imparting knowledge or developing skills. Examples include textbooks, audiovisual resources, computer programs, and laboratory supplies. (jw)

instructional objectives (See objective)

instructional reading level
The grade level at which a student can be challenged, but not frustrated, during reading instruction that assumes additional support. Although there is some variation in criteria, widely accepted standards are better than 95 percent accuracy in word recognition and 75 percent (or better) comprehension. (aw)

See also frustration reading level; independent reading level; informal reading inventory.

instructional rounds

An educational improvement strategy through which a network of educators (superintendents, principals, teachers, and central office staff) meet at regular intervals to observe teaching and learning in their schools and then debrief what they have seen, such as what students were asked to do and what they actually were doing; or the patterns of interaction. The network develops a problem of practice to focus observations and, after a debrief, determines the next level of work for the school they visited. (mf1)

instructional strategies

The overall planned procedures for implementing and achieving specific goals and objectives in teaching. Instructional strategies are ways the teacher can assist learners with their study efforts for each performance objective. The purpose of strategies is to outline how instructional activities will relate to the accomplishment of the objectives. Successful strategies for method and material presentation maximize the learning experience for all by planning and implementing an effective and efficient organization of methods, techniques, and information. (ce)

instructional technology

A field dedicated to the theory and practice of design, development, utilization, management, and evaluation of processes and resources for learning. The phrase also encompasses the application of technology to administrative functions of an educational institution. Technologies, primarily computer-based, integrated in classroom instruction for the purpose of providing a learning experience. Instructional technologies in teacher education address, in part, state and/or local guidelines for integrating technology into the classroom setting. (cf, clk)

instrumentation

The selection and combination of instruments in composition or performance of a musical work. For example, the usual instrumentation of a string quartet is two violins, one viola, and one cello. Interchangeable with orchestration, in which music is written especially with an eye to the various instruments in the orchestra and/or the specific instruments are chosen to play the music or comprise the orchestra. The skills of instrumentation or orchestration are usually reserved for conservatory-level education. (jbl)

intake

Process by which new adult students provide information about their learning needs, goals, and skills. Such information is generally used for placement and evaluation of program participation. (las)

intake interview

Involves gathering information and developing a therapeutic relationship with a client early in the treatment process, usually during the first session or two. The primary purpose of an intake interview is to collect information regarding the client's current presenting problem(s) or perceived difficulties. The interview also helps the clinician to formulate an initial diagnostic impression regarding a client's problem(s) or difficulties and to help ensure that the therapist is qualified to provide the type of treatment deemed to be most appropriate. Sometimes the person conducting the interview will be different from the person who treats the client. Intake interviews range from highly structured to unstructured. Frequently during the intake interview, a client's history is collected. Questions related to factors such as a person's family, psychiatric, medical, academic/work, military, social/marital, and legal histories are commonly asked. (kc, scmc, bdj)

INTASC (See Interstate New Teacher Assessment and Support Consortium)

integer

Any positive or negative whole number or zero; any number in the set $\{\ldots, -3, -2, -1, 0, 1, 2, 3, \ldots\}$. The positive integers, which are greater than zero, are also known as the natural numbers. The negative integers, which are less than zero, are $-1, -2, -3, \ldots$. Addition, subtraction, and/or multiplication of integers produce an integer; division of integers does not necessarily produce an integer. (kgh)

integrated academic and career-technical curriculum (See curriculum, integrated academic and career-technical)

integrated curriculum

A program of learning in which a topic or theme is studied from different disciplinary perspectives. In early childhood, this means that the theme of study is explored with materials that stimulate all the senses and appeal to different learning styles, and includes cognitive, physical, and social/emotional components. A model integrated curriculum for early childhood would explore the topic of "trees," for example, by planting seeds and observing their growth, painting on bark, pretending to grow like trees, reading books about trees, wearing gardening gear, collecting leaves, singing under the trees, and adopting a tree to observe through the seasons. An organization of the curriculum in which subject matters that are traditionally taught separately are combined. Instruction typically draws from two or more subject areas and focuses on a theme or concept. (ecr, bba)

integrated learning

The "horizontal" link across academic and vocational areas of the curriculum that offers students contact with different content areas and how to apply knowledge and skills associated with the areas. (jb)

Integrated Postsecondary Education Data System (IPEDS)

Started in 1986, IPEDS replaced HEGIS and became the core postsecondary education data collection program for the National Center for Education Statistics, in the U.S. Department of Education. The system collects institutional-level data that is used to discover and track trends in higher education at the institutional, state, and national levels. (cf)

integrated science

A grouping of all branches of science studied through a method that shows the interdependence, connections, and other relationships among the varied branches of science. For example, a study based on the sun could include concepts and processes from astronomy, biology, nuclear physics, the chemistry of photosynthesis and light, and so on. (tw)

integration

In the educational context, integration has a number of different meanings and can be implied at different levels in education. It is the act or process of forming, coordinating, or blending into a functioning or unified whole. Purposeful combination of at least one additional academic subject area with the teaching and learning of social studies, for example, literature and social studies, mathematics and social studies, sciences and social studies. Educational integration refers to the integration of educational leadership, management, curriculum, instruction, and assessment. Technology integration refers to technology used in a seamless manner to support and extend curriculum objectives, thus engaging students in meaningful learning. Social and cultural integration involves the incorporation of disparate ethnic or religious elements of the population into a unified society, providing equality of opportunity for all members of that society. Also, including students with various skill levels and abilities in the same classroom or program. Typically includes students with identified disabilities in a classroom setting with their nondisabled peers. (mm, sr, npg)

integrity

Literally, wholeness or oneness. Often used to mean "honesty"; entails a unity between a person's actions and words. Beyond the minimum of honesty, the person with integrity has a unity to his or her actions; there are some things that she or he must do, or must not do, in order to be the person she or he is. Integrity is thus more than honesty and entails a unity of the person as a whole. Some authors (e.g., Lynne McFall) claim that the principles around which identity forms must not only be unified, they must be worthwhile, for the person to possess integrity. (jc)

See also identity; self.

intellectual property

An idea or innovation that is created or discovered. This includes things that a person writes, designs, invents, sings, speaks, draws, discovers, and so on. Such property would include novels, sound recordings, software, trade secrets, a new type of mousetrap, or a cure for a disease. Intellectual property can be created by a person (or a person can pay someone to create it for them). Intellectual property is protected by patents, trademarks, and copyright laws. Each of these laws covers a specific type of intellectual property. (cf)

intellectualism

Intellectualism is the view that all human activities are governed by the intellect and thus can be influenced and studied by intellectual means. This theory has been questioned by researchers in the phenomenological tradition who have maintained that we must make a distinction between predicative and prepredicative activities. Predications occupy only a small part of our life and are explicit, intellectual activities like judgments, comparisons, inferences, attributions, and the like, whereas the most part of our activities are prepredicative in the sense that they precede all intellectual activities and are not themselves intellectual, but spontaneous and implicitly functioning. (jb1)

See also emotivism.

intelligence

For Deweyan pragmatists, intelligence is the ability to act intelligently (i.e., to shape one's actions in accordance with one's long-term ends); a set of capacities observable within human behavior, such as the ability to learn from experience, to make plans for the future and enact them, to learn and participate in practices of which one has previously been ignorant. It has been argued that there are many varieties of intelligence, of which standard academic forms (measured by tests such as the SAT, ACT, etc.) are merely a subset. These include moral, aesthetic, and emotional intelligence. The critical view is that intelligence is less a feature of the individual than a social construction that reifies certain socially desirable behaviors. A hypothetical mental force that is sometimes characterized as genetically inherited, unrelated to experience, and influencing an individual's level of achievement. Although there is little agreement about any single definition of intelligence, the term generally refers to an individual's potential to successfully comprehend mental abstractions. Currently, conceptions of intelligence are influenced by broader notions, such as Howard Gardner's Theory of Multiple Intelligences. Historically, intelligence has been measured by specifically constructed tests such as the Stanford-Binet. In the late 20th century, practitioners developed various assessments for a broad range of intelligent behaviors. (an, crl)

See also wisdom.

intelligence quotient (IQ)

A statistically derived measure of one's cognitive processing on a standardized test, such as the Stanford-Binet. Such tests are designed to measure one's percentile within an age-based group based on an assessment of cognitive tasks. The concept of an intelligence quotient, or IQ, has faced criticism because the tests, while correlating to some extent with factors such as academic performance and future success, are not measuring raw intelligence; they simply measure performance on one standardized test. In addition, testing of this manner has been criticized as having culturally value-laden items and for measuring only one type of intelligence, ignoring other strengths of the individual, such as musical or physical talents. Coined by William Stern in 1912, IQ is construed broadly as a measure of intelligence. It was originally defined as 100 times the mental age (determined by standardized tests) divided by the chronological age. It now represents a person's performance relative to peers. Both establish the average as 100, with the majority of people (approximately 68 percent) scoring between 85 and 115. (jcp, mkt)

See also intelligence; multiple intelligences.

intelligence test

One of a class of assessment instruments, or tests, that purport to measure intelligence. These tests assess cognitive abilities that are associated with success in academic or "real world," settings. Measures of verbal, mathematical, and perceptual skills are typically included. Generally, such tests consist of a graded series of tasks in the various aforementioned areas, each of which has been standardized with a large, representative sample of individuals. (mkt)

Intelligence Testing Movement

An early 20th-century development that advocated the use of standardized tests in public schools as a way of measuring intellect and sorting students into the appropriate curriculum. The World War I Army Alpha and Beta tests had opened the possibility of large-scale testing. Psychologists

and educators interested in linking scientific measurement to ideas of meritocracy viewed the public schools as an excellent arena for scientifically sorting students to be selected and educated for their proper future roles in society. Critics of the intelligence testing movement argued that minority and working-class children were at an unfair disadvantage and often sorted disproportionately into vocational and lower academic tracks. American psychologists Henry Herbert Goddard (1866–1957), Edward Thorndike (1874–1949), and Lewis Terman (1877–1956) are most closely associated with this movement. (vmm)

Intelligent Tutoring Systems (ITS)

A sophisticated implementation of computer-aided instruction that contains a knowledge of the domain to be taught, domain-specific pedagogical knowledge, and knowledge of the student to be taught. As the student interacts with the software, it updates its model of the student in order to select the most appropriate content and pedagogical style for that student, much as a human tutor would. The most sophisticated Intelligent Tutoring Systems provide features such as rich, configurable simulation environments, context-sensitive help facilities, lessons that appeal to different learning styles, and natural language interfaces. The ultimate goal for Intelligent Tutoring Systems is to provide active, scaffolded, highly contextualized learning with rapid feedback, which currently is available primarily through one-on-one interaction with an expert tutor. (eh)

intensive quantities

Numbers that arise through particular mathematical operations that cannot themselves be treated like extensive quantities; for example, price per pound or constant speed. These numbers express a multiplicative relationship between two other quantities, extensive or intensive. (amr)

intentionality

Intentionality is in the phenomenological tradition a theory of consciousness. According to this theory, consciousness is characterized by its directedness against something different than itself. Every kind of consciousness is correlated with its own particular object: perception with the perceived, thinking with the thought, feeling with the felt, dreaming with the dreamt, wishing with the wished, and so on. In other words, consciousness never exists alone as a pure state but always integrates subject and object in a unity. Intentionality should, however, not be confused with intentional, since not all kinds of consciousness are governed by intentions. (jb1)

interaction

An exchange between a person (child or adult) and one or more others, or between a person and materials or the environment. (db1)

interactionist perspective

A theoretical perspective that focuses on the consequences of social behavior. The interactionist perspective assumes the position that people exist and act, and that all other "structures" in society are simply human creations. For interactionists, society is constantly being created through people's communication and negotiation. (pmts)

interactive activity

An instructional design in which dialogue among the participants, teacher and learners, forms the core of the learning experience. It is a give-and-take of ideas in which all student contributions are accepted. In this type of instructional/learning setting, the learners' ideas are as important as the teacher's. The instruction is created with the students. This type of instructional activity is not top-down, but rather bottom-up. The learners are at the center and their voices direct the activities. (jls)

interactive audience response systems (See clicker technology)

interactive reading

Using interactive strategies, including asking open-ended questions and defining and discussing words, during book reading. Interactive book readings require the adult reader to actively facilitate the listeners' participation in the book reading. Dialogic reading is one type of interactive book reading. (jdc)

intercultural

Dynamic process of positive interaction between various identity groups of a society. It calls for an inherent interdependence beyond static descriptions and recognition of differences that can often result in the isolation and marginalization of groups into static ethnocentric identities. (hfs)

intercultural communication

Communication may be affected by the cultural and social background of the individuals involved. Intercultural communication occurs when individuals of differing backgrounds interact. In the classroom, an awareness of cultural differences in communication can assist a teacher in providing a supportive learning environment that meets the needs of each student. (jqa, npo)

intercultural education

A movement that began in the 1920s as a way to address the issues of cultural pluralism as a counter to assimilation. Also called "intergroup relations," its goal was to promote understanding among different racial and ethnic groups, while it sought to value the attributes of minority groups in mainstream society. Under the leadership of Rachel Davis DuBois, the Service Bureau for Intercultural Education (SBIE) was founded in 1934 to develop and disseminate curricular materials for schools. In the ensuing decades, intercultural education manifested itself through workshops, college courses, and K–12 curricular materials. It is considered to be the precursor to multicultural education. (caw)

interdisciplinary
In education, an approach to teaching that invokes more than one academic discipline to address a single problem or question. This practice of teaching promotes analysis of a single topic from perspectives in multiple subject areas. (clk)

interdisciplinary art education
The comprehensive or multifaceted approach to art education in which students experience and learn about art through multiple perspectives and disciplines. This approach was developed in reaction to the understanding that art is a source of knowledge, beliefs, and values and must be studied in a holistic way. (kf)

interdisciplinary curriculum
An instructional model whereby multiple disciplines are used to promote and/or enhance learning about a particular topic or skill. This supports the belief that students have greater focus and understanding when content is experienced in a variety of contexts. For example, learning shapes can be addressed through reading a book with examples of shapes in real life, playing with shape blocks, and walking along the perimeter of a shape. (db1)

interdisciplinary teaching and learning
Coordinated, systematic study drawing upon the disciplines of anthropology, archaeology, economics, geography, history, law, philosophy, political science, psychology, religion, and sociology as well as appropriate content from the humanities, mathematics, and natural sciences. Defined by the National Council for the Social Studies (NCSS), social studies is "the integrated study of the social sciences and humanities to promote civic competence." (npg)

interdisciplinary team
An organizational pattern of two or more teachers of different subject areas, who share the same students, schedule, and areas of the school to teach more than one subject. (bba)

interest
The state of having one's attention drawn to something; the desire to study a subject. It is at the root of motivation; students are more likely to learn that in which they have an interest. Something good for one is said to be in one's interest. These meanings are independent of each other; it is possible to take an interest in things that are not good for one or to not take an interest in learning the things that are in one's interest. The enduring problem of teaching is to get children to take an interest in that which it is in their interest to study. (jc)

interest inventory
Associated with career and technical or career guidance, an instrument on which the individual indicates a liking for or interest in various kinds of jobs, careers, or occupational activities. (db)

intergenerational literacy
Literacy programs that involve two or more generations in the acquisition and improvement of literacy skills. (jpc)

interiorization
Interiorization, from the socio-cultural theory of Lev Vygotsky, refers to the transition of cultural-cognitive tools from the external (cultural) plane to the internal (individual) plane of language and thought. Importantly, this internalization should not be considered a simple addition to existing cognitive structures or patterns of thinking, as if one has accrued yet another heuristic device or conceptual model. Rather, interiorization results in a transformation of the functioning of cognition, a revolutionary rather than additive structuring of mental activity that

results in the development of higher psychological processes. (tw1)

See also cultural-cognitive tools; sociocultural theory.

internal locus of control
The belief that events and reinforcers in life are due to internal factors that are under the direct control of the individual. Individuals with this type of belief often see themselves as responsible for events that occur, even when they have little control over those events. Individuals with an internal locus of control may feel more confident and in control of their life. (tsw)

International Adult Literacy Survey (IALS)
A survey of literacy skills, modeled on the National Adult Literacy Survey, which took place in several countries in the mid-1990s. (jpc)

See also National Adult Literacy Survey.

international education
The study of all aspects of society in other countries, including social, cultural, economic, and political, as they affect international relations. Such study often includes an examination of socioeconomic and political influences on education, as well as social and political structures. (jw)

International Literacy Day
Established by UNESCO as September 8 and celebrated around the world. (jpc)

international literacy prizes
A set of four awards administered by UNESCO and chosen by an international jury, which recognize people, programs, and countries that have achieved excellence in adult literacy education. The awards are the International Reading Association Literacy Award, the Iraq Literacy Prize, the Nadezhda K. Krupskaya Prize, and the Noma Prize. (jpc)

international phonetic alphabet
A standardized, widely used set of graphic symbols for transcribing speech sounds in any language in the world. (smt)

Internet
A global network connecting millions of independent computer networks to facilitate data transmission and information communication. It was originally constructed by the U.S. Department of Defense's ARPANET project in 1969 and has grown to become a highly commercial and widely accepted medium for a variety of online services. The initial ARPANET network connected computers at UCLA, Stanford Research Institute, UC-Santa Barbara, and the University of Utah in Salt Lake City. The basic structure of the network, which continues in today's Internet, was a distributed system. If any one site in the network malfunctioned, the other three sites could continue to communicate and share data. (hh, kg1)

See also extranet; intranet.

Internet addiction
A psychological dependence on the Internet that significantly interferes with one's normal daily activities, including relationships, social obligations, study habits, grades, and chores. It is characterized by an increasing difficulty in meeting educational or work obligations; longer Internet use with less enjoyment; spending more time online than intended; an inability to cut down, control, or stop use; and feelings of irritability or anxiety when not online. (ds)

Internet discussion lists
Internet discussion lists are used by groups of people with a common interest who share information on a regular basis. These lists appear in two forms. The first, an e-mail list used with a list-server, can be accessed by plain-text e-mail. Users sign up to be on a list; if one member sends mail to the list, every member receives it.

There are also Web services, often called bulletin boards, where users can access messages online using a graphical user interface. There are both moderated and unmoderated lists; some lists are by invitation only while others can be joined by anyone. (tll)

Internet safety

Some online events endanger the safety of children, youth, and adults. For instance, students who go online can be at risk for psychological harm from cyberbullying, exposure to pornography, or even physical harm from Internet predators. The Children's Internet Protection Act and the Protecting Children in the 21st Century Act were implemented by the federal government to protect children. Schools may be required to meet federal Internet safety standards by educating students about appropriate online behavior, using Internet filtering software to block inappropriate content from school networks, and securing student accounts to prevent unauthorized access. (jh)

Internet-Mediated Distance Learning (IMDL)

A general term of reference to use of computer networks in various forms of extra-classroom instruction. The latter part of the term, distance learning, is increasingly used for all forms of teaching-learning arrangements in which instructors and students communicate with each other from different locations. (cf)

internship

A period of supervised teaching, typically full-time, and often as the culmination of a teacher preparation program. The internship provides the intern socialization into the profession and an opportunity to develop her or his practice under the supervision of an expert. (dm2, eb)

internship coordinator (See coordinator, career)

interpersonal competence

A general term for the informed perceptions and expectations of others; often referred to as social intelligence, understanding, and communicating well with others; includes sensitivity to and appreciation of the activities, beliefs, and feelings expressed by others; can be learned, acquired, and improved through self-directed learning and professional development. (cf)

interpersonal feedback

Evaluative information given to an individual from an external source regarding a variety of behaviors; may include the feedback giver's reactions to the behavior(s). Interpersonal feedback may be used to develop, maintain, and/or change one's self-concept, to strengthen interpersonal bonds, and to develop empathy. (ktc)

interpersonal intelligence

One of Howard Gardner's (1993) multiple intelligences, the aptitude for social interaction characterized by charisma and group membership. The interpersonal learner usually has many friends and likes to talk to people. She or he learns best through cooperating with and teaching others. Teachers and political leaders often demonstrate high levels of interpersonal intelligence. (ecr)

interpersonal therapy

A nondirective and noninterpretive form of short-term psychotherapy that emphasizes interpersonal relationships. Clients are encouraged to reflect critically on their interaction patterns with others. They then learn adaptive behaviors to improve their interpersonal and communication skills. (jbb)

interpretation

Interpretation is in the hermeneutic tradition the work of explicating the meaning of human affairs in order to understand. (jb1)
   See also understanding.

interpreters

Hearing individuals who listen to a spoken message and communicate it in some way to an individual with a hearing impairment. (sr)

interpreting maps, charts, and graphs

The ability to use graphic forms of information to either identify specific data portrayed or to draw conclusions from the data concerning causes, effects, trends, or predictions. (jjc)

intersex

Intersex is a term that describes a range of physiological conditions in which the chromosomal, hormonal, external genitalia and/or internal reproductive organs do not conform to the sex categories of female and male. An intersex condition may or may not be evident at birth. There is currently considerable debate about the practice of physicians and/or parents "assigning" a male or female identity to an intersex infant, and performing surgical and/or hormonal interventions to support this assignment. Intersex advocates promote waiting until the child is old enough to express/identify a preferred identity. (jb2)

Interstate New Teacher Assessment and Support Consortium (INTASC)

An affiliation of state education agencies, higher education institutions, and national education organizations created in 1987. The consortium's work focuses on education program approval, teacher preparation, teacher licensure, and professional development. The consortium is dedicated to developing compatible educational policy between states and effective methods for maintaining quality teachers. INTASC has developed a set of model standards outlining what all new teachers should know in order to teach effectively; these standards act as a model for states to use as a basis in designing their own state standards for new teachers. (dek, cp)

intersubjectivity

Intersubjectivity is the state of opening the possibility of understanding and exchange between subjects. In this way intersubjectivity is a necessary but not sufficient condition for teaching and education. Intersubjectivity is also used in the sense of being available for or shared by several persons instead of being subjective or private. In this sense intersubjectivity is not only relevant for everyday reality, but is a common demand as well as claim in scientific research. (jb1)

See also communication; empathy; sympathy.

intervention

A planned action or process facilitated by a trained professional that is intended to alter the course of a potentially negative or suboptimal situation, primarily to improve it or prevent it from getting worse. For example, a special education teacher may use behavior modification with a student as an intervention to help the student stay on task during a reading assignment. An intervention can include, among other things, providing information/education, using therapeutic techniques in a counseling session, and/or providing medical attention. (sdc)

intradisciplinary curriculum

A curriculum that seeks to educate students about a single discipline by studying and integrating all of the areas that make up or are directly associated with the discipline. (ms)

intranet

Similar to the Internet in that it uses the same technology, but with limited accessibility. An intranet is owned by an organization and is accessible only internally within that organization. (hh)

See also extranet; Internet.

intrapersonal intelligence

According to Howard Gardner (1993), an aptitude for looking inside oneself for meaning. The intrapersonal learner usually follows his or her own instincts and is an original thinker. He or she learns best in solitary locations using individualized projects or self-paced instruction. Experts in intrapersonal intelligence might become, for example, spiritual leaders or psychotherapists. (ecr)

intrinsic reward

Refers to the psychological processes that motivate individuals to behave in a certain way and not in others; these are internal states that gratify the individual. For example, the personal gratification that comes with a job, although it does not pay well, is considered an intrinsic reward powerful enough for maintaining the job. (xss, yb)

introversion

A personality trait that describes an individual's preference for time alone, with one's own thoughts and feelings. These individuals prefer not to engage in social interactions and are not particularly motivated by external stimulation. Introverted individuals are often more quiet, reserved, deliberate, and unsociable, and prefer to work alone. They also tend to take positions of skepticism and often suppress feelings. (tsw)

See also extroversion-introversion.

intuition

Intuition helps us move through our thoughts and experiences and make sense of them. It is a source of insight, a direct responsiveness that helps us choose our ideas and pull them together. Historically, intuition is associated with insights, enlightenment, artistic expressions, and visions. Intuition is described by many cultures as a source of knowledge, although not necessarily true. It is described as nonrational, a form of nonreflective consciousness. Intuition seems to be personal, and subjective in quality. Whitehead described intuition in terms of

intrigue and romance. Kant described it in terms of direct contact, and Croce in terms of looking inward. (bt-b)

intuition in mathematics

A way of thinking that is characterized by self-evident statements that go beyond mere perception, or observable facts. Intuitive statements are accepted without the need for proof. An example of an intuitive statement is that for any two numbers, the numbers are either equal or one is larger and the other is smaller. An example of a nonintuitive statement is that the square of the hypotenuse of a right triangle is equal to the sum of the squares of the other two sides. (smc)

invented procedures

Before children are taught traditional algorithms, they often will invent their own valid procedures to solve computational problems. Some of these procedures include addition proceeding from left to right involving multiple partial sums (e.g., $32 + 69 = 30 + 60 + 2 + 9$), or multiplication by distribution (e.g., $4 \times 28 = 4 \times 20 + 4 \times 8$). (ey)

invented spelling

The result of children's attempts to spell words when they are learning how to write. Often the spelling is systematic and rule-governed. In the early stages, the spelling tends to be phonetic. For example, a child may write *littel* for *little*. (smt)

inverse operation

An operation that returns a result of an operation to the original number or entity. Addition and subtraction are inverse operations, as are multiplication and division (e.g., $3 + 5 = 8$ and $8 - 5 = 3$). (amr)

inverse word problems (See direct and inverse word problems)

invigilator (See proctor)

invisible college

A term first used to identify the informal association of gifted individuals with common intellectual interests. More recently the term refers to a group of scientists and/or scholars who collectively possess the talents, capabilities, and expertise of a college faculty but have not formalized their common interests and activities as an institution per se. (cf)

invisibility

In education, invisibility refers to the absence of specific cultures and ethnicities in teaching materials. This absence suggests that these groups are not important enough for inclusion and therefore do not merit consideration in many socioeconomic areas. (jqa, npo)

involuntary hospitalization

A judicial process imposed on a nonconsenting individual, primarily for the purpose of preventing harm to self or others, or of stabilizing an individual who is unable to care for him- or herself. An involuntary hospitalization may involve holding a client temporarily in a hospital setting (e.g., 72-hour hold) at the written order of a physician, due to a bona fide, high-risk concern or an identified imminent danger to self or others. This decision is often subject to administrative, judicial, and clinical review so that the individual's rights are not restricted beyond what is deemed absolutely necessary. (do)

involuntary minorities

Concept develop by John Ogbu to describe individuals and groups of individuals who have a single frame of reference in a society. The sole frame of reference is the dominant group in their society. These individuals are resentful, hostile, and disillusioned by the perception that they do not receive equitable or fair returns on their hard work in the workplace or in schools. A conclusion is drawn that putting faith, time, and effort in the pursuit of hopes for and gains in the future via education, or other sanctioned means, may not constitute a rational choice. (hfs)

IPEDS (See Integrated Postsecondary Education Data System)

ipsative assessment

The process of making a comparison against oneself. This can include measuring one's performance against one's own previous performance, such as how a person performs on a task relative to how they performed previously on the same task. It can also be how one's own preferences or experiences determine the order of a set, such as when a person selects their favorite among a list of objects. (ms)

IQ (See intelligence quotient)

IRE (initiate, respond, evaluate) (See recitation)

IRI (See informal reading inventory)

irrational number

A real number that cannot be expressed as a fraction. (kgh)

irregular words

Words in which the letters within the words do not follow typical sound-letter patterns (e.g., would, enough). Irregular words are not decodable and must be learned by sight. (rcr)

IRT (item response theory) (See item analysis)

isomorphism

A one-to-one correspondence between two sets A and B that is operation preserving. That is, the sets are structurally the same though their elements may be different. So, the result of an operation on two elements of a first set corresponds to the result of the same operation on the corresponding elements of the second set. (cmdv)

See also one-to-one correspondence.

issues-centered education
A popular pedagogical approach used in teaching social studies. The central focus of a unit of study in issues-centered education is an enduring public controversy. Teachers plan learning activities that relate to the focus of the unit. (cb)

ITA (See Initial Teaching Alphabet)

item
In any test or assessment procedure, the smallest unit of analysis, in the sense of analyzing a response from the test taker, can be called the test "item." This is the combination of what is presented to the test taker and their response format. In the traditional multiple-choice format, a test item is the question or statement given to the test taker, along with the three or four options from which they are to select their response. The test, in this case, is made up of a set of items. In the traditional essay test format, a test item is the topic, or prompt, given to the test taker, along with any specific instructions for the format and nature of their constructed response. (bkl)

item analysis
During test development and/or operational use, results on individual items can be analyzed and compared to results on other items or to subscores or total scores. This kind of analysis is very useful in deciding whether an item meets the objectives of the test developer. There are two major forms of item analysis: Classical Test Theory (CTT) and Item Response Theory (IRT). The former is over 100 years old and involves analysis of item pass rates (known as item difficulty) and agreement statistics between items and totals (known as item discrimination). The latter is about 40 years old and involves analysis of item response patterns using probabilistic models. Most modern testing companies use software that performs both CTT and IRT simultaneously. (fd)
See also item difficulty; item discrimination index.

item difficulty
In Classical Test Theory (CTT), item difficulty refers to the proportion of examinees who answered an item correctly. This proportion is also called the item's p-value. Easy items are indicated by large p-values, whereas difficult items are indicated by small p-values. The item difficulty in CTT is dependent upon the ability level of the sample of examinees being tested. Under Item Response Theory (IRT), item difficulty is expressed with reference to the ability scale. It refers to the location of an item on the ability scale where the probability of answering the item correctly is .50. (mj)
See also item analysis.

item discrimination index
Item discrimination refers to the ability of an item to differentiate high-performing and low-performing examinees on an entire test. In Classical Test Theory (CTT), an item discrimination index is commonly calculated by the correlation between the item score and the observed total scores. Large item discrimination indices indicate items with good discriminating power.

Under Item Response Theory (IRT), item discrimination is expressed in terms of the steepness of an item characteristic curve on the ability scale. It describes how rapidly the item characteristic curve changes with the examinee's ability level. (mj)
See also item analysis.

item response theory (IRT) (See item analysis)

iterable unit
A term used particularly in reference to a child's construction of 10. When a child has constructed 10 as an iterable unit the child can use a unit of 10 to measure out 10s, as in adding 10 to 37 to get 47. This is not always evident when the child counts by 10s as in 10, 20, 30, 40. Here the child might merely be reciting a standard number-word sequence he or she has learned to associate with particular items to be counted. (dc)

ITERS (See Infant/Toddler Environment Rating Scale)

itinerant teacher

Certified teacher with special education certification, who is not the teacher of record, but who instructs students who qualify for special education services. Other expectations include creating IEP reports, running meetings, mentoring students, tutoring, and other duties assigned to teachers. (jld)

Ivy League

A term used to describe a collection of elite academic institutions, including Brown, Columbia, Cornell, Dartmouth, Harvard, Pennsylvania, Princeton, and Yale. Used informally since the 1930s, this association was formally recognized in 1945 by university administrators seeking to reaffirm their common practices regarding academic standards, athletic eligibility requirements, and administration of financial aid for athletes. The association between the Ivy League and high academic standards and achievement is so strong that the term "ivy" can be used to denote high achievement among schools outside the actual league (e.g., "public ivies"). (ks2)

J

Jackson State Tragedy

A college demonstration held on May 14, 1970, at Jackson State College, protesting the U.S. invasion of Cambodia, turned violent when students clashed with city and state police and Mississippi National Guardsmen. Tragedy occurred when police fired rounds into a campus dormitory, killing two—a student and a local nonparticipant. (rih)

jargon

Unique language forms that people in certain professions or fields (e.g., academia, law, medicine, technology) use for efficient communication. Jargon is often incomprehensible to outsiders and is often referred to with negative connotations. Jargon may also be unintelligible utterances, usually associated with aphasia. Jargon can be either semantic or phonological; for example, a meaningless sequence of words or unconventional sound sequence. In language development of young children, the unintelligible strings of babbling with prosodic features that resemble adults' sentential intonations. Jargon appears before young children start to utter their first words in a more conventional way. An initial stage of a pidgin language, characterized with a large individual variation, reduced sentence structure, limited set of vocabulary, and simplified sound system. The mixture of two or more languages may lead to some incomprehensibility for the speakers of the original languages. (h-jk)

jazz

Often thought of as the one American contribution to the world of music, jazz is a 20th-century musical genre developed by African Americans (often trained musicians who were denied participation in classical venues) and featuring complex rhythms and artful improvisation done by solo or ensemble performers creating harmonic variations on chords or melodies. Modern jazz is jazz developed after the 1940s. While jazz has for a long time featured largely in community-based education, jazz groups and bands have only recently found their way into the musical offerings of those American secondary schools that have musical education programs. (jd)

Jeanes Fund

Also known as the Negro Rural School Fund, founded in 1907 by Anna T. Jeanes, a wealthy Quaker philanthropist, to improve African American schooling in the southern states. The fund is best known for training and supervising men and women known as "Jeanes teachers" to teach industrial education, promote home improvement work, establish clubs, improve health conditions, and extend leadership to raise money for new schoolhouses and materials. In 1937 the Jeanes Fund merged into the Southern Education Board, and the program finally ended in 1968. (vmm)

jigsaw technique

A specific procedure for cooperative learning. According to E. Aronson (1978), the originator of this term, jigsaw groups are made up of three to six members, with each student responsible for becoming an expert on a subtopic or theme. Members of other teams in the same classroom who are investigating the same subtopic may meet in expert groups to discuss what they are learning. Upon completion of the research, each member returns to the jigsaw group to present information on the subtopic to the other group members. This technique is especially helpful in preparation for unit examinations. (mje, jah)

Jim Crow Laws (See Civil Rights Act of 1964)

job breakdown

The complete analysis of the skill and knowledge components required in a specific job. (jm)

job coach

A person working with an individual with a disability on the job to assist with learning the skills needed to perform tasks, to identify aspects of the assignment that may require accommodations or adaptations, and to provide support and information to supervisors and coworkers. (sr)

Job Corps

A national program, funded under the Workforce Investment Act, that provides residential education and training to disadvantaged youth. (jpc)

job development

Provisions of satisfactory work opportunities through opening jobs to more people by removal of artificial barriers to employment and by job redesign or job creation. (jm)

job placement (See placement service)

job readiness

The knowledge, skills, and attitudes necessary for entering the workplace. This readiness may include general workplace skills and understanding (e.g., arriving on time, understanding and carrying out responsibilities, navigating the workplace, getting along with co-workers) as well as more specific skills that apply to particular positions. (las)

job redesign

Revision of a specific duty, role, or function of a worker in relation to the type or content of the job. (jm)

job rotation

Procedure in cooperative career and technical programs that encourages students to work in several different jobs with a cooperating employer during the school year in order to give them a wide basis of experience and training in the field. (jm, ea)

job satisfaction

The quality, state, or level of satisfaction that is a result of various interests and attitudes of a person toward a job. (jm)

job seeker

A person actively interested in finding employment. Includes the unemployed and may also include a person already employed but who is searching for another or better job. (jm)

job shadowing

Characteristically a part of career exploration in late middle and early high school. A student follows an employee at a business or industry for one or more days to learn about an occupation or industry. (db)

job task analysis (JTA)

Process by which the task requirements of a position are analyzed and outlined in order to identify the skills and knowledge necessary to perform that job effectively. An intensive examination of how people perform work to establish what a worker must know, do, or feel to learn specific work activities; conditions needed for competent performance; and minimum expectations for how well the job should be performed. JTA assists in identifying activities that may be simplified or improved. (las, sa)

job training

Vocational or career-technical instruction for a particular occupation. (jm, ea)

Job Training Partnership Act (JTPA)

U.S. legislation enacted in 1982 to provide job training to unemployed people so they could obtain unsubsidized employment. Among its most important elements were training for economically disadvantaged youth and adults, as well as summer youth employment and training programs. (las)

job-analysis technique

An approach to curriculum building based on the analysis of major and minor duties of a particular occupation and the knowledge, habits, and skills required for success in it, accompanied by the development of appropriate instructional units to train persons for the occupation in question. (jb)

jobber

An educational expert whose "profession" is securing employment. The word reflects the high level of mobility and frequency with which some educational experts change jobs. Also called ed-jobber. (lms)

job-embedded professional development

A model for in-service teacher development in which a small group of teachers study together at their workplace, over time, to investigate and address instructional problems by analyzing actual student "artifacts" such as essays, test scores, or videotapes of classroom instruction. These activities increase professional knowledge and skills of school faculty within the structure of their daily work activities and can foster both formal and informal learning opportunities, including but not limited to peer coaching, mentoring, inquiry, study groups, and action research. (cas, mrs, aa)

joint vocational school (See area vocational school)

Jones Survey (1917)

The official title of this report is *Negro Education: A Study of the Private and Higher Schools for Colored People in the United States,* but it is often referred to by the project facilitator's last name, Thomas Jesse Jones (1873–1950). The report is one of the first published surveys of schools serving racial minority groups in the United States, primarily African Americans. It was prepared for the U.S. Office of Education in cooperation with the Phelps-Stokes Fund and published by the Government Printing Office. (cm!)

Journal of Career and Technical Education

A nonprofit, international, refereed, scholarly journal serving the fields of vocational, career, technical, workforce, and career education. It is a publication of Omicron Tau Theta, the national graduate honorary society of career and technical education. (ea)

JTA (See job task analysis)

JTPA (See Job Training Partnership Act)

junior college

Two-year postsecondary institution that emerged in the early 20th century as an alternative to four-year undergraduate colleges. Founded in 1901, Joliet Junior College (Illinois) was the first public junior college in the nation. Originally intended to serve as feeder institutions for traditional colleges and universities, junior colleges began to offer terminal degrees (associate of arts) in the 1920s and 1930s. Junior colleges offered increased access to higher education and contributed to the substantial expansion of higher education enrollments, particularly in the early to mid-20th century. Today these institutions may also be referred to as "community colleges" or "technical colleges." (aja)

junior high school

An organizational model that emerged in the early 20th century creating a transitional period (typically seventh, eighth, and ninth grades) from the self-contained elementary school classroom to the subject-centered classrooms of the comprehensive high school. The new six-three-three configuration replaced the traditional six-six pattern and was designed to accommodate the developmental needs of early adolescents by providing students with opportunities to explore their interests and aptitudes. The junior high school quickly took on many of the characteristics of the subject-centered high school curriculum. Continued concern over the developmental needs of early adolescents precipitated the movement to create middle schools in the late 20th century. (wgw)

junto

A group of friends, convened by Benjamin Franklin in 1727, for the purposes of inquiry, debate, and personal improvement. Junto also is a term used for a discussion club that debated politics, morals, and natural philosophy. The term was later applied to a nonprofit organization founded in Philadelphia in 1941 to provide low-cost education to adults, combining learning and social activities. Any group created by members of a community, workplace, or the like, for self-directed learning in civic and other matters and for self-improvement may be called a junto. (chb)

justice

The concept of justice is closely related to the concepts of fairness, equity, and respect for rights and legitimate procedures. Justice demands fairness and respect for rights, substantively speaking, but in legal political contexts it also demands respect for legitimate rules of procedure. Political philosophers commonly distinguish among several forms of justice, including corrective justice, criminal justice, and distributive justice or justice in the distribution of fundamental rights, opportunities, and access to goods, including education. According to Aristotle there are two divisions of justice: distributive justice is the fair distribution of benefits and burdens across a society; commutative (or rectificatory) justice is that which is corrective in the transactions among people, maintaining or restoring balance. (rc, ewr)

See also rights.

just-in-time learning

Training, instruction, or information that is made available to the learner as close as possible to the time when the practical need for the learning has been identified or the time when the learning will be put into use. (chb)

K

K–16 bridge program

Programs that target the relationship between K–12 schools and higher education with a goal of improving the ability of students to transition from high school to college. These programs seek to align the curricular framework and instructional policies and practices employed in the K–12 systems with the requirements and achievement standards necessary for successful college enrollment and completion. (ms)

kanji

The set or a member of the set of ideographic characters, usually of Chinese origin and used predominantly for content words in standard Japanese script. (ml)

Kellogg Foundation

Founded in 1930 by W. K. Kellogg, the Foundation has become one of the largest philanthropic organizations in the world, and it was an early proponent of the adult and continuing education movement after World War II. Continuing Education Kellogg Centers have been constructed on 10 campuses in the United States, built in part with Foundation funds. (cf)

Kent State Tragedy

A university demonstration held on May 4, 1970, at Kent State University, protesting the presence of ROTC on campus, turned violent when nervous Ohio National Guardsmen began to shoot into the crowd. Four people died—two protesters and two nonparticipating students, one of whom was an ROTC cadet. (rih)

key informant

A person who has valuable perceptions and insights about a particular field or discipline, organization, or community, usually by virtue of his/her membership or leadership. Key informants can be useful in planning educational programs for adults. (chb)

key pal

The modern version of a pen pal. Instead of writing letters with paper and pencil, students correspond with one another via e-mail. (kg1)

See also e-mail.

key performance indicator (KPI)

A quantifiable measure, agreed to in advance, that reflects one or more critical success factors of an organization. KPIs operationally define an organization's high-priority strategic goals and objectives and help evaluate progress toward achieving them. They differ by organizational type and usually focus on longer-term considerations. Examples of KPIs used in the educational sector include student graduation rates, standardized test scores, sponsored research grants, and graduate school acceptance rates. (jz)

Keyes v. School District No. 1, Denver, 413 U.S. 189 (1973)

The first Supreme Court ruling on school segregation in the North and West and where no de jure segregation ruling had existed. The Court found intentional segregation in a portion of the district through racially isolated neighborhoods and gerrymandered attendance zones, which resulted in the entire school district presumed to be illegally segregated. In a significant precedent, this case recognized Latinos as a minority group that must be desegregated as well as African Americans. (ks2)

Kierkegaardian philosophy

Danish philosopher Søren Aabye Kierkegaard (1813–1855) is often referred to as "the father of existentialism." His key contribution to educational thought was his analysis of the relationship between teachers and learners as one of indirect communication. In order truly to learn something, argued Kierkegaard, learners must discover and appropriate the truth themselves instead of having it directly communicated to them by a teacher. Thus the task of the teacher is to lead students through a maieutic process of Socratic deliberation that "indirectly" brings them to an understanding of what the teacher wishes to communicate. Kierkegaard himself employed this method of indirect communication in his writings by using pseudonymous authorship and a variety of literary devices to obliquely communicate his message to the reader. (dd1)

See also Socratic method.

kindergarten

A term originally used by Friedrich Froebel to name his school for young children. Froebel believed that children were innately good and that he could create an environment in which their natural creativity would flourish. He used free play, singing, "gifts," and "occupations" as learning tools. Today, American schools use the term to describe any curriculum that is designed to prepare children for elementary grades. (jlj)

kinesiology

A discipline that focuses on physical activity and the science of human movement. (kpr)

kinesthesis

One's awareness of movement gathered from the senses; the ability to feel movements of the limbs and body and know the body's position in space. (rf)

kinesthetic learning

Skills and abilities gained through the sense of touch and the movement of self or objects. Young children especially benefit from kinesthetic experiences such as building with large and small blocks, creative movement with their bodies ("Let's make a train!"), and manipulating natural and/or fluid materials (e.g., sand, dried rice and beans, water). (ecr)

knowledge

As an intended educational outcome, knowledge is a collective term for concepts, principles, and practices in a particular field or professional specialty (e.g., a student's major field)—and the general data, information, and experience that are essential to effective performance in learning and applying what has been taught. (cf)

known fact procedures (See derived fact and known fact procedures)

Kodaly method

A method of teaching vocal music to young children in a school setting. The method was named for Hungarian music educator Zoltan Kodaly (1882–1967), based on his support of daily teaching of singing and music in select Hungarian elementary schools in the early 1950s. The method emphasized a sequential music curriculum for all children and utilized folk song and dance, a capella singing, hand signs coordinated with the solfege (do-re-mi) system, and careful attention to both the physical and intellectual developmental stages of the children. The results of this systemic practice of music education were so dramatic that the system was replicated throughout Hungary and later the world. Currently the method is often taught in combination with the Orff method as a means of integrating instrumental music experiences into the curriculum. (jbl)

See also Orff method.

KPI (See key performance indicator)

KWL chart

A three-column chart, developed by Ogle (1986), in which students organize information about the topic of a reading. In the "K" column, students list what they already know about the topic before reading, thereby activating their prior knowledge of the topic. In the "W" column, students list what they want to learn about the topic before reading, thereby setting a purpose for reading. In the "L" column, students list what they have learned about the topic after completing the reading, thereby reflecting upon and summarizing what they have learned. (jk)

L

Laban's Movement Framework
A systematic description that categorizes four aspects of movement: body, space, effort, and relationships. These aspects are further defined as what the body does, where the body moves in space, how the body performs, and what relationships occur. (rf)

labeling
A formalized process of designating an individual as having a condition or disability, such as mental retardation or a learning disability. (sr)

labor education
A specialized branch of adult education that attempts to meet the educational needs and interests arising out of workers' participation in the union movement. These needs may develop from the workers' membership and activity in the union or from their involvement as union members in the broader society. (jsj)

labor force nonparticipants
Persons who are not in the labor force, that is, who are neither working nor looking for work. Includes primarily those who work inside the home, are still in school, or are unable to work because of long-term physical or mental disabilities, and also retired persons and certain others who are not actively engaged in employment. (jb)

labor force participants
Persons who are in the labor force. (jb)

labor force participation
This term includes all of those who are either employed or who are unemployed and seeking employment. (jb)

labor market
The buying and selling of labor services—the supply of, and demand for, human resources in relation to a particular industry, area, or economy. The area from where a replacement worker for a given job would generally originate. (jb, ea)

labor market area
An economically integrated geographic area within which individuals can reside and find employment within a reasonable distance, or can readily change employment without changing their place of residence. Labor markets are classified as either metropolitan or nonmetropolitan (small labor market) areas. (jb)

laboratory, career-technical education (See career-technical education laboratory)

laboratory schools

Schools affiliated with and operated by colleges and universities that are designed to provide sites for research, development of exemplary practices of teaching, and opportunities for teacher education students to observe and participate in teaching. (bba)

LAN (See local area network)

Lancasterian system (See monitorial schools)

land ethic

In the mid-20th century, growing environmental challenges faced by the West created a need for a theory and practice of sustainable ethics related to land use. One of the most influential responses to date was the ecocentric ethic developed by Aldo Leopold (1887–1948) as described in his essay *The Land Ethic* and published in *A Sand County Almanac* (1949). Leopold called for a widening of respect for the natural world, with humans being "plain member and citizen of" an ecological community. An expanded discussion can be found *In Defense of the Land Ethic: Essays in Environmental Philosophy,* by J. Baird Callicott (1989). Leopold's *Land Ethic* continues to inform and support a variety of educational practices that encourage ecological and sustainable behavior (e.g., ecoliteracy, ecological education, environmental education, and place-based education). (vkh)

See also anthropocentrism; ecocentrism; ecojustice; environmental education; ethics; place-based education.

Land Grant Act (See Morrill Act of 1862)

land use

Relates to a spectrum of choices concerning what ends the land will serve. These choices frequently have been contested ones, especially in rural areas, when the proponents of recreational use, environmental preservation, and high-yield agriculture vie with decision makers for judgments in their favor. (lr)

land-grant institution

A college or university that has been designated by its state legislature or Congress to receive the benefits of the Morrill Acts of 1862 and 1890. The original mission of these institutions was to teach agriculture, military tactics, and the mechanical arts as well as classical studies so that members of the working classes could obtain a liberal, practical education. The Hatch Act of 1887 established the creation of the agricultural experiment station program, a key component of the land-grant system. (ch)

See also Morrill Act of 1862.

landscape

A painting, drawing, or other depiction of natural scenery; also, the background in a portrait or figure drawing. Often scenic vistas viewed from a distance. Landscapes are traditionally depicted from a single point of view and recede to a horizon. Schematic landscape details (e.g., rainbows, smiley suns, and a horizontal base line drawn as ground and/or sky) frequent the drawings of school-aged children. Due to the popularity of landscape as a genre in the visual arts, the term now applies to any tract of land with distinguishing features, and also to the horizontal orientation of any page or surface. (lj)

language barrier

A gap or barrier to communication that results from individuals speaking different languages. If a language barrier exists, it can thwart one's ability to communicate and to express oneself and may limit, or deny completely, one's ability for self-expression. (jbb)

language bias

In education, students experience language bias through exposure to teaching materials that use only masculine pronouns or Anglo names, practices commonly seen in older textbooks. The placement of nonnative-speakers of English in special education classes rather than in bilingual education or language immersion programs is another form of language bias. (jqa, npo)

language development
Refers to the development of a socially shared, systematic means of communication involving the representation of ideas, concepts, and feelings through the use of signs, sounds, gestures, or marks. Language develops from unintentional signals (cries, smiles, vocalizations) in early infancy, through the use of sounds, gestures, and expressions to the use of words and word combinations to communicate meaningful intentions. Language is dynamic and continues to develop throughout the life span. (vm)

Language Experience Approach (LEA)
An instructional method whereby students verbally dictate an experience as the teacher transcribes it. The dictation then becomes connected text to develop word recognition skills. (mmd)

language minority
People who have developed, or are developing, fluency in a home language that is not the dominant language of the wider society may be described as a language minority. The term language minority is not used to describe the level of fluency in the dominant language. In the United States, individuals whose first language is other than English are considered a language minority member. These students are often provided with intensive instruction in English as well as other standard education subjects. (jdc, jqa)

language-based learning disability
A language-based learning disability represents a spectrum of difficulties related to comprehension and use of spoken and written language. Language-based disabilities are generally thought to be due to a difference in brain structure; they can also be hereditary. (rcr)

laptop computer
A small computer designed to be portable. The monitor, keyboard, and central processing unit are combined into one machine the size of a notebook. Laptop computers can be easily transported around a school for use in various locations as needed. (kg1)
See also desktop computer.

large-group format
Any learning format in which ideas are presented to a full group (as distinguished from small-group formats, in which the large group is subdivided for different learning activities). Common formats include lectures and panels and plenary sessions at conferences. (chb)

latchkey kids
School-age children who do not have adult supervision after school hours. (bba)

latency period
The latency period, the fourth phase in Freud's theory of psychosocial development, begins at age six and lasts for about six years. During this phase, children are described as not being very interested in sexuality. Children's energy is focused on activities involving peers and opportunities for mastering cognitive learning and physical skills. (xss)

Latino studies
Latino studies is the interdisciplinary research and study of those people living in the United States whose origin is Latin America or the Spanish-speaking Caribbean. Social, cultural, historical, and linguistic aspects are just some of the areas included in Latino studies. (jqa, npo)

***Lau v. Nichols,* 414 U.S. 563 (1974)**
A Supreme Court decision that focused on the educational rights of children with

little or no English-speaking ability. The plaintiffs were non-English-speaking Chinese students who brought a class action suit against officials of the San Francisco (California) Unified School District. Plaintiffs claimed unequal educational opportunities under the Equal Protection Clause of the 14th Amendment and Title VI of the Civil Rights Act of 1964. The Court ruled in their favor, stating there was "no equality of treatment" by merely providing non-English-speaking students similar facilities, textbooks, teachers, or curricula. (gs)

Laubach approach

Reading instruction method developed by educator, sociologist, and minister Frank Laubach. The method is based on phonics, using "key words" for consonant and vowel sounds, and stresses decoding and structural analysis in a bottom-up approach to reading instruction. (las)

Law School Admissions Tests (LSAT)

A nationally used measure of potential success in professional schools of law; subject matter focuses on legal issues. Format is similar to other Educational Testing Service (ETS) measures for graduate admissions. (cf)

law-related education

An issues-centered social studies curriculum that focuses on the rules and regulations established by a government and applicable to a people. Support for teachers to establish law-related curricula in their classrooms is often connected to the state bar association of individual states. (cb)

LCDL (See culturally and linguistically diverse)

LEA (See Language Experience Approach)

leadership by domination

Leadership by domination occurs when a leader's desire for personal power overrides the organization's or group's collective goals. Usually, this type of leader makes decisions that will benefit himself/herself rather than the organization and/or the group. Under leadership by domination, a group typically does not cooperate fully with the leader because they feel they have been omitted during the decision-making process. Sometimes a group under leadership by domination refuses to cooperate at all. (tp)

League of United Latin American Citizens (LULAC)

Formed in 1929 in Corpus Christi, Texas, to advance the economic conditions, educational attainment, political influence, health, and civil rights of the Hispanic population of the United States. The aim of the organization is to use all constitutional means available to foster well-being through social action. One of the organization's major efforts is to promote learning and fluent use of the English language while maintaining Spanish and showing pride of heritage. LULAC is one of the oldest, largest, and most influential organizations representing Hispanics in the United States. (msb)

learner (See student)

learner-centered curriculum

A curriculum orientation that emphasizes the individual needs of students in planning, organizing, and delivering instructional programs. This approach focuses on student learning outcomes and gives learners the primary responsibility for their own learning choices. Learner-centered instruction is based on the needs and learning style of the student rather than on a prescribed curriculum and instructional approach. (bba, chb, jpc)

learning

Learning is a psychological process in which lasting changes in an individual's knowledge or behavior occurs as a result of experience. Explanations of how learning proceeds are influenced by philosophical, psychological, and sociocultural views of the learner and motivation. Such explanations typically emphasize the dynamics of either external behavioral changes or internal cognitive and emotional changes. Generally used to characterize a long-lasting change in knowledge, skills, attitude, or understanding of the world. Learning takes place as a result of interaction with the environment. Learning may occur either formally, as in a school or training course, or informally, as on the playground or at home. (prg, crl)

learning ability

The natural or acquired capacity to gain competency in a skill or understanding of content through instruction and/or introduction to new material and experiences. (jw)

learning activity centers (See learning centers)

learning centers

Popularized in the 1970s, learning centers are areas of the classroom devoted to specific learning activities, for example, art, writing, or mathematical calculations. These centers usually contain directions and learning materials that students can use independently to reinforce or practice curricular content. Typically, one or two students use a center at any one time, working at their own pace. (bba)

learning communities

Although there are a variety of models, traditionally learning communities have been most closely associated with cohorts of first- or second-year undergraduate students enrolled in the same group of courses and the faculty who teach those courses. A learning community might also take the form of a group of students who share common interests living in the same residence hall or floor of a residence hall, sometimes called a "learning-living community." Learning communities and learning-living communities are frequently theme-based and might be centered around a college major or a particular interest. The intent is that students will feel less isolation and be more engaged, more likely to be mutually supportive, and ultimately more successful. Faculty may also form learning communities, and again there are a variety of models. Faculty learning communities frequently, although not always, are interdisciplinary and are generally formed for designated periods of time. Centers for the advancement of teaching frequently adopt this model to support the enhancement of teaching and learning. (sn)

learning contract

A written agreement between teacher and student at the beginning of a unit of study that specifies the academic work the student is to accomplish at a particular level within a specified period of time. This contract subsequently serves as a reference for evaluating progress and the effectiveness of the learner's educational activities. In higher education, a learning contract is an agreement, usually one proposed by a learner and submitted for approval to a faculty member, that describes the learner's goals, means, and resources for study, the activities, duration, and output of the learner's study, the amount of credit sought, and the method of evaluation to be used. (bba, las, chb)

learning disability

Learning disability is a broad term that refers to a varied group of disorders manifested by significant impairment in a person's use of written or spoken language, reading, writing, reasoning, or math skills. In most instances, there must be a significant discrepancy between a person's overall cognitive ability and their achievement in one or more of these areas. Although many people consider these disorders to be due to some type of neurological dysfunction, there are scant data to support this view. Treatment of learning disorders involves modifying the instructional environment and measuring learning rates during different types of instruction in order to identify the most effective instructional strategy. (tsw)

learning effectiveness

The acquisition, assimilation, and application of knowledge, skills, or experiences given in a systematic way to facilitate constructive changes in the conceptual abilities of students, trainees, or learners. Learning effectiveness is demonstrated or inferred in tests, exams, or other methods of controlled observation by instructors. (cf)

learning environment

The characteristics related to providing a physical, intellectual, and sociopsychological environment that combine to either positively or negatively affect the educational process of the learner. (ch)

Learning in Retirement Institute

A continuing education program for adults of retirement age, part of a national network of over 200 programs around the United States. These are membership programs; members decide on the topics and activities, and programs are typically peer-led. Most are based at college or university campuses and do not award credits or lead to degrees. (chb)

learning management system (LMS)

Web applications for planning, delivering, tracking, and managing online courses and related learning events. For online education, commercial LMS (e.g., Blackboard and Desire2Learn) or open source LMS (e.g., Sakai and Moodle) can be used to deliver and manage online courses or enhance and support teaching and learning. (hh)

See also course management software.

learning objective

A statement of the desired outcome(s) of an educational activity, naming what learners can expect to gain or be able to do as a result of that activity. (chb)

learning organization

A term used in education when referring to a place where participants continually develop their capacities to create and achieve, where unique patterns of thinking are encouraged, where collective aspirations are fostered, where participants learn how to work together, and where the organization expands its capacity for innovation and problem solving. (mm)

learning outcomes measurements

Measures and describes what the learner will be able to do in behavioral terms in a particular course at specific levels (i.e., beginning, intermediate, advanced) once learning has been mastered. (pgg)

learning strategies

In higher education, these are methods, procedures, and techniques adapted and/or developed by college students in their acquisition of knowledge, competence, and understanding. In their development of learning strategies, college students are influenced in varying ways by a college education's intangible advantages and benefits, as well as its more explicit outcomes in the form of academic degrees, credits, grades, and honors. (cf)

learning style

A person's typical or preferred mode(s) of learning. The characteristic cognitive and affective behaviors that serve as relatively stable indicators of how a learner perceives, interacts with, and responds to the learning environment. Learning style can be influenced by intellectual preferences (e.g., multiple intelligences), family culture (e.g., interdependent vs. independent), psychological attributes (e.g., sensitivity to visual, auditory, or kinesthetic information), or sociological histories (the way the child has been socialized to think and behave). (chb, ecr)

learning-living community

A conception of education as a formal arrangement to integrate the learning experiences of students with their personal development and maturity. As loosely defined, the term implies a social or residential setting in which intellectual growth, personal development, and socialization are achieved as a unified effort. Specific disciplines such as foreign languages may use these arrangements to improve academic skills and promote cultural exchange. (cf)

least restrictive environment
An educational setting or program that provides a student with disabilities the opportunity to learn and work in the same setting as nondisabled peers by providing supports, accommodations, and adaptations as needed to meet the student's special needs. (sr)

lecture
A teaching format characterized by the presentation of information by a teacher to a group of learners. The lecture is an efficient way to distribute information to a large group of learners, to present new information, or to summarize information from many sources. (mkr)

left and right hemispheres of the brain
Like most of the body, the brain is symmetrical; it is made up of two (mostly) symmetrical hemispheres (each hemisphere then has four lobes). While some functions are localized in most individuals (for example, usually language processing is carried out mostly in the left hemisphere), many activities require the work of both hemispheres. Often, more detailed processing takes place in the left hemisphere, while "holistic" processing takes place in the right hemisphere. Each hemisphere contains a motor cortex and somatosensory cortex that correspond to the opposite side of the body (right hemisphere: left half of body; left hemisphere: right half of body). Most individuals have a dominant side (e.g., in a left-handed person, the right hemisphere motor cortex is dominant), but again most activity requires an integration of processing from both hemispheres, which are connected by a bundle of fibers called the corpus collosum. (pk1)

legal liability
Being obligated or responsible according to the law. This term is used to refer to a state of being held accountable, in part, through the application of legal statutes or sanctions due to acting/not acting in accordance with the law. (dd)

legislation
A term used in education that applies to the matter of business conducted or under the consideration of a legislative body. It includes the act or process of legislating, which may include making, passing, or enacting a prepared law or group of laws through the exercise of power by an official organization of a state or of another agency. In most states, legislation establishes and maintains the public schools and determines the responsibilities of state boards of education as well as the chief state officer and how they will be selected. Legislation also determines the curriculum, compulsory education requirements, the length of the school day and year, and whether there will be state community colleges and adult and vocational schools. (mm)

Lemon Grove Incident
Common name for the California case *Roberto Alvarez v. The Lemon Grove School* (1931), perhaps the first legal challenge to the segregation of Latino students in the United States. In 1931 the principal of Lemon Grove School near San Diego forced Mexican American students to attend a separate and unequal school facility from their Anglo peers. With the help of the Mexican Consul, the parents brought successful legal action against the school district and the children were allowed back into the school. (dwm)

LEP (See limited English proficiency)

lesbian
An identity label used to signify a woman who is attracted emotionally and/or sexually to members of the same sex. This term is used to refer to women, and the term "gay" is typically used to refer to men. The term "homosexual" is disliked by people who self-identify as lesbian or gay, in part because it overemphasizes the sexual aspect of sexual/affectional orientation and disregards the multifaceted nature of it. The origin of the term is from the female poet Sappho, who lived in a community of women on the Isle of Lesbos in ancient Greece. (ti, jb2)

lesson
A small segment of the curriculum, often focused on one topic or skill, that is normally a part of a sequence designed to improve or inform knowledge, attitudes, disposition, or behaviors. (rtc)

lesson plan
The organization of instruction for a particular lesson or period of time. Lesson plans often specify the objectives of the lesson, the instructional materials, and the procedures for teaching and assessing students. The plans may consist of a goal statement, learning objectives, preparation, introduction, teaching/learning activities, closing, and extension activities. Standards and assessment techniques are often included. For more efficient pacing of instruction, a contingency plan might also be stated. Basic lesson types are exposition, inquiry, discovery, induction, deduction, and research. (bba, mje, jah)

level 5 leadership
A term representing the highest level in a hierarchy of executive capabilities identified in the leadership research of Jim Collins (2001). Level 5 leadership blends extreme personal humility with intense professional will. The focused ambition found within Level 5 leaders is directed not at themselves, but at the success of the organizations or institutions of which they are a part. (jz)

leveled text
Short trade books sequenced by difficulty level determined by features such as picture support, type-token ratio, and sentence length. (mmd)

lexicon
A dictionary that contains information about syntactic properties and meaning. Any phonological representation of the words in a given language. (smt)

LGBT
Stands for Lesbian, Gay, Bisexual, and Transgender. It is an umbrella term that refers to the lesbian, gay, bisexual, and transgender community and may also refer to heterosexual allies of the group. Note that while the acronym LGBT is widely used in education, it is not a standard. It may include some (or none) of the following additions: "A" for ally, "Q" for queer or, less frequently, questioning, "P" for perceived to be gay, "I" for Intersex. For example, LGBTQ would likely signify for Lesbian, Gay, Bisexual, Transgender, and Queer. This flexibility allows individuals within the LGBT community to self-identify, that is, to choose term(s) that they feel represent them most truthfully. (acp)

See also LGBT studies; Gay, Lesbian, and Straight Education Network (GLSEN); gay, lesbian, bisexual studies.

LGBT studies
Lesbian, Gay, Bisexual, and Transgender (LGBT) studies is an overarching term for closely related fields of research and scholarship that examine the experiences and culture of LGBT lives. Emerging in the 1970s, LGBT studies programs are now found at most large colleges and universities. This interdisciplinary field of study often includes lesbian and gay studies, women and gender studies, queer studies, and/or sexuality studies. (acp)

LGBTIQQ alliance

A collective community of Lesbian, Gay, Bisexual, Transgender, Intersex, Queer, and Questioning individuals utilizing multifaceted approaches to facilitate the construction of a society conducive to the equitable existence of marginalized sexual and gender identities. (wpa, smh)

liberal arts

Comprising the basic disciplines in the natural sciences, social sciences, and humanities, liberal arts are the integrating forces in the total university community and are traditionally provided with a central position in the institution's structure, for they are the undergraduate mission of a university. Professional training, where these disciplines are to be applied, is exclusively a graduate-level responsibility. The traditional division of subjects into seven liberal arts goes back to Plato and Aristotle and was standardized by the middle of the first century B.C.E. The schools of the Middle Ages codified the seven liberal arts into the three literary arts of the Carolingian Trivium—grammar, rhetoric, and dialectic—and the four mathematical branches of the Quadrivium, arithmetic, geometry, astronomy, and theory of music. While this syllabus never claimed to embrace the totality of human knowledge, it did claim to provide an ideal of a general education suited to the whole person, and not just the professional training of the specialist—an ideal which continues to the present. (pk, jbh)

See also perennialism.

liberal arts college

An institution of higher education in which the principal emphasis is on a program of general undergraduate education leading to an BA or BS degree. Preprofessional and professional training may be offered, but not with primary emphasis. (cf)

liberal education

From Locke and Pestalozzi to Dewey and Bennett, there is a consensus that education should prepare the individual to live life to its fullest. This includes preparation for citizenship, work, and moral development. Since there is no single set of personality attributes, social abilities, or human interests, nor is there agreement about what such preparation entails, there can be no one set curriculum. Beyond the basics of reading, writing, and mathematical calculation, education will take different forms in various schools and cultures. Imposition of a single curriculum is a movement contrary to the direction of liberal education. Liberal education makes one free, liberates one. (sc)

liberal teacher education

A course of study for future teachers that emphasizes general, intellectual, and indirect thinking designed to produce self-reliance. A program of study that expects use of general intelligence to solve particular problems. (bjl)

Liberalism

Classical Liberalism is the belief that some scope of individual liberty should be protected against social and governmental constraints. Liberal philosophers of the Enlightenment argued that citizens possess natural rights (e.g., freedoms of religion, speech, and private property) that limit the authority of government; and that every citizen is entitled to as much personal liberty as is consistent with the same amount for every other citizen. Often contrasted to "conservatism," in that conservative educators emphasize education's role in socializing successive generations with the community's traditional beliefs and values, while liberal educators emphasize education's role in liberating new generations from many kinds of oppression, including some of the community's traditions. (mg)

See also communitarianism; individualism; person.

liberationist teacher education

An approach to preparing teachers that is based on the classical idea of a liberal education and proposes to develop teachers who serve as liberators in that they are developers of well-rounded, knowledgeable, rational, and moral human beings. (rtc)

library automation

Traditionally, the bibliographic database system that stores and maintains the library's records about the material it owns. The public utilizes this system for searching; the library uses it to track materials, to manage purchases, and to keep patron records. Increasingly, other systems are being added to library automation: citation linking mechanisms, interlibrary loan functions, services to search multiple databases at once, etc. These systems serve to support research and scholarship, making it easier for students to find and use information. (ac)

licensure

A system to ensure stakeholders that the teachers granted a license have met state requirements for teaching. The system provides the state authority to identify the minimum professional knowledge and skills necessary to acquire a teaching license. (clk)

Life Adjustment Movement

This movement grew out of a 1945 conference sponsored by the U.S. Office of Education, which concluded that a majority of secondary students were not receiving the basic life skills training needed for citizenship and adulthood. The reform movement designed by Charles Prosser in the late 1940s promised to increase the relevance of high school to the everyday lives of students and families via a focus on character education, the development of self-esteem, and practical social training. There was a particular emphasis on serving the needs of the 60 percent of students who could not be classified as either college preparatory students or vocational

education students. By increasing the pertinence and differentiation of school activities and lessons to the lives of students and the needs of a civil society, the movement sought to universalize attendance and decrease delinquency and the dropout rate among American high school students. Though proponents never settled on an exact definition, "life adjustment" generally referred to school training in areas such as domestic and civic life, mental and physical health, and use of leisure. Although popular with professional educators, "life adjustment" suffered a barrage of public attacks by critics who decried it as anti-intellectual. In the face of such controversy, the movement effectively lost steam by the end of the 1950s. (ag, hfs)

life drawing

The activity of drawing the human figure from a live model. Art classes often give students the chance to draw from a live model, often nude, so that students may learn to draw human features and form, and become acquainted first hand with capturing contour, gesture, and expression. Drawing from life is a requisite skill for artists and is demonstrated at its height in the work of Leonardo da Vinci, Michelangelo, Rubens, Hogarth, and Picasso. (ap)

life history

As collaboration between an ethnographer and a chosen informant, life history is the mediated portrayal of an individual life that emphasizes cultural context. Life history emphasizes the voice, agency, and perspective of the subject, paying keen attention to the cultural and historical processes that make up the context of the life. Anthropologist Caroline Brettell has astutely suggested that the use of life history leads to an "informed intersubjectivity." Paul Radin was the first professional anthropologist to explicitly champion the methodological significance of life history and thus to advocate explicitly an "insider's view" of culture. Many other notable anthropologists (including Elsie Clews Parsons, Edward Sapir, Oscar Lewis, Sidney Mintz, Barbara Myerhoff, and Marjorie Shostak) have followed suit. (jde)

life science
A grouping of sciences, including genetics, zoology, and botany, that studies the nature of living things. In education, a course in life science will incorporate ideas from several science branches, concentrating on general concepts and processes without the depth of study found in a specific study of the science branch. (tw)

life skills
Abilities and knowledge applicable to the performance of roles commonly assumed by adults in their lives, such as parent, worker, community member, or citizen. These tools help an adult to live and interact in a social context. (las)

lifelong learning
Learning throughout the lifespan, from infancy through old age; commonly used in the narrower sense of learning throughout the adult lifespan. The principle that people should have opportunities to learn, formally and informally, for personal growth and for acquisition of skills or competencies, throughout their lives. (chb)

Lifelong Learning Act of 1976
Legislation sponsored by Senator Walter Mondale and passed by the U.S. Congress, defining a broad scope of lifelong learning programs and calling for a clearinghouse to generate research on the barriers that hindered people's participation in learning. (Funding to implement this legislation was never appropriated.) (chb)

lifestory
A qualitative research technique that uses biography combined with story telling to record and interpret the real lives of educational leaders. (rbp)

lifetime activities
Sports or recreational activities that can be participated in throughout one's life. (rf)

lifeworld
A concept developed by Jürgen Habermas to explain the reservoir of implicitly known traditions, knowledge, or background and basic assumptions that are embedded in language and culture and are drawn upon by individuals in everyday life. As such, it is the context and background in which communicative action takes place and is formed by always unproblematic, taken for granted, convictions. Transformation in this background knowledge and set of assumptions involves changes in interconnected cultural, social, or personality dimensions. As individual personality is linked to society and culture as well as to the two differentiated elements of the system world (state and economy), all individual transformations have collective or social dimensions and implications. (hfs)

lighting
A key design element in performing and visual arts, lighting sets mood, creates atmosphere, enhances or communicates meaning, and serves to both illuminate and obscure specific aspects of a work. Indoor performances in theater, opera, and dance use hanging lights and spotlights for illumination; the earliest Greek theaters were designed to gain maximum effect from the natural light of the sun at various times of day. Photographers use artificial or natural light to create particular effects. Painters use shading and other visual techniques to represent the effects of lighting. (em)

limit
As values for x get closer to a given number c the function values of x get close to the limit, a number L. For example, as x values get close to a given number 2, x could take on the sequence of values 1.9,

1.99, 1.999, and so on. These values for *x* are getting close to 2. For a function $f(x) = 2x + 1$, when x is replaced with this sequence of numbers, the values of the function will get close to the number 5. The closer that the *x* value gets to 2 the closer function value will get to 5, which is the limit as *x* gets close to 2. Formally this means that for each positive ε there exists a positive δ such that the difference between L and the function of *x* is less than ε whenever the difference between *x* and *c* is less than δ. (rdk)

limit setting
Restricting an environment or behaviors, either spatially or with materials/equipment or by establishing rules to identify appropriate behaviors and restrict inappropriate behaviors. (db1)

limited English proficiency (LEP)
In the past, this term has been applied to adults and children who are not fluent in spoken and written English. The more neutral phrase, English language learners (ELL), has largely replaced "limited English proficiency" to describe this group of students. (acp)

limited English proficiency (LEP) students
Students for whom English is a second language and whose English is very limited. (bba)

LINCS (See Literacy Information and Communications System)

line and staff
Refers to a concept of organizational structuring that has a long history in military contexts. For example, the "line" represents the troops who will be directly engaged in facing the enemy. The "staff" represents those individuals and functions that "support" those troops. In education, the "line" consists of classroom teachers, principals, and any administrative officer through which principals must report. The staff consists of transportation, pupil services, food services, facilities, and everything else that is not directly instructional design or delivery. While there are other concepts of organizational structuring, the line and staff idea fits most bureaucratic contexts extremely well. (fwe)

line graph
A graph that displays data using points or dots that are connected together with lines to indicate the amount of data. (kr)

Line Graph

linear algebra

A branch of mathematics that studies the theory behind systems of linear equations. The study includes major topics such as vectors, vector spaces, linear transformations, matrices, and dimensions. (mlf, rlk)

linear equation

Any equation that can be put in the form $Ax + By = C$, where A, B, and C are real numbers with A and B not both zero; any equation where all the variables are to the first power only; any equation whose graph is a line. (rdk)

linearity

The property of being linear or well-behaved with regard to addition and scalar multiplication. Linearity is one-dimensional and is exhibited when a change in one quantity produces a directly proportional change in another quantity. (kva)

linguicism

This term refers to discrimination based on native language. In the classroom, linguicism may occur when nonnative-speaking students are provided fewer opportunities due to their lack of facility with the language of the dominant culture. (jqa, npo)

linguistic bias (See language bias)

linguistic intelligence

One of Howard Gardner's (1993) multiple intelligences, an aptitude for using and understanding words and the nuances of language. The linguistic learner likes to listen to stories read aloud and can repeat stories and conversations from memory. (Often, young children who exhibit large vocabularies and the ability to carry on conversation with adults are labeled "smart" by impressed adults.) Expert performers of linguistic intelligence include poets, authors, and public speakers. (ecr)

linguistics

The study of language or language communication, including its nature and structure. Subfields of linguistic inquiry include applied linguistics, psycholinguistics, sociolinguistics, and structural linguistics. (mc)

listening comprehension level

The grade level at which a student can comprehend at the 75 percent level when graded passages are read aloud in a naturally flowing manner. This level is usually higher than the instructional reading level and can be higher than the frustration reading level, as the oral vocabulary and discourse skills are typically stronger than the analogous reading vocabulary and comprehension skills. (aw)

listening to children

In education the teacher makes a conscious effort to hear and attend closely and respond to all students instead of ignoring them. In a classroom, a teacher may not be able to listen when being spoken to by a child. In this situation, it is necessary for a teacher to politely respond, "I can't listen right now. Can we talk later?" To take the time to listen to each and every child is fundamental to nurturing their self-esteem as well as providing a context where a teacher is able to learn from the student. In today's busy world, adults may overlook the importance of listening to a child speak. Often, there is no one who will take the time to listen and respond to a child. The act of speaking provides an opportunity for a child's oral language development. Furthermore, if in an educational setting a teacher fails to listen to students it is highly likely students will fail to listen to the teacher. The art of listening is a primary learning modality. One way to teach listening is by teacher demonstration—taking the time to listen to all voices. This simple human courtesy shows children how to listen as well as the importance of listening. When a teacher asks students to listen, then he/she must also listen to children. (jls)

literacy

Ability to read and write to a degree accepted by society, sometimes including the ability to perform arithmetic operations, enabling an individual to engage in activities with and effectively function in his or her group and community. Many literacy experts posit that there is not one single definition of literacy and, because of the breadth of concepts involved in literacy, some prefer the plural term "literacies." Recent applications include competency in a field of knowledge (as in computer literacy or media literacy). Types of literacy include functional literacy, such as skills in reading and writing, which, with numeracy, has traditionally been the essence of education. An extended meaning of literacy includes prose literacy (understanding literature, novels), document literacy (location and comprehension of information, forms, timetables), and quantitative literacy (discounts, bank balance). A higher level is critical literacy, when education is aimed not at rote memorization of the contents of books, but at critical knowledge of the axis of culture, looking for its foundations and awakening a personal position in the individual life and in activity as an engaged citizen. (mc, ji-m)

See also cultural literacy.

literacy circle

Also called a literature circle, this is a student-centered, cooperative reading activity designed to enhance and deepen students' reading of a text. Literacy circles begin with students' self-selection of a text from a variety of choices. After reading a specified portion of the text independently, students meet periodically in a small group with other students who have chosen this text. Within these literacy circles students discuss, respond to, and reflect upon what they have read. Each member of the circle is assigned a role that helps guide the group's discussion. As a result of the cooperative nature of literacy circles, students are exposed to a variety of readers' interpretations of a text, which serves to broaden each students' perspective on the text. (jk)

literacy education

Any program designed to teach basic reading, writing, and social skills to adults. Literacy education in the United States is provided in settings ranging from informal community-based initiatives to government-funded programs in technical institutions. These programs use a variety of instructional methods to address areas as diverse as GED preparation, workplace skills training, and ESL education. (dmv)

Literacy Information and Communications System (LINCS)

A web-based resource for adult literacy, supported by the National Institute for Literacy, that provides access to information useful to practitioners, adult students, teachers, policy makers, and researchers. (jpc)

literacy skills

Identifiable competencies that support the making and sharing of meanings through varying symbolic systems, usually but not restricted to print orthography. (mc1)

literal stage

A period of artistic development in middle childhood (ages 8 to 11) in which children's drawings appear to decline in terms of the expressivity found in the work of younger children. Children at this stage seem preoccupied with the desire to translate visually perceived images onto paper. Their drawings are often spatially constricted (i.e., older children do not make use of an entire drawing space as most young children do) and employ stereotypical, rather than personally conceived representations of individuals and objects. The frustrations of the literal stage cause many individuals to cease art making entirely. Some researchers defend the literal stage as a time of expanding repertoire rather than of the loss of early skills. (lw)

literate

To be able to read and/or write in a particular language or field (as in computer literate). (mc)

literate environment

A classroom in which literacy is valued and in which reading and writing take place frequently, routinely, and for a variety of purposes and audiences. (bba)

literature circle (See literacy circle)

lived ideologies

Fragmented composites derived from intellectual activities and knowledge that have been combined, integrated, and modified by cultural and personal experience, ideologies, and understandings manifested in the actions and behaviors of individuals. (hfs)

LMS (See learning management system)

lobes of the brain

Each hemisphere of the brain consists of four major divisions, or lobes (occipital, parietal, temporal, and frontal). The lobes are interconnected and anatomically continuous; landmark sulci (furrows) and gyri (ridges) are used to establish divisions between them. Many different functions are performed within each lobe; below are some salient examples, though not an exhaustive list.

The occipital lobe is the most posterior lobe of the brain, located near the back of the head. It is home to the primary visual cortex as well as processing many aspects of vision leading to visual perception (such as color, line, and motion).

The parietal lobe is anterior and dorsal to the occipital lobe. One of the well-known functions of the parietal lobe is a representation of space. The parietal lobe is also known for its integration of information from different senses (sensory association areas). Somatosensory processing leading to perception (i.e., information

about the position of the body in space as well as stimulation of the integument) also takes place within the parietal lobe.

The temporal lobes are the most lateral lobes of the brain. Primary auditory processing, as well as higher auditory processing leading to perception, are housed in the temporal lobe. Many functions related to object recognition, and naming and classification are performed in the temporal lobe. In most individuals, the left temporal lobe also has specialized areas for language and speech perception (Wernicke's area is located within the temporal lobe). Subcortical structures within the temporal lobe, including the hippocampus (sometimes referred to as medial temporal lobe) are critical for certain types of memory.

The frontal lobe is the most anterior lobe of the brain, located at the front of the head and above the eyes. Functions of the frontal lobe include motor planning and intentional body movements, and speech production (Broca's area is located within the frontal lobe). Additionally, a suite of functions referred to as "executive functions," including inhibition, attention, and working memory are thought to depend primarily on processing that takes place within the prefrontal cortex of the frontal lobe (i.e., the most anterior parts of the frontal lobe). (pk1)

local area network (LAN)

A group of computers within close proximity, such as in the same room or building, that are connected to one another. For example, machines in a computer cluster may be connected via a local area network so users have access to a shared printer or file server. Also known as a LAN. (kg1)

local wellness policy

Local wellness policies promote health and wellness in school districts. Public Law 108-265, passed in 2004, requires each local educational agency that is part of the National School Lunch Program to establish a local school wellness policy. The policy must include goals for nutrition education, physical activity, and other school-based activities that are designed to promote student wellness. (kpr)

locomotor skills

Movement skills that require the body to move from one place to another (traveling). It involves changing the base of support and possibly losing contact with the ground (i.e., jumping, skipping, hopping, rolling, running). (rf)

locutionary meaning

The literal meaning of an utterance. For example, if Person A asks Person B who is in the same room: "*Are you too warm?*" the locutionary meaning of the utterance is to question whether Person B is comfortable with the current temperature in the room. (smt)

logarithm

A function that transforms multiplication into addition: the log of a product equals the sum of the logs. Using this definition, it turns out that the logarithm is the integral of the function 1/x; this is called the natural logarithm. The natural logarithm is also the inverse of the exponential function. (smc)

logic

The normative study of valid, or correct, reasoning, and the rules that govern it. Logic concerns itself with whether an argument is valid; with whether, if one accepts the premises or assumptions made in the argument, one must accept its conclusion on pain of irrationality. When an argument is valid, its conclusion is said to follow logically from, or to be a logical consequence of the premises. The central aim of logic is to accurately and systematically explain what this relation of logical consequence amounts to. (gu)

See also critical thinking; reason.

logical thinking

Science of reasoning dealing with a criteria of valid thought, necessary or expected because of what has gone before. In an instructional setting, the process (sequential reasoning) is as important as the product (possible answer). In other words, the step-by-step process a learner uses to arrive at an answer illuminates the thinking process and cognitive development. This insight allows a teacher to adapt curricula to meet students' developmental levels. One way a teacher may encourage a learner's logical thinking is through the use of the terms such as first, second, then, and finally. In a writing workshop, the learner is asked to write about a personal experience. Within this context, the teacher recommends to each learner to identify what happened first, what happened next, then what happened, and the final happening of the personal experience. (jls)

logical-mathematical intelligence

The ability to understand and use numbers and mathematical concepts and create and follow logical arguments. One of Howard Gardner's multiple intelligences. (jwc)

logicism

The science of correct reasoning. Reasoning is best defined as the drawing of inferences or conclusions from known or assumed facts. (kr)

logico-mathematical knowledge

Piaget proposed that mathematical learning could be divided into three types of knowledge: physical knowledge from experience with the physical world (the bead is hard and has a hole in it), social knowledge constructed by social environments (the bead is red and inexpensive), and logico-mathematical knowledge of relationships of concepts and skills (this bead is larger and brighter than another). (ey)

logistics

In testing, logistics are the various activities involved in planning and carrying out a test administration. The logistics of testing include procuring any necessary test materials (test papers, audio or videotapes, pencils, score cards, and so on) and organizing the details of test administration, from scheduling the test and arranging for testing rooms and proctors to hiring and training raters. Also included under the general rubric of logistics is the consideration of diverse practical problems such as disseminating test results, storing test records, and maintaining test security. Specifying in detail the logistics of test administration is an essential aspect of determining the practicality of a given testing method. For example, logistical considerations may be important in deciding between multiple-choice or open-ended questions in testing reading comprehension. (scw)

LOGO

A programming language created by Seymour Papert at MIT in 1967. Designed as a tool for learning, it features modularity, extensibility, interactivity, and flexibility. Since its inception, LOGO was intended to be part of an environment in which a wide range of users could constructively explore sophisticated and complex problems and projects in mathematics as well as language, science, music, robotics, and others. While most LOGO environments originally included the robotic Turtle that could be directed to move about the floor by typing commands into the computer, the Turtle has now evolved into a computer graphic that moves on the computer screen. (slr)

long vowel

Vowels with longer duration of vowel sound. The vowel sounds that are also the names of the alphabet letters a, e, i, o, u. For example, the *a* in *cape* and *o* in *cold* are long vowels. They may also be denoted by two vowels, such as *ai* in *rain* and *ee* in *meet*. (yu)

long-term potentiation (LTP)

Long-term potentiation describes the increased sensitivity of a neuron to fire in response to the input of another neuron.

It is also expressed as a "strengthening" of neuronal connections. Several mechanisms of LTP have been proposed: the receiving (or postsynaptic) neuron may modify the shape of its dendritic spines to facilitate greater propagation of the signal; the receiving neuron may increase the number of active synaptic receptors; the receptors in turn may be modified to remain open for a longer period of time; the receiving neuron may send a signal back to the sending (or presynaptic) neuron to stimulate a stronger signal. Synaptogenesis and neurogenesis are other mechanisms sometimes associated with LTP. The general interest in LTP is in its role as an explanation for aspects of memory and learning. (dh)

looping

The practice of assigning the same teacher to a group of students for two consecutive academic years, or grade levels; in the third year, the teacher begins teaching a new group of students at the lower grade level. For example, a teacher might teach a group of first graders in year one, teach the same group of students for second grade in year two, and then begin teaching a new group of first graders in year three, staying with them through second grade in year four. The purpose of looping is to increase the efficiency and effectiveness of instruction by eliminating, in the second year, the period of time required for teachers, students, and parents to become familiar with each other. (bba)

loose-knit groups

Centers of social interaction characterized by a great deal of permeability, fluid and developing social expectations (behaviors, attitudes, obligations, etc.), as well as the presence of acceptable boundary crossing. (hfs)

low arts (See fine arts)

lower division

The freshman and sophomore years of a baccalaureate degree program organized to provide the general education portion of a student's curriculum in the first two years of a four-year program. (cf)

lower-order questions
Questions requiring only the recall of specific information rather than engagement in complex or abstract thinking. (bba)

low-incident population
In bilingual education, this term is used to identify a group of speakers of a language other than English too small to be entitled to a bilingual program. In those situations, such students may be placed in an English as a second language program. (jqa, npo)

low-literate adult
A term used to describe adults whose literacy skills are limited. (jpc)

loyalty oath
During the post–World War I era, and then after World War II, nearly every state and the federal government required its employees to take loyalty oaths affirming their loyalty to the government and laws of the United States. While loyalty oaths had been a routine feature during wartime and were required of military and high-ranking government personnel, Cold War loyalty oaths were unique in both their scope (as many civilians, most notably teachers and professors had to take them); and the level of allegiance they demanded. Often educators refusing to take these oaths out of personal or political convictions faced termination, nonemployment, and professional ostracism. (ah)

LSAT (See Law School Admissions Tests)

LTP (See long-term potentiation)

LULAC (See League of United Latin American Citizens)

lyceum
A community-based adult education organization in which the members, often working people, are both learners and teachers. The lyceum focuses on the dissemination of mainstream culture and values, typically through lecture and/or discussion. The first lyceum was created by Josiah Holbrook in 1826 in Massachusetts. Lyceums spread throughout New England, the South, the Midwest, the Atlantic states, and even to England. The Lyceum Movement was named for the school formed by Aristotle in ancient Greece. Lyceums disseminated political information, provided adult instruction, and encouraged social reform through public lectures and debates during the 1830s through the 1860s. (js, dwm)

M

MACOS (See Man: A Course of Study)

macroculture

The predominant culture of a society is the macroculture. In the United States the macroculture has a white-Anglo-Saxon-Protestant tradition, although there are influences from many microcultures. (jqa, npo)

macrosystem

In an ecological model of child development (Bronfenbrenner, 1979), a macrosystem is the largest context in which a child lives in his or her society. Society is systematically created by broad entities, such as government, religion, and ethnicity, that influence the beliefs, values, and actions of human beings. Children are socialized into the macrosystem day by day as they live in the society. (ecr)

magna cum laude

Latin phrase meaning "with great praise," used as a designation for a college or university honor graduate of higher attainment than *cum laude* and less than *summa cum laude*. (cf)

magnet school

A school that draws students from an entire school district rather than from a specific geographical location. Magnet schools typically have special themes (e.g., art, music, drama, technology) or curriculum areas (e.g., science, mathematics) that attract students and their families to the school. Magnet schools are defined in Sec. 3005 of Title III of the Elementary and Secondary Education Act (ESEA), as amended through December 31, 1990, as schools or education centers that offer a specialized curriculum capable of attracting substantial numbers of students of different racial backgrounds. Magnet schools were started as a means of achieving desegregation and are characterized by student and parent choice, enrollment beyond geographical bounds, and a curriculum based on a special theme or method of instruction (e.g., computer science or performing arts). Today, however, magnet schools are being used to combat rising absenteeism, dropout rates, and academic failure in traditional schools. As a strategy for addressing these problems, magnet schools allow for the voluntary reassignment of children or faculty to reduce, eliminate, or prevent these problems in one or more K–12 schools of a local education agency. In the context of school-to-work, magnet schools specialize in certain professions or career centers that train students for entry-level jobs in career and technical fields. (bba, jb, wg, dm)

Magnetic Resonance Imaging (MRI)

MRI is a neuroimaging technique that uses magnetic fields to visualize the structure of the brain. MRI has good structural resolution and can produce very clear pictures of both surface and deep brain structures. In research, MRI is sometimes used in conjunction with functional imaging methods to relate mental activities to particular brain structures; on its own, MRI images structure only, giving no information about brain activity. In medicine its primary application is in the identification of brain damage or disease. (mt)

magnetoencephalography (MEG)

MEG is a functional neuroimaging technique that records the magnetic fields produced by electrical activity in the brain. MEG uses extremely sensitive devices to directly measure currents formed by groups of active neurons. The primary use of MEG is in the measurement of the time course of an activity, because MEG has excellent temporal resolution and can resolve events within milliseconds. Although the spatial resolution of MEG is better than EEG, it is not as good as MRI, and MEG recording is limited to activity of brain areas close to the brain's surface. (mt)

magnitude

A property that can be quantitatively described or measured. Thus, the length of a vector—regardless of its position—is known as its magnitude, or the volume of a sphere is its magnitude. Magnitude also refers to the intensity of an earthquake, generally given in the Richter scale. (dbc)

maieutic (See Socratic method)

mainstream Americans

A label for legal residents of the United States who have characteristics of the dominant ethnic and cultural groups. Typically a mainstream American is a white Anglo-Saxon Protestant and has middle or higher social-class status. (jqa, npo)

Mainstream English Language Training (MELT)

A project designed to provide consistency among English-language programs funded by the Office of Refugee Resettlement of the U.S. Department of Health and Human Services. In addition, it sought to provide continuity between domestic and overseas training programs and provide guidance for curriculum development, establishing instructional levels and assessment. Among the products of the project are the widely used Basic English Skills Test (BEST) and its Student Performance Levels (SPL). (las)

mainstream-centric curriculum

A mainstream curriculum presents information and concepts from the point of view of the dominant social class. Typically in the United States, this is the perspective of white Anglo-Saxon Protestant males. (jqa, npo)

mainstreaming

The process of providing opportunities for students with disabilities, assigned to separate settings, to participate in programs with typical peers for a designated period of time. (sr)

maintenance bilingual approach

Using the student's native language as a basis for instruction, the student is encouraged to use and develop native-language skills while mastering a second language. Both native and second languages are used in the instructional process. (jqa, npo)

MALDEF (See Mexican American Legal Defense and Educational Fund)

Male-to-Female (See transsexual)

malingering
Deliberate and intentional feigning of physical or psychological symptoms, dysfunction, and/or impairment (e.g., illness, disability, or incompetence). Involves attempting to paint a more negative clinical picture than actually exists, usually in an attempt to gain an external goal or benefit of some sort. (kab)

malpractice
A situation in which a person in a professional position engages in behaviors that are unethical, incompetent, and/or negligent. It is an act or behavior of a professional that does not meet the standards of his profession. Malpractice can be an unintentional or intentional act and may or may not lead to legal action. Reported cases of malpractice are almost always investigated by the governing body of that profession. (tsw)

Man: A Course of Study (MACOS)
A curriculum project developed in the 1960s that was part of the "new social studies" movement. Based upon the work and ideas of psychologist Jerome Bruner, MACOS was a middle-grades curriculum project in which the disciplines of anthropology and biology helped students discover the similarities and differences between humans and animals. By 1975, MACOS was used in over 1,700 schools, but later its funding was cut severely after controversy erupted, and conservative groups charged MACOS with cultural relativism and environmental determinism. (cb)

Management by Objectives (MBO)
An administrative process that identifies and accomplishes organizational purposes by joining superiors and subordinates in the pursuit of mutually agreed goals that are specific, measurable, time bound, and joined to an action plan. Management by Objectives is a system for motivating and integrating the efforts of school personnel toward common objectives. (ly)

management of decentralization
Management of decentralization is a management and organizational strategy whereby decentralized, highly involved teams of individuals provide products and/or services, such as in a school setting, and have decision-making authority during the process. Typically, with management of decentralization, four key resources are necessary for successful management: power, knowledge and skills, information, and rewards. (tp)

management revolution
The term used in referring to the adoption of business management concepts and principles in the administration and governance of American colleges and universities in the 1960s and 1970s; sometimes dated from the introduction of planning programming budgeting systems during Lyndon B. Johnson's presidency. (cf)

manga
A kind of comic book produced in Japan containing cartoon characters drawn in a particular style: with wide foreheads, pointed chins, oversized eyes, jagged stylized hairdos, and small noses and mouths. The themes of manga range from sentimental to sensational (e.g., stories about two cuties finding true love or a wronged hero gaining robotic powers to conquer evil) and many Japanese school children draw proficiently in the manga style. Indeed, the production and sale of youth-created manga is serious business (inviting early entrepreneurship and involving great sums of money) that has captured the interest of youth culture researchers in this country and abroad. (jd)

manipulative play
Free choice activities engaging children with hands-on materials that promote fine motor development, often with creativity and applying problem-solving techniques. Examples of manipulative play are activities with puzzles, various construction materials, blocks, stringing beads, or lacing cards. (db1)

manipulative skills

The ability to handle objects to send them away, gain possession, or maintain possession. These skills include throwing, striking, catching, trapping, carrying, and dribbling. (rf)

manipulatives

Items used by students to help them better understand mathematics concepts by manipulating, grouping, or moving them to derive a desired outcome. Any object used by students that enables them to develop strategies for problem solving and/or promotes a better understanding of the mathematics concept under investigation. (vdf)

Manpower Development Training Acts

A series of U.S. federal laws passed in 1962, 1963, and 1965 designed to provide funding for education and training for youth. (las)

manual training

A course or training to develop skill by using the hands in the practical arts (such as woodworking and metalworking). (jb)

marginalization

The treatment of some person, group of people, or ideas as if they are insignificant and unimportant. To be marginalized is to be devalued and treated as inferior and inconsequential, or even to be treated as invisible and not noticed at all. An example of marginalization is when policy is designed to recognize certain minority groups, such as African Americans, but others, such as Latino Americans, are not included in the policy. When a person contributes an important idea to scholarship but that contribution is not cited and is thus forgotten, that person and the idea become marginalized. (bt-b)

marketing education

Major educational program area in career and technical education, designed to provide students with the attitudes, skills, and knowledge to be successful in postsecondary education, the workforce, and as consumers through classroom instruction, experiential education, student internships, and through leadership and personal development by participating in student leadership organizations. Course-work competencies focus on marketing, management, entrepreneurship, promotion, communications, and distribution. (ea)

marital therapy

Therapy that attempts to stabilize and improve the relationship of two individuals who regard themselves as marital partners. Although there are many forms of marital therapy, their common goal is to improve the interactional and behavioral patterns of the couple as well as any underlying individual problems that are impacting the marriage. In contemporary society, this form of therapy has expanded from clients who are husband and wife to unmarried or homosexual couples who are cohabitating. (tsw)

marketplace of ideas

Concept that a college campus community may host forums for speakers who may hold controversial views on issues; that freedom of speech includes the consideration and rejection of some positions or concepts. (cf)

Marxism

Marxism is distinct from Marx's social theory. There is not one Marxism but multiple interpretations of Marx's beliefs, such as Leninist, Stalinist, Maoist, Sandanista, Castroist, and Feminist Marxism. All are applications of Marxist theory to particular local conditions that share basic Marxist theoretical perspectives, including his materialist analysis of social life: the facts of social organization can be explained by the ways in which the needs of society are produced, and the relationships individuals and groups have to the means of production. Marxisms usually have both action components for social change and theoretical components for creating policies and practices to bring about such change. (db-j)

mascot
A symbol used by a place of higher education, often most associated with the athletic departments and teams of that college or university. (jbm)

master schedule
The listing of the locations, meeting times, and teachers of each section of a course or class that is taught in a school. The master schedule is usually developed in a matrix format, designed to focus on resource allocations. Depending on the school size and number of course offerings, this process can be as simple as writing names on a class roster or as complex as one requiring sophisticated computing software. When the master schedule is complete a school should have the most efficient use of personnel in creating sections of classes to meet the interests and needs of students. The process of developing a master schedule is independent of the type of instructional structure that a school utilizes (e.g., traditional schedule, block schedule, etc.). (ly)

master teacher
An instructor who is recognized as possessing exceptional teaching ability. This recognition may be the result of professional preparation, experience, or superior skills. This label is sometimes used to distinguish those educators qualified to assist new teachers or interns, or to host student teachers. (jw)

master's degree (See degree, master's)

mastery learning
An instructional strategy in which students are expected to reach a certain level of proficiency. Students study material at their own pace, receiving the assistance they need in order to meet the predeter-mined level of mastery, which is typically set at 80 percent on an objective test. (bba)

MAT
Master of Arts in Teaching degree. (clk)

mathematical learning potential
A level at which students are striving to achieve their full potential, in order to participate in a high-quality discussion within the classroom. This is done by creating mathematical goals for oneself. (jmg)

mathematical model
The representation of phenomena through mathematical relations and expressions. Mathematical models are typically created and applied by interpreting abstract deductive theories and their connection with phenomena of the physical world. (gtm)

mathematical purpose
The reason behind the manipulation of procedures and the derivation of their use. The focus is on why a procedure works and the mathematical approach for the "why" behind the actual methods used. (jmg, ldz)

mathematical reasoning
A type of reasoning that involves constructing the relationship between mathematical ideas, and being able to reason logically, to clearly express mathematical thoughts, and to recognize and use patterns, generalizations, and abstractions. (smc)

mathematical symbol systems
These systems are of two kinds: symbols that stand for quantities and symbols that stand for relationships between quantities. An important goal in mathematics education is for students to establish meaning for these symbol systems, to make connections between mathematical symbols and the mathematical objects they reference. (amr)

mathematical system of organization

A way of thinking that allows for formulating methods in which to create connections with previous mathematical knowledge to generalize topics in order to deepen the student's core structure of knowledge. This in turn will provide a structured system of thought. (jmg)

mathematical task

A problem that engages students in mathematics and allows them to explain their thought process while building from their current knowledge. Tasks that permit this allow for perturbation to occur, which motivates the students, and allows them to create their own connections and meanings. (jmg)

mathematics

The science dealing with quantities and form, and their relationships, by use of numbers and rigorously defined symbols; an activity of construction patterns and relationships in number and form. (dc)

mathematics anxiety

A sense of apprehension and fear regarding mathematics, often characterized by one or more of the following: an inability to rationally evaluate one's mathematical knowledge or skill; actual difficulty learning or mastering mathematical content; physiological signs such as sweating, increased pulse, tension, and loss of memory that develop while discussing or doing mathematics; an inability to perform according to one's abilities during mathematical activity (e.g., quizzes, tests, and oral discussion). (cmdv)

matrix structure

A matrix structure is the result in which a new "team" of persons is formed to resolve an issue. Participants of the team occupy two roles, one on the team and one in the formal structure. Many situations in the real world do not lend themselves to the stability or rigidity of a formal bureaucracy. Such situations are often character-ized by the need for a highly innovative or unusual response on a short time line and are not part of a system's normal behavior and/or issues within the existing structure, which make it impossible or highly improbable to attain a satisfactory outcome. In such a case a temporary structure may be created around the special need or "project." (fwe)

Matthew Shepard Act

The 1998 murder of Matthew Shepard (December 1, 1976–October 12, 1998), a gay college student from Laramie, Wyoming, received national media attention and transformed the cultural discourse on GLBTQ issues. Shepard's death was labeled a hate crime, and after more than 10 years of highly contentious debate, Congress passed and President Obama signed into law a hate crimes bill bearing Shepard's name that extends protection to gay people. There have been protests in some U.S. school districts in response to student productions of *The Laramie Project*, a play by Moises Kaufman based on the response of Laramie townspeople to Shepard's murder. (jb2)

MBO (See Management by Objectives)

MCAT (See Medical School Admissions Tests)

McCarthy Era

The name given to a period of time (1950–1954) that represented one of America's most politically repressive eras. The era is best known for an anticommunist hysteria, and it routinely featured government hearings investigating alleged communist behavior and/or sympathizers. The academy and the secondary classroom did not escape the ravages of McCarthyism, and countless educators saw their careers and lives ruined by the often baseless claims alleging communist sympathies. The period came to an unceremonious end in December 1954, when the U.S. Senate voted to censure Joseph McCarthy, the Wisconsin senator for whom the period is named. (ah)

McCollum v. Board of Education, School District 71, 333 U.S. 203 (1948)

A Supreme Court case that upheld the separation of church and state. In 1940 the Council on Religious Education in Champaign, Illinois, offered religious classes during the school day. Students were not forced to attend and permitted to go elsewhere during the classes. Vashti McCollum, a parent and atheist, claimed the program violated the Establishment Clause of the First Amendment. In a majority six-to-one opinion Justice Hugo Black argued that the classes were "utilization of a tax-established and tax-supported public school system to aid religious groups to spread their faith." (vmm)

McGuffey Readers

First developed by William Holmes McGuffey (1800–1873) in 1836, *McGuffey's Eclectic Readers* were the most popular schoolbooks of the 19th century. Using a mixture of moral and religious lessons, the *Readers* provided literacy instruction as well as an introduction to middle-class social and political values. For a country entering the industrial age, the *Readers* provided millions of American children with an introduction to modern values, work habits, and social relations. It is estimated that 40 million *Readers* were sold in the 1850s and 1860s alone, and that over 122 million were sold overall, with the release of the final edition in 1901. (mkw)

McLaurin v. Oklahoma State Regents, 339 U.S. 637 (1950)

A U.S. Supreme Court case decided the same year as *Sweatt v. Painter,* in which the Court ruled that racial segregation within an educational institution violated the equal protection clause of the 14th Amendment. McLaurin had been admitted into the University of Oklaho-ma's PhD program in education but was physically separated from his classmates by being required to sit, study, and eat in "segregated facilities" within the university. While *McLaurin,* like *Sweatt,* did not overturn the doctrine of "separate but equal," it was an important step toward its demise. (alw)

MCT (See minimum competency testing)

mean

Mean is one of the measures of central tendency of scored distribution. Two other measures are median and mode. The mean is commonly known as arithmetic average. It is computed by dividing the sum of all scores in the distribution by the number of scores. As compared to median and mode, the mean is more affected by outliers (extreme values) in the distribution. (jx)

See also median; mode.

mean length of utterance (MLU)

A basic measure of a speaker's linguistic development and productive language ability. MLU consists of the ratio of the average number of morphemes in an utterance to the number of utterances in a corpus. (jrk)

See also morphemes.

meaning

As a technical philosophical term, meaning refers to words and propositions that have sense. We grasp the sense of a word or proposition when we know what to do with it, and know how to use it in the language we use, and more broadly in the practices we engage in. Some philosophers believe that meanings are real objects, residing in a real domain (e.g., conceptual space), while others reduce meanings to modes of behavior that are recognized as signaling understanding. Thus, meaning as discussed in metaphysics and the philosophy of language. In another sense, philosophers use the term meaning as practically synonymous with "purpose," as in "the meaning of life." (an)

measurement

In mathematics, measurement is the practice of quantifying. It involves identifying an attribute to be measured, choosing an appropriate unit of measure, and comparing that unit to the object being measured. This can be done through direct means, such as measuring the length of an object using a meter ruler, or through the use of derived formulas, for example, calculating the area of a rectangle using the conventional formula, length times width. (amr)

measurement division (See quotitive division)

mechanical drawing (See drafting)

media

The collection of methods used to deliver mass communication: newspapers, television, film, radio, the Internet, and so on. Media can also be used to describe the materials and methods used in an artistic endeavor. For example, some artistic projects use "mixed media," which might include acrylic paint, found objects, and collage. (ewr, npo)

media literacy

Of or pertaining to the process of critically thinking through how media depicts and represents ideas and groups. Becoming media literate means to understand how the media functions as a type of cultural imperialism that influences society. Since media serves the interests of those in power, the notion of an awareness/consciousness about how this occurs is crucial if we are to live in a truly democratic society. This is taken from Freire's notion of *conscientizacao,* which is defined as "the process by which students, as empowered subjects, achieve a deepening awareness of the social realities that shape their lives and discover their own capacities to re-create them" (Darder, Baltodano and Torres, 2002, 15). In other words, an exploration as to how media shapes public lives. (sb1)

See also Freirian.

media multitasking

The ability of a student to do more than one task at the same time, for example, typing a paper while simultaneously accessing social networking websites and listening to music on a portable media device. (rsd)

median

Median is one of the measures of central tendency of score distribution—the other two measures are mean and mode. It divides a distribution exactly in half so that 50 percent of the scores fall at or below this value. Hence, the median is also called 50th percentile. To obtain the median, scores are first ordered from lowest to highest. When there is an odd number of score points, the median is the middle number among the ordered score points; when the number of score points is even, the median is the average of the two numbers in the middle of the ordered score points. Compared to the *mean,* the median is less affected by outliers in the distribution. For this reason, it is the preferred measure of central tendency when outliers are observed. (jx)

See also mean; mode.

mediation

Under the guise of socio-cultural theory, mediation is the means by which learners adopt the social and intellectual apparatus of their culture. Mediation comes in two broad categories: a student's contact with experts such as teachers and more learned or able peers, and the use of particular psychological tools that allow learners to master and control their own mental functions. Of central importance to both are the ideas that learning is fundamentally social in nature, and that it is through the appropriation and interiorization of cultural goods that learners come to possess higher psychological processes. (tw1)

See also interiorization; socio-cultural theory.

Medical School Admissions Tests (MCAT)

The nationally administered test for admission to medical school, with format and subject matter directed to medical theory and practice. (cf)

medium

The material, method, or form used in an artistic endeavor. In painting, for example, the liquid material with which color pigments are mixed (e.g., acrylic, oil, water, etc.) is the medium. As a method, the medium is the specific use, for example, of lithography in print making; and, as a form, the use, for example, of dance as the "medium" of expression for a given emotion or theme. While the term "medium" has other uses in scientific and psychic realms, in art education, it is generally used as described herein. (km)

See also media; mixed media.

MEG (See magnetoencephalography)

MELT (See Mainstream English Language Training)

melting pot

A term used for the assimilation of immigrants to the United States into the mainstream culture. Immigrant groups were expected to blend into the dominant culture rather than retain strong aspects of their ethnic or racial cultural heritage. Other metaphors are currently used, such as the "salad bowl," society in which each culture provides its own unique, distinctive contribution, making a diverse and better society. These changing perspectives are reflected in teaching materials provided in classrooms, with more sensitivity to diverse cultures apparent now than in previous decades. (npo)

member check

A technique to address the validity of a qualitative study. The researcher solicits feedback from the research participants concerning the accuracy and completeness of the researcher's analysis, interpretation, and understanding of the data. Also known as "participant feedback." (mas)

memoing

Used in qualitative data analysis, memoing is a technique whereby researchers record their reflections on some aspect of the analytic process. Memoing originated as a means for researchers, who were developing grounded theory, to reflect on the processes of coding data. The process is now more generally applied to writing memos that may range from a single sentence to several pages and that record the researcher's thoughts about any aspect of the analytic process. Memos may address personal, methodological, or theoretical issues. (rws)

memory

The ability to store, retain, and recall new information relies on a set of systems; together these are referred to as memory. These systems include working memory and long-term memory. Long-term memory has both implicit/procedural (nondeclarative) and explicit aspects. Explicit aspects cover both semantic and episodic memory. The best-defined type of short-term memory is known as working memory: working memory is known to have an extremely limited duration, and to have a capacity of roughly five to seven items for most people. Working memory is part of an interrelated group of cognitive abilities known as executive function, which include attention and aspects of decision making and is a robust predictor of academic success across domains and disciplines. Information moves from working memory or other short-term memory systems into long-term memory via a process of consolidation. Within long-term memory systems, the most salient distinction is between implicit (or nondeclarative) forms of memory and explicit (or declarative) forms of memory; implicit memory can be thought of as memory for "knowing how" and explicit for "knowing what." Implicit memory is used for skills that require procedural learning, not well transmitted by words (for example, imagine teaching someone to ride a bike through only words). Implicit learning can take place without consciousness or attention and often occurs through trial-and-error and practice. Explicit memory is used for things we are aware (conscious) of and able to discuss. The primary distinction within explicit memory systems is between semantic and episodic memory. Semantic memory is memory for facts and concepts; episodic memory is memory for episodes or events in one's life. (pk1)

Mendez et al. v. Westminster School District of Orange County, CA, 64 F. Supp. 544 (1946)

Landmark desegregation case in which Judge Paul J. McCormick found that school districts in the Ninth Federal District Court of Los Angeles had denied Mexican children their constitutional rights by being forced to attend separate schools. The court ruled that segregation of children based upon their "Latinized" appearance violated the 14th Amendment and the ratification of the Treaty of Guadalupe Hidalgo, which had guaranteed Mexican Americans equal rights in the United States. (vmm)

mental ability

Natural potential or capacity to acquire or retain knowledge. The gauge of one's ability to respond to intellectual stimulation in relation to previously obtained information or skills. (jw)

mental age

A performance level determined by academic, behavioral, or cognitive assessment. Usually used for those with developmental delays or retardation, the level indicates at what relative age the individual's mind is functioning. (jcp)

mental arithmetic

Involves solving mathematics tasks mentally. For example, a teacher may ask students to calculate mentally an addition, subtraction, or multiplication task such as $28 + 32$, $50 - 12$, or 12×25. Students are then asked to share their solution methods with the class. The focus of mental arithmetic is upon development of meaningful and proficient methods of computation rather than simply upon speed and memorization of facts that may not necessarily have meaning for students. (sdt)

See also mental computation.

mental computation

The intellectual execution of a problem by the use of cognitive reasoning and perceptions without the aid of pencil and paper or other external devices. It involves the use of number sense, personal algorithms, and regrouping numbers into "friendly numbers." (vdf)

See also mental arithmetic.

mental health

Commonly used to describe the well-being of individuals as conceived by themselves as members of a particular social environment. The concept of mental health is normative, as it is a social concept influenced by cultural mores and societal rules. (crl)

mental modeling

Also called "think aloud," this is an instructional technique in which the teacher explicates the internal process involved in thinking through a problem or applying a strategy. Mental modeling reveals the internal metacognitive processes of skilled readers so that students may emulate these processes. (jk)

mental retardation

Significant subaverage general intellectual functioning existing concurrently with deficits in adaptive behavior and manifested during the developmental period. IQ measurements are below 70, with several levels of retardation based on the severity of cognitive impairment. (sr)

mental status exam

A brief assessment of a patient's current cognitive and emotional functioning. The mental status exam (MSE) includes an interview and an evaluation of the individual's appearance, motor functioning, speech, affect and mood, thought content, thought processes, perception, intellect, and insight. There are two forms of the MSE, a brief version and a more lengthy MSE. The more lengthy MSE may include formal tests and procedures to augment or clarify information obtained through other sources. (tsw)

mentor

An experienced guide who offers knowledge, insights, support, and wisdom that is useful to a protégé over an extended period of time in order to teach necessary knowledge, skills, and abilities the protégé needs to achieve life or career goals. In the context of teacher education, a mentor may be an experienced teacher who is an integral part of the teacher induction process through his or her work with beginning teachers. (jb, clk)

mentoring

Mentoring, which in Greek means "enduring," is typically defined as a nurturing relationship between an instructor and a learner, or, in other words, one person helping another. Typically, the instructor guides, assures, and assists the learner through the challenges of mastering a skill and/or enhancing his/her knowledge base. Sometimes mentoring takes the form of peer mentoring, with one learner instructing another learner. Educational mentoring helps mentored youth improve academic understanding and achievement. Career mentoring helps mentored youth develop the essential skills to pursue

a career pathway. Personal development mentoring helps mentored youth during times of personal and/or social stress to enhance their decision-making processes. The mentoring process can be formal or informal and can occur in a variety of settings, including business, professional settings, and academia. (tp, chm)

merit-based financial aid

Financial aid awarded upon the basis of academic achievement. Determinations may be based upon grades, test scores, or in some cases the special talents, abilities, or personal qualifications of the applicant. (sn)

meritocracy

A system of social, educational, or governmental placement, advancement, and access to opportunity that putatively refers to individual human merit as opposed to characteristics over which a given individual may have less or no control. The term often implies a role for testing; that is, if a particular university makes extensive use of entry and placement testing in its admissions decision, it is said to be meritocratic. The term evolved to contrast with nepotism or legacy, as when candidates are accepted to universities solely or largely based on family membership. (fd)

mesosystem

The interaction between the microsystems to which a child belongs. A child's family interacts with his/her school, for example, and with his church; the child's school has points of intersection with his/her community. According to the ecological model of child development (Bronfenbrenner, 1979), how these microsystems interact influences the child's development. (ecr)

See also microsystem.

metacognition

The act of thinking about thinking. For example, when a student is taking a test, metacognition refers to thinking about the process of responding, that is, thinking of mnemonic devices or organizational strategies, rather than the content of what is being tested. Metacognition has been shown to be an effective tool for academic success as well as psychological well-being, as when it is used as a treatment for depression. Current models of metacognition encompass both the metacognitive knowledge that results from thinking (i.e., knowledge of facts, tasks, and goals, and problem-solving strategies), and metacognitive activity (i.e., the use of self-monitoring to adapt and apply strategies to solving new problems). Both metacognitive knowledge and activity are important components of current literacy-learning strategies. (jcp, jrk)

metadiscourse

In writing, metadiscourse refers to words and phrases that go beyond the content of the writing to comment on how the text should be read. Metadiscourse often gives clues to the structure of the text (first, next, finally), the writer's confidence in his assertions (perhaps, certainly), or directions for the reader (to summarize, therefore). In general, metadiscourse showcases the writer's expertise and gives the reader information about how the text should be read. (cld)

metaevaluation

The evaluation of an evaluation. Scholars have recently encouraged this practice to assure quality and accurateness of evaluation of educational programs. (sd)

See also program review.

metalinguistic awareness

The awareness and the ability to reflect on one's language use and knowledge. It is usually developed in the process of learning a second language, either simultaneously with one's native language (e.g., simultaneous bilingualism) or in succession (foreign language learning). (smt)

metaphor

In language (especially poetry), a word or expression ordinarily associated with one meaning (e.g., "loud") used deliberately to explicate another (e.g., "face"), thus making an implicit comparison (i.e., between verbal and visual expression) that crosses boundaries (here, those of sound and sight). Distinguished from *simile* (explicit comparison, e.g., "she looks like she sounds"), metaphor occurs in any art form when symbolic structures (like bold lines in painting or exaggerated movements in dance) create new meaning through unexpected association. Young children frequently use metaphors ("I'm melting") but are not expected to understand and consciously master the technique until adolescence. (kb)

metaphysics

The study of those questions that cannot, even in principle, be resolved by the scientific method, though increasingly the question is whether there are any such questions. According to Aristotle, metaphysics is both the science of God and the science of Being. As a science of God, metaphysics for Aristotle amounted to what philosophers now describe as "natural theology," the use of reason to understand as much as we can about divinity (e.g., the first, uncaused cause of things). As a science of Being, metaphysics, or ontology, studied in various ways what Dewey referred to in *Experience and Nature* as "the generic traits of all existence." (an)

methodology

The application of principles, practices, and procedures to a problem, project, course of study, or given discipline. The theories and techniques used in teaching. (jw)

methods class

A course in the teacher education curriculum focusing on the development of instructional strategies often linked to a particular discipline. This course draws on the knowledge base underpinning teaching practice in general or in a specific discipline to help educators learn instructional strategies and skills. (clk, dm2, eb)

metonymy
Greek, meaning change of name. Figure of speech in which the name of an object or concept is replaced with a word closely related to or suggested by the original, as crown for king (e.g., the power of the crown was mortally weakened). While metaphor unites unexpected terms to create meaning, metonymy uses associated terms to extend meaning. In journalism the White House may stand for the president of the United States. In art, works may be referred to by their artist (e.g., "The Tate has a collection of Turners," rather than "The Tate has a collection of paintings by Turner"). (kpb)

metric system of measure
A system of measure based on powers of 10. Whereas the customary system is more widely used in the United States, the metric system is the standard or accepted system internationally. (dbc)

Mexican American Legal Defense and Educational Fund (MALDEF)
Founded in 1968 by Pedro Tijerina in San Antonio, Texas, MALDEF is a national nonprofit organization whose mission is to protect and promote the civil rights of Latinos in the United States. MALDEF was aided at its founding with a $2.2 million grant from the Ford Foundation for civil rights legal work. The organization has actively been involved in educational civil rights cases, including bilingual education through litigation, advocacy, community education, collaboration with public and private agencies, and scholarships. (vmm)

Mexican American studies
Programs of study, usually at the higher education level, that promote understanding of the history, culture, socioeconomic status, and politics of Mexican Americans in the United States, and their contributions to American culture. (jqa, npo)

Meyer v. Nebraska, 262 U.S. 390 (1923)
U.S. Supreme Court case that overturned lower-court decisions convicting Meyer of breaking a 1919 Nebraska state law banning foreign language instruction to students in private schools and to those who had not yet completed the eighth grade. The Supreme Court reasoned that the conviction of Meyer detrimentally affected the instructional opportunities of citizens and deprived the plaintiff of his 14th Amendment rights. The case has also been interpreted as setting limits to state control in regulating private schools. (dwm)

MI (See motivational interviewing)

microcounseling skills
A series of specific, relationship-building techniques utilized by a mental health practitioner. It is designed to be brief, cost effective, and flexible in its application. There are four basic components of microcounseling: written and/or video models; role-play practice; observer feedback; and remediation practice. Some microcounseling skills include techniques that focus on active listening, reflection of feelings, paraphrasing, asking open-ended questions, summarizing, and increasing culturally appropriate attending behaviors (i.e., eye contact, body language), establishing rapport, and identifying counseling goals. (tsw, lbl, tvh)

microculture
Cultural groups that have unique values and aspects that are distinctively different from the larger society are microcultures. (jqa, npo)

microethnography
A postpositivist research tool to comprehend how particular cultural events or goals are accomplished on a daily basis. The methodology asserts that cultural

meaning must be investigated through particular interchanges and uses detailed transcripts of words and actions to ask the question, "In what moment is understanding created?" Microethnography is linked to other methods that seek to understand process, as opposed to those explaining global or fixed cultural systems or beliefs (e.g., macroethnography), including conversation analysis (Emmanuel Schegloff, Harvey Sacks), the ethnography of speaking (Dell Hymes), culture as practice (Pierre Bourdieu), and culture as created by discursive actions (John Gumperz). (sw)

microsystem

A small unit of society in which the child holds membership. In an ecological model of child development (Bronfenbrenner, 1979), the child belongs to several microsystems, including its family, school, church, and community. The content and tone of the microsystem sets a template for the child to imitate and thus socialize into its behavioral and attitudinal structures. (ecr)

microteaching

A practice of teaching a lesson to a small group for a designated time period, targeting a specific objective or practicing a skill for the purpose of developing teaching technique. For example, a preservice teacher would teach a short lesson to a group of peers or students and then analyze it. In some cases, video or audiotape is recorded to facilitate the process of analysis. (clk)

middle school

An organizational model that emerged in the late 20th century in response to dissatisfaction with the earlier junior high school model. Renewing the focus on providing an educational program appropriate to the developmental needs of early adolescents, the middle school typically provides a range of organizational arrangements, including team teaching and block scheduling, a comprehensive program of academic, vocational, and guidance counseling, and a professional staff committed to meeting the unique emotional, physical, social, and intellectual needs of early adolescents. Middle schools typically include grades six through eight but may range from grades five through nine in various combinations. (ljm)

migrant education

Educational programs and services for children of migratory workers. Because migrant children and their families do not have long-standing ties to a community, opportunities for education are often sporadic or limited in scope. Migrant education programs were developed to provide equitable educational opportunity. (jqa, npo)

migration

The tendency of people to move from place to place in search of better employment, schooling, and quality of life. Migration has long been a feature of American society. One particular type of migration has been the steady movement of people away from rural areas to urban or suburban ones. (lr)

migratory child

A child who is, or whose parent and/or spouse is, a migratory worker and is temporarily enrolled in a school during seasonal work and who is not a permanent resident of the community where temporarily enrolled. (ms)

milieu teaching strategies

A group of language intervention procedures that are arranged to teach functional language skills in social contexts. Children are taught these skills in conversation-based strategies within the context of everyday interactions and routines. (xss)

milieu therapy

Form of therapy based on modifying an individual's current environment to elicit more adaptive ways of functioning. This might involve altering the social and/or physical components such that healthier patterns of behavior will emerge. Treatment in an inpatient setting is often referred to as milieu therapy when attention is placed on establishing routines, such as exercise, eating, sleep hygiene, and taking medication. (tsw, mjs)

millennial generation

A term referring to individuals born between 1982 and 1992. The children of the Baby Boomer generation, millennials are characterized by having had protected childhoods, and by their facility with technology, openness to diversity, self-confidence, high expectations, and optimism. As with Generation X, the generation immediately preceding them, millennials have become the subject of study because of their significant impact on the dynamics of college campuses and the work place and their interaction with other generations. (lcf)

Milliken v. Bradley, 418 U.S. 717 (1974)

U.S. Supreme Court decision that struck down a lower court order to integrate the suburban schools of Detroit, Michigan, with its inner-city schools. This was the first case in which the majority of the Supreme Court overturned a lower court that had sought greater integration. The Court drew a distinction between de facto segregation, usually unintended separation not maintained by force of law, and de jure segregation, a separation mandated and enforced by law. Chief Justice Burger wrote in his opinion that de facto segregation is beyond the jurisdiction of the courts. (dwm)

mimetic

Greek *mmtikos*, from *mmsis*, mimicry. Imitative, having to do with mimicking or imitation. Imitation as a form or agent of the arts as in a mimetic dance, work of art, or artistic performance where the form of representation is actual imitation of the subject. Mimes use mimetic techniques to deliver their portrayals without words. Some educators believe that children see the function of art to be mimetic, to imitate rather than interpret objects or events in life. (jd)

minds-on learning

Learning in which students are intellectually engaged and actively thinking about what they are learning. (bba)

miniature

A visual representation of something—an object, person, or sometimes place—that is smaller than traditional representations of the same subject. Miniatures are often associated with book art and illuminated manuscripts. (ap)

minimalism

Refers to a 20th-century school of art in which works of art, music, and language are spare, employing very few lines, shapes, colors, textures, notes, or sounds. Monochromatic palettes and anonymous styles are the hallmarks of this movement, which is imprinted with similar simplicity of elements on music, literature, and design. Also called ABC art, minimal art, reductivism, and rejective art. Traditional modes of reference and expression are ignored in pursuit of minimalist objectives. (jd)

minimum competency testing (MCT)

Criterion-referenced testing designed to assess whether students have reached a predetermined level of competence. The minimum competence is designed to identify those individuals who did not reach a certain standard of achievement. Results communicate sufficient competence rather than excellence. (clk)

minority group

Any subgroup of people having special characteristics within another group that is dominant politically, economically, ethnically, or religiously. Such subgroups are often bound together by special ties that distinguish them from the other group. Minority groups often establish their own cultural or ethnic identities and may have a sense of occupying a subordinate political or economic status. (hrm, ew, jkd)

minuend
The number from which another number (the subtrahend) is to be subtracted. (amr)

mirror neurons
Mirror neurons are a specific type of neuron that is active both when observing an action being performed by others as well as for performing the action oneself. These neurons were first discovered in the 1990s in the lateral ventral premotor cortex of monkeys, and they were firing when the monkey was grasping a grape as well as when he saw a human experimenter or another monkey grasping a grape. Mirror neurons have been speculated to exist in humans as well, but the proof of their existence is still missing, since it would require single-cell recording in the human brain—an invasive procedure that is considered unethical. Nevertheless, neuroscientific experiments using noninvasive technologies such as fMRI and showing activation in brain regions that are part of the motor system, both when observing and performing an action, have been interpreted as showing activation of mirror neurons. Mirror neurons are assumed to play an important role in social cognition by enabling us to understand others' actions through a process of simulation, that is, by mapping their actions onto our own action system and observing its embodied effect. (mf2)

miscue
An error made when reading orally. A miscue can include repetitions, substitutions, insertions, omissions, or no responses. Hesitations that hinder the flow of passage reading can also be considered miscues. (aw)

miscue analysis
The systematic analysis of the miscues a student makes when reading orally to determine strengths and weaknesses in background knowledge and language proficiency. (aw)

miseducation
The introduction of formal academic and/or physical training during the early childhood period. According to David Elkind (1988), the mind of the preschool child is not ready for formal instruction. If perpetually pressured to overachieve, a child can develop neuroses and chronic stress responses such as violence and teen pregnancy. (ecr)

Missouri ex rel. Gaines v. Canada, 305 U.S. 337 (1938)
During the 1930s, the NAACP began to legally challenge the doctrine of "separate but equal" in regards to graduate and professional education for blacks. In order to circumvent the enrollment of blacks at white institutions, southern states adhered to the practice of awarding out-of-state scholarships to encourage blacks to enroll at northern institutions. In this case Lloyd Gaines sued the University of Missouri for admission to its law school. The court ruled that awarding out-of-state scholarships violated the Equal Protection Clause of the Constitution. The decision enabled the NAACP to undertake a full-scale assault on segregation in southern institutions of higher education. (jrb)

mistakes (as learning opportunities)
As children make mistakes or behave in culturally inappropriate ways, teachers, parents, and caregivers can use those behaviors or instances as teachable moments. Mistakes or behaviors that are viewed as "problems" will naturally occur as a part of growth and development and can be used to gently guide the child toward more acceptable behaviors through explanation and redirection. (kdc)

mixed age grouping (See Multilevel teaching)

mixed media
The use of more than one kind of method, form, or substance in the creation of an artistic piece. In visual arts, for example, the use of paint and collage. In the performance arena, for example, a piece that combines theater, visual arts, and music. Mixed media productions are often explored in schools in order to combine/integrate various disciplines and to showcase/make use of different artistic talents. (km)

MLU (See mean length of utterance)

mnemonic
Any strategy used to help with memory. In school, mnemonic devices can be taught as a method of studying and retaining information. (jcp)

mobility
Refers to the willingness to move from place to place in search of employment, schooling, and an enhanced quality of life. This tendency has been accelerated in rural areas since World War II and has resulted in a changing rural population marked by fewer agriculturally based families. The decade of the 1990s witnessed a significant increase in nonfarm rural dwellers. (lr)

mode
Mode is one of the measures of central tendency of scored distribution. Two other measures are mean and median. The mode is defined as the most common or frequent score in the distribution. Different from mean and median, the mode is a useful measure of central tendency when data in the sample or population are nominal or categorical, for example, gender, marital status, or level of education. (jx)
See also mean; median.

model minority
Stereotyped term for Asian American students who are often portrayed as excelling in school. While many Asian Americans perform well in the classroom, others do not, and all may be subject to racist attitudes. The term "model minority" creates expectations that anyone of Asian heritage will be successful and not subject to discriminatory practices, thereby ignoring the reality of racism. (jqa, npo)

modeling
A teacher's demonstration, by words and actions, of the behaviors, skills, or competencies that students are to learn. Typically, the acting out of a desired behavior by a more mature person provides a learner with an opportunity to learn the desired behavior through observation. However, children may also learn about inappropriate behaviors modeled by older peers or adults, usually unplanned by the older peers or adults. In teacher education, modeling is used to facilitate the development of a preservice teacher's practice, utilizing those techniques derived from theories of practice studied in the teacher education curriculum. (bba, kms, yb, clk)

modeling of students' mathematical thinking
Mathematics education researchers in the constructivist tradition are concerned with how research participants make sense of their mathematical thinking and how the researchers make sense of what the participants present to the researchers. In an effort to be clear and somewhat efficient about whose sense making is being referred to, researchers refer to those models constructed and presented to the researcher by the participant as first-order models and those that are constructed and presented to the research community by the researcher as second-order models. (smts)

moderate-to-vigorous physical activity (See MVPA)

modern art (See contemporary art)

modern dance

A uniquely American creation of dance pioneered in the 1920s. Also called contemporary dance, it replaced the old rules of the controlled movements and precision of ballet with barefooted dancers introducing spare, stark, angular movements, and blunt gestures. Seminal choreographers and dancers Martha Graham, Merce Cunningham, Erik Hawkins, and many others worked independently developing distinctive personal styles that explored serious themes of modern life. As the art form matured throughout the 20th century contemporary dancers have mixed impulsive gestures from folk and street dance while retaining the visual poetry of classical dance, both European and African. (kbc)

modern math (See New Math Movement)

modernism

Historical period dating from the European Enlightenment into the mid-20th century. Modernism is the specific ideology undergirding Western society. The ideology of modernism includes: truth is absolute and the same for everyone under all circumstances; knowable order exists in both the natural and social worlds; truth and order are based on eternal laws; truth and order are attributes of a material reality composed of essential characteristics. This ideology also states that science and/or science-like approaches are the prime avenues for uncovering truth, order, and essence; all inquiry should be scientific in character; the human condition can be steadily improved and social progress can be made by applying understandings gained through scientific practice to all things. In a literary context, modernism refers to the use of language, themes, and styles characteristic of modern times, such as teen angst writings. Literary modernism, however, addresses a loss of belief and faith in society and self, and the consequent search for meaning in more abstract, symbolic, mystical sources. An art movement of the 20th century that departed from those traditions of art and literature that featured realistic representation. Often identified as abstractionism, the modernist focus was on abstractions of reality that expressed emotion and/or imagination with less obvious or no apparent reference to physical reality. Where narrative painting, for example, was easily "read" by the viewer, modernist work sought to demand more from the viewer—the need to "figure" out the work. When children's early artistic productions are likened to the work of professional artists, the comparison is often said to express a modernist view. (db-j, npo, jd)

See also Enlightenment; postmodernism.

modules

Modules are intact, skills-based units of instruction within competency-based teacher education. In general, modules refer to specific instructional units with assessment incorporated into the educational experience. These units typically last for a limited duration of time and may build upon one another into an overall instructional program. (rtc, npo)

monitorial schools

A system of schooling that used older and more advanced students to teach younger and less able students. The system was devised in the early 1800s by Joseph Lancaster and Andrew Bell. Typically, all students met in a single room on benches, with monitors assigned to groups of 10 students. The teacher instructed the monitors, who then instructed the younger students. The system fell out of use in the mid-1800s when the more modern system of grouping by age level came into use. Recent interest in the monitorial system has emerged due to dissatisfaction with current educational practices. Also referred to as the Lancasterian system, Lancastrian system, or mutual instruction. (npo)

monochromatic

Consisting of only one or variations of one color. Artistic pieces are considered monochromatic if they employ tones of one color or are in black and white. In art education, monochromaticism can be a useful way of exploring lights and darks, contour, and shading. In general education, monochromaticism can serve as a practical way of explaining the physics of wavelengths. Something is monochromatic if it employs light or radiation of a single wavelength or frequency. (km)

monoglot

A person who knows only one language, usually his or her native language. (acp)
    See also monolingualism.

monolingualism

Ability to speak a single language only, usually one's native language, with some degree of proficiency. An individual may still be considered monolingual despite having some knowledge of or instruction in another language, as long as it is not enough to achieve fluency. (acp)
    See also monoglot.

monologue

A dramatic convention in which one character speaks at length, giving a speech or a soliloquy either to other characters or to the audience. In addition to advancing the plot, the monologue is often used to communicate a character's inner thoughts. Stand-up comics use the monologue as their primary means of entertaining audiences. Monologues from plays can usually stand alone from the rest of the text, providing good material for work in acting classes or for memorization exercises in school literature courses. Often auditions—for plays or acting programs—require the preparation of a monologue. (em)

monosexism (See homophobia)

montage

A single pictorial, musical, or cinematographic composition made by juxtaposing or superimposing several different elements. The term also applies to a pictorial technique in which cutout illustrations, or fragments of them, are arranged together and mounted, and to the picture so made. Ready-made images alone are used, and they are chosen for their subject and message. In both these respects montage is distinct from collage and papier colleé. Photomontage uses photographs only. In cinematic usage, the term "montage" refers to the assembling of separate pieces of film into a sequence or a superimposed image. (kpb)

Montessori method

A philosophy and strategy of teaching based on Dr. Maria Montessori's belief that children learn best by doing things on their own. In a multiage classroom, children at various stages of development actively learn from, and with, each other. Dr. Montessori, a former engineer, physician, and educator in the 19th century, designed a learning environment in which children are supported to work according to their innate passion for learning, engaging in spontaneous and purposeful activities guided by a trained adult, and progressing according to their individual capabilities. Using developmentally appropriate materials developed by Dr. Montessori, teachers create dynamic, interactive learning environments that encourage each child to reason, negotiate, collaborate, cooperate, and understand, leading to the development of an autonomous individual, competent in all areas of life. The Montessori method is built on the belief that children learn best through sensory explorations such as seeing, hearing, smelling, tasting, and kinesthetic experiences. The method supports the pursuit of many different experiences, including physical, social, emotional, and cognitive. Designed to enable students to maximize their full potential through purposeful activity, the method is based on interactions between three elements of learning: the student, the learning environment, and the teacher. Students learn through active engagement with a variety of "self-correcting" materials guided by the passive support of a teacher whose primary role is to organize a painstakingly "prepared environment" and observe and direct student development within that environment. In recent years several modifications have been made to the Montessori method to continue to adapt to student needs. In the United States, children typically begin Montessori at age three, because the ages of three to six are considered to be the prime time for establishing the foundation for later academic and social success. (mc, jc2, ba)

mood disorder

A mood disorder is a psychiatric disorder characterized primarily by a disturbance in mood. This term includes the depressive disorders, bipolar disorders, mood disorders due to a general medical condition, substance-induced mood disorders, and mood disorders not otherwise specified. The disturbance in mood can occur at both ends of a continuum ranging from severe depression to excessive euphoria. (tsw)

moral development

Moral development refers generally to growth in understanding of right and wrong in individuals, but also metaphorically in cultures. Following Alfred North Whitehead and John Dewey, the term took on specialized meaning under the research of David Krathwohl and Benjamin Bloom (taxonomy of affective development) and Lawrence Kohlberg (stages of moral development). These researchers, and those influenced by them, believed that moral development occurs, or can occur, in tandem with intellectual and psychological development, and education is properly directed at this aspect of the child's development as well. The family, religion, and public forums of politics, law, the press, and so on are institutions, together with education, of moral formation. Lawrence Kohlberg theorized that individuals went through a sequential series of stages in developing moral consciousness. These stages proceed from a basic level of doing what is socially correct because there are negative consequences, to good citizenship behavior to maintain social norms, to the higher levels of moral behavior based on personal principles and the greater welfare of humanity. Robert Coles developed a psychosocial theory of moral development that did not necessarily follow the same stages as cognitive development. Moral development has applications in educational settings as a part of character and citizenship education. (sc, npo)

moral education

The process of teaching people to be good. Moral education differs from moral philosophy in that it is less concerned with the nature of good character than the question of how anyone comes to have one. Some philosophers have argued that since morality is subjective or "ideological," and education must be rooted in rationality, all moral education must really amount to indoctrination. On the other hand, there are many (e.g., Kohlberg) who would promise the means by which students could be made to act better, or at least to think more truly (or at least carefully) about ethics. (an)
   See also education.

morpheme

The smallest unit of language that carries information about meaning or function (e.g., the following words consist of two morphemes: desks = desk + s; flying = fly + ing; worked = work + ed). Morphemes can be free (can be a word by itself, e.g., plane, jump) or bound (must be attached to another element, e.g., the plural –s, past tense –ed). Morphemes are important units in literacy, particularly in nonalphabetic writing systems, where morphemes are common building blocks. Finally, the order of acquisition of different morphemes reveals important milestones in the process of child language development and foreign language learning. (smt)

morphology
The study of the structure of words. The component of grammar that includes the rules of word formation and interpretation, such as derivation and inflection. The classification, in linguistics, that deals with the internal structure and forms of words. A morpheme is a word or part of a word that conveys meaning. Morphemes may be free or bound. A free morpheme denotes meaning by itself, while a bound morpheme denotes meaning when attached to a free morpheme. For example, the word "cat" is a free morpheme. The morpheme "cats" is two morphemes: cat is a free morpheme while the s is a bound morpheme. (smt, jls)

Morrill Act of 1862
The Morrill Act of 1862, also known as the Land Grant College Act, established institutions in each state with the purpose of educating people in agriculture, home economics, mechanical arts, and other practical professions. The Land Grant act was introduced by Justin Smith Morrill, a congressman from Vermont who wanted to assure that education would be available to those in all social classes. The Morrill Act of 1862 was passed by Congress and signed into law by President Lincoln legislating that each state receive 30,000 acres of land for each senator and representative. The land grants were to be devoted to the establishment of colleges concentrating on the study of agriculture and mechanical arts, but not confined to this curriculum. These grants made possible the establishment of new colleges and the improvement of existing ones. A second Morrill Act, passed in 1890, provided further annual funding for the growing institutions and also provided for the development of several universities for black students. Since 1890, both acts have been amended to establish land-grant colleges in U.S. territories and for Native American tribal colleges. (ch, cf, mb)

motherese (See child-directed speech)

motion geometry (See transformation geometry)

motivation
Motivation is viewed generally as a powerful force that drives learning, although its source is debated. To some, action is impelled purely by stimulation and satisfaction of impulse. For many traditional educators, extrinsic motivation compels behavior with the prospect of reward or punishment. Rousseau asserted, however, that motivation to learn is inherent in the nature of humans, due to innate biological drives. Progressive educators have argued that education should therefore be tailored to the intrinsic interests and readiness of the learner. Others posit that motivation is less a result of any "force" than of more or less conscious choice and social agency. (rt)

motivational interviewing (MI)
A client-centered, yet directive counseling style for eliciting behavior change by helping clients explore and resolve ambivalence. Counselors who use this style act collaboratively, express empathy, avoid arguing, manage resistance without confrontation, and support the self-efficacy of the individual, using techniques such as open-ended questioning, reflective listening, summarizing, and affirming. Studies have supported the efficacy of MI among problem and dependent drinkers, for whom this approach was first developed by William R. Miller and Stephen Rollnick in the early 1990s. It has since been used with diverse clinical populations and applied to a variety of problem behaviors. (sdc)

motor control

The neural control associated with muscles that allows for the development of motor skills. (rf)

motor development

Development of motor skills is usually divided into at least two general categories, gross motor skills and fine motor skills. Gross motor skills refer to activities that involve the use of the large muscles of the neck, trunk, arms, and legs. The development of some of these skills includes progression in lifting of the head, rolling, sitting up, crawling, creeping, and walking. Fine motor skills involve movements of the small muscles, especially those of the eyes, speech musculature, hands, fingers, feet, and toes. The development of these skills includes progression in grasping, writing, cutting, and picking up small objects. (vm)

motor dyspraxia (See motor skill disorder)

motor learning

Changes that occur in motor skills as a result of practice. (rf)

motor skill disorder

A motor skill disorder occurs when an individual lacks the motor coordination necessary to perform tasks that, given normal intellectual ability and the absence of other neurological or psychological disorders, are considered to be appropriate for his/her age. Motor skill disorders are sometimes also termed developmental motor coordination disorders, clumsiness, dyscoordination disorders, or motor dyspraxia. (jbb)

motor unit items (counting)

Actual objects need not be present during the counting activity. The touching or pointing movement itself is the thing being counted. (amr)

See also children's counting schemes.

movement

Primarily physical motion, the movement of the body in the creation or performance of art. An obvious element of dance and theater. In music, a movement refers to one part of a whole musical composition, independent with respect to tone, structure, key, and tempo. In painting and sculpture, movement can refer to the representation or suggestion of motion through the relation of artistic elements. In literature or poetry, movement refers to the qualities of the piece that engage and transport the reader from start to finish, as in a moving poem. In classrooms, movement activities offer students the opportunity to stretch and relax and experience their own mattering space. (km)

See also genre.

movement approach

An approach to curriculum based on Laban's Movement Framework in which the curriculum is divided into Educational Dance, Educational Games, and Educational Gymnastics. (rf)

See also Laban's Movement Framework.

movement education

Learning experiences in which children participate in activities applying large or gross muscles. This can be free and creative, sometimes to music or rhythm, or directed by another in order to promote kinesthetic development. (db1)

MRI (See Magnetic Resonance Imaging)

multiactivity model

A traditional physical education instructional model used in many secondary schools to expose students to a variety of activities. Units of instruction are identified by the sport or the activity that is their focus (i.e., soccer, yoga, weight training). The model is characterized by the use of short activity units and often with large portions of class time devoted to learning and practicing skills and drills in isolation that are not easily transferred into game play or performance. (kpr)

multiage grouping

Multiage grouping is an arrangement that brings students from more than one age cohort together around a common educational activity. This activity could be focused narrowly (such as grades one through three grouped together) or broadly (such as involvement by students of all ages in the operation of a school's food service). (lr)

multiage teaching (See multilevel teaching)

multicultural awareness

Refers to the processes through which an individual learns about people from other cultural backgrounds. Usually the processes include exploration of other people's cultural values and beliefs, parenting styles, family structures, traditions, religious beliefs, historical past, or contemporary issues. Theoretically, multicultural awareness is required in achieving multicultural competence. (xss, yb)

multicultural education

The enactment and study of educational policies and practices that seek to create equitable educational opportunities for all groups of students. Multicultural education is designed to help all students acquire the knowledge, skills, and attitudes necessary for high academic achievement and critical functioning in a pluralistic, democratic society. Multicultural educators recognize that education is part of a larger sociopolitical context and believe that teaching must be grounded in a commitment to social justice and critical approaches to teaching and learning that explicitly address race, ethnicity, language, social class, sexual orientation, ability, and other diverse markers of cultural identity. (sld, ddr)

multicultural literacy

The development of capacities that allow and promote multiple and diverse languages and understandings, so that individuals can communicate across borders of cultural difference, histories, perspectives, conceptions, and experiences. (hfs)

multicultural literature

A category of literature that depicts individuals from different cultures. Showing both the unique traditions and perspectives of diverse cultures, and the similarities common to humanity, multicultural literature is particularly effective in raising awareness of the diversity in society. Multicultural literature includes all genres. Educators use multicultural literature to teach about different cultures and to encourage interactions among students of dissimilar backgrounds. (jqa, npo)

multicultural teacher education (MTE)

Refers to efforts to infuse teacher education with multicultural training in order to adequately prepare teachers to teach in culturally diverse classrooms. (acp)

multiculturalism

The study of various cultures and ethnic groups of peoples, with an effort to understand and appreciate their diversity. There are levels and degrees to this kind of study, so that, at a beginning level, other cultures besides one's own are recognized. Later, students are invited to participate and contribute at a more advanced level by examining other cultures in order to transform their own cultural views, and vice versa. On the one hand, multiculturalism is criticized for insufficiently centering the contributions of Western civilization; on the other hand, multiculturalism has come under criticism for not offering a critical enough perspective, for not being more antiracist in its approach to the study of cultures and ethnicities. This is an evolving definition, with some experts defining multiculturalism exclusively in terms of racial and ethnic diversity, and others expanding the definition to include gender, socioeconomic class, sexual/affectional orientation, ability and disability, and religious diversity. (bt-b, llf, emm)

See also cultural diversity; ethnicity; pluralism.

multidigit

A numeral that contains more than one digit. For example, 746 and 91.27 are multidigit numbers. (kva)

multidisciplinary teaching and learning

Promotes knowledge of civic issues and involvement in civic activities. Extending from the interdisciplinary nature of learning in the social studies, multidisciplinary learning focuses on civic issues such as health care, crime, education, and foreign policy in a sociocultural context and the processes for developing resolutions through social action outcomes. (npg)

multidisciplinary team

A group of professionals from various disciplines, such as educators, psychologists, and physicians. (sr)

Multilevel teaching

The mixing or integration of students of different ages, working at different levels, in one classroom or learning setting. (bba)

multilingualism

Ability to speak two or more languages in addition to one's native language with some degree of proficiency. (mc)

multimedia

An item composed of several different forms of media, such as text, images, audio, and video. Some websites and educational software programs use multimedia. Students can also create their own multimedia products, such as slide show presentations. (kg1)

multimedia annotation

Multimedia annotations refer to digitalized visual or aural materials provided in addition to text in order to facilitate or enhance learning. These materials, often in the forms of pictures, video clips, audio recordings, and Flash animations, illustrate the complicated ideas and concepts in reading in an easy-to-understand way. The purpose of providing the multimedia annotations to learners is to increase their chance of learning. According to the Cognitive Theory of Multimedia Learning, learners understand and retain information better if they build meaningful connections between textual, visual, and aural information (Mayer, 2001). Many empirical studies in second language learning have shown that difficult words are better learned by English as a second language readers if these words are annotated by pictures and videos (Xu, 2010). (jx)

multimodal therapy

A form of cognitive behavioral therapy that rests on the assumption that most psychological problems are multifaceted, multidetermined, and multilayered. A primary goal of this therapy is to assess the various dimensions in which individuals operate, called "modalities," that exist in a state of reciprocal transaction and flux and are connected by complex chains of behavior and other psychophysiological processes. (jbb)

multiple

A product of two factors, whether arithmetic or algebraic, is a multiple of those factors. For example, in $3 \times 4 = 12$, 12 is a multiple of the factors 3 and 4. (kva)

multiple causation

An empirical principle stating that for any observable event there are generally several independent causes. In education, multiple causation states that any change in a child's behavior, achievement, or attitude may be a result of several distinct factors operating simultaneously. For example, a change in a child's academic performance might be related to diet, stress, health, instructional methods, social pressure, teacher expectations, and a host of other factors. (crl)

multiple exits

The idea that once a student chooses a career pathway there are many jobs they can achieve depending on the level of education required and how far they want to go (e.g., a student in health careers can "exit" the pathway after high school and obtain an entry-level job in the health field, or they can earn a one-year certificate for the next level of jobs, a two-year associates degree, and so on). (rz)

multiple intelligences

A theory, popularized by Howard Gardner, proposing that intelligence is not a unitary trait, but rather a collection of several quite different abilities. The multiple intelligences—verbal-linguistic, logical-mathematical, bodily-kinesthetic, musical, spatial, naturalistic, existential, interpersonal, and intrapersonal—have neurological foundations. It is Gardner's claim that the nature of schooling gives privileges to the linguistic and logical-mathematical traditions and that other intelligence goes largely unidentified and uneducated. (bba, ecr)

multiple perspectives

The ability to view a situation from a variety of viewpoints. By presenting multiple perspectives, teachers extend and broaden interpretations of what is currently taught in schools. Examples may include global perspectives, cultural diversity, and environmental education. (mje, jah)

multiplicative conceptual field

Term used by Gerard Vergnaud to define situations for which one usually needs to use multiplicative reasoning: linear and n-linear functions, vector spaces, dimensional analysis, fraction, ratio, rate, rational number, and multiplication and division. (amr)

multiplicative inverse

The number that when multiplied by the original number creates a product of one; for example ¼ is the multiplicative inverse of 4 because $4 \times ¼ = 1$. (ps)

multiplicative reasoning

Involves constructing the interrelationship between multiplication and division and developing appropriate multiplicative strategies to use when solving problems involving proportion, ratio, rational number, rate, and other multiplicative settings. Students can use more primitive additive reasoning (e.g., repeated addition) in some situations; however, there are other settings where additive reasoning will not work (e.g., proportional settings). The student must have developed multiplicative thinking to be successful in these settings. (smc)

multiply disabled

Having more than one impairment, the combination of which adversely affects an individual's ability to function. (sr)

multipotentiality

The ability to choose and pursue a career in a wide array of specialty fields. This ability is most typically associated with intellectually gifted, or academically talented, high school or college students. These students may experience difficulty choosing a college major or an occupation, in part, because they have the potential to perform well in multiple academic disciplines and career fields. (sc)

multisensory

Involving more than one of the senses. (sr)

multiuser virtual environment (MUVE)

An educational technology that enables multiple simultaneous participants to access virtual spaces configured for learning. Learners represent themselves through graphical avatars that communicate and interact with other avatars, computer-based agents, digital artifacts, and virtual contexts. This technology-enhanced learning environment provides diverse and immersive activities in support of classroom curriculum. (jz)

mural

From the Latin *murus,* wall. An image painted or applied either to an interior or an exterior wall, often in a public space. Designed and executed by individual artists or collaboratively created, murals often communicate a social, historical, or political aspect of the community in which they are placed. This is in the tradition of political and historical Mexican murals by early 20th-century artists such as Diego Rivera and Jose Clemente Orozco. In education, mural making provides authentic encounters with project-based collaborative work, whether in decorating the walls of the school or out of school in arts initiatives that serve community development and social reconciliation. (ap)

museum curator

From the French "to care," the curator is the guardian of the collection of a museum. In an art museum, the curator is responsible for the content and presentation of exhibits in the museum. Curators decide what works of art will be presented, how they will be arranged (e.g., chronologically, by artist, and/or by theme), and what information will be included in labels and other resources (curators often write guides to exhibits) that accompany a show. While curators are most often associated with art museums, they have counterparts in all museum settings. (yjl)

museum education

The field of education within museums. While museums may be thought to be inherently educational by virtue of their cultivating and maintaining collections of important cultural artifacts and works of art, the institution and development of educational programming in the context of the museum is what is designated as museum education. Children's and history museums have traditionally focused on educational programming, but art museums seriously began to do so only within the last decades of the 20th century. A report by the American Association of Museums, *Excellence and Equity: Education and the Public Dimension of Museums,* in 1992 was pivotal in this change, charging art museums to embrace education in their mission statements. (jd)

See also museum educator.

museum educator

Responsible for the oversight and programming of educational activities in the museum. Through visits for school-aged children to a variety of adult activities, the museum educator enhances the reach of the museum by linking resources to educational theory and practice, forging collaborations with schools, training museum docents and classroom teachers, and assessing the educational effectiveness of all these opportunities. The museum educator helps to develop audiences by considering issues of diversity and access in the production of educational materials. Museum educators can help classroom teachers plan visits to the art museum that will be tailored to their curricular needs. (yjl)

music

Sound and silence intentionally ordered and presented in such a manner as to evoke an aesthetic response in the listener. Derived from the Greek *muse,* it originally was inclusive of all art forms represented by the nine muses but eventually became associated primarily with Polyhymnia, the muse of many songs. Music is one of the art forms that is most frequently (after visual arts) taught in schools. Its study has been associated with positive effects in nonarts subjects. (jbl)

music education

Distinguished from "art education," which is usually associated with visual arts, or "arts" education, which broadly includes training in the many art forms (visual, music, drama, dance, etc.), music education refers to teaching and learning how to play a musical instrument (as in private lessons or the school band), voice training (singing in class or school choirs), music theory (notes, rhythm, pitch, etc.), and, less frequently in public education, to the acquisition of compositional skills, that is, the tools and time to create one's own music. (jd)

music therapy

Music used as a clinical intervention (by trained professionals) in treating emotional, physical, or physiological challenges, including learning disabilities. Therapeutic use may include structured listening, moving to or improvising music, and the thoughtful discussion of lyrics. (jd)

musical/rhythmic intelligence

The special ability to find rhythmic and tonal patterns in everyday life. According to Howard Gardner (1993), the musical learner likes to listen and respond to music and may sing well and/or play an instrument. Children with musical intelligence may make up their own tunes or like to perform music, and learn best by singing and rhythmic chanting. (ecr)

musicology

The systemic study of music as a branch of knowledge apart from those elements of music related to composition or the actual physical/technical aspects of performance. The field is often divided into two subgroups: primarily historical or theoretical studies of Western classical and popular music, and comparative study of non-Western and/or indigenous music, commonly known as ethnomusicology. (jbl)

mutual instruction (See monitorial schools)

mutuality

Occurs when a person simultaneously maintains a sense of self but remains open to a range of ideas and possibilities from another person. Mutual interactions may guide both people to have increased feelings of liveliness and energy. It can also increase the clarity of one's own, as well as the other's, thoughts, feelings, and needs. Mutuality can enhance relational growth and self-growth for both participants. Within group therapy, members make gains mutually though providing and receiving feedback. (tsw)

MUVE (See multiuser virtual environment)

MVPA

A common acronym for the phrase "moderate-to-vigorous physical activity," which describes exercise intensity that raises the heart rate up to a level that can enhance fitness. Recommendations for quality school-based physical education programs include that 50 percent of class time spent is spent in MVPA. (kpr)

N

naming

Names applied to ethnic and cultural groups have a powerful impact, particularly based on the source of the name. Names chosen by the group itself may empower, while names applied by the dominant group may demean or belittle, even when the names are not clearly offensive. When groups choose to rename themselves it offers the opportunity to take control of how they are viewed in the larger society and to demonstrate how they perceive themselves. (jqa, npo)

narrative

A story, the telling of a story, or the representation of a story. In visual art, drama, or dance, the narrative elements are those aspects of the work, play, or performance that help tell the story. Narrative poetry and narrative art are distinguished by the ways in which they focus on the telling of stories through the particular art form. School children in the middle years (ages 8 to 12) frequently produce narrative art in drawings that tell stories or in comic-book-like depictions of their daily lives and struggles. Some forms of educational and social science research, such as portraiture, use narrative as an integral part of the presentation of the research. (em)

narrative research

A type of inquiry within qualitative research. A narrative is a story of an individual's firsthand experience, often organized in a sequence or chronology of events. Narrative research focuses on describing the personal experiences of one or more individuals related to the phenomenon under investigation. Narratives may be analyzed for content, such as setting, characters, plot, problem, and resolution, or for function and purpose, such as moral tales, success stories, and story as oral performance. (mas)

narrative text

Text that employs storytelling techniques possibly including plot development, character development, and literary style or tone. Fictional texts are often referred to as narrative texts, as opposed to nonfictional texts such as news stories, critical essays, and science reports, which might emphasize facts over literary style or tone. (za)

NASDCTEc (See National Association of State Directors of Career Technical Education Consortium)

NASPE (See National Association for Sport and Physical Education)

NASPE content standards in physical education

Six national content standards that help define what a person should know and be able to do after completing a quality K–12 physical education program. (rf, kpr)

Nation at Risk, A

Subtitled *The Imperative for Educational Reform*. Report issued by the National Commission on Excellence in Education in 1983. This report examined academic outcomes of U.S. education in comparison to that of other countries and concluded that American schools were contributing to a "rising tide of mediocrity that threatens our very future as a nation and a people." The report's concerns and its recommendations to improve academic standards in American public education significantly contributed to the educational reform movement of the 1980s and 1990s. Recommendations from this report were eventually incorporated into the 1994 legislation, Goals 2000: Educate America Act. (vmm)

National Academic Advising Association (NACADA)

Established in 1977 and now including over 10,000 members, NACADA is an international association for persons in higher education who work in the field of academic advising. It promotes and supports quality academic advising by sponsoring numerous events, publications, scholarships and awards, and by providing a variety of web-based resources. (sn)

National Adult Literacy Database (NALD)

A website maintained by the Literacy Board of Canada that provides access to information, documents, curricula, and materials useful to adult educators in Canada. (jpc)

National Adult Literacy Survey (NALS)

A 1992 assessment of the literacy skills of the U.S. adult population. NALS tested 26,091 adults (16 and older) and assessed literacy on three scales—prose, document, and quantitative—each of which had scores of between 0 and 500. Based on these results, adults in the United States were assigned to one of five NALS Levels. Level one represents very limited literacy skills. Level two represents limited literacy skills. Level three represents sufficient literacy skills to accomplish most literacy tasks that occur in daily life and work. Level four represents strong literacy skills, and Level five represents a high level of skills attained by only about 5 percent of the U.S. population. (jpc)

national arts standards

National standards for arts education were agreed upon and published in 1994, marking the inclusion of the arts in the nine core subjects officially recognized for a complete education for American children. Developed by a consortium of national arts education associations, the standards outline what every young American should know (both content and process-based knowledge) in visual arts, dance, theater, and music, organized on three levels (grades K–4, 5–8, and 9–12). The standards are voluntary and offer frameworks—not curriculum content—for individual state design. The inclusion of standards for the arts as part of the core curriculum is considered by advocates a step in rewriting the wrong of the original Goals 2000: Educate America Act, which omitted the arts in its Five New Basics but finally included them in 1994. (jd)

National Assessment of Adult Literacy (NAAL)

A 2002 assessment of the literacy skills of the U.S. adult population that is modeled on the National Adult Literacy Survey. (jpc)

National Association for Sport and Physical Education (NASPE)

One of six associations within the American Alliance for Health, Physical Education, Recreation, and Dance (AAHPERD). (rf)

National Association for the Education of Young Children (NAEYC)

NAEYC is an advocacy organization promoting quality services for children through better training for professionals, improved public policies, and building a united network of stakeholders for voicing and disseminating information. Commensurate with its advocacy goals, the organization publishes position statements and sets guidelines for direct service and teacher preparation programs. NAEYC is perhaps best known for the establishment of standards for "developmentally appropriate practice" and "accreditation," a voluntary system for the evaluation of quality in early child-care settings. (jlj)

National Association of College and University Business Officers (NACUBO)

Founded in 1962, after evolving from a network of regional associations started in 1909, NACUBO is a national higher education association, representing chief administrative and financial officers, formed to promote sound management and financial practices in colleges and universities. (cf)

National Association of Industrial and Technical Teacher Educators (NAITTE)

Founded in 1937, NAITTE promotes cooperation among educators engaged in the preparation of teachers in technology education, trade and industrial education, and technical education. The Association's goal is to advance and promote excellence in industrial and technical teacher education and trainer training in all settings. (sa)

National Association of State Directors of Career Technical Education Consortium (NASDCTEc)

Washington, D.C.–based professional society founded in 1920. Committed to leadership and results, membership is made up of state and territory agency heads responsible for career and technical education. (sa)

National Association of State Universities and Land-Grant Colleges (See Association of Public and Land-Grant Universities)

National Board Certification

National Board Certification is earned by experienced teachers who undergo a review of their knowledge and skills as evidenced in four portfolio submissions. Three of the entries are classroom based and the fourth is related to accomplishments outside of the classroom. Portfolio entries are built around five Core Propositions established by the National Board for Professional Teaching Standards, the organization that awards the National Board Certification. The Core Propositions are as follows: teachers are committed to students and learning; teachers know the subjects they teach and how to teach those subjects to students; teachers are responsible for managing and monitoring student learning; teachers think systematically about their practice and learn from experiences; teachers are members of learning communities. (dek, cp)

See also Take One!

National Board for Professional Teaching Standards

This group was founded in 1987 on the basis that teaching and learning can be improved through the development and implementation of quality professional teaching standards. Based on the standards established, the board creates assessments of and certifies teachers who meet their standards and includes them in educational reform efforts. (ms)

National Center for Education Statistics (NCES)

Part of the U.S. Department of Education, and the primary federal entity for collecting, collating, analyzing, and reporting data that are related to the condition of education in the United States and other nations. (cf)

National Center for Higher Education Management Systems (NCHEMS)

The national center was originally founded in 1969 to develop and disseminate information systems for use in reporting institutions' data to federal and state governments. Currently NCHEMS is a private nonprofit organization whose mission is to assist colleges and universities as they continue to improve their management information capabilities. (cf)

National Commission on Social Studies

A 33-member panel of teachers, scholars, and policy makers that met in 1989 and issued a report, "Charting a Course: Social Studies for the 21st Century." The panel called for reform of the social studies curriculum and recommended that

geography and history be at the center of social studies instruction, but advised that concepts from other social sciences should also be integrated. The most unusual aspect of the report was the recommendation that U.S. history not be taught separately but integrated into a three-year world history course. (cb)

National Community Service Trust Act (See AmeriCorps)

National Council for Accreditation of Teacher Education (NCATE)

The accreditation agency, which has emerged as the primary accrediting agency for professional teacher education programs in the United States, recognized by both the U.S. Department of Education and the Council for Higher Education Accreditation. NCATE was founded in 1954 by a coalition of five key groups representing the teaching profession: the Council of Chief State School Officers (CCSSO), the National Education Association (NEA), the National School Boards Association (NSBA), the American Association of Colleges for Teacher Education (AACTE), and the National Association of State Directors of Teacher Education and Certification (NASDTEC). (dek, cp)

National Council for the Social Studies (NCSS)

Founded in 1921, NCSS is the largest organization in the United States devoted solely to social studies education. NCSS supports and promotes the teaching and learning of social studies through a variety of forums. Such venues include the publication of several journals, particularly *Social Education,* the hosting of an annual conference, and NCSS's affiliation with state, local, and regional councils and associated groups. (cb)

national curriculum

Curriculum standards establishing what students should know and be able to do that are developed at the national level by a board of political, business, and education leaders. (bba)

National Education Association (NEA)

Founded in 1857 in Philadelphia, the NEA is active on local, state, national, and international levels. It is a volunteer organization that assists with the betterment of education for students as well as teachers, faculty, administrators, and others who are involved in the process. The association resides in Washington, D.C., and is a large lobbying force for public education. A professional body committed to the welfare of its members, the NEA also involves itself with many aspects of public education, including partnerships and campaigns to facilitate student safety and health, as well as education. (rih, tp)

National Endowment for the Arts (NEA)

An independent agency of the federal government created by Congress in 1965 to foster the excellence, diversity, and vitality of the visual, literary, and performing arts. The NEA augments access to and appreciation of the arts for all Americans and supports arts activities of merit through grant making; leadership initiatives; partnerships with state arts agencies, regional arts organizations, other federal agencies and the private sector; research; and public information. The NEA seeks to increase nonfederal contributions to the arts through both its funding and advocacy. The agency serves as a catalyst and partner with those who support the arts and does not direct the creative activities of artists or arts organizations. (kf)

National Endowment for the Humanities (NEH)

As part of the National Foundation on the Arts and Humanities, a federal agency created in 1965, NEH supports activities that promote the humanities, making grants to institutions, groups, or individuals. The endowments support both research and the development of experimental projects to support and integrate the humanities in many areas of American society. (cf)

National Institute of Education (NIE)

Established as part of the Education Amendments of 1972. Its purpose was to provide federal support to basic and applied research in education that would alleviate systemic problems such as the lack of equality of educational opportunity, as well as promote new models of pedagogical practice. NIE was established in the wake of earlier federal efforts to support education research (e.g., the Cooperative Research Act of 1954) and absorbed a number of programs formerly administered by the U.S. Office of Education Bureau of Research. NIE was absorbed into the U.S. Department of Education Office of Educational Research and Improvement (OERI) in 1985 and disbanded as part of the Higher Education Amendments of 1986. (sw)

National Instructional Materials Access Center (NIMAC)

A repository for electronic files that have been created by publishers following the National Instructional Materials Accessibility Standard (NIMAS). Created under IDEA 2004, the NIMAC receives source files in NIMAS format from textbook publishers. The NIMAC then makes these files available for download from an online database to authorized users in the United States and its territories. Downloaded files are used to create specialized formats, such as braille, audio, or digital text, in order to assist qualifying blind, visually impaired, or print-disabled students in elementary or secondary schools. (jg1)

National Instructional Materials Accessibility Standard (NIMAS)

A nationally recognized technical standard that guides the production and electronic distribution of digital versions of textbooks and other instructional materials so they can be more easily converted into accessible formats. Textbook publishers send NIMAS files to the National Instructional Materials Access Center (NIMAC), when requested to do so through a state textbook adoption or purchase order from a school district. The NIMAS files can then be used to produce specialized formats, including Braille, large print, digital text, and audiobooks, for students with print disabilities. Educators and administrators seeking accessible instructional materials for their students with disabilities can locate NIMAS and Accessible Instructional Materials (AIM) information on their state department of education website or at http://aim.cast.org. (jg1)

National Literacy Act of 1991

Federal legislation that amended the Adult Education Act by shifting the focus of federal funding to target the least educated students, rather than GED-level students. (las)

National Network for Educational Renewal

A membership network founded by John Goodlad. The focus of the network is on the renewal of both schools and the institutions that prepare the teachers and administrators. School/higher education partnerships and collaborative practices are emphasized to support the work of the network and to improve education. (ms)

National Occupational Competency Testing Institute (NOCTI)

A leading provider of high-quality occupational competency assessment products and services to secondary and postsecondary educational institutions in the United States and around the world. (sa)

National Reporting System (NRS)

A system for states to report statistics about their adult basic education programs funded under the Workforce Investment Act. The NRS requires states to report data on the number of adults

served, average hours of instruction for each participant, learning gains as measured by objective tests, and impact of participation on employment. (jpc)

National Research Center for Career and Technical Education (NRCCTE)

Funded by the Office of Vocational and Adult Education, the Center generates and disseminates scientifically based knowledge and provides technical assistance to improve career and technical education in the United States. (sa)

National Research Council (NRC)

The National Academy of Sciences founded NRC in 1916 as a means of fostering collaboration between academic and industrial elites to enhance scientific military efforts and advise the federal government. During World War I the NRC aided in the development and production of optical glass, nitrates, poison gas, and other materials. Today the NRC is the principal operating agency of the National Academy of Sciences and the National Academy of Engineering. It provides services to the government, the public, and the scientific and engineering communities. (vmm)

National School Reform Faculty

An initiative begun in 1995 at Brown University that focuses on improving student achievement through the development of educational professionals. Utilizing facilitative leadership and critical friendships, the initiative seeks to develop learning communities of adult learners who can work together and support each other to improve their schools. (ms)

National Science Foundation Act, 1950

Legislation signed into law by President Harry S. Truman, that established the National Science Foundation, an independent federal agency responsible for the initiation and support of basic research in all scientific disciplines in the United

States. An important part of its charter was the promotion and support of science education as a key means of enhancing the research potential of the country as a vital national resource. This was accomplished through the provision of grants, loans, and other forms of assistance for, among other things, graduate fellowships, teacher training institutes, and course content improvement projects. (jlr)

National Student Federation of America (NSFA)

A liberally oriented national organization of student governments in the United States, which grew out of a concern for the League of Nations, the World Court, and other questions of foreign policy in 1925. The organization survived until 1946 and served as the model for the National Student Association. The NSFA officially formed out of the union of two separate efforts, the Intercollegiate World Court Conference held at Princeton in December 1925, and students from seven Western universities who had come together in January 1925 to form a group they called the National Student Federation of America. Delegates from the two groups met in Ann Arbor on December 2–4, 1926, to officially form the National Student Federation of America (NSFA). The NSFA was not a mass-membership organization, but rather a federation of student governments. During the late 1920s and early 1930s, the NSFA was considered by most university administrators and others as the legitimate voice of the American student community. (nt)

National Survey of Student Engagement (NSSE)

Started in 1999, NSSE (pronounced nessie) is an annual national survey to determine the level of student engagement and learning in four-year colleges and universities. College freshmen and seniors are randomly surveyed to determine satisfaction with the educational programs and activities offered at their college or university. Survey questions are tied to five benchmarks of effective educational practice. The benchmarks are level of academic challenge; active and collaborative learning; student-faculty interaction; enriching educational experiences; and supportive campus environment. NSSE provides an alternative to rankings such as those provided by *U.S. News & World Report*. (pw1)

National Teacher Corps (See Teacher Corps)

National Youth Administration (NYA)

A federal program established in 1935, designed to provide funds for part-time employment of students between the ages of 16 and 24 and employment opportunities in community projects for other youth not enrolled in school. The program was established by an executive order of President Franklin D. Roosevelt and was heavily influenced by the involvement of Eleanor Roosevelt, Harry Hopkins, then head of the Work Progress Administration (WPA), and Aubrey Willis Williams, Hopkins's deputy administrator and later head of the NYA. Originally an agency within the WPA, it was moved to fall under the Federal Security Agency (FSA) during a major governmental reorganization in 1939. Mary McLeod Bethune, director of NYA's Division of Negro Affairs, was responsible for developing special programs for African American youth and for enlarging the numbers of African Americans in master's and doctoral programs. By 1940 the NYA had provided part-time work for more than 2 million students and employment for an additional 2.6 million nonstudent youths. NYA was terminated by Congress in 1943 during wartime budget restrictions and a shrinking unemployment problem; however, it served as a forerunner for similar federal programs, such as the National Youth Corps and the college Work-Study Program. (nt)

nationalism/patriotism
Devoted and faithful love, support, and defense of one's nation, country, or political entity. (cb)

Native American Studies (See American Indian Studies)

native language literacy
Literacy instruction in which learners develop literacy in their first language prior to learning to read in a second language. The approach is based on the assumption that literacy acquisition proceeds more smoothly in a first language and that skills from the native language literacy can be transferred to literacy acquisition in the second language. (las)

Native Schools
A set of common schools established chiefly in the Reconstruction period following the Civil War, although many schools were established earlier in the 1800s. The schools were funded, constructed, staffed, and maintained solely by African Americans in order to increase numeracy and literacy among the formerly enslaved Africans. As they were supported entirely by African Americans, they are distinct from government-supported Freedmen's Bureau schools of that era, which served similar communities in the South. (hfs)

natural numbers (See integer)

naturalism
A philosophical doctrine centered upon two ideas: the metaphysical idea that only the things studied by the natural sciences exist; and the epistemological idea that the methodology used in the natural sciences must be used to examine all objects. While some philosophers believe that the metaphysical idea is primary and the epistemological idea is a consequence of it, others claim that the converse is the case. Naturalism can be seen as setting the boundaries of education by limiting the types of things that exist and restricting the things that can be known. (rk)

See also empiricism; foundationalism; idealism; positivism; realism.

naturalistic
The intention in literature and visual art to represent things in their natural state, as things realistically exist in nature. Artists who create in a naturalistic style seek to represent their subject as closely to its actual existence as possible, as it has been observed in a natural setting. Naturalistic landscape paintings, for example, are often depictions of a scene at a particular time of day so that the light, shade, plants, clouds, and colors appear similar to the way they appear in nature. (ap)

naturalistic inquiry
A holistic approach to the study of social behavior in the settings in which the behavior naturally occurs. Naturalistic inquiry holds that social behavior is time and context bound and therefore is best studied in natural rather than contrived settings. Naturalistic inquiry is distinguished from naturalism, which posits that the social sciences can be studied in the same manner as the natural sciences. (rws)

naturalistic intelligence
According to Howard Gardner (in Checkly, 1997), a sensitivity to the patterns in the natural world. Naturalists are quick to identify and discriminate (e.g., classify) among living things. Children with naturalistic intelligence learn by working directly with living things and by making connections between the world of nature and the world of artifice. Expert naturalists include botanists, taxonomists, and veterinarians. (ecr)

NCA (See North Central Association)

NCATE (See National Council for Accreditation of Teacher Education)

NCES (See National Center for Education Statistics)

NCHEMS (See National Center for Higher Education Management Systems)

NCLB (See No Child Left Behind Act)

NCSS (See National Council for the Social Studies)

NEA (See National Education Association)

NEA (See National Endowment for the Arts)

need-based financial aid
Financial aid awarded on the basis of financial need. The Free Application for Federal Student Aid (FAFSA) is generally used for determining federal, state, and institutional need-based aid eligibility, although additional determinations may be used. (sn)

needs assessment
Any process through which the learning needs of a group are analyzed. This information is generally ascertained through observation, interviews, surveys, and/or documentation reviews. Conducted prior to the development of an instructional program, a needs assessment allows the program to be designed based on identified needs. (mkr, ch)

negative freedom (See freedom)

negative peace
A concept that emphasizes the elimination or absence of overt violence. (hfs)

negative recognition
Rejection of anyone based on appearance, including dress, physical characteristics, language, and socioeconomic status. (jqa, npo)

negative space
The space not occupied by (surrounding) the subject of a composition. Negative space is defined by both the positive space (the subject) and the frame (the outside border) of a composition. In art education, negative space, and the shapes created in its relation to the positive space, are generally taught as simultaneously defining and defined by the positive space of a piece. For example, a composition may be created by drawing the negative space only, thereby defining the positive. In teaching writing, notions of negative and positive space may inform the importance of backdrop or context as a positive force on what is featured. (km)

neglect
Generally, this terms means to underserve, give insufficient attention to, or leave unattended a person who has a legitimate claim or right to such attention. In professional or educational contexts, this refers to providing inadequate attention or service to a client or student. Such inattention may imply a lack of respect. (dd)

neglected majority
A term coined by Dale Parnell, past president of the American Association of Community Colleges, to describe secondary students in the two middle quartiles on academic ability who are often overlooked by educational reforms focused on the highest- or lowest-performing students. (db)

NEH (See National Endowment for the Humanities)

Nelson Amendment (1907)
This amendment to the Morrill Act of 1862 increased the federal appropriations for each land-grant school. The amendment also stipulated that a portion of the increased appropriations be used to offer teacher education courses in agriculture and the mechanical arts/engineering. (klj)

neoconservativism
Neoconservativism is a right-of-center political and philosophical doctrine that

emphasizes tradition, an active military, a moralistic worldview, and strong family values. Primarily rooted in the United States, it has become increasingly prominent in politics in recent decades, particularly under President George W. Bush. The emphasis on military strength and hegemonic assertiveness has led to a large military and "Hawkish" or neo-Realist positions on global politics. While neoliberalism values the market, individualism, progress, and deregulation, neoconservatives may in fact be willing to accept a welfare state and strong corporate regulations if seen as a means to protect traditional values, the American way of life, or the traditional family. For a more in-depth discussion of the relationship between neoliberalism and neoconservativism see Apple (2006). In education we can see the influence of neoconservativism in various forms of "Back-to-Basics" reforms, the emphasis on a common curriculum as found in E. D. Hirsch's *Cultural Literacy,* the celebration of the Western Canon such as Allan Bloom's *The Closing of the American Mind,* and increasingly close links between the military and schools and colleges in the form of recruitment and research. (tn)

See also back-to-basics; democracy; ideology; neoliberalism.

neoliberalism

With roots in classical liberalism, neoliberalism has become the dominant political ideology in recent decades. Most commonly identified with the rise of political leaders such as Margaret Thatcher and Ronald Reagan, neoliberalism emphasizes individualism, the market, economic and technological progress, deregulation and privatization, unhindered entrepreneurial innovation, and the importance of rational self-interest. It elevates the market above other forms of social and political order such as the nation-state. Sometimes called "market fundamentalism" or laissez-faire economics, neoliberalism claims that all social, economic, and political problems

are best resolved through the free market. It is to be differentiated from neoconservativism, which instead emphasizes tradition, family values, nationalism, and military strength. The impact of neoliberalism on education can be observed in the expectation that education serve as an economic investment, such as the production of human capital for the knowledge economy (with due expectations of return on investment); in the growth of privatization and promotion of school vouchers and school choice; high stakes testing and accountability; and, corporate funded research for commercial application. Its most vocal critics in education come from movements such as critical theory, postmodernism and postcolonialism, and feminist and anti-racist education. (tn)

See also consumerism; commercialization of education; liberalism; critical theory; anti-racist education.

nervous system

The nervous system has two major divisions, the central nervous system and the peripheral nervous system. The central nervous system is made up of the brain and spinal cord and occupies the processing space between stimulus and response. Sensory input from the peripheral nervous system is processed in the central nervous system, and instructions for action (e.g., movement) originate in the central nervous system and are carried to the muscles and other effectors by peripheral nerves. The peripheral nervous system is made up of nerves exiting and entering the spinal cord that carry instructions from the brain to various parts of the body and carry sensory information from the body to the brain. (pk1)

net-price calculators

Designed to help students and their parents estimate the true cost of an institution of higher education. Colleges and universities will be required to post a net-price calculator on their websites by August 2011. Net price is defined as the average yearly price charged to aided full-time, first-time undergraduates after grant aid has been subtracted from the cost of attendance. For public institutions, the net price, tuition and fees, and cost of attendance will be based on in-state rates. (sn)

neural architecture

Architecture is a metaphor useful in describing the structures that are created by networks of neurons. These structures of neurons, or the neural architecture, can be modified through experience and take on different characteristics of shape, size, and density. (dh)

neuroconstructivism

Neuroconstructivism seeks to make a direct connection between cognitive development and brain development. Specifically, the "-constructivism" identifies the increasing complexity of representations, as well as the skills and adaptations that they engender, as an individual develops. The "neuro-" recognizes that this increase in cognitive and representational complexity is related to an elaboration of neural structures. This developmental process is embodied in the sense that the mind, brain, and body interact with and adapt to the environment. It is embedded in the social and cultural milieu that makes up much of intellectual and emotional life. (dh)

neurogenesis

Essentially the creation of new neurons and other types of nerve cells in the brain. It was believed for years that this process did not occur in the adult brain, but recent findings have indicated otherwise. While not a very common occurrence, it appears that the growth of neurons derives from the modification of residual progenitor or stem cells, although other mechanisms may exist. (dh)

neuroimaging

Neuroimaging is the use of tools to create a representation of the structure (structural imaging) or function (functional imaging) of the brain. The applications of neuroimaging are mainly in research, in which neuroimaging techniques are used to learn more about the human brain, and in medicine, in which neuroimaging can help reveal and identify brain damage and disease. Widely used examples of neuroimaging tools include MRI and EEG. (mt)

neuroleptic

A category of psychotropic medication. From the Greek "stopping of the neurons," this term is synonymous with antipsychotic drugs. Neuroleptics are prescribed with the intent of ameliorating cognitive and behavioral symptoms of psychoses, such as confusion, psychomotor agitation, delusions, and hallucinations. (cap)

neuron

These specialized nerve cells are the basic building blocks of the brain, the spinal column, and the nervous system. They receive, process, transmit, or conduct electrical impulses over long distances throughout the body's nervous system and can be the longest cells known. Neurons consist of a cell body with one or more dendrites and a single axon, which can be several meters long. Neurons are excitable cells, cells in which there is action potential. A neuron may receive impulses from sensory cells (sensory neurons) or other neurons and send impulses to muscles through motor neurons (motoneurons). Neurons that connect only with other neurons are called interneurons. (ns)

neuroplasticity

Neuroplasticity describes several mechanisms by which structural changes take place in the brain. Neuroplastic actions include the remapping of function within regions of cortex, long-term potentiation, synaptogenesis, neurogenesis, and other physical changes in the axonal and dendritic projections of neurons. (dh)

neurostimulants

A type of pharmaceutical that increases neuronal activity. Common types include methylphenidate and dexamphetamine. Neurostimulants are often used in the treatment of ADHD. (sd1)

New England Primer

Second only to the Bible in colonial New England, the *Primer* was the most prevalent textbook in America during the 17th and 18th centuries. The small textbook (usually 3.5 by 4.5 inches) blended reading instruction with religion, and two to three million copies of its more than 360 editions were sold while it was in print (1685/90–1886). Perhaps most famous for its verse "In Adam's Fall/We Sinned All," the *Primer* typically included an illustrated alphabet, spelling and syllable lessons, moral stories, and prayers, verses, and portions of the Bible to be learned by heart. The *Westminster* or *John Cotton Catechisms* were generally reprinted as part of the *Primer*. (jlw)

new literacy studies

A theory, promoted by Brian Street and James Gee, that conceptualizes literacy as a social practice, rather than a set of skills. (cas)

New Math Movement

Also known as modern math, this method of teaching mathematics in the 1960s and 1970s dealt with a greater emphasis on mastering mathematical concepts, such as set theory, number bases, and laws of arithmetic, such as the distributive law, associative law, and commutative law, and less emphasis on practicing computation skills. (kgh)

new social studies

The Cold War era and the launching of *Sputnik* in 1957 ushered in a wave of reform in the American educational system. The federal government sponsored much of the reform, and by the mid-1960s an unprecedented period of curriculum innovation developed. Curriculum projects, which included the "new social studies," focused on inquiry methods and the structure of the disciplines. During this time period, 50 major new social studies curriculum projects were developed. Despite these efforts the legacy of the new social studies is that the scope, sequence, and content of the social studies curricula across the United States did not change substantially. (cb)

NFE (See nonformal education)

NGO (See nongovernmental organization)

NIE (See National Institute of Education)

nihilism

The belief that there is no meaning in or purpose to life. With the success of modern astronomy, physics, and Darwinian biology, purpose (teleology) was slowly read out of nature. Nihilism is simply the name for the constellation of views that take Nietzsche's claim that any meaning we find for our lives in the universe is merely the projection of our own wishes, fantasies, and self-images onto the objective world. (an)

NIMAC (See National Instructional Materials Access Center)

NIMAS (See National Instructional Materials Accessibility Standard)

NLD (See nonverbal learning disorder)

No Child Left Behind Act (NCLB)

Federal law signed by President George W. Bush in 2002, reauthorizing the Elementary and Secondary Education Act of 1965, which laid a framework of accountability, choice, and flexibility to ensure no child was left in a failing educational system. NCLB provided for the following provisions:

- States must set higher standards for reading and mathematics and establish testing to determine the level at which the standards are met. Actions may be taken against schools failing to meet state standards, with recognition going to those that do close their achievement gap.
- Parents are given increased rights to transfer their child from a low-performing school to a higher-performing school or receive additional public or private supplemental educational support from an approved provider and receive Title I funds in order to do so.
- States agreeing to greater accountability measures are given greater flexibility in how they apply federal grant funds for education, including the option for consolidation of local educational agency funds in order to achieve higher performance results.
- Funding provided for the establishment of the Early Reading First and Reading First programs to support reading instruction. (ms)

NOCTI (See National Occupational Competency Testing Institute)

nominal group process
A process designed to help a group establish priorities. This technique is often used in adult education, whereby individuals are asked to respond to a question in writing. Responses are then read and discussed by the group. A facilitator helps to classify, order, and synthesize the final conclusions of the group. Also called nominal group technique. (chb, las)

nominal numbers
Numbers used to name objects, as in house numbers or postal codes. (amr)

noncredit course
A course offered by an academic institution for which that institution does not offer academic credit. Noncredit courses are typically offered by continuing education or extension units in colleges and universities; these courses are often job- or career-related, or are focused on recreational rather than academic learning. (chb)

non-Euclidean space
N-dimensional spaces exhibiting constant nonzero curvature. Non-Euclidean spaces are analogous to Euclidean space except for the existence of parallel lines; the fifth axiom (the parallel postulate) is negated by two cases. Elliptical (spherical) space contains no parallel lines, has constant positive curvature, and can be modeled in three dimensions by a globe. Hyperbolic space contains multiple parallel lines, has constant negative curvature, and is used as the basis for current theories of the universe. (ey)

nonexpansive character education
First proposed by McLaughlin and Halstead (1999), this term refers to forms of character education often associated with conservative ideology and pedagogical approaches. Nonexpansive character education is, for example, associated with direct instruction. Prominent proponents include Thomas Lickona (1996), William Bennett (1994), and Edward Wynne and K. Ryan (1997). (dpb)

See also expansive character education.

nonfarm residents
Nonfarm rural residents make up an increasing proportion of the rural population. The growth of this group is a product of several forces, including increased industrial relocation, the emergence of the kind of home-based employment made possible by technology, the availability of cheaper housing, and the flight from urban crime, pollution, and deteriorating schools. (lr)

nonformal education (NFE)
A term used to describe educational programs in the Third World that are

organized educational activities that happen outside the formal education system. (jpc)

nongovernmental organization (NGO)
An organization that is not entirely funded by the federal government of a country and the mission of which usually involves a social or community-oriented task. (las)

nongraded instruction
An instructional approach in which students proceed through a sequence of content and skills in a subject area at their own pace rather than moving through traditional grade levels at an established pace. (bba)

nonlinear equation
Any equation in which the terms contain more than one variable or the variables have a power other than one; any equation whose graph is not a line; any equation that is not linear. (rdk)

nonlocomotor skills
Movements that are performed in one space that don't require a change in the base of support or traveling (e.g., bending, stretching, twisting, pushing, pulling). (rf)

nonmathematical reason
A mathematical concept that is applied to a real life application involving the context of one's personal life, where the actual mathematical use is not relevant. (jmg)

nonreader
Person who is unable to read at all or who has a reading level corresponding to first or second grade. (las)

nonrepresentational
A work of art is nonrepresentational if it has no identifiable references to an object, person, or place in the natural world. Nonrepresentational art may more fully represent feelings and concepts in lieu of recognizable objects of representation. Much of contemporary art is nonrepresentational, including the work of Mark Rothko and Jackson Pollock. Educational researchers question whether the nonrepresentational drawing of young children results from a different aesthetic or understanding of the functions of graphic symbolization or merely a lack of representational skills. (ap)

nonroutine problems
Mathematical tasks that do not simply involve a student mechanically repeating a known procedure or method. A nonroutine problem may involve students finding the height of a person given a footprint or figuring out the number of buses needed for a field trip for their class. If methods and procedures for a task are specifically prescribed and students simply mimic these, then a nonroutine task may become a routine problem or exercise. Nonroutine problem solving provides opportunities for students to understand and learn mathematics. (sdt)

nonsexist education
Instruction that incorporates recognition of the achievements of women and men alike is considered nonsexist. In addition, such instruction addresses the needs of female and male students, avoids use of sexist language and pronouns in educational materials, encourages equal aspirations in both sexes, and promotes equality of educational experiences. (jqa, npo)

nonstandard English
If it is assumed that there is a single standard dialect of English, then all the other speech varieties of English are labeled as nonstandard. Modern linguistics takes special care in describing these variations as equal in status to the standard dialect. Most commonly, speech varieties of English are categorized based on the region in which the speakers live, namely regional dialects (e.g., Southern American dialect, Philadelphian dialect, Boston

dialect, etc.) or on the social status of the speakers, namely sociolects (e.g., jargon, slang), which are usually determined by the speakers' socioeconomic status, gender, ethnicity, age, occupation, and so on. (smt)

nonstandard mathematics problem

Sometimes referred to as a nontrivial or nonroutine task. These problems cannot be solved in a simple algorithmic manner. Students may be asked to use multiple approaches or different representations to solve the problem and should be able to justify their solutions. These problems tend to be more engaging for students. Problem-solving skills and higher-level thinking are necessary due to the complexity of the task. (mlf, rlk)

nonstandard/standard measure

Standard measure is a type of measurement established by authority, custom, or general consent as a model or example. Examples are rulers, scales, thermometers. Nonstandard measure is nonconforming to what is commonly used to measure a specific mathematical situation. (jdk)

nontenure track

A type of position wherein tenure (and its incumbent security) or the tenure process is not offered as a condition of employment. Sometimes this designation is abbreviated NTT. Faculty hired as non tenure track often serve at the rank of lecturer or instructor. (jbm)

nontraditional

In career education, a reference to an individual pursuing occupations not customary for members of their gender, race, or other category. Also used to refer to older students enrolled in programs. (jb)

nontraditional education

Any education designed to be delivered to learners other than "traditional" postsecondary learners (18 to 23 years old), especially in formats other than the traditional

full-time sequence of daytime courses. With the increasing numbers of adult students on U.S. campuses and an increasing variety of delivery formats for learners of all ages, the distinction between traditional and nontraditional education began to blur by the 1990s. (chb)

nontraditional students

Individuals who enter or return to university or college beyond the typical age (mid-twenties). The term also applies to ethnic minorities, women with dependent children, underprepared students, and other groups less commonly represented in postsecondary educational institutions. (las, ch)

nonverbal communication

Refers to a form of communication that is expressed through behaviors and actions rather than through words. It is considered by many to be an important, clinically meaningful form of communication. Parsons and Hughes (1975) referred to it as "leakage" and believes that it provides insight into how a client is really feeling. Because clients are frequently more aware/cognizant of their words than they are of their behaviors and actions, nonverbal communications may be useful for assessing congruence between verbal and nonverbal communications (e.g., client says he or she is happy; however, he or she is sitting slumped over, is noticeably tearful, and is staring blankly at the floor). (ksp)

nonverbal learning disorder (NLD)

A learning disability affecting approximately 6 percent of American children, characterized by poor numerical, spatial, and conceptual performance, poor social perception, and the inability to adapt appropriately to novel situations and information. In contrast to their mathematical difficulties, these children read and spell accurately, due to their excellent rote verbal memory skills and advanced phonemic awareness. However, while their decoding skills are proficient, NLD children have trouble with reading comprehension. NLD is associated with increased risk of clinical depression. These children are socially and physically clumsy and have difficulty modulating their voices as well as interpreting facial expressions, negative social feedback, and linguistic tone. (mhi-y)

nonvocational

A term used to describe practical arts activities valued for their contribution to general education rather than designed to train persons for wage-earning occupations. (jm)

norm

As a scientific concept, norm is the conceptual equivalent of average and represents statistical frequency. As a philosophical concept, norm is defined as a standard, or rule, used for judging and guiding conduct. As a philosophical concept, norm is irreducible to objective measurements obtained through scientific methods. However, a norm identified through statistical methods can become a norm for judging and guiding conduct when it is accepted as a norm for social practice. (lkk)

See also normation.

norm referencing

This is both a form of test development and of score usage. Results from norm-referenced tests are interpreted as the test taker's rank among peers. The group on whom the test is developed is often called the "norm group," and the published rankings, by which the score is interpreted, are often called the "norms." (fd)

See also criterion referencing.

normal school

Refers to institutions dating back to 1838 in the United States that were established to prepare teachers for the nation's common schools. The generally accepted explanation for the origin of the term "normal" is that it comes from France, where *école normale* was the name given to schools that were created to train teachers for the Republic. After 1900, most normal schools evolved into colleges or universities, and the term has fallen into general disuse. (sn)

normalization

A process of integrating individuals with developmental disabilities into the general community. (sr)

normalized child

Maria Montessori believed that each child enters the classroom with some form of deviation from the norm. She based her educational system on the assumption that exposure to the order, tranquility, and harmony within the Montessori classroom allows the child to gain self-confidence and inner discipline, leading to internalizing 10 characteristics of a "normalized" individual. These characteristics include: love of order, love of work, profound spontaneous concentration, attachment to reality, love of silence and working alone, sublimation of the possessive instinct, obedience, independence and initiative, spontaneous self-discipline, and joy. (nrs)

normation

Normation is the process by which social norms become standards in judging one's own performance as well as the performance of others. It differs from what is often called "socialization," because it affords a contrast between the existing social community and the community as it would be if it were all that its members think it ought to be. Hence, normation includes the acquisition of ideals and thus provides room for the social criticism of social norms. Normation is the central educational concept in Green's *Voices: The Educational Formation of Conscience*. (tfg)

See also norm.

norms

Acceptable behavior, beliefs, and values by most of the members of the society. A cultural unwritten rule with social consequences, but not a law. Many members of society conform and follow the accepted behaviors in hopes of fitting into society. They assist in defining and maintaining the parameters of being an insider, compared to an outsider. These behaviors vary from culture to culture but they are not fixed; they change and adapt according to fluctuations in society. (kf1)

North Central Association (NCA)
Founded in 1895 as a membership organization of educators for the accreditation of schools and colleges in 19 states. In November 2000 accreditation of higher education institutions was moved to the Higher Learning Commission, a newly incorporated organization. (cf)

Northwest Ordinance of 1787
The principle concern of the Ordinance of 1787 was the establishment of a process for carving new states out of the Northwest Territory. For the first time, Congress stated that education was foundational to the government of the new states. "Religion, morality, and knowledge being necessary to good government and the happiness of mankind, schools and the means of education shall be forever encouraged." Building on the Ordinance of 1785, which required that the 16th lot of every township be set aside to support public schools, the Ordinance of 1787 was an important first step toward federal support for education. (lg)

notation
The system of symbols used to represent numbers, objects, and operations. (rdk)

novice teacher
An untenured teacher who is just beginning to work in a classroom, often having just completed a teacher preparation program. (rtc)

NRC (See National Research Council)

NRCCTE (See National Research Center for Career and Technical Education)

NRS (See National Reporting System)

NSSE (See National Survey of Student Engagement)

nucleus
A voiced element (usually a vowel) that forms the core of a syllable (e.g., the vowel "a" is the nucleus in the first syllable of *napkin*). (smt)

null curriculum
Content, skills, and/or dispositions entirely absent from the explicit curriculum, operationalized curriculum, and hidden curriculum. Examples include the absence of women composers in a music program (content), the absence of mentioning Jews in the U.S. Revolutionary War (content), the absence of discussing Arabic contributions to mathematics (content), the lack of opportunities to create rap music or hip-hop music (skill), or the absence of presenting controversies in science (disposition). (db-j)

See also explicit curriculum; hidden curriculum; operationalized curriculum.

number concepts
The realization and cognitive understanding of what numbers mean. It involves the development of number relationships, namely one-to-one correspondence, more, less, and same. (vdf)

number decomposition/ recomposition
Decomposition refers to the ability to separate numbers into component parts in order to perform some operation on those numbers. For example, a person might think of 27 + 35 as (20 + 7) + (30 + 5). These parts are then recombined as (20 + 30) + (7 + 5), which in turn is recombined as 50 + 12 or 62. Research has highlighted the importance of these

abilities for fluency in estimation and mental arithmetic. (cmdv)

number learning
Number learning is the act or experience of one who is attaining knowledge of numbers, or learning a skill related to numbers. Number learning is knowing what numbers are and how they relate to one another in a mathematical sense. (jdk)

number line
A line of infinite extent whose points correspond to the real numbers according to their distance in a positive or negative direction from a point (usually zero). Number lines are used primarily for addition and subtraction of positive and negative numbers. They can determine distance, continuum, and relative position. (jdk)

number sense
An intuitive feeling for numbers and their various uses and interpretations; an appreciation for various levels of accuracy when figuring; an ability to detect arithmetical errors; a commonsense approach to using numbers; having an awareness of multiple relationships among numbers. (dc)

number systems
Our base 10 number system is built on place values of increasing powers of 10. Other number systems exist based on increasing powers of 2 (computer binary) or 12 (clock) or 20 (Mayan). (ey)

number theory
The study of natural or counting numbers (1, 2, 3 . . .) and integers (. . . –2, –1, 0, 1, 2 . . .). Some of the major topics include prime and composite numbers, factoring polynomials, divisibility, congruence, and modular arithmetic. (mlf, rlk)

numeracy
The ability to use numbers and apply math processes to solve work and daily life problems. Numeracy is marked by the ability to think and express one's own thoughts quantitatively. Skills a child uses in counting, performing number operations, comparing numbers, and sensing the size of numbers. Numeracy skills developing in the preschool period include counting, cardinality, and conservation of number. (wja, jpc, vm)

numerate
Term to describe someone who can use numbers and apply math processes to solve work and daily life problems. (jpc)

numeration
The symbol systems and rules used for recording numbers in a particular number system. (dc)

numerical composite
Used in explaining the child's construction of 10 as a unit. At this level the meaning given to the set of 10 is as 10 ones or a single entity, but it is not both simultaneously. (amr)

numerical data
Information in the form of real numbers or constants, such as 2 or π, that are used as a basis to interpret, calculate, discuss, or reason about the event from which the data were drawn. (gtm)

O

obedience

Compliance with the expressed wishes or orders of those in authority regardless of one's own judgment or wishes; a virtue in institutions that are unabashedly hierarchical, but of questionable value in democratic institutions committed to the principles of individual autonomy, social and political equality, and shared responsibility. The central educational problem in a democracy is how to make the transition from being ruled by others to ruling over oneself while remaining within the expectations and need of a social order. (nl)

object method (See Oswego Movement)

object permanence

The concept that an object is in existence even when it cannot be perceived through use of the senses. For example, children who continue to search for the object after it is hidden are thought to possess object permanence. This is a component of Jean Piaget's developmental theory and is thought to be mastered during the sensory-motor stage of cognitive development. (mf)

object relations theory

A contemporary variant of psychoanalysis that minimizes the focus on the individual as isolated and at the mercy of instinctual drives. Rather, the focus is on interpersonal relatedness, as reflected in one's mental representations of the self and other. The object through which gratification is sought is usually a person, some aspect of a person, or a symbolic representation of a person. It is toward these "objects" that an individual directs her or his desires or behavior. (rnp)

object teaching

An approach to educating children popular in the mid-19th century, rooted in the theories of Johann Pestalozzi and popularized in the United States through the teacher education provided in normal schools, especially the Oswego (New York) State Normal and Training School. Object teaching focused on building lessons around objects familiar to the child (e.g., plants, animals) as a means of stimulating his or her interest in learning. Object teaching represented an early effort to define a systematic approach to pedagogy and represented a move away from complete reliance on textbooks for classroom content and conduct and toward an appreciation for the child as an active participant in the educational process. (sw)

objective

A clear statement of what students are supposed to know or be able to do as a consequence of instruction (usually a lesson or a series of related lessons). The objective may be a specified cognitive, affective, behavioral, or expressive outcome. (bba, ja)

objective, career

The individual's ultimate workforce goal, on which course work, effort, and resources are directed and focused. (ea)

objective test

An assessment procedure or test that consists of structured, fixed items that are administered, scored, and interpreted in a standardized manner and do not require the subjective evaluation of the examiner. An example of an objective test is a multiple choice exam, whereas an example of a subjective test is an essay test. The primary purpose of objective tests is to measure an individual's characteristics or responses in a way that is independent of rater bias and other types of assessment errors. Objective tests and procedures tend to be more reliable and valid than projective or subjective tests. (tsw)

See also subjective test.

objectivity

Stresses impartial judgment and the existence of a world independent of consciousness. It assumes that a distinction between appearance and reality can be made, which is fundamental to its opposition to subjectivity and mind-dependent judgment. Objectivity is defined both epistemologically and ontologically. Epistemologically, objectivity occurs with interpersonal, impartial judgment, in contrast to the intrapersonal, biased judgment of subjectivity. Ontologically, objective entities are the propositional truths and empirical facts identified as existing independently of consciousness. Objective entities are distinguished from consciousness-dependent phenomena such as sensations, dreams, memories, and aesthetic properties, which are associated with subjectivity. (lkk)

observation

A social science methodology for gathering information about a subject by watching, noting, and describing the interaction of an individual or group within a given social context. (jjc)

observed score

An observed score on a test is the number of points obtained by an examinee on the test. The observed score is mainly influenced by the examinee's true ability, but also by other random events such as test environments or the examinee's psychological and physical factors. In Classical Test Theory (CTT), observed score (X) is viewed as a combination of true and error scores, both of which are unobservable. (mj)

See also true score.

occipital lobe (See lobes of the brain)

occupational adjustment (See adjustment, occupational)

occupational analysis

Process by which the task requirements of an occupation are analyzed and outlined in order to identify the skills and knowledge necessary to perform effectively in that occupation. This information can then be used to guide training and education activities. (las)

occupational competencies (See competencies, occupational)

occupational growth

Growth of learners in maturity of career and technical understanding and in development of attitudes in harmony with the changing demands of modern social and economic life. (jm)

occupational guidance

A function of a vocational or career guidance program, which supplies individuals with an inventory of their abilities, aptitudes, and interests as they relate to occupations of interest to them. Presents facts about jobs and occupational fields, requirements of various occupations, and employment possibilities. This activity may include arranged experiences in order to help students select a vocation more intelligently. (jm)

occupational literacy

Ability to read materials required in the workplace. Recently, the term has been expanded to comprise the capacity to listen, speak, and write as necessary in a workplace context. (las)

occupational mobility

The pattern of changes in occupation taking place in society. These include changes between the occupation of parent and child, movement in and out of an occupational position, changes from one job to another within a community, from one job to another between communities, and from one type of job to another within or between communities. (jm)

occupational skill standards

Performance-based statements that specify the knowledge, skills, and abilities a worker must possess to be competent and successful in an occupation. (jb)

occupational standard

An established measure for judging the quality of work performed in a trade or occupation. (jb)

occupational study

The exploration of jobs and careers by students through participation in career and technical education, vocational and career guidance, or some other occupationally related educational endeavor. (ea)

occupational survey

An investigation and evaluation to gather pertinent information about industries or occupations in an area, to determine the need for training, and so on, for the purpose of improving or developing a career and technical program. (db, ea)

See also employment survey; vocational education survey.

occupational therapy

A therapy or treatment provided by an occupational therapist, focused on sensory integration, coordination, and fine motor skills. (sr)

occupations

In the context of early childhood education, occupations are materials designed by the "Father of Kindergarten," Friedrich Froebel, to develop children's psychomotor skills and to be intrinsically appealing and therefore engaging to the children. The occupations in his "child's garden" included, among others, sewing boards, clay work, bead stringing, and working with paper. (ecr)

off-campus programs

Educational programs affiliated with a particular college or university, but held in a location remote from the main campus. Often these programs are part of an institution's goal to attract new students or to meet community needs. Off-campus programs can offer full degrees or can offer specific courses to fulfill the education requirements of the community in which they are located. For accreditation purposes, an institution must demonstrate that they have sufficient resources to adequately maintain the program. (cf)

Office of Apprenticeship

A division of the U.S. Department of Labor that connects job seekers looking to learn new skills with employers looking for qualified workers. (sa)

Office of Educational Research and Improvement (OERI)

An agency of the U.S. Department of Education that provides national leadership for educational research and statistics. In its stated mission to promote excellence and equity in American education, the agency funds grants to help improve education, collects statistics on the status and progress of schools, and provides technical assistance to those working to improve education. With the signing of the Education Sciences Reform Act of 2002, OERI ceased to exist and was replaced by the Institute of Education Sciences. (cf)

Office of Vocational and Adult Education (OVAE)

The Office of Vocational and Adult Education is a federal agency within the U.S. Department of Education. It administers and coordinates programs that are related to adult education and literacy, career and technical education, and community colleges. (sa)

Official English

An umbrella term used by individuals and organizations that intend to make English the official language of the United States; may also be known as English Only. Two key groups promoting this movement are U.S. English and English First. As their names imply, these groups argue that since English is the primary language for communication, no other languages should be used—in schools, in government, and so on. They also claim that the English language is being lost due to bilingual education programs and increased immigration. Supporters urged the passage of Proposition 227, a 1998 California law, which attempted to ban bilingual education in public schools across the state. These groups are not related to English Plus, which, in contrast, believes that the United States would be better served if individuals are not only proficient in English but also have skills in other languages. Each represents a point of view in the ongoing debate in the United States around the escalating globalization of society and the abilities needed to flourish in the multicultural world community. (acp, jqa)

oil painting

The product or process of using an oil-based medium—a paint created from ground pigments suspended in oil—which is then applied to a prepared surface. The use of oil paint became widespread in the Italian Renaissance and remains the preferred type of paint for many contemporary artists. Oil paintings are durable and lend themselves to the creation of a range of interesting surface textures. The process takes a long time to dry, requires technique to master, and involves messy substances for brush cleaning and mixing; as a result, oil painting is almost never introduced in art programs for very young children. (ap)

OJT (See on-the-job training)

Old Deluder Law

A law enacted by the Massachusetts General Court in 1647 that required towns with 50 households or more to appoint a person to teach reading and writing. All towns with 100 households or more were required to set up a grammar school to prepare students for university. The law levied a fine on towns who failed to meet these requirements, the first law of its kind. The name comes from the preamble, which states, "it being one chief project of that old deluder, Satan, to keep men from the knowledge of the Scriptures." (clp)

old field school

A type of school typically found in the American South in the antebellum period. Old field schools were built by neighboring farmers on land (old or fallow fields) donated by the landowner, for the purpose of providing schooling to the neighborhood children. Teachers were hired by the parents on a per term contract basis and parents paid a subscription to send their children. Parents provided additional support to the school by often building the schoolhouse and providing firewood. Textbooks were often whatever the pupils had at home. (jg)

one-room schools

Once the norm throughout the United States, these small, one-teacher schools were found primarily in the rural areas until the mid-20th century. Rural school consolidation, centralized state control, and the decrease in rural populations caused the number of one-room schools to decrease through the late 19th and 20th centuries. Peer tutoring, small class size, and local control and ownership are positive attributes of one-room schooling, while isolation, poorly trained teachers, and widely disparate funding and quality were reasons cited for its demise. In 1997, there were fewer than 500 one-teacher schools in the United States, down from a peak of 119,001 in 1937. (jv)

one-stop career centers

Centers funded through the U.S. Department of Labor aimed at consolidating programs, resources, and services that link employers with job seekers. Services available at the centers include Internet access and workshops related to the job search process, a variety of job-related training, and referral to adult basic skills programs. Although they were initially implemented earlier, these centers are part of a one-stop system mandated by the Workforce Investment Act of 1998. (las)

one-to-one correspondence

A pairing of the elements in a set A with the elements in a set B such that every element in set A is paired with exactly one element in set B, every element in set B is included in a pair, and no two elements from set B are paired to the same element in set A. (cmdv)

See also isomorphism.

online education

Use of the Internet and various types of information communication technology (ICT) to support the learning process to deliver educational materials and experiences. Also known as e-learning, student-teacher interaction occurs primarily through web-based synchronous and asynchronous interactions because the teacher and students are in different physical locations. (eh1, eb)

online tutorial

An online program designed to teach specific skills or competencies. Online tutorials may incorporate a variety of technologies, including sound and animation, and are commonly found in database packages, course management systems, and computer software programs. Online tutorials are effective and efficient methods of teaching sequential skills. (pw1)

onset

Within a syllable, the longest sequence of consonants to the left of each nucleus that does not violate the pronunciation constraints of the language in question (e.g., [st] forms the onset of the second syllable in *lobster*). (smt)

on-the-job training (OJT)

A form of workplace training designed to allow the individual to receive training, acquire knowledge, and/or develop required skills while doing his/her work. Such training usually involves acquisition of skills and knowledge about a task, opportunities to practice applying those skills and knowledge until a standard is met, and recognition of achievement of each standard. (jsj, las)

ontology

In metaphysics, the study of being and existence, an attempt to accurately and systematically explain what there is and what there is not. The term "ontology" is sometimes used to refer to the range of entities whose existence is acknowledged by a philosopher or presupposed by a theory. Thus one speaks of the ontology of a theory, and a philosopher is sometimes said to be committed to such-and-such an ontology; for example, an ontology of material objects and sets. (gu)

opaque

From the Latin *opacus,* meaning shaded or dark. The quality or state of being impervious to rays of light. One cannot see through something that is opaque, as there is no light to see through to the other side. In painting, opacity refers to the power of a pigment to cover or obscure the surface to which it is applied. Opaque is the opposite of transparent. The term is sometimes used across domains. For example, one might say, "That poem is opaque," and mean it was impossible to "see through," or literally, to understand. (kf)

open access

Free online access without copyright or licensing restrictions to scholarly articles and scientific literature produced by faculty and researchers at colleges and universities. The open access movement was driven by advances in Internet technology and by steep price increases in print journal subscriptions. Open access models are defined as either green or gold. Green open access occurs when an author publishes a scholarly article or scientific report in a traditional subscription-based journal and also deposits a copy of the work in one or more open access digital repositories. Gold open access occurs when an author publishes a scholarly article or scientific report in an open access online journal free of any access fees or barriers. (pw1)

open admissions

College or university policy that admits all students on a first come, first served basis with minimal or no entry requirements. Critics argue that the original goal of providing postsecondary education to the talented disadvantaged has been subverted, and the policy is now abused by many students and has resulted in lowered academic standards. Proponents cite success rate of graduates and favor policy reforms and increased support for public schools to improve student preparation. (nc)

open campus

A school policy that allows students to leave school grounds when not engaged in a structured school activity. Policies differ from school to school. In some, students are allowed to leave school property whenever not assigned to a class; others permit leaving the school site only during lunch. (jw)

open classroom

An instructional approach that emphasizes more student choice, individual and small-group work, curriculum integration, and flexible use of space. (bba)

open educational resources (OER)

Educational materials and content that are usually free and offered under various open licensing structures that allow the materials to be used, redesigned, and redistributed as needed. The term is often shortened to OER, and the philosophy surrounding open educational resources is similar to that of open source software. Examples of open educational resources include courseware, textbooks, learning objects, modules, and journals. (sds)

open enrollment plan

A system for enrolling students in schools based on the choice of parents or guardians. Most open enrollment plans allow students to enroll at any schools within a district, although some plans allow students to attend schools in another district. (bba)

open entry-open exit

Policy often applied in adult education programs whereby learners may enter or stop attending a class at any time. (las)

open house

An opportunity, usually in the early fall, for parents to visit their children's classrooms and meet the teachers. Typically, teachers describe their goals and plans for the year and give an overall picture of the curriculum they will follow. (bba)

open number sentence

An equation where one number is not provided and is usually replaced by "__," e.g., 3 + __ = 7. Usually used with students in the early years before the use of standard algebraic symbolism. This permits students to use the numbers that they comprehend the meaning of while they are engaged in a particular mathematical operation. (vdf)

Open School Movement

Refers to a period of elementary education reform that flourished in the 1960s and 1970s. Inspired by practices in England and Great Britain, the movement championed a system of education that responded to students' individual achievement levels, characteristics, and behaviors. In the United States, Charles E. Silberman was a leader through his 1970 classic *Crisis in the Classroom*. While proponents adhered to no standard curriculum, common practices followed the principles of open education, in which students select activities and learn at their own initiative. Teachers employed informal styles of instruction, moving freely about the classroom, guiding student work and recording progress. (ljl)

open skill

A motor skill that is performed in an environment that changes. (rf)

Open University

A distance education institution in the United Kingdom providing university and professional education to adult students in the United Kingdom and throughout the world since 1969. Curriculum is delivered through radio and television broadcasts, audio and videotapes, and computer software, supported by personal contact with locally based tutors and a network of regional study centers. Originally conceived to democratize higher education, the program features an open admissions policy. (dmv)

open-ended

Not closed to possibility, free from restrictions; free to argument, not settled; open to new ideas. In education, a type of questioning to encourage divergent thinking. When a teacher asks a question, is there only one right answer or more than one? A teacher supports his or her students' cognitive development/problem solving by considering a range of possible answers/responses. Children in a learning setting where there is usually only one answer tend to guess what answer/response the teacher wants. An open-ended approach to instructional practice and instruction encourages learners to consider multiple possibilities. (jls)

open-ended materials

Teaching resources that allow for multiple uses and/or individual interpretations, encouraging creative exploration and divergent experiences and expression. (db1)

open-ended question

Questions for which there are many correct or acceptable responses. In counseling, this is a specific type of question that allows a counselor, or therapist, to influence the quantity and quality of a client's response. Typically requires/encourages a longer, more detailed answer. "In what way was that hurtful?" is an example of an open-ended question. If used appropriately, these types of questions can help a counselor focus a conversation, explore a client's thoughts and feelings in depth, and clarify any misunderstandings. They can be particularly helpful with clients who are reluctant to disclose personal information. (ksp, bba)

operation

A mathematical action on one or more members of a given collection that results in a member of the given collection. Operations can be performed on real numbers, imaginary numbers, sets, vectors, polynomials, and functions. Operations can be designated by written notation. Examples: absolute value and square root are operations that can be performed on real numbers. Binary operations such as addition and multiplication combine two real numbers to yield a single real number. (ey)

operationalized curriculum

The explicit curriculum as presented, with changes made consciously and unconsciously. These may include (but are not restricted to) leaving out portions of, rearranging content sequences in, utilizing materials other than those stipulated in the explicit curriculum, and/or communicating attitudes about the explicit curriculum. These alterations are made based upon, among other things, personal dispositions toward the curriculum and/or subject area, notions of teaching and/or knowledge that differ from those instantiated in the explicit curriculum, or selecting ways of teaching and knowledge that become available in the teaching setting but are not accounted for in the explicit curriculum. Also known as taught curriculum. (db-j)

See also explicit curriculum; hidden curriculum; null curriculum.

oppositional ethnic behavior

A set of demeanors and attitudes that represent attempts from subdominant ethnic minority groups to distinguish themselves from the controlling majority mainstream culture, and in doing so, to resist the dominance of that culture. These differences can be constituted in language, dress, comportment, walk, and carriage, among other manifestations of identity. Relatedly, as autonomous cultural identities they represent challenges to the power and authority of the dominant culture. Such behaviors are considered representations of a culture that has arguably been ignored and rendered invisible in schools and the larger society. (hfs)

oppositional frame of reference

A strategy used by minorities to protect their cultural identity and to establish and maintain boundaries from the dominant social group. The division of social groups in school cafeterias may be seen as an instance of oppositional frame of reference. (jqa, npo)

oppression

Systematic, institutionalized mistreatment of one group of people by another. The oppressing group is viewed as having resources that enable them to impose their beliefs and values on others. The oppressed, not having similar resources, are subject to unfair treatment, ridicule, and potential internalized feelings of worthlessness. Bullying in schools can be viewed as one type of oppression. (jqa, npo)

optics

The branch of physics that studies the physical properties of light, its behavior, propagation, and interactions with matter. Optics can be considered as a subdivision of electromagnetism, as light is a form of electromagnetic radiation. The quantum nature of light also makes it part of the study of quantum mechanics or modern physics. (tw)

optimal period (See critical period)

oral examinations

A general term for the efforts of universities to review or appraise student achievement prior to certification or graduation; at the doctoral level, a typical "oral" would be a two- or three-hour session in which students are questioned by senior faculty who represent their various disciplines. (cf)

oral history

A method of preserving and recording personal accounts, past experiences, and events by interviewing subjects in order to record information that would not ordinarily appear on official documents. Oral history is the oldest form of recording history, predating the written word, and it emerged into an entire movement in 1948, when interviews were first recorded by use of tape recorders and transcribed for historical use. The modern form of oral history is a discipline in the field of history. (jrm)

oral language

Oral language development is generally referred to as a naturally occurring process. Oral language skills develop as children interact with their parents and others and develop understandings about the purposes and appropriate use of language. Oral language skills include two main components: knowledge of the structure of language, and the ability to use language in communication. Knowledge of the sound structure of spoken language, vocabulary skills, syntactic understanding, the ability to gain meaning from context, and skills in the social process of communication are all components of oral language. Oral language skills are often considered to be the basis for literacy skills; it has been found that oral language skills of children are predictors of reading achievement. (rcr)

oral phase

First phase in Freud's theory of psychosocial development, the oral phase begins at birth and lasts about 12 months. During this phase, the infant seeks gratification through oral stimulation and engages in such activities as sucking, biting, and swallowing. (xss)

oral rehearsal

A technique to improve writing in which students discuss and practice their ideas aloud before writing them. This technique has been shown to result in higher-quality writing. (cld)

orals (See oral examinations)

orchestra

From the Latin *orchstra*, the space in front of the stage in Greek theaters where the chorus performed. The area in a theater or concert hall where musicians sit (and just behind) is still called the orchestra, but the term more usually refers to a large ensemble including a full complement of string instruments (violin, viola, cello, bass, and occasionally harp) along with woodwinds, brass, and percussion instruments. The number of instruments included in each section can be used to identify a type of orchestra (symphony, philharmonic, or chamber); however, other than the chamber orchestra as the smallest group, there are no standardized rules regarding the use of such designations. (jbl)

orchestrated immersion

Process by which the learner is fully immersed into an environment created to allow the learner to fully experience all facets and stimuli associated with an event, activity, culture, concept, or idea. (ms)

ordinal number

This is the result of imposing an ordering on a group of objects; for example, the months of the year are ordered from the first month, January, through the twelfth month, December. (amr)

Orff method

"Orff Schulwerk." A method of teaching music and movement developed by German composer and music educator Carl Orff (1895–1982). The foundation of the method is the combination of music and movement into a playlike atmosphere that emphasizes learning music by hearing and making music first, through rhythmic movement and improvisation. This is followed by learning to use traditional notation to compose original music. Special child-sized xylophones with removable bars are used to facilitate improvisation and limit the opportunities to play wrong notes. Currently it is often taught in combination with the Kodaly method to ensure proper vocal training. (jbl)

See also Kodaly method.

organic chemistry
The branch of chemistry that studies compounds containing the element carbon. (tw)

organic inquiry
A qualitative methodology that places the stories of participants and researchers at the focal point of study. Participants give voice to the content and meaning of their experience, rather than researcher analysis, perspective, and understanding. (hfs)

organic intellectuals
Individuals who are the clerisy and organizing element of a given sociopolitical class. Their functionality is central to their identity as intellectuals. While all individuals are intellectuals, not all individuals serve in that capacity in either a sociopolitical class or in a larger society. Their function is to direct, develop, and articulate the modes of thought (political, philosophical) and aspirations of their distinct class, and in this way particularize their class. (hfs)

organizational behavior
How people as individuals and groups act within an organization. Organizational behavior in the context of a school is the culture, policies, and traditions that make up an educational enterprise. The key elements in organizational behavior are people, structure, and technology and the environment in which it operates. The behavior of an organization is often evaluated and analyzed in terms of four models: human resources, contingency, productivity, and systems. The human resources model looks at how employee growth and development is nurtured and supported. The contingency model examines how different behaviors are required by different environments for effectiveness. The productivity model focuses on how organizational behaviors are assessed in terms of their efficiency. The systems model describes how all parts of an organization interact in a complex relationship. Leadership roles, communication, and decision-making processes are frequently mentioned facets of organizational behavior that determine the ability of an organization to learn and improve. Three organizational behaviors that are thought to lead to and foster learning within an organization are openness to new experiences, encouragement of responsible risk-taking, and a willingness to acknowledge failure and to learn from failure. (ly)

organizational discrimination (See institutional discrimination)

organizational intelligence
The factual data, information, and knowledge that are selected and stored for use in appraising trends, developments, crises, and related events reflecting an organization's past and providing counsel and advice for planning in the future. (cf)

organizational politics
A term used in education when referring to the realities of organizational life that often undermine rationality. Coalitions of individuals and groups bargain to determine the distribution of power in organizations. They can be destructive or constructive. Ingratiating, networking, information management, impression management, coalition building, and scapegoating are common political tactics used by members to gain advantage. Political games are played to resist authority, to counter the resistance to authority, to build power bases, to defeat rivals, and to produce organizational change. Organizational politics can be successfully

managed through collaboration, accommodation, or compromise. (mm)

organizing data or information
Organizing information for future use requires knowledge and decision making in the determination of meaningful classifications for easy retrieval and application. The computerized database allows for quick retrieval of only the information that meets particular criteria by enabling the user to delete, combine, broaden, or narrow a category of data at will. Databases are useful to educators in teaching logical thinking, problem solving, and information handling, while students are taught to build their own databases or use the ones provided. (igb)

orientation
Activities that take place at the start of a course of study designed to help students become familiar with the learning institution. In adult education programs, orientation generally addresses program and teacher expectations, clarification of learner goals, and identification of strengths and needs. (las)

orthographic depth
The degree of correspondence between the letters and phonemes of a language. Shallow orthographies have close to one-to-one letter-phoneme correspondence, while deep orthographies do not have one-to-one correspondence between letters and phonemes. Languages such as English and Hebrew are orthographically deep, while Spanish and Finnish are relatively shallow. (cld)

orthography
A set of standard accepted conventions for the usage of written or printed symbols to represent the sound or meaning units of a language within a given writing system. The study of the established usage conventions of writing systems. The art of using the symbols of a writing system according to established conventions. (ml)

Oswego Movement
Educational movement based on the principles of Johann Pestalozzi's "object method." Edward A. Sheldon of Oswego, New York, and Margaret Jones of England created a training school in 1861, which became the Oswego State Normal and Training School in New York (1865). The method focused on the acquisition of knowledge through interaction with natural objects, observation, inquiry, and use of the five senses. The movement was most prominent between the years 1861 and 1886. Teacher training through the Oswego program helped to popularize the practice by taking the methodology across the country and through adaptation at other normal schools. (ljl)

See also object teaching.

othering
A process that distinguishes, marks, and names those thought to be different from one's identity, particular collective, or community, often through comparative devaluation and judgment. In this way, one's identity is affirmed as normal. (hfs)

outdoor education
Broadly refers to all aspects of education about, for, and in the natural environment. The term may also refer to a distinct field of education that assumes that the best way to learn about the environment is through direct contact with nature. Direct experiences in the outdoors provide for both the identification and resolving of "real-life" problems. Other related terms include adventure learning and environmental education. (hrm, ew, jkd)

outdoor play
Refers to opportunities to play outside of the classroom or home. Usually scheduled as part of daily routines in the classroom setting, outdoor play can help children develop gross motor skills, social skills, and vivid imaginations. Special precautions, such as fencing, padded surfaces under structures where children fall, close

supervision, and careful maintenance of equipment must be observed. (jlj)

outreach
The extension of university resources and services in the form of professional knowledge and expertise to the general public and its constituencies, and to assist in the amelioration of societal problems. (cf)

outsourcing
Obtaining resources or contracting work from sources outside an institution or area. (ja)

OVAE (See Office of Vocational and Adult Education)

overachievement
Accomplishment beyond the level expected. Performance that exceeds the level predicted by previous assessments of potential. (jw)

overexcitabilities
An aspect of Polish psychiatrist Kazimierz Dabrowski's (1902–1980) Theory of Positive Disintegration, which has drawn particular attention from educators of "gifted" students. Dabrowski posited that some individuals were prone to a more intense and longer than normal physiological response to stimuli. He identified five forms of these overexcitabilities: psychomotor, sensual, imaginational, intellectual, and emotional. He argued that overexcitabilities are central to both the psychological development and life experience of those who experience them. In Dabrowski's theory, overexcitabilities are understood as a neurological difference from the norm. Though overexcitabilities are based in the nervous system, through the development of structures that reflect the emergence of a sense of self, they come to be expressed psychologically. In Dabrowski's work with 80 gifted children and young people in the late 1960s, he found that all of them exhibited at least some of the five overexcitabilities. The concept of overexcitabilities has since been utilized by educators to support assertions of developmental difference and account for variance in social behavior, and it has been extended as a basis for assessing potential among gifted students. (bda)

See also positive disintegration.

overt behaviors (See covert/overt behaviors)

P

papier-mâché

An artistic process whereby paper strips (often newspaper) are soaked in a mixture of flour and water (flour paste) and layered on to a base (e.g., a balloon, an imprint of a face for a mask) to create a firm hard substance. A frequent and popular school art medium, papier-mâché seems to children as the process of turning paper back into wood. (jd)

paradigm

A set of beliefs accepted without question and used as a frame for seeing the world. Originally applied to scientific work (see Kuhn, *The Structure of Scientific Revolutions*, 1996), the term now is applied more generally. Kuhn proposed that "paradigm shifts" occur when one way of looking at the world is replaced rapidly by another, a decision made outside the bounds of evidence. This revolutionary replacing of one scientific theory with another is in contrast to what he called "normal science." Kuhn's thesis directly challenged a central assumption of logical positivism, which considered such changes rational and therefore susceptible to mathematical modeling. Paradigm is used in educational research to refer to the complex set of fundamental beliefs that contribute to decision making about research. Specifically, a paradigm dictates one's reasons for doing research, the types of questions asked in research, the methodology used to conduct the research, the relationship of the researcher to the participant, as well as the final form of reporting the research. Identifying a particular paradigm requires that a person address issues of ontology, epistemology, methodology, and axiology. The term "paradigm" is often coupled with words like qualitative, quantitative, positivist, postpositivist, interpretivist, and constructivist. Each term when paired with the word paradigm reflects a particular way of viewing the world that includes what one believes about reality, knowledge, inquiry, truth, and relationships. (grw, als)

See also philosophy of science.

paradigm pioneer

A paradigm pioneer is one who realizes the importance of the opportunity at hand, visualizes its far-reaching potential, and accepts the challenge of taking the new paradigm, or mindset, from concept to application. Paradigm pioneers typically share three characteristics: intuition, courage, and long-term commitment to change. (tp)

paradoxical intention/technique

A therapeutic procedure whereby an unwanted behavior is eliminated or reduced by prescribing its performance or by magnifying some aspect of the behavior. This technique is particularly useful for clients who are resistant to therapeutic advice, who are noncompliant with treatment, and who have anxiety disorders. This technique may also serve to help clients distance themselves from their problematic behavior and gain a different perspective on the actual consequences associated with the behavior. (tsw)

paraeducator (See paraprofessional)

parallel curriculum
Curriculum models offered at several levels for teaching in heterogeneous classrooms by offering alternative tracks to enable students to acquire the basic and more advanced skills. (sr)

parallel instruction (See parallel curriculum)

parallel postulate
The fifth axiom of Euclidean geometry. It can be stated: given a line and a point not on the line, exactly one line can be drawn through the given point parallel to the given line. When challenged, alternate postulates can be constructed that define internally consistent non-Euclidean geometries such as spherical geometry (no parallel lines exist) and hyperbolic geometry (many parallel lines exist). (ey)

parallel thinking
A process of thinking in which both sides of an argument are considered at the same time. In contrast to the Socratic method of analysis, argument, and judgment, parallel thinking allows for the nonjudgmental consideration of both, or more, sides of an issue or dilemma, leading to resolution. (jwc)

paraphrase
A specific type of listening response that involves summarizing or restating the content, or "essence," of a client's comments,

so as to verify the accuracy of a counselor's perceptions and/or to bolster a client's confidence that the counselor is, indeed, hearing accurately what he or she is saying. (bmm)

See also restatement.

paraprofessional
In education, paraprofessional refers to those who do not have a teaching certificate but who work with children in the classroom with and under the supervision of a certified teacher as teacher aides, instructional aides, or assistants. They work in the educational setting to assist teachers in making instruction more effective and more efficient. Several areas in which paraprofessionals may work include: preparation of classroom materials, tutoring students, supervision of small groups or individual students, clerical duties, operation of equipment (audiovisual, computers). Job requirements and training vary by state and by duty assigned, with some states requiring special licensing or certification for paraprofessionals. (bba, bs)

parent education
A structured program that teaches the skills, knowledge, and attitudes assumed to be important in the raising of children. These programs often utilize curriculum to teach parents how to care for their child, including feeding and diapering, child development, discipline, meaningful activities, health/medical care, bonding, and a variety of specialized topics requested by the parents or deemed necessary by the professional. Parent education programs are as varied as parents are themselves. Some are voluntary, while the courts or child protective agencies mandate others. Some are center/office-based while others are home-based. The goal of parent education programs, however, is universal in that parent education is designed to teach, inform, and guide parents in their role as caregivers. (kdc, jpc)

parent involvement

The involvement and support of parents or guardians in the schooling and care of their children. Parent involvement entails honest, open, and frequent communication and cooperation between parents and teacher. Extensive parent involvement facilitates information exchange that can better meet the individual needs of children and families. Examples of parent involvement activities include parents as classroom volunteers, special events such as holiday parties, luncheons or picnics, parents as field trip chaperones, and parent inclusion in management groups. (bba, jlj)

Parent Teacher Association (PTA); Parent Teacher Organization (PTO)

An organization, at the school or district level, of parents or guardians of children enrolled in the school or district. These organizations have regularly scheduled meetings and annual fundraising events to serve the needs of the school or district. The parents typically do the greatest amount of work on the committees, although teachers are usually represented as well. (bba)

See also parents' organizations.

parentocracy

Set of relationships whereby an individual child's education becomes increasingly dependent upon the economic characteristics and ambitions of parents, rather than intrinsic student ability or effort. In addition, such an arrangement reflects a change in educational decision making and parental involvement from a collective sensibility to a more individual consumerist, or free market, sensibility. (hfs)

Parents, Families, & Friends of Lesbians and Gays (PFLAG)

PFLAG is a global grassroots organization committed to support for Lesbian, Gay, Bisexual, and Transgender individuals and their families, friends, and allies through educational and political advocacy. Founded in New York in 1972 as a haven for parents of lesbian and gay children, the organization has since expanded in reach and mission. PFLAG has initiated a number of legal campaigns, including the expansion of the Title IX ruling in the 1990s to include protection of lesbian and gay students from harassment in educational programs in the United States. (smh, wpa)

parents' organizations

Generally, a volunteer group of parents organized to improve education by strengthening communication and collaboration between the home and school. Activities of parents' organizations may include fundraising, community service projects, parent education programs, or support of school activities. Usually parents join together not only to exercise some control over the business of the school, but also to meet one another. The most common parent organization in the United States is the Parent Teacher Association, which was formed in the late 1800s. By 1954, the National Parent Teacher Association had grown to 7.5 million members. By the mid-1980s, it had declined considerably. Early names for this organization were Home-and-School Associations, Parent-Teacher Associations, The National Congress of Mothers, and The National Congress of Parents and Teachers. (jr)

See also Parent Teacher Association.

parent-teacher conference

A meeting between a teacher and a student's parent(s) or guardian(s) for the purpose of discussing the student's performance and progress in areas such as academic achievement, social and emotional issues, attendance, attitude, work habits, special aptitudes, or other characteristics or activities. Usually lasting 15 to 30 minutes, parent-teacher conferences may be scheduled at regular times during the school year or can be initiated by school personnel or the parent. (ba)

parietal lobe (See lobes of the brain)

participant feedback (See member check)

participant observation
The hallmark of ethnographic fieldwork, participant observation is the standard methodological technique employed, whereby to the extent welcomed by informants and made practical by circumstances, an ethnographer lives in and experiences directly the life and culture being studied. By engaging in participant observation, the ethnographer hopes to understand in greater depth what it feels like and means to be a native. It provides what Clifford Geertz has called the ethnographic authority of "being there." (jde)

participant-centered learning
A form of learning that takes place when there are peer-to-peer discussions of real-world problems, organizations, and situations. Learning takes place in an environment that is created by both those who are learning as well as the teacher. By working together, the students create their own knowledge. A form of experiential learning that employs case methodology. (ms)

participatory democracy
Sometimes known as "direct democracy," participatory democracy emphasizes the importance of ongoing, direct, active involvement by citizens in the fundamental dimensions of their democratic life. While liberal approaches emphasize protecting the sphere of autonomous individuals who engage in politics only to preserve their privacy, participatory democracy is based on and also promotes a vibrant and lively public realm or civil society in which citizens engage in politics as a fundamental dimension of life. While proceduralism emphasizes the administrative dimensions of democracy, such as voting, electoral reforms, governmental structures, administrative processes, and so on, participatory

democracy is more robust and comprehensive, akin to Dewey's description of democracy as a "way of life" (1916). In his *Strong Democracy* (1984), Benjamin Barber articulates the limitations of representative democracy due to its overemphasis on the importance of elected representatives as the primary democratic agents rather than an engaged and active citizenry in participatory democracy. As a political and social movement, it is a product of student, feminist, ecological, and community movements beginning in the 1960s and continuing into the 21st century. (tn)
See also democracy; democratic education; civic education.

participatory education
An approach to instruction that involves students as active partners in the design and implementation of their own learning and where teachers act as facilitators. (las)

participatory research
A type of research in which the researcher is part of the process being studied. Researchers identify the research question through a problem or issue that arises in their work. This research strategy includes a variety of methods focused on developing challenges to social, political, and economic power through the shared, reciprocal, and intentional breaking of traditional paradigms of objective researcher/researched roles and the development of new investigative paradigms. The researched assume responsibility for shaping the research agenda, tools of inquiry, analysis, and dissemination of findings along with the researcher. Any such process should consist of three conjoined features: research, education, and action. The intent is to coconstruct knowledge that could facilitate change and transform circumstance. (las, hfs)

particularist
An approach to social diversity that holds that basic differences exist among

individuals across various ideologies, social locations, and aspects of identity. In certain cases, these perceptions and constructions of difference could be used to subordinate others, while in other cases the differences could be used as instruments of liberation. (hfs)

partitive division
A form of intuitive division in which objects or a collection of objects are separated into a number of equal groups or smaller collections. The divisor should be a whole number and smaller than the dividend; the quotient must also be smaller than the dividend. This model of division is often termed sharing division. (slr)

partnership
In education, joint ventures created by school system staff to promote school-community cooperation, provide incentives for students, supplement curriculum and staff, and obtain equipment. Business and industry achieve improved public relations and enhanced community image from these relationships. In teacher education, a collaboration among different institutions, including but not limited to schools, social service agencies, cultural institutions, businesses, industries, and institutions of higher education, for the purpose of improving teacher education and student outcomes. This approach allows different organizations to pool resources to address institutional and community needs. (jb, clk)

part-whole
The fractional portion or ratio of a selected amount in comparison to the total amount. How the portion of the whole relates to the whole. The relationship between the whole amount and the part. The part-whole interpretation of fractions is the one highlighted in many elementary mathematics programs. (vdf)

PASS (See Planning, Attention, Simultaneous, Successive theory)

passport, career (See career passport)

patriotism (See nationalism/patriotism)

patron
A patron is someone who pays for the production or performance of a piece of art or writing. An art patron may also commission, or request the production of a specific and completely new work of art. Patrons may also support art institutions rather than specific works or artists. Because they lend vital support to art making, patrons may also have some control over what kind of art is made or performed, although usually this control is demonstrated through preferences rather than actual censorship or dictation of exactly what an artist does or makes. (ap)

pattern
A form, shape, or figure proposed for imitation. Patterns can be chance or natural configurations and have observable characteristics. Patterns can be units of units, a sequence, or grouping that can be repeated. (jdk)

pauper schools
Also called "charity" or, in the northern states, "free" schools. Pauper schools were made available to orphaned, poor, or homeless children during the last of the 18th and first part of the 19th centuries. Usually supported by charitable contributions, but sometimes with state or local funds, the schools taught basic literacy, numeracy, and Christian beliefs, often using the Lancastrian or monitorial method. The association of pauper schools with the new public schools of the mid-19th century often delayed the common school movement, particularly in the southern states. (crsg)

PBL (See problem-based learning)

PDA (See handheld computer)

PDP (See professional development points)

PDS (See professional development schools)

Peabody Education Fund
Named for its benefactor, George Peabody (1795–1869), who originally donated $1 million to the southern states in 1867 "for the promotion and encouragement of intellectual, moral or industrial education." The fund was administered by Barnas Sears, former president of Brown University, from 1867 until his death in 1881, and by an advisory board of 15 members. The Peabody Fund created matching grants for public school systems in the southern states and provided extensive funds, first for teacher training institutes and later for normal schools throughout the South. At the end of the fund in 1914, it had distributed $3.4 million to aid schooling and had established the George Peabody College for teachers at Vanderbilt University. (vmm)

Peace Corps (See AmeriCorps)

peace education
Education for peace is based on a commitment to nonviolence as a political and social tool to solve conflicts. Its primary aim is to reduce structural violence and create social justice. Other overlapping topics are international studies, global education, and education for world citizenship. Peace education implies drawing out of people their desires to live in peace and emphasizes peaceful values upon which society should be based. Peace educators warn about the hazards of violence broadly construed—wars, civil strife, domestic conflict, and environmental destruction. Peace education has three stages: identification of the problems of violence; instruction about alternatives to violence; and a commitment to take action to address some of problems identified in stage one. It fits within the tradition of education for social responsibility, in which teachers ask their students to address urgent problems. (cd, ih)

pedagogical content knowledge
A term introduced by L. S. Shulman (1986) to denote teachers' knowledge about the nature of children's minds, how those minds work when learning takes place, and the role instruction plays in fostering learning. It also includes the teacher's knowledge of subject matter and the most effective way to introduce it to the student. (ja)

pedagogy
Refers to the art and profession of teaching. It stands for how a teacher teaches, the methodology one uses as a teacher, and the style of teaching a teacher chooses. It also refers to the preparatory training or instruction would-be teachers acquire in teacher education programs. (bt-b)
See also teaching.

pedagogy of place
Pedagogy of place refers to knowledge and practice about the art of teaching that supports the creation of a curriculum of place. This knowledge is based on a recognition of the need to connect instruction to the day-to-day lives of young people and to contextualize instructional goals in the places in which students live. (lr)
See also curriculum of place.

pedagogy of poverty
Teaching practices identified by Haberman, which are responsible for maintaining low levels of academic achievement among poor students. There are 14 of these practices, including, but not limited to, giving information, giving tests, punishing noncompliance, and giving grades. It is both the combination and preponderance of these activities to the exclusion of all other practices that is particularly devastating and troubling. Students are locked into traditional pedagogies and

curricula that do not allow for creativity or alternate modes of learning. (hfs)

peer coaching
An instructional setting in which teachers work together to develop and improve teaching practice, often including collaborative goal setting, observations of one another's teaching, and formative feedback on progress toward meeting goals. (rtc)

peer debriefing
A technique to address the validity of a qualitative study. The researcher meets with one or more external reviewers or colleagues for the purpose of reflecting on the process of the research, in particular, the researcher's effect on the research. The peer debriefer acts as devil's advocate and provides feedback concerning the accuracy and completeness of the researcher's design, data collection, and analysis procedures. (mas)

peer review
Process by which manuscripts are sent to experts in a discipline for review before being accepted for publication. In most cases, reviewers do not know the author of the manuscript, a process called "blind" or "masked" peer review. When two or three reviewers who do not know the identity of the author are required, the process is referred to as "double blind" or "triple blind" review. There are different levels of peer review, and some periodicals consider editorial review to be a form of peer review. Not without controversy, the peer review process has been criticized for being unacceptably slow and because even with multiple reviewer there have been some highly publicized instances of inaccurate and/or fraudulent information being published. (sn)

peer teaching
A method wherein prospective teachers practice lessons or teaching strategies using other prospective teachers as both a surrogate class and a source of feedback. (rtc)

peer tutoring
The assignment of students to assist one another in learning tasks either on a one-to-one basis or in small groups. Such assistance is provided by a fellow student competent in the curriculum. Three types of peer tutoring models exist: older students tutor students in lower grades, usually outside of class; students tutor other students within the same class; and two students help each other as equals in the learning situation. (bba, sr)

Pell Grant
Financial aid in the form of grants provided by the federal government to low-income undergraduate students and postbaccalaureate students in certain programs. Eligibility is determined based upon expected family contribution, cost of attendance, enrollment status (full- or part-time) and length of attendance (full or partial year). These grants differ from loans in that they do not need to be repaid by the student. Established in 1972 as part of the reauthorization of the *Higher Education Act of 1965,* Pell Grants were originally called Basic Educational Opportunity Grants (BEOGs). They were later renamed Pell Grants in honor of Senator Claiborne Pell, Democrat from Rhode Island, who was a major proponent of the legislation to establish these federal grants for low-income students. (pw1)

Pensionado Act of 1903
Legislation enacted by the Second Philippine Commission under the direction of William Howard Taft during his term as the first civilian American governor-general of the Philippines. The act created a program, known as the pensionado program, which financed the studies of selected Filipino students in the United States. The program ran from 1903 to 1928, and it was commonly viewed as a method to foster goodwill between Filipinos and Americans after

the annexation of the Philippines by the United States in 1899. Many in the U.S. government also felt the program would contribute to the eventual independence of the Philippine islands, which came in 1946. The first 100 pensionados were selected from approximately 20,000 applications from 37 provinces within the Philippines. Pensionado students came from the top Philippine elite families, and many later became national leaders in government, education, and business upon their return to the Philippines. Being selected for the pensionado program was very prestigious, as the original criteria included moral and physical qualifications as well as high social status. (nt)

people of color

A term used to refer to individuals identifiable because of physical characteristics, often including skin color. People of color often face discrimination in various forms and are easily targeted. Historically, educational institutions routinely segregated or provided inequitable learning opportunities to people of color. (jqa, npo)

percent correct score

Percent correct score is the proportion of items that are answered correctly on a test. It is computed by dividing the number of correct answers by the total number of test items, and multiplying the result by 100. It ranges from 0 to 100. Because the percent correct score is a standardization technique that takes into account differences in scale and the total number of items between tests, it allows a comparison of test-takers' performance across different measures of the same construct, assuming these measures have similar difficulty levels. However, if two tests have different overall difficulty level or different distributions of item difficulties, the percent correct score may become misleading. (gl)

percentile ranking

Percentile ranking is the percentage of examinees in a group that have lower test scores than a given examinee. When the sample is large and representative, percentile ranking provides useful information about the individual's performance compared to the rest in the group. However, percentile ranking is sample dependent and can be misleading if the sample is small with a heavily skewed distribution. (gl)

perception

An awareness of the elements of the environment and self through sight, sound, taste, smell, or touch. This information is used to acquaint one with the world, and it is an important source of ideas. Empiricists hold that these ideas are the building blocks of language and give meaning to words. Others argue that perception, since it is mediated by the senses, is undependable as a source of knowledge. Meaningful objects, such as trees, faces, books, tables, and dogs, are normally seen rather than separately perceived as the dots, lines, colors, and other elements of which they are composed. In the language of Gestalt psychologists, immediate human experience is of organized wholes, not of collections of elements. Behavioral psychologists tend to dehumanize perceptual theory and research. When attention is limited to objective stimuli and responses, parallels can readily be drawn between perceiving (by living organisms) and information processing (by such devices as electronic computers). (kpb, rk)

perceptual learning

A type of learning that involves interactions with the environment that lead to a change in perception. Perceptual learning may also be an improvement in perceptual understanding of some activity or object with practice and repetition. An example of perceptual learning might be developing an appreciation that was previously lacking for a style of music. (npo)

perceptual unit items (counting)

Things that can be seen and touched as they are being counted, such as beads or fingers. These items have to be in the child's perceptual field. (amr)

See also children's counting schemes.

percipience

The power of perceiving especially keenly and attentively. Associated by art philosophers like Ralph Smith and Harold Osborne with perception of objects and experiences in the world of art. Smith sees percipience as the goal of arts education—to imbue students with the heightened capacities of intellect and sensitivity required to make and find understanding in the worlds of art and culture. (jd)

See also aesthetic education; perception.

percussion

The family of instruments that produce sound by being shaken or struck in some manner. Instruments may be divided into two categories: membranophones, instruments with a natural or synthetic skin that vibrates to produce sound, generically known as drums; and idiophones, instruments of solid construction that produce sound when hit, shaken, or rubbed, such as gongs, bells, wood blocks, maracas, and the like. A second manner of categorizing percussion instruments is that of fixed pitch (e.g., xylophone, piano, tubular bells) or indefinite pitch (e.g., gong, cymbal, snare drum). Modern composers have expanded the definition of percussion to include such found instruments as metal garbage cans and lids, brake drums, basketballs, and children's toys. (jbl)

perennialism

The view that truth is permanent and lasting and that education should pass on those truths that human experience has already proved and proved to be worth knowing. Like essentialism, perennialism argues for a curriculum that should be taught to everyone, but in contrast to essentialists, perennialists argue that there are things worth knowing for their own sake. In strong contrast to progressives,

perennialists oppose all forms of vocational education. (jc)

See also essentialism; progressivism.

perennialist curriculum

Program of study that assumes the possibility and existence of universal and absolute truths. It is based on the assertion that all students must accept the same cultural premises and perspectives as objective truths despite any differences in either individual or collective cultural identity. (hfs)

performance

A public presentation in front of an audience of, for example, a play, dance piece, musical composition, or opera; also, the work of any individual in that presentation. Performance can be seen as a craft unto itself, with a set of skills—including, for example, awareness of self on stage, understanding of relationship to audience, and use of body and voice (or musical instrument)—applicable to presentational work across arts dimensions. In nonarts education, performance-based assessment is judged on this sense of a demonstration of skills in action. (em)

performance art

A hybrid art form, making use of a variety of arts and media (including dramatic monologues, comedy, dance, music, film and video, painting, found objects), with the central element being presentation for an audience. Artistically close to experimental theater, contemporary performance art is rooted in the spontaneous happenings popular in the mid-20th century and the use of real events as artistic performance. More recent performance art pieces are often rehearsed and scripted. Performance art includes interpretive, abstract, nonrepresentational pieces and often is underpinned by sociopolitical critique, commentary, or deconstruction of convention. (em)

performance assessment

Analysis of an individual's or group's performance in order to identify discrepancies that can be addressed through education. A measure of academic achievement that offers an alternative to standardized tests. Such assessments measure how well students apply knowledge to the real world. Performance assessments are best known in the form of portfolios or projects that allow children to demonstrate their skills by completing a certain task or activity. An important advantage of performance assessments is that they allow teachers to measure student growth over time. Within teacher education, performance assessment is an analytical and judgmental analysis of teaching practice based on observations of actual classroom behavior. (aw, chb, rtc)

performance feedback

Evaluative information given to an individual from an external source regarding how well a person is performing specific tasks or behaviors; may include the feedback-giver's perceptions of the effects of those tasks or behaviors. (ktc)

performance IQ

Derives from a weighted average of a subject's raw scores on five of the performance subtests that are part of the battery of subtests that constitute the Wechsler Scales of Intelligence. A performance IQ is heavily influenced by a person's immediate problem-solving skills and correlates with most activities that are more valued in our society as "spatial perceptual." The performance IQ is perceived to be a numerical measurement of a person's "performance and visual discrimination intelligence," which are psychological constructs and can therefore never be proven. (aw)

performance simulation

An artificially created activity that invites an individual to perform certain tasks or roles in a lifelike situation and lends itself to the establishment of standards for assessing that performance. Techniques include structured interviews, in-basket exercises, case studies, and live interactions. (chb)

performance-based education

A form of teaching and learning that emphasizes the performance of skills and knowledge as evidence of learning. (las)

performing arts

Artistic domains that are based on presentation in front of an audience (e.g., drama, dance, and music). Distinguished from other art forms (e.g., literature, visual arts including painting, photography, and sculpture) by virtue of the action in time of the performance (as opposed to a work that can be revisited numerous times) and the relationship with a live audience (as opposed to encounters with readers or viewers who are unknown to the artist). Performance in front of a live audience has traditionally provided a powerful and memorable experience for school children developing a sense of themselves and their relation to/impact on others. (em)

peripheral nervous system (See nervous system)

Perkins Act (See Carl D. Perkins Vocational and Applied Technology Education Act Amendments of 1990 and 1998; Carl Perkins Vocational Education Act of 1985)

perlocutionary act

The response (usually an action) of the hearer to the utterance. For example, if Person A asks Person B: "Are you too warm?" and in response Person B stands up and opens a window, the perlocutionary act of the utterance is the physical act of opening the window. Person B's action is a direct result of the illocutionary force of Person A's utterance. (smt)

permeability

Refers to school-to-work transition systems and the ability of students to easily move from one location in the system or program to another and change direction at any time. (hfs)

permissive discipline
A plan of discipline in which the adult consistently permits the child to make his or her own choices, intervening little in the child's development. This method is child-centered, but because the adult is nondemanding and accepts the child's impulses, children frequently learn to be impulsive and aggressive, and in addition less self-reliant and explorative than their peers. (ecr)

per-pupil cost
Accounting for expenses by dividing costs by number of pupils being served. (sr)

perseverate
To repeat persistently for no apparent reason. (sr)

persistence
In adult education, the combination of intensity (usually hours per month) and duration (usually total months) of study by adults to accomplish a personal goal, which is usually expressed as the total number of hours of study within a 12-month period. Also, a process in which adult students study in class, study on their own when they are not able to attend class, and then reenter class when they are again able. (cas)

person
A term with various technical and semi-technical usages in philosophy and law. In law, person refers either to human beings who are capable of rights and duties, or to entities, such as corporations, created by law and given certain legal rights and duties of a human being. Person has a particular importance in moral philosophy. Person can be distinguished from such related terms as human being, individual, homo sapiens, man, self, and so forth. The locus of the distinction is that person connotes reason and intelligence. (pk)

See also individualism; liberalism; self.

personal learning environment
The way in which a student creates his/her place within the virtual learning community of an online course. The student picks the online course tools that will help him/her to interact efficiently and effectively within the online course, while also promoting optimal personal learning according to his/her learning style. (mkrf)

personal response system (PRS)
An educational technology through which learners in a classroom setting use remote control devices (often referred to as "clickers") to answer questions posed by the instructor. This technology consists of an integrated system that uses software and remote control devices to gather, tally, and display audience responses. Instructors have the opportunity to poll learners to gain immediate input, and each learner has the opportunity to interact within a large classroom setting. (ln)

See also clicker technology.

personalism
An approach in philosophy many centuries old, holding that the cosmos is ultimately personal. For some this entailed a god, or God. For others it meant that, since the nature of all things is ultimately personal, our human systems (e.g., government, education, social systems) need to take into account persons and aspects of humanity to be effective and holistic. A more formal system called personalism was developed by Walt Whitman and Borden Parker Bowne, among others, at the end of the 19th and beginning of the 20th centuries. (sc)

personality disorder
A category of mental disorders characterized by pervasive and persistent patterns of maladaptive interpersonal behavior that deviate markedly from the expectations of an individual's culture. The enduring behavior pattern is inflexible and pervasive across a broad range of personal

and social situations and invariably leads to clinically significant distress or impairment in important areas of functioning (e.g., school, work). Considered to be an aberration of "normal" personality development, often involving early, fixed, and maladaptive ways of relating to self and others. (do)

personality test
One of a class of assessment instruments designed to evaluate an individual's personal traits or characteristics. These instruments may be theoretically based or atheoretical, may utilize objective or projective techniques, and may range from assessing normal interpersonal functioning to psychopathology. A variety of personality tests are used in mental health, medical, vocational, and educational settings. Uses for personality tests include assessing strengths and weaknesses, assisting with diagnosis, predicting response to treatment, and/or enhancing self-understanding. (cap)

person-environment fit (P-E Fit)
According to Holland, P-E Fit is the match between an individual's personality traits (i.e., person) and work-setting characteristics (i.e., environment). Personality traits and work settings are classified as Realistic, Investigative, Artistic, Social, Enterprising, and Conventional (RIASEC). Others such as Rene Dawis define P-E Fit slightly differently, that is, as the interaction between an individual's needs (reinforcers) and work-setting requirements (skills). (sc)

perspective
Linear perspective is a system of drawing or painting in which the artist attempts to create the illusion of depth on a flat surface. The lines of objects in a picture are slanted inward, making them appear to extend back into space. If lengthened, these lines will meet at a point along an imaginary horizontal line representing eye level. Each such imaginary line is called an orthogonal. The point at which such lines meet is called a vanishing point. This system will work only if one is parallel and perpendicular (90-degree angles) to the objects that one is drawing. (kpb)

perspective transformation
A term introduced by Jack Mezirow that describes an impact of adult education in which the student develops a more inclusive way of interpreting experience. (jpc)

Pestalozzianism
Educational philosophy of Swiss teacher Johann Heinrich Pestalozzi (1746–1827), which rejected traditional 18th-century teaching methods based on rote memorization and corporal punishment. Pestalozzianism is founded on the idea that children learn best by observing and analyzing the objects in their world under the guidance of professionally trained teachers. Pestalozzianism also holds that children require an emotionally secure school/home environment in order to develop intellectually, morally, and physically. Pestalozzianism was introduced to the United States in the early 19th century and gradually gained in acceptance, particularly through the Oswego Movement. (nc)

See also Oswego Movement.

PET (See Positron Emission Tomography)

PFLAG (See Parents, Families, & Friends of Lesbians and Gays)

phallic phase
The third phase in Freud's theory of psychosocial development is the phallic phase that begins at age three and lasts for about 24 to 36 months. During this phase, children aim to resolve their sexual identities and seek gratification through their sex organs. Freud theorized that children develop conflicting feelings and become sexually interested in the parent of the opposite sex in this phase. (xss)

phase theories of adult learning

Theories that emphasize the skills and roles to be learned at certain age-related phases of an adult's development. The theories center on the content and essence of the task at hand rather than on the changing nature of the individual's capabilities or psychological structures; no phase is judged to be better or more mature than any other phase. (jwg)

See also stage theories of adult learning.

Ph.D. (See degree, doctor's)

Phelps-Stokes Fund

A nonprofit foundation founded in 1911, whose mission is to improve educational opportunities of African Americans, Native Americans, Africans, and the rural and urban poor. It was established by the will of Caroline Phelps Stokes (1854–1909), a New York philanthropist. The Fund's early policies emphasized agricultural and industrial education for southern blacks and was exported to British colonies. The Fund also sponsored landmark reports on African American education (1916), education in Africa (1922 and 1924), and Native American education (1928). Today the Fund continues its mission with several centers and collaboration with public and private agencies. (clp)

phenomenology

A form of British empiricist philosophy. A philosophic method developed by Edmund Husserl. In educational research circles, a form of educational inquiry devoted to explicating the "lived experience" of people in learning situations (not restricted to schools). A descriptive practice, the phenomenologist's interest is in understanding both the essential characteristics of experience that transcend local conditions and the structures of consciousness whereby experience is possible. (db-j)

phenotype

The observable, outward characteristics of an individual organism. One's phenotype is influenced by one's genotype and interactions with the environment. (sd1)

Phi Beta Kappa

Phi Beta Kappa, with the initials PBK of the Greek motto *Philosophia Biouy Kubernetes* (Love of wisdom, the guide of life), is an honor society with a purpose to recognize and foster excellence in the undergraduate liberal arts and sciences. Founded on December 5, 1776, at the College of William and Mary in Williamsburg, Virginia, its insignia of a golden key became recognized as a symbol for the highest academic achievement. (ks2)

philosophical fieldwork

An approach to research described by Elizabeth Kamarck Minnich (2005) that is concerned with thinking about and through meaning systems and questioning how meaning systems can inform and deform our relationships, including our relationships with one another. Philosophical fieldwork acknowledges that both formalized research methods and informal interactions with others contribute in important ways to research and inquiry, and aims to hold horizons open through thinking through and beyond that which we think is known. (dn, asf)

philosophy

The pursuit of wisdom and the study of ideas upon which all beliefs and practices are based. From the Greek words *philos* and *sophos* meaning the love of wisdom, philosophy investigates questions through systematic methods and reasoned argument. Philosophy is an academic discipline of the social studies comprising logic, ethics, epistemology, aesthetics, and metaphysics, and accounting for thinking about all other academic disciplines of the social studies. (npg)

philosophy of education

Most obviously, philosophical reflection upon the practice of teaching and learning, both in and outside of schools. During the latter half of the 20th century, when philosophy was thought to be the study of concepts, philosophy of education was supposedly concerned with concepts such as "teaching," "education," "indoctrination," and "curriculum." Since philosophers generally stopped dichotomizing concepts and facts, philosophy of education is more involved with the matter than simply the form of things. For example, in the philosophy of education, political philosophy studies the nature and possibility of truly democratic education; epistemology studies the ways in which teaching transmits or makes possible the acquisition of knowledge; ethics, the possibility of properly educating as opposed to brainwashing. (an)

philosophy of science

Broadly concerns two kinds of questions: whether we are justified in accepting scientific theories or the methods deployed in scientific reasoning, and, if so, just how to resolve ontologically puzzling features of scientific theories (e.g., Quantum Indeterminacy) or concepts fundamental to the entire enterprise (e.g., causality, probability). Remarkable advances in mathematical logic and physics at the turn of the 20th century gave rise to logical positivism, a philosophical movement committed to empiricism and formal logic, which dominated the field until the mid-1960s. Key projects begun under the positivists, such as mathematical modeling of scientific inference, have matured into research areas within philosophy, logic, and artificial intelligence. (grw)

See also logic; paradigm.

phoneme

The smallest unit of sound in language. It does not carry meaning on its own, but different phonemes alter the meaning of a word. For example, if we change the final phoneme in the word *bat* from /t/ to /d/, the meaning of the word, as well as its part of phonology speech, change completely. The word *bat* is a noun and means

a type of flying rodent, or an instrument used in baseball to hit the ball, while *bad* is an adjective and means the opposite of *good*. In writing, phonemes are represented with phonetic symbols, and the most commonly used system for phoneme representation is the International Phonetic Alphabet. (smt)

phoneme-grapheme correspondence

The relationship between a grapheme and the phoneme(s) it represents; letter-sound correspondence, as the grapheme/letter c represents the phoneme/sound /k/ in the word *cat* and the phoneme/sound /s/ in the word *cent*. Technically, graphemephoneme correspondence refers to how letters correspond to sounds, not vice versa. Phonics as a teaching technique in reading instruction utilizes graphemephoneme correspondences—that is, how to pronounce words seen in print. Grapheme-phoneme correspondence is a particularly useful teaching tool in reading instruction in languages that have shallow orthography, that is, where there is one-to-one mapping of letter to sound (e.g., Spanish, Russian, Hungarian, Bulgarian). It is a less useful tool in languages with deep orthography, where one letter could represent multiple sounds (e.g., English, French). (smt)

phonemic awareness

The conscious awareness that words are made up of segments of speech (phonemes) that are represented with letters in an alphabetic orthography (i.e., a vowel sound or vowel-consonant pair). (smt)

phonetics

The branch of linguistics that studies the content and structure of the sounds of all human languages. It aims at analyzing and describing all possible human sounds and utilizes the International Phonetic Alphabet to uniformly represent these sounds. It consists of three main branches: articulatory phonetics, which studies the anatomical structures and physiological mechanism of speech production; auditory phonetics, which studies the structures and mechanisms of speech perception; and acoustic phonetics, which concerns the measurement and analysis of the physical properties of the sound waves produced when a person speaks. (smt)

phonics

The association of letters with the sound system of a language. Phonics is part of the phonology of the language. Phonics is the basis for one method of teaching early reading skills in which letters and letter combinations are associated with speech sounds and used to decode the meaning of written words. Instructional practices for early literacy that focus on breaking the orthographic code by stressing the systematic relationship between the sounds of speech and spelling. (vm, jrk)

See also direct code; whole language approach/instruction.

phonological awareness

The conscious knowledge of all levels of the speech sound system (word boundaries, stress patterns, syllables, phonemes, etc.). It is usually developed in the process of learning to read, when the typically unconscious phonological knowledge becomes conscious and the person is aware of it. Phonological awareness allows a speaker to, for example, intentionally produce sounds that form meaningful utterances, make up new words, add the appropriate phonetics segments to form plural and past tense, and know what is or is not a sound in one's language. (smt)

phonological processing

Refers to the identification and manipulation or use of phonological information in written or spoken language. There are three interrelated components of phonological processing, including phonological sensitivity (sometimes called phonological awareness), phonological working memory, and phonological access to lexical storage (rapid naming). Phonological

processing skills in young children are related to later word decoding skills. (rcr)

See also phonological awareness; rapid naming.

phonology

The component of a grammar made up of the elements and principles that determine how sounds vary and pattern in a specific language. The study of the smallest units of sounds (phonemes) that reflect a difference in meaning in a language. Rules pertaining to the structure, distribution, and sequencing of speech sounds within a language are included in phonology. (smt, rl)

phonosyntactic disorder (See specific language impairment)

photography

Process of recording the image of an object by exposure to light or other related radiation on a sensitive material (such as film) usually, but not necessarily, through a lens in a camera. Derived from the Greek *photos* (light) and *graphein* (to draw), photography was first used by the scientist Sir John Herschel in 1839. Widely regarded as art, it is also challenged as mechanical reproduction—a passive record of reality—because of its dependence on technology. Cameras are often used in art education as tools with which students can place aesthetic frames around their lived worlds and learn formal properties such as composition through the framed view of the camera lens. (yjl)

phronesis

In classical Greek, signifies practical wisdom, good judgment, or practical intelligence, a dominant aim of higher education in the Greek and early modern European traditions. It was identified as both a "cardinal" virtue, a capacity and disposition to judge and choose well in disparate circumstances, in matters both domestic and civic, and as an element essential to the possession of any other genuine virtue. Aristotle (384–322 B.C.E.) regarded phronesis as both presupposing and completing moral virtue, and as involving both a "universal" component consisting of systematic knowledge of human affairs, and a perceptual component that enables one to discern with subtlety the particulars of the situation at hand. (rc)

See also practical wisdom.

physical abuse
Any nonaccidental physical injury to a child by a person responsible for a child's welfare (e.g., parent, caretaker, teacher) or by a person who is in a position of power over a child. It is not necessary for the individual to intend to injure the child (e.g., injury resulting from unusual or extreme discipline; physical punishment not appropriate to age or developmental level). Although a physical indicator is usually present, the injury may have occurred in the past or not be readily detected, as in an internal injury, a bruise covered by hair or clothing, or evidence of a healed wound. (llf, emm)

physical education
Traditional physical education instruction is focused on the development of skill and technique, sometimes called the skill-drill approach. Students learn skills before strategies and tactics and apply that knowledge in game play at the end of a unit of instruction. (kpr)

physical play
Free choice activities in which gross motor abilities are utilized and developed. (db1)

physical science
A grouping of sciences, including physics and chemistry, that studies the nature of nonliving matter and energy. In education, a course in physical science will incorporate ideas from several science branches, concentrating on general concepts and processes without the depth of study found in a specific study of the science branch. (tw)

physical therapy
Treatment of physical disabilities provided by a trained therapist focused on gross motor skills, movement, and posture. A physician often prescribes physical therapy. (sr)

physics
The branch of science that studies matter and energy and the interactions between matter and energy. Divisions include subjects such as motion studies, electricity and magnetism, optics, thermodynamics, and modern physics. (tw)

physiology
The branch of biology that studies the processes, functions, and activities of life or living matter. (tw)

Piagetian theory of cognitive development
Jean Piaget developed theories related to the stages of cognitive development in children. These included four stages: sensory-motor, preoperational, concrete operational, and formal operational development. His theories have greatly affected instructional practices in the classroom. In each stage of development, the child exhibits specific characteristics and learning stages that can be utilized by a teacher to maximize learning. (npo)

See also concrete operational development; formal operational development; preoperational development; sensory-motor development.

PIC (See private industry councils)

pidgin
A simple (very limited lexically) but rule-governed speech variety developed for communication among speakers of mutually unintelligible languages who come into contact to conduct business, usually trade. Pidgin is often based on one of those languages. There are a number of such speech varieties in the world today,

including a large number of English-based pidgins (e.g., *Tok Pisin,* in Papua New Guinea; *Chinook Jargon,* in the Northwest of the United States; *Hawaiian Pidgin,* in Hawaii; etc.). (smt)

pie chart (See circle graph)

pie graph (See circle graph)

Pierce vs. Society of Sisters, 268 U.S. 510 (1925)
This landmark U.S. Supreme Court case ruled that a 1922 law in Oregon requiring parents to send their children only to public schools "unreasonably interferes with the liberty of parents and guardians" to direct the upbringing of their children if they choose private education. It further argued that the state may not compel students to receive education only at public, state-supported schools, as to do so would endanger the business rights of private schools. (djr)

place value
The value given to a digit due to its location in a numeral with respect to the units place. The place value of each location is determined as a power of the numeral base system. For example, using the numeral 214, the 4 represents the units place (4×10^0), the 1 represents 1×10^1, and the 2 represents 2×10^2 in the base 10 numeral system. In base 8, the 4 represents the units place (4×8^0), the 1 represents 1×8^1, and the 2 represents 2×8^2. (kva)

place-based education
An approach to education that focuses on the learner's immediate locale. This includes both the local human (cultural, economic, sociological) and nonhuman (environmental, ecological) communities. As such, the content and the pedagogy are rooted in the unique histories, people, ecosystems, arts, cultures, and so on of a particular home-place. Often involves project-based, hands-on, real-world ac-

tivities that make use of the resources beyond the limits of the school itself. (sb1)
See also pedagogy of place; curriculum of place.

placement
The decision to place a student in the appropriate course or section on the basis of his or her proficiency in the subject matter. Criteria for placement include scores on institutional placement tests, scores on standardized aptitude or achievement tests, and, in higher education, years and content of high school instruction in the subject. (cf)
See also examination, placement.

placement counselor (See counselor, placement)

placement service
An essential element of the guidance program, concerned with assisting students to progress in employment or further education. Occupational placement involves both part-time placement for those still in school and full-time placement for those who leave school. Educational placement has to do with specialized and technical training opportunities as well as with academic institutions. The service is offered both in secondary schools and in institutions of higher education. (jm)

planned variations
Intentional extensions for learning activities that facilitate individualization, leading experiences to branch into intentional learning most appropriate for each individual child, relative to differing abilities and/or interests. (db)

planning
Process of consciously formulating public, corporate, or institutional policy and the specification of means by which policy can be implemented. Planning is often advocated as an effective means of adopting/ changing environmental and/or cultural conditions. (cf)

Planning, Attention, Simultaneous, Successive (PASS) theory

Based on the work of A. R. Luria, PASS is an intelligence theory developed by Canadian psychologist Jagannath P. Das and colleagues that suggests that intelligence can be divided into four distinct yet interconnected cognitive processes:

- Planning—the extent to which the mind is able to use information from its knowledge base and feedback stimulus to problem solve, make decisions, act, and react.
- Attention and Arousal—the extent to which the mind is able to focus on the task, object, and information, and is directly impacted by the degree of importance and interest placed by the learner.
- Simultaneous Processing—the extent to which the mind is able to acquire information from multiple sources of stimuli simultaneously and cohesively integrate them.
- Successive Processing—the extent to which the mind is able to acquire information in a sequential or successive order (ms)

planning programming budgeting systems (PPBS)

Business management concepts and principles initiated in industry and the Department of Defense. This system is advocated in colleges and universities as a systematic structure for making decisions on policy, strategy, and the development of capabilities to accomplish stated missions. It is regarded by its advocates as a cyclical process containing three distinct, but interrelated phases of planning, programming, and budgeting institutional operations. (cf)

planning time

A regularly scheduled time during the school day when teachers can plan lessons, evaluate student work, or engage in other activities to support their instruction. (bba)

Platonism

Originally, Plato's (427–348 B.C.E.) position that reality is different from the sensible world. For Plato there are eternal, perfect, unchanging, nonphysical objects (the Forms), which are the true objects of knowledge. Sensible objects are poor copies of the real objects. In contemporary metaphysics, Platonism is the position that there are universal concepts, properties, or objects that exist independently of particular, sensible objects. (ec)

Platoon School Plan (See Gary Plan)

play

A written work for the theater. Play is also what actors (who play roles) or musicians (who play instruments) do in performance. Play can also be a broad term encompassing games, activities, and actions that children and artists engage in to explore, experiment, and stimulate the imagination. It is critical in its many forms (dramatic, improvisational, pretend, group) for the development of children cognitively, socially, and creatively. For artists, play can be experimentation with ideas, improvisation with characters or musical instruments, or exploration of new techniques, all serving the creative process. From Old English *plegian*—to exercise oneself. Play refers to physical, intellectual, or creative exercise. (em)

play group

An adult-supervised social cluster of children whose members are gathered for the purpose of fun, entertainment, and pleasure. (db1)

Play Movement

Refers to efforts beginning in the late 19th century to provide opportunities for creative and educational play for children under the aegis of institutions such as public schools or civic organizations. Playgrounds established both in parks and schoolyards were designed to protect children from urban cultural influences and to provide a respite for children growing up in an increasingly complex Industrial Age. Reflects the increasing responsibility taken by the school and allied social institutions for the extracurricular education of children during the Progressive Era of the late 19th and early 20th centuries, and the perceived association between physical education and fitness and moral training. (sw)

play therapy

A treatment approach that is used widely with children. It incorporates therapeutic interventions within the context of play. Through play, therapists are able to establish a therapeutic relationship with the child, assess the nature of the child's difficulties, permit the child to reenact anxiety-provoking experiences, help the child find meaning in those experiences, provide the child with alternative coping strategies, and facilitate the development of preventative strategies. There are many theoretical approaches to doing play therapy. Some of the more common approaches include psychoanalytic, humanistic, cognitive-behavioral, Adlerian, and filial therapy. (kc, scmc, bdj)

PLC (See professional learning community)

Plessy v. Ferguson, 163 U.S. 537 (1896)

The U.S. Supreme Court case that solidified the "separate but equal" standard by which it was permissible to provide separate facilities for whites and African Americans if these accommodations were of equal quality. The case grew out of a railway car incident in which a black man insisted upon remaining in the white car. *Plessy* was eventually used throughout the South as the basis to justify separate schools for black and white children and was not overturned until *Brown v. Board of Education* in 1954. (dwm)

pluralism

The rejection of the idea that there is one best way of life or one path to truth, or even that there is a unitary truth to be found. Pluralists accept the incommensurability of different systems of values and beliefs, different ways of life. The root of pluralism may be that there is no way to adjudicate between the value of different ways of life or, more strongly relativistic, that no way of life is better than any other. (jc)

See also ethnicity; ethnocentrism; multiculturalism; tolerance.

Plyler v. Doe, 457 U.S. 202 (1982)

This U.S. Supreme Court decision stemmed from a Texas law that excluded undocumented immigrant children from the right to a free public education. The Court ruled that the law was a violation of the Equal Protection clause. As a result, schools are prohibited from: denying admission based on undocumented status, treating undocumented students differently from others to determine residency, requiring disclosure of documentation status, making inquiries designed to expose documentation status, requiring Social Security numbers, and taking actions designed to "chill" school access. "Chilling" was defined as taking actions designed to create fear among undocumented persons. (mg1)

podcast

A combination of iPod® and broadcast. It consists of audio or video files made available through a syndication format called a podcatcher. The most popular is iTunes. The first podcasts appeared in 2004. Podcasts allow an individual to create and share audio or video recordings, including instructional material, lectures, or other learning objects. (gle)

poetry

A piece of writing or the art of writing that has aesthetic or artistic features that transcend and deliver the meaning of the words. Poetry has been compared to music because of the rhythm and meter of lines (even when rhyme is not a feature) and the harmonious arrangement of sounds. Poets select their words like painters select their images; indeed some poems are shaped like objects one can see in the world. A particular attention to the sound and form of language is the work of a poet, as is the expression of emotion beyond the content of the literal meaning. Young children love poetic language and especially enjoy creating rhymes of their own design. (jd)

point
The value awarded for successful completion of a test item or task. Points are typically summed to create a total score on a test. (fd)

policy
A general conception in academic administration and governance pertaining to institutions and organizations in all phases of their operation; a broader, more inclusive concept than law, rules, regulations, decisions, procedures, and operations (as being more specific or routine). Policies are often stated succinctly as "the reasons for" general characteristics, operations, and procedures. (cf)

policy analysis
The intensive study of alternatives in policy decisions and their various consequences; often mistaken for policy research, in which control is more likely and predicted consequences may be confirmed or refuted. Such analysis is sometimes regarded as rational rather than empirical. (cf)

policy research
The study of policy antecedents, alternatives, and expected consequences under conditions permitting a more systematic analysis of expected outcomes or results. On many occasions the better control of extraneous variables permits an explanation of outcomes in terms of their antecedents or determinants. (cf)

policy studies
The systematic analysis and interpretation of national, state, or institutional policies in terms of their antecedents, consequences, determinants, and effects. Policy studies are the investigation of policy as guidance or direction of administrative decisions and actions. These studies may include comprehensive overview of laws, rules, and regulations as they affect institutional administration and governance. (cf)

policy-related research
The study of antecedents, process, and consequences with expectations of identifying more effective policies. In this effort, the object of research is policy itself and the desirability of change or modifications. (cf)

See also theory-based research.

political correctness
An attitude reflecting broad social, political, and educational change, especially to redress historical injustices in matters such as race, class, culture, gender, and sexual orientation. Such attitudes often require a rigid affiliation to progressive compliance and develop a coded language that seeks not to offend certain ethnic, racial, cultural, and gender groups. Politically correct attitudes can nonetheless mask many true feelings and inner hostilities of people. (hrm, ew, jkd)

political parties
Distinctive social organizations whose principal objective is to place their avowed leaders into the offices of government. Political party systems are almost always in some interlocking relationships with other political institutions: as managers of election systems, as controllers of military and other national bureaucracies, as coalition builders among organized interest groups, as communicators with and through the media, and as civic educators. (cd)

political science
The study of the theory and practice of politics, the investigation of political behaviors, and the analysis of political

systems comprising history, law, policy, institutionalism, national foundations, international relations, global concerns, and comparative politics. Political science attends to issues of power and control, decision making, governance, and leadership. (npg)

political socialization

A process of learning political attitudes and behaviors through social interaction. Family, education, media, peers, groups, and organizations facilitate the acquisition of this knowledge. (cd)

political theory

The analysis of the normative, empirical, and conceptual aspects of political life. This analysis involves the examination and interpretation of ideas such as justice, freedom, authority, obligation, and so on, and applying these ideas to institutions. Matters such as the justification for the state and other institutions, the role of conceptions of the good in politics, and the place of education in a just society are typically addressed by political theories. (rk)

politically relevant teaching

Educational philosophy whereby teachers are mindful and aware of the cultural identities, norms, values, and practices of students, as well as of the political realities of inequality, power, and disfranchisement in the lives of students. This knowledge and awareness can serve as elements of personal and professional agency as well as guide educational decision making concerning pedagogy, curricula, and the relationships formed with students. Centered upon a belief in schools and the process of education as engines of social justice, uplift, and change. (hfs)

politics of knowledge

This is the notion of understanding knowledge as "cultural capital," that is, as knowledge, values, and attitudes that accrue to individuals as members of groups based on social class, race, ethnicity, and gender. As a basic operating component of the hidden curriculum, cultural capital effectively determines the experience of any given individual within the educational system, and, ultimately, serves to reinforce and continue existing inequalities of opportunity within the larger society. (ks1)

polyglot

A person who knows several languages. Usually the term is used to refer to a person who knows how to speak, write, and understand several languages. Derived from the Greek words *poly* = many, and *glotta* = tongue. (smt)

polynomial

The sum, or difference, of one or more terms made up of numbers, variables, or the product of numbers and variables possibly raised to some power. The following are examples of polynomials: $2x + 1$, $3x^5$, $x^2 - 2x + 5$. (rdk)

popular culture

Low, as opposed to high, culture. With the increasing economic power of the middle- and lower-income populace in Europe and the United States since the beginning of the Industrial Revolution in the 19th century, artists have created works with the aesthetics of this population in mind. Comic books, film, television, advertising, and collectibles are just a few of the artistic media often placed in the realm of popular culture. The splatter-painted canvases by abstract expressionist Jackson Pollock and the silk-screened paintings by Andy Warhol of soup cans and celebrities signaled unprecedented fusions between high and low art and the transition to the postmodern age. (kf)

popular education

A form of adult education that is developed by and for disadvantaged people, usually with a political element to the curriculum. It is often characterized by horizontal relationships between facilitators and participants, the involvement of community groups in identifying and finding solutions to local issues, and acknowledgement of the community itself as a source of knowledge. (las)

See also community-based education.

Port Huron Statement

A political and social treatise written in 1962, which can be considered the seminal intellectual document of the New Left movement. The *Port Huron Statement* was an incisive analysis of the state of American culture in the early 1960s, and the alienation that some younger Americans felt from it at that time. Drafted by Tom Hayden, the eventual leader of Students for a Democratic Society (SDS), the *Port Huron Statement* advocated the search for a meaningful life beyond the pursuit of material wealth, and democracy by individual participation. (ah)

portfolio

In education, portfolios are purposeful, collaborative, self-reflective collections of work, which are one way to provide a more complete, situated view of teacher or student skills, knowledge, and commitments. A portfolio is a thematic collection of artifacts to demonstrate the growth and accomplishment of an individual over an extended period of time, including (but not limited to) work samples, projects, performance pieces, reflective journals, and peer review notes. Multiple sources allow association and juxtaposition of related tasks. Unlike traditional testing instruments, portfolios capture individuals' authentic learning performance, keep track of individuals' development, and provide longitudinal evidence for feedback on learning. Essential portfolio design concerns include content, organizing principles, time frame, and involvement of the individuals around whom the portfolios are centered. In art education a portfolio is a folder or flat suitcase that contains a compilation of samplings of the general

work or representations of the best work of an artist. Portfolios are used for evaluation purposes, and students applying to art schools are regularly asked to submit a portfolio of their work for review in the admissions process. The notion of portfolio assessment, making judgments across a representative sampling rather than on the basis of one piece of work, has become a standard evaluative process in many schools. It is an example of pedagogy that is based on the practices of professional artists. (ja, tc, ap)

portfolio assessment

Assessment of a learner's knowledge or competence based upon evidence (records, examinations, papers, videotapes, transcripts, reviews of performances, etc.) gathered and submitted by the learner. This organized collection of representative samples of student work is designed to illustrate a student's accomplishment and represent progress made toward reaching specified goals and objectives. (chb, bba)

portmanteau word

A word originating from Lewis Carroll's *Through the Looking Glass* (ch. 6): "you see it's like a *portmanteau*—there are two meanings packed up into one word." Such words take form and meaning from blending two or more distinct words or parts of words. Typical examples include the word "smog," which is derived from smoke and fog, or the word "brunch," which is formed from breakfast and lunch. (h-jk)

portrait

Most often associated with visual art, a portrait is a representation of a person or group of people, usually created as a painting or sculpture. The features of the person or group that are represented usually concern physical appearance, but a portrait can also include or consist of an object or abstraction that symbolizes or encapsulates some essential aspect of the subject/s. Portraits are created in other art forms such as literature (e.g., Joyce's

Portrait of the Artist as a Young Man). There is even a research methodology called portraiture that tries to capture the aesthetic aspects of portrait making. (ap)

position paper
A position paper is an instrument for policy formation. The purpose of a position paper is to present a stance as a means of providing information for administrators. The components of a position paper include an introduction of the issue, a presentation of logical reasons and/or evidence to support the position, as well as a conclusion. In educational arenas, position papers are typically associated with policy development. (tp)

positionality
This concept issued from feminist scholarship that states that an individual's gender, class, and race fix the relational position within society and influence any work or ideas produced. Knowing the role of both the source of ideas and the person discussing them aids in understanding the relative context. Because of the multiple roles that each individual has, positionality is a fluid concept. (jqa, npo)

positive disintegration
Kazimierz Dabrowski's (1902–1980) theory of personality development based on the notion that growth happens through psychological tension and anxiety. Rather than viewing crisis as negative force, Dabrowski suggests that the "disintegration" or collapsed functioning of one level of development opens to the emergence of the next level. Unlike other developmental theories, Dabrowski's model is not based on stages that correlate with age and assume universal progression. Dabrowski is concerned with "developmental potential" (DP). One aspect of his DP model is the concept of "overexcitabilities," which has been particularly taken up by advocates of gifted education as means of understanding student variance. (bda)

See also overexcitabilities.

positive freedom
A process whereby individuals develop an awareness of, as well as name, obstacles in their everyday lives. These obstacles can be personal, institutional, or societal. Individuals become aware and awake to possibilities, including the malleability of circumstance. The concept also involves an element of praxis, or active work, toward the realization of envisioned alternatives. (hfs)

See also freedom.

positive peace
A concept that emphasizes the dialectical relationship between the twin and interdependent aims of peace and social justice, whereby peace cannot be achieved without social justice. (hfs)

positive psychology
The branch of psychological inquiry that focuses on human growth and optimal human functioning, including such areas as creativity, wisdom, giftedness, talent, responsibility, spirituality, and general well-being. Positive psychology can be differentiated from other branches of psychology in that it does not focus on psychopathological processes. It is related to humanistic theories of personality that emphasize growth and self-actualization, such as Carl Rogers's phenomenological approach and A. H. Maslow's hierarchy of needs. (jih)

positivism
A philosophical movement that began in the mid-19th century. It identified science as the sole kind of genuine knowledge and advocated employing it to improve social life. In the early 20th century, logical positivism emerged. It preserved the commitment to the centrality of science but significantly shifted the focal point of inquiry. The task that logical positivists set for themselves was elucidating and improving the explanatory and predictive machinery of science in terms of mathematical logic. Their primary focus was

physics, which, embracing the thesis of the unity of science, they believed could serve as the model for all science. The foremost principle of logical positivism was verificationism: in order for a claim to be meaningful—cognitively significant—its truth (or falsity) must be capable of determination either by (a) specifying the relevant observational test, of (b) deriving its truth (or falsity) from definitions or logic. Logical positivism jettisoned metaphysical claims (e.g., God exists) and value claims (e.g., abortion is morally wrong) from the domain of things that could be established (or refuted) because they could not be rendered cognitively significant. Although positivism in its various forms has been under intense criticism since the mid-20th century, it still exerts a quite powerful influence, particularly in the social sciences. (kh)

See also empiricism; naturalism.

positivism in educational administration

A dominant paradigm that influences educational organizations, positivism reinforces the notion of education being run as a machine or in assembly-line fashion. Positivism is characterized by: top-down management; linear, sequential curriculum; strict time schedules; and departmentalization. (bs)

Positron Emission Tomography (PET)

PET is a functional neuroimaging technique that uses nuclear signals to produce a three-dimensional image of brain activity. A radioactive tracer is injected into the bloodstream and radioactivity in the brain is measured based on the assumptions that more active brain areas will have higher blood flow and areas with more blood flow will have higher radioactivity. From this information, brain activity can be indirectly recorded and imaged. The principle application of PET is in human brain mapping research, where PET information is often combined with MRI to give both structural and functional information.

PET was once the most widely used functional neuroimaging tool but has recently given way to fMRI due to fact that PET requires a radioactive injection. PET gives only an indirect measure of brain activity and is a correlational tool only. (mt)

postcolonialism

An area of thought that is a critical response to the global impacts of colonialism and colonization. Well-known figures in postcolonialism are Frantz Fanon (1925–1961) (*Black Skin, White Masks*, 1967, and *The Wretched of the Earth*, 1961) and Edward Said (*Orientalism*, 1978) in his later influential work. Postcolonialism recognizes that although sovereignty is gained through decolonization, strong relationships of colonization remain through cultural, educational, migratory, political, and socioeconomic structures. Former colonies will often have marginalized populations that have limited access to educational, socioeconomic, and political spheres. One such example is indigenous and Afro-Brazilian peoples having marginalized status within Brazil as compared to Portuguese-Brazilians. Postcolonialism is also critical of hierarchical dualisms. The imbalanced dualism is between the colonizer being viewed as superior and civilized compared to the colonized peoples being viewed as inferior and uncivilized. (vkh)

See also decolonization; dualism; colonialism; colonization.

postmodernism

An intellectual and cultural movement that challenges norms of rationality, knowledge, justice, beauty, and so on that Enlightenment-era or "modernist" thinkers believed to be objective and universal. Postmodernists take such norms to be the beliefs and values of powerful ethnic, class, and gender groups. Postmodernist critiques of hierarchical power structures (oppression) focus more on cultural arenas like language, sexuality, and consumerism than on military and economic affairs.

A common form of postmodernist criticism is a "genealogy" or "archaeology" of the historical and cultural factors that led to the construction of a traditional norm, in order to discredit its objectivity and/or universality. A positive form of postmodernist work is to explain and defend the perspectives of marginalized groups, as occurs in the new academic disciplines of women's studies, African studies, and queer theory. Postmodernist educational theorists advocate multicultural curricula, local standards, and critical or liberationist pedagogy. In art, literature, or architecture, postmodernism reacts against earlier modernist principles (characterized by the deliberate departure from tradition) by reintroducing classical elements of style or exaggerating modernist preoccupations. Postmodernism deconstructs (delves below the surface to find debilitating contradictions) the authoritative voice and single path of modernism. The importance of creative originality, paramount in modernism, is supplanted by issues of identity, incorporating feminist, racial, sexual, and environmental concerns. In postmodernism, reality and its representation overlap and are characterized by pastiche, irony, and intertextuality. Collage/montage, installation, performance, and earth and body art are examples of postmodern discourse. (mg, kpb)

postsecondary career education
Educational programs offered after high school graduation, usually at the 13th and 14th grade levels, provided in occupational and/or technical fields by community and technical colleges and other postsecondary institutions offering adult and post-high school instruction and credentials. (db)

postsecondary education
Learning activities that take place beyond a high school level. In the United States, postsecondary education takes place in two- and four-year colleges and universities, as well as training institutions that require at least a high school diploma or equivalent for entrance. (las)

postsecondary occupational education (See postsecondary career education)

postsecondary technical education (See postsecondary career education)

postsecondary vocational education (See postsecondary career education)

poststructuralism
Widely interpreted as a movement of thought and interdisciplinary style of philosophizing and writing arising out of France in the 1960s in response to the essentializing, totalizing, and reductive thought, methods, and practices characteristic of structuralism. Frequently conflated with postmodernism, it is characterized by a socially and culturally constructed subject created through discourse, ideology, and language. Through deconstruction, poststructural forms of analysis expose how contingency and ambiguity contribute to the destabilizing, or decentering, of meaning that is understood to be shifting, multifaceted, and perspectival. Jacques Derrida and Michel Foucault are considered two of its most notable thinkers and writers, though they would reject any such label. (jm1)

See also structuralism; deconstruction.

posttest
Any assessment designed to provide information on the skills or abilities of test takers following instruction or an experimental procedure, often compared with pretest results. (scw)

See also pretest.

potential
Predicted peak level of capacity. (sr)

pottery
The activity, skill, or result of making objects by hand out of clay that are then baked at various temperatures in a kind of oven called a kiln. In its raw form, clay is malleable and offers a delightful tactile experience for students of art education. Upon exposure to heat, the clay hardens and becomes inert. A potter's wheel is a machine with a horizontal spinning disc on which clay is shaped into decorative or useful objects. The term "ceramics" is derived from the Greek *keramikos,* of pottery, and, in spite of certain technical differences, is used interchangeably with the term "pottery." (kf)

poverty
The shortage or absence of common and necessary goods and services such as food, clothing, shelter, and safe utilities including water, heat, and sewage. Poverty is experienced and reported in terms of absolute poverty and relative poverty; poverty can be situational and short-term or generational and long-term. Victims of poverty tend to experience reduced health care, education, and job opportunities along with increased homelessness and crime. (npg)

power
Power is the ability to produce an effect, maintain a structure, or institute change. In education, power implies having the necessary consensus, resources, leadership, participation, and authority to maintain existing educational structures or to enforce change and modification of those structures. Some forms of power include: legislative, founded in legal or governmental guidelines; expert or referent, founded on the knowledge base of a particular person or organization; and symbolic, founded in cultural traditions. Power can be exerted through political action, public discourse, or modification of social structures. (tm)

powerful teaching and learning
Authentic teaching and learning that is meaningful, integrative, values-based, challenging, and active as defined by the National Council for the Social Studies (NCSS). Teaching and learning must be relevant to and connected with the learner; experiences must be combined within the social studies and across the curriculum. Social studies content and processes must convey affective outcomes of responsible citizenship. Experiences must engage learners and advance their thinking. (npg)

PPBS (See planning programming budgeting systems)

practical life
One of the areas of the Montessori classroom, which provides the child with fine-motor activities, is called practical life. These activities include pouring liquid and dry ingredients, scooping, and using practical tools such as funnels, tongs, basters, and the like. These activities encourage the development of order, concentration, coordination, and independence. (nrs)

practical wisdom
In recent educational theory this term refers, often with explicit reference to the Greek term *phronesis,* to good judgment or practical rationality, considered as a dominant aim of teacher education and pedagogical and curricular inquiry. The appearance of the term in these contexts is often associated with a resistance to conceiving of teaching and teacher education simply in terms of the acquisition and deployment of discrete skills, or in terms of the formulation, assimilation, and application of theories, on the grounds that the deployment of skills and theories must be guided by good judgment. (rc)
See also phronesis.

practicality (See logistics)

practice
Practice is originally a Greek term with the meaning of doing, performance, action, and it has been in theoretical use

since Aristotle, who regarded practice as one of the basic activities of human beings. The other two were theoria (theory) and poiesis (skillful making). The relation between theory and practice has in modern Western thought resulted in opposed positions, giving priority either to theory or practice. Two examples are Marxism and pragmatism. In Marxism practice is the primal force in society and the vehicle for changing it. Pragmatism has stressed the importance of activating the pupils in order to learn. Practice can also take the form of habitualized and institutionalized ways of doing something. This applies to all professional activities (e.g., teaching). (jb1)

practice effect

The influence of any type of practice on test performance (positive or negative) on subsequent performance. (yu)

practicum

A course of instruction aimed at closely relating theoretical-based study to practice through a supervised practical experience. In teacher education, this is typically an on-the-job experience for students studying to become teachers and/or clinicians. A practicum involves the practical application of the theory studied in the classroom. Student teaching experiences are considered practicums. (cf, ja)

practitioner

In teacher education, one engaged in the practice of the teaching profession for the sake of acquiring or retaining skills. (ja)

practitioner inquiry

A process in which practitioners identify questions or issues of concern in their work, conduct research around these issues, and incorporate findings of their research into their work. This type of inquiry may be undertaken individually or in conjunction with a group of practitioners pursuing related research questions. (las)

pragmatics

A branch of linguistics concerned with the use of language as distinguished from its meaning or formal properties. Subtopics in pragmatics address the effective and appropriate use of language in daily life and include but are not limited to: culturally determined rules for using speech (e.g., politeness); the genre-specific organization of discourse; the appropriate and effective linguistic expression of communicative intent (see speech act theory); and the rules that govern conversational appropriateness and skill. (jrk)

pragmatism

Pragmatism is a form of philosophy that "takes the continuity of experience and nature as revealed through the outcome of directed action as the starting point for reflection" (Seigfried, 1996). Pragmatists reject the central problems of modern philosophy as presupposing false dichotomies (e.g., mind/body, reason/will, thought/purpose, reason/emotions, self/others, belief/ action, theory/practice). They favor a description that emphasizes a primal, integral, relational unity. Pragmatists believe that human action can improve the human condition and that the results of inquiry are the measure of the theory. Pragmatists deny the possibility of attaining knowledge that is certain or universal. (bt-b)

praxis

An active, continuous process of critical action and reflection upon accepted knowledge, experiences, and perceptions of reality in order to transform reality. A cyclical acknowledgement that human beings shape, create, and maintain both the conditions of the world, and the world itself, requiring that human beings similarly work to change the world. Paulo Freire used the term "praxis" to describe a process by which a group of adult literacy students begin to act upon the forces that control their lives. The process involves a cycle of reflection and action based on that reflection, followed by further reflection. (hfs, jpc)

Praxis Series™

Teacher assessment exams developed by Educational Testing Services (ETS) that measure teacher knowledge and skills. There are three tests in the Praxis series, each measuring a different aspect of teaching. Praxis I assesses a teacher candidate's preprofessional skills, Praxis II assesses content-specific knowledge, and Praxis III evaluates teaching performance. Many states require scores on at least one of these measures for teacher licensure and certification. (sld, ddr)

preemployment counseling (See counseling, preemployment)

preemployment education

Educational activities that seek to prepare unemployed individuals for the workplace. This type of education may include development of basic skills, job search skills, and other skills and knowledge needed to function in a workplace context. (las)

preferred knowledge

Those attitudes, norms, and information that students and teachers construct and for which each is subsequently rewarded. Absent the presence of any alternative understandings in classrooms, it legitimizes existing social and power relationships in schools and society. (hfs)

prejudice

Any opinion or attitude that is formed without regard to factual information. Prejudice is usually a preconceived opinion or bias against a person or group of people. Prejudice is characterized by stereotypical or even ignorant beliefs that are not critically examined, but rather are formed as a result of prior assumptions, opinions, values, and beliefs. Such assumptions, opinions, beliefs, and values are usually negative and can be used to justify political, economic, and social policies. Nonetheless, it is possible to have a positive, but prejudiced, attitude or belief. (crl)

prejudice reduction (See anti-racist education)

preliminary examination (See examination, preliminary)

prelims (See examination, preliminary)

prenatal development

Consists of three periods: germinal (first two weeks, characterized by rapid cell division), embryonic (weeks three to eight, characterized by development of several major organs; embryo grows to about one inch long), and fetal (week nine to nine months, characterized by reflexive and voluntary movements, and brain activity). (xss)

prenatal stage

It refers to the ontological (human being) stage of development before the child is born. Begins at the time of conception to right before delivery. (xss)

preoperational development

In Jean Piaget's theory of cognitive development, the preoperational stage occurs during the second stage of a child's development, from approximately two through seven years of age. During this stage a child rapidly develops language ability as well as an understanding of symbolism. The child is also able to represent things symbolically, but from an egocentric perspective. Behaviors that are considered preoperational are those that rely less on the application of consistent problem-solving strategies and more on intuition. The use and manipulation of symbols in language, simple problem solving, and play situations are some of the behaviors shown by preoperational children. (npo, vm)

prepared environment

The Montessori classroom, as prepared by the teacher, is called a prepared environment. It includes a variety of materials, allowing the student to learn at his/her own pace. Each set of materials, referred to as "work," includes a work cycle and an inherent control of error, allowing the child to perceive if and when an error occurs and then make the corrections on his/her own. The work is designed in an orderly fashion that allows for concentration, coordination, and stimulation of the senses through hands-on learning. (nrs)

prereferral intervention

Provision of special services before completion of the eligibility for special education services. (sr)

prerequisite

Academic course or class or experience requiring successful completion prior to the enrollment in a subsequent, more advanced academic course or class; implies a linear acquisition of knowledge. (cf)

preschool

Care and curriculum designed to meet the needs of children ages three to five years. Ideally, preschool learning is carefully planned and coordinated to prepare children for the transition to kindergarten. Curriculum may include block play, science, arithmetic, pretend play, arts and crafts, constructing with manipulatives, and gross motor activities. (jlj)

presentational

The manner in which something is presented. The way in which a symbol or image represents something or the way in which something is set forth for the attention of the mind. An immediate object is presentational inasmuch as it evokes a perception, cognition, or memory. In experimental work, the act of placing a stimulus before a subject is presentational. In social interactions, the manner in which a person expresses oneself is a presentational ritual.

In symbol system theory presentational symbols are those that require interpretation in terms of their own presentation (e.g., downward lines representing sorrow) as opposed to notational symbols that somewhat arbitrarily represent that to which they refer (like the notation "2"). (kpb)

preservice teacher

A person who is actively engaged in a teacher education program or alternative certification program with the goal of becoming a prekindergarten through twelfth grade teacher. This designation includes those who are just beginning a teacher education or alternative certification program through those who are student teaching or interning but are not yet employed as teachers. (kmt, nfd)

president (See chancellor)

President's Commission on Campus Unrest

Republican Governor William Scranton (Scranton Commission) undertook this report, which President Nixon commissioned in June 1970 in response to the violent catastrophes at Kent State University and Jackson State University. The Commission reviewed various outbreaks of violence throughout the nation on college campuses, particularly in response to the U.S. invasion of Cambodia and the Kent State and Jackson State shootings. The report contained recommendations for governmental and university officials, as well as the public at large, on how to defuse campus outbursts before turning violent. (rih)

pretend play

A specific form of play that children engage in, in which children take on roles and improvise situations by themselves or with others, sometimes using dolls or stuffed animals as well, or in which children take objects and imagine they are other things (a towel is a magic carpet, a bandanna is a leash to walk an imaginary dog). Many educators and theorists believe that pretend play is a crucial aspect of children's development intellectually and socially. It is through pretend play that children try on, experience, and come to understand the roles and relationships of the adult world that they are preparing to enter. (em)

pretest

Any assessment designed to provide information on the skills or abilities of test takers before instruction or an experimental procedure. Pretest results are frequently compared with posttest results to investigate the effects of instruction or experimental procedures. Used as a verb, pretest means to administer test items on a trial basis to a sample of test takers before the test is administered operationally. Pretesting is conducted to provide a check on the quality of test items and clarity and suitability of administrative procedures. Quantitative data from pretesting (e.g., item facility and discrimination indices) can be used to determine whether items are functioning as intended, while qualitative data (e.g., test-taker interviews) can provide insights into test takers' affective reactions to the test items, whether they found them difficult, confusing, and so on. (scw)

See also posttest.

prevention

Preventive actions taken to reduce or control for the occurrence of negative experiences upon children's growth and development. These may be organized into three levels: primary, secondary, or tertiary. (xss, yb)

See also primary prevention; secondary prevention; tertiary prevention.

prevocational education

An educational program, usually in middle or junior high school, providing general introductory instruction about technologies for career exploratory and guidance purposes rather than preparation for a specific occupation. Prevocational education is intended to lay a foundation for future vocational career choice. The first phase of a work-study program that offers students the opportunity to evaluate their abilities as workers and to become familiar with job requirements. (db)

primary colors

The three primary colors (those that cannot result from the mixture of any two colors) are red, blue, and yellow. When two of the primaries are mixed together, the result is known as a secondary color (red and yellow making orange, red and blue making purple, yellow and blue making green). With the aid of black and white, primary colors can be mixed to create the total spectrum of possible colorations. Mixing colors is a joyful exercise for young children and an important aspect of the work of professional painters. (jd)

primary prevention

This level focuses on avoiding negative experiences that impact children's lives from ever occurring. At this level physical environmental alterations may be made, as may discussions of potential harmful causes and experiences, raising community awareness about these potential causes, and providing training or other supports to counterbalance the possible negative effects. Community values are addressed at this level of prevention. (xss, yb)

primary School

Historical term that denotes schools that provide basic education for a child in kindergarten through grade three. The school must be licensed or certified and provide appropriate instructional programs including literacy, basic skills acquisition, and preparing children for adulthood. Currently the term "elementary school," meaning grades K–5, is more commonly utilized. (lcw)

primary sources

The raw materials of research such as artifacts, maps, pictures, original texts of books, plays, diaries, people, letters, journals, school records, oral testimony by an eyewitness, and the like. These sources are firsthand, independent, original, and form the foundation upon which historical research is constructed. From exposure to primary sources, students are provided with the opportunity to experience the past more directly than otherwise possible. (igb)

prime

A natural number greater than one (i.e., an element from the set {2, 3, 4, 5, . . .}) whose only positive divisors are one and the number itself. The integer 1 is not considered prime. It is considered a unit. (cmdv)

prime factorization

When a number is written as a product of its prime factors. (ps)

primitive reflexes

Reflexes stimulated by touch, present at birth, and that gradually disappear during the first years of life. Early neurological problems are suspected if these reflexes are abnormal, absent, or persist for an extended period of time. Examples of the primitive reflexes are grasping, swimming, sucking, rooting, and stepping reflex. (mc2)

principal

The school principal is the instructional leader, manager, director, and chief executive officer of the school. The duties of the principal include, but are not limited to, approving the appointments of teachers and campus staff; setting specific educational objectives for the campus; developing campus budgets; and assigning, evaluating, and promoting campus personnel. Principals are also charged with assuming the administrative responsibility and instructional leadership for campus discipline. (ly)

print concepts

An understanding of how print works; that print represents speech, that there is a certain direction to read, and knowledge of book parts. (mmd)

printmaking

The creation of multiple impressions on paper from greasy pigment applied (sometimes with the help of a press) repeatedly to the same plate, block, stone, screen, transfer paper, or film negative. Main processes include: relief, where nonprinting areas are etched away (e.g., woodcuts, photoengraving); intaglio, where printing areas are recessed (e.g., etching, engraving, drypoint); and planographic, involving a flat surface (e.g., lithography). Educators often employ simple techniques requiring minimal equipment such as wood cutting, using a spoon to press on the paper, and potato printing, in which potato halves are carved, dipped in paint, and pressed onto paper. (lj)

prior learning assessment

Assessment of learning gained prior to matriculation in a postsecondary institution, usually with the goal of awarding credit in recognition of that learning. The learning may have been gained through training courses, work experience, voluntary activities, reading, and so on. Assessment may be done through examination, review of products or a portfolio, interviews, and the like. (chb)

prison art programs

Collaborations between prisons and individual artists in which practicing visual artists, dramatic artists, or poets spend time working with incarcerated individuals. Such programs are designed for both inmate artists and nonartists, allowing artistically inclined inmates to hone existing artistic skills and allowing all inmates an opportunity for self-reflection, self-expression, and the growth of self-esteem. (lw)

private education

Educational institutions and programs supported primarily by nonpublic funds are considered private. These schools and colleges are administered by the private sector with limited or no governmental oversight, allowing for specific types of educational philosophies and practices to be used in the classroom. (npo)

See also public education.

private industry councils (PIC)

Advisory groups, created through the Job Training Partnership Act, that bring together representatives from business and industry to oversee local efforts in the areas of occupational training and adult literacy development. (las)

private schools (See private education)

private space

Refers to area or areas in the home, school, or familiar place where a child may relax and feel comfortable. The area or space may be visible by others, but there is an explicit understanding that others in the larger setting should not interrupt the child's activities in the space. This area may house quiet activities such as reading books, playing with toys, resting, or other individual or very small group activities. (at)

private university

Unlike state-funded universities, private universities depend on student tuition as well as income from endowments and contributions from individuals and companies for funding. Consequently, private universities are usually more costly than state universities for students who attend college in their state of residence. Students with few financial resources who want to attend private universities often apply for scholarships, financial aid, work-study, or student loans. (cf)

privatization

The encroachment of the corporate private sector and big business into schools through a variety of methods, whether it is through the sponsorship of athletic teams, technologies, food, curricula, or advertisement. Some corporations have developed their own charter schools. Some schools have contracted out school services in order to make limited public funds stretch further. Many educational theorists, researchers, and commentators have critiqued this trend, expressing deep concern over the effects of such influence on truly public education. The controversial topic of vouchers is often included in discussions of privatization as well. (lev)

privilege

A special advantage or benefit enjoyed by an individual or socioeconomic class. Privilege can be consciously used, or can be assumed as a right by the privileged group or individual. In common usage, privilege is often expressed as an advantage based on status or rank that is used to maintain the social status quo. Sociologists point to examples such as male privilege, white privilege, and heterosexual privilege, all of which have implications for education. (jqa, acp)

privileged communication

Any document, statement, or other form of communication that is not open for public examination or scrutiny. Within traditional psychotherapy settings, this refers to material that is produced or disclosed within a bona fide therapeutic relationship. Privilege enables mental health professionals to protect clients' confidentiality in a legal setting, though specific laws regarding privilege vary from state to state. (mkt)

probability

The branch of mathematics concerned with analyzing the possibility of a particular event occurring. Probability is computed on the basis of observing the number of actual outcomes and dividing that number by the number of possible outcomes. (kr)

probes (See probing questions)

probing questions
Teacher questions or statements immediately following a student's response that are designed to encourage the student to think more deeply and respond more thoroughly, usually by clarifying, elaborating, or extending the initial response. (bba)

problem of practice
Statement of a current dilemma or challenge related to student learning. In the context of instructional rounds for school improvement, developed by researchers at the Harvard Graduate School of Education, the problem of practice is an instructional problem that the host team in a district-wide network wants to solve in order to improve student learning. It focuses on the instructional core, is directly observable, actionable, connects to a broader strategy of improvement in the school or education system, and is high-leverage (i.e., if acted on, it would make a significant difference for student learning). (mf1)

problem posing
Problem posing involves students taking a mathematics problem or task and generating their own set of questions or tasks. Nonroutine problems or problems that have more than one solution provide more opportunities for students to become engaged in problem posing. (sdt)

problem posing education
A term used by Paulo Freire to describe and discuss a problem that is important to their lives. This active and continuous process of education allows teachers and students to critically identify contradictions,

questions, circumstance, and issues that arise in social reality. The development of a critical consciousness in both student and teacher is central to the process. The roles of teachers and learners meld, as all participants take on the dual roles of learner and educator. The shared and individual knowledge and perceptions subsequently become the focus of study through inquiry designed and redesigned to facilitate action in, with, and upon the social reality of the world. (jpc, hfs)

problem solving
A strategy used to apply all previously acquired knowledge and experience to new situations and challenges. Education increasingly focuses on the teaching and reinforcement of individual problem-solving skills as a priority area separate from the imparting of accumulated knowledge. In educational psychology, this is a counseling strategy to resolve a situation or question that is causing client distress. Five phases are involved in problem solving: defining the problem, identifying possible solutions, choosing an effective solution, implementing the solution, and evaluating the outcome. In mathematics education, problem solving is a mathematics task in which the solution is not known. Problem solving is not applying a known procedure to a task that would simply be an exercise (or routine problem). The focus of problem solving is for students to understand and learn mathematics. Many researchers equate mathematics with problem solving. The determination of a problem is particular to an individual. For example, to a young student, 28 + 56 may be a problem, if she/he has no algorithm to apply. George Polya (1887–1985) was known for a four-step linear method for problem solving, but current research shows that problem solving is a more complicated recursive process. In educational administration problem solving involves identifying, constructing, and developing solutions to conceptual,

organizational, and technical problems that influence administrative effectiveness in various situations and under particular conditions. (cd, sc, sdt, cf)

problem-based learning

An instructional approach that organizes the curriculum around loosely structured problems that students attempt to solve by using knowledge and skills from several disciplines or subject areas. In higher education this instructional method or curricular framework uses complex and compelling problems as the context and stimulus for learning. Faculty members work as facilitators, guides, and coaches, and students take some ownership of the learning process as they work to seek viable solutions to the problem. (bba, cf)

problem-centered learning

An instructional approach for mathematics classrooms described by Wheatley, which has three components: tasks, groups, and sharing. The teacher is first responsible for choosing tasks that will likely be problematic. After choosing potentially problematic tasks, students then work in pairs or groups (collaboratively) to solve the task. The third component involves students sharing with the class their thinking and ideas about the mathematical tasks. Problem-centered learning focuses upon students understanding and making sense of mathematics and is in direct contrast with a teacher-directed classroom, which focuses primarily upon students repeating prescribed procedures that are dictated by the teacher. (sdt)

procedural mathematics knowledge

A student who possesses just procedural mathematics knowledge is able to use the procedure or algorithm in a very limited way to solve routine tasks. These tasks must be presented in a situation that is identical to the way in which it was learned. These students are usually unable to solve nonroutine problems since they do not possess a deep understanding of the underlying concepts involved; they only possess "how-to" knowledge. For example: a student who has only procedural knowledge of "average" would be able to say the average of {1, 2, 3} is equal to 2 but would not be able to list three numbers whose average is equal to 2. (mlf, rlk)

See also conceptual mathematics knowledge.

process approach

A method of teaching that focuses on procedures rather than the final product. Skills obtained, although learned through study of a specific subject, are often transferable to other topics and situations. Processes taught include communication, inference, measurement, observation, and so on. (jw)

process drama

Developed and advanced by drama educators such as Cecily O'Neill and Dorothy Heathcote, process drama, designed specifically for work in classrooms, is a structured method of using improvisation within curricular lessons in order for students to discover knowledge as they proceed. Students engage by playing roles pertinent to the lesson and improvising within the situation; the teacher guides, questions, and adds new information by taking roles as necessary within the classroom drama. A lesson on fossils might have students playing archaeologists, historians, politicians, and biologists, while the teacher-in-role guides both the drama and the learning that emerges from it. (em)

process mapping

A management practice or technique in which a series of organizational activities is elaborated in stepwise detail, using various symbols, to delineate and outline the constituent elements, actions, actors, and timeframe in which the activities are taking place to better understand relationships between these parts. This practice is generally used to develop clearer understanding among multiple parties involved in a particular activity, improve efficiency in accomplishing the activity, and/or document institutional knowledge. (sh)

process reflection

An examination of *how* individuals perform the functions of perceiving, thinking, feeling, or acting. It also includes an assessment of efficacy in performing each in isolation and in totality. (hfs)

process writing

A top-down, student-centered approach to writing in which writing instruction focuses on the process of creating writing rather than on the end product, and in which content and self-expression are emphasized over grammatical and lexical accuracy. The process writing approach views writing as a recursive endeavor that incorporates stages of prewriting, drafting, revising, editing, and publishing. (jk)

processfolio

A term conceived by Project Zero, a research group at the Harvard Graduate School of Education, as part of their 1980s curriculum and assessment project Arts PROPEL. While a portfolio is traditionally a collection of completed products, a processfolio contains works in progress that reflect a student's learning over time. Invented for use with the arts (e.g., visual arts or music), processfolios can be used in any classroom where students are asked to assess individual examples of their work, not as "good, better, best," but as interrelated developing steps in their overall learning. (jd)

proctor

A person whose duty is to watch over examinees during a test. Responsibilities of a proctor may include seating examinees, distributing and collecting test materials, checking identification, and monitoring examinees to prevent cheating. Proctors may also be called upon to certify the identity of examinees, for example, if a test is administered via the Internet rather than at a central testing site. As a verb, to supervise a test ("to proctor"). (scw)

prodigy

A person with special, extraordinary, or unusual artistic ability well beyond what might be gained by training—usually refers to a child. Like genius, the label "prodigy" can suffer from overuse and misuse, applied widely to anyone demonstrating ability and used for promotional purposes rather than description and understanding. Derived from the Middle English word for portent production (*prodige*) and the Latin word for omen or monster (*prodigium*), prodigy originates as a word signifying a sign of things to come, an indication of the future. Educational researchers have noted that prodigiousness seems to fall in one area (e.g., chess) rather than being global. (em)

production

The creation, presentation, and/or performance of a work of art (e.g., visual art, literature, drama, music, opera, dance, or film). A theatrical production refers to both the performance itself as well as the whole process of creating the final presentation. In film, production refers to the stage during which the primary shooting of scenes takes place (preceded by the planning and writing during preproduction and followed by the editing and finishing work of postproduction). Often, production is used to indicate the whole artistic project, as in "That was a beautiful production of Swan Lake." From a cognitive perspective, production (the making of a work) is often distinguished from perception (the perceiving of a work) even though both processes require meaning making through an artistic medium. (em)

productive noise

The sounds (e.g., speech, manipulation of equipment) made by students who are actively engaged in a cooperative or collaborative learning activity. Productive noise is considered to be a natural, positive by-product of active learning rather than the sign of a poorly managed classroom in which noise interferes with effective instruction. (bba)

professional degree (See degree, professional)

professional development

Any activity designed to help an adult, especially a professional, to become current or remain current in his/her field; to develop and enhance skills and knowledge; or to increase the breadth and depth of understanding that can lead to improved practice. In education, professional development encompasses the intentional, ongoing, and systemic processes and activities designed to enhance the professional knowledge, skills, and attitudes of educators so that they might, in turn, improve the learning of students. While there is not total agreement on the major models of professional development, there is some agreement on the following: training, observation/assessment, involvement in a development/improvement process, study groups, inquiry/action research, individually guided activities, mentoring. In higher education professional development activities foster faculty members' increasing sophistication in their academic discipline, and they usually take the form of sabbaticals for scholarship, research grants, or support for travel to conferences in the discipline. (chb, bs, cf)

professional development points (PDP)

Units measuring ongoing education required of educators and administrators in public school settings in order to maintain professional educator certificates or licenses issued by state departments of education or the National Board for Teaching Standards. These points may be earned through a variety of activities including degree course work, professional education programs, and mentoring. May also be referred to as continuing education units (CEUs). (ln)

See also continuing education unit.

professional development schools

Schools focused on the development of novice professionals, continuing development of experienced professionals, and research and development of the teaching profession. Professional development schools are usually affiliated with an institute of higher education in order to fulfill the goals of preparing all teachers to teach all students; meeting the diverse needs of children and families; collaborating as a community of learners; and conducting research and development of the teaching professional and school reform. The aim is to transform the educational enterprise by changing teaching, schooling, and teacher education simultaneously. (mrs, aa, bba, ja)

professional knowledge

Empirically grounded reflective process related to one's expertise. In education, professional knowledge refers to application of theory and practice in the classroom by the teacher. (bjl)

professional learning community

A group of teachers and administrators within a school who create a collaborative work culture, continuously seek and share learning, and then act on their collaborative learning. Professional learning communities are an organizational strategy for professional development, school change, and improvement. Effective professional learning communities focus on the goal of examining their daily practice in order to improve the learning of their students. (mrs, aa)

See also communities of practice.

professional practice

In education, the integration of theory and practice to create an individual pre-service and in-service teacher's approach to dissemination of information in the classroom. (bjl)

professional practice doctorate

The professional practice doctorate was proposed in order to reinvent a doctorate that focuses on preparing practitioner leaders in the field of education. While some aspects of a professional practice doctorate could be similar to the research doctorate, it should stand on its own as a rigorous preparation for leaders who are engaged in the practice of education. (eh1, eb)

professional semester

In a teacher education program, usually the final 16 weeks of study in which a pre-service teacher is placed in a supervised practice arrangement in order to develop expertise as a teacher under the guidance of an in-service teacher and a teacher education supervisor. (bjl)

professional sequence

In education, a step-by-step procedure in which one level is built upon another in turn until the ultimate goal is reached (i.e., certification, licensure, higher education degree, etc.). (bjl)

professional standards

In the field of Pre-K–12 education, a common set of knowledge, skills, and values expected of teachers, administrators, school counselors, and other educators. Developed by state boards of education as well as the National Board for Teaching Standards, these standards must be met by educators in order to achieve and maintain educator certificates awarded either by a state or the National Board for Teaching Standards. (ln)

professionalism

The conduct, aims, or qualities that characterize or mark an occupation or a person working in a particular occupation. (bjl)

professoriate

A collective term for the thousands of scholars, scientists, professionals, and specialists who hold faculty rank in American colleges and universities. (cf)

proficiency-based education

An approach to education that emphasizes the demonstration of skills and knowledge as evidence of learning. (las)

profile scores

Profile scores refer to a set of standardized scores based on a set of variables or measures. Typically profile scores are plotted together in one chart with three types of information: level, dispersion, and shape. Level information indicates a standardized score average across variables for an individual examinee, assuming these variables measure similar constructs. Dispersion defines how widely the values of these variables deviate from the level score. Dispersion information is normally dependent on correlations among the set of variables. Shape information of profile scores informs the ups-and-downs of the values on the set of variables. The shape of profile scores indicates strength and weakness of an individual examinee on the set of variables considered. (gl)

program approval

In teacher education this is the process by which an accrediting agency evaluates the scope, sequence, and quality of a teacher education program in order to award accreditation or license to prepare educators. (rtc)

program articulation

The process of arranging the instructional programs of the successive grades and divisions of the educational system so that a closely interlocking, continuous, and consistent learning environment is provided as learners progress through the system. It is also the degree of continuity, consistency, and interdependence in the offerings of the successive grades and divisions of the educational system. (db)

program design

The arrangement of educational or other activities with specific objectives related to curriculum and instruction. The design of a program will affect its implementation and the outcomes. (npo)

program evaluation (See evaluation; program review)

program review

Process in which academic programs are appraised in terms of criteria chosen to judge their effectiveness. Program review occurs at various levels. Colleges may have their own program review procedures, and various programs may hold discipline-based accreditation. There are also six accrediting agencies: Middle States Association of Colleges and Schools, New England Association of Schools and Colleges, North Central Association of Colleges and Schools, Northwest Commission on Colleges and Universities, Southern Association of Colleges and Schools, and Western Association of Schools and Colleges. (sn)

programmed instruction

A method of instruction that presents subject matter to a student in a sequence of small, controlled steps through which a student proceeds at his or her own pace. Using a computer or workbook, the student is asked one or more questions at each step and is provided answers upon completion of each. In addition to the correct answer, additional information may be provided at the conclusion of each step. (jw)

progressive adult education

An educational philosophy that values learning derived from observation and experience rather than from tradition and authority. The progressive philosophy of adult education emphasizes democracy and creativity in the classroom. It focuses on the learner's experience and practical problem-solving methods. Educators facilitate learning rather than teach so that the relationship between educators and learners is codependent and collaborative. (jwg)

progressive education

An educational reform movement of the late 19th and early 20th centuries that gathered momentum with the formation of the Progressive Education Association in 1919. The philosophy emphasizes learning by doing, adaptation of the curriculum and instruction to student needs and interests, cooperative learning, the introduction of real-life issues into the curriculum, and the use of the school to address social, political, and economic problems. Progressive education is typically contrasted with traditional education, which emphasizes teacher- and discipline-centered instruction. While the first two decades of the 20th century were the heyday of progressive education, its influence is evident in the work of modern educators and educational theorists as well. Individuals closely associated with this movement included John Dewey and Francis W. Parker. Begun as a reaction to the industrial, assembly-line model of teaching and learning, which lifted up the values of efficiency, compliance, and standardization, progressive education emphasized individual differences and the learner's overall development in the social-emotional realm as well as the physical and intellectual ones. Progressive educators have sought to reform education to make it a vehicle for the empowerment of students from all backgrounds, rather than an instrument of their social control and stratification. Progressive education is generally student-centered, favoring, for example, critical thinking over rote learning, student-teacher dialogue over lecture, immediate over delayed relevance of curriculum, learning by doing over reading textbooks, and the strengthening of moral judgment over conformity to dominant ethical norms. (cd, hv, ecr, mg)

See also progressivism; traditional education.

progressivism

Progress means improvement of some kind. Progressivism was a pluralistic reform movement in the United States in the late 19th and early 20th centuries (the Progressive Era) based on the conviction that the underprivileged status of groups such as blacks, immigrants, and women was attributable to social and political oppression rather than to a lack of intelligence or ambition. Thus, progressive psychologists, philosophers, and social scientists worked for the reform of social institutions, including education, to make them serve the purpose of improving the lives of individuals from all segments of society. (mg)

See also essentialism; perennialism; progressive education; vocational education.

Project Adventure

An experiential program that utilizes physical activity, risk, trust, adventure, problem solving, and hands-on learning. Project Adventure is a registered trademark. The corporation is a leader in adventure education. It offers training and consulting for businesses, human service organizations and educational groups, publications, equipment, and design and installation of challenge ropes courses. (rf)

See also adventure education.

project approach (See project-based learning)

project method

Popularized in the United States by William Kilpatrick in 1918, the project method is teaching and learning in which students engage in activities or carry out projects that they themselves regard as purposeful and interesting. Kilpatrick proposed several projects, each with a different type of purpose: in Type I, the purpose is to embody some idea in external form (to produce a play, for example); in Type II, to enjoy an aesthetic experience (for example, to listen to music); in Type III, to solve some problem; and in Type IV, to gain some particular knowledge or skill (to learn French irregular verbs, for example). (hv)

project training

A participative experience that combines career or vocational-technical instruction in the classroom with supervised and coordinated laboratory activities. (jm)

Project Zero

A research center founded in 1967 at the Harvard Graduate School of Education by Nelson Goodman. Initially intended to focus its efforts on the improvement of arts education, the project was codirected by Howard Gardner and David Perkins from 1972 to 2000. Project Zero now conducts research in the areas of human cognitive development, creativity, thinking, and other disciplines related to learning. In 2000, Steven Seidel was appointed director, and the project continues to be at the forefront of research in the field of education. (jwc)

project-based learning

An instructional approach in which students are allowed to engage in a long-term, complex project where they must spend time asking and debating questions and ideas, investigating by designing plans and experiments, collecting and analyzing data, asking more complex follow-up questions, and possibly concluding with creating artifacts that represent their learning or making a presentation. In this environment, the student is given the opportunity to connect what is covered in the curriculum with real-world experiences through extended inquiry. The project exploration and direction is strongly controlled by the student's own choices and motivations. In career education, project-based learning encompasses participative educational experiences that combine career and technical instruction in the classroom with supervised and coordinated laboratory or work-based learning activities. (ms, ea, jm)

projective test

One of a class of personality assessment techniques that involves a relatively unstructured verbal-response task. Only brief and general instructions are provided so as to maximize the free play of fantasy. Consistent with this aim, the test stimuli are usually vague and ambiguous. The underlying "projective hypothesis" is that the structure that the subject imposes on the ambiguous task and the perceptions and interpretations of the stimuli will reveal fundamental aspects of psychological functioning. Representative instruments include the Rorschach Inkblot Test, the Thematic Apperception Test (TAT), and the various incomplete sentences blanks, among others. (rnp)

proof

The logical step-by-step arguing of a proposition from axioms, assumptions, or previously proved propositions by direct or indirect methods. Evidence or argument that persuades the mind to accept the asserted idea or thought as true. Also, a proof may be a convincing or persuasive demonstration. (wja)

propaganda

Any association or concerted movement whose aim is the spreading of ideas, information, or misinformation for the purpose of helping or injuring an institution, cause, doctrine, practice, or person. Through the mass media, the primary target of propaganda is the political class (or social managers), that is, the minority of population that is educated, articulate, and expected to play some role in decision making. (ewr)

PROPEL (See Arts PROPEL)

proportional reasoning

Proportions are equivalent ratios (see ratio). Multiplicative thinking is needed in order to be able to solve proportional tasks meaningfully. Piaget's clinical interviews, reaffirmed in later studies, highlighted the difficulty many adolescents and adults have in successfully reasoning in proportional situations. (amr)

proprietary schools

For-profit institutions such as business schools, trade and technical schools, and cosmetology and correspondence schools. As an alternative to college, they provide opportunities for adults to improve their skills or change careers, especially adults without a high school diploma. (las)

proscenium arch

The arch that frames the stage in a traditional theater, marking the separation of the often elevated performing area from the audience. Viewed as a way of making theatrical performances stylistically similar to paintings (i.e., providing something to look at within a frame). The proscenium arch highlights the distance between actors and audience both physically and dramatically, separating the unreal (action on stage) from the real (lives of the audience). An extension of the stage, called an apron or thrust, in front of the proscenium arch, brings dramatic action closer to the audience. (em)

prose literacy

Defined in the National Adult Literacy Survey as the knowledge and skills needed to understand and use information from texts that include editorials, news stories, poems, and fiction. (jpc)

pro-social skills

Teaching children social competency and fostering peer acceptance by developing skills in such areas as friendship, problem solving, anger management, and overall self-esteem. (sr)

prosody

A component of reading fluency that relies on reading with expression. Prosody can relate to various aspects of the reading, including tempo or pace, rhythm, stress, pitch, intonation, emphasis, and appropriate phrasing. (cld)

Prosser Resolution

Popular name for *Vitalizing Secondary Education: Education for Life Adjustment* (1951), the final report of a conference of educators that had been held in 1945 to discuss a U.S. Office of Education study on vocational education. Made famous by author Charles Prosser's assertion that 60 percent of high school students were not having their needs for "life adjustment education" met by existing academic and vocational education programs, this report provided the spark that ignited the life adjustment education movement. This movement later became the target of savage criticism by supporters of rigorous intellectual standards in education, such as Arthur Bestor. (sw)

protocol

A facilitation tool with guidelines for group discussion designed to ensure that each participant has the opportunity to speak and to listen. Widely used in professional development for educators and applicable to many types of discussion, such as participant introductions, reflection, or idea generation. Protocols provide a safe structure in which to ask challenging questions of colleagues and ensure equity and parity in terms of each individual's needs. Typically used as vehicles for building the skills and culture necessary for collaborative work, protocols force transparency by segmenting elements of a conversation whose boundaries might otherwise blur. These segments include talking and listening, describing and judging, and proposing and giving feedback. (mf1, mrs, aa)

provost

A university or college senior campus administrator reporting to the president of the institution, often overseeing the work of the campus's deans, and providing the academic direction of the institution. Some provosts retain faculty status. (jbm)

proxemics

The study of personal and cultural spatial needs and consequent influences on interaction and communication with others. A typical example is an individual's comfort zone in his or her proximity to another speaker, and how that affects the ensuing dialogue. (jqa, npo)

proximal processes

Core to human development, proximal processes are the forms of interaction that occur in a person's immediate environment repeatedly over a long period of time. Such interactions occur between a parent and child, between children, and between student and teacher or coach when learning an activity, sport, skill, or technique. One's own characteristics, interests, talents, and abilities can impact the extent of impact and form of the proximal process. (ms)

PRS (See personal response system)

pseudowords

A string of letters that appears to be an actual word in a language because it follows the rules of that language. Vatch is an English pseudoword; cvtah is not. (mmd)

PSOC (See Psychological Sense of Community)

psychoactive drug

Term used for medications that affect people psychologically by altering mood, anxiety, cognitive processes, or behavior. They are often useful in treating, among other problems, depression, anxiety, insomnia, psychosis, or mania. Psychoactive drugs do not necessarily affect the underlying causes of these problems but can provide symptomatic relief. (sdc)

psychoanalytic therapy

An insight-oriented therapeutic approach that relies principally on introspection and that has been modified conceptually and technically from Freud's original formulations on psychoanalysis. This approach relies upon two fundamental hypotheses: the principle of psychic determinism, or causality, and the proposition that unconscious mental processes exert a frequent and significant impact on normal and abnormal mental functioning. Commonly employed interventions include interpretation, but, in contrast to formal psychoanalysis, there is less systematic analysis of the transference and of underlying dynamics, and sessions are conducted face-to-face. (rnp)

psychodrama

Therapeutic approach developed by J. L. Moreno that uses theatrical techniques as a way of gaining insight, changing undesirable behaviors, and increasing self-expression. A psychodrama consists of a protagonist (the client whose problem is the focus of the group), auxiliary people (group members that represent significant players in the protagonist conflict), the audience (group members who observe and provide reactions to the drama), and the director (the group therapist/psychodramatist). Psychodramas usually follow a sequence of events: the theme is identified by the director, a protagonist is chosen, the protagonist and auxiliary members act out the problem and explore different solutions, and the audience discusses their reactions. (tsw)

psychoeducational assessment

A series of standardized tests evaluating a student's level of perceptual, social, and academic functioning that culminates in a clinical report that includes a psychological and academic profile identifying any needs for special education placement and services for school-aged children. (ecb, nl1)

psychological assessment

The use of procedures, tests, and techniques to evaluate specific areas of psychological functioning, including the individual's abilities, behaviors, and personal qualities. Psychological assessments often include an interview with the client, psychological measurements of behavior, and systematic observations of client behavior and functioning. This information is combined with corroborating data and is used to gain a better understanding of client characteristics, diagnose specific mental disorders, and make recommendations to help the client function more effectively. (tsw, lbl, tvh)

Psychological Sense of Community (PSOC)

Seymour Sarason (1974) defined PSOC as: "The perception of similarity to others, an acknowledged interdependence with others, a willingness to maintain this interdependence by giving to or doing for others what one expects from them, and the feeling that one is part of a larger dependable and stable structure" (p. 157). (cma)

psychological test

An objective and standardized measure of a sample of behavior. Responses are scored and interpreted using a standard set of rules. If possible, scores are compared to norms that match the client in terms of age, grade level, or level of psychological functioning. These norms then allow for an understanding of how an individual's scores compare to others that have similar characteristics. Psychological tests evaluate many areas of functioning, including traits, aptitudes, personalities, behaviors, or needs at the particular time of testing. (tsw)

psychomotor stimulant

Considered to be any stimulant that has a mental effect that encourages a bodily motor response. Such stimulants include substances ranging from caffeine to cocaine. The well-known drug Ritalin, a psychotropic medication, is an example of a psychomotor stimulant. Touches and sensations that elicit reflexive responses (e.g., the sucking reflex in infants in response to a touch on the cheek) are also considered psychomotor stimulants. (mkt)

psychosis

Any severe disorder in which an individual loses contact with reality. Most typically, psychosis involves serious disruptions in a person's perception, cognition, affect, and emotions. It may be characterized by hallucinations, delusions, and disorganized speech and behavior. Gross impairment of reality testing interferes with the ability of the individual who is actively psychotic to accurately perceive and draw inferences from external reality, as well as evaluate one's own thoughts and perceptions. (tsw, rnp)

psychosocial development

Describes an individual's process of maturation in psychological and social areas. This process usually evolves from an infant's focus on self to awareness of others as individuals. The development process changes as the individual begins to interact more fully with others, until such interactions incorporate complex relationships in adolescent and adult years. Various theorists have proposed different models of psychosocial development. Freud identified several stages of psychosocial development with a psychosexual focus; Erik Erikson emphasized interactions between the physical and social environment with the individual; and Lawrence Kohlberg focused on aspects of moral development. (npo)

psychosomatic illness

Any mental disorder with somatic or bodily manifestations that is assumed to arise, at least in part, from cognitive and/or affective processes. Stated differently, any mental disorder with accompanying physical symptoms that arise from psychological causes. (kab)

See also somatoform disorder.

psychotic disorder

A category of mental disorders that have as their primary feature gross impairment in reality testing, typically characterized by symptoms such as hallucinations, delusions, disorganized or disordered thought or speech, disorganized behavior, or catatonic behavior. (jih)

psychotropic

Mind altering. Usually in reference to drugs affecting behavior or perception. (jwc)

PTA (See Parent Teacher Association)

PTO (See Parent Teacher Association)

public art

Any artwork made for and located in a place of access to a public audience. Graffiti or murals on the sides of building walls (often depicting historical elements or community aspirations), sculptures (from statues memorializing famous figures to works of abstract art), and aesthetic displays of landscape architecture are all regarded as public art. Public art ranges from art that is simply placed in a public space to art that is intended to provoke public conversation about a controversial issue. In community arts education, the collective enterprise of creating public art is thought to promote community development. (ap)

public education

In the United States public education is available "free" to the children of American citizens who are eligible to attend kindergarten through twelfth grade. There is no tuition charged directly to students attending; the cost is paid through local school, city, state, and federal taxes. However, there can be hidden costs such as instructional materials. Public schools are often referred to as "state schools," for they must follow federal and state guidelines, such as not discriminating against students based on gender, race, or physical disability. (bt-b)

See also private education.

public ivies

Term originated by Richard Moll in 1985 in his book *Public Ivys: A Guide to America's Best Public Undergraduate Colleges and Universities*. Moll named eight public universities that he felt offered an Ivy League education at a public school price: College of William & Mary, Miami University, University of California, University of Michigan, University of North Carolina at Chapel Hill, University of Texas at Austin, University of Vermont, and University of Virginia. More recent authors have expanded this list. (sn)

Public Law 78-346 (See Serviceman's Readjustment Act of 1944)

Public Law 89-10 (See Elementary and Secondary Education Act)

Public Law 89-329 (See Higher Education Act of 1965)

Public Law 92-318 (See Education Amendments of 1972)

Public Law 93-638 (See Indian Self-Determination and Education Assistance Act)

Public Law 94-142 (See Education for All Handicapped Children Act of 1975)

Public Law 96-88 (See United States Department of Education)

Public Law 101-542 (See Student Right-to-Know and Campus Security Act)

Public Law 103-227 (See Goals 2000: Educate America Act)

public Schools (See public education)

public service

Concepts and principles identifying the various ways in which colleges and universities meet their responsibilities to community, state, society, and nation as well as their numerous constituencies. This service ranges in form and fashion from traditional extension programs to more recent outreach and engagement activities and efforts. (cf)

public sphere

Public spaces where, because of their potential for equality, critique, accessibility, reflexivity, and problematizing the unquestioned, individuals can communicate without fear of censure. The ideal of a public sphere asserts itself as a safeguard against the systematizing and hegemonic effects of the state. Such spaces may also promote full and dynamic participation by citizens, ensuring movement toward a participatory democracy. (hfs)

public universities

Public or state universities are partially subsidized by the state as part of its public education system. The amount of the subsidy varies from university to university and from state to state, but the intent is to make higher education affordable for more students and less expensive than private universities. (sn)

public values (See values)

pull-out programs

A way of providing additional services to exceptional students by removing them from their regular classroom and placing them in a special class with a special education or resource teacher. (bba)

pupil (See student)

pupil-teacher ratio (PTR)

"The number of students in a school or district compared to the number of teaching professionals" (McRobbie et al. 1998, 4). In some venues all educators are part of the computation, including counselors, administrators, and so on. In this formula, the divisor (number of educational personnel) is very important. PTR is a way to assure equitable distribution of funds and is important to administrators, policy persons, and others. The difference between PTR and class size in U.S. elementary schools is about n = 10 (Achilles and Sharp 1998). PTR is a formula and administrative process for allocation of resources; class size is an organization for providing instructional and educational services to clients. Data generally available in large databases are PTR data. Valid and reliable ways to get class-size data are to count students in a class and/or to establish class sizes and monitor them, as in Tennessee's STAR study. Surveys and databases usually generate PTRs. (cma)

puppetry

The making and/or manipulation of puppets for use in some kind of theatrical show. A puppet is a fabricated doll-like representation of an animal or human, usually with a hollow cloth body in which the puppeteer's hand is inserted and a wooden or papier-mâché head. In Europe, China, India, Java, and elsewhere in Asia, there are ancient traditions of puppet theater. It is assumed that puppet theater has everywhere antedated written drama and, indeed, writing of any kind. A popular activity in kindergarten classes, puppetry is historically one of the earliest of art forms. (kf)

purposeful teaching and learning

Applying cognitive processes in setting goals, planning the procedures, implementing activities, engaging the teachers and learners, connecting the outcomes, and assessing the events so they are meaningful and relevant. Purposeful teaching and learning provides a framework to involve teachers and learners throughout the process, giving each of them voice, choice, and ownership. (npg)

purposive (or purposeful) sampling

Sampling in which particular settings, persons, or events are selected deliberately in order to provide information that cannot be gotten as well from other choices. This is an alternative to both probability sampling and convenience sampling and is the most common form of sampling in qualitative research. (jam)

Pygmalion effect

Usually regarded as synonymous with self-fulfilling prophecy. The Pygmalion effect suggests a strong link between expectation and outcome; in particular, the influence of teacher expectation on student achievement. For instance, if teachers have high expectations of students, they in turn yield high performance (as exemplified by George Bernard Shaw's *Pygmalion*), and the reverse is true. The Pygmalion effect came from an ancient myth. The sculptor Pygmalion, a prince of Cyprus, wanted to create an ivory statue of the ideal woman. He did so and named her Galatea. She was so beautiful that Pygmalion fell desperately in love with her and prayed to the goddess Aphrodite to bring her to life, and so she did. (mc)

Q

quadrivium

Four (*quad*) subjects or "ways" (*via*) to truth; the second level of course work offered in the 12th-century European cathedral schools, and later, in altered form, in European medieval universities: arithmetic, geometry, music, astronomy. (bgr)

See also trivium.

qualitative research

The term "qualitative research" became widely used in the late 1980s to describe a range of research methods and techniques, which were central to anthropology and qualitative sociology, and that had been covered by the more specific term ethnography. Since that time there has been a dramatic expansion of qualitative inquiry into other research domains including education. This expansion has brought with it considerable controversy about the extent and meaning of qualitative research in terms of both its epistemological foundations and its methods and strategies. Despite the controversy over the proper application of the term, qualitative research can best be defined as a form of social inquiry that takes reality as socially constructed rather than given and where the data are primarily textual rather than numerical. Qualitative research is conducted in naturalistic settings where the researcher, who is the instrument of research, pays close attention to context and to the meanings participants attach to social behavior. Qualitative research tends to be inductive and holistic, and analysis is interpretive rather than statistical. (rws)

quantitative history

An approach to historical research in which one makes use of information technology to collect, manipulate, and analyze large sets of data. Unlike social history, which is a term used to describe an approach to the choice of topic for historical inquiry, quantitative history is a term that simply implies that the historian has chosen to base his or her arguments in whole or in part on an analysis of quantitative (i.e., numeric) data. Quantitative analysis of historical information such as census data, racial and ethnic representation in a community, or the percentage of children in a school eligible for free lunches can be used to bolster an argument regarding the experience of schooling at a specific time and place. (sw)

quantitative literacy

Defined in the National Adult Literacy Survey as the knowledge and skills required to apply arithmetic operations, either alone or sequentially, using numbers embedded in printed materials. (jpc)

quantitative research

A numerically based analysis that utilizes scientifically gathered data from tests, measures, formulas, and calculations in order to answer a question or prove a hypothesis by establishing a statistically significant relationship between variables. (ms)

quantitive reasoning

Having an understanding about quantities and relationships between quantities. Research indicates the importance of the development of quantitative reasoning to the study of algebra. (dc)

quarter (academic calendar)

Universities and colleges adopting a quarterly system divide the calendar year into four quarters, with each quarter typically being 10 weeks long. Three quarters are required to complete one academic year. For purposes of transfer, three quarter hours equal two semester hours. (sn)

queer

Originally meaning odd, queer became a derogatory term to describe GLBT people in the 20th century. The term is now used to describe those who see their own identity as not fitting with contemporary "norms" of gender and sexuality. Most often used by academics, political progressives, and young people; some GLBT people still consider the term queer offensive and do not use it to self-identify. (jb2)

See also gender queer; queer theory.

queer pedagogy

The implications of queer theory for the practice and study of critical pedagogy encompass queer pedagogy. Queer theories are not unified propositions, but generally refer to a constellation of analytical tools and strategies used to disrupt discursive productions of the "normal," with particular, albeit not exclusive, attention to sex/gender binaries. Queer theories draw from poststructuralist destabilization of the subject and are generally suspicious of the role "community" plays in identity production, even if the community's stated claims take a liberal stance. In this way, queer theories arise both out of and against the more assimilationist aspects of lesbian, gay, bisexual, transgender (LGBT) studies and civil rights movements. The aim is not to reconcile the tensions between the binary oppositions of "homosexual" and "heterosexual," or "gay" and "straight," but rather to exploit the tensions between "queer" and "normal" as a means of opening a larger critique of power and identity politics. Advocates of queer pedagogy suggest strategies to stimulate rethinking issues such as the student/teacher binary, classroom identity politics, and the function of the erotic in education. Queer pedagogy is ultimately focused on confronting educational processes that assume heterosexuality is universal, natural, and normative; critiquing the ways that other knowledges are produced in relation to those assumptions (such as race, class, and nation); and questioning the ways that schooling historically has been used to consolidate power structures through the production and propagation of heteronormative discourse. (bda, npo)

queer studies

Queer studies is an emerging interdisciplinary field whose goal is to analyze a wide variety of sexual identities, performances, discourses, and representations and to call into question the notion of normative sexuality and gender. (jb2)

See also gay, lesbian, bisexual studies.

queer theory

Queer theory is less a theory and more a collection of approaches to studying and questioning assumptions about sex, gender, and sexuality. These approaches mainly flow from intellectual traditions in feminism and lesbian and gay studies.

Queer theory and, with it, queer studies emerged in the early 1990s and entered the field of education shortly after. (acp)

See also LGBT studies; queer studies.

questioning

Part of the GLBTQ acronym that describes those who are unsure of their gender identity and/or sexual identity and may or may not be in a deliberate process of exploring these aspects of their identity. (jb2)

questioning techniques

Employed by teachers to assess students' knowledge, direct a discussion, stimulate inquiry, and challenge ideas, assumptions, or biases when discussing controversial issues. The quantity and quality of learning is impacted by the frequency, type, and level of questioning that takes place between a teacher and students in a classroom. A variety of category systems are available for assessing the levels of questions and responses. Among these are Benjamin Bloom's "Taxonomy of Educational Objectives: Cognitive and Affective Domains," J. B. Guilford's "Structure of Intellect" model, and Kohlberg's "Developmental Stages of Moral Reasoning." (igb)

quiet area

Area that is physically and psychologically comfortable and inviting for children who prefer to be away from the group to gather their thoughts. Rules for behavior may be established for proper use of the area. For example, rules may be developed together with children concerning the number of children who may use the area at any one time and the type of activities that are permissible. (at)

quilting

The making of quilts or coverlets, in which two layers of cloth are filled with padding and held in place by ties or stitched designs. Quilts are distinguished by their patchwork designs, which are often geometrically complex and highly decorative. Once one of the few avenues for women to express political or religious views, quilting continues to be a form of artistic expression and, because of its patchwork quality, lends itself well to collaborative work (e.g., the AIDS quilt). It is popular in schools, where students use the quilt to create individual squares or patches around a common theme. (lj)

Quincy Plan

School design developed in Boston's Quincy Grammar School in the mid-19th century in which students were divided into grades, promotions were based on a system of requirements, and the facilities consisted of a square, four-story building with each grade occupying a separate floor, an auditorium on the fourth floor, and the administration occupying the basement. The Quincy Plan aided in the standardization of design and administration of schools from coast to coast in the late 19th century. (dwm)

quiz

An exercise used to assess knowledge or skills. Often a relatively short or informal set of questions intended to test given information, such as a completed chapter or recently completed unit of study. (jw)

quotitive division

A form of intuitive division in which one attempts to determine how many times a smaller quantity is contained within a larger quantity. The divisor must be smaller than the dividend. This model, often termed "measurement division," may be seen as repeated subtraction in cases where the quotient is a whole number. (slr)

R

race

A socially constructed category classifying groups of people according to selected physical and inherited characteristics. Skin color and hair texture, but not eye or hair color, are used in the assignment of race. The concept of race has become questionable, as science has demonstrated that all humans share about 97 percent of their genes. (jc)

See also culture; ethnicity.

race-based admission

The practice of acceptance and entrance to a school or university of an individual who belongs to a distinct ethnic group. Although other requirements such as standardized test scores, academic records acceptable to the school or university, class ranking, and writing instruments that assess one's knowledge are considered in the admission process, race can be the determining factor that permits entry. (jt)

racism

A type of destructive prejudice that involves the unequal treatment of a particular group of individuals because of social, physical, economic, linguistic, or other characteristics that socially define a particular race. Racism involves a belief system whereby one racial category (or several) is considered to be superior or inferior to another. Racism can be expressed at an individual level, when a person expresses hatred or fear against others who are perceived as differently "raced"; at a cultural level, when a group of people of common heritage hold racist views such as the Nazis held against Jewish people; at a political level, when a society creates laws that are racist, such as that it is illegal for blacks to own property; and at an institutional level, when seemingly neutral criteria favor members of one race over another. (cd, bt-b)

radical adult education

Education based on the premise that, in order for people to exercise their power and participate in the political process, knowledge and learning must come first. It assumes that members of a community can learn both to understand the problems of their communities and to find the best solutions. Social action and transformation of communities are seen as the direct result of actively considering issues of power and oppression as root causes of community problems. (chm)

radical democracy

"Radical" democracy insists that all people need to live in a society where decisions are really made by the people. The position is that a society where these conditions do not exist requires the need to replace, transform, and rebuild social institutions so that all people can decide their destinies. This belief in the need for critique and transformation of society, rather than simple amelioration, is what makes the democratic ideal "radical." Radical democratic theory is nonfoundational, fallibilistic, and contingent; it is historically situated, rooted in particular times and settings. It relies on a qualified relativistic view of truths. (bt-b)

See also democracy.

radical sign
The symbol, √, used to name roots. (ps)

rap/rap music
Rap (1960s slang for conversation) has developed into a contemporary musical genre, often called hip-hop, consisting of rhythmically chanted, often improvised poetry sung/spoken on its own or along with selections from popular music. Often critical of mainstream culture, rap reflects a social and political awareness that appeals to and gives voice to youth who, for a myriad of reasons, may have been placed at risk. Feared by some as promoting violence and misogyny, rap represents a range of voices that resist categorization. Rap has been embraced by popular culture, incorporated into the repertoire of many performing artists, and frequently used or featured in movies. Some educators see the rhythm and appeal to youth of rap music as a vehicle for teaching and learning. (jd)

See also hip-hop.

rapid naming
Sometimes referred to as rapid automatic naming or lexical retrieval. It is the ability to efficiently retrieve phonological information from long-term memory and is often measured by determining the amount of time needed to name a series of familiar objects, colors, digits, or letters arranged on a page. It is generally accepted that slow rapid naming speed characterizes at least a subset of children with reading disabilities and is a predictor of reading success. However, researchers are divided over whether rapid naming is a component of phonological skills or whether they represent separate cognitive processes. The double deficit hypothesis proposed by Maryanne Wolf suggests that the readers with the most significant disabilities are those who demonstrate weaknesses in both rapid naming and phonological processing, while other individuals with reading disabilities show deficits in only rapid naming or phonological processing. (rcr)

rate
The speed of reading, often measured as the number of words per minute (wpm) or the number of words correctly read per minute (wcpm). (mmd)

rate of change
A measure of how quickly a quantity is changing with respect to another quantity. An example is the behavior of an object under gravity. For each second that the object is falling, the distance it travels every second changes. So the distance the object is falling changes with respect to time. The instantaneous rate of change of an object can be found by calculating the slope of the tangent line of the trajectory of the object; in other words, derivatives can be used to find rates of change. (smc)

ratio
The comparison of two quantities. This comparison can be a part-whole comparison, expressed as a fraction, a/b, or a part-part comparison expressed in the form a:b. (ps)

rational counting
Counting discrete objects with meaning. This involves being able to organize the objects in some way so that a one-to-one match can be made between the

objects counted and the standard number word sequence. Also, there is a realization that the last number named represents the total number of objects in the set. (dc)

rational emotive behavioral therapy (REBT)

Originally called RET (Rational Emotive Therapy) by Albert Ellis, REBT is a cognitive-behavioral therapy in which the therapist challenges and questions the client's irrational ideas. An assumption is that emotional and behavioral responses are an outgrowth of faulty cognitions. REBT can best be understood in an *ABC framework. A* represents an *activating* event related to an important desire, goal, or preference. *B* is the *belief,* usually related to failure to attain the goal that follows the activating event. The belief determines *C, consequences,* such as feelings of anger, anxiety, and depression. (tsw)

rational number

A real number that is in the form a/b where a and b are integers and $b \neq 0$; a real number that can be expressed as a fraction, for example, $a/1$ is a rational number and is written as a; a real number that is a repeating or terminating decimal. Another notation used to express a/b is (a, b). (kgh)

read aloud

An instructional method designed to develop students' language and comprehension skills by listening to and discussing books read by the teacher. (mmd)

readability

The quality and clarity of a piece of written work. Writing that can be understood by those for whom it is written. (jw)

reader response theory

A teaching approach that emphasizes the reader's experience interacting with a text as opposed to the intention of the author or the text itself. Thus, teachers using this approach are concerned with the student's subjective thoughts on the text, and not with any particular objective interpretation of the text. (za)

reader's workshop approach

Reader's workshop consists of three instructional approaches: independent reading, guided reading, and literature study. During independent reading, students read books on their own that they can comprehend successfully without support from the teacher. During guided reading, children are grouped by reading level or the skill they need to work on; they read books at a slightly more advanced level with support from the teacher. In this approach, the teacher works on developing particular skills students need to become better readers. In contrast, during literature study, children are grouped heterogeneously according to their interests. They read books and engage in discussion with peers who are reading the same text. (jas)

reading

The construction of personal meanings from the use of available language systems (grapho-phonemics, syntax, semantics, and pragmatics). (mc1)

reading motivation

A multidimensional construct that is often considered to involve self-efficacy and the belief that one can be successful in reading. Reading motivation encompasses involvement in purposeful reading, extrinsic motivation related to goal orientation, and intrinsic motivation related to reading as a social activity. Reading motivation tends to differ, on average, by gender and by ethnicity, and tends to decline as children advance through the grades in school. (rcr)

reading readiness

The conceptual and affective preparedness for formal instruction in reading (and usually writing). (mc1)

reading recovery

A program of individualized support for struggling beginning readers based upon the work of New Zealander Marie Clay. (mc1)

reading strategies

The conscious, purposeful evocation and application of reading behaviors that, when used automatically and unconsciously, are considered skills. Reading strategies are valuable in particular situations in which skills cannot be automatically invoked, such as during initial learning, when unexpected breakdowns in comprehension occur, and in situations in which a task is too difficult to be processed adequately by the reader's present skills. (jk)

REAL (See Responsible Education About Life Act)

realism

The philosophical position that the world exists independently of our perceptions or theories of it. Although realism is a prominent position in current philosophy of science, it has had little influence on qualitative research, which is usually seen as based on some form of constructivism. (jam)

realistic mathematics

Based on Hans Freudenthal's view of mathematics, which is that mathematics is a human activity and should be connected to reality. In realistic mathematics, students are given context-based problems, which may be based in real life but may also be based on problem situations that students can imagine. By solving context-based problems, students are able to develop mathematical tools and understanding, creating models that may help solve other related problems. (kgh)

reality

Most simply, that which exists. Ever since Plato, reality has been understood as the opposite of "mere" appearance. Hence, for Plato (and for some 20th-century physicists) the world ordinarily grasped by the five senses is merely the reflection of something more permanent, more substantial. The attempt has been made to replace the illusion of appearances with knowledge of true causes and entities that embody them, which would constitute reality. Kant, among others, thought this search for reality perfectly hopeless insofar as it involved the use of terms such as "cause" well beyond their appropriate bounds. (an)

reality therapy

This type of therapy emphasizes that individuals can control their own behavior and that behavior is determined by choices made in order to meet the five basic needs. It focuses on teaching individuals how to direct their own lives and to make effective decisions and how to deal with stressors. In order to be able to meet future needs successfully, the effectiveness of what the client is currently doing should be emphasized and evaluated. (tsw)

really simple syndication (RSS)

A technology that allows individuals to receive instant updates of information. The process requires an individual to subscribe to a source of web-based information (such as a news website) via a "feeds" button that appears on the website. When the content of the website is updated, the information is automatically transferred to the user's computer and is accessible from a single point of reference (usually the "feeds" button is located on the Internet toolbar). Individuals can subscribe to multiple sources of information, all of which are aggregated and available through the RSS "feed" on the toolbar. Educators commonly subscribe to news websites, websites containing videos and photos related to curriculum, and teaching blogs. Also known as RSS or an RSS feed. (sm)

reason

The ability to assess and consider a situation in its various aspects. Reason can also be the explanation for a particular choice or behavior. (npo)

reasonableness

The quality of rationally determining whether your thinking and the answer to a problem is able to be justified to yourself or to another person. Using estimation strategies to assess whether a result of computation is appropriate. (vdf)

reasoning

Typically considered problem solving, reasoning can involve either inductive or deductive thinking. Using logic, reasoning is part of the cognitive process that uses available information to develop new ideas or information. (npo)

REBs (See regional employment boards)

REBT (See rational emotive behavioral therapy)

recertification

In education, renewing a credential in the area of competence in which a state department of education endorses the teacher to be qualified to teach. The credential or teaching certificate authorizes an agency to hire a teacher in accordance with state standards at the professional level. (bjl)

recession

The common term used for the contraction phase of the business cycle; a general period of declining economic activity during which the real gross domestic product declines by approximately 10 percent, the unemployment rate rises, and inflation tends to be low or nonexistent. Recessions generally last from 6 to 18 months, with one year most common. (mkg)

reciprocal teaching

A form of collaborative teaching in which teacher and students share the teaching responsibility by taking turns as leaders in discussing a reading selection. As they discuss the reading, the students, as well as the teacher, engage in four reading comprehension strategies—asking questions, clarifying areas of confusion, predicting upcoming content, and summarizing reading material. (bba)

reciprocity

In teacher education, an interstate certification agreement with other states signed by the state board of education in which a teacher is certified; the agreement recognizes the teaching certificate earned and, with proof and optional testing, will issue a teaching certificate in the states that have signed the agreement. (bjl)

recitation

Question and answer discourse in which the teacher asks questions and students respond. Recitation follows a pattern known as IRE (Initiate, Respond, Evaluate): The teacher asks a question; the student responds; the teacher evaluates the response. Recitation is typically used to review and assess student understanding and recall after a reading assignment or lecture. Teachers usually ask convergent questions (questions having specific predetermined answers) focusing on literal-level understanding and recall. (ba)

recomposition method (See number decomposition/recomposition)

reconceptualism

Name given to a significant historical movement in curriculum studies in the 1970s that saw its origins in conferences first at the University of Rochester and then at Bergamo Center in Dayton, Ohio. Begun by a diverse group of scholars, unified only by their opposition to the then dominant managerial and prescriptive approaches to curriculum development and instruction, reconceptualism shifted the focus from traditional, quantitative, behavioral models, such as the Tylerian Rationale, toward reconceptualized understandings of the various philosophic, social, political, cultural, psychological, artistic, and economic dimensions of curriculum and teaching. Explorations into race, class, gender, sexuality, ecology, aesthetics, and democracy typify this movement, though the forms of analysis, critique, and description are varied, complex, and often interdisciplinary. The emphasis is on autobiographical and phenomenological, internal experiences rather than external objectives, such that the curriculum is the interpretation of lived experiences. William (Bill) F. Pinar, Paul Klohr, Janet Miller, Maxine Greene, Henry Giroux, Elliot Eisner, Philip Jackson, and William Reynolds are recognized as some of its most notable contributors. (jm1)

Recording for the Blind and Dyslexic

A not-for-profit organization that has a free library of over 55,000 digitally recorded books. They will also read any book into an audiobook format if requested by a student who is vision impaired or has dyslexia. (ab1)

See also audiobook.

rectificatory justice (See justice)

recursive problem solving

Involves finding a solution to a mathematical task by returning or turning back to steps already taken. For example, when problem solving one may initially attempt various strategies for finding a feasible solution. Then, one will step back to reflect upon the task and strategies applied. This process may continue through several iterations before a solution may be found. (sdt)

redirection

Using positive, nonpunitive guidance to refocus a child's interest before or after an undesirable behavior occurs. The use of this technique requires keen observation by the teacher or caregiver to anticipate a child's actions and emotions, or quick response from the teacher or caregiver to resolve conflicts without reinforcing the use of the undesirable behavior. The teacher or caregiver acts calmly in order not to create a disturbance in the environment or setting. (at)

reductivism (See minimalism)

reentry courses

Courses designed to allow adults to enter higher education programs without needing to pass through lower levels of the educational system. (las)

reentry student

Individuals who return to an educational program after a prolonged absence. Typically these are students who, after enrolling in a postsecondary institution and then abandoning their studies, matriculate again in a postsecondary institution. (las, chb)

referral

The process by which a person is recommended to receive services different from those currently being provided. Students may be referred for counseling, psychological or educational testing, medical examinations, and so on. A referral is typically made when the present array of services is not meeting the needs of the student. Referrals involve identifying a need for a referral, finding an appropriate referral source, and preparing the client for the experience of being referred. (tsw)

reflection

According to John Dewey (1910), reflection is "the active, persistent, and careful consideration of any belief or supposed form of knowledge in the light of the grounds that support it and the further conclusions to which it tends." Reflection is in its literal sense self-reflection, a bending back on itself, but it is also used in the sense of thinking in general. In philosophy reflection has always had a central place in this double sense. First of all, philosophy can to a large extent be determined as reflection in the sense of thinking. Second, self-reflection has played a decisive role in modern philosophy (i.e., from the Renaissance, as a means for finding an absolute foundation of knowledge), but also as a way of differentiating consciousness from the material world. In contemporary discussion of professional competence and vocational education, reflection has played a prominent role. In counseling, reflection is a specific type of listening response that involves commenting on/identifying the affect (i.e., feelings) associated with a client's comments. This method is used to increase a client's self-awareness, to encourage him or her to experience his or her feelings more deeply, and to bolster his or her confidence that the counselor is, indeed, understanding accurately what he or she is experiencing emotionally. (bjl, jb1, bmm)

reflective decision making
The process of examining the merits and problems of the situation under consideration in a deliberate and careful way, considering both the past and future while assessing potential outcomes. (cd)

reflective inquiry
A process that calls for careful description of a problem with all its contributory elements, including self-evaluation and examination of the participant's own contributions to the problem. A consideration of the "why" as well as the "what" of a problem. Often traced back to John Dewey's conceptualization of "active, persistent and careful consideration of any belief or supposed form of knowledge in the light of the grounds that support it and the further conclusions to which it tends" (1910, 9). Reflective inquiry is a cornerstone of a constructivist approach to the teaching of social studies, as opposed to the traditional "knowledge transmission" approach. Historically, U.S. schools have undertaken democratic education as a social studies focus; as democracy is predicated upon critical analysis of accessible information, this perspective advocates the teaching of social studies as an exercise in reflective inquiry. (cd, ks1)

reflective practice
A concept introduced by Donald Schön in 1983. In reflective practice, a person learns by looking at their past experiences and the successes, failures, outcomes, thoughts, emotions, individuals, and events that surround the experiences. The process may be facilitated by another who has competency in the area being reflected on and is meant to help the learner improve by reflecting on what happened in the past. A teacher/practitioner engages in continual assessment of the improvement of practice by examining and analyzing actions, motives, student outcomes, and education policies. (ms, rtc)

reflective teacher education
An approach to teacher education that emphasizes the development of deliberative and analytical thinking about and improving upon one's teaching based on student outcome data, on desirable teaching practices, or on moral principles in teaching. (rtc)

reflective teaching
Teachers' continuous self-monitoring and thoughtful deliberation about the effectiveness of their teaching in an attempt to improve learning in their classrooms. (bba)

reflexivity
The idea that the researcher is an involved participant in and cannot be detached from the social world that one is studying. There is a mutual influence process occurring among the researcher, the research participants, and the research setting. Also, includes the practice of becoming

aware of, monitoring, and understanding this mutual influence process and its effects upon the research. Similar to the concept of "researcher subjectivity." (mas)

reform

In education, may be a legislative act, a process, and/or a social movement to bring about change. (bjl)

refresher course

A course that helps adults relearn and/or update skills and knowledge that they have acquired previously but no longer possess. (jpc)

refugee resettlement programs

Programs geared toward preparing refugees for resettlement in a new country. Components of these programs include instruction in the new country's language and customs, immigration information, and employment skills. (las)

regalia

Academic garb typically worn by students and professors in higher education at academic occasions such as convocation and commencement. Gowns, hoods, and caps (typically either tams or mortarboards) are designed based upon the degree conferred, with specific regalia for bachelors, masters, and doctoral degrees. Colors in the regalia typically denote the institution where the degree was conferred and the subject area of the degree. Some colleges and universities have signature regalia designed specifically for their institutions. (pw1)

regent (See trustee)

Regents of the University of California v. Bakke, 438 U.S. 265 (1978)

U.S. Supreme Court decision that considered the case of a white applicant (Allan Bakke) who was denied admission to the University of California at Davis Medical School. Several minority applicants with lower scores were admitted to the same program, and a divided Court ruled against using only racial quotas as the basis in the admissions process. However, the Court did allow that race could be used as a factor, as long as it was not the only factor. (mc3)

Reggio Emilia

A city of 130,000 people in the Emilia Romagna region of northern Italy in which the municipal early childhood system has evolved a distinctive and innovative set of philosophical assumptions, curriculum and pedagogy, method of school organization, and design of environments. This approach fosters children's intellectual development through a systematic focus on symbolic representation. (bjl)

regional educational laboratories

Regional educational laboratories are 10 federally created nonprofit agencies that link educational practitioners with relevant research, information resources, technical assistance, development opportunities, and evaluation services. (lr)

regional employment boards (REBs)

Regional entities that provided coordination and oversight to ensure access to training opportunities for workers as well as the availability of a trained workforce able to meet employer needs. The REBs were created under the Job Training Partnership Act and became Local Workforce Investment Boards under the Workforce Investment Act. (las)

regional school district

A form of public school organization used in some geographic areas marked by low populations and great distances. Such a district includes schools (normally a number of them) from more than one community in an attempt to achieve critical mass with regard to resources and programs. (lr)

register

In the context of language and linguistics, register is a variant of language typically used to communicate in a particular setting or context, such as the legal register. (cld)

registered apprenticeship

Programs that meet specific federally approved standards designed to safeguard the welfare of apprentices. Programs are registered with the Bureau of Apprenticeship and Training (BAT), the U.S. Department of Labor, or a State Apprenticeship Agency or Council approved by BAT. (jm)

See also apprenticeship.

registrar

The official responsible for maintaining and overseeing admissions and other student records in a school or university. Registrars maintain vital statistics on students, determine eligibility for enrollment, and maintain cumulative data records from prior school years. The registrar is the chief custodian of student grade information and often is responsible for overseeing and distributing student extracurricular eligibility information. Additionally, the registrar is responsible for handling student withdrawal from school procedures and communicating and transferring necessary student information between districts or colleges. (tm)

registrar, office of the

An office supporting the educational process by record keeping. The official student's educational record or transcript is maintained in this office. (cf)

registration

The procedure by which students are assigned to class. It includes approval of courses to be taken by the student, organization of sections, and assessment and collection of fees. (cf)

regression

Regression, often referred to as linear regression, is a statistical procedure that is used to predict one variable (i.e., dependent variable) on one or several variables (i.e., independent variables) that are assumed to have linear relationship with the dependent variable. Regression analysis results in a regression equation in which the predicted value of a dependent variable is expressed as a weighted combination of independent variables. The distances between the predicted values and observed values of the dependent variable are called regression errors. Fitting a regression model is to minimize the regression errors based on an estimation method. The regression line based on an ordinary least square method can be drawn by connecting the mean values of the dependent variable conditioned on the values of the independent variable or variables. A fitted regression model in most cases supports more of a correlational relationship than a causal relationship between the dependent and independent variables. (gl)

regrouping

Rearranging numbers to make computations easier. The structure of our number system, based in tens, along with the commutative and associative properties, allow for regrouping and reorganizing of numbers. For example, given an addition problem, a child might think of 347 + 28 as 34 tens and 7 ones plus 2 tens and 8 ones. (mlf, rlk)

regular words

A word that is decodable because all of the letters or groups of letters within the words (e.g., digraphs, blends) represent their most common sound. There are words that are regular for both reading and spelling and words that are regular for reading only, because there is more than one possible way to represent the sounds present within the word (e.g., *train* is regular for reading, but it could be also be spelled as *trane*). Readers can generally process regular words more easily than they can irregular words. (rcr)

regular/irregular shapes

Regular polygons have congruent sides and congruent angles, for example, the equilateral triangle and the square. Regular polyhedra have congruent regular polygons as faces, with congruent edges and congruent solid angles. Three-dimensional regular polyhedra are limited to the five Platonic solids (tetrahedron, octahedron, icosahedron, hexahedron, and dodecahedron). Irregular shapes include at least one side, edge, or angle that is not congruent to another. (ey)

rehabilitation

The process of restoring an individual to a designated level of capacity, typically as part of treatment for an injury or illness. (sr)

rehabilitation therapy

Treatments aimed at facilitating recovery from injury or disease, encompassing a broad spectrum of domains, such as physical, occupational, speech, vocational, recreational, and psychological therapies. Rehabilitation therapy entails improving an individual's physical, sensory, and/or cognitive abilities that have declined from previous baseline levels. Treatment is designed to restore as much functioning as possible, to compensate for deficits that cannot be reversed, and to assist individuals to achieve optimum levels of independence in their daily lives. (cap)

rehearsal

In the performing arts, sessions in which director, cast, and crew practice and prepare for the public performance of a work. The rehearsal period is a process in which every aspect of the production is worked on: the abstract (coming to an understanding of the meaning of a work), the concrete (creating the look of the production), the physical (staging the work), and the technical (lights, sets, and costumes), and, finally, the putting together of all the pieces. Rehearsals provide wonderful opportunities for teaching and learning about the art of performance, the collaborative dimension, and the artistic process. (em)

reification

In mathematics, reification refers to the ability to conceive of the result of a process as a permanent entity, or as an object. The same mathematical concepts can be interpreted at times as objects and at other times as a process. For example, $\sqrt{-1}$ can be seen as an abstract object, i, or as the result of the process of taking the square root of negative 1. Similarly, $2x$ can be seen as an object, $2x$, or it can be seen as the process of doubling a number. (smc)

reinforcement

Refers to the "schedule" that delivers a reinforcer in order to increase or decrease the probability of occurrence of a target behavior. Reinforcers may be delivered on a fixed-ratio or variable-interval schedule, depending on the target behavior. (xss, yb)

See also reinforcer; target behavior.

reinforcer

Any event or experience that follows a behavior and results in the desired behavior. (xss, yb)

rejected children

A category of student with extremely poor peer relationships, including those students who are actively and explicitly disliked or forsaken by their peer group. Even as these students enter into new social relationships and peer groups where they are unknown, they often quickly reestablish their prior status as socially undesirable. Such students often have increased rates of delinquency and criminality when compared with other students. Their status often remains stable at home and in school settings over time, although this is not necessarily a permanent condition or state. (hfs)

rejective art (See minimalism)

related services

Transportation and developmental, corrective, and other support services that a child with disabilities requires in order to benefit from education, including speech/language pathology and audiology, psychological services, physical and occupational therapy, recreation, counseling services, interpreters for those with hearing impairments, medical services for diagnostic and evaluation purposes, and assistive technology devices and services. (sr)

relatedness

Having multiple problems and finding ways to make connections between them to find the solution. (ldz)

relation

In mathematics, relation is a pairing that matches each element of the domain with at least one element in the range. A relation is a set of ordered pairs where every x corresponds to some y. (ps)

relational/instrumental understanding

Terms first used by Richard Skemp in explaining two contrasting views of mathematics learning. Instrumental understanding focuses upon students following prescribed rules and procedures or rules without reason. By contrast, relational understanding focuses on making sense of the problem and procedures for solving a mathematics problem. Some researchers question whether instrumental understanding is truly understanding, while recognizing relational understanding as "understanding." (sdt)

relationships

Finding connections between mathematical problems and real-world situations by taking the real-world situations and using them to help solve a mathematical problem. (jmg, ldz)

relatively prime

A relationship between two integers in which the only divisor common to both integers is 1; in other words, two integers are relatively prime if their greatest common divisor is 1. (cmdv)

relativism

The belief that truth is subject to the influence of human beings, that truth is personal and subjective. Such a view of truth implies that there can be no means for us to determine what is right or wrong, for there are no objective, neutral, universal standards we can rely on to help us make sound judgments. Some philosophers argue that such a description of relativism is naive and simplistic. They argue that relativism can be qualified to allow for the possibility of solving our problems to our satisfaction and warranting our assertions to the best of our abilities without having to rely of a concept of absolute truth. (bt-b)

See also truth.

relaxed alertness

An instructional technique where a highly challenging learning environment is created that allows students to openly explore new thoughts and ideas and is also free of fear. (ms)

reliability

In a theoretical sense, reliability indicates the correlation between observed and true scores. In measurement theory, all measures or tests are assumed to have measurement errors. When measures have large measurement errors, observed scores will deviate further from a person's true scores, resulting in a low reliability or correlation between observed and true scores. In practice, reliability refers to the consistency of a measure or test. Because a true score is not observable, reliability indicates how replicable observed scores on the test are if the same person repeats the test an infinite number of times. It is a quantitative indication of test quality. (hl)

See also observed score; true score.

religion

The study of a structured or formalized approach to spirituality based on a higher power or supernatural quality that gives meaning to the follower. Considered belief systems or faiths to which individuals ascribe and follow through a set of beliefs, practices, guidelines, and symbols, religions are organized into groups to which individuals belong and share in their ideologies and practices. (npg)

religious education

This term refers to the teaching-learning process centrally concerned with development of religious faith and commitment. Thus, it focuses on the understanding and belief in religious doctrines and practice. In *Schempp v. Abingdon* (1963), the Supreme Court distinguished between religious education and teaching about religion, ruling that teaching religion ("religious education") is constitutionally not permissible, while teaching about religion is not only permissible, but a necessary component of a worthwhile general education. (wl)

remedial adult education

Education offered to adults with academic skill insufficient to be successful in postsecondary education. In community college settings, this type of education refers to classes and other instruction aimed at strengthening learners' skills in reading, writing, and math, as well as study skills, to prepare them for participation in regular classes. More recently, the term has been replaced with "developmental education." (las)

remedial education (See developmental education)

remedial instruction

Teaching designed to help a student or group of students overcome a learning deficiency in a given subject. Instruction designed to improve skills found deficient through formal assessment. (jw)

repertoire

The collection of skills, techniques, or specific works that an artist is ready to use or perform—for example, a singer's repertoire consists of the songs she/he has rehearsed and can sing in performance, as well as the styles in which she/he performs. Also can apply to the works that an organization has worked on and can perform—for example, a theater company's repertoire includes the plays that it performs. Some researchers take a repertoire approach to children's acquisitions of artistic skills, envisioning each stage in development as an opportunity to acquire new modes of expression. (em)

repertory

The operational mode of a performance company (theater, dance, opera, music), in which a number of works are in production, alternating performances, while new works are simultaneously in rehearsal. For example, a repertory theater might have one show in rehearsal, two others rotating in performance, and another in the planning stages. The same company of actors performs in all productions. The advantage for actors is the range of roles they get to perform simultaneously; the advantage for the theater is the broad audience base that such production variety can attract. (em)

replete

A symbol or work of art is thought to be replete when it is complex and dense in construction and meaning. The philosopher Nelson Goodman, in his historic work *Languages of Art*, describes relative repleteness as the situation in which aspects of the construction of a work (like reproduction theory   399

the thickness, thinness, or direction of lines) are intricately tied to its meaning. Relative repleteness is one of Goodman's symptoms of the aesthetics. Rejecting the question "what is art?" for a more transient view of "when is art?" Goodman posited various criteria for conditions that hold when something is considered to be art. (jd)

representation

An image, likeness, or reproduction of a person, object, place, or event. The act of one thing standing in for and referring to another. For example, a story can be represented by a play; a person by a character, a painting, or a sculpture; and an event by a dance or piece of music. While ideas and emotions can of course also be represented in works of art (as in other venues), we tend to designate that type of representation (beyond the representation of tangible entities in the physical world) as expression or symbolism. In mathematics, representation conveys mathematical ideas in ways that others will understand. According to the National Council of Teachers of Mathematics, it refers to process and product: the act of capturing a mathematical concept or relationship in some form and to the form itself. Some forms of representation are graphs, symbols, and diagrams. (tkb, dc)

See also expression/expressivity; symbol.

re-presentation

Re-creating mentally an experience or mathematical idea; a mental act that brings a prior experience to an individual's consciousness; to replay one's mental thoughts (including senses) about a particular experience; revisiting mentally. This re-creation is never exactly as it was when previously experienced, having been changed and influenced by other experiences in the intervening time. The term is used particularly in radical constructivism to distinguish this mental activity from "representation." (dc)

representational

A work of art is representational if it has identifiable references to an object, person, place, or event in the physical world. Representational art is thought to look like what it depicts as opposed to nonrepresentational or abstract art, which often has little about it that is recognizable as depicted form. Representational art has traditionally been so valued in schools and society that young children frequently grow impatient with their developing graphic skills because they cannot realistically draw what they see. Many arts educators advocate introducing children to other aesthetic qualities (like expression, composition, etc.) that they may more easily achieve in their artistic productions and of which they can rightly be proud. (jd)

reproduction theory

A theoretical construct attempting to explain how schools, through curricular and pedagogical practices, reproduce learners into their social classes. It has been developed by Marxist theorists (such as Herbert Gintis, Samuel Bowles, and Jean Anyon), ethnographers (Paul Willis), and others (Pierre Bourdieu and Jean-Claude Passeron, Basil Bernstein). Examples include: (1) Working-class students receive teaching and curricula that are purposefully rote, dedicated to developing learners who (a) are willing to do boring, meaningless work, (b) are prepared to accept external authority's demands, and (c) see culture as something they do not have but which belongs to other classes who thus deserve their higher status in society. (2) Upper-middle-class students receive education dedicated to (a) being creative, (b) aspiring to professional life (lawyers, artists, teachers, doctors, engineers), and (c) adding to the culture without challenging the cultural prerogatives of the social hierarchy. Reproduction theory is closely associated with the hidden curriculum, as both reference the ways in which schools reproduce in students dispositions toward conventional notions of social life, gender, sexuality, and so forth. (db-j)

See also critical theory; resistance; resistance theory.

Republic, The

The title of Plato's most famous book, and one of the most famous books to be found in the history of philosophy. Alfred North Whitehead once said that all subsequent philosophy is a footnote to Plato, and most of Plato's best-known beliefs and problematics are to be found in *The Republic*. Most obviously the book is a discussion of the nature of the just government, but it also is deeply concerned with the nature of the human person, morality, epistemology and metaphysics, and so on, essentially the nature of human good. *The Republic* is still perhaps the best introduction to philosophy for the literate person. (an)

reruralization

This term describes the proposed return of large numbers of people in search of social stability and an agricultural way of life to the rural areas of the Great Plains. It has been proposed by a number of social and educational reformers (e.g., David Orr and Paul Theobald), who see rural life as capable of competing with urban centers in terms of quality of life. (lr)

research

Study or investigation, in an organized and thorough manner, to establish concepts, principles, and facts. Basic research is designed to test a theory but may have no immediate application. Applied research, on the other hand, is designed to solve problems rather than deal with theoretical assumptions. Pure research addresses the theoretical issues and is not expected to have any immediate benefit to society. The systematic study of a problem or issue may be undertaken in a variety of methods. For example, scientific methods include observation and experimentation, while market research includes surveys, opinion polls, and focus groups. Research is an active part of the learning process, and so critical to education. (npo)

research assistant (See graduate assistant)

research fellowship (See fellowship, research)

research university

Institutions nationally recognized for their extensive research and scholarship in the arts and sciences and the excellence of their graduate and undergraduate programs; includes the top 50 or 100 institutions, depending upon how they are assessed. This term is applied to universities that typically include a wide range of undergraduate programs but are committed to graduate education and research. Faculty at these institutions are expected to create and produce scholarly works, with the university supporting their research by providing space, extensive libraries, laboratories, support facilities, studios, museums, schools, hospitals, equipment, support staff, and other amenities. (cf, lcw)

researcher subjectivity

The influence of the researcher on the research. The influences may include the researcher's personal characteristics, values, beliefs, knowledge, and/or experiences. These influences may affect the research in positive or negative ways. This is similar to the concept of reflexivity. (mas)

researcher-as-instrument

A central characteristic of qualitative research. This idea highlights the personal role of the researcher in ensuring the quality of all aspects of the research. Implies the need for disciplined training and practice in the skills of qualitative data collection and analysis. Also suggests the need for the researcher to adapt to circumstances of the research and, in this sense, is related to the concept of emergent design. Also connotes the need for the researcher to be aware of how one's characteristics may affect the research, and, in this sense, is related to the concept of researcher subjectivity. (mas)

resegregation
Despite desegregation efforts, some schools have reverted to segregated schools due to urban flight, poor implementation of desegregation plans, and local housing issues. Because of funding formulas, segregated/resegregated schools suffer from fewer resources than schools in wealthier communities. Resegregation may occur through tracking of students into special programs, as well as through population changes. (jqa, npo)

residency requirement
Policy of some educational institutions that a certain number of academic credits be earned at and be granted by the degree-granting institution. Residency requirements at some institutions mandate that a student be present in on-campus classrooms for a stated number of academic terms or a period of time. (cf)

resident teacher (See apprentice teacher)

resilience
Refers to the ability of a child to recover from stressful or harmful experiences. While there is a biological component to the development of resilience, supportive family and caregivers are crucial to the development of resilience in children. Families and caregivers help children build resilience by providing consistent, nurturing caregiving and guidance that promote positive problem-solving skills, responsibility, and a bright outlook for the future for the children. (kdc)

resistance
The process and means by which learners in schools work against the effects of the hidden curriculum and social reproduction (as understood through reproduction theory). Resistance is distinguished from oppositional behavior. Oppositional behavior references behavior that only opposes a situation but without a conscious social, political, cultural, and/or economic critique. Resistance behavior is critically aware oppositional behavior in which the individual works to change the underlying conditions and assumptions that structure the present situation. (db-j)
   See also critical theory; hidden curriculum; reproduction theory; resistance theory; social reproduction.

resistance theory
Theory that focuses on the resistance that women and minorities adopt in order to create meaning in an education system and society that promotes existing power relations of white male dominance. Three central themes in the theory are: all people have the capacity to create and produce meaning in their lives and to resist forces of oppression; forms of resistance are influenced by factors of oppression, which include race, class, gender, ethnicity, age, and sexual orientation; and the forms of resistance may sometimes lead to other forms of oppression or domination of those involved in resistance of others. (las)

reskilling
Learning opportunities for adults through which they may acquire new skills for their current job or gain skills for a new occupation. (las)

resource person
A knowledgeable person who is available to be consulted during a training program. (jpc)

resource teachers
Professionals who have received some type of specialized training that prepares them to work with specific types of exceptional students. For example, resource teachers may provide assistance in materials,

planning, and instruction for students who have emotional and physical handicaps, students who are gifted and talented learners, or students who have difficulty reading. (bba)

respect

The act and attitude of treating another human being with behavior and communication that conveys acknowledgement that the other person has worth, value, and dignity and is deserving of nonjudgmental, courteous, and responsive interaction. In working with a child, a professional must treat the family and the child, as well as other professionals, with respect. Respect may also represent the courtesy to refrain from intruding upon or interfering with, which has a two-directional meaning in the classroom: respect of the teacher by students, and respect of students by the teacher. (kdc, ce)

Response to Intervention (RtI or RTI)

The goal of RtI is to ensure success for all students and prevent students from being unnecessarily assigned to special education programs. The most dominant RtI model consists of three levels or "tiers." In tier 1, schools provide screening, progress assessment, and research-based interventions for all students in order to ensure schoolwide academic success. Tier 2 instruction involves providing more practice and review in small groups for learners in need of additional attention. Tier 3 instruction provides individualized support for students with significant learning problems who have been identified as not responding to the extra help provided in Tier 2. Tier 3 consists of an organized plan to pair individualized or small group academic assistance (the intervention) with a systematic study of that assistance in order to provide research-based support to student(s) who are experiencing academic difficulty or delay. Each attempted intervention is studied to see if a student is able to make academic gains on her or his own. (kmt, nfd)

responsibility

An action or expectation that is presumed to accompany a person's social, political, or economic status, such as a citizen's responsibility to pay taxes. (jjc)

Responsible Education About Life Act

A bipartisan bill (S.611/H.R.1551) introduced in 2005 that calls for federal funding to support comprehensive sexuality education in schools. The bill is in response to long-standing federal funding for abstinence-only-until-marriage programs that have been seen as ineffective in preventing adolescents from engaging in harmful sexual behavior. To date, the bill has not left the subcommittee to which it was referred. (jb2)

responsive teaching

Sensitive interpersonal adaptations between teacher and pupil; a large web of interconnections among individuals, cultures, languages, and schooling. (bjl)

restatement

Repeating, either verbatim or in concise own words, information that a client has just conveyed to a counselor. Restatements are useful for demonstrating that a counselor is listening attentively, for anchoring a client's comments, and/or for encouraging the client to elaborate/consider the topic area further. (bmm)

retraining

The learning of new skills when the skill demands of work change. (jpc)

reverse discrimination

When a dominant group loses privileges due to the implementation of affirmative action and other policies to encourage diversity, it is labeled reverse discrimination. This controversial issue arises because some view diversity policies as discriminating against the formerly privileged group, while others view them as redressing inequities and providing opportunities to all. (jqa, npo)

reverse transfer students

Students who transfer from four-year to two-year institutions of higher education. Some definitions include students who attend two-year colleges at the same time they are enrolled at a four-year institution, and students who attend two-year colleges after graduating from four-year institutions. (sn)

revolution

A term with multiple meanings in a social studies context. In geography, it pertains to the orbit of the celestial bodies. In government or history classes, the definition provided by the 2001 *Oxford English Dictionary,* "A complete overthrow of the established government in any country or state by those who were previously subject to it; a forcible substitution of a new ruler or form of government," is most appropriate. (cd)

rezoning

Rezoning involves making a change in an existing zone or section for a specific purpose. When rezoning is discussed with regard to public schools, it is typically because attendance zones must be redrawn. Generally, attendance zones have to be restructured when there is a major population shift in a particular area or when new schools are built to ease overcrowding in existing schools. Many times the rezoning efforts involve shifting the attendance of several schools in order to achieve the needed balance. Rarely is rezoning without controversy, because most people do not want to change from their current school to another. (bs)

rhetoric

One of the seven liberal arts. Defined as the "art of persuasion," rhetoric can be traced to the Sophists of ancient Greece, who gradually codified general rules that could serve as a basis for a systematic training in the art of public speaking, a crucial skill for taking part in the political life of ancient democracies. The perfect Sophist had to demonstrate a universal competence and be able to hold his own on any subject whatsoever. Rhetoric was the core of advanced education in the ancient and medieval world. While classical rhetoricians were primarily concerned with formal speech rather than ordinary talking or writing, modern rhetoricians stress that the development of both speech and writing are central to a liberal arts education. (pk)

See also communication.

rhyme

The nucleus and the coda of a syllable taken as a whole (e.g., [_uts] is the rhyme of the syllable *nuts*). Its name is derived from the fact that in poems and children's rhymes, in order to create the rhyme, the nucleus and coda of the final syllable are identical (e.g., *Moses supposes his toeses are roses*). (smt)

rhythm

The means by which time is organized and expressed in music. Standard music notation includes symbols that signify either fractions or extensions of beats, which communicate to the performer when each sound should occur relative to those around it. In drama, rhythm may be used as a synonym for timing or the speed and manner with which lines are spoken, or, in the case of plays, when events occur on stage. Rhythm may be expressed in the visual arts by the use of repeating pattern or form, or in poetry by the pattern of regularity of beats in a line. (jbl)

Right, The

Ethical theories may be divided into two kinds: those which posit the priority of The Good, and those which posit the priority of The Right. Unlike theories that advance the idea that ethical conduct consists in promoting some good or another, theories of The Right do not depend on the furtherance of any particular value or end. Instead, they posit as the political ideal a set of regulative principles that, in themselves, do not presuppose advancing any determinate theory of The Good. Such regulative principles must conform to a concept of right, a moral category given prior to and independent of The Good. Theories of The Right thus seek to affirm the primacy of justice and the sanctity of individual rights. Hence the concept of justice, understood as a neutral, procedural framework, and derived independently of any determinate conception of The Good, is seen as morally overriding. (pk)

See also Good, The.

rights

That which is due to anyone by just claim, legal guarantees, or moral principles. Teaching about rights is a common aspect of the social studies curriculum. In the United States the Bill of Rights and subsequent amendments guarantee fundamental rights under the Constitution. These rights include freedoms, securities, and guarantees of equal treatment before the law. For example, freedom of speech is protected by the First Amendment. One account of rights relates them to claims that are, or at least can be, upheld and justified by the law. Another account specifically relates rights to concurrent duties that the law obliges us to perform. The concepts of natural rights and natural law, however, refer to moral rights, duties, and obligations, rather than legal claims. Natural rights arose from ancient and medieval conceptions of what is reasonable and fair, and they have evolved into the modern notion of human rights, such as those of liberty, equality, due process, and self-determination. This notion of human rights as inalienable and universal has gained currency and, in 1948, the Universal Declaration of Human Rights was adopted by the United Nations General Assembly. (cb, psc)

See also justice.

rime

In a word or syllable, the rime is the vowel sound and the consonant sound at the end of a word. For example, in the word split, *spl* is the onset and *it* is the rime. Often groups of words with the same rime are referred to as word families. (cld)

risk

Risk is typically defined as the possibility of loss, danger, or injury. Within the field of education, particularly experiential education, the duality of risk as both hazard and adventure is a primary catalyst in the journey between ignorance and knowledge. The potential for this event to have a negative, neutral, or positive outcome is determined by the context, motivation, and agency of the learner. This multidimensional process can occur physically, psychologically, emotionally, intellectually, and spiritually. Also, risk is the possibility of an undesired outcome of a given action and the effect of uncertainty on educational objectives. (ahs, bhg, pbc)

risk management

The careful accounting of possible negative outcomes, combined with actions taken to mitigate risks, as well as the calculus of balancing risk and reward. Risk management entails assessing various potential outcomes and predicting likely results. Risk management is the practice of handling and controlling factors that could cause suffering, harm, loss, or danger. In education this can be applied to activities that occur on institutional premises during extracurricular events as well as regular programs. (ahs, bhg, jt)

Ritalin

A psychomotor stimulant often used to treat those with hyperactivity disorders. There is controversy surrounding the use of Ritalin with students, particularly young children. Ritalin may be prescribed for treatment of Attention Deficit Disorder whether or not hyperactivity is associated with ADD. (npo)

See also psychomotor stimulant.

Roberts v. City of Boston, 59 Mass. 198 (1849)

An early racial segregation case in which an African American child, Sarah Roberts, sued Boston's Primary School Committee for forcing her attendance at a black-only school, although several white schools were nearer her home. A passionate defense by Charles Sumner raised the issues of "equality before the law," separate but equal schools, and principles of local control. In a climate of increasing nativism, the Massachusetts Supreme Judicial Court ruled against Roberts. However, in 1855, the state created the first nondiscriminatory school law. (le)

role play

The taking on of a character, the assumption of a part, or the representation of a type in a pretend situation—the foundation for all dramatic work. Educational drama work frequently involves improvisational role play, in which both teacher and students take on roles to explore an issue or topic. Though the word "role" is based in theater (evolved from the original French word for a roll of parchment, on which an actor's part was written), role plays are now used in a variety of settings for purposes ranging from job training to conflict resolution. Young children play roles (note the authentic performances in the kindergarten pretend play space) to try on and come to understand better the roles and responsibilities of the adult world. The process allows students to experience issues both affectively and cognitively and serves as the basis for subsequent analysis and discussion. Role play enables participants to engage in higher-order reasoning and judging activities through interaction that encourages choice. Elements often provided are jobs and roles, character specifications, scripts, and directions. Participants are given the opportunity to gain a sense of perspective as they work from inside a character or problem and can be given varying degrees of latitude in defining characters and/or scripts. Role play is intended to stimulate creative and critical thinking in students. Variations on traditional role-play techniques include role reversal, multiple role play, and self-confrontation. (em, las, igb, mkr)

romancing

The term used for those occasions when young children are asked what their scribbles represent. As they come to understand that adults expect drawings to be something or tell a story, they respond appropriately. Pointing at a tangle of lines, they may say, "That's me and Daddy taking a walk." Researchers doubt the intention of children when making the drawings and call the after-the-fact naming of the image romancing. (jd)

romanticism

A cluster of ideas and attitudes exhibited in works of philosophy, literature, history, art, and music from the late 18th to mid-19th centuries. Romantics repudiated many of the ideas and attitudes characteristic of the Enlightenment, exalting passion over reason, imagination over intellect, the subjective over the objective, individual creativity over adherence to formal rules, the organic over the mechanical, nature over culture, and provincialism over cosmopolitanism. Rousseau applied romanticism to education, celebrating nature and passion rather than culture and intellect. As a general philosophical movement, "romanticism" is most often associated with the initial phase of German Idealism. (mbm)

root (See square root)

rooted curriculum

Rooted curriculum is a variant of curriculum of place. When teachers design a curriculum that is rooted, it means that they relate curriculum closely to the places in which their students live. They use the community as a resource and the curriculum that it informs as a way of strengthening the community. (lr)

ropes course

A series of low-to-the-ground or high-in-the-air elements constructed from rope, metal cable, wood, trees, and other materials designed to physically, mentally, and emotionally challenge individuals. The challenges may involve risk taking, problem solving, or cooperative learning in order to complete the task. (rf)

Rosenwald Fund

Philanthropic fund established by Julius Rosenwald, president of Sears, Roebuck and Company in 1917 for "the well-being of mankind." Influenced by Booker T. Washington's philosophy of self-help, Rosenwald concentrated much of the Fund's activities toward blacks in the southern United States. Between 1928 and 1948 (when the Fund closed), the Fund's resources were dispersed through initiatives in education, health, fellowships, and race relations. The hallmark of the Fund, however, was the rural school-building program. From 1914 to 1932, a total of 4,977 schools were built throughout 15 southern states. The fund required that white and black communities match the amount provided by Rosenwald and that schools be incorporated into the public school system. (jrb)

rotation

The action of moving an object on its axis or center. The axis, or turning point, may be inside the object, on the object, or outside the object. The object itself is not distorted by the rotation. (jdk)

rote counting

The reciting of the standard number word sequence in proper order: "one, two, three, four, five. . . ." This is done in isolation without actually counting any objects. Young children can often recite the sequence of numbers without actually being able to count rationally. (dc)

See also rational counting.

rough and tumble play

Refers to active, physical play that appears aggressive but is not mean-spirited or confrontational. Children typically do not use their full strength or try to hurt one another. Examples include play fighting and wrestling. (at)

rounding

To give an approximation of a number to a specified decimal place. Simple rounding rules are as follows: if the digit in the specified place has a value of five or greater, increase that digit by one and replace all digits to the right of that digit with zeros; if the digit in the specified place has a value of less than five, replace the digits to the right of this digit by zeros. Rounding skills are used frequently in determining estimates for computations. (amr)

routine problems

Sets of mathematics tasks or exercises used as vehicles of instruction or as means of practice. Often these problem sets do not fit the definition of problem solving as it is understood in recent research in mathematics education. (sdt)

See also nonroutine problems; problem solving.

RSS (See really simple syndication)

RTI (See Response to Intervention)

rubric

A set of guidelines for scoring a subjective assessment. The instructional component of an exam as opposed to the actual test items or tasks (e.g., the printed advisory at the bottom of a test booklet that states: "Do not turn the page until told to do so"). (fd)

Rudolf Steiner education (See Waldorf education)

running record

Running records are often used by classroom teachers to assess students' reading accuracy and fluency in reading short, new, or familiar texts. To take a running record teachers work with a copy of the same text that the student is reading. The teacher marks his or her copy using a system of check marks and error marks as the student reads. Generally teachers mark the text with a check as a word is read correctly and with other marks for omissions, substitutions, additions, and self-corrections. In addition, teachers often time students as they read. Teachers also determine students' reading rate and accuracy. They can then use this information to inform instruction and determine students' reading levels. (rcr)

rural brain drain

The outward migration of rural people, especially young ones in search of better educational and vocational opportunities, to urban and suburban areas. It is an ongoing rural issue, and it results in smaller populations, reduced social capital, and diminished economic capacity. It is complicated by school consolidation and open transfer policies, as well as by larger economic policies. (lr)

rural capacity building

Efforts to strengthen the ability of grassroots leaders and community-based organizations to advocate for policies and practices that improve educational opportunities and outcomes in vulnerable rural communities. It is seen as the key to viable and sustainable rural communities and usually involves educational as well as economic dimensions. Such efforts occur in most parts of the world. (lr)

rural development

Rural development is an example of a multivalued social goal, one that contains several dimensions of value, all of which are important, but none of which are dominant. The improvement of rural communities is based on economic growth, the fulfillment of basic social needs, the achievement of equity, and the creation of a fuller participation in decision making. Increasingly, rural development is not merely an economic goal. (lr)

rural extension

Rural extension is the collective name for a range of outreach activities of county governments and land grant universities that aim at disseminating knowledge and leadership techniques to improve agriculture and strengthen rural communities and families. Extension agents, specialists, and educators, working with county agents, provide rural people with nonformal learning opportunities based on the latest research. (lr)

Rural School and Community Trust

Successor to the Annenberg Rural Challenge, a national advocate for rural educational reform and capacity building. It produces research studies of special interest to rural schools and communities, serves as a rural-oriented educational policy analysis group, and provides a national platform for the discussions of rural school issues through its publications and meetings. (lr)

Rural School Consolidation Movement

Spurred by social and economic changes in the late 19th and early 20th centuries, the closure of rural schools to consolidate them into bigger district or township schools resulted in there being a tenth of the number of school districts in 1998 than there were 60 years before. The depression of the 1890s and the concerns of the Progressive movement were precipitants of consolidation, seen as a means to lessen the disparities between rural and urban education, in addition to being more economical due to larger tax bases and economies of scale. Consolidation of schools occurred most rapidly at the turn of the 20th century, and again from the 1940s to the 1960s. (jv)

rural schools

Schools that are found in rural communities. Use of the term rural is complicated by the breadth and diversity of rural America. No single definition of rural suffices, though statistics for student population are used to apportion state funding formulae, just as student population statistics are used to define metropolitan or nonmetropolitan status. (lr)

rural sociology

Can be best understood as the systematic study of people within groups that operate in rural settings. Many of the groups studied (churches, schools, businesses) are similar at first glance to those in urban settings but function in ways that are interestingly different given their relatively greater importance due to the scarcity of social capital in rural settings. (lr)

S

Sabbath School

A school for religious and moral instruction of the populace, which is typically held on the Sabbath and associated with a church or other religious institution. In poorer areas, the instruction may also include lessons on reading in order to facilitate reading of the Bible. (ms)

sabbatical

A paid leave of absence for faculty from their regular teaching and advising duties. Faculty will typically conduct extensive research, write books or articles, develop courses or curricula, return to their field of practice, or engage in artistic endeavors while on sabbatical. The primary purpose of a sabbatical is to provide time away from teaching for the faculty members to rejuvenate themselves and to reinvigorate their teaching. Universities have different criteria and requirements established for faculty to apply for and be granted a sabbatical leave. (pw1)

SACS (See Southern Association of Colleges and Schools)

SAE (See Standard American English)

Safe Schools Coalition

An organization that originally emerged from hearings conducted by the Seattle Commission on Children and Youth in 1988 to determine the needs of gay and lesbian youth. Now an international public-private partnership that works to reduce bias-based harassment in schools and help schools better serve gender-variant children, gay families, and GLBTQ youth. (jb2)

SAIR (See Southern Association for Institutional Research)

sampling distribution of a statistic

The probability distribution of all values of a statistic when all possible samples of the same size n are taken from the same population. The sampling distribution depends on the underlying distribution of the population, the statistic being considered, and the sample size used. This distribution is typically represented as a probability distribution in the form of a table, probability histogram, or formula. (pmts)

sampling error

Sampling error, often known as sample to sample variation, is an error that is caused by estimating a statistic (e.g., mean, correlation, or percentage) based on a sample instead of the whole population. Although in most cases it may not be known for sure for a given population, sampling error is empirically estimated using the variation associated with a given sample; and greater sampling errors are typically associated with a small sample size and a less representative sample. Sampling error is often considered as random error comparing with systematic error. (gl)

San Antonio Independent School District v. Rodriguez, 411 U.S. 1 (1973)

After a walkout by Mexican American students at Edgewood High School in 1968 over a lack of supplies and qualified teachers, parents started a class action suit invoking the U.S. Constitution's 14th Amendment equal protection clause. They hoped to force the reallocation of supplemental property taxes and equalize public school funding across Texas. The U.S. Supreme Court rejected the suit, 5–4. Justice Powell's majority opinion rejected the "poor" as definable class appellees and stated that "despite . . . inherent and somewhat obvious imperfections," Texas's school funding system "did not impinge on any fundamental right," thus excluding education as such a right. (salb)

San Francisco School Board Segregation Order

In 1906, anti-Japanese agitation in San Francisco led its school board to order Japanese and Korean students to join their Chinese counterparts in a segregated school in Chinatown. Strong protests from Japan, a rising international power recently victorious in the Russo-Japanese war, forced President Theodore Roosevelt to intervene. The school board rescinded its order after Roosevelt promised to end Japanese immigration. As a result of this compromise, the United States and Japan negotiated the Gentlemen's Agreement of 1907–1908, which ended the flow of Japanese male laborers to the United States. (eht)

San Francisco State College Strike of 1968–1969

On November 6, 1968, a coalition of minority student groups at San Francisco State College declared a campus-wide strike. They presented the administration with a list of demands, mainly concerned with creating or enlarging ethnic studies programs and increasing minority student admissions. San Francisco State faculty members also began their own strike in early 1969 to address administrative and personnel issues and demand a resolution to the student strike. The faculty strike was resolved February 24, 1969. The student strike was settled on March 21, 1969, with many student demands met completely or in part. (nc)

SAT (See Scholastic Assessment Test)

satellite campus

A campus that is physically removed from a larger, main campus. Satellite campuses are generally not residential and are primarily used to house courses taken by students who commute. (sn)

satire

The use of sarcasm, irony, parody, or wit, primarily in literature (including dramatic literature), to ridicule, critique, or harshly criticize social conditions, human behavior, and/or moral beliefs. Distinguished from burlesque by its harsh rather than loving/playful intonation. The intention of satire is to provoke audiences/readers to both laugh and think; satire uses humor purposefully to confront the audience/reader with important ideas in an entertaining way. Educational researchers note that the ability to use or understand irony or satire comes with development and experience. (em)

scaffolding

Based on Vygotsky's (1978) zone of proximal development, this concept emphasizes the importance of supportive activities by an adult (e.g., a teacher), in which such assistance may be kept or removed during the learning process, based on the learner's potential level of development. The gradual withdrawal of adult support is generated through instruction, questioning, modeling, feedback, and so on, which leads to a more autonomous learner/child. A distinction is often made between *scaffolds* and *supports,* the latter referring to environmental aids such as graphic organizers and technological tools (cf. Fischer and Bidell, 1998). (mc)

student rather than a bully for aggressive behavior would be an example of scapegoating. Schools themselves can be scapegoats when deemed responsible for social problems such as violence and other disruptive behaviors. (jqa, npo)

scatter plot

A graph that displays data using dots or points to indicate the amount of data. Depending on the amount of points, the data can look scattered, which indicates the name "scatter plot." (kr)

Scatter Plot

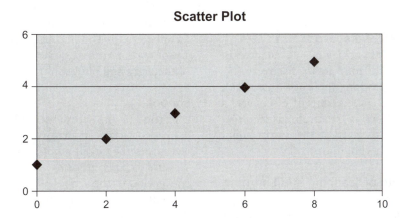

scaling

The process of applying a specific ratio or scale factor to an object in order to expand or reduce its dimensions in proportion. For example, a scale factor would be used in scaling an architectural design to fit the dimensions of blueprint paper. (kva)

SCANS (See Secretary's Commission on Achieving Necessary Skills)

scapegoat

Displaced blame and anger are directed to a more vulnerable but innocent person or group in the scapegoating process. Minority groups often experience this phenomenon. While this is a common behavior, it can cause great damage. Within the school setting, blaming the weaker

scene

A unit of dramatic action, usually occurring within one setting and over a continuous time, that contains a beginning, middle, and end. Most often, scenes are the building blocks of a larger play (though they can also be performed alone). For analytic and dramatic purposes, scenes can be subdivided into smaller units, beats, which function much like bars in music notation and performance. Scene may also refer to the setting of a play—including time and place—as depicted through scenery and lighting, or to images (e.g., landscape) in the visual arts. (em)

scholarly research

The systematic and objective search for evidence that will substantiate, verify, or refute previous findings, interpretations, or explanations within a specified academic discipline. Recognized by scholars by its particular emphasis on style, method, and purpose—as in historiography or literary analysis. Scholarly research is often referred to as disciplined inquiry as opposed to subjective or impressionistic analyses and interpretations that do not reflect scholarly traditions. (cf)

scholarship

The quality of a student's achievement in his or her studies. A scholarship may also be a financial grant that does not involve repayment. (cf)

scholarship of discovery

Scholarship is achieving excellence in one or more of four areas: discovery (research), integration, application (service), and teaching. Scholarship of discovery is a major aspect of research institutions, where it forms part of the institutional mission. (cma, rbp, npo)

Scholarship of Teaching and Learning (SoTL)

A movement that conceptualizes teaching as scholarly work. SoTL builds on the 1990 report, *Scholarship Reconsidered*, by Ernest Boyer, and involves the formal study of teaching and/or learning and the scholarly communication of such work. (sn)

scholastic achievement

The degree of success attained by a student in academic endeavor, based on past academic performance or on tests designed to determine mastery of subject matter. (cf)

See also academic achievement.

Scholastic Assessment Test (SAT)

Formerly called the College Board Scholastic Aptitude Test, the SAT is promoted as an assessment instrument and used with other data and information to select applicants who are well suited for academic achievement. (cf)

scholasticism

The philosophy practiced in medieval universities. Although scholasticism represents a heterogeneous admixture of concerns and antecedents (significant contributions were made by Greco-Roman as well as Arab and Jewish scholars), the center of its inquiries might be broadly interpreted as an attempt to reconcile philosophy (which Aquinas maintained supplied premises from nature) with Christian revelation. It is the juxtaposition of reason and faith that provided scholasticism with both its driving force and distinctive voice. Scholasticism has come to be identified with the central phase of Western Latin medieval thought and reached its apogee with Thomas Aquinas's *Summa Theologica*, a reconciliation and synthesis of theology and philosophy. (pk)

school

The root of the word "school," and its equivalent terms in many languages, derives from the Greek *scholé*, which means "leisure." This informs the traditional conception of the school as a place of liberal education within which there is freedom from considerations concerning the world of work and earning a living. There are two critical responses to this view of the school. One is the instrumentalist response that envisages the school as an arena in which young people are prepared for work and for life in society. The other is the radical response that perceives the learning promoted in school as a means of socioeconomic domination by the rich and powerful. (kw)

school art

The kind of art work that children are asked, encouraged, and/or taught to do in school. Educational researchers like Brent Wilson have studied the phenomenon of school art, which is often quite disparate from the sort of art work that children and older youth do on their own. For example, the narrative comic book drawing so important to many American preadolescents (and also the Manga drawings of Japanese youth) are often very personal, self-directed, and quite removed from the traditional drawing exercises that students are assigned in art classes. (jd)

school choice

A somewhat controversial educational reform strategy that has gained popularity since the late 1980s. Proponents believe that allowing parents to choose a school for their child promotes greater parental involvement in education. They also argue that the competition for students forces schools to improve to retain their current students and to attract new students. Choice opponents argue that less desirable schools will neither improve nor close due to lack of resources, but that students in those schools will have access to fewer resources than before. (ks)

school climate

A term that refers to perceptions of the general environment of the school; the formal organization, informal organization, personalities of participants, and organizational leadership. The set of internal characteristics that distinguish one school from another and influence the behavior of each school's members is the organizational climate of the school. (jt)

school community relations

Unlike public relations, which is a one-way process, effective school community relations seek to establish effective two-way communication channels between school and community in order to achieve consensus with respect to the role of the school. School community relations may involve school to community, school to parent, or community to school involvement programs. It may also involve partnerships of school and community working together cooperatively and financially. An example of this could be in the school receiving funds from organizations/businesses in the community, or in the community benefiting from the use of school facilities. Programs that are created as a result of school community relations might be tutoring or after-school programs, parent education programs, adult education or literacy programs, learning service programs in the school, or community education programs. (jr)

school consolidation

The process of merging small schools into larger organizations. The number of school districts in the United States has decreased from a peak of 150,000 in 1900 to less than 15,000 today. Their average size has increased by 15 to 20 times since 1930. There is significant disagreement about the effects of consolidation. It has been supported because of its fiscal advantages and opposed because of its social and economic effects on rural communities. (lr)

school counselors

A school counselor is an individual charged with various student-centered responsibilities in a school environment. Among many duties, school counselors are responsible for preparing and managing student schedules, overseeing student fulfillment of graduation requirements, dispersing college and career information to students, certifying transcripts, and assisting with college admissions. In many cases counselors also serve as therapists, assess and diagnose students for placement, manage programs, provide guidance, or administer standardized tests. (tm)

school culture

The beliefs, attitudes, and values held by the members of a school. (bba)

school district

A school district is a legal entity charged by the state with the task of providing and managing public education within a prescribed geographic boundary. School districts can be of various sizes and may spread across county and municipal borders. A school district is normally supervised locally by a school board of publicly elected trustees, but in some cases a school district may be directly managed by a state board of education. (tm)

school improvement plan

A plan, often mandated by state departments of education and local school districts, designed to improve how a school functions and operates in order to enhance teaching and learning. (bba)

school nurses

The primary caregiver of first aid and medical screening on most school campuses. The school nurse can be employed by the school district or by a local agency contracted by the local education agency (LEA). Trained nurses can provide immediate first aid and health care services. School nurses are often involved with health education issues with students and provide screening for vision, hearing, spinal curvature problems, and pregnancy-related concerns. Trained staff are involved with the administering of student medications and analysis of possible conflicts and behavior concerns. Qualifications and duties ascribed to school nurses vary in almost all LEAs. Some require nurses to hold a degreed registered nurse license, while others require only a licensed vocational nurse status, and some LEAs do not provide for a formally trained medical staff person at all. (ly)

school restructuring

In research, schools are said to have both structures and cultures. A school's culture is usually defined as the taken-for-granted beliefs about what is important in the school and how things are done. Because it has to do mainly with beliefs and values, school culture is said to be mainly in people's minds. School structure, on the other hand, is considered to be less of a mental phenomenon and more of an objective reality or realities. Generally, a school structure is a set of rules for how time, people, and space will be apportioned. The school schedule, for example, is considered an aspect of structure because it divides the day into various periods, and these, in turn, determine who will be where at any given moment. Grades and grade levels are another important aspect of structure, because children are divided according to their ages into learning groups. The architectural plan and design is a structure because it determines the spaces in which children will work. School restructuring is changing the rules for how time, people, and space should be divided (e.g., changing such things as the school schedule; going from a six-period day to a block schedule). School restructuring always holds implications for school culture and vice versa. Sometimes, school cultures undermine or make difficult attempts to restructure. (cl)

school-based management (See site-based management)

schooling

In its most usual sense of age-specific, organized learning, schooling has two principal aims and one significant consequential feature. First, schooling aims to develop understanding and other human capacities, and this is its peculiarly educational dimension. Second, it aims to provide socialization, that is, preparation to live in, and contribute to, society. But the institution has a third feature that seems an unavoidable consequence of schooling in almost any society. This is its facilitation of positional advantage (i.e., the labor market advantage conferred by the exchange value of education). (kw)

school-linked services

A system of social programs focused on poverty alleviation, developed first in 1960s America. These programs sought to center the schools as institutions of change and development in the lives of families and communities. Programs such as free breakfast for students, health clinics, and others were based in school facilities and paid for by compensatory education funds until the middle of the 1980s. (hfs)

schools of choice (See open enrollment plan)

School-to-Career System

The School-to-Career System comprises three components—school-based learning, work-based learning, and connecting activities—that are designed to better prepare students with various academic abilities and employability skills for the demands of the workplace. School-based learning is supposed to involve classroom instruction utilizing high academic standards, as well as occupational skill standards as developed, jointly, by educators and employers via various state departments of education and labor. Work-based learning consists of mentoring, training, and working opportunities for students so they can develop a range of skills in a given industry. Connecting activities are those activities that students participate in that help connect the classroom experience to the work experience, such as being matched with jobs, and having training supervisors and/or worksite mentors. With these opportunities, students' work-based learning can be integrated into the school curriculum. Overall, the School-to-Career System's purpose is designed to improve the workplace readiness of all students entering employment. (tp)

See also education to careers; school-to-work.

school-to-employment (See education to careers; school-to-work)

school-to-work

A system for youth to advance easily from school to work by creating relations between education and career. The system links elementary and secondary education, vocational-technical education, and higher education to engage all youth in the lifelong learning of knowledge, skills, and attitudes essential to pursue career pathways into college and high-skill, high-wage jobs. (jb)

See also education to careers.

school-within-a-school model

An organizational model in which a smaller autonomous educational unit is set up inside a larger school. The school-within-a-school will have its own teachers and students and design its own educational program, although it may share facilities such as libraries, athletic facilities, and cafeterias with its host school. The smaller unit seeks to replicate the advantages of a smaller school environment in order to achieve increased student achievement, well-being, and sense of community. (ms)

SCI (See student centered instruction)

science

A method or process of evolving or developing an explanation of a phenomena or idea based on observation, identification, description, and experimental investigation using the best and most currently available information. A series or system of investigative activities designed to lead to an explanation or to further knowledge of a subject. In teaching, a set of information concepts and the study of the processes used to develop and understand these concepts. (tw)

science, technology, and society strand

The impact of science and technology on society. This thematic strand was introduced widely by the National Council for Social Studies in *Expectations of Excellence: Curriculum Standards for Social Studies* (1994). The theme calls for examination of social issues resulting from advances in science and technology. (cd)

science club

A group of students or other interested people who gather to study, explore, explain, and take part in activities that relate to science. (tw)

science fair

A gathering of displays showing various science projects completed by groups of students. Science fairs are frequently judged as to the outstanding project(s) according to established criterion. (tw)

science laboratory

A room or building equipped for performing scientific experiments or investigative procedures or for teaching science using the equipment and procedures. An academic time period set aside for laboratory work. (tw)

scientific notation

A way of expressing any finite decimal number as a product of a decimal number between 1 and 10, and a power of 10. (wja)

scientifically based research (SBR)

Research that involves the application of rigorous, systematic, and objective procedures to obtain reliable and valid knowledge relevant to education activities and programs. It includes research that: employs systemic, empirical methods that draw on observation or experiment; involves rigorous data analyses that are adequate to test the stated hypotheses and justify the general conclusions drawn; relies on measurements or observational methods that provide reliable and valid data across studies by the same or different measurements and observations, and across studies by the same or different investigators; is evaluated using experimental or quasi-experimental designs; ensures that experimental studies are presented in sufficient detail and clarity to allow for replication or, at a minimum, offer the opportunity to build systematically on their findings; and has been accepted by a peer-reviewed journal or approved by a panel or independent experts through a comparably rigorous, objective, and scientific review. (cma)

Scopes Monkey Trial

A landmark and polarizing 1925 legal case in Tennessee that tested the First Amendment constitutionality of the prohibition regarding the study of evolution in the classroom. The Butler Act of 1925 had made it an offence to teach in publicly funded schools and universities any theory that denied the divine creation of man as taught in the Old Testament, or to teach, instead, that man had descended from a lower order of animals. Despite becoming the focus of national ridicule, the State of Tennessee convicted John Scopes of having taught evolutionary theory and ordered him to pay a $100 fine. This conviction was later set aside *nolle prosequi* on the grounds of legal technicality, but the Butler Act remained in place until 1967. Although the facts regarding the actions taken by Scopes were never contested, this ground-breaking trial pitted Christian Fundamentalist groups against the American Civil Liberties Union and demonstrates the social division still present in the creation–evolution debate. (tw1)

See also academic freedom.

score

The numerical value that results from the assessment of an assignment or examination. The act of grading. (jw)

Scranton Commission (See President's Commission on Campus Unrest)

screening

In early childhood education, screening is a brief procedure for identifying children who may be at-risk for developmental delays. Screening procedures and results do not provide comprehensive information about the developmental status of a child, but they play a critical role in identifying children who need additional evaluation. (xss, yb)

screening test
One of a class of assessment instruments designed to measure and identify a subset of characteristics from a larger group of characteristics, primarily for the purpose of differentiating individuals according to, for example, their aptitudes, skills, personality, or psychological symptoms. (kab)

scribbling
Originally from the Latin *scribere,* to write. Writing or drawing that is hastily and often illegibly executed. Loose or exploratory marks such as words dashed off on a sticky note or marks made on a dinner napkin while pondering an idea. Distinguished from rapid sketching, which deliberately captures a subject's characteristic lines and feeling, scribbling need not be representational or lead to any final product; however, it often articulates an early stage of invention. Scribbling has been studied by educational researchers as an early stage of children's drawing in which media, mark making, and symbolic function are explored. (lj)

sculpture
A sculpture is a work or the discipline concerned with works of visual art crafted in three dimensions. The process of shaping figures or designs in the round or in relief, as by chiseling marble, modeling clay, or casting in metal. Sculptures may be crafted out of fragile materials like paper. The activity of making sculpture helps children grasp an understanding of three dimensions as represented in life and in art. (ap)

SCUP (See Society for College and University Planning)

SDS (See Students for a Democratic Society)

search engine
A web-based computer program that enables users to locate information on the Internet. Some search engines ask users to input a query in the form of keywords or phrases. The search engine then returns a list of websites that contain the specified keywords. Other search engines organize websites into categories, enabling users to browse by subject area for websites that contain their desired information. Using a search engine to locate information on the Internet can be a powerful way for students to conduct research online. (kg1)

search string
The terms or phrase entered into a search engine in an attempt to locate a relevant website. When searching for information for research projects, two approaches for constructing search strings are effective: (a) representing the research topic using a single term or question, and (b) representing the research topic and a focus area using discrete terms or a natural language phrase (Guinee, 2007). When looking for a constrained answer, questions and other strings that use specific terms to represent the research topic and focus area are most effective. Students' literacy skills, web experience, and grade influence their ability to construct effective search strings (Guinee, 2007). (kg1)

seating chart
A diagram of the classroom showing the location of student desks or seats and the name of the student who regularly occupies each seat. (bba)

seatwork
Academic work that students complete individually and independently at their desks or seats in the classroom. Typically, seatwork involves practice of newly learned content, skills, or strategies. (bba)

secondary education
The years of education that follow elementary school, typically for students

ages 11 or 12 through 17 or 18. Secondary schools may include middle schools, junior high schools, and senior high schools. The instructional focus moves from the mastery of basic skills to the use of these skills in exploring and developing complex ideas. Secondary education may be either terminal or preparatory to further education. (jw)

secondary prevention

The identification of negative causes and experiences that impact children's lives. Identification occurs through activities such as developmental, mental health, and physical health screenings in communities and schools. Referrals to appropriate agencies providing services may also be considered secondary prevention. (xss, yb)

secondary school (See secondary education)

secondary sources

Books and articles written by someone who reports information or findings based on primary sources in the form of a quotation from or reference to the primary source. These written documents or oral reports are removed from the original fact or event by at least one level. (igb)

Secretary's Commission on Achieving Necessary Skills (SCANS)

Commission formed in 1990 by the U.S. Secretary of Labor to examine how well America's youth are prepared to meet the demands of the workplace. The 1991 report released by the Commission indicated that job performance requires five competencies (identifying, organizing, planning, and allocating resources; working with others; acquiring and using information; understanding complex interrelationships; and working with a variety of technologies). In addition, a three-part foundation of basic skills (reading, writing, math, listening, and speaking), thinking skills (including thinking creatively,

making decisions, solving problems, visualizing, knowing how to learn, and reasoning) and personal qualities (responsibility, self-esteem, sociability, self-management, and integrity and honesty) are required competencies. (las)

sedative hypnotic

A type of psychotropic medication that depresses activity to the central nervous system, reduces anxiety, and induces sleep. The distinctive characteristics of sedative hypnotics are their ability to achieve their effects without affecting mood or reducing sensitivity to pain. Two of the most commonly prescribed sedative hypnotics are benzodiazepines and barbiturates. Sedative hypnotics decrease time to fall asleep, decrease awakenings, and increase total sleep time but also decrease time spent in stage four and REM sleep. After discontinuing medication, a "rebound effect" of increased REM sleep may occur. This may include several weeks of bizarre, vivid dreams, restlessness, and awakenings. These drugs are often recommended for short-term use because they can be habit-forming and can cause withdrawal symptoms. (tsw)

See-the-Sound (See visual phonics)

segregation

Isolation or separation of one group from another group. Often this separation is based on race, ethnicity, or gender, but it may also be based on socioeconomic class, ability, or language proficiency. Within education, segregation in schools led to unequal learning opportunities. Federal legislation currently prohibits racial segregation. (jqa, npo)

self

Most generally the self can be thought of as whatever marks the center of human personality, the locus of human freedom, reason, and individual identity. In the philosophy of Descartes, the self, or ego, is a purely mental substance, a thinking thing.

This modern conception of the self is at odds with the prevailing medieval view, in which self is inherently mental and physical (i.e., embodied form). The idea of a unitary self is challenged by some who claim that we inhabit multiple, or "fractured," identities. (an)

self-actualization

The need to develop one's full potential by maximizing one's talents and abilities. Abraham Maslow believed that this need for self-actualization exists in everyone but is often thwarted by the environment. When our basic needs are met, energy is available for use in striving for greater understanding of ourselves and our surroundings. Self-actualization is considered the highest level of Maslow's hierarchy. Because our struggle to satisfy needs that are lower in the hierarchy is a continuing one, only a small number of people achieve self-actualization. (tsw)

self-assessment

Process for measuring one's own progress and accomplishments. An individual can conduct self-assessments on one's knowledge, skills, and/or dispositions before the learning as a preassessment, during the learning as a formative assessment, or after the learning as a summative assessment. Self-assessments provide insights about an individual to better understand one's strengths, weaknesses, and behaviors. Self-assessments can be conducted on a regular schedule to note change over time and to analyze the effectiveness of various interventions and treatments. (npg)

self-concept

A person's perception and evaluation of his or her abilities, attributes, and characteristics. This view can be positive or negative, singular or multifaceted, can change over time, and is largely dependent upon context. Discrepancies between self-concept and a person's goals and their actual skills, abilities, and

characteristics can lead to problems such as anxiety or depression. (tsw)

self-contained

In special education, a homogeneous setting in which individuals with like disabilities are separated from their nondisabled peers. (sr)

self-contained classroom

An organizational plan commonly used in elementary schools in which one teacher teaches all or most subjects to the same group of children in a single classroom. (bba)

self-control

Refers to the ability of a child who, when faced with a frustrating situation and feeling out of control, can display the appropriate reaction or engagement in problem-solving techniques related to the frustrating situation. (at)

self-correction

A correction to an error made in reading that is initiated by the student with no assistance or prompting from another person. In many measures of reading accuracy, self-corrections do not count as errors because they are quickly caught and corrected by the reader. (cld)

self-directed learning

Learning that is initiated and carried out by the learner, independent of formal academic structures. The student designs and implements the curriculum and instructional process, with or without the assistance of a trained adult educator. Some theorists treat self-directed learning as a desirable goal of adult learning (i.e., the ability to learn without support or direction from traditional educational institutions). (las, chb)

self-disclosure

An individual's decision to share personal information about oneself to another person. As both an intrapersonal and interpersonal process, self-disclosure is viewed as important in self-understanding and in establishing relationships. It has been suggested that mutual self-disclosure in relationships is optimal because it deepens trust and helps both people better understand each other. A balance of self-disclosure should be found; too much or too little self-disclosure has been found to inhibit relationship development. (tsw, med)

self-efficacy

Beliefs that build the foundation for a person's motivation and confidence in achieving a desired outcome. Self-efficacy beliefs are judgments about ones' capabilities and influence how a person thinks, feels, and behaves. The term self-efficacy was first coined by Albert Bandura, who stated that strong efficacy beliefs enable one to persist in accomplishing challenging tasks even when faced with pressing situational demands. In teacher education, self-efficacy is a positive self-view as a competent professional, including self-confidence in the authentic professional mastery of educational material. (sld, ddr, mlp, reb)

self-esteem

Self-esteem is the degree to which the evaluation of oneself as part of overall self-concept is positive. Self-esteem may influence both mood and behavior and may impact a range of personal and social behaviors. Low self-esteem is generally considered maladaptive and is often related to a number of negative psychological attributes and outcomes, such as susceptibility for depression, low academic achievement, and behavior problems in school. Individuals with low self-esteem may have trouble dealing with problems, be overly self-critical, and become passive. High self-esteem is often related to success and a number of positive psychological attributes and outcomes. Individuals with high self-esteem are usually more adept at handling conflicts and

making friends. However, excessively exaggerated self-esteem may be associated with violent, antisocial, or sociopathic behavior. (tsw, db1, fa)

self-expression

A process in which an individual is able to communicate one's own personality/ way of being through varying media. Howard Gardner's Theory of Multiple Intelligences identifies different ways to learn and to represent thinking/learning. Each individual has contrasting life experiences influencing how they may interpret an event. In an instructional setting, for example, the teacher may read a storybook to a group of children. In follow-up discussion she encourages/allows students to think of a variety of ways to demonstrate their interpretations, rather than requiring only one way to respond to the plot line. Divergent thinking/questioning is promoted and individual differences are valued. This type of learning environment fosters each learner's cognitive, social, and emotional development. A fundamental characteristic of encouraging individual self-expression is acceptance. This acceptance creates a learning situation in which differences are valued. (jls)

self-fulfilling prophecy

Term used to indicate that a belief that something will happen actually causes it to happen. In education, a teacher with preconceptions about a student's ability may cause that student to live up or down to those expectations. When students are labeled as slow or troublesome, the teacher treats them accordingly based on this theory, leading the student to fulfill the expectations. (jqa, npo)

self-portrait

When an artist or writer creates a portrait of him- or herself, it is called a self-portrait. The activity of making self-portraits through literary or visual artistic modes is popular with students of all ages and an apt vehicle for exploring self-expression through various artistic media. (ap)

See also portrait.

self-reflection

The practice of individual introspection, involving active analysis of past situations, events, and products with the inherent goals of critique and revision for the purpose of achieving an understanding that can lead to change in thought or behavior. (mf1)

See also reflexivity.

self-regulated learning

A proactive learning process in which learners regulate their own motivation, learning methods, behavioral performance, and use of environmental resources in order to improve and enhance their academic performance. This form of learning occurs in response to the feedback the learner receives from self-monitoring current learning processes and resultant outcomes. (ms)

self-study

Learning activities that individuals pursue on their own, outside the context of an organized educational setting. This type of study comprises a variety of activities, including reading, listening to audiotapes, working with workbooks, watching educational television programs, or working with computerized educational materials. (las)

semantics

A branch of linguistics concerned with the meaning and interpretability of language. Broadly, meaning is encoded in two different but related levels of language. At the lexical level, meaning is represented in the denotations and associations of individual words, and by the conceptual contrasts, similarities, or fine distinctions evident among words (e.g., synonymy, antonymy, polysemy). At the phrase or sentence level, meaning and interpretability are governed by syntax, and by the relationship among the grammatical elements of the phrase or sentence. (jrk)

semester

A period of time that is approximately one-half of a 9- to 10-month academic year. From the Latin *semestris,* meaning "half yearly." Also refers to an academic calendar of two terms, starting in August and ending in May to comprise an academic year. This calendar is commonly used by American colleges and universities. (cf)

semi-literate

Term referring to individuals who possess rudimentary literacy skills but whose proficiency is limited to simple reading and writing tasks. (las)

seminar

A group of limited size gathered for the purpose of advanced study under the direction of an instructor. A class of graduate-level or college students focused on intense study of a particular subject or engaged in focused research. A meeting for the presentation and exchange of content and ideas. (jw)

seminary (See academy)

semiotics

The study of signs and symbols and their relationship to referents, that is, the things to which they refer. A philosophic field enriched by such thinkers as Charles Sanders Peirce, Ferdinand de Saussure, Umberto Eco, and Roland Barthes, its implications have been profound for researchers into cognition and the arts. Considering various art forms as different symbol systems (e.g., music as a system made up of notes, visual arts of marks, dance of gesture), the production and perception of a work of art can be thought of as triumphs of thought (as opposed to the transference of emotion). Arts education advocates have embraced this reconceptualization of art making and perceiving, hoping it will help the arts to be taken more seriously in school. (jd)

semiskilled trade (See trade, semiskilled)

senior high school
A school that typically ranges from grade 9 or 10 through grade 12. A secondary school that follows a junior high or middle school and offers courses through those required for graduation. (jw)

sensitive period
A sensitive period is a length of time during which neuronal development is especially sensitive to environmental and experiential input. The sensitive periods of specific regions of the brain can take place at different times throughout the life span. At the conclusion of the sensitive period, the neural system in question typically becomes far less malleable and, while neuroplasticity endures throughout the life span, it can require a greater investment of time and effort to achieve changes within the system. (dh)
    See also critical period.

sensitive periods
According to Dr. Maria Montessori, a child passes through "sensitive periods" during which he/she is drawn to certain kinds of "work" over others. These include sensitive periods for movement (at 0–1 ½ years), an interest in small objects (1 ½–5 years), order (2–4 years), grace and courtesy (2 ½–4 years), refinement of the senses (2 ½–6 years), language (0–6 years), writing (3 ½–4 ½ years), reading (3–5 ½ years), and spatial relations (4–6 years). The work provided in a Montessori classroom coincides with these time periods. (nrs)
    See also critical period.

sensory-motor development
The period in infancy before the acquisition of language, when information about the surrounding environment is gained through the use of senses and motor actions. Mental representations of objects in the environment are gained through behaviors that include grasping, mouthing, gazing, banging, and reaching. In this first stage of a child's development, according to Jean Piaget, the child responds to and is strongly influenced by external stimulation. This stage occurs during the first two years of life. (npo, vm)

separation anxiety
Anxiety or disturbing feelings a child expresses when a familiar adult leaves the child's field of vision, temporarily or for an extended period of time. (kms)

sequence
In mathematics, a sequence is an orderly progression, a set of quantities that are arbitrarily ordered in some way. Alternately it can be a function whose domain is the positive integers (i.e., the infinite sequence). In teacher education, the connected series of courses a preservice teacher takes to satisfy the academic requirements dictated by the institution in which a culminating degree is being sought is a sequence. (kva, bjl)

sequence multiunits
Multiunit chunks within the number sequence, involving the skill of skip counting by tens, hundreds, etc. For example, being able to count 10, 20, 30, . . . or 13, 23, 33, . . . Initially the child might be simply reciting a pattern word sequence. For it to be useful in developing multiunit addition and subtraction strategies, these counting activities must be associated with the mathematical objects being counted. (amr)
    See also collected multiunits.

series
A sequence of numbers that are added/summed, which is often denoted by the capital Greek letter sigma (Σ). The series may or may not be infinite. The finite sequence $(1, 3, 8, 13, 20)$ is the series $(1 + 3 +$

$8 + 13 + 20$) and the infinite sequence (1, 2, 3, 4, 5, 6, ..., ∞) is the series (1 + 2 + 3 + 4 + 5 + 6 ...). (dbc)

service learning

A learning situation that incorporates community service projects with classroom instruction. Service learning is appropriate for students in all grade levels, from kindergarten to the university level, and any number of students can work on a given service project, from a single student to the entire school. Service learning projects allow students to apply what they learn in the classroom to solve real-world problems. Service learning teaches students to be active in their community as they create projects that often deal with issues in education, the environment, and public safety. Career and technical students organizations (CTSOs) are one type believed to be related to positive social and academic outcomes, including lower rates of school failure, suspension, and dropout, as well as improved grades, self-concept, and attitudes toward society. Rooted in the community schools movement of the 1920s and 1930s, service learning's goal is to develop democratic mindsets, a sense of community, enhance self-esteem, and connect learning to life experiences for students. (kmt, nfd, sa, cf, jrs)

Serviceman's Readjustment Act of 1944 (Public Law 78-346)

More commonly known as the "G.I. Bill," this act provided all veterans of World War II, regardless of gender or race, an opportunity to study at higher education institutions by providing governmental stipends for tuition, books, and housing. Over two million veterans embraced this chance to attend higher education, swelling college and university enrollment. Although the federal government had provided support to higher education through the Morrill Acts of 1862 and 1890, the G.I. Bill established the precedent of federal aid directly to students, a

role that it expanded greatly during the late 20th century. (rih)

Seven Sister Colleges

A group of East Coast colleges originally created for women, but now encompassing a range of single-sex, coeducational, and reciprocal campus arrangements. The seven are Barnard, Bryn Mawr, Mount Holyoke, Radcliffe, Smith, Vassar, and Wellesley colleges. All were founded in the 19th century to provide classical education opportunities for women, and each bears a history of strong philanthropy on behalf of women's education. The colleges' presidents created the term "Seven College Conference" in 1926 to enhance their networking opportunities. (le)

severe disabilities

Disabling conditions that require ongoing support in one or more major life activities, such as mobility, communication, self-care, and learning. (sr)

sex education (See human growth and development)

sex or gender bias

The act of ascribing roles, behaviors, expectations, and aspirations to individuals or groups primarily on the basis of gender. (ch)

sexism

The belief that one sex is superior to another. In most cultures throughout time sexism has favored men over women, boys over girls. Examples of sexism can be found in the desire to have male children over female and giving males an education better than girls, or denying females an education altogether. As part of the hidden curriculum, sexism teaches that girls are not as important as boys by centering men over women in texts and by giving more attention to boys than girls in class. Paying one sex less for equivalent work, or denying personal or political rights based on sex is sexism. (bt-b)

sex-role conflict

A conflict that occurs when an individual holds attitudes or engages in behaviors that are perceived to be incompatible with socially proscribed sex-role norms. Traditional, stereotypic examples include a man who may cry or a woman who may express an interest in auto mechanics. Such conflicts may be internal, due to personal sex-role beliefs, or external/interpersonal, due to attitudes or beliefs held by others. (dd)

sexual abuse

This term typically refers to the abuse of a child by an adult who derives sexual gratification through physical contact with prepubescent children, though adults can also become victims of sexual abusers. At the core, sexual abuse is the sexual mistreatment of another person. Such abuse includes any act of sexual exposure or sexual contact and can range from inappropriate touching and fondling to rape. (mkt)

sexual harassment

Sexually harassing behaviors encompass a broad range of actions, including, for example, unwelcome sexual advances or requests for sexual favors when the acceptance or rejection of such actions serves as a basis for academic or employment decisions. Sexual harassment behavior also includes conduct that interferes with a student's or employee's performance by allowing the existence of a hostile working or learning environment. (ti)

sexual identity

This term has two meanings. It may be used to signify sexual/affectional orientation (e.g., gay, lesbian, bisexual, heterosexual), or it may refer to a person's sense of belonging to a particular sex category (e.g., male, female, transgender). To avoid confusion, the former is sometimes referred to as "sexual orientation identity" and the later is sometimes referred to as "gender identity." (ti)

sexual orientation

The direction of one's emotional and/or sexual attractions toward members of the same sex, the other sex, or both sexes. This construct is made up of many dimensions (e.g., sexual attraction, emotional preference, self-identification, sexual behavior) and may be described along a continuum. In other words, someone does not have to be exclusively attracted to women or men but may feel varying degrees of attraction to both sexes. Sexual/affectional orientation develops across a person's lifetime—different people realize at different points in their lives that they are heterosexual, gay, lesbian, or bisexual. Sexual orientation is distinct from other components of sex and gender, including biological sex, gender identity, and gender role. (ti, jb2)

sexual orientation identity (See sexual identity)

sexuality education (See comprehensive sexuality education)

shadow drama

Originating in Asia, specifically Bali, Thailand, and China, and traced as far back as the 12th century, a performance art in which flat, cut-out puppets (made of materials like leather or paper) are manipulated behind a screen (either rice paper or a white sheet). Lighting from behind the puppets projects the silhouettes on to the screen, so, to the audience, the puppets appear as shadows. Shows using shadow puppets may focus on contemporary society, religion, or local issues, and may be serious or comedic. Shadow drama provides wonderful classroom theater opportunities to children of all ages. (em)

shame (See guilt/shame)

shared governance

A term used to denote cooperation between administrators and faculty members in meeting their respective responsibilities in institutional governance. (cf)

shared vision

In education this term refers to a set of goals or aspirations arrived at from a collective image of the future. The development of a shared vision is usually the primary task of leadership through the participation of many individuals. It fosters a genuine commitment and enrollment that permeates the organization with a sense of commonality, giving coherence to diverse activities. (mm)

sharing division (See partitive division)

SHEEO (See State Higher Education Executive Officers)

sheltered English

A method of instructing English language learners in which teachers use simplified English vocabulary to teach subject matter. (yu)

shopping mall high school

A descriptive term used to represent the variety of academic courses, extracurricular activities, and specialized services available to high school students, and the opportunity students have to select the classes and activities to participate in based on their own interests. The student acts as the consumer of the system's educational products, which the school works to provide in order to keep the students engaged, learning, and developing. (ms)

short course (See course, short)

short vowel

Vowels with shorter duration of vowel sound. The vowel sounds of the alphabet letters *a* (as in *cat*), *e* (as in *met*), *i* (as in *sit*), *o* (as in *pot*), and *u* (as in *cut*). (yu)

sight word

A word that children recognize as a whole, rather than decoding it and/or sounding it out. Often sight words are frequently used words and do not follow phonetic rules.

For example, *the, are, eight,* and *because* are sight words (from the Dolch Sight Word List). (yu)

sign

From the Latin *signum;* a mark, token, sign, or image. Any item that stands for something other than itself. An act or a gesture used to convey an idea, a desire, information, or a command (e.g., a thumb up to indicate success). A conventional figure or device that stands for a word, a phrase, or an operation (e.g., a red light signifying stop). The nature of the sign itself as well as its relationship to its referent (the object to which the sign refers) and to its interpreter (the individual finding meaning) determine whether the sign is an icon, index, or symbol. Sign also means to use the hands in an intentional, conventional, verbal manner to express linguistic meaning analogous to that conveyed by speech. Signs are described by hand configuration, location with respect to the body, and action. Signs are unlike gestures in that gestures are ad hoc, ungrammatical, and comparatively limited in number and meaning. (kpb, mhi-y)

sign language

A form of communication primarily used by deaf and hard-of-hearing individuals using the fingers and hands to form symbols and gestures to represent letters, words, and concepts. The most prominent sign language in the United States is American Sign Language (ASL), although there are many natural and mutually unintelligible sign languages in the world. (sr, mhi-y)

signature pedagogy

A systematic, shared set of practices that distinguishes preparation programs in a particular profession. Coined by Lee Shulman, the term is used to capture the idea that certain teaching and learning practices in specialized professions such as medicine distinctively define the student learning experience within those professions. Because researchers have described few distinct practices for preparing teachers, Shulman argues for signature pedagogy in teacher education. (eh1, eb)

similarity

The property of being similar (i.e., one object exhibits similarity to another if it can be scaled to match). More specifically, a transformation of Euclidean space in which any two points, A and B, and their transforms, A' and B', are related by a factor, k. $|A, B| = | k A', k B'|$. (kva)

simile (See metaphor)

simulation

Any imitation or representation of real-life interpersonal or other dynamics, including artifacts, rules, consequences, and so on, designed to help participants understand the dynamics of a complex situation. Common simulation formats are in-basket exercises, games, role plays, and computer simulations. For classroom use of simulations, limitations must be imposed due to factors such as safety, age appropriateness, time, and resources. Some of the most powerful simulations are computerized versions such as "The Oregon Trail" and "Where in the World Is Carmen Sandiego?" (chb, mje, jah)

Single Photon Emission Computed Tomography (SPECT)

SPECT is a functional neuroimaging technique that uses nuclear signals to indirectly measure blood flow and brain activity. A gamma-emitting radioactive tracer is injected into the bloodstream, and radioactivity in the brain is measured based on the assumptions that more active brain areas will have higher blood flow and areas with more blood flow will have higher radioactivity. From this information, brain activity can be imaged. SPECT is very similar to PET but it is more widely available because it is less expensive than PET. SPECT gives only an indirect measure of brain activity and is a correlational tool only. (mt)

Sipuel v. Board of Regents of the University of Oklahoma, 332 U.S. 631 (1948)

A U.S. Supreme Court case that ruled, following *Missouri v. Gaines,* that the State of Oklahoma must provide opportunities for graduate and professional education within its borders equally to both black and white students. The Court rejected the state's hasty establishment of a "law school" for blacks, which consisted of three rooms in the state capitol, three faculty members, and access to the state law library. Facing the choice of admitting Sipuel or ceasing enrollment of white students in the University of Oklahoma Law School until the new program met the legal test of "separate but equal," the state chose to grant her admission. (alw)

site-based management

An approach to school management that shifts responsibility for the governance and control of schools from the central school district authorities into the hands of teachers, administrators, community members, and others at the level of the individual school. The rationale for this approach is that those most affected by school-related decisions should participate in making them. Site-based management provides teachers an opportunity to assume leadership roles in decision-making processes that impact their educational organization, curriculum development, discipline, professional development, and student learning, as well as many other educational issues. The scope of the local empowerment varies across school districts. One characteristic that sharply distinguishes a school district's degree of implementation of site-based management is the extent to which parents and community members are involved as true partners in school decision making. (bba, tp)

site-based teacher education

That portion of the preservice teacher education program that occurs on a public or private school campus, often associated with instruction in professional development schools. (rtc)

situated cognition

Theory that learning is influenced by context. Cognition exists in the relations among people. Learning and knowing do not exist independently but are structured by interpersonal interactions and attempts to solve real-life problems in everyday settings. The physical and social experiences, as well as situations in which learners find themselves and the tools they use in that experience, are viewed as integral to the learning process. (las, chb)

situated learning

An approach to learning that incorporates realistic tasks found in everyday situations rather than focusing on abstract concepts. This approach also addresses how knowledge is acquired in the real world to resolve problems. In everyday life, situated learning is generally unintentional rather than deliberate. (npo)

situational teaching

Curriculum-based instruction using applied, real-life circumstantial knowledge constructed by the individual student. (bjl)

skepticism

Originally a school of philosophy in ancient times claiming that no beliefs could be known to be true, though some could be seen as more probable or rational than others. A stronger view held that no belief could be shown even to be more or less probable than others. Modern skepticism stems from the writings of Descartes, in which the arguments of the ancient schools clear away all that could be doubted so that knowledge can be built upon a sound foundation. Philosophers such as Hume adopted more or less skeptical doctrines once it was decided that Descartes's technique of raising doubts through skeptical argument was more effective than his positive attempts to refute doubt. (an)

sketch

A preliminary drawing, model, performance, or the like. A sketch is often coarsely executed and captures the essential elements of the work, neglecting details. In the visual arts, a sketch may be a rapid note, done from life or nature; an embodiment of the artist's ideas, useful for apprentices in the workshop; or an early stage of work, such as an underdrawing. In literature, a sketch is a short composition that is discursive in style and familiar in tone. In drama it is a slight theatrical scene such as a comic variety act; and in music, a brief instrumental composition, frequently for the piano. (lj)

skill

Something one knows how to do. In education, skill is often related to reading, addition, driving, accounting, and plugging in formulas. Skill is attained by practice and can have many components. (bjl)

See also skills.

skill standards

Standards that define the work to be performed, how well the work must be done, and the level of knowledge and skill required within a specific industry sector. These specifications have been developed by business and industry-based organizations, educational organizations, individual states, or a combination of these. (sa)

skill training

Career and technical courses or portions of courses that have as their principal objective the development in the student of certain specific abilities that have marketable value in business and industry. (jm)

skilled trade (See trade, skilled)

skills

"Skills talk" is ubiquitous in education, and there is a widespread tendency to indiscriminately identify every type of human ability and competence with a corresponding skill. Thus while some insist that "skills" imply repetitive and mechanical tasks unconnected with knowledge and understanding (e.g., typing skills, fine motor skills), others are equally insistent that we can identify and teach those very general skills that are integral to any enterprise (e.g., the skills of teaching, the skills of critical thinking, the skills of successful parenting). Because of such wide-ranging and wholesale use, "skills" has effectively become little more than a synonym for "ability." (pk)

See also skill.

skills certification

Certification of an individual's knowledge and skills in a specified occupation or occupational specialty, usually for a specified period of time. Can be classified into two areas: certifications issued by industry that are product-related; and certifications issued by organizations or professional associations. (jac)

skip counting

Refers to counting by multiples of a particular number (e.g., counting by twos or by fives). (amr)

skit

A short dramatic scene, most often written or performed as comedy (e.g., in the style of satire, slapstick, or burlesque). Skits may also be called sketches, as in sketch comedy, the style employed by many comedy troupes and on American television shows such as *Saturday Night Live*. The brevity of skits makes them an ideal vehicle for student education in writing and performing dramatic scenarios. (em)

sleep disorder

A category of mental disorders characterized by a significant departure from the normal sleep-waking cycle. Four main types of sleep disorders have been identified: sleep disorder related to another medical disorder (often related to a mood or anxiety disorder), sleep disorder related to a general medical condition (due to direct physiological effects of a medical condition), substance-induced sleep disorder (as a result of the use or disuse of a substance, including a medication), and primary sleep disorders, which are caused by none of the aforementioned etiologies. Subcategories of primary sleep disorders include dyssomnias (disorders involved with initiating or maintaining sleep, or with excessive sleepiness; sleep disturbed in amount, quality, or timing) and parasomnias (characterized by abnormal behavioral or psychological events occurring with sleep, specific sleep stages, or sleep-wake transitions, including nightmares and sleepwalking). (mkt)

SLI (See specific language impairment)

Sloan Consortium (Sloan-C)

An organization that promotes the use of online education in higher education. Originally funded by the Alfred P. Sloan Foundation, Sloan-C is now a nonprofit, member-sustained organization that hosts workshops and conferences and offers degree and certificate programs. Sloan-C publishes *The Journal of Asynchronous Learning Networks, The Sloan-C View,* and numerous books and reports. (sn)

small-group format

Any learning format in which a large group of learners is divided, temporarily, into smaller sections, often with some shared background or interest. Small groups commonly focus on discussion and analysis of ideas. (chb)

SMART Board®

A large touch-sensitive monitor. The SMART Board enables interactive multimedia learning experiences. Instead of displaying content on a computer monitor, it is displayed on a large white board attached to a projector. The touch-sensitive screen is used to manipulate displayed items or to enter information into the computer. Users can also use colored pens to write on the screen, which can then be converted into digital text. The SMART Board technology was developed by SMART Technologies, Inc. (ab1)

SMART goal

A term traditionally used in the business community, recently applied to achievement-based goals in public education. SMART is an acronym for "strategic and specific, measurable, attainable, results-oriented, and timebound" (DuFour, DuFour, Eaker, and Many 2006). These goals are generally set as a building or grade level in order to foster collective responsibility for the success of all students. An example would be "85 percent of fourth graders will achieve at a level of proficiency on the state test in reading in the spring of 2015." (dlt)

smart pen

A pen with a small computer inside. Smart pens are used with a special paper that contains microscopic dots used to record information. The pens record audio, which corresponds with written notes made on the special paper. Students can use smart pens to listen to the audio associated with their notes. One smart pen manufacturer is developing a smart pen to convert handwritten notes to digital text. (ab1)

Smith-Hughes Act (1917)

The Smith-Hughes Act was intended to provide funds for training people who had entered or who were about to enter the workforce on the farm. The legislative intent was to support programs that provide students 14 and older with the skills necessary to gain employment in industry, agriculture, commerce, skilled trades, or home economics. Widely supported at

passage, the legislation helped legitimize the idea that schools should help prepare students to enter the job market, and it has been cited as one of the first important instances of direct federal support for local educational programs. This act was the first vocational education act to be passed in this country and is considered to be the foundation for the promotion of vocational education in the United States. The requirements of the bill, however, are thought to have provided the basis for isolation of vocational education from the remainder of the curriculum in many schools. Some of those requirements are: establishment of a separate state Vocational Education Board, salaries for teachers, restrictions placed upon students, and curriculum segregation. (bs, mkw)

Smith-Lever Act (1914)

Federal law creating the Cooperative Extension Service, the agency of the U.S. Department of Agriculture that, in cooperation with state and local agencies, educates people about research generated by the land grant colleges. Located in every county in the United States and its territories, Cooperative Extension has grown beyond its original emphasis on farming and home economics to assist urban and rural people with practical application of land-grant college-generated research. The legislation also created the Federal Board for Vocational Education. (mb, las)

SMS (See status mobility system)

SNCC (See Student Non-Violent Coordinating Committee)

snowball technique

Teaching technique whereby a question or problem is addressed individually, then discussed in pairs, then in groups of fours, and continuing on in ever larger groups. The process may be used as an ice-breaker, for problem solving, or for consensus building. (las)

social action outcomes

Endeavors conducted by individuals and groups to assist other individuals and groups. Social action outcomes tend to occur after individuals and/or groups increase their own awareness and knowledge associated with a particular situation and then modify their behaviors to offer assistance in the forms of emotional, physical, and/or financial help. (npg)

social agency

The ability to function freely and with ownership within a given structure to achieve specific individual outcomes. (npg)

social bookmarking

A way to store favorite sites, articles, or other information on the Internet, organize that content, and share it with others. Social bookmarking uses tags or keywords to classify saved bookmarks. In addition, social bookmarking sites typically allow users to track the most popular bookmarks for a given tag, annotate content, or search for other users with similar interests. Teachers and students may use social bookmarking for collaboratively sharing relevant information found on the Internet. The ability to access bookmarks from any computer is useful for doing research at home, school, and the library. (kd)

social capital

Social capital refers to treating human resources (e.g., social knowledge, networks of social relationships, civic involvement) as a form of capital for the purposes of economic growth. The term was proposed by James Coleman in 1988 as a way of reconciling sociology's focus on understanding how social relationships shape action with economics' assumptions about rational decision making and objective predictors of action. Social scientists have utilized the construct of social capital to describe intangible resources existing between individuals and groups. The core idea behind social capital theory is that social networks have value. In the realm of education, networks of mutual obligation and trust nurture the intellectual and interpersonal development of individuals and gain them access to material and social resources. Within an invisible economy of social exchanges, social capital supplies important resources (information, knowledge, and skills) related to the academic advancement of individuals and groups. (lr, adj)

social change

Transformation or restructuring of the political, economic, and social relations and dynamics in a given community or society at the institutional level. (hfs)

social cognition

Social cognition is present whenever social information is interpreted and thought about. It is crucial when understanding oneself or any member of the same species, but given that human beings as well as a wide range of other animals live in social environments, it can be analyzed from the perspective of any of these species. In fact social cognition is so important that in extreme cases, the continued absence of social interaction can lead to severe developmental deficits and even to death. Social cognition can operate consciously, such as when realizing that a friend is smiling broadly and seems to be in an exceptionally good mood, as well as unconsciously, as is the case for many stereotypes and attitudes. The way social information is understood is influenced by internal factors such as the perceiver's emotional state (which is variable in the short run) and personality (which is somewhat more stable over time), as well as by external factors such as the social situation itself. The study of social cognition lies at the intersection of several disciplines, including psychology, biology, anthropology, and sociology. (mf2)

social construction of knowledge

The idea that children learn through interaction with more competent adults or peers, using feedback to help develop new ways of thinking about their worlds. For example, followers of Piaget believe that one way learning occurs is through discordant episodes, in which two actors disagree on the content being shared. (aw)

social development theory

Constructed and popularized by Lev Vygotsky (1978), social development theory asserts that social interaction influences cognitive development in powerful ways and takes place continually throughout one's life. Vygotsky's theory describes a Zone of Proximal Development—a place where social interaction and learning occurs. This theory has profound implications for schools as places of social interaction and learning and for teachers as facilitators of learning through their creation of collaborative learning environments. (jwc)

social efficiency (See social reproduction)

social efficiency approach

A teaching philosophy that places an emphasis upon the capacity of a teacher to apply an established, research-driven knowledge base in his/her practice (instructional decisions, pedagogy, curricula, etc.). (hfs)

social facting

The theory developed by Emile Durkheim of the process by which a society, or its social institutions, exerts and places influence, constraints, and expectations upon individuals in order to encourage or forbid certain behaviors and activities. (hfs)

social history

An approach to historical research that became popular in the latter half of the 20th century. Whereas older traditions in historical research focused on the study of elite groups such as politicians and eminent citizens, social history became characterized by a focus on the history of "everyday life," on the historical experience of marginalized groups (e.g., women, children, racial minorities), and on topics related to broader issues in the social sciences (e.g., social mobility). A social history of education might focus, for example, on the relationship between race, ethnicity, or class, and access to public schooling. Because of its focus on chronicling the history of marginalized groups, this has also been referred to as "history from the bottom up." (sw)

social justice

A civic duty to address the needs of all members of a society. Social justice requires that equality and fair treatment of all individuals occurs in social, economic, educational, and other situations. (jqa, npo)

social learning orientation

A focus on the individual's ability to learn vicariously by watching others. Derived from Bandura's Social Learning Theory, which emphasizes individuals' ability to learn by observing other people's behavior and its consequences and then making decisions about their own behavior. (mkr)

social mobility

The ability of members of a society to change and alter their social strata of classes. This movement can be in either direction, moving up the class ladder or down. How social class position is measured varies from culture to culture. Typically two types of mobility occur: structural mobility, caused by a change in occupation, and circulation mobility, any other change resulting in class movement. (kf1)

social networking website

Websites, such as MySpace, Facebook, and Twitter, that enable online interactions among Internet users. The basic features of social networking sites include presenting personal profiles, writing blogs, e-mailing, and sharing multimedia files. Social networking has positive (e.g., reducing perceived loneliness and enhancing offline friendships) and negative (e.g., cyberbullying, spreading incredulous or hostile gossip online) impacts on society in general and on education in particular. To protect students' online safety, many school districts have stringent rules against accessing social networking sites while in school. (lll)

social organization

Institutions and structures created and organized within society that enforce norms, such as schools and churches. Social organization can also be thought of as groups of individuals coming together for common interest, with no monetary incentive. (kf1)

social protest

Movements that use or create events to express political ideas about social issues. Notable social protest movements include student protests about the Vietnam War in the 1960s. (jqa, npo)

social reconstruction

A curriculum movement from the 1930s and 1940s developed by, among others, George Counts and Harold Rugg. Politically left-leaning, social reconstructionists prescribed that schools should be institutions for social change and reformation, building a new society defined by increased social justice. Two examples are George Counts's essay and subsequent book *Dare the School Build a New Social Order?* and Harold Rugg and Lawrence Krueger's social studies curriculum entitled *Man and His Changing Society*. Social Reconstruction was a thread in Progressivism and developed through the Progressive Education Association. (db-j)

See also social reproduction.

social reconstructionist

A teaching philosophy that places an emphasis upon the capacity of teachers to apply their knowledge of the sociopolitical implications of their practice. Additionally, they must understand both the social context of their practice and the contributions their teaching make toward justice, equality, and the establishment of more humane conditions in schools and the larger society. (hfs)

social reconstructionist teacher education

An approach to teacher education that emphasizes and develops teachers abilities to see the social and political forces upon and implications of their actions and to assess the importance of changing policies, teaching practices, or both. (rtc)

social reproduction

A curriculum movement in the early 20th century dedicated to differentiating the curriculum in accord with various learners' likely social destinies (tracking and guidance counselor practice developed out of this movement). The general notion that the job of schools is to reproduce the social, political, and economic status quo of society. This theory is also known as social efficiency. Social reproduction theories elaborate upon the premise that schools are key sites for the maintenance of social, cultural, and economic inequality. Reproductionists claim the role of schools is to sort individuals and groups according to the hierarchical division of labor in society via social, cultural, and economic processes, which largely go unnoticed and play powerful roles in shaping the behavior of individuals and their educational trajectories. Reproduction theories have been categorized by Aronowitz and Giroux (1993) into three models, which explore the maintenance of inequality in the following spheres: the economic reproductive model (Bowles and Gintis), the cultural reproductive model (Bourdieu), and the hegemonic-state reproductive model (Antonio Gramsci). (db-j, adj)

See also critical theory; reproduction theory; social reconstruction.

social roles

A set of behaviors, attitudes, and actions by individuals within a society. This triad is usually defined by a series of factors all bearing down on the individual in creating his or her position in a society. These factors consist of perceived norms of the society, interactions with others, one's self-esteem, and one's status. Income and level of education influence the status one assumes in his/her immediate environment. In addition, this position in society is determined by how individuals perceive themselves based on acceptance by those already admitted into the social position. (kf1)

social stratification

The classification of people based on income, education, occupation, inherited wealth, and power in society. May also be called social class. (jqa, npo)

social studies education—as a conserving force

A perspective that emphasizes the role of education, particularly social studies education, in maintaining the status quo in society. This view of the social studies holds that through the operation of both the formal and the hidden curriculum, existing sociopolitical roles and expectations for the various groups (social, economic, gender, political, etc.) within a society are maintained and perpetuated. (ks1)

See also three traditions of social studies education.

social studies education—as disciplinary study vs. integrated field of study

This issue is at the crux of the debate concerning the definition of the social studies. On one side of the debate are advocates who support the teaching of individual disciplines of study that parallel college course subjects (e.g., history, geography, economics). On the other side are advocates of a unified field of social studies consisting of knowledge and skills drawn from the various disciplines while ignoring disciplinary boundaries, the focus of which is a systematic study of the needs of students and society, especially civic needs. (ks)

social studies education—as social critique

A perspective that contrasts with the view of social studies education as a conserving force. This view, with its basis in critical theory, advocates the role of social studies in critically examining existing social and political structures toward the goal of social action and reform. (ks1)

social studies teacher education

Traditionally, elementary teachers are certified as elementary generalists, often with little or no specific coursework in social studies. Secondary teachers have typically been specialists in a particular discipline; if certified as composite social studies, course work is still normally in distinct and often unconnected fields of study. Both approaches face criticism for inadequately preparing teachers who are interested in and capable of teaching dynamic, integrated, and essential social studies courses for K–12 students. (ks1)

social studies teachers—as curriculum theorizers

The loose structure and wide-ranging goals of social studies as a field of study encourages teachers to take ownership in deciding the organization and purposes of their curriculum. Hilda Taba and others advocated teachers' involvement in curriculum development. Collaboration between classroom teachers and university faculty in the development of social studies curriculum is a growing trend in the field. (jrs)

social studies teachers—disciplinary knowledge

Drawing from such diverse fields of study as anthropology, archaeology, economics, geography, history, law, philosophy, political science, psychology, religion, and sociology, social studies instruction requires a broad range of disciplinary knowledge. This diversity is most pronounced in elementary school social studies, which seeks to integrate many fields of study in thematic units or into an "expanding communities" design, while secondary social studies is organized according to discrete social science disciplines. Teachers generally major or concentrate in only one social science field. (jrs)

See also expanding communities.

socialism

Any system of social organization in which the means of production and the distribution of wealth are subject to social control, or any political movement advocating the institution of such a system. Socialists may disagree about the extent to which the means of production should be socialized, the principle whereby wealth should be distributed, and the nature of the social control that should be exercised. (mbm)

socialization

The process of acquiring the knowledge, skills, attitudes, customs, and values of a culture. In the United States, the schools are increasingly involved in the socialization of children. Schools are charged with helping students acquire democratic values and practices, work-related skills, the ability to work cooperatively in groups, and other cultural elements. (jrs)

Society for College and University Planning (SCUP)

Founded in 1965, SCUP is a higher education association organized to focus on planning at all levels and in all contexts in the academy. The group promotes the advancement and application of effective planning to assure the health, vitality, and quality of higher education, especially during times of significant change. (cf)

sociocentric view of knowledge and learning

Theory that holds that an individual's interactions with others are major determinants of both the substance and process of education and knowledge construction. Knowledge, understanding, perspective, and the resultant expression of ideas are therefore relational, and not solely individual, as they are the by-products of the interactions of groups of people across time. (hfs)

sociocultural context

The environment or milieu of an individual or group described in terms of common or shared cultural characteristics and/or social roles. Members of the same social environment will often think in similar styles and patterns even when their resulting conclusions differ. (npg)

socio-cultural theory

Socio-cultural theory is, properly speaking, a collection of principles about learning and psychological development that stress the predominant role of language and culture in the formation of individual consciousness. Premised in the work of Vygotsky and Luria, these theories emphasize the dialectical relationship between the individual and their broader social-cultural environment, whereby the individual interiorizes (internalizes/adopts) cultural modalities of thought. Such interiorization is accomplished by way of the mediation made available through more experienced, expert relationships and the utilization of cultural-cognitive tools. In a broad sense, this may be viewed as an inversion of much Piagetian thinking: whereas Piaget stressed the necessity of developmental readiness before specific learnings could properly commence, Vygotsky posited that through the invocation of cognitive tools and expert relations, learning can actually lead ahead of, and draw forth, development. (tw1)

See also cultural-cognitive tools; interiorization; mediation.

sociodrama

A form of improvisational role-playing developed by Jacob Levy Moreno, used to explore how people interact in social situations and solve conflict within groups and organizations. In a classroom, sociodrama might help examine how students of different racial backgrounds interact with each other. Employing specific techniques, including role reversal (participants switch roles to gain new perspective and understanding) and soliloquy (action freezes and one participant speaks her/his inner thoughts), sociodrama can be either enacted by participants working through a particular issue or performed for a group that then uses the sociodrama as the basis for work on an issue. (em)

socioeconomic status

A category developed in the combination of the position, or score, of persons on criteria such as income, amount of education, occupation, or neighborhood type. Scores are then divided so as to create divisions such as upper class, middle class, and lower class which are articulations of life chances and opportunity. (hfs)

sociology

The study of individuals and groups and the ways they interact within society. The basis of social studies, sociology examines all topics and issues that describe how individuals treat themselves, how people interact with one another, how organizations function, how cultures operate, and so forth. Sociology not only investigates the question of how; it also probes the question of why, to offer purpose and rationale from many different perspectives. (npg)

socio-mathematical norms

Classroom norms that involve the evaluation of insightful solutions or mathematically elegant explanations and argumentations; identifying what counts as a mathematical explanation and what counts as a mathematically different strategy. The constituted norms depend on the students' understanding, attitudes, willingness, and mathematical development. (dc)

Socratic method

A method of teaching that explores topics or seeks to enhance understanding through question asking and dialogue, rather than through didactic presentation. These educational practices are based on the belief that all humans, particularly children, hold knowledge and/or truth within them. This method is attributed to the Greek philosopher Socrates by his student Plato. The Socratic method is also sometimes called "maieutic" because the teacher works "like a midwife." Proponents of dialogical pedagogy have found different techniques used by Socrates for different purposes, including the following three: to induce puzzlement in students (by challenging the adequacy of their beliefs) that will turn into a humble willingness to learn; to prompt students to figure out for themselves answers the teacher has in mind, by asking them a series of leading questions; to engage with students in open-ended inquiry on a topic with the expectation that the beliefs of the teacher and the students will likely be changed in the process. (alm, bgr, mg)

See also dialogue.

soft skills (See employability skills)

solfège

A method of singing and/or teaching music (the production of music and the reading of notational music) that employs syllables (do, re, mi, fa, sol, la, ti) to represent pitches with a single syllable (from sol-fa) corresponding to a single note. Taught in schools of music with young children and at the conservatory level. (jd)

Solipsism

Solipsism (from Latin *solus,* alone, and *ipse,* self) exists in two main forms: ontological and epistemological. The ontological solipsism maintains that I and my own states of consciousness are all that exist. The epistemological solipsism expresses a belief that it is only possible to have knowledge of myself and my states of consciousness. Solipsism does not need to be an explicitly formulated theory but can also be the consequence of a more general ontology or epistemology. (jb1)

solution-focused therapy

A type of brief therapy proposed by de Shazer in which identifying a solution is more effective than dwelling on the problem or gaining insight. The therapist helps the client focus on the here and now instead of the past. A particularly powerful tool in solution-focused therapy is to ask the "miracle question," in which the client pretends that a miracle has occurred and the problem has gone away. They must then describe specific differences that would be noticed if the problem miraculously disappeared. Focus is then placed on defining these changes and making them a reality. (tsw)

somatoform disorder

A category of mental disorders in which there are physical symptoms suggestive of a medical condition. However, these physical symptoms cannot be explained by a general medical condition, by the effects of any substance, or by another mental condition. There is typically a strong presumption on the part of medical professionals that the symptoms are linked to mental and emotional factors, and that they serve psychological purposes. Symptoms of such a disorder can range from a preoccupation with the idea of having an illness, resulting from the misinterpretation of bodily symptoms, to severe pain that has no physical cause. (mkt)

sophistry

Subtly deceptive argumentation. Sophistry is a way of making a rhetorical point by pandering to the desire of those who seek information but who do not have any knowledge of the topic under consideration. In this way, the ignorant wish to become informed, but they are also easily led to conclusions that are misleading because of their ignorance. Advertisements are sometimes examples of sophistry. Schools promote sophistry, too, when teachers act as sophists rather than seekers of wisdom and regard students as "customers" rather than as learners and also seekers of wisdom. (drb)

See also sophists.

sophists

Fee-charging itinerant teachers from around the fifth century B.C.E. Contemporaries of Socrates, sophists were generally regarded by philosophers (e.g., Plato) as charlatans because their goal was to earn money teaching people to speak well. Rhetoric at the time was valuable, as Athens was becoming increasingly litigious. As dispensers of information, especially in the area of ethics and in the relationship between customs (*nomos*) and nature (*phusis*), sophists like Protagoras (ca. 490–ca. 420 B.C.E.) and Gorgias (ca. 483–376 B.C.E.) emphasized the idea that different people have different virtues. Since sophists recognized that opinion was more action-guiding than truth, they argued that those who could change opinions had ultimate power. (drb)

See also sophistry.

SoTL (See scholarship of teaching and learning)

sound quality (See timbre)

soundness

In philosophical logic, soundness is a quality or property of arguments that are not only valid but also have true premises. Since the premises of a sound argument are true, and the steps upon which the conclusion is inferred are logically acceptable, the conclusion will be true also. (an)

See also validity.

Southern Association for Institutional Research (SAIR)

This professional organization supports institutional research programs at colleges and universities in the South. The professional activities, publications, and collegial network provided by SAIR are designed to support the successful and effective practice of higher education throughout the region. (cf)

Southern Association of Colleges and Schools (SACS)

This association accredits more than 12,000 public and private educational institutions, from prekindergarten through the university level, in 11 southeastern states and Latin America. Member institutions regularly perform comprehensive self-evaluations to assist them in planning for improvement and to assure the public of their overall quality. (cf)

sparsity factor

State educational funding formulae, especially in the Great Plains states, that provide additional funding for rural school districts that are geographically isolated and that meet minimum standards for student numbers and land mass. Generally such districts are too far from neighboring districts to make consolidation and busing attractive alternatives. (lr)

spatial awareness

Demonstrated when the child becomes aware of his/her own body as a physical object, knows to look for people and objects out of immediate sight, and begins to learn how to find other places in the physical environment. (vm)

spatial intelligence (See visual-spatial intelligence)

spatial reasoning

Relates to the properties of space. The understanding of space and what can or cannot occupy a given amount. The ability to make inferences, conclusions, and judgments in regard to the concept of space. (vdf)

spatial sense (See spatial reasoning)

spatial visualization

The ability to imagine, manipulate, measure, and compare geometric shapes or situations, mentally or with a drawn figure. (ey)

special education

Educational help designed for students who have been identified with specific disabling conditions. (sr)

special populations

Those students who may require certain services or accommodations due to their disability, limited English, poverty, or the like. Important for career and technical teacher training because of the prevalence of these students in CTE courses. (rz)

specialist degree (See degree, specialist)

specialized high school (See high school, specialized)

specialty teachers (See resource teachers)

specific job competencies (See competencies, specific job)

specific knowledge

Information used to interpret, explain, and participate in repetitious situations. Specific knowledge gives the individual the ability to process information faster and make decisions when involved in similar situations. (jqa, npo)

specific language impairment (SLI)

Also called phonosyntactic disorder, SLI is the most common childhood language disorder, indicated by difficulties with inflectional morphology (e.g., word endings that specify number and tense) and syntax. SLI children usually begin to talk at the same age as nonimpaired children but progress more slowly. Such children have difficulty learning new words from context clues and often struggle in learning to read and write. However, SLI children are typically not cognitively impaired or autistic. (aw)

specific occupational competencies (See competencies, occupational)

specification

A generative blueprint or plan for a test; the word is often used in the plural, as when referring to "the specifications for" a particular test. A "table of specifications" is a table, chart, or some other organizational graphic that shows the various content areas to be covered in tests and the number of items or tasks associated with each area. At a lower level of specificity, particular test tasks can be further specified (often in documents separate from the table) as to how those tasks should be written. In many test development systems, specifications are not written down but rather exist in the shared consciousness of the team of people who work (often over many years) to develop those tests. That phenomenon, coupled with a natural desire for reduction in cost and stability of test development, often makes it difficult to change test specifications—and hence difficult to change the actual tests that they generate. (fd)

SPECT (See Single Photon Emission Computed Tomography)

speech act theory

A sociolinguistic theory concerning the communicative function of interpersonal speech. Broadly, speech is seen as a system of conventionalized expressions that are meaningful within a given speech community and that accomplish social acts (e.g., greeting, requesting, promising, warning). Central to this view of communication is the dynamic relationship between a speaker's intent and an interlocutor's understanding of an utterance, given the sociocultural context of their interaction. (jrk)

See also illocutionary force; locutionary meaning; perlocutionary act.

speech and language disorder

Problems in communication and related areas, including delays and disorders in the areas of articulation, voice, fluency, form, content, and effective use of language. (sr)

speech code

A rule or policy designed to protect individuals from speech that could embarrass, humiliate, ridicule, or somehow victimize or stigmatize based on an individual's race, ethnicity, religion, sex, sexual orientation, creed, national origin, ancestry, age, marital status, handicap, and/or veteran's status. The courts have created a fine line between permissible speech codes and those that infringe on an individual's free speech rights. (cf)

speech to text

A form of voice recognition software. Often used as an assistive technology by students with dysgraphia, this software enables users to convert spoken words into digital text. Through repetitive exercises the software is formatted to learn a particular user's voice. The user then speaks into a microphone and printed text appears on the screen as he/she talks. (ab1)

speedness

Speedness concerns the time examinees are allowed to complete a test. Typically, large-scale standardized tests are administered with a time constraint. However, having a time constraint on a test task should not be confused with a test being speeded. Although many large-scale tests have time constraints, they are not speeded because they can be completed by a majority of test takers. When tests are speeded, it indicates that a majority of test takers cannot complete the test in the allocated time. (jx)

spell check
A computer utility that verifies the spelling in a digital text document. Spell check programs generally identify misspellings and suggest possible correct spellings. Students can use spell check programs to verify and correct spelling in their written work. (kg1)

Spencer Foundation
Established in 1968 by Lyle M. Spencer, of Science Research Associates, to "investigate ways in which education can be improved around the world." The Foundation has made grants totally approximately $250 million since that time period. (cf)

spina bifida
Cleft spine, in which there is an opening in the spinal column. There are three general types of spina bifida: Spina Bifida Occulta—an opening in one or more of the vertebrae without apparent damage to the spinal cord; Meningocele—the meninges, or protective covering around the spinal cord, has pushed out through the opening in the vertebrae; Myelomeningocele—the most severe form of spina bifida, in which a portion of the spinal cord itself protrudes through the back. (sr)

spiral curriculum
A school or district's sequence of courses and content that includes the same topics of study at several different grade levels. At each new interaction with the topic, the level of depth and sophistication increases. (jw)

spiritual education
Education attentive to the nonrational, nonphysical part of human nature. Spiritual education is an attempt to address some of the concerns traditionally addressed by sectarian religions in a nonsectarian way. Those interested in returning religious values to the public schools often try to avoid church–state conflicts through the enactment of programs of spiritual education. However, a number of philosophers have insisted that spirituality is best understood as located within some religious practice or another and that the idea of spirituality dislocated from a religious context is essentially problematic. (an)

spiritual formation
A general term often employed in religious education referring to any intentional strategy intended to deepen faith commitments or nurture "spiritual growth." Spiritual formation depends on a broad array of pedagogical strategies that may include one-on-one spiritual direction or companioning, formal class settings, and other educational endeavors. Central to the concept of spiritual formation is an assertion that one's development of an interior life in relation to some concept of the transcendent is crucial to one's overall development and maturation. (bda)

spirituality
Functions as an umbrella term for the consideration of a wide array of issues and themes, which range from morality and character building to ontology and afterlife, but largely is concerned with humanity's relationship to each other, the larger creation, and the transcendent. In popular rhetoric, the term is often used in opposition to religion, which is depicted as constrained by dogmatic concerns. Yet, simultaneously, "spirituality" is used within theological studies in reference to those aspects of religious life that are most intimate, self-implicating, and transformative. Advocates of including spirituality in the education discourse argue that

it provides a more holistic approach that results in the healthier development of the student, and thus ultimately, the society. Critics contend that spirituality is inherently tied to theological claims, and the nebulous use of the concept only functions to obscure those claims. (bda)

SPL (See student performance level)

splitting conjecture
Related to the development of multiplicative thinking. A term used by Jere Confrey to explain students' intuitive and primitive actions that are not reliant on counting and repeated addition, actions such as sharing, folding, dividing symmetrically, and magnifying. (amr)

sponsor teacher (See cooperating teacher)

sponsored mobility
Process or system of sorting whereby elite status and attendant power is controlled by the established elites or their agents and can be granted by only those parties. A recognition of certain desirable and shared qualities in the recruits presages selection and induction into the privileged. Elite status can never be attained or earned without their assent. (hfs)

sport education model
A physical education instructional model developed as an alternative to the multiactivity model. The goals of sport education are to educate students to be skilled games players and to help them develop as competent, literate, and enthusiastic sportspersons. The hallmarks of sport education include: long units of instruction called seasons, affiliation as a team member for the entire season, competition, culminating events, and a festive atmosphere. (kpr)

sport management
A field of knowledge dealing with the application of business principles to the sport industry. (kpr)

sport pedagogist
A person who specializes in the art and science of teaching and coaching. (rf)

sports medicine
A field of knowledge dealing with the care, prevention, treatment, and rehabilitation of people who participate in sport and fitness activities. (rf)

Sputnik
Soviet satellite launched on October 4, 1957, which marked the beginning of the Soviet–American Space Race, an aspect of the Cold War in which each side tried to show superiority in space-related technologies. The effect upon American education was passage of P.L. 85–864, also called the 1958 National Defense Education Act, which funded increased use of math and science in curricula across grade levels, and the National Defense Student Loan Program (1958), designed to increase enrollment in science and engineering programs in higher education. (dwm)

square root
The reverse process of squaring. The square root of a number is a number, that when squared, is equivalent to the number under the radical sign. (ps)

stage theories of adult learning
Theories that stress an established sequence of developmental change over time, typically hierarchical, from lower to higher stages of functioning. Development is characterized by increasing complexity and flexibility; at each new stage of development, the individual displays patterns or capabilities of which he/she would not have been capable previously. The application of stage theories in adult education implies that adults may revisit earlier stages to resolve conflicts from earlier periods in different ways. (jwg)
See also phase theories of adult learning.

staging (See blocking)

Standard, occupational (See occupational standard)

Standard American English (SAE)
An idealized dialect of English that is considered by some language purists to be the proper dialect. SAE is not defined precisely, and thus, in real life, no one speaks it. Some consider the dialect used by political leaders and the upper socioeconomic classes, the dialect used for literature and in formal writing, the dialect taught in schools and used by national news broadcasters to be the correct form of language. However, today on all of these levels, regional/ethnic dialects tend to prevail and the notion of SAE is slowly becoming obscure. (smt)

standard deviation
Standard deviation is a statistical term referring to the dispersion of statistical population or data. It is the measure of variation most commonly used in statistics and indicates how data points are spread around the mean. The standard deviation of a set of sample values, denoted by *s,* is a measure of the variation of values about the mean. (It is calculated by taking a square root of variance.) Interpretation of standard deviation assumes the normal distribution of data where 68 percent and 95 percent of data points fall within one standard deviation and two standard deviations of the mean, respectively. When a study reports a standard deviation of 2.3 and a mean of 56 on a test and the normal distribution can be assumed, it shows that 68 percent of the test scores are between 53.7 and 58.6 (i.e. 56 ± 2.3). (hl)
    See also variance.

standard error of measurement
The standard error of measurement (SEM) is an estimate of measurement error in using an examinee's test score. The *Standards for Educational and Psychological Testing* (1985) defines SEM as "the standard deviation of errors of measurement that is associated with the test scores for a specified group of test takers" (94) The SEM is calculated by the formula: $S_x \sqrt{(1-r_{xx'})} = \text{SEM}$ where S_x is the standard deviation of the observed scores of the test and $r_{xx'}$ is the reliability coefficient of the test. There is a reciprocal relationship between the reliability and SEM. The larger the test reliability, the smaller the SEM. The SEM indicates a range of scores examinees can receive on the test after taking into account measurement errors. (mj)

standard measure (See nonstandard/ standard measure)

standard setting
Standard setting is the general term for a variety of systematic procedures with the shared goal of defining the minimum test score or a cut score that separates one level of performance (understanding, competence, expertise, or accomplishment) from another. For example, in tests used for occupational credentialing, a minimum score differentiates between failing and passing; in state-based student testing, minimum scores differentiate among multiple performance levels, such as basic, proficient, or advanced. Standard setting is a judgment-based process, in which one or more committees of experts defines the knowledge and/or skills expected of a test taker who just meets a performance level, and may review test questions, responses to questions, and item and test data to decide on the score needed to reach a level. Popular standard setting methods include Angoff, Bookmark, Body of Work, and Contrasting Groups. (rjt)
    See also cut score.

standardized test
An assessment instrument that utilizes fixed, unchanging procedures for administration and scoring. The results, or test scores, have been shown to be reliable and valid through empirical study. Using consistent, set procedures eliminates variables affecting test performance, including

variations in instructions, scoring procedures, time limits, or procedural order. Results obtained may then be compared to other scores from the same test. Because the standardization procedures help eliminate possible confounding influences, any differences in scores may, at least theoretically, be attributed to true differences in performance. Standardized tests may be used in areas such as intellectual, cognitive, or personality assessment, behavioral observations, or interviews. Standardized tests are published or issued by testing companies or agencies (sometimes governmental) and are intended to provide comparable information about test takers' abilities across a range of settings or geographical areas. Standardized tests are written by trained test writers according to explicit specifications, and information about their reliability, validity, and comparative norms is usually published in a technical manual that accompanies the test. Standardized tests generally (though not always) consist of multiple-choice questions. Tests are usually administered on a large scale by an education agency to measure student achievement in a well-defined curricular domain, mainly for accountability purposes. Standardized tests are often viewed as objective, efficient, and cost-effective. However, standardized tests are also seen as having some flaws. First, standardized tests often reveal little about student thinking processes and problem-solving techniques. Second, the norming process, content selection, and types of items raise accusations of linguistic and cultural bias against low socioeconomic or bilingual students. Third, standardized test scores often reshape curricula and cause teachers to teach to the test. (lbl, tvh, scw, al)

standards in testing

Codes of ethical or good practice as, for example, the published standards of conduct issued by a given testing company or governmental agency. Expected levels of performance or skill mastery as, for example,

state, national, or international standards against which test items and tasks are developed. Statistical norms are also used as a form of standards in testing. (fd)

See also standard setting.

standing committee

Committees written into institutional bylaws to assure continuity in their specific commitments. Members are elected annually for various lengths of service. (cf)

standpoint epistemologies

Standpoint epistemologies do not claim to know what is absolutely true for all people and all times. It is possible to find feminist, Africana, and Native American epistemologies, for example, that present theories of knowing from within the context of particular worldviews. To further illustrate, feminist standpoint epistemologies emphasize that individual knowers are limited, situated, partial knowers. They emphasize the fallibility of criteria and standards and insist on the need to include others, especially outsiders, into the discussion of what are truths in order to help us enlarge our views and compensate for our own limitations. (bt-b)

See also epistemology.

state accountability systems

Organized efforts at the state level to develop useful measures, indicators, and other information to review and appraise the effectiveness of institutions of higher education in using state or public resources. (cf)

state board for vocational or career-technical education

A board created by a state legislature to cooperate with federal authorities in administering provisions of the federal and supplementary laws in regard to career and technical education. (jm)

state education agency

State education agencies are charged with promoting leadership for learning in order to improve student achievement. Most state education agencies today seek to allocate funds, build capacity, establish challenging standards, assessments, and accountability systems through using new technologies to provide resources to those students who are least likely to succeed, to strengthen efficient and effective administration, and to improve community involvement. They are in charge of early childhood, elementary, secondary, and higher education at the state level. (cl)

State Higher Education Executive Officers (SHEEO)

This nonprofit, nationwide association of chief executive officers serves statewide coordinating boards and governing boards of postsecondary education. Its objectives include the interests of states in quality higher education, and in promoting the importance of state planning and coordination as the most effective means of gaining public confidence in higher education. Forty-nine states and Puerto Rico are SHEEO members. (cf)

state literacy resource centers

Federally funded centers established to encourage the coordination of literacy services, enhance the capacity of state and local organizations to provide literacy services, and serve as a link between literacy educators and the National Institute for Literacy for the sharing of information, expertise, and resources related to literacy. (las)

state mandate

A term used in education that refers to an authoritative command, order, or commission from a state official or agency whose power has been granted by the state. It may be given in the form of a formal order, legislation, or authorization to act given by a state court or official to a less powerful body or individual. An example would be the legislature of a state mandating a specified amount of staff development for personnel each year. (mm)

state plan

In career and technical education, a state plan is an agreement between a state board of vocational or career-technical education and the U.S. Department of Education, describing the vocational education program developed by the state to meet its own purposes and conditions and the conditions under which the state will use federal vocational education funds. Such conditions must conform to the federal acts and the official policies of the U.S. Department of Education before programs may be reimbursed from federal funds. (jm)

state university

An institution under state control and offering courses, programs, and continuing education opportunities, with a strong emphasis on practical or applied subjects. (cf)

statewide planning

Refers to interinstitutional studies and recommendations of governing boards, coordinating boards, commissions, task forces, or other agencies authorized by state governors or legislatures. (cf)

statistical literacy

A term used to describe a person or group's ability to understand statistics. Statistical models help to identify critical survival skills for both students and adults. Students are primarily learners of statistics, but they can also be consumers of statistics in making decisions on what to buy, or producers of statistics if they are working on a research project. Adults are often in job situations in which they are producers of statistics. (pmts)

statistical reasoning

A term used to describe the way people reason with statistical ideas and make sense of statistical information. Models of statistical reasoning help clarify how people are thinking about statistics, what they seem to know and understand, and where they have difficulty. (pmts)

statistical thinking

A philosophy of learning and action predicated on the following fundamental principles: all work occurs in a system of interconnected processes; variation exists in all processes; and understanding and the reduction of variation are key to success. Statistical models help teachers and researchers attend to important concepts and processes in the teaching and learning of statistics and reflect what learners, consumers, and producers of statistics should know. (pmts)

statistics

Application of the theories of probability to problems involving sets of data and other related questions. The discipline that provides methods to help make sense of data. Also, the analysis of characteristics of a population by observing characteristics of a smaller random sample of the population. These characteristics of the sample are then used to summarize or describe the whole population. (wja)

status

Social position in a society or organization that affects relationships, power, and identity. (jqa, npo)

status mobility system (SMS)

Strategies for achieving success that are culturally and socially acceptable. In the United States education is viewed as one such system for achieving success. (jqa, npo)

stereotypes

Fixed or general patterns, such as mental pictures or representations, held by an individual or by members of a group. These thought patterns represent an oversimplified opinion, attitude, or uncritical judgment. Stereotypic misinformation exists concerning ethnicity, religion, race, and gender. (mje, jah)

stereotyping

The act of ascribing roles, behaviors, expectations, and aspirations to individuals or groups primarily on the basis of gender, race, culture, religion, and sexual orientation. (ea, ch)

still life

A pictorial representation of objects that are inanimate (not alive) or animate only in the sense of vegetative life. The term derives from the 17th-century Dutch *stillleven*, meaning a motionless natural object (dead pheasants or fowls are sometimes included in still life paintings, as are fruit or vegetables) or objects (containers like bowls that hold the fruit or tables with cloths on them). Exercises in still life painting or drawing are particularly instructive for art students mastering techniques of light and shadow as necessary for replicating, for example, the folds in a tablecloth, because the object of representation does not move or change and can be revisited on numerous occasions. (jd)

stochastics

A term used to include related branches of mathematics, namely statistics and probability. (amr)

stop-out

Term applied to adult learners who, because of life circumstances, stop attending classes with the intention of returning at some later point in time. Often during such a hiatus from organized learning, stop-outs may engage in self-study or other forms of informal learning. (las)

strategic planning

Strategic planning is a process that people engage in to define an achievable and sustainable future for the institution or organization. School leaders are occupied with planning for a shared vision of the future in light of societal changes and the internal issues of the school (financial stability, demanding parents, children with special needs, gender equity, diversity, new technology, etc.) In order to successfully plan strategically, institutions and organizations are now shifting toward a more participatory planning process and to creating a school climate that is open to considering innovation. Some aspects that should be considered when creating a strategic plan are: examination and analysis of internal data, building consensus, developing recommendations for guiding policy goals, specific sequential implementation supported by financial projections, and broad participation and communication. (cl)

stress management training

A combination of techniques and strategies, usually cognitive, behavioral, and educational, that is implemented to help reduce and prevent the physical and psychological effects of stress and stressful situations. Some typical strategies include teaching healthy eating and exercise habits, examining and modifying dysfunctional beliefs, relaxation training, deep breathing, and time management. (tsw, fa)

structural assimilation

When dominant and subordinate groups begin to interact, intermarry, and become equal in a society, structural assimilation has occurred. (jqa, npo)

structural equation modeling

Structural equation modeling (SEM) is a statistical procedure that can be used to model complex relationships among observed and latent variables. Types of SEM include path analysis, regression, factor analysis, latent variable models, and mixture models. SEM can be used to test existing theories about the relationship among variables (confirmatory perspective) and to explore and refine new theories about the relationship among variables (exploratory perspective). SEM is also known as the analysis of covariance structure since it is primarily based on the covariances of a set of observed variables, although in some cases the analysis can also be conducted based on a correlation matrix. When the model-implied covariance matrix has an acceptably small distance from the observed covariance matrix, the proposed model will be accepted as a plausible model with a satisfactory model-data fit. (gl)

structural neuroimaging (See neuroimaging)

structuralism

An intellectual movement and approach to human and social sciences that seeks to describe how humans make sense of the world. It reached its peak in Europe in the mid to late 20th century. Structuralism posits a human-constructed reality structured by and in binary opposites (e.g., nature/culture, male/female, white/black). These oppositions, in turn, structure meaning and reveal the hidden, unconscious "grammar," or logic, of a system. Structures, while commonly misunderstood to be concrete manifestations, are actually cognitive models. Prominent structuralists include the founder of structural linguistics, Ferdinand de Saussure, who proposed a scientific model of language as an objective, closed system of rules and universally held sets of relations held in common by both authors and readers. Other theorists then sought to uncover and describe invariant structures in culture, society, the human psyche, consciousness, and history. After de Saussure, notable structuralists included, for example, Claude Lévi-Strauss (anthropology), Louis Althusser (sociology), Jacques Lacan (psychoanalysis), and Roland Barthes (literary and cultural criticism). (jm1)

structured activities

Activities that have been planned to enhance children's practice and use of specific skills. These activities usually require children to follow specific directions or instructions to complete task(s); teachers may also provide verbal guidance, modeling, or physical help as the children complete the task(s). Structured activities can be implemented in large groups, small groups, or on an individual basis. (at)

student
An individual to whom instruction is being delivered. The student may be any age, and instruction may be delivered in a variety of settings, using different methods and technologies. Instruction may even be self-directed. Typically students in the United States have a mandated number of years of school attendance in recognized educational institutions. Mandatory schooling terms vary among states. The term "pupil" is correctly applied to students at the elementary level but is commonly used at all levels. Current use of the term "learner" reflects the increased interest in lifelong learning. In the broadest sense, a student is someone who seeks knowledge and understanding in any setting. (npo, jwc)

student advocate
A leader who makes educational decisions based on the needs of the student, demonstrating empathy and a willingness to deal with students on an individual basis, placing high importance on helping the student achieve appropriate levels of success. (djl)

student affairs
Division of university or college governance that includes areas related to student life. It could include such areas as academic advisement, financial aid, health services, new student orientation, residence hall life, international services, career centers, disability concerns, and student activities. On smaller campuses, athletics may fall under the office or division of student affairs. (sn)

student blowouts
A term used to describe massive student demonstrations associated with the Mexican American (or Chicano) civil rights movement of the 1960s. Blowouts, also called walkouts, in Los Angeles, Denver, San Antonio, and elsewhere during 1968–1969 demonstrated student unhappiness with discriminatory practices in the schools and expressed support for programs such as bilingual education and Mexican American cultural programming in the schools, such as Chicano studies. (sw)

student-centered instruction (SCI)
An instructional approach employing creative methodologies in which students become the center of the learning process by influencing the content, activities, materials, and pace of learning. If properly implemented, the SCI approach strengthens retention of knowledge and increases motivation to learn. (cf, bba)

student engagement
Generally encompasses students' active participation, their willingness to exert extra effort, and in some cases, their involvement in planning their curriculum or learning experience. Some definitions specify only a student's willingness to complete basic school tasks. The term is used with all levels of education. In higher education, it frequently involves some type of extracurricular or community service and is often associated with the National Survey of Student Engagement (NSSE). (sn)

student exchange programs (See exchange programs)

student follow-up (See follow-up, Completer)

student government
An organization of representatives from the student body charged with responsibilities, as authorized by school administration, ranging from the creation of student conduct regulations to overseeing student organizations and activities. (jw)

Student League for Industrial Democracy (SLID)
College student section of the socialist-inspired League for Industrial Democracy (LID). LID was established in 1921 as the successor to the Intercollegiate Socialist Society (founded in 1905). In 1933,

the LID student section renamed itself the Student League for Industrial Democracy in order to emphasize its place within a broader student protest movement. The economic crisis of the Great Depression contributed to SLID's expanded membership, along with similar organizations such as the Young People's Socialist League (YPSL) and the National Student League (NSL). In 1935, SLID and the NSL combined to form the American Student Union. (aja)

student learning center

As recent additions to institutions of higher learning, these campus facilities advance student learning in a technological era and enhance the quality of learning in many ways using the various concepts, principles, and methods of assessment. These centers typically provide academic support services to students needing assistance with course work or the transition to college-level requirements. (cf)

student management system

Software used to manage typical day-to-day operations for a school and can include: processing student admissions; enrolling new students; storing student grades, academic progression and performance; and maintaining attendance records and other administrative functions. (pgg)

Student Non-Violent Coordinating Committee (SNCC)

Black student organization founded in Raleigh, North Carolina, in 1960 for the purpose of ending segregation through nonviolent action. Founders included Ella Baker of the Southern Christian Leadership Conference and divinity student James Lawson. During the early 1960s SNCC engaged in many nonviolent actions throughout the south, including sit-ins, Freedom Rides, and voter registration drives. In 1966, SNCC shifted to a militant, confrontational approach under the leadership of Stokely Carmichael. By the late 1960s membership had rapidly declined. (nc)

student performance level (SPL)

Provides a description of an adult learner's language abilities along a scale of 0 to 10. This level is correlated to score ranges on the Basic English Skills Test (BEST). (las)

student portfolio

A tool for personal development. An evolutionary collection of student goals, action plans, reflections, and work samples that document and direct the student's progress in achieving increasing levels of competence in certain critical areas. It is not merely a binder of random documents; it is a capsule that represents the whole of a student's college experience. It is a documentation of curricular and extracurricular learning. (cf)

Student Protest Movement of the 1960s

Phrase used to describe college and university student activism directed at a broad range of issues, most notably civil rights and the Vietnam War. Groups involved include the Student Nonviolent Coordinating Committee (SNCC), Students for a Democratic Society (SDS), and the Weather Underground. The movement's legacies include: greater diversity in faculty and student bodies; creation of Chicano, black, and women's studies departments; and a relaxation of student regulations. (egh)

student response systems (See clicker technology)

Student Right-to-Know and Campus Security Act (Public Law 101-542)

Passed in 1990 by Congress to increase disclosure of information by institutions of higher education. This legislation required that the graduation rates of athletic scholarship recipients be disclosed, and that campus crime statistics be reported and made available to students and parents. The Campus Security Act is now named for a former victim, the "Jeanne Clery Disclosure of Campus Security Policy and Campus Crime Statistics Act." Current amendments to the "Clery Act" require broad reporting obligations from campus and community personnel and have extended the area to include property surrounding the campus. (djr)

student teacher
An apprentice elementary or secondary school teacher who, as a college or university student, is fulfilling experiential degree requirements. (cf)

student trainee
A regularly enrolled secondary school student participating in a cooperative program of training in an occupation with related classroom instruction. (jm)

student-centered curriculum (See learner-centered curriculum)

Students for a Democratic Society (SDS)
Organization focused on political and social change, generally thought of as being the cornerstone of the student protest movement of the 1960s. In 1962 students from several universities met in Port Huron, Michigan, and drafted the famous political manifesto, the *Port Huron Statement*. SDS chapters sprang up on campuses throughout the United States, with an estimated 30,000 to 100,000 student members. SDS was involved in a range of civil rights and anti-Vietnam War activities. It finally dissolved in 1969, but some of its work was continued through splinter groups such as the Weather Underground. (egh)

student-teacher ratio
The relationship between the number of students in a given institution or district and the number of teachers. A school with 300 students and 10 teachers would have a student-teacher ratio of 30 to 1. Written as 30:1. (jw)

study abroad
Educational programs designed to offer students (high school, undergraduate, and graduate) opportunities to study and live outside of their home country. Such programs vary in duration, ranging from several weeks to a year or more. Study abroad encourages knowledge development of a country or region through engagement with language and culture. Curricular elements of study abroad programs may include direct enrollment in a college or university, research, fieldwork, internship, or service learning in the host country. Programs are offered in diverse geographical locations all over the world. (ebd)

study circle
A learning process in which a group of adults meet to learn something together in a democratic process that encourages participants to be both teachers and learners. Study circles were first organized in Sweden in the early 20th century. (jpc)

style
From the Latin *stylus*, an instrument for engraving. Style is the imprint of the artist as if engraved on the work of art. It is a coherence of aesthetic properties indicative of the hand and/or mind of the artist. In visual arts and literature, it is the constant form—and sometimes the constant elements, qualities, and expression—in the art of an individual or group. Style is the product of artistic devices and may involve modulation of line, voice, rhythm, tone, and structure; or use of cliché, allusion, metaphor, irony, and the like. An area of debate in aesthetics, it can also be synonymous with fashion, originality, loftiness, or attractiveness. Very young children are sensitive to (can recognize) the artistic style of other children in their classrooms. (lj)

sub-baccalaureate degree

Postsecondary technical training less than a bachelors degree, such as certificate programs, associate degrees, and apprenticeships; also refers to the labor market that requires this level of training, which may be the fastest-growing segment of the economy. (rz)

subemployment

A summary measure of the total problem of unemployment and low earnings, designed to represent its compound impact on disadvantaged groups and its effects in preventing several million workers and their families from sharing in the nation's economic prosperity. Subemployment can be expressed in absolute numbers or as a rate. (jm)

subitizing

The skill to recognize a quantity in a group without counting. (amr)

subject matter

A course or area of studying a particular branch of knowledge. The subject represents the core or substance of that which is being examined or discussed. A subject-centered curriculum is organized with subject matter as the center and surrounded by activities and content that reinforce the learning of subject matter. (ce)

subject matter (content) knowledge

Typically the knowledge of the content, methods of inquiry, syntax, and structure of an academic discipline such as biology, history, music, or literature. (rtc)

subject-centered curriculum (See subject matter)

subjective test

Subjective refers to any scoring procedure in which the scorer must use his or her own judgment to determine the acceptability of a response to an item. The most common use of subjective scoring is the use of a rating scale to judge oral or written responses to test items. While subjective scoring is generally less reliable than objective scoring, the use of clearly articulated scoring rubrics and rater training have been shown to bring subjective scoring procedures up to acceptable levels of reliability. (scw)

See also objective test.

submersion bilingual education

Sometimes called "sink or swim," this form of education places a bilingual student in an English-speaking-only classroom with no special assistance or guidance. Such programs are considered illegal based on the court case decision of *Lau v. Nichols.* (jqa, npo)

subsistence level

The economic level at which only the minimum necessities of life (such as food and shelter) can be provided. The amount of money a person must earn in order to sustain a minimal standard of living. (ewr)

substance abuse

The misuse of mind- and/or mood-altering substances, whether legal or illegal, culminating in negative effects on oneself and/or others, and impairing one's ability to successfully adapt to and meet role requirements at, for example, home, school, or work. Substance abuse may involve continued use when it is physically hazardous, or when an individual has already developed legal, social, or interpersonal problems as a result of past persistent and hazardous use of a substance. (do)

substance-related disorder

A category of mental disorders that is etiologically related to the misuse of legal or illegal substances (e.g., drugs, medications, toxins, etc.). Substance-related disorders include substance-use disorders (e.g., substance dependence and substance abuse) and substance-induced disorders (e.g., substance intoxication, substance withdrawal, substance-induced delirium, substance-induced mood disorder). (do)

subtest

A subtest is a subcomponent of a larger test that consists of measures (or subcomponents) of different, but related constructs. It usually assesses a particular skill or construct of interest. For example, the Graduate Record Examination (GRE) General Test includes three subtests: Verbal Reasoning, Quantitative Reasoning, and Analytical Writing. A good subtest, like any other test, has items with high internal consistency reliability. (jx)

subtractive schooling

A concept advanced by Chicana sociologist Angela Valenzuela, subtractive schooling describes the structural and cultural processes by which U.S. public schools divest immigrant and U.S.-born Latino youth of important social and cultural resources, leaving them progressively vulnerable to academic failure and reproducing them as a monolingual, English-speaking, ethnic minority, neither identified with Mexico nor equipped to function competently in America's mainstream. Building upon the concept of subtractive assimilation, Valenzuela developed the term "subtractive schooling" to bring the school more clearly into focus in the broader Americanization project. She suggests that schools may be subtractive in ways that extend beyond the concept of subtractive cultural assimilation to include the content and organization of the curriculum. (adj)

subtrahend

The number being subtracted from another number (the minuend). (amr)

success course

Course designed by a college or university, generally by a two-year or community college, to help assist in increasing retention rates and/or transfer rates from two-year schools. The course generally covers topics such as college life, goal setting, study skills, stress management, and cultural competencies. (kku)

summa cum laude

Latin phrase meaning "with highest praise," used as a designation for college or university honor graduates and their academic attainment. (cf)

summative evaluation

The process of collecting, analyzing, and reporting data about instruction, training, or programs for the purposes of decision making. Educators and educational program developers employ summative evaluations at the end of an instructional cycle to determine the extent to which students mastered the learning objectives. Similarly, facilitators use summative evaluation at the end of training workshops to determine program efficacy and to provide data that can be used to recommend continuation or discontinuation of the program. Summative evaluation can be contrasted with formative evaluation. Summative evaluations collect data *after* a program has been implemented; formative evaluations collect data *during* the development of a program in order to improve the design. (sm)

superintendent

In education, the superintendent is the educational leader and the chief executive officer of the school district. The superintendent is charged with assuming administrative responsibility and leadership for the planning, operation, supervision, and evaluation of the education programs, services, and facilities of the school district. Superintendents are also charged with preparing and submitting the district budget to the board of trustees. They must prepare recommendations for policies to be adopted by the board of trustees and oversee the implementation of adopted policies. The political nature of the role of the superintendent has resulted in an increase in the turnover rate among superintendents. (ly)

supervision

A general term used to denote any process whereby a less experienced person is learning and training under the guidance of someone who has exhibited a specified level of mastery in the area in which they are supervising. Professional supervision typically involves five steps: problem identification, diagnosis, planning, implementation, and evaluation. Supervision can be used to facilitate skills in such diverse areas as consultation, counseling, and administration. (tsw)

supervisor

In education, one who supervises a school unit or operation working to improve instruction. Supervisors may develop and evaluate objectives related to existing programs or develop and manage new programs. They may have roles that are either assistive (providing direct or indirect services) or administrative (providing administrative or evaluative services). Assistive supervisors may assist teachers by establishing communication, aiding and supporting them, and offering expertise in specific areas, providing both direct and indirect services. Administrative supervisors may manage and control instructional programs as well as evaluate teachers for personnel decisions. (bs)

supplemental educational services

Providers of additional academic instruction designed to increase academic achievement in low-income students under the terms of the No Child Left Behind Act of 2001. Instruction is provided outside the regular school day and is expected to be research-based as determined by the standards of the U.S. Department of Education. (lr)

support group

A group typically composed of individuals with common life issues or problems. Group members help each other reduce psychological stress and make desired life changes. They share their experiences, make suggestions, and encourage each other. Support groups are often led by individuals struggling with similar or identical issues, rather than by a counseling professional, although counseling professionals may be used as consultants. Support groups may be organized informally or more formally through an organization. Individuals meeting to support each other through divorce, or through writing a thesis are examples of support groups. (sdc)

survey, employment (See employment survey)

survey, occupational (See occupational survey)

survey, vocational education (See vocational education survey)

survey course (See course, survey)

suspension

A school's disciplinary action in which a student is removed from a class or school for a fixed period of time as a result of an illegal activity, history of misconduct, or acts that threaten the safety of another student, teacher, or school staff person. Suspended students also may not be allowed to attend school-sponsored activities. Students required to attend an alternate class during suspension are said to be in "in-school" suspension. Certain conditions may be required before a student is able to return to his/her normal schedule. (ms)

Suzuki method

Approach to teaching music to very young children, developed in Japan by Shinichi Suzuki. Emphasizes learning based initially on rote and consistently on repeated listening, for example, to recordings of folk songs for beginners and baroque and classical music for older students. The Suzuki method has gained a worldwide following and has been expanded to include instruments that can be scaled down to an appropriate size for a child, including viola, cello, bass, harp, flute, guitar, and piano. It has been credited for producing child prodigies and criticized for appearing to produce mechanical performers who lack music theory and sight-reading skills. (jbl)

Swann v. Charlotte-Mecklenburg Board of Education, 402 U.S. 1 (1971)

Landmark U.S. Supreme Court decision in North Carolina, which held that school authorities are responsible under the 14th Amendment for developing a plan for racial integration. The Court upheld the district court's county-wide busing order. *Swann* became a hallmark of school desegregation, requiring court-ordered busing programs throughout the urban United States and subsequently triggering protests to busing measures to achieve racial integration. (mc3)

Sweatt v. Painter, 339 U.S. 629 (1950)

A U.S. Supreme Court case that ruled that the University of Texas's separate law school for blacks was unequal to its law school for whites. Looking at tangible resources such as faculty and libraries, as well as intangibles such as academic reputation and prestige, the Court decided that the State of Texas had not met its obligations to provide a separate but equal education for black law school students in the state. *Sweatt* built on the success of *Missouri ex rel Gaines v. Canada* (1938) to challenge the notion of "separate but equal" in professional and graduate education. (alw)

Sweezy v. New Hampshire, 354 U.S. 234 (1957)

U.S. Supreme Court decision that overturned the contempt of court conviction of University of New Hampshire professor Paul Sweezy. In this Cold War–era academic freedom case, Sweezy was interrogated in the New Hampshire state legislative hearings on subversive activities and refused to answer questions regarding

the Progressive Party and his lectures. The Court ruled that the university is protected under the 14th Amendment to decide who may teach, what may be taught, how it shall be taught, and who may be admitted to study. (mc3)

syllable

A unit of linguistic structure composed of one or more phonemes. (smt)

See also coda; nucleus; onset; rhyme.

syllabus

A brief statement or outline of the objectives and/or schedule of a course of study, lectures. (jw)

symbol

A form, image, object, act, sound, or other entity that stands for or represents something other than itself. Symbols are usually associated with their referents (that which they represent) by reason of relationship, convention, or accidental resemblance (e.g., a horse running wild symbolizing freedom). Symbols are sometimes studied in terms of their cultural significance or connection to something repressed in the unconscious mind. Educational psychologists have studied children's developing expertise in using and understanding different systems of symbols (e.g., language, music, gesture, visual arts) and noted that development with one set of symbols does not predict proficiency in another. (kpb)

symbolic manipulation

Changing the form of a symbolization without affecting its meaning. For example, $0.5b = b/2$, $t^3 = t \times t \times t$, or $1G = 9.8$ m/s^2. (kva)

symbolic play

Symbols used by children to represent different objects or materials in their play. In the child's mind, a verbal description usually accompanies the symbol used in play. The younger the child, the more closely related the symbol would be to the real object. For example, a younger child may use a toy truck to represent the family car. As children get older, the verbal descriptions become more complex. Older children may use a wooden block as the family car or a spoon as an airplane. (at)

symbolic violence

The covert, or hidden, ways in which the powerful assert their domination over the less powerful in the development of norms, attitudes, values, and behaviors. The phenomenon occurs when one group is presumed to have the legitimate power and authority to enforce norms and to covertly punish transgressions. (hfs)

symbolism

The use of symbols in art, literature, films, and so on, to represent ideas. A type of art and literature that originated in France and Belgium in the late 19th century that favored the expression of states of mind over the representation of reality. Influenced by Romanticism and the Pre-Raphaelite Brotherhood, its symbols were meant to be mysterious, ambiguous suggestions of meanings. Many Symbolists dealt with the macabre, the mysterious, and the morbid. Adolescent artists seem ready to consciously employ symbols in their own art work and writing and to appreciate Symbolism in works of art. (kpb)

symmetry—line/rotational

Also called axial symmetry. Line or rotational symmetry refers to symmetry with respect to a specific line or axis. To exhibit symmetry, each point on one side of the line is balanced by a point in an identical mirrored position on the other side of the line (i.e., the image on one side can be rotated 180 degrees about the line to exactly match the image on the other side of the line). (kva)

sympathy

Sympathy is a phenomenon in which the emotion of one person induces the same emotion in another merely by its presence. The word "sympathy" comes from the Greek *paéthos,* meaning suffering, and *sym,* with or together. Like the sympathetic vibration that a plucked guitar string draws from adjacent strings, human emotions also vibrate with those of others. Contagious laughter is an example of a sympathetic response. (sv)

See also compassion; empathy; intersubjectivity.

symposium

An educational format in which two or more speakers are utilized, to present differing information or points of view on a given subject. Speakers are introduced by a moderator, who (after the individual speaks) summarizes and opens the program to questions from the audience. (cf)

symptom-based test

One of a class of assessment instruments designed to measure cognitive, emotional, and/or behavioral manifestations of a specific psychological disorder or a specific aspect of psychopathology. Symptom-based tests are typically administered using a client self-report format, with clients endorsing items they deem to be consistent with their experiences. Such tests may assess symptoms related to a particular disorder, such as depression (e.g., Beck Depression Inventory) or symptoms related to multiple disorders (e.g., Symptom Checklist-90-Revised). (cap)

synaesthesia

From the Greek *syn-,* union, and *aísthesis,* sensation. The ability or tendency to translate experience perceived in one sense almost automatically into another (e.g., the sound of a musical note makes a particular color appear). The condition has been linked with particular artists and with artistry in general, but it affects just as many nonartists as artists (though more women than men). Synaesthesia also includes the description of one kind of sense impression through vocabulary of another (e.g., harmony or brilliance both of musical sounds and colors) and is thereby linked to metaphor. Howard Gardner has noted that many preschool children (perhaps because of their less differentiated developmental stage) seem to have synaesthesia. At four or five, "the age of Synaesthesia," children associate freely across, rather than express confusion about, boundaries between sensory domains. (tkb)

synaptogenesis

Synaptogenesis is the creation of a new synapse through the process of increased branching of axonal projections from the sending (presynaptic) neuron to the dendrites of the receiving (postsynaptic) neuron. (dh)

synchronous discussion

A discussion or conversation in which all participants are present and together at the time the discussion is occurring. The participants include both active discussants and observers, and they may be together in the same place or connected online such as in an online group chat. (ms)

synchronous learning

A learning process in which instructor and students interact simultaneously via an online program. It takes place in a virtual classroom through video conferencing or web-based real-time broadcasting. (hh)

See also asynchronous learning.

syntax

The study of the structure of phrases and sentences; the component of the grammar that includes the rules of sentence formation. (smt)

synthesis

The process by which one draws data from a variety of sources and is able to use it in producing a new explanation or description of an event, trend, or phenomenon. (jjc)

system of measurement

A set of reference samples used to compare length, time, mass, volume, and temperature. Two of the most commonly used systems are the Metric and English systems. (kva)

system of reasoning

Developing a logical outcome that conveys the meaning of a mathematical concept or equation. This encourages students to understand the main ideas of the concept and to create connections that allow them to justify their answers. (jmg, ldz)

systematic instruction

Defined by Katz and Chard (1989) as instruction of an individual or a small group of children who require adult assistance in learning a specific skill and subskills involved in areas such as literacy and numeracy. (kms)

systematic observation

Refers to collecting data in the form of observation on a consistent basis to use in program development and evaluation. (kms)

T

TABE (See Test of Adult Basic Education)

table top art

A term describing art that is done in the nonarts classroom and is constrained by the limits of size of student desktops and the constraints of classroom tidiness. Table top art is most often the sort of activity done with precut paper shapes glued and colored at holiday time or "color within the lines" assignments done on photocopied work sheets. By contrast, artwork done in studios and art classrooms is often large in scale and dependent on rich and messy media of expression. (jd)

tactical restrictions

Limiting and giving guidelines to refine the student's use of technology within the classroom through close monitoring. Encouraging the manipulatives to be used as an aide as opposed to being completely dependent on the tools when working toward a solution. (jmg, ldz)

tagging

The process of using digital technology to bookmark a web page. In order to "tag" content, an individual may subscribe to a social tagging service (e.g., delicious or Diigo). The subscription allows individuals to download a set of tagging tools that appear below the Internet browser bar. Individuals can click on a page, bookmark the page, and tag the page for reference. Users can then add labels to the tag with keywords related to the topic and share the tagged page with others. For instance, students in a science course might tag articles about weather patterns and share the information with the group. The labels individuals include as part of tags become part of an ever-growing database that categorizes information. (sm)

Take One!

Connected to the National Board Certification process, Take One! is a job-embedded program offered by the National Board for Professional Teaching Standards to pre- and in-service teachers, administrators, and professors in education that can act as a tool for professional development or as a preliminary step toward National Board Certification. This video-based portfolio program helps teachers improve teaching practices and student learning. The program is designed for use either with individual teachers or schoolwide implementation and is available in 25 different certification areas. (dek, cp)

See also National Board Certification.

taken-as-shared consensual meanings

A term coined by Cobb and Yackel (1996), used to refer to meanings that are assumed by those in the sharing group to be the same. In certain situations, taken-as-shared consensual meanings can be transitory. Such a situation would occur if a member in the sharing group develops a difference in a meaning that all in the group had assumed to be shared among themselves. When that adjusted meaning is presented to the group by the dissenting member, the group can no longer make an assumption of shared meaning. Thus, the group no longer possesses the assumed-to-be-agreed-upon meaning they previously shared before the difference in meaning was made known. Such is a case of a transitory taken-as-shared consensual meaning. (smts)

talent

Ability, skill, capability, or aptitude in the arts or other fields. Usually describes ability or skill that a person possesses naturally, rather than the result of study or training, though talent may be enhanced or discovered through training. Though possible to recognize talent to some degree, talent is not clearly and specifically defined. It is virtually impossible to measure, and conceptions of what constitutes talent can differ from person to person. Considering the work of children across various artistic domains, talent may be easier to recognize in music than in other artistic domains. (em)

talented students (See gifted students)

tap dance

A form of dance, with African origins, in which the rhythm is tapped out by metal taps attached to the heels and toes of the dancer's shoes. Tap dance can be done with or without accompaniment (the tapping makes the music to and through which the dancer dances). While tap is a very appealing art form to young children, it is primarily taught in out-of-school settings, notably in urban community centers. (jd)

Tape v. Hurley, 66 Cal. 473 (1885)

A case in which the California Supreme Court affirmed the right of an American child of Chinese descent to attend public school. A principal had refused to admit eight-year-old Mamie Tape, an action supported by the San Francisco superintendent and the school board. When the Supreme Court upheld a lower court's decision to allow Tape to attend the school, the California legislature passed a law that permitted local school boards to establish segregated schools. The San Francisco school board responded by establishing the Chinese Primary School, in which Tape was enrolled. (eht)

Tarasoff Decision (See duty to warn/protect)

target behavior

Typically a desired behavior for a child to initiate, engage in, or master that furthers growth and development. The behavior is described in detail and an intervention plan developed to increase the behavior. May also refer to a behavior deemed inappropriate, with an accompanying intervention plan designed to reduce it. (kms, yb)

targeted employment programs

Subsidized employment programs designed to offer assistance to workers having unusual barriers to employment, including commonly discriminated populations, older workers, homemakers returning to work, migrant and seasonal farm workers, and workers with difficult job histories. (ea)

Targeted Reading Intervention (TRI)

A rural early literacy initiative developed for K–1 classrooms by the National Research Center of Rural Educational

Support to meet the needs of districts affected by geographic isolation and limited resources. Such efforts are designed to offset the economic barriers rural districts face when considering in-service training options. (lr)

task analysis
The process of breaking down a skill or activity into its component parts to teach it in smaller increments. (sr)

taught curriculum (See operationalized curriculum)

tax abatement
A term used in education in reference to a decrease or reduction in the amount of taxation assessed against a corporation by a school district, city, or county. This is a popular method of attracting corporations to an area with a promise of no *ad valorem* taxes for a period of time (*ad valorem* means "according to value," a phrase that is used when a duty or tax on an item is levied as a percentage of the value of the item, rather than at a flat rate). However, the property remains on the tax rolls of the school district. (mm)

taxonomies
From the field of biology, the term "taxonomy" refers to an orderly classification of information. Examples of educational taxonomies include the cognitive domain, the affective domain, and the psychomotor domain. Well-known taxonomies in the field of education include Benjamin Bloom's for the cognitive domain, David R. Krathwohl's for the affective domain, and T. C. Barrett's for levels of questioning. (mje, jah)

Teach for America
An organization, founded by Wendy Kopp in 1990, that enlists college graduates from any field and varying degree levels to teach in low-income communities, in both rural and urban settings across the United States, for a two-year period. The program provides initial training and ongoing support in all 35 regions for teachers throughout their two-year commitment. (dek, cp)

teachable moments
A spontaneous discovery, question, or wonderment on the part of the child that allows for instruction and guidance by the teacher to introduce new concepts or reinforce those concepts already explored. The teacher may make comments, ask questions, and provide additional opportunities to expand on the children's inquiries or interests. (kdc)

teach-back
An interactive form of learning in which learners "teach-back" to others what they have learned. Specific applications of this technique vary depending on the educational setting in which it takes place. In some situations, students are asked to instruct fellow students on what they themselves have just learned. Teach-back supports the notion that the best way to learn anything is to teach it. (jwc)

teacher
One whose occupation is to instruct. Today's expectations for an effective teacher typically involve command of subject matter and the ability to teach it to diverse students. Other expectations may include managing and monitoring student learning, understanding how students develop and learn, thinking systematically about what is practiced, and working collegially to enhance learning. (ks)

Teacher Corps
Modeled on the Peace Corps and created under Title III of the Higher Education Act of 1965, this federally funded domestic program specifically recruited and trained teachers, frequently attracting underrepresented minorities to the field, to address educational deficits in underserved minority and low-income communities. Teacher education programs in universities were

enlarged, teacher interns employed, and communities involved in decision making at the school. Working with a master teacher, interns were recruited to work for two years in the inner city, rural Appalachia, Indian reservations, and other underserved areas. At the conclusion of two years of study and community service, the intern received a teaching certificate and Bachelor's Degree in Education. The program evolved during subsequent reauthorization to include troubled youth, and students with disabilities. By the year 1980, 13,000 interns had been trained. In 1981, President Reagan removed funding to end the program in his effort to decentralize education. (reb, djr)

teacher education

The intentional and unintentional curricula, instructional settings, and experiences that enable teachers to promote learning and change in others. (rtc)

teacher educator

An individual involved in the preservice preparation and the continued in-service training of educators. (jw)

teacher empowerment

Concept that holds that the reform efforts and initiatives of teachers can and will revitalize educational institutions. Furthermore, a freeing of teacher capacity, agency, interests, and ability can substantially improve education from within, when compared with solutions imposed on teachers. (hfs)

teacher institute

An early form of teacher education, teacher institutes were popular in the antebellum United States as a means of bringing new teachers into the profession and as a means of providing intensive instruction in pedagogical techniques. The first teacher institute was organized by Henry Barnard in Hartford, Connecticut, in 1839, but the model quickly spread across the United States by building on the popular model of the evangelical revival. Although teacher institutes were largely replaced by normal schools as the preferred means of formal preservice teacher education, they remained popular as an in-service educational model into the 20th century. (sw)

teacher leader

An educator who holds a position of leadership or influence in a school, but not through a certified administrative position. The defining activity of a teacher leader is influencing school policy and/or practices beyond that teacher's individual classroom. A teacher leader operates on a continuum from informal roles (e.g., leading a study group) to formal roles (e.g., department head). While not functioning as an administrator, a teacher leader may seek advanced certification, such as National Board of Professional Teaching Standards certification. (dlk)

teacher power movement

Refers to the period during the 1960s and 1970s when teacher unions such as the American Federation of Teachers became increasingly militant in their demands for teacher rights in areas such as salary negotiations, classroom size, and professional counseling and supervision. Not strictly related to union membership or activities, the teacher power movement represented a broad-based effort by teachers to assert their rights as professionals and to gain greater influence over educational policies and practice. (sw)

teacher preparation

A specified program of curricular and cocurricular experiences designed to prepare people to become teachers. (rtc)

teacher unions (See unions)

teacher-centered instruction

An instructional approach in which the teacher controls the content, the activities, the materials, and the pace of learning.

This traditional learning model generally is associated with passive rather than active learning. (bba, cf)

teacher-coordinator

In fields such as business and office education and distributive education, a member of a school staff who teaches the related and technical subject matter involved in work experience programs and coordinates classroom instruction with on-the-job training. In cooperative office education, this position is responsible for administering the program and may or may not be responsible for the adult program in distributive education. (jb)

teacher's aide (See paraprofessional)

Teachers of English to Speakers of Other Languages (See TESOL)

teaching

Teaching can be defined as actions by which one person intends that another person learn a certain content of knowledge. Teaching occurs in everyday situations in the family or in the street, but most teaching occurs in institutionalized settings with a predefined curriculum. The most common teaching institution is the school, but teaching is also an institutionalized activity in hospitals and companies. In English, the study of teaching is called pedagogy; in many languages it is called didactics, and this discipline includes empirical as well as philosophical investigations. (jb1)

See also pedagogy.

teaching assistant

Work position generally contingent upon enrollment as a postbaccalaureate student. Typically a teaching assistant assists a professor by teaching classes, grading, and other activities related to instruction. (cf, npo)

teaching effectiveness

The presentation, dissemination, and appraisal of subject matter to be learned in training, teaching, educating, or developing knowledge, competence, or understanding; the guidance and directions given learners under conditions of supervised practice. (cf)

teaching fellowship (See fellowship, teaching)

teaching for understanding

An educational framework that focuses educational practice on developing student understanding and flexible knowledge. Researchers have collaborated with many experienced teachers to develop, test, and refine this approach. Key components are generative topics, understanding goals, performances of understanding, and ongoing assessment. (mf1)

Teaching Games for Understanding (TGFU)

A physical education instructional model that was developed in response to the traditional approach to teaching games, which focused on the development of skill and technique to the detriment of knowledge and understanding. TGFU is a constructivist approach to teaching games that involves setting and solving problems in modified game play as a central focus of each lesson. (kpr)

teaching methods

The exercises, lessons, and materials used to teach. The techniques used to impart knowledge or develop skills. The tools and strategies of instruction. (jw)

teaching objectives

Statements of learning outcomes for students. These goals may be formulated as broad, general statements or in terms of specific, observable learner behaviors (i.e., behavioral objectives). Objectives may be classified according to cognitive, affective, and psychomotor domains. (mje, jah)

Teaching Personal and Social Responsibility Model (TPSR)

TPSR is a physical education and youth development instructional model. The model focuses on teaching life skills and values integrated with physical activity. Students become responsible for their own behavior and well-being and then become more aware of and responsive to the needs of others. The TPSR Model emphasizes effort and self-direction as essential to the achievement of personal well-being; respecting others' rights, considering others' feelings, and caring about others as necessary for the achievement of social well-being. (kpr)

teaching portfolio

In higher education, a collection of work produced by a faculty member designed to document, over an extended period of time, the faculty member's strengths and accomplishments as a teacher. Typically, the teaching portfolio is relatively short (6–8 pages) and contains some standardized material, such as student evaluations of teaching. It also commonly contains distinguishing information such as teaching responsibilities, philosophy, goals, and accomplishments as a teacher. This collection of documents not only represents the best teaching but also provides the occasion to reflect on teaching. (cf)

teaching styles

Methods, procedures, and strategies in instruction and interpersonal relations that have developed and matured through years of personal and professional experience. Teaching style should not be confused with instructional strategies with explicit objectives, supervised practices, and behavioral expectations that are better suited for industrial or military training. (cf)

teaching team

A cross-disciplinary faculty group in which teachers with separate areas of expertise agree to work together to design and implement instruction. This method is used frequently when special education faculty work with subject-matter-oriented or grade-level-oriented faculty. (rtc)

teach-ins

A nonviolent type of demonstration created during the early years of the student movement of the 1960s at the University of Michigan. This forum-type protest comprised mostly students and faculty members and spread rapidly across college campuses. The teach-ins assisted in getting people's opinions on various subjects related to the movement out into society. The teach-in form gained national attention when a nationwide teach-in was televised in 1966. (rih)

team planning

Planning by a group organized to work together in a collaborative manner. Team planning may refer to student teams (group projects) or teacher teams (interdisciplinary unit of study). Either type of team must first determine objectives and the means (activities, methods, and techniques) for attaining the objectives. (ce)

team teaching

Two or more teachers, typically at the same grade level, who collaborate to provide instruction to a group of students. (bba)

tech prep (See technical preparation)

techbook

Similar to a textbook, as it is a manual of instruction or a standard book within a field of study. Its format is entirely online. Educational institutions instruct students to purchase online access, in order to read the required course material. (mkrf)

technical colleges

Institutions concentrating on technical and/or vocational education and offering an associate degree in arts (AA); formerly known as technical/vocational schools. (cf)

technical education (See career and technical education)

technical preparation (tech prep)

Educational programs originating through the Carl D. Perkins Vocational and Applied Technology Act of 1990, creating articulated and integrated academic and career-technical curriculum linking the last two years of high school with the first two years of college. This term also refers to academic and career-technical curricula supported by formal articulation agreements between secondary schools, two-year colleges, and sometimes also four-year colleges and universities. (db)

technical teacher education

An approach to teacher education that emphasizes the acquisition and application of specified teaching behaviors or strategies. (rtc)

technical theater

The areas of theater production that focus on stagecraft: sets, lighting, sound, props, special effects, stage management. Though the spotlight in dramatic performance is generally on the performer, the technical side is crucial to the overall success of a production. The importance of this expertise is evidenced by the number of degree-granting programs (undergraduate and graduate) in technical theater. "Techies" is the affectionate name for backstage technicians. In school productions, invisible to the audience, techies enjoy backstage camaraderie as they gain important knowledge and shoulder great responsibility, often with little public acknowledgment for their work. (em)

technique

Derived from the Greek *tekhne* (art, craft, skill) and *tekhnikos* (of art). Describes a method (e.g., syncopation in music), the medium (e.g., documentary film), or the skill (e.g., ballet dancing) used to create a work of art. Can be taught, learned, observed, practiced, studied. Despite the strong link, based in the Greek roots of technique, between art and skill, the question across all arts domains is: what constitutes proper technique? In the visual arts, realistic representation or abstract expression? In music, playing notes precisely or expressing the mood of a piece? In theater, Stanislavski's method or classical acting? Some artists and critics suggest that technique must be acquired if only to be overcome. Picasso is known for saying, "I painted all my life like Raphael so that one day I could paint again like a child." (em)

technology

The practical apparatus, methods, and systems with which a material enterprise or purpose is carried out. The term "technology" comes from the Greek word *têchnê*, which is essentially similar in meaning to the Latin word *ars*. Both designate practical activities involving knowledge as well as manipulation of some sort. Thus medicine is *têchnê* as much as painting and oratory and teaching. The construction and use of machinery of any sort, such as armaments, computers, and automobiles, represents similar forms of *têchnê* and make up modern technology. In education, the term is often synonymous with computer applications in teaching and learning. Technological literacy, or the acquisition of computer skills, is an increasingly common curriculum component. (jrs, ig)

technology education

The application of scientific principles to designing and implementing instructional systems with emphasis on precise and measurable educational objectives, learner-centered rather than subject-centered orientation, strong reliance on educational theory to guide educational practice, validation of educational practices through empirical analysis, and extensive use of audiovisual equipment media in instruction. Also used in a more limited sense to describe a reliance on equipment or technology-oriented instructional technique strategies such as computer-assisted instruction, simulators, multimedia presentation, and media-based self-instruction. (jb)

techspert

This recently coined word is used to identify a class of individuals who are experts when it comes to educational technology. Expert in this case refers to awareness and the "how to" when it comes to technology old and new. It does not necessarily mean that they are experts in terms of pedagogy, management, or professional development. (rsb)

telecollaboration

Sharing academic tasks across distances using electronic communications media. Educators and students use teleconferencing, Internet communications, e-mail, instant messaging, and other means to work cooperatively from geographically separate locations. The Internet was developed for this type of information sharing. (jrs)

temporal lobe (See lobes of the brain)

tenure

Tenure, in education, is a guarantee of position permanence, after successful completion of a probationary period of service, in a school, college, or university. Proponents of tenure assert that tenure protects a teacher's/professor's academic flexibility and/or freedom of instruction, as well as longevity of employment, while critics argue that tenure either shields or prolongs the release or dismissal of an inept, unqualified, or incompetent teacher/professor. In most tenure cases, an educational institution may release or dismiss a tenured teacher/professor for just cause after due process or as a result of financial exigencies. (tp)

termination

In counseling, termination is the end of a therapeutic relationship between a counselor, or mental-health professional, and a client. Termination may be planned or unplanned (i.e., the client drops out of treatment). Unplanned termination is typically called "premature termination." Planned termination anticipates the end of the relationship and allows the counselor and client to discuss issues surrounding termination fully prior to its occurrence. (mkt)

tertiary education

The third level of education following primary education and secondary education. Tertiary education also is called higher or postsecondary education. (cf)

tertiary prevention

This level of prevention focuses on reducing or eliminating negative experiences for children for whom developmental harm already exists. Direct services to those identified are provided through intervention and compensation programs, in which the focus is on enabling and optimizing the children's developmental and educational progress. (xss, yb)

TESOL

Teachers of English to Speakers of Other Languages (TESOL) is a national organization for professionals who teach English to nonnative speakers within the United States or throughout the world. (acp)

test

An exercise used to assess knowledge or skills. Often a formal set of questions or tasks intended to generate a quantitative representation used to determine if a student possesses certain abilities or comprehends given information. Tests can be used to compare individuals to groups or populations or can be used to gauge individual development. (jw)

test bias

Properties of an assessment instrument that yield significant differences between groups (i.e., sex, race/ethnicity, students with disabilities, limited English proficient students) that are not due to actual differences in the construct being assessed. Test bias impairs the validity (content, construct, predictive, consequential) and the fairness of the measurement. The differences are systematic and not due to chance. Test bias may result in inappropriate or unwarranted interpretation of a given individual's test score. (tsw, fg, mgg)

See also differential item functioning (DIF).

test coaching

Test coaching refers to the various ways in which people can be instructed on how to take tests. This can take the form of teaching general test-taking skills and strategies, or can be focused on a particular test instrument. There is some controversy over whether test coaching can actually improve individual scores on particular tests. A more benign view of this practice, perhaps, would be that it allows test takers to become more familiar with test format and process and, thus, reduce the effect of test method on the estimation of test-taker ability. (bkl)

test interpretation feedback

A multistep, interpersonally based process that involves, among other things, synthesizing and making sense of a client's test results, presenting the results and their implications to a client, and collaborating with a client to construct meaning/new self-understanding based on the results. (kab)

Test of Adult Basic Education (TABE)

A norm-referenced test that measures reading comprehension by asking students to answer multiple-choice questions about what they have read. The reading passages are both literary and related to daily life and employment situations. The TABE is the most commonly used test of achievement in adult basic education programs. (jpc)

Test of English as a Foreign Language (TOEFL)

An international examination that assesses the ability to understand spoken and written English. This test is used to evaluate English proficiency of international students planning to study in countries where English is the language of instruction. The test is designed primarily for students entering colleges and universities or pursuing graduate studies, who are not native English speakers. Initially developed for use in Canada and the United States, this test is now used worldwide by institutions and organizations concerned with assessing English proficiency. (jpc, npo)

Test of Functional Health Literacy in Adults (TOFHLA)

An assessment designed to measure literacy related specifically to health. The TOFHLA tests match ability and reading comprehension using actual health care materials, such as consent forms and prescription vials, and is available in English and Spanish. (las)

Test of Spoken English (TSE)

Test that measures the oral communication skills of nonnative speakers of English. During the 20-minute test, test takers respond orally on tape to a range of printed and recorded information. The test is used by many U.S. colleges and universities in selecting international students and teaching assistants and by other institutions to certify English-language ability. (las)

Test of Written English (TWE)

Test given to nonnative speakers of English to assess their ability to perform writing tasks comparable to those required of students in universities in North America. Skills tested include the ability to generate and organize ideas, support ideas with evidence or examples, and respond to an essay question. The test is a requirement for individuals who take the paper format of the TOEFL exam, though a separate TWE score is recorded. (las)

text

While text traditionally refers to the body of words that comprises a written tome, text is also used more broadly (e.g., within the context of semiotics) to refer to the content of a work of visual art, or music, dance, or even a product of the media. This broader view of text and the notion of "reading a text" as an act of interpretation is attributed to the French philosopher Roland Barthes. Any stand-alone entity that has been constructed out of symbols (like words, notes, gestures) that we seek to understand, interpret, or place in some context, can be thought of as a text. (jd)

textbook

A book used in a particular branch of study. Textbooks are most often used to assist the teacher in content area subjects, including social studies, science, language arts, and mathematics. Effective textbooks assist students through the use of text organizers, pattern guides, and glossaries. (ce)

text-to-speech

A utility program that speaks digital text aloud. Students with visual impairments or reading disabilities can use text-to-speech to access digital text. With the use of an optical character recognition scanner, handwritten or printed text can be converted to digital text and read aloud. In addition, students can use text-to-speech utilities to verify text they have written by hearing it read aloud. (kg1, ab1)

texture

The actual or simulated surface quality (imagined feel) of an art object, such as its roughness or smoothness. Actual textures, such as the surface of a smooth marble sculpture can be touched and felt by the fingers. Simulated textures are those found in paintings in which the viewer does not actually touch the surface but can visually perceive its texture as a physical sensation suggested by the way the artist has painted certain areas of a picture, such as the lushness of fabrics depicted in Renaissance paintings. (kf)

theater

From the Greek *theatron*, a place for seeing, especially for dramatic representation. A building, designated room, or outdoor space dedicated to the presentation of plays, films, or other dramatic performances. Also used to refer to theatrical performances, or drama, as to the action that is put up in showcases entitled theaters. The most basic interdisciplinary arts curriculum can be found in the painting of sets to be used in a school theatrical production. (em)

See also drama.

theater games

Originated by Viola Spolin, theater games are short, structured improvisational activities that have been used in environments ranging from classrooms to acting workshops to theater rehearsals. In the classroom, games are designed to tap into a student's sense of creativity, imagination, and spontaneity, pushing students to explore their environment, their interactions with others, and the world around them; learn to communicate, concentrate, and solve problems; and take an active part in their own learning. By using games that are documented or inventing new ones, teachers can use theater games as building blocks for lessons or projects in their classes. (em)

theater of the absurd

A form of theater that envisions human experience as absurd, isolated, and/or meaningless and captures that perspective in nontraditional incoherent dramatic presentation employing nonsensical and repetitive dialogue, ludicrous and puzzling situations, purposeless plots, and meaningless conclusions with purposeful disregard for traditional narrative and theatrical coherence. Educators often cite Eugene Ionesco and Samuel Beckett as representative writers, and Beckett's play *Waiting for Godot* (1953) as a prime example of theater of the absurd. Though it has never been a formal theater movement, with the style originating from post–World War II French writers, most nonrealistic drama is tagged as theater of the absurd. (kc)

theater of the oppressed

Developed in the 1960s by Augusto Boal, then director of the Arena Theatre in Sao Paulo, Brazil. In this theatrical genre, the audience takes an active role in the creation of the onstage drama, turning from "spectators" into "spect-actors." In a version often used in classrooms, actors dramatize a social problem or oppression and audience members then freeze the action, step in for one of the actors, and, in character, offer ways to deal with the issue. Boal intended to use theater for social, political, and educational purposes by breaking down its dominant hierarchical traditions into accessible participatory forms. (em)

theater-in-education
(See drama-in-education/
theater-in-education)

theater-in-the-round

A style of theater driven by the shape of the performance space, in which the audience surrounds the stage entirely or almost entirely. A reaction against the reliance on proscenium stages, in which the audience and actors are often separated by physical and dramatic distance, theater-in-the-round allows for more intimacy and a reduction in distance between actor and audience. Though true in all performance spaces, the director and performers in theater-in-the-round must be acutely aware of staging and the actors' positions in relation to the audience because of conflicting and overlapping sightlines, and the omnipresence of the audience. (em)

theatrical genres

Continuously evolving forms in which theater is performed and presented, driven by style, time period, societal values, consciousness of audience, economics, performance space, the need to create new forms, and other factors. Some (e.g., tragedy, comedy) have existed since the beginning of theater. Others emerged at particular points in time: for example, melodrama (carried through in contemporary soap operas), naturalism and realism (efforts to depict real life on stage), absurd and avant-garde theater (reactions against society and convention), and theater of the oppressed (sociopolitical consciousness-raising and activism through theater). (em)

thematic planning

The organization of subject matter around unifying topics or themes. This teaching strategy organizes classroom instruction by relating textbooks, class activities, and experiences together by a topic. Thematic planning can include a set of lessons around a particular theme, or different subjects can be planned and connected by the theme. (ce)

theology

Literally meaning the study of God (from the Greek *theos,* meaning God; and *logos,* meaning knowledge), "theology" refers to the study of religious philosophies, practices (individual and corporate), beliefs, sacred texts, and spirituality (here referring to systems of making meaning of experiences deemed sacred). Often in academic contexts theology is constructed as being concerned with validating or supporting the specific faith claims of a given religious tradition, whereas "religious studies" is assumed to set aside personal investment in the faith claims of the religious subject. In education discourses, the consideration of the curriculum as a theological text suggests that the epistemological assumptions of any (or no) religious tradition implicates the learner's engagement with other knowledge. (bda)

theorem

The resulting statement of a formal proof, an assertion that can be formally proved. (kva)

theory

An account of a domain that identifies or clarifies the nature of the objects in that domain and their relationships to one another, formulated and justified through reasoning and evidence, generally with the primary aim of expressing the truth or providing understanding of the domain, but sometimes in order to guide practice. Among the former sorts of theories are number theory and scientific theories. Among the latter are moral theories, which are concerned with the nature of moral concepts and judgments and the relationships among them, and educational theories, which have both descriptive and normative components and are intended to guide educational practice. (rc)

theory, critical (See critical theory)

theory of action

A commonly held understanding of a presumed set of actions by which an individual or organization plans, develops, executes, and evaluates an activity or course of action. Developed in many forms, the purpose is to document in narrative or charted form an agreed upon series of steps through which an idea or objective will be accomplished and verified. (sh)

theory-based research

The testing or investigation of hypotheses that explain observed outcomes in theoretical or cause-and-effect terms. Quite often this form of research leads to further research that explicitly affirms or refutes the theory as presently stated. (cf)

See also policy-related research.

thick description

This term was originally coined by the philosopher Gilbert Ryle, in his book The Concept of Mind (1949), and was applied to ethnographic research by Clifford Geertz in a classic essay, "Thick Description: Toward an Interpretive Theory of Culture" (1973). Thick description, for Geertz, is meaningful description, description that incorporates the intentions of the actors and the codes of signification that give their actions meaning for them, what anthropologists call an emic account. However, the term is widely misused to refer to "rich" or detailed description. (jam)

think aloud (See modeling)

think tank

Independently standing organized body of scholars who investigate topics and create reports to inform the public about issues of the day. Examples of think tanks include the American Heritage Foundation and the Brookings Institution. (cf)

thinking

For Descartes, thinking is a purely mental event (i.e., an event that occurs outside of any spatial location, solely within the mind). In contrast, Wittgenstein points out in his later philosophy that thinking is more public than Descartes allows, though more than merely behavioral capacities, dispositions or habits. (For example, thoughtfulness is more than the ability or disposition or habit to act in such and such a way, in such and such a situation.) Current efforts are to avoid defining it as totally private or totally public. (an)

See also constructive thinking; critical thinking.

thinking, critical (See critical thinking)

thinking strategies

In mathematics, children use thinking strategies to figure unknown number combinations through the use of known combinations, through the development of number sense and number relationships.

Three commonly used strategies are double ± 1, for example, figuring 6 + 7 by using a known combination, say 6 + 6 and adding 1 to that result; making 10, for example, figuring 7 + 5 by thinking of 5 as 2 and 3, thus 7 + 3 = 10, 2 more gives 12; and compensation, for example, in solving 9 + 7 by moving 1 from the 9 and adding it to the 7 to form a known double, 8 + 8. (amr)

think-pair-share
A method of informal cooperative learning in which the teacher poses a topic, question, issue, or problem; allows time for students to think individually; has students pair off and discuss their ideas with their partners; and has students share their thoughts with the whole class. In a variation, a student pair may share with another student pair before sharing with the rest of the class. (bba)

third age learning
Educational activities geared toward people who have retired. (jpc)

third culture kids
Term used to describe children, whose parents are from one culture, that spend a significant amount of time in a second culture as a result of their parent's employment. As a result of the exposure to the two different cultures, the children develop a third culture that integrates aspects of both cultures. This term was first coined by sociologist Ruth Hill Useem in the 1950s. (ms)

threaded discussion
A web-based asynchronous discussion in which participants' contributions are organized as statements and responses. Each message and its associated responses forms a thread. Software for threaded discussion normally gives the reader visual cues about the relationships between messages and allows the reader control over how threads are displayed. Threaded discussion is a common component of courseware products. Students may use threaded discussion to participate in an extended conversation. Because messages are organized by threads, students need not contribute sequentially; discussion can move forward on multiple topics simultaneously. (ac)

three traditions of social studies education
The core subjects of social studies instruction in the schools: history, geography, and civics (political science). The vast majority of social studies concepts taught in schools come from these three fields, in part because of widespread consensus that schools should help children understand their heritage, the world around them, and their rights and responsibilities as citizens in a democratic republic. (jrs)

three-period lesson
An individual or small group lesson provided by a Montessori teacher during the preschool ages is called a three-period lesson. The simply ordered lesson includes three steps designed to provide the student with the language and vocabulary associated with particular objects. First the teacher states the name of an object once and then repeats its name. The teacher then asks the student to repeat the new vocabulary and finally verifies that learning has taken place by asking the student to identify the object on his/her own. (nrs)

tier-two words
Words that are neither simple nor easily learned through oral language (in contrast with tier-one words that generally can be easily taught and understood, such as table); nor are they technical and specific in meaning (as with tier-three words such as neuroplasticity). Tier-two words are high-frequency and used in a variety of domains (for example the word *compromise* is a tier-two word). Tier-two words are frequently targeted for vocabulary instruction, especially in elementary school. (jdc)

tight-knit groups

Centers of social interaction characterized by a great deal of permanence, fixed social expectations (behaviors, attitudes, obligations, etc.), and stable group boundaries. These centers and sets of relationships are also known as home groups or core membership groups. (hfs)

tiling

A covering of a flat region with repetitions of a particular shape with no overlapping. Tiling activities require the coordination of a covering and a patterning activity and as such can lead to the development of many geometric ideas and support students' unitizing activity. (amr)

timbre

A distinctive tone, identified with a particular musical instrument or individual voice, produced by musical overtones (i.e., the harmonic tones surrounding a core note). Each musical instrument or human voice produces a unique and distinctive resonance, such that a listener can distinguish among instrument groups and individual artists. Often referred to as "sound quality." (lw)

time

For Augustine, time was some essential quality or property of things, which belongs to some specific genus and species and therefore should be open to philosophical definition. For some, time has been equated with duration; for others time is a form of consciousness the mind projects onto a thing that is timeless in itself. Metaphysicians have long argued about the reality or unreality of time, a debate that may take on new significance in light of recent developments in physics. For many, knowledge of time is actually no more or less than the ability to participate in certain human practices such as the intelligent use of clocks and calendars. (an)

time out

A management technique providing a period of time for an individual to be alone or away from a social setting. In an educational setting the procedure is used as a method of classroom management. A teacher may remove a disruptive child from a group activity to provide the child with time to focus and gain perspective. When a teacher uses time out as a management strategy, it is important that she/he talks with the child to maximize the potential of modifying inappropriate behaviors. (jls)

Tinker v. Des Moines Independent Community School District, 393 U.S. 503 (1969)

A U.S. Supreme Court case that held that students are considered "persons" under the Constitution and are entitled to freedom of expression of their views unless doing so would substantially interfere with the operation of the school and the rights of other students. The case involved three public school students suspended for wearing black armbands to class in order to protest U.S. policy in the Vietnam War. The Supreme Court reversed the decision of the lower courts, stating that "it can hardly be argued that either students or teachers shed their constitutional rights to freedom of speech or expression at the schoolhouse gate." (gs)

Title IV, Civil Rights Act of 1964

Titled "Desegregation of Public Education," this section of the Civil Rights Act of 1964 authorized the U.S. attorney general to file lawsuits against school districts that refused to integrate or continued patterns of racial discrimination against students. It also encouraged enactment of the desegregation law by offering cooperative school districts teacher training, technical support, and funding for integration programs through the U.S. Department of Education. (acp)

See also Civil Rights Act of 1964.

Title VI, Civil Rights Act of 1964

Title VI of the Civil Rights Act of 1964 states that federal funds cannot be used to finance programs or activities where there is "discrimination on the grounds of race, color, or national origin." The threat of losing this critical funding source persuaded many segregated public schools across the United States to comply with the Act and integrate their schools. (acp)

See also Civil Rights Act of 1964.

Title IX

Part of the Education Amendments approved by Congress in 1972, this clause prohibits the discrimination, based on sex, of anyone wishing to participate in an institution or program that receives federal funds. Title IX extends to educational institutions, both public and private, and includes participation in athletics. The regulations contained in Title IX were signed by President Ford in May of 1975 and sent to Congress for review prior to official adoption of the legislation. (aku)

TMS (See Transcranial Magnetic Stimulation)

toddlers

Young children who have recently begun to walk. Usually considered between the ages of one and three years. Toddlers are discovering new independence and are typically egocentric. (jlj)

TOEFL (See Test of English as a Foreign Language)

TOFHLA (See Test of Functional Health Literacy in Adults)

tolerance

Tolerance, the willingness not to use force against people whose beliefs or actions we abhor, is the chief virtue of liberal communities, or those committed to protecting individual freedom of conscience. Tolerance does not imply acceptance or promotion of the belief or behavior tolerated, as is often misunderstood when governments protect hate speech and religious expression. The principle of tolerance is incoherent (requiring tolerance of intolerance) without the "harm principle": all expressions and actions must be tolerated except those that harm others. In liberal democracies public schools are legally bound to accommodate students and teachers with religious and cultural differences. Beyond that, tolerance is often promoted in schools as a civic virtue, which leads to two difficulties. First is the controversy about what "harmful" speech or acts will not be tolerated in the school. Second is that tolerance is sometimes taught as the avoidance of criticizing certain points of view, which is incompatible with criticism and inquiry as educational objectives. (mg)

See also pluralism.

tone

A vocal or musical sound of a specific quality (i.e., high, low, etc.), manner of expression, or pitch. In music, the interval of a definite pitch or vibration, generally a major second (e.g., C-D). In the dramatic arts, a vocal sound that indicates meaning, expression, or mood. A style or manner of expression in writing. In the visual arts, tone refers to the value or color quality of a piece as determined by light, shade, and color. (km)

top-down vs. bottom-up cognition

This subtle concept expresses the modulation or refining activity that expectations (the "top") have on sensory input (the "bottom"). The context of a situation, the memories stored of similar situations, and the conceptual frameworks operating on experience serve to modify, clarify, and analyze the "raw" data received through the senses. As sensory data travels from the bottom up, it is filtered through the lenses of higher-order cognitive processes imposed from the top down. Simple illustrations of this are the well-known duck-rabbit and old woman-young woman diagrams/illusions, in which the ambiguity of the image must be sorted out by higher-level processes.

While trivial, these examples identify a process that commonly occurs in many acts of perception. (dh)

topology
The study of the properties of geometric figures that remain unchanged when the figure is stretched, bent, or twisted; the family of subsets of a given set that contains the set itself as well as the empty set and all open subsets of the given set. The union of any two sets in this family is in the family, and the intersection of any sets in the family is also in the family. (rdk)

tort
The term is derived from the Latin word *tortus,* meaning "wrong," and refers to that body of the law that allows injured individuals to obtain compensation, "damages," from the person causing the injury. There are three major categories of torts: intentional interference; strict liability; and negligence. School districts and personnel may be faced with a tort if inadequate supervision or maintenance of equipment causes injury to a student. Relief may be obtained in the form of damages or an injunction. Cases of intentional interference and strict liability are rare. A legal cause for action in tort can be established if four essential elements are present: an individual has the duty to protect others against unreasonable risks; the individual fails to exercise an appropriate standard of care; the negligent act is the proximate cause of an injury; and a physical or mental injury, resulting in actual loss or damage to the person, exists. (mm)

TOT (See training of trainers)

total quality management (TQM)
Focuses upon an organized process to continuously innovate and improve systems, products, and/or services, while capitalizing upon stakeholder empowerment, via teamed efforts, to exceed customer expectations. W. Edwards Deming (1900–1993), American statistician and quality-control expert, greatly influenced the development of the basic philosophy and principles of total quality management. The practice of total quality management within an organizational culture supports the constant goal of attaining customer satisfaction through an integrated management approach of empowerment, teamwork, continuous improvement, and customer satisfaction. This process is cyclically adopted by educational institutions, often in response to external criticism. (tp)

total village
A term derived from the African proverb, "It takes a whole village to raise a child." It refers to the network of relationships that support and affect the lives of children and implies that such relationships should be considered more thoughtfully so that they can reinforce one another. (lr)

TPSR (See Teaching Personal and Social Responsibility Model)

TQM (See total quality management)

tracking
The voluntary or involuntary practice of placing students in different programs or courses according to their ability and prior academic performance. In elementary schools, lower-performing, average, and higher-performing students are typically placed in separate classrooms. (bba)

trade
A central topic in the social studies curriculum involving concepts such as exchange transaction, comparative and absolute advantage, international tariffs and trade barriers, cultural differences, and others. Normally embedded in the elementary social studies curriculum and in secondary school history courses, trade is taught formally in the secondary economics course. In career education, a trade is an occupation requiring specific manual or mechanical skills and training. A craft is one in

which only skilled workers are employed. (jrs, jb)

trade, semiskilled

An industrial occupation requiring skill in a limited range of activities. (jm)

trade, skilled

An occupation requiring a high degree of skill, usually in a wide range of related activities, and secured through a combination of job instruction, trade instruction, and work experience, such as apprenticeship or a cooperative industrial program. (jm)

trade and industrial education

An educational program designed to teach the skills required for careers in various trades, including carpentry, masonry, cosmetology, culinary, and so on, and includes instruction to develop basic manipulative skills, safety judgment, technical knowledge, and related occupational information. (jb, ea)

trade school

A public or private career and technical school that trains youth and adults in skills, technical knowledge, related industrial information, and career decisions necessary for success in one or more skilled trades. (jm)

trade secrets

This intellectual property involves keeping secret a certain formula, recipe, design, or the like. The secret can be kept by persons signing papers agreeing to keep the secret or by admitting that this is a trade secret. An example would be the recipe for a food product. (cf)

traditional education

The underlying idea of traditional education originated with Plato. Formulated broadly, its central tenet is that there is a reality that is knowable through the use of reason. Students study a curriculum arranged in a series of stages by which they gain a rational, privileged view of reality.

By immersing the mind in increasingly abstract subject matter, the student learns to distinguish between social convention and what is ultimately real and true. Traditional educators emphasize the relevance of eternal and lasting truths, rather than content relevant to particular times and places. The teacher ideally embodies those moral and intellectual virtues that the subject matter is intended to impart. (pk)

See also essentialism; perennialism; progressive education; vocational education.

traditional patterns of social studies instruction

Instructional approaches to the teaching of social studies consisting primarily of methods of information transmission, emphasizing breadth over depth of coverage. These approaches emphasize teachers, texts, and assessment as the key elements. (ks)

tragedy

A theatrical or literary format concerning human pain, demise, and death. In classical Greek theater, tragedy relies on a character held in high regard who, because of a tragic flaw (often hubris or willful resistance or fate), falls into despair and destruction. It was thought that the identification with the tragic hero both elevated the self-esteem of the audience and allowed for a catharsis or release of deep emotion. Western art forms may draw on Greek tragedy, but the tragic in art is more broadly based on human suffering and differs across time, culture, and circumstance. (kbc)

trainee

A person being trained. (jpc)

trainer

A person directing or teaching in a training program. (jpc)

training

Instruction that is planned and focused on the acquisition of skills and knowledge for a specific task or purpose. The establishment of routines and habits (e.g., Aristotle's view that virtues arise from habitual behavior). Providing an individual with the know-how to perform a particular task. In the latter sense, training commonly suggests vocational preparation lacking theoretical knowledge (e.g., cooking, plumbing, mechanics), but we also speak of training doctors, lawyers, and historians. In contrast to education, training is undertaken for extrinsic purposes and practical ends (e.g., career preparation), while education is intrinsically valuable and is lifelong and continuous. Moreover, while education is about the development of the mind, training frequently involves the imparting of routine, mechanized skills, a distinction highlighted by contrasting the implications of "sex education" and "sex training." (jpc, pk)

training and development
Learning opportunities that enhance the skills and knowledge of employees for the purpose of improving work performance as well as for individual growth. (alm)

training cycle
Cyclical process surrounding the development of training programs. It consists of four stages: needs assessment, planning, implementation, and evaluation. (las)

training of trainers (TOT)
The process of training people who will, in turn, provide training to others. (jpc)

training program
A detailed set of directions covering the procedures for organizing and conducting an occupational course of training. Includes statements covering location of classes, selection and number of trainees, description and length of courses, instructor selection, physical facilities and supplies, and supervisory duties. The responsibility of coordination for program training between business, industry, and educational institutions is clearly defined. (db)

transactional analysis
A form of psychotherapy developed by Eric Berne. Drawing from a specific body of theory and techniques, it is practiced in a relatively straightforward manner, in both individual and group settings. Its primary goal is for clients to develop a realistic, mature approach to life. As stated by Berne, it is to "have the adult ego state maintain predominate influence or authority over the impulsive child state." (dd)

transcendental numbers (See irrational number)

Transcranial Magnetic Stimulation (TMS)
A noninvasive tool used to excite neurons in the brain. Unlike neuroimaging techniques, TMS interferes with brain activity rather than merely recording it. During TMS, a weak electric current is induced in the brain to temporarily "knock out" a particular brain area. This technique is important in human brain mapping research because it can directly demonstrate causality: if a subject performs worse on a cognitive task when activity in a particular brain region is interfered with, it may be assumed that the brain region is causally involved with the task. TMS is considered safe in subjects without preexisting brain conditions such as epilepsy. (mt)

transcription
The process of making a written record of data obtained from audiotaped or videotaped interviews or observations. The usual practice is a verbatim transcription, that is, an exact, word-for-word record. This is augmented by descriptions of paralingual expression such as dialect, pauses, tone of voice, word stress, pitch, and so on, and nonverbal behavior such as gestures, facial expressions, body language, who is talking to whom, and so on. (mas)

transfer
The concept that some reading skills in one language are available to a student

when learning to read in an additional language. Skills that have been shown to transfer are phonemic awareness and print concepts. (mmd)

transfer function
The practice of continuing enrollment at a college or university other than the one in which a student is currently enrolled; generally documents that a student has completed up to two years of full-time lower-division university-parallel college course work for a selected degree program. (pgg)

transfer of learning
The effective application of knowledge and skills gained in one context in a new and different context. Learning or problem-solving experiences derived from one setting or event influence learning or problem solving in a subsequent setting or event. Transfer may be to a similar situation or to new and different situations. (alm, vm)

transfer student
A student who has withdrawn from one institution or program and has been enrolled in another. (jw)

transferable skills
Skills acquired in one context that can be applied in another. (jpc)

transference
In psychoanalytic theory and therapy, this term refers to the patient's positive or negative emotions, especially those experienced in childhood, that are reproduced or relived toward the therapist. This is believed to reflect the patient's relationship to a significant person outside of therapy. It includes rational and adaptive aspects as well as irrational distortions that arise from unconscious struggles. This repetition in transference involves elements in both the past and the present and tends to reflect persistent experiences with other important authority figures. (tsw)

transformation, graph
Transformations of graphs occur as two basic types. Rigid transformations are those in which the shape of a graph is not changed, but only its position. These include moving the graph horizontally or vertically or reflection about an axis. Nonrigid transformations are those in which the shape of the graph is changed. These include stretching or shrinking the graph. (rdk)

transformation geometry
Three types of rigid transformations of a shape are possible: rotation, or a turning of a shape around a point that may be on, inside, or outside the shape; translation, or a sliding of the shape from one position to another without rotating the shape; and reflection, or flip of the shape about (a) a line on the figure, (b) a line not on the figure, or (c) a line intersecting with a vertex of the shape. (amr)

transformational leadership
Transformational leaders build commitment to the organization's (school's or district's) objectives and empower followers (teachers and administrators) to achieve these objectives. These leaders are expected to: define the need for change; create new visions and commitment to the visions; concentrate on long-term goals; inspire followers to pursue higher-order goals; change the organization to accommodate their vision rather than work within the existing one; and mentor followers to take greater responsibility. As a result, followers become leaders, leaders become change agents, and ultimately the school or district is transformed. (jt)

transformational learning (See transformative learning)

transformative intellectuals
Critical thinkers who are simultaneously engaged in the processes of inquiring about, reflecting upon, and changing the world in which they live. (hfs)

transformative learning

Learning characterized by self-reflection and self-examination; especially learning designed to lead to a clearer understanding of oneself through the identification of assumptions, acquired earlier in life, that affect functioning in adulthood. A learning theory first developed by Jack Mezirow that results in deep change or a transformation of tacitly acquired frames of reference—composed of sets of assumptions and expectations—that determine, filter, and often distort thought, emotion, decision making, and action. Assumptions are beliefs about reality that are taken for granted and not usually reflected upon or questioned. The concept also involves reflective and cyclical processes of engagement in, and disposition for, discourse and dialogue in order to arrive at tentative best judgments upon which to act until new perspectives, evidence, or arguments are encountered that are found to be more justified and reasonable. Also called transformational learning. (chb, hfs)

transformative pedagogy

A critical orientation toward teaching/ curriculum committed to social equality and justice; a continuation of the social reconstruction tradition. Its main exponents include Paulo Freire, Henry Giroux, bell hooks, Peter McClaren, and Ira Shor. Approaches include: joining phenomenological and existentialist philosophy with leftist politics to promote a critically reflexive examination of individuals' social lives (Freire); applying concepts of hegemony and resistance to curriculum analysis, developing the notion of "teacher as intellectual," and using culture studies to examine the concept of "border identities" (Giroux); applying feminist theory to transformative pedagogy (e.g., bell hooks); mixing critical theory with cultural studies (McClaren); and promoting transformative classroom practices (Shor). Also called critical pedagogy. (db-j)

See also critical theory; hegemony; phenomenology; reproduction theory; resistance; resistance theory.

transgender

An umbrella term used to describe a wide variety of people whose gender identity or gender expression differs from conventional gender norms associated with their biological sex and includes, among others, transsexuals, transvestites, and people who do not identify with a singular gendered label. Many transgender people live part-time or full-time as members of their affirmed gender. Transsexuals and cross-dressers fall within the transgender category, but not everyone whose appearance or behavior is gender-atypical will identify as transgender. Being transgender does not imply any specific sexual orientation. Students who identify as transgender experience high levels of harassment and victimization in schools. (jb2, ti)

transition programs (See bridge programs)

transition services

Programs or courses designed to assist students with disabling conditions to move from school to adult life, jobs, or additional education. (sr)

transitional bilingual approach

Programs that assist students in moving from instruction in their native language to classes that are taught entirely in English are called transitional language programs. They may be directed to bilingual students or those learning English as a second language. (jqa, npo)

transitional education (See bridge programs)

transitional knowers

Students who accept that some knowledge is uncertain and recognize that learning is more complex than the simple acquisition of knowledge. These students prefer to collect the ideas of others and use them to understand, as well as clarify, their ideas through debate. (hfs)

transnational studies

A disciplinary field of study engaging issues of globalization, nation states, geographies, and culture across multiple borders. Literature in this field interrogates established relationships between first and third worlds, as well as assumptions of inferiority and superiority of place, people, or custom. It examines the way capitalist societies in the West have the power to name, designate as visible or invisible, or otherwise label different ways of life and thinking. Transnational studies also address the West's complicity in maintaining these differences and allocating resources selectively as sustainable means of survival. (lev)

transnumeration

A term, put forth by Chris Wild and Maxine Pfannkuch (1999), in which a particular representation of data can reveal entirely new or different features that were previously hidden. These hidden features may have a major impact on how one interprets the data in that particular context. This term goes beyond the mere transformation or re-representation of the data, so as to identify instances in which striking features of a context are suddenly revealed. (pmts)

transparency

Referring to school-to-work transition systems and the ability of students to plot a course from their present location and circumstance to a distant future goal. (hfs)

transparency (language)

The degree of correspondence between phonemes and the letters that represent them. In a transparent orthography, the sound-to-symbol correspondence is predictable and one-to-one (e.g.,

Serbo-Croatian, Spanish). Opaque orthographies have a lower correspondence between sounds and their symbols, as the pattern and meaning layers of the language are more prevalent (e.g., English). Differences in the transparency could lead to differences in reading acquisition. (mmd)

transportation

Transportation can be defined as the business of moving passengers, goods, or materials. The state board of education and the local school district provide the opportunity for safe and efficient transportation to all eligible students. Rules and regulations concerning eligibility vary in each state and local school district. (jt)

transsexual

Transsexuals are transgender people who live or wish to live full-time as members of the gender opposite to their birth sex. Biological females who wish to live and be recognized as men are called female-to-male (FTM) transsexuals or transsexual men. Biological males who wish to live and be recognized as women are called male-to-female (MTF) transsexuals or transsexual women. Transsexuals usually seek medical interventions, such as hormones and surgery, to make their bodies as congruent as possible with their preferred gender. The process of transitioning from one gender to the other is called sex reassignment or gender reassignment. (jb2)

transtheoretical model of change

An empirically derived, multistage, sequential model of general change proposed by Prochaska and others in the 1980s. A primary contribution of the transtheoretical model of change is finding a successful self-changer by drawing upon strategies across psychotherapeutic approaches to achieve goals. This model does not offer one approach but allows for multiple approaches to be organized in order to understand and facilitate change. Behavior change is accomplished through a series of five stages: precontemplation, contemplation, action, preparation, and maintenance. The first three stages are concerned with introspection about change, whereas the last two stages are concerned with actual observable change. (tsw, med)

traumatic brain injury
An acquired injury to the brain caused by an external physical force, resulting in total or partial functional disability or psychosocial impairment, or both. The term applies to open or closed head injuries. (sr)

treatment fidelity
Educational research strategy in which an intervention, practice, process, model, or treatment is employed consistently and as outlined over time across subjects or environments. (ms)

TRI (See Targeted Reading Intervention)

triangulation
A process used to support the validity of a study. Data are collected using a variety (not necessarily three as the name implies) of techniques. Findings are enhanced by using data gathered from techniques such as: multiple human sources (e.g., roles/positions of people related to the issue), multiple methods (e.g., observations, focus groups), multiple investigators, archival records (e.g., student records, written policy), and/or multiple theoretical perspectives. (jrj)

trigger event
Moments and occurrences when previously held views must be discarded in light of new information or experience, and as a result new perspectives, understandings, and assumptions emerge. These events may provoke learning activities. For example, the loss of a job may be the

motivation (trigger) for a person to enroll in a program in order to learn a skill and be able to find a new job. (hfs, jwg)

trigonometry
The study of the properties of trigonometric functions (i.e., the function of an angle expressed as a ratio between two sides of a right triangle). (amr)

trimester
An academic calendar whereby the 12-month calendar year is divided into 3 academic terms of about 15 weeks each. (cf)

trivium
First level of course work offered in 12th-century European cathedral schools: grammar, dialectic, and rhetoric. These three (*tri*) "ways" (*via*) were believed to create paths in the mind to attain truth. The trivium and quadrivium nominally formed the Faculty of Arts (general or core) curriculum of medieval (13th-century) European universities. (bgr)
    See also quadrivium.

truancy
Being absent without permission. Deliberate absence of a student from school without the consent of parents, guardians, or school authorities. (jw)

truant
One who is absent without permission. A student who is absent from school without the consent of parents, guardians, or school authorities. In some states, the label of truant is placed on a student following a legally set number of days absent without permission. (jw)

true score
In Classical Test Theory (CTT), all tests are viewed as having measurement errors due to random events. A true score is defined as a person's true ability on a test that is free from such errors. Because the true score is not observable, it is defined as the expected score of a probability

distribution of all possible observed scores. (mj)

See also observed score.

Truman Commission Report

Produced by a special commission at the request of President Harry S. Truman to determine the status of higher education in the United States and its potential to play a strategic role in the support of democracy. The 1947 report, *Higher Education for American Democracy,* challenged the current state of higher education and the barriers it created that prevented equal access, while promoting the importance of universal education to democracy. The creation of the community college system was promoted by the report and led to its establishment by enabling the creation of supportive legislation. Financial aid programs established by the Higher Education Act of 1965 are also a legacy of the report and its efforts to promote access. (ms)

trustee

Trustees are persons elected or appointed to governing boards. This term is more often used by private institutions than public institutions, where the term *regent* may be used for the same purpose. (cf)

trustworthiness

Term was coined by E. Guba (1981) as an alternative to "validity," which he saw as intrinsically positivist in its implications, for naturalistic research. Trustworthiness refers to the credibility or persuasiveness of an account, and Lincoln and Guba (1985) developed alternative criteria for establishing trustworthiness in naturalistic research. However, Guba and Lincoln (1989) later stated that these criteria were themselves too positivist and proposed an additional set of authenticity criteria, which they felt were fully compatible with constructivism. (jam)

truth

Truth has been understood as a "correspondence" between some proposition and some fact or facts in the real world. Thus a person's claim that "it is raining in my backyard" is true if, and only if, in fact it is raining in his backyard. Philosophers such as Nietzsche and William James have been said to reject the correspondence theory. But for James, at least, perhaps the point is better put in the following way: The correspondence view is at best trivial, for it never tells us what kind of property correspondence is; "it is raining" might picture, or refer to, or be directly caused by the fact that it is raining. But what of "2 + 2 = 4," "murder is wrong," and "the South lost the Civil War?" (an)

See also relativism.

TSE (See Test of Spoken English)

tuition

Payments charged by an educational institution for academic instruction, not including materials, books, or laboratory fees. Historically tuition was charged only by private educational institutions, but, with the advent of current school reform programs and programs such as the school-choice movement or voucher system, it has come to refer to public school costs as well. More specifically, tuition is the cost associated with educating one student. Some states have a "no or minimum tuition" policy defined by law. For that reason, "student fees" are often used synonymously with tuition when student costs are increased. (rsb, dm)

tuition guarantee

Usually refers to an institution's guarantee that the annual cost for tuition will not increase between the first year a student is enrolled and the student's senior year. Guarantees are generally valid for four or five years. (sn)

t-unit

A linguistics term for the smallest grammatically complete sentences that text can be divided into; often a simple sentence or a main clause with all subordinate clauses attached. A t-unit is often used to measure the complexity of texts or student writing. (cld)

tutor

In Britain, most colleges and universities assign students a staff member who takes responsibility for the students' welfare by guiding them through their academic program. This tutor is expected to facilitate the students' personal development, monitor their academic progress, and serve as a liaison between the students and the higher education administration. In the American South, well-to-do rural families during the 19th-century antebellum era often hired tutors to teach their children academics and manners. (lcw)

tutoring

A form of individualized instruction in which a teacher, another adult, or a fellow student provides special assistance to a student or small group of students. (bba)

TWE (See Test of Written English)

21st century skills

With today's students growing up in a postindustrial information- and knowledge-based era, 21st century skills are those abilities students must acquire in order to function as citizens in a global, technology, and digitally enhanced modern world. According to Wagner, 2008, these skills include critical thinking and problem solving; collaboration and leadership; agility and adaptability; initiative and entrepreneurialism; effective oral and written communication; accessing and analyzing information; and curiosity and imagination. Such organizations as the Partnership for 21st Century Skills seek to support the incorporation of 21st century skills and standards in education. (ms)

twice exceptional

A term used in gifted education in reference to students who are identified as both academically gifted and learning disabled. Twice exceptional students can present challenges to identification measures, as the disability can mask academic performance. Appropriate service models, addressing multiple needs for differentiation, can call into question core assumptions about the construction of both "gifted" and "learning disabled" programs. (bda)

two-way bilingual education

A program in which students learning English are placed with students learning a different second language. Students are expected to learn one another's native language, develop proficiency, and gain a greater understanding of each other's cultures. (jqa, npo)

two-year college

An institution providing two years of instruction beyond the secondary level. The two-year college takes several forms, including the junior college, the community college, and the technical college. (cf)

Tylerian rationale

An outcome-based curriculum development theory influenced by the scientific, social efficiency, and behaviorist approaches of Franklin Bobbitt and B. F. Skinner. This dominant approach to curriculum development, promoted by Ralph Tyler in his influential book, *Basic Principles of Curriculum and Instruction* (1949), is organized around four categories: defining learning objectives through the identification of socially valued knowledge and skills; organization and selection of experiences for achieving the stated objectives; development of curriculum, or units of study; and evaluation of learning outcomes using objective instruments to gather behavioral evidence. These manifest in schools as, variously, goals, purposes, learning objectives, lesson plans, scope and sequence guides, and standardized tests. In this model, the emphasis is on control of students and their environments. (jm1)

U

UCD (See user-centered design)

u-curve in artistic development
The nonlinear developmental trajectory identified by cognitive developmental psychologists that places early artistry (drawing/graphic symbolization) at one end of the u, balanced at the other by the mature state of professional artists. The trough of the u is occupied by children between the ages of 8 and 11 (in the literal stage) whose drawings have been viewed as less expressive than those of five-year-olds, artist adolescents, and adults. U-shaped development is noted in other cognitive processes but is usually resolved by the reclaiming of early skills. In drawing, children more often abandon the activity by adolescence. Some educators believe that consistent arts training throughout early schooling would reverse the downward curve. (lw)

UCWHRE (See University Council for Workforce and Human Resource Education)

UD (See Universal Design)

UDL (See Universal Design for Learning)

UI (See user interface)

unconditional positive regard
A psychotherapeutic technique in which the therapist accepts the client without judging, evaluating, or disapproving of characteristics or behaviors. The therapist expresses a willingness to listen without interceding, thereby creating a positive relationship in which the client feels free to express feelings without fear of judgment or rejection. (tsw)

unconscious
The part of the mind containing the psychic material of which the ego is unaware. These mental processes and properties are unavailable to conscious recall but nevertheless are believed to have a profound effect on thoughts, feelings, and behaviors in everyday life. (rnp)

underachievement
Accomplishment below the level expected. Performance that falls below the level predicted by previous assessments of potential. (jw)

understanding
Understanding is the spontaneous grasp of the meaning of human affairs (for instance, the meaning of language, music, and pictures), of human behavior, or of human artifacts. Understanding is a key

concept in hermeneutics, but there are different theories of what it takes to understand. As an intended educational outcome, understanding is the modifications that reflect the individual's comprehension of knowledge and development of competence. Understanding implies a difference in appreciation as the result of comprehension, development, and experience. (jb1, cf)

See also interpretation.

UNESCO

The designated mission of the United Nations Educational, Scientific and Cultural Organization, which has 188 member states, is to contribute to peace and security in the world. Adopting its constitution in November 1945 at the London Conference, UNESCO has as its purpose the advancement of universal respect for justice, for the rule of law and human rights, as well as respect for fundamental freedoms, without distinction of race, sex, language, or religion. Five principal functions claimed by UNESCO are the exchange of specialized information, the transfer of knowledge, the development of policy, the preparation of international instruments and statutory recommendations, as well as prospective studies relative to tomorrow's world. (tp)

UNICEF (See United Nations Children's Fund)

unified/integrated teacher education

A type of preservice teacher education program that combines general teacher preparation content with special education content to enable preservice teachers to successfully work in inclusive classrooms where special education students work alongside general education peers. (kmt, nfd)

Uniform Resource Locator (URL)

An address for specifying the location and name of a document accessible via the Internet. Also known as a URL. URLs consist of several pieces of structured information: the protocol, the domain, any necessary path information, and the document name. The U.S. House of Representatives member list can serve as an example: http://www.house.gov/house/MemberWWW.html. The protocol is the first element; the URLs for web pages usually use the protocol "http:", which tells the browser to utilize the hypertext protocol. The second element is the domain, which indicates which server stores the document. For example, "www.house.gov" indicates the server for the House of Representatives web site. On complex websites, documents are organized into folders and subfolders. This organization structure is called a path. Here the path is "/house/." The final element of the URL is the name of the document itself: "MemberWWW.html." (ac)

unions

In education, organizations composed of teachers or other employees, focused on workplace issues of salaries, benefits, physical settings, conditions, and professional standards. Unions are found in all states of the United States, with the primary distinguishing feature among them being the right to conduct legal strikes or work stoppages. The activities of unions are also directed to political issues that members determine to be important to the teaching profession. The issues often involve federal and state decisions affecting funding (e.g., vouchers and charter schools). Unions are also active in curriculum and instructional issues that the organizations deem to be important to students and to teachers. (ly)

unit

A single item or a group counted as a single entity. (dc)

See also units.

unit, vocational

A financial unit and program of study approved by the state department of education in accordance with the state's plan for career and vocational-technical education. (jm)

United Nations Children's Fund (UNICEF)

A nonprofit organization founded by the United Nations in 1946 to be responsible for improving the welfare of European children who were victimized by World War II. Since 1950, UNICEF has provided food, clothing, and rehabilitative programs to ensure that the nutritional, health, and educational needs of children in more than 140 nations are met, as well as to promote their developing potential. Globally, UNICEF community-based educational services teach community leaders how to improve sanitary living conditions and how to become better parental caregivers and providers by means of area-specific job skill enhancement programs. In the United States, UNICEF has targeted inner-city children as its focus for assistance. In 1965, UNICEF received the Nobel Prize for International Peace. (tp)

units

Collections of related lessons organized around a topic or theme. The learning activities may include content, information, skills, and concepts. In addition, assessment strategies are necessary in a unit plan. Length of units may range from one week to one semester. (mje, jah)

See also unit.

units of measure

These quantities determine the outcome of measurement. They may be length, time, heat, or value. The measurement or amount of something is determined through a particular unit of measure. (jdk)

unity

The condition of being one in number, or the harmonious combination of parts into one whole. One of three principles of the Aristotelian canon of dramatic composition, interpreted by French classical dramatists in the 16th and 17th centuries, which says that a play must represent a single action occurring in a single setting during the course of a single day. In the visual arts, unity is seen as an artistic quality characterized by balanced composition. Interestingly, young children create unified compositions that are visually pleasing, and their work tends to become more differentiated with development. (lj)

univalence

A function that is considered to have univalence is a one-to-one function. Therefore, the function has an inverse. (mlf, rlk)

See also one-to-one correspondence; inverse operation.

Universal Design (UD)

A philosophy for designing products and services so they are usable by all people to the greatest extent possible. The term "universal design" was first coined by the architect Ronald L. Mace in the 1980s and calls for the design of products and structures that anticipate the needs of individuals with disabilities and accommodates these needs from the outset. Examples of universal design include installing curb cuts into sidewalks, installing handles on drawers that require no gripping, and captioning on video and television. The Individuals with Disabilities Education Act of 2004 references universal design, particularly as it relates to assistive technology as a means for students with disabilities to gain physical access to the general curriculum. (jg1)

See also Universal Design for Learning.

Universal Design for Learning (UDL)

An educational framework based on research in the learning sciences, including cognitive neuroscience, that guides the development of flexible learning environments to accommodate individual learning differences. The UDL framework, first defined by the Center for Applied Special Technology (CAST) in the 1990s, calls for creating curriculum that provides the following: multiple means of representation that give learners a variety of ways to acquire information and knowledge (e.g., text, images); multiple means of expression that provide learners with alternatives for showing what they know (e.g., writing, speaking); and multiple means of engagement that appeal to diverse learners' interests, challenge them appropriately, and motivate them to learn (e.g., project choices, scaffolded support). One central idea of UDL is that as new curricular materials and learning technologies are developed, they should be designed to be flexible enough to accommodate the unique learning styles of a wide range of individuals. UDL recognizes that increasing physical access and eliminating physical barriers to education is an essential step in universal design, but genuine learning requires much more than physical access—it requires cognitive (or intellectual) access, too. UDL is based on the Universal Design movement in architecture, which emphasizes the need to make buildings accessible to all people through supports such as wheelchair ramps, Braille, and closed captioning. A definition and provisions for UDL are incorporated into the Higher Education Opportunity Act of 2008. (jg1, jok)

universalist

An approach to social diversity that holds that a basic similarity exists among individuals regardless of group affiliation, or that people are initially quite different but are capable of developing similarities if properly instructed as a central tenet. (hfs)

university

An institution of higher learning with baccalaureate programs in general education, the liberal arts, behavioral and social sciences, and the physical and biological sciences; graduate programs in advanced or specialized fields of study; and professional programs in traditional fields of knowledge (e.g., law, medicine, engineering, journalism, education, business, etc.). (cf)

University Council for Workforce and Human Resource Education

Organized in 1976, the Council is a non-profit organization representing the nation's leading universities. UCWHRE provides leadership for teaching, research, and service initiatives in career and technical education (CTE) and human resource development (HRD). The Council's mission is to shape the future of CTE and HRD through improving the policy and practices of education in the United States toward the betterment of individuals and the larger society. (sa)

university extension

Term used to describe nonagricultural adult education activities based at universities. In more recent usage, the term has been replaced by "continuing education." (las)

University of Maryland v. Murray, 169 Md. 478 (1936)

African American applicant Donald Murray sued the University of Maryland Law School after being denied admission to the all-white school. With the help of the NAACP and lawyer Thurgood Marshall, Murray won admission by arguing under the equal protection clause of the 14th Amendment. The order was upheld in the Maryland Court of Appeals one year later. (dwm)

unpack

A process by which an individual or group arrives at a more complete understanding of a statement, belief, or situation by clearly elaborating unspoken contextual references, often as widely held social, political, scientific, or cultural considerations. (mf1, sh)

urban

Characteristic of the city, city life, and/or distribution of people living in the city. Urban schools in the United States of the late 20th century were often characterized as enclaves for low-income, often minority, students. (kf1, msb)

urban Education

Urban education encompasses the teaching and learning processes that occur within an urban environment. It includes those aspects of the urban school system, the community and cultures, the administrators, teachers, students, and the political and economic variables that directly impact those processes. (ms)

urban teacher residency

A means of preparing teachers for urban classrooms. The purpose of urban teacher residency programs is to build effective partnerships among school districts, higher education institutions, and nonprofit organizations; enlist and coach teachers to meet specific district needs; sustain residents once they are hired as teachers of record; and support cohorts of high-quality, diverse teachers who are committed to careers in marginalized school settings. Residents are chosen according to criteria aligned with the needs of the district. Master's-level course work is tightly integrated with an intensive, full-year classroom residency alongside a qualified, veteran mentor. Following this experience, residents become the teacher of record and continue to receive skilled mentoring. (dm2, eb)

URL (See Uniform Resource Locator)

U.S. Department of Education (ED)

The U.S. Department of Education was established on May 4, 1980, by Congress in the Department of Education Organization Act (Public Law 96-88 of October 1979). ED is responsible for coordinating federal programs related to education, for collecting and disseminating information on American schools, and for sponsoring and disseminating the results of research into the nature, quality, and conduct of American education. ED was created to replace the U.S. Office of Education (USOE), originally established in 1867, and the National Institute of Education (NIE), established in 1972.

ED has been responsible for distributing monies attached to federal programs such as the National Defense Education Act (NDEA) and the Elementary and Secondary Education Act (ESEA), as well as for spearheading debate over educational reform through the publication of reports such as *A Nation at Risk* (1983). (sw, dm)

U.S. Office of Education (See United States Department of education)

U.S. v. Fordice, 505 U.S. 717 (1992)

A lawsuit filed by a group of African Americans against the State of Mississippi in federal court in 1975. The suit's intent was to create a more equitable system of higher education by requesting increased funding for the state's three historically black colleges. Twelve years later when the case went to trial the court found a number of discriminatory practices in college admissions and funding but concluded that the state's desegregation policies were intended to assure that race-neutral policies were practiced. As long as those policies did not contribute toward the racial identification of specific schools, there was no violation of federal law, according to the district court. This decision was upheld by the U.S. Court of Appeals for the Fifth Circuit. However, the Supreme Court found that the lower courts had not applied the correct legal standard to Mississippi's higher education system. The majority opinion written by Justice White held that the adoption and implementation of race-neutral policies is not sufficient to indicate the state has met its duty under the equal protection clause and Title VI to eliminate aspects of a dual system. If policies related to the prior dual system were still in place and have discriminatory implications, they must be changed to create equal educational opportunity. Although the Supreme Court did not mandate that Mississippi provide resources to improve its three historically black universities, it did state that the dual system being practiced had to be addressed. (jqa, npo)

usability

The ease with which the target user of a product can successfully complete appropriate tasks with that product. Tools should be designed to integrate seamlessly with a user's task such that the person can focus on solving the problem at hand rather than how to work the tool. In order to be usable, products must be designed with the users' goals in mind and with minimal room for error. (tll)

USB flash drive

A portable device for storing computer data. The flash drive is the functional successor to the diskette or floppy disk. Flash drives are useful for storing and transporting files. Students and teachers can save a file onto a flash drive from their home computer and then work on it using a computer at school or the library and vice versa. (kg1)

user interface (UI)

The part of a product or piece of software with which a human interacts. This is an umbrella term that can include the graphical interface to an electronic book, the control panel on a copy machine, or the buttons on a TV remote control. Two common computer user interfaces are command line (text only) and graphical user interfaces, also known as GUI (images, buttons, and toolbars). Some corporations and other organizations offer user interface guidelines to assist in the production of effective user interfaces. (tll)

See also human factors engineering.

user-centered design (UCD)

An approach to design that is based on the notion that the customer or "user" has particular needs, which should be considered and used as the basis for the development of a product (including curriculum). User-centered design relies on a variety of methods (including focus testing, surveys, and usability testing) to collect input from users. Often educational publishers and software developers employ user-centered design methods during the analysis, design, and development of new products in order to learn more about the features and ease-of-use options that users desire. This approach improves the likelihood that the final product is a solution tailored to how individuals actually use a product. (sm)

user-generated content

Content created by the end-users of the Internet rather than institution administrators. Wikis, such as Wikipedia, blogs, discussion boards, podcasts, and digital video are examples of publicly available user-generated content. Some sites, like Amazon.com, present a combination of administrator- and user-generated content. A benefit of user-generated content for education is the opportunity for multiple viewpoints and perspectives to be represented. (kd)

See also Web 2.0.

utilitarianism

A form of consequentialism. Act utilitarianism asserts that an act is right if it produces at least the same proportion of good over bad as any available alternative act for all people affected by the act. Rule utilitarianism asserts that an act is right if it follows a rule that generally produces at least the same proportion of good over bad as any alternative rule for all people affected. Classical utilitarians consider pleasure to be the greatest good, and right acts are those that bring about more pleasure than pain for as many people as possible. Some utilitarians recognize a plurality of goods, such as pleasure, knowledge, and virtue. (mhs)

See also consequentialism.

V

validity

In testing, validity represents claims to the trustworthiness or credibility of qualitative or quantitative data gathered for the purposes of making decisions or drawing inferences. The evidence needed to establish validity has been associated with typological distinctions such as content (the match between the actual content of the test instrument and what it intends to measure), criterion-related (the match between scores on the test and other measures), and construct (the match between the test and the underlying construct or trait being measured). Currently, construct validity is seen as the unifying concept for test validity. New approaches to establishing validity are being considered, as assessment has expanded beyond strictly quantitative approaches to gathering information, and embracing forms such as portfolio assessment, where results are reported as qualitative profiles. In logic, validity refers to a quality or property of arguments. A valid argument is one that meets the following criterion: if the premises are true, so is the conclusion. In other words, in a valid argument the conclusion (whether true or false) follows, by legitimate logical steps, from the premises (again, independently of their truth value). Sometimes the term "valid" is applied to theses, as in the claim "you have a valid point," that is, your thesis is reasonable, plausible, true (i.e., to be commended). (bkl, an)

See also soundness.

value

As a noun, value means worth. As a verb, value means to consider something as important. Questions regarding matters of valuation have much to do with the source of the worth of the quality, attribute, or consideration valued. Some hold that value is subjective, that a thing is of worth because someone values it. Others hold that there are things that are of intrinsic value and worth valuing, whether or not one sees the worth. In art, value is the degree of light or dark in a scale of grays. In the visual arts, that is the relative tone of color in each distinct section of a picture (e.g., if the artist uses two grades of dark, the white of the page may furnish a third value). In music, similarly, it is the relative length of duration of a tone signified by a note. The value of art, a subject of interest and debate in art education, refers to its real or perceived worth in society. (jc, lj)

See also values; values clarification; virtue.

values

Values are qualities based on normative judgments of good and bad, and in which there is an emotional investment. They may be moral or nonmoral in nature and may be judged on instrumental or intrinsic grounds. Values may be held consciously or unconsciously by groups or individuals, and they tend to influence behavior. Private values are internal principles, which one establishes in order to evaluate and critique the actions, ideas, and practices of one's self and others. These standards are not fixed but are in flux and changeable. Values are acquired or learned through a complex set of influences, usually over a long period of time. Public values are necessary for the common good in a pluralistic society, allowing for diversity and individualism to exist and influencing how people interact with each other. Public values are a set of overarching beliefs that all groups within a society or nation endorse to maintain societal cohesion. The acquisition of values and value systems is a significant goal of educational practice, and a variety of theories concerning the acquisition of values exist. These include values clarification, character education, cognitive developmentalism, and Robert Coles's psychosocial theory of moral development. (prg, kf1)

See also cognitive development; moral development.

values clarification

A pedagogical strategy by which an educator leads a student to a greater and deeper personal understanding of his/her beliefs by engaging the student in a series of activities designed to focus on a particular moral or ethical value. Values clarification is one of several theoretical and methodological frameworks for developing thoughtfulness about and awareness of values. Sidney B. Simon and Louis E. Raths, in particular, developed "values clarification" as a specific strategy for the development of this awareness. They contended that public schools were not justified in inculcating specific virtues or ethical commitments in children. Schools should help students develop a set of personally meaningful values. Values clarification was popular for several years but fell into disfavor, criticized as subjectivistic, relativistic, secularistic, and individualistic. Nonetheless, some of the strategies and vocabulary of values clarification are incorporated in much educational practice. (wl, jjc)

See also value; values.

van Hiele levels

These describe discrete levels of geometric thinking, as proposed by Pierre M. van Hiele. The levels are characterized by an absence of memorization, sequential progress through the levels (i.e., no conceptual level may be omitted), and the facts that the levels are context independent, learners do benefit from being taught at a higher conceptual level, and progression is mainly due to teaching and learning experiences rather than maturation. Initially, five levels were proposed, although some authors conflate levels three through five. (kva)

variable

A symbol, usually a letter of the alphabet, that represents one or more numbers. A placeholder for a specific unknown number, for example, as in $n + 5 = 12$; a representative of values, as in $3t + 6$; to state properties or generalizations, for example, $a + 0 = a$; used in formulas to express relationships, as in $A = LW$; and to describe functions or sequences. (kgh)

variance

Variance is a statistical notion that indicates the variability of data. It is calculated by averaging the squares of the deviations of the observed values from its expected value (or mean). (mj)

verbal IQ

Derives from a weighted average of a subject's raw scores on five of the verbal subtests that are part of the battery of subtests that constitute the Wechsler Scales of Intelligence. A verbal IQ is heavily influenced by a person's experiences and correlates with most activities that are more valued in society as "academic" and therefore very important to our culture's school-aged population. The verbal IQ is perceived to be a numerical measurement of a person's "verbal intelligence," which is a psychological construct and can therefore never be proven. (aw)

verbal unit items (counting)
Items counted are not present in the child's perceptual world. The act of counting involves the coordination of the utterance of a number word and the mental production of a unit item. (amr)

See also children's counting schemes.

verbal-linguistic intelligence
One of Howard Gardner's multiple intelligences in which an individual exhibits exceptional ability to use and understand words and language. (jwc)

verisimilitude
The closeness in nature and/or presentation of a work of art, literature, or theater to reality; the representation of truth, real life, or commonly recognizable scenes and events through art. Verisimilitude is often described in terms of degrees (e.g., how realistic or lifelike a work of art is). (em)

vertical articulation (See articulation, vertical)

vertical staffing (See horizontal staffing)

VESL (See vocational English as a second language)

virtual globe
A three-dimensional software version of the globe that combines satellite imagery with multimedia and virtual simulations. Virtual globes, such as Google Earth, allow users to view the Earth from many perspectives. Content is enhanced so users can view details such as streets and buildings, including virtual tours. Virtual simulations display more abstract concepts, such as weather patterns, environmental issues, and population densities. (kd)

virtual learning community
A type of environment within the modality of distance learning. This type of learning environment fosters active and collaborative learning while emphasizing inquiry, independent use of information resources, case study approaches, and individual and small-group problem solving and decision making. (mkrf)

virtual learning environment (VLE)
A computer-generated interactive learning space that allows for innovative teaching and learning activities (e.g., conducting a virtual fieldtrip through an interactive learning website or running a chemical experiment via a three-dimensional simulation). A VLE can exist on multiple platforms, including microcomputers, handheld computers, game consoles, interactive television, and proprietary systems. Common features include interactive environments sustained through electronic communication, computer simulation, and file sharing between individual learners. (jh)

virtual reality (VR)
A term reputedly coined by Jaron Lanier, head of Virtual Programming Language, Inc. It is usually taken to refer to a computer-mediated simulation that is three dimensional, multisensory, and interactive, so that the user's experience is "as if" inhabiting and acting within an external environment. There are at least two deeper issues obscured by this definition, however: first, it tends to focus on the technology of VR, and not on VR as a subjective experience of immersion (reading a novel or watching a film and

becoming engrossed in them are also VR experiences); second, the "virtual" is often opposed to the "real," whereas in fact VR is a hybrid or medial concept between the imaginary and the real—it challenges that sharp distinction. The most promising applications of VR technologies for education include: exploratory simulations or models with which learners can interact and study change over time; collaborative spaces in which social coconstruction of knowledge is mediated by a shared virtual space; and multidimensional and multisensory representations of data that allow learners to observe, analyze, and manipulate the data in various ways. (nb)

virtual schooling

An institution or program that teaches K–12 courses entirely or primarily online. Virtual schools may offer full-time or supplemental programs and may be operated by traditional public schools, districts, states, consortia, private schools, or for-profit corporations. Cyber charter schools are a type of virtual school. (eh1, eb)

virtual university

Describes institutions or entities that provide their programs or courses of study exclusively through the use of technology. Some virtual universities are divisions of an existing physical campus, while others provide only online programs. (sn)

virtue

Sometimes translated from the Greek *arete* as "excellence," virtues are traits of character thought indispensable to human well-being. The whole constellation of virtues (and vices) a person possesses constitutes that person's character. Aristotle defined virtue as the predisposition to do the right thing, in the right way, at the right time, for the right reasons. (sr1)

See also value; values.

virtue ethics

An Aristotelian approach to ethics that gives primacy to the practice and development of virtue(s) rather than to the commitment to the good or to duty. The key question for virtue ethicists is how one recognizes the practice of a virtue apart from reference to some concept of the good or of duty. (jc)

See also deontological ethics; ethic of care; ethic of responsibility; ethics.

visiting lecturer

A faculty member who has been invited to deliver a lecture on a particular topic of general interest in the academic community. Visiting lecturers may also be asked to deliver a series of lectures over a varying period of time. (cf)

visiting scholar

The temporary or short-term appointment of a well-known faculty member to discuss specific topics, issues, concepts, or research findings. Visiting scholar appointments are frequently used as a means of stimulating or renewing interest (student and faculty) but are also used to examine without commitment a colleague for permanent appointment. (cf)

VISTA (See AmeriCorps)

visual art

The imitation or invention of objects and/or ideas in visible form. While it can be a component of other art forms, such as choreography or furniture making, the term is usually associated with traditional arts such as painting, engraving, sculpture, and architecture. In colloquial speech it is common to use art and visual art interchangeably; however, this is misleading. It is increasingly important to specify the range of artistic forms, including music, dance, theater, literature, and visual art, that are captured under the heading of art. In schools today, visual art is most commonly taught to children by art specialists, visiting artists, and classroom teachers. (lj)

visual culture

The world of visual images that surround us, from children's book illustrations to art in the museum to iconic symbols (like Barbie and Bart Simpson) to the products of digital technologies such as the action figures interacting in a video game. Arts educators are divided as to whether the range of images from pop to high culture are equally worthy of curricular inclusion; proponents argue that the study of how images reflect the values of an era help students to become critical consumers of visual culture. (jd)

visual impairment

Used to describe individuals who are partially sighted, low vision, legally blind, or totally blind. Partially sighted indicates some type of visual problem; low vision generally refers to a severe visual impairment, such as individuals who are unable to read a newspaper at a normal viewing distance even with the aid of glasses or contact lenses; legally blind refers to a person with less than 20/200 vision in the better eye; and totally blind refers to absence of light perception. (sr)

visual learner

An individual who attends most closely to the visual in any experiential realm and therefore is thought to learn most effectively through modes of observation and response to what is seen rather than heard or read. While visual perception and processing of visual stimuli is part of everyone's mode of and repertoire for learning, visual learners are those who favor and find most success in this realm. While an obvious vehicle for visual learning would be heavily illustrated texts, the study of works of art as agents of history, philosophy, psychology, and the like is an ideal venue. (jd)

visual literacy

The ability to read, decode, code, and encode visual imagery and messages. Visual imagery builds methods of communication, interrogation, and reification of ideologies, philosophies, norms, and interaction. Visual literacy prepares students to understand the saturation of visual imagery surrounding them and builds on their concurrent relationship to text. (lev)

visual phonics

Also called "See-the-Sound," visual phonics uses hand-shapes and written symbols to represent the sounds of English for students who may not have access to them in other ways (students with speech or hearing disorders, for example). The goal of visual phonics is to help students learn to spell and sound out words using these hand signals and written symbols. (jas)

Visual Thinking Strategies (VTS)

Based on the work of educational researcher Abigail Housen and museum educator Philip Yenawine, Visual Thinking Strategies (VTS) is an approach to looking at art, usually in the context of museums or galleries, in which the viewer is asked to respond to the question, "What do you see?" and defend responses by referring to the work at hand ("Why do you say that?"). This inquiry-based approach has been useful to art museums attempting to transform learning in the museum from an information/empty-vessel-based approach, to one more interactive and empowering for the viewer. (ap)

visual-perceptual abilities

A set of skills that are used to take in visual information and integrate that information with other sensory information to construct meaning. Visual-perceptual abilities include skills such as visual discrimination, visual memory, visual closure, visual spatial relationships, figure-ground discrimination, visual-auditory and visual-motor integration, and visual association. In numerous studies, visual perceptual abilities have been shown to be statistically significant in regard to reading achievement. (rcr)

visual-spatial intelligence

Described by Howard Gardner in his Theory of Multiple Intelligences as the ability to think using mental images and pictures. The ability to understand visually represented images. (jwc)

Vitalizing Secondary Education: Education for Life Adjustment (1951) (See Prosser Resolution)

VLE (See virtual learning environment)

vocabulary

The words used in a language or a particular book or branch of science, or the like, or by a particular author. The range of words known to an individual. Vocabulary size is an important measure of a person's literacy level; it generally reflects the amount of reading a person has done and is commonly used in standardized measures of intelligence. In educational research, it is used as a measure of the level of a child's language development, degree of bilingualism, and level of second-language learning. (smt)

vocalization

The process of articulating a consonant as a vowel sound. The process of using vowel indicators in writing systems that do not use vowels, as in Hebrew. The utterance and formation of vocal sounds. Sound made through vocal fold vibrations and modified by the resonance of the vocal tract. (mc)

vocation

From the Latin *vocare*, which translates as "to call." Though often used secularly in reference to professional identity, the term maintains religious undertones bespeaking its association with divine call to some form of work understood as ministry. Theologically, the valuing of particular work as a vocation, as opposed to simply a job, implies a deeper spiritual conviction and commitment to the role the work plays in one's self-understanding. In some contexts, particularly Roman Catholic and Orthodox Churches, the term is used specifically in reference to participation in a religious order or ordained ministry. Thus vocation is understood as larger than the work itself and includes a commitment to a purpose or way of life. The implicit cosmological claim is Platonian: that each person has a specific role to play in the universe, and the objective of education is to assist in discerning that role and to prepare the student to play it out well. In secondary schools the adjective form "vocational" has been used to describe curricula emphasizing the preparation for a skilled labor position (e.g., mechanic, welder, carpenter, technician) deemed "nonacademic" or in contrast to "college preparatory." (bda)

vocational

Pertaining to a vocation or occupation, including all gainful occupations and homemaking. (jm)

vocational adjustment (See adjustment, vocational)

vocational adult education

Education aimed at training or retraining adults to aid them in obtaining employment or advancing in their careers. (las)

vocational advisor (See advisor, vocational)

vocational aptitude

Innate or acquired capacity for a vocation or occupation, indicated by the ability to develop specific skills and to acquire knowledge and information that enable the learner to prepare for or to be more proficient in a chosen trade, occupation, or profession. (jm)

vocational center (See area career center)

vocational clinic

A conference of a counselor and other specialists (such as psychologists) to consider the case data and problems of a person relating to the selection of an occupation and adjustment to it. (jm)

vocational course (See course, career-technical or vocational)

vocational curriculum guidance

Guidance through the systematic arrangement of courses and learning experiences that are designed to help students as they make choices of occupations, work activities, and training that are suitable to their abilities, interests, and needs. (jm)

vocational education

The development and enhancement of the human capacities necessary for work and earning a living, and most accurately understood as one aspect or subset of education in its general sense. Sometimes a very sharp distinction is made between vocational education, with its applied and instrumental orientation, and liberal education, with its exclusive focus on the pursuit of knowledge for its own sake (i.e., for pure or noninstrumental reasons). Yet vocational purposes fall legitimately within the domain of education because of work's potential contribution to human flourishing and the complex and intellectually challenging character of higher-level vocational skills. More narrowly, vocational education is a form of education that provides training for a specific occupation, particularly in agriculture, trade, or industry. Originally carried out through apprenticeship and the home, and evolving into the 19th-century manual training movement, vocational students were trained for jobs in separate schools and as part of the secondary school curriculum in courses like metalworking and clerical skills. The federal Smith-Hughes Act (1917) provided states with funds for agricultural, industrial, and home economics education. In the last half of the 20th century the U.S. Congress continued to authorize workforce training acts. Currently, vocational education is used to indicate an organized educational program, or series of programs, directly related to the preparation of an individual for paid or unpaid employment, or for additional preparation for a career that may or may not require an advanced/college degree. (kw, lh, sc, jb)

See also career and technical education; civic education; essentialism; perennialism; progressive education; traditional education.

Vocational Education Act of 1963

Federal legislation, known as the Perkins Act, designed to extend present programs and develop new programs of vocational education; encourage research and experimentation; and provide work-study programs to enable youth to continue vocational education. This was the first federal legislation allowing funding for vocational education beyond high school. (jb)

vocational education survey

A study to obtain necessary information as a basis for the proper development of programs of vocational education. (db)

See also employment survey; occupational survey.

vocational English as a second language (VESL)

Type of instruction in English for speakers of other languages that is focused on language used in occupational contexts. (las)

vocational goal (See goal, career)

vocational guidance

The process by which persons are assisted in selection of a vocation and of adequate vocational training or retraining that is realistic in light of actual or anticipated opportunities for gainful employment. In each case this guidance is situated to the counselee's interests, needs, and ability to benefit from such training. (jm)

See also occupational guidance; vocational curriculum guidance.

vocational high school (See high school, specialized)

vocational school

A school that is organized separately under a principal or director for the purpose of offering training in one or more skilled or semiskilled trades or occupations. (jb)

See also area vocational school.

vocational training

Sometimes used to designate short-term courses dealing with entry-level skills only. On-the-job training and experiences that contribute to the student's preparation for occupational adjustment. (jm)

See also vocational education.

vocational unit (See unit, vocational)

vocational-technical education program (See Career education program)

voice

The sound produced by the vocal chords, in speaking, singing, or other utterances. It is a form of expression and medium of art, usually referring to individuals, but also to inanimate objects like musical instruments, invisible or guiding spirits, political parties, and the like. To have voice is to have the privilege of speaking, and more broadly, to have agency or power. In language, voice is the form of a verb in which the relation of subject to action is indicated (i.e., active, passive, or middle voice). It is also the disposition that infuses a piece of writing with idiosyncratic style (e.g., the voice of Faulkner) or the state of knowledge, perspective, or preoccupations of an educational researcher documenting pedagogy. Voice may mean the presence of the narrator as speaker, writer, or researcher in a piece of work. In addition to aspects of culture, race, class, and gender, voice typically reveals the personality or personality characteristics of the researcher and his/her subjects and gives flavor to the research report. Qualitative researchers often discover their own voices while listening to the voices of those they are interviewing. The term is often associated with silence due to the power of a voice that may be withheld. (lj, baw)

volition

An act of will that displays rational inclination when performing a perceived good. Seeking the *good*, happiness, is the formal objective of volition, besides an ineluctable human characteristic. Good volition is facilitated with intact practical reasoning of respective merits of particulars (i.e., aim, circumstance, values, premises, evidence, imagination). Virtuous habits of will (e.g., prudence, temperance, courage, and justice) are conditions for effecting good volitions. Defective deliberation and the vices influence acts of bad volition. (dv-l)

See also determinism; freedom.

voluntary minorities

Concept developed by John Ogbu to describe individuals and groups of individuals who voluntarily immigrate to a host society, providing them with a dual frame of reference. This frame comprises a sense of the conditions of those in their society of origin, as well as the conditions, perspectives, and experiences of other group members in the host society. The duality of their identity can generate optimism concerning their future opportunities despite real barriers to their success. Contrasted with involuntary minorities. (hfs)

volunteerism

One of the three basic forms of collective action. It involves the formation of voluntary associations to provide social services and support mechanisms such as education or housing that other forms of collective action (governments and markets) are unable or unwilling to provide. (lr)

voucher

A document usually issued by a state or federal government that can be used by parents to pay tuition at an out-of-district public school, a private school, and/or a religious school. The term is also used more broadly to describe school-choice proposals in which states would help pay tuition for children attending private or religious schools. Some critics of public schools believe tuition vouchers that could be used for private schools or that allow parents to choose which public school their child could attend would bring the free market system to education, forcing public schools to improve in order to stay competitive. Some argue that vouchers would subsidize the wealthy while siphoning money away from the public schools. Others suspect that vouchers would produce a large underclass of students, including many of those with special education requirements, trapped in a system without enough resources to meet their needs. Important questions about accountability to the public for expenditure of public money, the constitutionality of using public money for religious schools, regulation of the schools both private and public, adequate transporta-

tion, and equitable access are still causes for debate. (dm)

voucher plan

A plan for funding education in which parents or guardians receive a voucher, or tax money, that they can use to pay for the education of their child at a school of their choice. The selected school then uses the voucher to pay for educational services delivered to the child. (bba)

vowel

A speech sound that is produced with little obstruction in the vocal tract and that is generally voiced (vocal cords are closed and vibrating during the sound production). A letter that stands to represent the sounds described. (smt)

VTS (See visual thinking strategies)

vulnerable adult

A person 18 years old or older who is unable to care for him/herself or to fully protect his/her rights and interests due to physical, cognitive, mental, and/or emotional impairment. This would encompass, for example, adults with developmental disabilities or with legal guardians, elderly adults who have become incapacitated, or those living in extended-care facilities or receiving services from an agency or individual provider due to an inability to care for themselves. (llf, emm)

W

wait time

A pause or period of silence between a teacher's question and a student's response (wait time one) and between a response and the teacher's feedback or follow-up question (wait time two). Average teacher wait times are about one second, but research has shown several beneficial effects on student responses when teachers increase wait time to three to five seconds. (bba)

Waldorf education

Founded in Stuttgart, in 1919, by Austrian philosopher Rudolf Steiner, this educational philosophy and methodology is based upon a spiritual and psychological view that understands child development as moving through three major stages: early childhood, in which learning experiences are provided so that the child can encounter and imitate that which is good in the environment using sensory and practically based activities; elementary years, in which a feeling for beauty is engendered though artistic and harmonious methods of learning; and secondary years, when cognitive depth, healthy judgments, living concepts, and a search for truth are striven for. This holistic teaching practice is derived from more than 90 years of practical experience. For the kindergarten years, a natural environment is created in which rhythms of the week and year are fostered through bread baking, imaginative play with natural materials, traditional and made-up fairy stories, and the fostering of a breathing rhythm between teacher-directed and child-initiated activities. Reverence, wonder, and healthy social relationships are nurtured. In the elementary years, a distinctive feature is the class teacher, who may remain with the same group of children and parents for much or all of the primary years. Human cultural history is given via stories and artistic activities, beginning with ancient cultures and moving through the Middle Ages and Renaissance and on into modern times. Waldorf education in non-European countries uses corresponding features of these epochs in their own cultural history. Science is taught by encouraging students to observe carefully and make exact descriptions rather than using theories. In secondary Waldorf education, students encounter qualified specialists in the various fields of knowledge. High standards of academic, artistic, and social interactions are aimed for. As in the elementary school, topics are taught in the first two hours each morning, for about three to four weeks, before another topic is taken up. There are currently some 1,000 independent Waldorf/Rudolf Steiner schools in 60 countries worldwide, 1,000 kindergartens, plus institutions for special education, Waldorf teacher training colleges, and university degree programs. (nc1)

War on Poverty

American movement triggered by the civil rights era of the 1960s and promoted by Presidents John F. Kennedy and Lyndon B. Johnson. The War on Poverty aimed to eradicate the inequity in social and economic conditions. Under programs of the War on Poverty initiative, job training and education programs flourished. The Head Start program was created as part of the War on Poverty. (jlj)

washback

Washback refers to the impact of a test on society at all levels from individuals to its value system. Particularly, the term denotes the effects of a test on examinees and teaching. Washback effects are often discussed as part of test quality and validity. (jx)

WASP

An acronym for White Anglo-Saxon Protestant. Typically this designation is used for the group that is considered to be the main contributor and dominant culture in the United States. Historically, White Anglo-Saxon Protestant figures and achievements were included in standard classroom materials. Currently, contributions from the many cultures that have played an active role in American development are included in teaching materials. (jqa, jrw)

Weather Underground

A radical, militant student protest organization that formed following the demise of Students for a Democratic Society (SDS) in 1969 with the overriding purpose of defeating U.S. imperialism. The Weather Underground took its name from a Bob Dylan song and was alternately known as the "Weathermen" and the "Weather People." The organization began a clandestine guerrilla war campaign in 1970. Tactics included violent confrontation and the deployment of time bombs. The organization declined by the 1970s but continued to operate in secrecy. (egh)

Web address (See uniform resource locator [URL])

Web page

A digital document composed of some combination of text, graphics, sound, video, and hyperlinks. A web page can be a public document accessible via the World Wide Web, a semiprivate document accessible via an Intranet, or a private document on a local machine. For instance, a teacher can create a web page about a particular topic and post it on the World Wide Web, making it accessible to her students and other students via their home computers. Or, the teacher can store the web page as a local file on her classroom computer where only her students can access it while in her classroom. (kg1)

Web survey

Web surveys allow individuals to collect data via the Internet. The survey creator uses a software program (e.g., Survey-Monkey, Confirmit, Psychdata) to design the survey and then send invitations to respondents who log onto a website to complete the survey. The survey creator can then use the software program to analyze or download the collected data. Students can use web surveys to collect data for school projects. Teachers and administrators can use web surveys to gather information from students, parents, or teachers. (wf)

Web 2.0

Refers to the evolution of technology surrounding Internet use and represents the second generation of the web, which emphasizes interactivity with other users rather than information retrieval. The term was first used in 2004. The metamorphosis of the web from a read-only medium, where consumers went to get information, into a read-write medium, in which consumers also participate in creating the content directly, impacts education by providing authentic opportunities for performances of understanding. In addition, the collective intelligence created through user-generated content can help students to better understand how historians might construct history. Blogs, podcasts, social networks, wikis, and video hosting are examples of web 2.0 activities. (gle, kd)

See also user-generated content.

Web-based communication

A communication method that involves interaction conducted via the Internet. It may consist of discussion postings, transmission of assignments via the Internet, and synchronous chat sessions among groups of participants in real time. (mid)

Web-based course

A course that is delivered mainly through a connection to the World Wide Web. The course may reside on a server and be accessed by students through a web browser, or may be downloaded onto student computers. (cf)

Web-enhanced instruction

Web-enhanced instruction allows an instructor to create a web page (or pages) with relevant links for the class. Web-enhanced instruction is generally designed as a supplement to on-campus/on-site instruction. (mid)

Website

A website is an integrated collection of web pages created by a person or organization. Within the site, web pages are organized hierarchically, with a home page serving as the initial access point at the top of the hierarchy and additional web pages forming branches. Hyperlinks connect related web pages within the site. In

an educational setting, school districts, schools, teachers, or students may all have websites for displaying information. (kg1)

See also home page; hyperlink; web page.

WEEA (See Women's Educational Equity Act)

welfare-to-work

Term applied to programs that are designed to prepare welfare recipients to enter for the first time, or to reenter, the workforce. Such programs may provide basic skill instruction as well as training in how to obtain and hold a job. (las)

wellness

A positive approach to health that promotes a healthy lifestyle by maintaining physical, social, emotional, spiritual, occupational, and intellectual well-being. (kpr)

wellness coordinator

A person within the local educational agency or school who is charged with the responsibility for making sure that each school fulfills the district's local wellness policy as required by Public Law 108-265. (kpr)

Wernicke's area

An area in the temporal lobe known to be important in speech perception is called Wernicke's area. First reported by Carl Wernicke in the late 1800s as part of his case study of a patient with damage to this area who had trouble with speech perception but not speech production. The discoveries by Broca and Wernicke led to an early understanding of dissociation of functions, in this case, the dissociation between speech production and speech perception. (pk1)

See also Broca's area.

Western Interstate Commission for Higher Education (WICHE)

This regional organization was created in the 1950s by the Western Regional

Educational Compact, adopted by Western states. WICHE thus is an interstate compact created by formal legislative action of 15 states and the U.S. Congress to facilitate resource sharing among the higher education systems of the West. (cf)

Wheeler-Howard Act (See Indian Reorganization Act [1934])

whistle blower

In education this term refers to a person using a strategy designed to use inside information about a particular behavior that is believed to violate an important norm or law. An external authority is informed of the violation. The person attempts to keep the contact secret due to circumventing the legitimate channels of control and fear of reprisal. A person may employ this tactic if they believe that a deliberate attempt has been made to "cover up" a violation of the law. (mm)

White Anglo-Saxon Protestant (See WASP)

White Citizens' Councils

Founded in rural Mississippi in 1954 in response to federal school integration mandates, White Citizens' Councils rapidly spread beyond Mississippi into other parts of Dixie. Typically, local membership rosters comprised a veritable who's who list of a community's civic and businesses leaders whose opinions strongly influenced their white, prosegregation constituencies. The Councils' preferred methods of defying federal will to integrate local schools varied from locale to locale but generally included petitioning and devising harsh and targeted economic reprisals against local civil rights activists. Despite their routine outward denunciation of Klan violence, many Councils fostered clandestine relationships with Klan members. Such support helped to sustain the South's efforts to resist school integration. (ah)

white flight

A term used to describe the departure of white families from housing and schools in areas that are becoming desegregated, or from programs that will require their children to be bused into a school formerly associated with minority group children. Historically associated with changes that came about following *Brown v. Board of Education,* white flight results in a situation where schools that have been desegregated become resegregated as minority families become the majority of those willing to live in a neighborhood or send their children to neighborhood public schools. Voluntary desegregation programs such as magnet schooling have been seen as a solution to the problem of white flight. (sw)

white matter

White matter is tissue in the brain that consists mostly of bundles of myelinated fibers (axons) that carry nerve impulses between neurons and that connect various gray cell areas (nerve cell bodies). The myelin sheath provides an insulation that helps to conserve the electrical impulses traveling through the axon fiber and is important for processing information quickly. White matter tissue does not contain cell bodies and appears pinkish white to the naked eye in a freshly cut brain, because the myelin sheath is mainly lipid (fatty) tissue veined with capillaries. It is situated between the brainstem and cerebellum and consists of structures at the core of the brain such as the thalamus and hypothalamus. The expression of emotions, the release of hormones from the pituitary gland, and the regulation of food and water intake are related to certain nuclei within the white matter considered to be part of the limbic system. The basal ganglia, involved in movement control, are found in white matter beneath the cerebral cortex. White matter continues developing into adulthood. (ns)

whiteness theory

The study of "race" as a socially constructed category that varies in different historical and cultural settings. White- ness theory makes "race" an explicit cat- egory that no longer assumes whiteness as the norm against which all other "races" are judged. Whiteness theory calls on the majority culture, whites, to critique their positions of privilege and power and at- tempt to refuse such positions, as a means of problematizing and actively seeking to remove such privilege and power. At the same time, it is important for whites to acknowledge the privileges they are awarded, even against their wills, by liv- ing in racist societies. (bt-b)

whole language approach/instruction

A set of instructional practices for early reading and writing that emphasizes the importance of children's construction of meaning. It is both a theoretical perspec- tive and a professional movement. The three characteristics of the whole lan- guage approach grow from this ideol- ogy: phonics instruction is embedded in meaningful reading and writing activi- ties; teachers are viewed as facilitators of learning rather than directors; and portfolios and other performance-based assessments, as opposed to skill-based assessments, are the preferred methods of measuring progress. Whole language is usually taught to lower grades even though whole language advocates recom- mend it for all levels. Different interpreta- tions of whole language instruction lead to considerable variation in the range of practices that are identified as whole language. Whole language instructional methods tend to provide learners with an immersion in language learning— listening, speaking, reading, and writing— learning by doing. The whole language approach to teaching respects the abil- ity of learners to set and determine their own purposes. The wholeness in whole language instruction typically refers to working with the whole child's needs: cognitive, emotional, physical, and spiri- tual. The language of whole language fo- cuses on an indirect approach to teaching

specific skills as they are needed by a learner. (jrk, mc, jls)

See also indirect code; phonics.

whole number

A subset of real numbers, consisting of the natural or counting numbers as well as 0 (0, 1, 2, 3 . . .). (jmg)

WIA (See Workforce Investment Act)

WIBs (See workforce investment boards)

WICHE (See Western Interstate Commission for Higher Education)

Wiki

A wiki is a website that allows users to add, delete, or revise content on the site using their own web browsers. This is made possible by wiki software that runs on the web server. Wikis are created mainly by a collaborative effort of the site visitors that allow them to work together to create knowledge repositories, usually united around a central topic. An example of a large wiki is *Wikipedia,* a free ency- clopedia in many languages that anyone can edit. Wikis can also be used privately within a course management system to fa- cilitate collaborative learning. The term "wiki" comes from the Hawaiian phrase, "wiki wiki," which means "super fast." A wiki exemplifies the potential for thou- sands of users adding content to a website on a regular basis, making the site grow "super fast." (mid, ab1)

Winnetka Plan (1919)

An early example of individualized in- struction. Instituted in 1919 in Win- netka, Illinois, by Carleton Washburne, it allowed students to progress at their own pace using self-instructional materi- als. Instead of letter grades, dates of suc- cessful mastery were recorded on "goal cards." Equally important as the mas- tery of common learning objectives was the time devoted to creative and group activities, which Washburne believed nurtured individuality and responsible citizenship. (af)

Wisconsin Idea

The concept that the public university should provide practical adult education programs, focusing on industrial and agricultural training, on a nondegree basis, thereby connecting the university to all constituent groups and areas in the state. Developed in 1911, it was the precursor to the Cooperative Extension Service. The concept that the university serves the educational needs of the public by sharing the intellectual wealth of the university across the entire state, not just among students and faculty of the university, is attributed to John Bascom (University of Wisconsin president, 1874–1887), Charles McCarthy (*Wisconsin Idea*, 1912), Charles R. Van Hise (university president), and Robert M. La Follette (Wisconsin governor). Direct results were the nation's first educational extension program, shaping of legislation by university faculty, and formation of commissions active in state government and private enterprise. These efforts continue today and are augmented by programs that continue the tradition of the Wisconsin Idea. (chm, srd)

Wisconsin v. Yoder, 406 U.S. 205 (1972)

Addressed the conflict between compulsory education laws and the First Amendment right to free exercise of religion. In *Yoder* the U.S. Supreme Court held that members of the Amish religion could withdraw their children from the final two years of compulsory schooling. Claiming that the Amish "way of life and religion were inseparable," the Court found that additional schooling would endanger Amish religious beliefs. (sw)

wisdom

A combination of intelligence, knowledge, and practical wisdom; awareness or knowledge of what life is really about, what our purpose (or purposes) as sentient creatures is, as well as the liberation that comes not merely from understanding but from enacting our accumulated understanding. Philosophy, as the love of wisdom, is not merely a science, like physics, which seeks in a detached methodical way objective theories of its proper objects of study; it is the search for theoretical knowledge of God, the soul, and the meaning of life. (an)

See also intelligence.

womanist/womanism

Coined by Alice Walker, this term is used to refer to a black feminist or feminist of color. Feeling alienated from the feminist movement that focused on white female perspectives of discrimination, those who describe themselves as a womanist incorporate the many aspects of black womanhood's response to racism and sexism. A womanist is a strong, outspoken woman who cares about other women of color, their philosophies, and the way they are treated. In higher education, feminists of color often form alliances because they feel left out of the predominantly white feminist movement. (jqa, npo)

Women's Educational Equity Act (WEEA)

First enacted in 1974, promotes educational equity for women and girls who suffer discrimination based on gender. The law provides financial assistance to enable educational agencies and institutions to meet the requirements of Title IX. The Women's Educational Equity Act was reauthorized and passed within the Improving America's Schools Act of 1994 as Public Law 103-382. The program's scope was expanded and includes support for implementation activities and funds for research. The 2001 reauthorization of the Elementary and Secondary Education Act contains the same provisions for research and implementation in WEEA. (wg)

women's studies

Typically a course of study in higher education, women's studies have also trickled into the secondary curriculum. These courses address the academic, cultural, and economic contributions made by women to society. In higher education, entire departments may be focused on women's studies, with degrees offered. At the secondary level, a unit or series of lessons on women's contributions is more common. At both levels, not only the contributions but the development, achievements, and discrimination experienced by women at various times are addressed. Current elementary-level instructional materials increasingly include information about the contributions of women to the United States. (jqa, npo)

word bank

A storage place for written words that beginning readers can reference as needed to increase their ability to read them. (mmd)

word family

A group of words that closely relate to one another in form and/or meaning. A group of words that have the same base or root word but different inflected forms and derivations. The group includes all the inflected and derived forms from which the meaning can be inferred by an individual through the base word and his or her knowledge of derivations and inflections (e.g., pitch, pitcher, pitched). A group of words that have related meanings (e.g., fast, quick, speed). Teaching form-based word families can help improve children's phoneme awareness as well as their decoding and spelling skills through the use of patterns (e.g., if children learn to decode and spell the rime–at, they can then be taught to read and spell words in the same family, including s-at, m-at, and p-at). Meaning-based families can be used to help children expand their vocabularies and infer meanings. (rcr)

word prediction

A word processing feature that employs algorithms to suggest the word a user is typing or may type next. Word prediction can be used for convenience (e.g., by users of handheld computers) but may also serve as an assistive technology for students with composition or handwriting disabilities. (kg1)

word problem

A mathematical question posed in written form that requires the reader to determine pertinent relationships and decide on appropriate procedures to employ in order to arrive at a solution. (kva)

word study

An approach to spelling instruction that, rather than focusing on the memorization of individual words, introduces students to sounds and spelling patterns. In word study programs, students often move through the curriculum in stages of development, from initial understandings of sounds and spelling patterns to a more complex understanding of Greek and Latin root words. (jas)

work experience

Employment undertaken as part of the requirements of a school course, designed to provide experiences in the chosen occupation, which may or may not be supervised by a teacher, coordinator, or employer. (db)

work-based learning

Learning activities that take place in a work setting. (las)
  See also School-to-Career System.

workbooks

Commercially published materials accompanying textbooks that are designed to provide students with additional practice and application of content and skills taught in the textbook. Students typically complete workbooks independently in the classroom. (bba)

workforce development

Programs that concentrate on specialized study that develops, complements, or expands an employee's or individual's existing knowledge and skills to put emphasis on real-world skills that can be directly applied in the workplace to achieve increased productivity for an employer. System of efforts designed to enhance the capacity of workers to fill the range of labor market needs. Workforce development is the educational aspect of human resource and organizational development that designs programs to improve work environments and manage human capital effectively in organizations. Training programs are aligned with organizational goals to improve both worker and organizational performance. (jb, las, dmv)

workforce education

Workforce education is that form of pedagogy that is provided at the prebaccalaureate level by education institutions, by private business and industry, or by government-sponsored, community-based organizations, in which the objective is to increase individual opportunity in the labor market or to solve human performance problems in the workforce. (kg)

Workforce Investment Act (WIA)

Federal legislation enacted in 1998 that replaced the Adult Education Act and included a focus on employment. The WIA consolidated employment, training and literacy programs into state block grants for adult education and family literacy, disadvantaged youth, and adult employment and training services. Intended to encourage greater collaboration and coordination among employment and training agencies and adult education programs, the act created an integrated "one-stop" system of workforce investment and education activities for adults and youth. Title II of the WIA established an accountability system to measure state performance in adult basic education. (las)

See also Adult Education and Family Literacy Act.

workforce investment boards (WIBs)

Regional boards established within states and certified by governors to set policy for local workforce investment systems. WIBs are composed of representatives from business, local educational institutions, labor, community-based organizations, economic development agencies, and representatives from one-stop career systems. With the advent of the Workforce Investment Act in 1998, WIBs were created to replace private industry councils. (las)

workforce readiness credential

A certificate of readiness for success in entry-level jobs in the United States. Adults take a web-based assessment, demonstrating competence in four areas: situational judgment, oral language, reading with understanding, and using math to solve problems. The certificate demonstrates to potential employers that certificate holders have the critical skills needed to start in nonsupervisory, nonmanagerial, nonprofessional positions across a wide range of careers. (cas)

working alliance

A multidimensional, relationship- and process-oriented construct that involves the degree to which a client and a counselor, or therapist, are able to connect emotionally, to develop mutually agreed-upon treatment goals, and to work together purposefully in a therapeutic setting. (ktc)

Workingmen's Education Movement

During the 1820s and 1830s workingmen's political parties advocated tax-supported common schools. Workingmen, such as skilled journeymen, artisans, and mechanics, felt that public education would help level divisions between social and economic classes and enable the children of working families to protect their own interests, particularly economic and political exploitation, and exercise democratic political power. (crsg)

WorkKeys®

Job skill assessment system created by ACT, Inc. Used by businesses to assess employees and applicants, and for job analysis to benchmark skill levels; more recently used by high schools for curriculum development and job readiness. (rz)

workplace education

Educational activities that are offered to incumbent workers. These learning opportunities range from basic skills instruction to job-related training and may be provided by internal and/or external staff. (las)

workplace educator

Individual involved in the organization and delivery of workplace education programs. The term applies to instructors, curriculum developers, and program coordinators, as well as those who serve as liaisons between business and educational programs. (las)

workplace literacy

Literacy instruction that takes place at a work site and that emphasizes literacy skill development for application in the workplace. (las)

worksheets

Commercially or teacher-prepared materials, one to a few pages in length, that are designed to provide students with additional practice and application of content and skills learned in the classroom. Students typically complete worksheets independently in the classroom. (bba)

workshop

An educational program designed to bring together persons interested in a specific field, for cooperative participation in educational experiences, and to provide new knowledge and skills, develop plans and programs, and reassess attitudes. The major work in developing learning experience is provided by the participants themselves. (cf)

Work-Study Program

In higher education, this program was begun under the Higher Education Act of 1965, providing federal funds for part-time work opportunities for college students needing financial aid to begin or continue their education. Usually these programs are aimed at the postsecondary-level student who has demonstrated financial need to assist in paying for tuition and room and board. At the secondary level, a work-study program is an educational experience in which the student spends a certain number of hours a day in classes, acquiring basic learning, and a specified number of hours working for an employer, generally on a salary basis. The actual work experience is administered jointly by the educational institution and the employer. (lcw, jm)

World Bank

The World Bank was founded in 1944 and is the largest development-assistance source, providing loans to developing countries. Its objective is to help those countries develop into a path of stability, sustainability, and equitable growth in order to diminish poverty. This institution offers different services to implement its poverty-reduction activities in its member countries. Some of the services are financial, analytic and advisory, and capacity building. Poverty reduction is the most urgent task for the World Bank. Through sustainable growth and investment in people, including education and training activities, this institution has the mission to reduce poverty and improve living standards. (cl)

World Wide Web

One component of the Internet consisting of a series of publicly accessible web pages connected by hyperlinks. The World Wide Web, also known as the web, contains varied and diverse information "published" by organizations and individuals. Students can use the web as a source for retrieving information or publishing their work. (kg1)

See also hyperlink; web page.

worldview

In general, the lens through which an individual perceives, interprets, and makes sense of the world. It is moderated by the attitudes, beliefs, values, and learned assumptions that have developed over time, through an individual's personal experience of culture and cultural identification. Worldview is multidimensional. Common dimensions include: beliefs about human nature (e.g., good, bad), preferred relations with nature (e.g., scientific, harmonized), activity orientation (e.g., doing, being), time orientation (e.g., past, present), and preferred ways of relating to one another (e.g., individualistic, collectivistic). (cag)

writing center

That part of an instructional setting that offers a wide range of supplies for the creation and composition of written materials. The supplies are likely to include many kinds, sizes, and colors of paper and stationery, all manner of writing and drawing implements, and a range of equipment like staplers, hole punches, and string that can be used to bind or display that which is written. (mc1)

www (See World Wide Web)

X

xenophobia

Fear and hatred of strangers and foreigners is known as xenophobia. This may be directed to entire cultures and countries, or to immigrants with different traditions. In education, xenophobia creates resistance to multicultural policies and cooperation and collaboration among different cultural groups. (jqa, npo)

Y

year-round schools

Schools that are in session through the summer months as well as during the traditional academic year. Students attend school the same total number of days in year-round and traditional schools; however, rather than one long summer break, year-round schools have shorter breaks regularly scheduled throughout the year. A major purpose of year-round schools is to reduce the amount of reteaching that needs to be done each fall as a result of students' forgetting, over the long summer break, some of what they have learned the previous year. (bba)

Young Adult Literacy Survey

The first national survey of adult literacy, conducted by the National Center for Education Statistics in 1985. The survey assessed the literacy skills of young adults ages 16 to 25 along a continuum of skills used to process written materials encountered by adults in a variety of contexts. (las)

young adult literature

Texts in which the story lines, characters, and reading levels are appropriate for teenage readers. Classic young adult novels include S. E. Hinton's *The Outsiders*, Harper Lee's *To Kill a Mockingbird*, Robert Cormier's *The Chocolate War*, Anne Frank's *Diary of a Young Girl*, and Maya Angelou's *I Know Why the Caged Bird Sings*. (za)

Young Americans for Freedom (YAF)

A politically conservative organization for university students and youth, founded in 1960 from the union of members of the Youth for Goldwater for Vice-President Committee and some members of the Young Republicans. The organization officially began at a conference held at the family estate of William F. Buckley Jr. in Sharon, Connecticut, on September 10–11, 1960. The conference, attended by approximately 100 delegates from 44 colleges, drafted the Sharon Statement to articulate the group's principles, which included beliefs in a free-market economy and the importance of an American victory over communism. The organization began publishing the magazine *New Guard* later that year. In congruence with the organization's founding, YAF was heavily involved with the 1964 presidential campaign of Barry Goldwater. YAF continues to exist on various college campuses in some form. In 2000, Erik Johnson of Yale University assumed national chairmanship of YAF and opened a new YAF headquarter office in Wilmington, Delaware. (nt)

Young People's Socialist League

Also known as YPSL, a socialist organization officially founded in 1915 for youth between the ages of 15 and 30. The active membership before World War I (estimated between 5,000 and 10,000) was decreased due to government repression. In the early 1920s it was reorganized under Harvard student Albert Weisbord. During the Great Depression of the 1930s its activities engaged labor and unemployment movements. YPSL encountered competition from Communist Party youth movements but is credited with being a key predecessor of the student movement of the 1960s. By 1972 it had virtually stopped all activities and in 1977 was officially disbanded. (vmm)

youth apprentice

A young person who, with approval from a parent or guardian, has entered into an agreement with the school and an employer under which the employer provides an opportunity for the apprentice to learn a skilled trade or occupation as part of a formal school-to-work learning opportunity. (db)

See also apprentice.

youth apprenticeship program

Normally a multiyear program that merges work- and school-based learning in a particular occupational area or career cluster and is intended to directly lead into either an associated postsecondary program, entry-level job, or apprenticeship program. (jb)

youth leadership development programs (See ASPIRA)

YPSL (See Young People's Socialist League)

Z

zero-based budgeting
A budgeting process that begins each year's budget at zero and requires the budgeting unit to justify its entire budget each year. Initiated by Texas Instruments, Inc., the term was often associated with the federal government during Jimmy Carter's presidency. (cf)

zone of proximal development
Proposed by Lev Vygotsky (1978), it is the distance between a child's actual developmental level, which is determined by independent problem solving (e.g., tests), and the level of potential development by the same child, determined through problem solving and guided by an adult or in collaboration with more capable peers. A child's actual developmental level refers to functions that have already matured and are therefore the end products of development. On the contrary, the zone of proximal development refers to functions of the child that have not yet matured but are in the process of maturation under adult guidance, in collaboration, and/or in groups. The concept of zone of proximal development is a major component of social-constructivist theories of human development and learning. (mc)

See also social development theory.

zoology
The branch of biology that studies animals. (tw)

z-score
A z-score, also known as a standard score, indicates the location of a raw score (as a direct result of measurement) within a given distribution in terms of standard deviation. To convert a raw score into a z-score, the mean of the data is subtracted from the raw score, and the result is divided by the standard deviation of the data. The sign of the z-score tells whether the raw score is below ($-$) or above ($+$) the mean. Like the raw scores, the z-scores also have a distribution called z-distribution, z-score distribution, or standardized distribution. Such a distribution is normal (i.e., in the shape of a bell curve) with a mean of 0 and a standard deviation of 1. (jx)

See also standard deviation.

Bibliography

Abdul-Haqq, I. "Constructivism in teacher education: Considerations for those who would link practice to theory." (ERIC Document Reproduction Service No. ED426986), 1992.

Abdul-Haqq, I. "Infusing technology into preservice teacher education." *ERIC Digest.* Washington, DC: ERIC Clearinghouse on Teaching and Teacher Education (ERIC Document Reproduction Service No. ED389699), 1995. http://www.ed.gov/databases/ERIC_Digests/ed389699.html.

Academic press dictionary of science and technology. 2001. http://www.harcourt.com/dictionary/def.html.

Achilles, C. M., and M. A. Sharp. "Solve your puzzles using class size and pupil-teacher ratio (PTR) differences." *Catalyst for Change* 28, no. 1 (1998): 5–10.

Adams, D. W. *Education for extinction: American Indians and the boarding school experience, 1875–1928.* Lawrence: University of Kansas Press, 1995.

Adams, J. Q. *Dealing with diversity study guide.* 3d ed. Dubuque, IA: Kendall/Hunt, 2001.

Advocates for Youth. "Creating safe space for GLBTQ youth: A toolkit." Glossary. http://www.advocatesforyouth.org/index.php?option=com_content&task=view&id=607&Itemid=177.

Advocates for Youth. *Sex education resource center.* http://www.advocatesforyouth.org/index.php?option=com_content&task=view&id=84&Itemid=123..

Agar, M. *The professional stranger: An informal introduction to ethnography.* New York: Academic Press, 1980.

Aggarwal, S. "Total Quality Management—technique." *Business Horizons* (1993): 66. http://deming.ces.clemson.edu/pub/tqmbbs/prin-pract/qwkguide.txt.

Albert Ellis Institute. "REBT definition." http://www.rebt.org/about/whatisrebt.asp.

Alexander, P. A., and T. Jetton. "Learning from text: A multidimensional and developmental perspective." In *Handbook of Reading Research,* vol. 3, edited by M. L. Kamil, P. B. Mosenthal, P. D. Pearson, and R. Barr, 285–310. Mahwah, NJ: Lawrence Erlbaum, 1984.

Alkin, M., ed. *Encyclopedia of educational research.* 6th ed. New York: Macmillan/Maxwell Macmillan International, 1992.

AllBusiness, Business Glossary. "Asynchronous discussion." http://www.allbusiness.com/glossaries/asynchronous-discussion/4946115–1.html.

Allen, K. E., and L. R. Marotz. *Developmental profiles: Pre-birth through eight.* Albany, NY: Delmar Publishers, 1999.

Allison, P. C., and K. R. Barrett. *Constructing children's physical education experiences.* Boston: Allyn & Bacon, 2000.

Altbach, P., and G. Kelly. *Education and colonialism.* New York: Longman, 1978.

Altenbaugh, R. J., ed. *Historical dictionary of American education.* Westport, CT: Greenwood Press, 1999.

American Association of Colleges for Teacher Education. "Alternative preparation for licensure." http://www.aacte.org/press_room/alt_prep_licensure.htm.

American Association of School Administrators (AASA). *AASA Online.* http://www.aasa.org.

American Council of Education. "ACE analysis of Higher Education Act Reauthorization." Washington, DC: ACE, 2008. http://www.acenet.edu/e-newsletters/p2p/ACE_HEA_analysis_818.pdf.

American Educational Research Association. http://www.aera.net.

American Educational Research Association, American Psychological Association, National Council on Measurement in Education. *Standards for educational and psychological testing.* Washington, DC: American Psychological Association, 1985.

The American Heritage dictionary of the English language. 3d ed. Boston: Houghton Mifflin, 1992.

The American Heritage dictionary of the English language. 4th ed. Boston: Houghton Mifflin, 2000.

American Psychiatric Association. *Diagnostic and statistical manual of mental disorders: DSM-IV.* 4th ed. Washington, DC: American Psychiatric Association, 1994.

American Psychiatric Association. *Diagnostic and statistical manual of mental disorders: Text revision: DSM-IV-TR.* 4th ed. Washington, DC: American Psychiatric Association, 2000.

American Psychological Association. *Answers to your questions about transgender individuals and gender identity.* Washington, DC: APA, 2006. http://www.apa.org/topics/sexuality/transgender.aspx.

American Psychological Association. *Answers to your questions for a better understanding of sexual orientation & homosexuality.* Washington, DC: APA, 2008. http://www.apa.org/topics/sexuality/orientation.aspx.

Amos WEB*LLC. "Amos web economic gloss'arama, 2001." http://www.amosweb.com/gls/.

Anastasi, A., and S. Urbina. *Psychological testing.* 7th ed. Upper Saddle River, NJ: Prentice Hall, 1997.

Anderson, J. *The education of blacks in the South, 1860–1935.* Chapel Hill: University of North Carolina Press, 1998.

Anderson, T. H. *The movement and the sixties: Protest in America from Greensboro to Wounded Knee.* New York: Oxford University Press, 1995.

Angus, D. L., and J. E. Mirel. "Equality, curriculum, and the decline of the academic ideal: Detroit, 1930–68." *History of Education Quarterly* 33, no. 2 (1993): 177–207.

Answers.com. *Sci-Tech dictionary.* "Mathematical model." http://www.answers.com/topic/mathematical-model.

Anttila, E. "Children as agents in dance: Implications of the notion of child culture for research and practice in dance education." In *International Handbook of Research in Arts Education,* edited by L. Bresler, 865–879. Dordrecht, The Netherlands: Springer, 2007.

Appalachia Educational Laboratory (AEL). http://www.ael.org.

Apple, M. W. "The hidden curriculum and the nature of conflict." In *Educating the democratic mind*, edited by Walter C. Parker, 173–200. Albany: State University of New York Press, 1996.

Apple, M. W. "Understanding and interrupting neoliberalism and neoconservatism in education." *Pedagogies: An International Journal* 1, no. 1 (2006): 21–26.

Arbuckle, D. S. *Counseling: Philosophy, theory, and practice.* Boston: Allyn & Bacon, 1965.

Arizona Department of Education. "Capacity Building Coaches." http://www.ade.az.gov/.

Arizona State University. *Student code of conduct and student disciplinary procedures.* http://www.asu.edu/aad/manuals/sta/sta104–01.html.

Aronowitz, S., and H. Giroux. *Education under siege: The conservative, liberal, and radical debate over schooling.* South Hadley, MA: Bergin and Garvey, 1985.

Aronowitz, S., and H. Giroux. *Postmodern education: Politics, culture and social criticism.* Minneapolis: University of Minnesota Press, 1993.

Aronson, E., N. Blaney, C. Stephin, J. Sikes, and M. Snapp. *The jigsaw classroom.* Beverly Hills, CA: Sage, 1978.

Arum, R., and I. R. Beattie, eds. *The structure of schooling: Readings in the sociology of education.* Mountain View, CA: Mayfield, 2000.

Asante, M. *The afrocentric idea.* Philadelphia: Temple University Press, 1987.

Asante, M. *Afrocentricity.* Trenton, NJ: Africa World Press, 1992.

Ascher, C., and E. Flaxman. *A time for questions: The future of integration and tech prep.* New York: Institute on Education and the Economy, Teachers College, Columbia University, 1993.

Association for Supervision and Curriculum Development. http://www.ascd.org.

Association Montessori Internationale, 2002. http://www.montessori-ami.org/ami.htm.

Association of College and Research Libraries. *Information literacy competency standards for higher education.* Chicago: American Library Association, 2000. http://www.ala.org/ala/mgrps/divs/acrl/standards/informationliteracycompetency.cfm.

Association of Delaware Independent Schools. http://www.advis.org.

Austin, L. *The counseling primer.* Philadelphia: Accelerated Development, 1999.

Baars, J. "Concepts of time and narrative temporality in the study of aging." *Journal of Aging Studies* 11, no. 4 (1997): 283–288.

Bacciocco, E. J. *The new left in America: Reform to revolution, 1956–1970.* Stanford, CA: Hoover Institution Press, 1974.

Badway, N., and W. N. Grubb. *Curriculum integration and the multiple domains of career preparation: A handbook for reshaping the community college.* Berkeley: National Center for Research in Vocational Education, University of California at Berkeley, 1997.

Baker, C., and S. P. Jones. *Encyclopedia of bilingualism and bilingual education.* Philadelphia, PA: Multilingual Matters, 1998.

Baker, F. B. *The basics of item response theory.* 2d ed. College Park, MD: ERIC Clearinghouse on Assessment and Evaluation, 2001.

Bakhtin, M. M. *The dialogic imagination: Four essays.* Austin: University of Texas Press, 1981.

Balanced Score Card Institute. http://www.balancedscorecard.org.

Baldwin, J. W., and R. A. Goldthwaite, eds. *Universities in politics: Case studies from the late Middle Ages and early modern period.* Baltimore, MD: Johns Hopkins University Press, 1972.

Ball, L., and K. Stacey. "Teaching strategies for developing judicious technology use." In *Technology-supported mathematics learning environments*, edited by William J. Masalski, 3–15. Reston, VA: National Council of Teachers of Mathematics, 2005.

Bandura, A. "Self-efficacy: Toward a unifying theory of behavior change." *Psychological Review* 84 (1997): 191–215.

Bank, Barbara J. *Gender and education: An encyclopedia.* Westport, CT: Praeger, 2007.

Bank Street College of Education. http://www.bnkst.edu.

Banks, J. A. "Multicultural education: Historical development, dimensions, and practice." In *Handbook of research on multicultural education*, edited by J. A. Banks and C. A. McGee Banks, 3–24. New York: Macmillan, 1995.

Banks, J. A. *Teaching strategies for ethnic studies.* 5th ed. Boston: Allyn & Bacon, 1991.

Banks, J. A., and C. McGee Banks, eds. *Handbook of research on multicultural education.* New York: Macmillan, 1995.

Banks, J. A., and C. McGee Banks. *Multicultural education: Issues and perspectives.* 3d ed. Boston: Allyn & Bacon, 1977.

Baptiste, H. P., Jr. *Developing the multicultural process in classroom instruction: Competencies for teachers.* Washington, DC: University Press of America, 1997.

Barber, B. R. *Strong democracy: Participatory politics for a new age.* Berkeley: University of California Press, 1984.

Barksdale-Ladd, M. A., J. Isenhart, and A. R. Nedeff. "PDS collaboration in the design and delivery of a reading and language arts methods course." *Reading Horizons* 38, no. 2 (1997): 31–53.

Barlow, T. A. *Pestalozzi and American education.* Boulder, CO: Este Es Press, 1977.

Barnard, H. *Normal schools, and other institutions, agencies, and means designed for the professional education of teachers.* Hartford, CT: Case, Tiffany and Company, 1851.

Barnes, N. "The fabric of a student's life and thought: Practicing cultural anthropology in the classroom." *Anthropology and Education Quarterly* 23, no. 2 (1992): 145–159.

Barrow, R., and G. M. Barrow. *A critical dictionary of educational concepts: An appraisal of selected ideas and issues in educational theory and practice.* New York: Teachers College Press, 1990.

Bartlett, F. C. *Remembering: A study in experimental and social psychology.* New York: Macmillan, 1932.

Bartlett, T., and P. Wasley. "Just Say 'A': Grade Inflation Undergoes Reality Check." *Chronicle of Higher Education* 55, no. 2 (September 5, 2008): A1.

Bartuska, T. J., and G. L. Young, eds. *The built environment: A creative inquiry into design and planning.* Menlo Park, CA: Crisp, 1994.

Baruth, L. G., and E. D. Robinson III. *An introduction to the counseling profession.* Englewood Cliffs, NJ: Prentice Hall, 1987.

Baumgarten, S., and T. Langton. *Elementary physical education: Building a solid movement foundation.* Champaign, IL: Stipes, 2006.

Bauwens, J., J. J. Hourcade, and M. Friend. "Cooperative teaching: A model for general and special education integration." *Remedial and Special Education* 10 (1999): 17–22.

Beauboeuf-LaFontant, T. "A movement against and beyond boundaries: Politically relevant teaching among African-American teachers." *Teachers College Record* 100, no. 4 (1999): 702–723.

Beck, L., and J. Murphy. *The four imperatives of a successful school.* Thousand Oaks, CA: Corwin Press, 1996.

Beder, H. *Adult literacy: Issues for policy and practice.* Malabar, FL: Krieger Publishing Company, 1991.

BehaveNet, Inc. http://www.behavenet.com.

Belkin, G. S. *Introduction to counseling.* 3d ed. Dubuque, IA: Wm. C. Brown Publishers, 1988.

Bell, E. T. *The development of mathematics.* New York: Dover Publications, 1992.

Belvin, J. "How college financial aid works." *How stuff works,* 1998–2000. http://www. howstuffworks.com/college-financial-aid1.htm.

Bendick, J. *Mathematics illustrated dictionary.* New York: Franklin Watts, 1989.

Bennett, W. J. *The de-valuing of America: The fight for our culture and our children.* Colorado Springs, CO: Focus on the Family, 1994.

Bergin, A. E., and S. L. Garfield. *Handbook of psychotherapy and behavior change.* 4th ed. New York: Wiley & Sons, 1994.

Berk, L. E., and A. Winsler. *Scaffolding children's learning: Vygotsky and early childhood education.* Washington, DC: National Association for the Education of Young Children, 1995.

Berlowitz, M. J. "Urban educational reform: Focusing on peace education." *Education and Urban Society* 27, no. 1 (1994): 82–95.

Bern, R. M. *Child, family, school, community: Socialization and support.* Orlando, FL: Harcourt College Publishers, 2001.

Bernard, J., and R. K. Goodyear. *Fundamentals of clinical supervision.* 2d ed. Needham Heights, MA: Allyn & Bacon, 1998.

Berne, E. *Transactional analysis in psychotherapy: A systematic individual and social psychiatry.* New York: Grove Press, 1998.

Bestor, A. *Educational wastelands: The retreat from learning in our public schools.* 2d ed. Urbana: University of Illinois Press, 1985.

Betz, N. E. "Self-efficacy theory as a basis for career assessment." *Journal of Career Assessment* 8 (2000): 205–222.

Birt, R. "Existence, identity and liberation." In *Existence in black: An anthology of black existential philosophy,* edited by Lewis R. Gordon, 205–213. New York: Routledge, 1997.

Bisexual Resource Center. "Bisexuality." http://www.biresource.org/pamphlets/bisexuality. html.

Blacker, D. "Allowing educational technologies to reveal: A Deweyan perspective." *Educational Theory* 43, no. 2 (1993): 181–194.

Bloom, B. S. *Compensatory education for cultural deprivation, [A report] based on working papers contributed by participants in the research conference on education and cultural deprivation.* New York: Holt, Rinehart and Winston, 1965.

Bloom, B. S., ed. *Taxonomy of educational objectives: The classification of educational goals: Handbook I, Cognitive Domain.* By a Committee of College and University Examiners. New York: Longmans, Green, 1956.

Blumenfield, P. C., J. J. Krajcik, R. W. Marx, and E. Soloway. "Lessons learned: How collaboration helped middle grade science teachers learn project-based instruction." *Elementary School Journal* 94, no. 5 (1994): 539–551.

Blythe, T. *The teaching for understanding guide.* San Francisco, CA: Jossey-Bass, 1998.

Boehm, M. "To be banned in Burbank." *Los Angeles Times,* May 27, 2008. http://articles. latimes.com/2008/may/27/entertainment/et-laramie27.

Boesel, D., and L. McFarland. *National assessment of vocational education: Final report to Congress,* vol. 1, *Summary and conclusions.* Washington, DC: U.S. Department of Education, Office of Educational Research and Improvement, 1994.

Bogdan, R., and S. Biklen. *Qualitative research for education.* 3d ed. Boston: Allyn & Bacon, 1998.

Bohan, J. S. *Psychology and sexual orientation: Coming to terms.* New York: Routledge, 1996.

Bohm, D. *On dialogue.* New York: Routledge, 1996.

Boles, H. W., and M. F. Seay. "Community education leadership: A theory." In *Community education: A developing concept,* edited by M. F. Seay and Associates, 85–116. Midland, MI: Pendell, 1974.

Boles, H. W., and M. F. Seay. "Institutions, communities, and the agencies of community education." In *Community education: A developing concept,* edited by M. F. Seay and Associates, 49–81. Midland, MI: Pendell, 1974.

Bond, K. E., and J. Deans. "Eagles, reptiles and beyond: A co-creative journey in dance." *Childhood Education* 73, no. 6 (1997): 366–371.

Bondy, E., and D. D. Ross, eds. *Preparing for inclusive teaching: Meeting the challenges of teacher education reform.* New York: State University of New York Press, 2005.

Booth, W. *The craft of research.* Chicago: University of Chicago Press, 1995.

Bossert, J., ed. *Glossary and tables for statistical quality control.* 3d ed. Milwaukee: ASQC Quality Press, 1996.

Bott, E. *Family and social network: Roles, norms, external relationships in ordinary urban families.* New York: The Free Press, 1971.

Bottoms, G., A. Presson, and M. Johnson. *Making high schools work.* Atlanta, GA: Southern Regional Education Board, 1992.

Bourdieu, P. *Outline of a theory of practice.* Cambridge: Cambridge University Press, 1977.

Bowe, F. G. *Birth to five: Early childhood special education.* Albany, NY: Delmar Publishers, 1995.

Bowers, C. A., and D. Flinders. *Culturally responsive teaching and supervision: A handbook for staff development.* New York: Teachers College Press, 1991.

Bowles, S., and H. Gintis. "Can there be a liberal philosophy of education in a democratic society?" In *Critical pedagogy, the state, and cultural struggle,* edited by H. A. Giroux and P. L. McLaren. Albany: State University of New York Press, 1989.

Boyer, Ernest L. *Scholarship reconsidered: Priorities of the professoriate.* Princeton, NJ: Princeton University Press, 1990.

Boyer, P. S., ed. *The Oxford companion to United States history.* New York: Oxford University Press, 2001.

Boyle, K. *The long walk at San Francisco and other essays.* New York: Grove Press, 1970.

Bragg, D. D. "Linking high schools to postsecondary institutions: The role of tech prep." In *Education through occupations in American high schools,* vol. 2, edited by W. N. Grubb, 191–211. New York: Teachers College Press, 1995.

Bragg, D. D. "Opportunities and challenges for the new vocationalism in American community colleges." (New directions for community colleges, no. 115). In *The new vocationalism in community colleges,* edited by D. Bragg, 5–15. San Francisco: Jossey-Bass, 2001.

Bragg, D. D. *Promising outcomes for eight local tech prep consortia: A summary of initial results.* St. Paul: National Research Center for Career and Technical Education, University of Minnesota, 2001.

Bragg, D. D., R. E. Hamm, and K. Trinkle. *Work-based learning in two-year colleges in the United States.* Berkeley: National Center for Research in Vocational Education, University of California, Berkeley, 1995.

Bragg, D. D., J. Layton, and F. Hammons. *Tech prep implementation in the United States: Promising trends and lingering challenges.* Berkeley: National Center for Research in Vocational Education, University of California, Berkeley, 1994.

Bragg, D. D., and W. Reger. *New lessons about tech prep implementation: Changes in eight local consortia since reauthorization of the federal tech prep consortia in 1998.* St. Paul: National Research Center for Career and Technical Education, University of Minnesota, 2002.

Brameld, T. *Toward a reconstructed philosophy of education*. New York: Dryden Press, 1956.

Bransford, J., S. J. Derry, D. Berliner, K. Hammerness, and K. L. Beckett. "Theories of learning and their roles in teaching." In *Preparing teachers for a changing world: What teachers should learn and be able to do*, edited by L. Darling-Hammond and J. Bransford, 40–87. San Francisco, CA: Jossey-Bass, 2005.

Brantlinger, E. "Adolescents' interpretation of social class influences on schooling." *Journal of Classroom Interaction* 28, no. 1 (1993): 1–12.

Bredekamp, S., ed. *Developmentally appropriate practices in early childhood programs serving children from birth through age 8*. Washington, DC: National Association for the Education of Young Children, 1987.

Bredekamp, S., and C. Copple, eds. *Developmentally appropriate practices in early childhood programs*. Washington, DC: National Association for the Education of Young Children, 1997.

Brems, C. *Basic skills in psychotherapy and counseling*. Belmont, CA: Brooks/Cole, 2001.

Brennan, R., ed. *Educational measurement*. 4th ed. Westport, CT: American Council on Education/Praeger, 2006.

Brenner, C. *An elementary textbook of psychoanalysis*. Rev. ed. New York: International Universities Press, 1973.

Brill, Stephanie, and Rachel Pepper. *The transgender child: A handbook for families and professionals*. Berkeley, CA: Cleis Press Inc., 2008.

The British Dyslexia Association. http://www.bda-dyslexia.org.uk/.

Bronfenbrenner, U. *The ecology of human development: Experiments by nature and design*. Cambridge, MA: Harvard University Press, 1979.

Brown, A. L., A. S. Palincsar, and B. B. Armbruster. "Instructing comprehension-fostering activities in interactive learning situations." In *Theoretical models and processes of reading*, 4th ed., edited by R. B. Ruddell, M. R. Ruddell, and H. Singer, chap. 36. Newark, DE: International Reading Association, 1994.

Brown, R. "Administration of technology: Teaching, learning and resource management." In *Technology leadership for school improvement*, edited by Rosemary Papa, 45–59. Thousand Oaks, CA: Sage, 2009.

Brown, R., P. Noble, and R. Papa. *So you want to be a higher education academic administrator? Avoid crossing to the dark side, or, what they don't tell you in leadership institutes*. Lancaster, PA: Pro.Active Publications, 2009.

Bruess, C. E., and J. S. Greenberg. "Resolving ethical issues when conducting sexuality education." *American Journal of Sexuality Education* 3, no. 4 (2008): 313–322.

Brunner, H. S. *Land-grant colleges and universities*. Washington, DC: U.S. Department of Health, Education and Welfare, 1962.

Bryn, A., and D. Bryne. *Counseling skills for health professionals*. South Melbourne, Australia: Macmillan Education Australia Pty Ltd., 1997.

Buber, M. *Between man and man*. London: K. Paul, 1947.

Buber, M. *I and Thou*. New York: Scribner, 2000.

Buber, M. *The knowledge of man*. New York: Harper & Row, 1965.

Buber, M. *Pointing the way: Collected essays*. New York: Harper, 1957.

Buhle, M. J., P. Buhle, and D. Georgakas, eds. *Encyclopedia of the American left*. New York: Garland, 1990.

Buis, A. G. "An historical study of the role of the federal government in the financial support of education, with special reference to legislative proposals and action." PhD diss., Ohio State University, 1953.

Buker, E. A. *Talking feminist politics: Conversations on law, science, and the post modern.* Lanham, MD: Rowman and Littlefield Publishers, 1999.

Bullough, V. L. "Transgenderism and the concept of gender." *The International Journal of Transgenderism* 4, no. 3 (2000). http://www.wpath.org/journal/www.iiav.nl/ezines/web/IJT/97–03/numbers/symposion/bullough.htm.

Burg, D. F. *Encyclopedia of student and youth movements.* New York: Facts on File, 1998.

Business Majors Web site. "Decision-making in organizations." http://businessmajors.about.com/education/.

Bussmann, H. *Routledge dictionary of language and linguistics.* Edited and translated by G. Trauth and K. Kazzazi. New York: Routledge, 1996.

Cade, B., and W. H. O'Hannon. *A brief guide to brief therapy.* New York: Norton, 1993.

Calhoun, C., and A. Finch. *Vocational education: Concepts and operations.* Belmont, CA: Wadsworth Publishing Company, 1976.

California Safe Schools Coalition. *Safe place to learn: Consequences of harassment based on actual or perceived sexual orientation and gender non-conformity and steps for making schools safer.* Davis: University of California, 2004.

Callahan, R. E. *Education and the cult of efficiency.* Chicago: University of Chicago Press, 1962.

Callan, E. *Creating citizens: Political education and liberal democracy.* Oxford, UK: Clarendon Press, 1997.

Callicott, J. B. *In defense of the land ethic: Essays in environmental philosophy.* Albany: State University of New York Press, 1989.

Cambridge international dictionary of English. Cambridge: Cambridge University Press, 1995.

Cameron, B. D. "Trends in the usage of ISI bibliometric data: Uses, abuses, and implications." *Portal: Libraries and the Academy* 5, no. 1 (2005): 105–125.

Cannella, G. S. *Deconstructing early childhood education: Social justice and revolution.* New York: Peter Lang Publishing, 1997.

Career Services—KIWI Careers. "Admissions officer." http://www.careers.co.nz/jobs/3g_had/j51713a.htm.

Carkuff, R. R., and W. A. Anthony. *The skills of helping: An introduction to counseling skills.* Amherst, MA: Human Resource Development Press, 1979.

Carlson, R. V. *Reframing & reform: Perspectives on organization, leadership, and school changes.* White Plains, NY: Longman Publishers, 1996.

Carnevale, A. *Community colleges and career qualifications.* Issues Paper No. 11. Washington, DC: American Association of Community Colleges, 2000.

Carnoy, M. *Education as cultural imperialism.* New York: David McKay, 1974.

Carnoy, M. "Education, state, and culture in American society." In *Critical pedagogy, the state, and cultural struggle,* edited by H. A. Giroux and P. McClaren, 3–23. Albany: State University of New York Press, 1989.

Carpenter, C. *History of American schoolbooks.* Philadelphia: University of Pennsylvania Press, 1963.

Carpenter, H., and M. Prichard. *Oxford companion to children's literature.* Oxford: Oxford University Press, 1999.

Carr, D. *Educating the virtues: An essay on the philosophical psychology of moral development and education.* London: Routledge, 1991.

Carr, D. "Varieties of incontinence: Towards an Aristotelian approach to moral weakness in moral education." In *Philosophy of education,* edited by F. Margonis, 130–138. Urbana, IL: Philosophy of Education Society, 1996.

Carr, J. F., and D. E. Harris. *Succeeding with standards: Linking curriculum, assessment, and action planning.* Alexandria, VA: Association for Supervision and Curriculum Development, 2001.

Carson, C. *In struggle: SNCC and the black awakening of the 1960s.* Cambridge, MA: Harvard University Press, 1995.

Castro, T. *Chicano power: The emergence of Mexican America.* New York: Saturday Review Press, 1974.

Cazden, C. B., V. P. John, and D. Hymes. *Functions of language in the classroom.* New York: Teachers College Press, 1972.

The Center for Applied Special Technologies (CAST). http://www.cast.org/about/index.html.

Center for Coaching & Mentoring, Inc. (CCMI). http://www.coachingandmentoring.com.

Center for Education Reform. http://www.edreform.com.

Center for Teaching Quality (CTQ). http://www.teachingquality.org.

Chaiklin, S., and J. Lave, eds. *Understanding practice: Perspectives on activity and context.* Cambridge: Cambridge University Press, 1996.

Chang, H. "Serving ethnically diverse communities." *Education and Urban Society* 25, no. 2 (1993): 212–221.

Chaplin, J. P. *Dictionary of psychology.* 2d ed. New York: Laurel, 1985.

Checkly, K. "The first seven . . . and the eighth." *Educational Leadership* 55, no. 1 (1997): 8–13.

Chen, A., and C. D. Ennis. "Content knowledge transformation: An examination of the relationship between content knowledge and curricula." *Teaching and Teacher Education* 11, no. 4 (1995): 389–401.

Children's Defense Fund. http://www.childrensdefense.org.

Christensen, C. M. *The innovator's dilemma: The revolutionary book that will change the way you do business.* New York: HarperCollins, 2003.

Christensen, C. M., M. B. Horn, and C. W. Johnson. *Disrupting class: How disruptive innovation will change the way the world learns.* New York: McGraw-Hill, 2008.

Chubb, J. E., and T. M. Moe. *Politics, markets and America's schools.* Washington, DC: Brookings Institution, 1990.

City, E. A. *Instructional rounds in education: A network approach to improving teaching and learning.* Cambridge, MA: Harvard Education Press, 2009.

Clapham, C., and D. Corson, eds. *Encyclopedia of language and education,* vol. 7, *Language testing and assessment.* Boston: Kluwer Academic Publishers, 1997.

Cobb, P., and G. Wheatley. "Children's initial understandings of ten." *Focus on Learning Problems in Mathematics* 10 (1988): 1–28.

Cobb, P., and E. Yackel. "Constructivist, emergent, and sociocultural perspectives in the context of developmental research." *Educational Psychologist* 31, no. 3/4 (1996): 175–90.

Cobb, P., and E. Yackel. "Constructivist, emergent, and sociocultural perspectives in the context of developmental research." In *Classics in mathematics education research,* edited by T. P. Carpenter, J. A. Dossey, and J. L. Koehler, 208–226. Reston, VA: National Council of Teachers of Mathematics, 2004.

Cochran-Smith, M., D. Davis, and K. Fries. "Multicultural teacher education: Research, practice, and policy." In *Handbook of research on multicultural education.* 2d ed., edited by J. A. Banks and C. A. McGee Banks, 931–975. San Francisco, CA: Jossey-Bass, 2004.

Cochran-Smith, M., and K. Fries. "Research on teacher education: Changing times, changing paradigms." In *Handbook of research on teacher education,* edited by

M. Cochran-Smith, S. Feiman-Nemser, and J. D. McIntyre, 1050–1093. New York: Routledge, 2008.

Coffey, A., and P. Atkinson. *Making sense of qualitative data: Complementary research strategies.* Thousand Oaks, CA: Sage, 1996.

Cohen, L. G., and L. J. Spenciner. *Assessment of children and youth with special needs.* Boston: Pearson Education, 2007.

Cohen, S., ed. *Education in the United States: A documentary history.* 5 vols. New York: Random House, 1974.

Coie, J. D., K. A. Dodge, and H. Coppotelli. "Dimensions and types of social status: A cross-age perspective." *Developmental Psychology* 18 (1982): 557–570.

Collins, A., J. Hawkins, and S. Carver. "A cognitive apprenticeship for disadvantaged students." *Center for Technology in Education Technical report no. 10.* Washington, DC: U.S. Office of Educational Research and Improvement, 1991.

Collins, A., J. Hawkins, and J. R. Frederiksen. "Three different views of students: The role of technology in assessing student performance." *Journal of the Learning Sciences* 3, no. 2 (1993): 205–217.

Collins, J. *Good to great: Why some companies make the leap . . . and others don't.* New York: HarperCollins, 2001.

Collins, P. H. *Black feminist thought.* London: HarperCollins Academic, 1990.

Colman, A. M. *A dictionary of psychology.* New York: Oxford University Press, 2001.

Colorado Department of Education. "School finance web index." http://www.cde.state. co.us/cdefinance/sfcateg.htm.

Colorado's Communications for a Sustainable Future Web Site. "Re: Cost-benefit versus cost-effectiveness." http://csf.colorado.edu/clim-econ/current/0027.html.

Comings, J., B. Garner, and C. Smith. eds. *Annual review of adult learning and literacy,* vols. 1–2. San Francisco: Jossey-Bass, 2000/2001.

Compayre, G. *Abelard and the origin and early history of universities.* New York: Charles Scribner's Sons, 1910.

Computer User. http://computeruser.com.

Connell, R. W. "Teaching the boys: New research on masculinity and gender strategies for schools." *Teachers College Record* 98, no. 2 (1996): 206–235.

Continuous Quality Improvement (CQI) Server. Department of Industrial Engineering, Clemson University. "TQM—The most asked questions." http://deming.eng.clemson. edu/pub/tqmbbs/prin-pract/questns.txt.

Cook, R. E., A. Tessier, and M. D. Klein. *Adapting early childhood curricula for children in inclusive settings.* Upper Saddle River, NJ: Prentice Hall, 2000.

Cooke, B. D., and D. Buchholz. "Mathematical communication in the classroom: A teacher makes a difference." *Early Childhood Education Journal* 32, no. 6, (2005): 365–369.

Cooney, T. J. "Research and teacher education: In search of common ground." *Journal for Research in Mathematics Education* 25, no. 6 (1994): 608–636.

Copleston, F. C. *Medieval philosophy.* New York: Harper & Row, 1961.

Corey, G. *Theory and practice of counseling and psychotherapy.* 5th ed. Pacific Grove, CA: Brooks/Cole, 1996.

Corey, M. S., and G. Corey. *Groups: Process and practice.* 3d ed. Pacific Grove, CA: Brooks/ Cole, 1987.

Cormier, S., and B. Cormier. *Intervention strategies for helpers: Fundamental skills and cognitive behavioral interventions.* Pacific Grove, CA: Brooks/Cole, 1998.

Corporation for National and Community Service. "What is service-learning?" http:// www.learnandserve.gov/about/service_learning/index.asp.

Corsini, R. J. *The dictionary of psychology.* Philadelphia: Brunner/Mazel, 1999.

Corsini, R. J. *Encyclopedia of psychology*. New York: Wiley & Sons, 1984.

Corsini, R. J., and A. J. Auerbach, eds. *Concise encyclopedia of psychology*. 2d ed. New York: Wiley, 1996.

The Cost-Effective Organization. "Buy your way to cost control." http://members.aol.com/thehickel/costef7g.htm.

Council of Chief State School Officers. http://www.ccsso.org/intasc.html.

Council of Chief State School Officers. "Interstate New Teacher Assessment and Support Consortium (INTASC)." http://www.ccsso.org/Resources/Programs/Interstate_Teacher_Assessment_Consortium_(InTASC).html.

Council on Teacher Education. "Certification information." http://www.ed.uiuc.edu/cte/cert/index.html.

Counts, G. S. *Dare the school build a new social order?* New York: John Day, 1932.

Covey, S. R. "Principles of total quality." In *Principle-centered leadership*, by S. R. Covey, 250–260. New York: Simon and Schuster, 1992.

Cranton, P. *Understanding and promoting transformative learning*. San Francisco: Jossey-Bass, 1994.

Cremin, L. A. *American education: The colonial experience, 1607–1783*. New York: Harper & Row, 1970.

Cremin, L. A. *The transformation of the school: Progressivism in American education 1876–1957*. New York: Vintage Books, 1961.

Crenshaw, K., N. Gotanda, G. Peller, and K. Thomas. *Critical race theory: The key writings that formed the movement*. New York: New Press, 1995.

Creswell, J. W. *Educational research: Planning, conducting, and evaluating quantitative and qualitative research*. Upper Saddle River, NJ: Merrill/Prentice Hall, 2002.

Creswell, J. W. *Qualitative inquiry and research design: Choosing among five traditions*. Thousand Oaks, CA: Sage, 1998.

Crocco, M. S., and O. L. Davis Jr., eds. *Bending the future to their will: Civic women, social education, and democracy*. Lanham, MD: Rowman and Littlefield, 1999.

Crotty, M. *The foundations of social research: Meaning and perspective in the research process*. London: Sage, 2003.

Crystal, D. *The Cambridge encyclopedia of language*. 2d ed. Cambridge: Cambridge University Press, 1997.

Crystal, D. *An encyclopedic dictionary of language and languages*. Cambridge, MA: Blackwell Publishers, 1992.

Culp, B. O., J. R. Chepyator-Thomson, and S. Hsu. "Pre-service teachers' experiential perspectives based on a multicultural learning service practicum." *The Physical Educator* 66, no. 1 (2009): 23–36.

Cunningham, D., and G. Hall. *Teacher education: Meeting the challenges of the future*. http://www.aare.edu.au/00pap/cun00359.htm.

Curran, B., C. Abrahams, and T. Clarke. *Solving teacher shortages through license reciprocity*. Denver, CO: State Higher Education Executive Officers, 2001.

Curren, R., ed. *Philosophy of education*. Urbana: Philosophy of Education Society/University of Illinois at Urbana–Champaign, 1999.

Dabrowski, K. *Positive disintegration*. Boston: Little Brown & Co., 1964.

Dacey, J. S., and J. F. Travers. *Human development across the lifespan*. 3d ed. Madison, WI: Brown & Benchmark, 1996.

Damon, W., ed. *Handbook of child psychology*. New York: John Wiley & Sons, 1998.

Dana, N. F., and D. Yendol-Hoppey. *The reflective educator's guide to classroom research: Learning to teach and teaching to learn through practitioner enquiry*. Thousand Oaks, CA: Corwin Press, 2008.

Dana, N. F., and D. Yendol-Hoppey. *The reflective educator's guide to professional development: Coaching inquiry-oriented learning communities*. Thousand Oaks, CA: Corwin Press, 2008.

D'Andrea, M., and J. Daniels. "Promoting multiculturalism and organization change in the counseling profession: A case study." In *Handbook of multicultural counseling*, edited by J. G. Ponterotto, J. M. Casas, L. A. Suzuki, and C. M. Alexander, 17–33. Thousand Oaks, CA: Sage, 1995.

Danforth, E. Jr. *Colleges for our land and time: The land-grant idea in American education*. New York: Harper, 1957.

Danielson, C. *Teacher leadership that strengthens professional practice*. Alexandria, VA: Association for Supervision and Curriculum Development, 2006.

Danzberger, J., C. Bodinger-deUriarte, and M. Clark. *A guide to promising practices in educational partnerships*. U.S. Department of Education, Office of Educational Research and Improvement, 1996. http://www.ed.gov/pubs/PromPract/.

Darder, A., M. Baltodano, and R. D. Torres. *The critical pedagogy reader*. New York: Routledge, 2002.

Darling-Hammond, L., M. Bullmaster, and V. Cobb. "Rethinking teacher leadership through professional development schools." *Elementary School Journal* 96, no. 1 (1995): 87–106.

Darwin, C., and A. Wallace. "On the tendency of species to form varieties; and on the perpetuation of varieties and species by natural means of selection." Presentation to the Linnean Society, London, July 1, 1858.

D'Augelli, Anthony R., Arnold H. Grossman, and Michael T. Starks. "Childhood gender atypicality, victimization, and PTSD among lesbian, gay, and bisexual youth." *Journal of Interpersonal Violence* 21, no. 11 (2006): 1462–1482.

David, M. E. "Parents, gender, and education." *Educational Policy* 7, no. 2 (1993): 184–205.

Davis, O. L., ed. *NCSS in retrospect*. National Council for the Social Studies, Bulletin 92. Washington, DC: National Council for the Social Studies, 1996.

Davis, S., and P. Lawrence. *Matrix*. Reading, MA: Addison-Wesley, 1977.

d'Eaubonne, F. "The time for ecofeminism." Translated by R. Hottell. In *Ecology: Key concepts in critical theory*, edited by C. Merchant and R. S. Gottlieb, 174–197. Atlantic Highlands, NJ: Humanities Press International, 1994.

Debo, A. *A history of the Indians of the United States*. Norman: University of Oklahoma Press, 1970.

Decker, A. F. *A handbook on open admission: Success, failure, potential*. Boulder, CO: Westview Press, 1976.

DeGeorge, R. T. *American freedom and tenure: Ethical issues*. Lanham, MD: Rowman and Littlefield, 1997.

Dei, G.J.S. "Crisis and adaptation in a Ghanaian forest community." *Anthropological Quarterly* 62, no. 1 (1988): 63–72.

Dei, G.J.S. "The renewal of a Ghanaian rural economy." *Canadian Journal of African Studies* 26, no. 1 (1992): 24–53.

Dejnozka, E. L., and D. E. Kapel. *American educators' encyclopedia*. Westport, CT: Greenwood Press, 1991.

Delaware Technical & Community College (DTCC), Student Services. "Success course." http://www.dtcc.edu/services/pdfs/college_success_courses.pdf.

Delgado, R. *Critical race theory: The cutting edge*. Philadelphia: Temple University Press, 1995.

del Pilar O'Cadiz, M., and C. A. Torres. "Literacy, social movements, and class consciousness: Paths from Freire and the São Paulo experience." *Anthropology and Education Quarterly* 25, no. 3 (1994): 208–225.

D'Emilio, J. *The world turned: Essays on gay history, politics, and culture.* London: Duke University Press, 2002.

Deming, W. E. *The new economics for industry, government, and education.* Cambridge: Massachusetts Institute of Technology Center for Advanced Engineering Study, 1993.

Denzin, N., and Y. Lincoln. *Handbook of qualitative research.* 2d ed. Thousand Oaks, CA: Sage, 2000.

Denzin, N. K. "Evaluating qualitative research in the poststructural moment: The lessons James Joyce teaches us." *International Journal of Qualitative Studies in Education* 7, no. 4 (1994): 295–308.

DeRosier, M. E., J. B. Kupersmidt, and C. J. Patterson. "Children's academic and behavioral adjustment as a function of the chronicity and proximity of peer rejection." *Child Development* 65, no. 6 (1994): 1799–1813.

De Shazer, S. *Keys to solution in brief therapy.* New York: W. W. Norton, 1985.

Deskbook encyclopedia of American school law. Rosemount, MN: Informational Research Systems, 1998.

DeSoto, M. "Defining argumentation." *English 101 first year composition.* http://glory. gc.maricopa.edu/mdinchak/eng101/a_define.htm.

De Villiers, J. "Specific language impairment (SLI)." In *Gale encyclopedia of childhood & adolescence.* Detroit: Gale Research, 1998. http://www.findarticles.com/cf_dls/ g2602/0004/2602000494/p1/article.jhtml?term.

Devore, J. L., and R. Peck. *Statistics: The exploration & analysis of data.* 3d ed. Belmont, CA: Duxbury Press, 1997.

Dewey, J. *How we think.* Boston: D.C. Heath, 1910.

Dick, W., and L. Carey. *The systematic design of instruction.* 4th ed. New York: Harper-Collins, 1996.

Dictionary of Education P.L.U.S. http://dictionary.soe.umich.edu.

Dictionary.com. http://dictionary.com.

Dictionary.com. "Tactical online." http://dictionary.reference.com/browse/tactical+.

Dilworth, M. E. *Diversity in teacher education: New expectations.* San Francisco: Jossey-Bass, 1992.

Dirven, R., and M. Verspoor. *Cognitive exploration of language and linguistics.* Philadelphia: John Benjamins Publishing Co., 1998.

Dolch Word Lists. http://www.theschoolbell.com/Links/Dolch/Dolch.html.

Dottin, E. S. "Utilizing the concept of 'conceptual framework' in national accreditation" (ERIC Document Reproduction Service No. ED429062), 1999.

Doucette, D. *Community college workforce training programs for employees in business, industry, labor, and government.* Mission Viejo, CA: League for Innovation in the Community College, 1993.

Dougherty, K. J. *The contradictory college: The conflicting origins, impacts, and future of the community college.* Albany: State University of New York Press, 1994.

Downey, C. J., F. W. English, L. E. Frase, W. K. Poston, and B. E. Steffy. *The three-minute classroom walk-through: Changing school supervisory practice one teacher at a time.* Thousand Oaks, CA: Corwin Press, 2004.

Downs, R. B. *Heinrich Pestalozzi, father of modern pedagogy.* Boston: Twayne, 1975.

Drucker, P. *Management: Tasks, responsibilities, practices.* New York: Harper and Row, 1974.

Dubois, R. D. *All this and something more: Pioneering in the intercultural education movement: An autobiography.* Bryn Mawr, PA: Dorrance, 1994.

Dufficy, P. J. "The pedagogy of pre-service TESOL (Teaching English to Speakers of Other Languages) teacher education." *Journal of Education for Teaching: International Research and Pedagogy* 19, no. 1 (1993): 83–96.

Dufour, R., R. Dufour, R. Eaker, and T. Many. *Learning by doing: A handbook for professional learning communities at work.* Bloomington, IN: Solution Tree Press, 2006.

DuFour, R., R. Eaker, and R. DuFour. *On common ground: The power of professional learning communities.* Bloomington, IN: Solution Tree Press, 2005.

Duke, D. L. *The retransformation of the school: The emergence of contemporary alternative schools in the United States.* Chicago: Nelson-Hall, 1978.

Dunn, F. "The educational philosophies of Washington, Du Bois, and Houston: Laying the foundations for Afrocentrism and multiculturalism." *Journal of Negro Education* 62, no. 1 (1993): 24–34.

Dunn, T. "Understanding and coping with CBTE limitations." *Journal of Teacher Education* 31, no. 4 (1990): 27–33.

Dupre, J. *Out of the past: The struggle for gay and lesbian rights in America.* (DVD). New York: A-Pix Entertainment, 1998. http://www.pbs.org/outofthepast.

Education Development Center (EDC). Center for Science Education. http://www.cse.edc.org.

Education Week on the Web. http://www.edweek.org/.

Educational Facilities Laboratories. *Learning about the built environment: A report.* New York: National Association of Elementary School Principals, 1974.

"Educational programs for students at risk." http://www.looksmart.com.

Educational Testing Service (ETS). *Praxis series.* http://www.ets.org/praxis.

Edwards, C., L. Gandini, and G. Forman, eds. *The hundred languages of children: The Reggio Emilia approach to early childhood education.* Norwood, NJ: Ablex Publishing Corporation, 1993.

Edwards, V., and D. Corson, eds. *Encyclopedia of language and education,* vol. 2, *Literacy.* Boston: Kluwer Academic Publishers, 1997.

Egan, G. *The skilled helper: A problem-management approach to helping.* 5th ed. Pacific Grove, CA: Brooks/Cole, 1994.

Eisenmann, L., ed. *Historical dictionary of women's education in the United States.* Westport, CT: Greenwood Press, 1998.

Eisner, E. W. "The uses and limits of performance assessment." *Phi Delta Kappan* 80, no. 9 (1999): 658–660.

Elkind, D. *The hurried child: Growing up too fast too soon.* Cambridge, MA: Harvard University Press, 1988.

Elkind, D. *Miseducation: Preschoolers at risk.* New York: Knopf, 1987.

Ellis, A. K. *Teaching and learning elementary social studies.* 6th ed. Boston: Allyn & Bacon, 1998.

Encyclopedia Britannica. http://www.Britannica.com.

Encyclopedia.com. http://www.encyclopedia.com.

English, F. W. *Deep curriculum alignment.* Lanham, MD: Scarecrow, 2001.

English, F. W. *The postmodern challenge to the theory and practice of educational administration.* Springfield, IL: C.C. Thomas, 2003.

English, F. W., and W. Poston. *The curriculum management audit.* Lanham, MD: Scarecrow Education, 1995.

Ennis, C. "Teachers' responses to noncompliant students: The realities and consequences of a negotiated curriculum." *Teaching and Teacher Education* 11, no. 5 (1995): 445–460.

Erikson, E. H. *Childhood and society.* 2d ed. New York: Norton, 1963.

Ernst, B., and D. R. Wagner. *Academic freedom: An everyday concern.* San Francisco: Jossey-Bass, 1994.

Ernst, G., and E. L. Statzner. "Alternative visions of schooling: An introduction." *Anthropology and Education Quarterly* 25, no. 3 (1994): 200–207.

Ettling, D. "The praxis of sustaining transformative change." *Teachers College Record* [online]. 2002, no. 1088. http://www.tcrecord.org/Content.asp?ContentID=10881.

Evans, R. J. *In defense of history.* New York: W. W. Norton, 2000.

Evans, T., and M. Grace. "Distance education as the gendered privatization of learning." *Journal of Curriculum Studies* 27, no. 3 (1995): 299–315.

Everett, J., M. Gershwin, H. Hayes, J. Jacobs, and R. Mundhenk. *How should "quality" technical education and training be defined?* Washington, DC: Office of Vocational and Adult Education, U.S. Department of Education, 2002. http://www.ed.gov/offices/OVAE/HS/everett.doc.

Family Educational Rights and Privacy Act Regulations (FERPA). 34 CFR Part 99 Family Educational Rights and Privacy. http://ed.gov/policy/gen/reg/ferpa/index.html.

Fanon, F. *Black skin, white masks.* New York: Grove Press, 1967.

Fanon, F. *The wretched of the earth.* New York: Grove Press, 1961.

Farber, P. "The politics of teacher authority." *Educational Foundations* 5, no. 1 (1991): 75–88.

Farris, P. *Teaching, bearing the torch.* Boston: McGraw-Hill College, 1999.

Fausto-Sterling, A. "How to build a man." In *Constructing masculinities,* edited by M. Berger, B. Wallis, and S. Watson, 127–134. New York: Routledge, 1995.

Fausto-Sterling, A. *Sexing the body.* New York: Basic Books, 2000.

Federal Communications Commission. *Children's educational television: FCC consumer facts.* http://www.fcc.gov/cgb/consumerfacts/childtv.html.

Feinberg, R. C. *Bilingual education: A reference handbook,* Santa Barbara, CA: ABC-CLIO, 2002.

Feltham, C., and W. Dryden. *Dictionary of counseling.* London: Whurr Publishers, 1993.

Ferfolja, T. "Schooling cultures: Institutionalizing heteronormativity and heterosexism." *International Journal of Inclusive Education* 11, no. 2 (2007): 147–162.

Ferrari, M., and R. J. Sternberg. "The development of mental abilities and styles." In *Handbook of child psychology,* vol. 2, edited by D. Kuhn and R. S. Siegler, chap. 18. New York: John Wiley & Sons, 1998.

Finch, C., and J. Crunkilton. *Curriculum development in vocational and technical education: Planning, content, and implementation.* 5th ed. Needham Heights, MA: Allyn & Bacon, 1999.

Finn, J. D. "Withdrawing from school." *Review of Educational Research* 59 (1998): 117–142.

Finn, J. D., and K. E. Voelkl. "School characteristics related to student engagement." *Journal of Negro Education* 62, no. 3 (1993): 249–268.

Fischer, K., and T. Bidell. "Dynamic development of psychological structures in action and thought." In *Handbook of child psychology,* vol. 1, edited by R. M. Lerner, 467–561. New York: Wiley, 1998.

Fiske, E. B. *Smart schools, smart kids: Why do some schools work?* New York: Simon & Schuster, 1991.

Fleming, T. "Habermas on civil society, lifeworld and system: Unearthing the social in transformation theory." *Teachers College Record* [online] 2002, no. 10877. http://www.tcrecord.org/Indexing.asp?.

Flemming, A. S. "The philosophy and objectives of the National Defense Education Act." *Annals of the American Academy of Political and Social Science* 327 (1960): 132–138.

Flexner, A. *Medical education in the United States and Canada: A report to the Carnegie Foundation for the Advancement of Teaching.* New York: Carnegie Foundation for the Advancement of Teaching, 1910.

Flores, A. "Pythagoras meets van Hiele." *School Science and Mathematics* 93, no. 3 (1993): 152–157.

Foner, E. *The new American history.* Philadelphia: Temple University Press, 1997.

Foner, E., and J. Garraty, eds. *The reader's companion to American history.* New York: Houghton Mifflin, 1991.

Forester-Miller, H., and T. Davis. "A practitioner's guide to ethical decision making." *American Counseling Association.* http://www.counseling.org/resources/pracguide.htm.

Foster, M. "Savage inequalities: Where have we come from? Where are we going?" *Educational Theory* 43, no. 1 (1993): 23–32.

Fox, D. C. "The outdoor education curriculum at the elementary school level." *Journal of Educational Sociology* 23, no. 9 (1950): 533–538.

Francis, B., and C. Skelton. "Men teachers and the construction of heterosexual masculinity in the classroom." *Sex Education* 1, no. 1 (2001): 9–21.

Frankenberg, R. *White women, race matters: The social construction of whiteness.* Minneapolis: University of Minnesota Press, 1993.

Franklin, K. J. "K. L. Pike on etic vs. emic: A review and interview." Summer Institute of Linguistics, 1996. http://www.sil.org/klp/karlintv.htm#Abstract.

Franklin, V. P. *Black self determination: A cultural history of African American resistance.* 2d ed. Brooklyn, NY: Lawrence Hill Books, 1992.

Franklin, V. P. "They rose and fell together: African American educators and community leadership, 1795–1954." *Journal of Education* 172, no. 3 (1990): 39–64.

Freeman, J., ed. *Women: A feminist perspective.* 5th ed. Mountain View, CA: Mayfield, 1995.

Freiburg, J. H. "The federal government as a change agent: Fifteen years of the Teacher Corps." *Journal of Education for Teaching* 7, no. 3 (1981): 231–245.

Freire, P. *Education for critical consciousness.* New York: Continuum, 1996.

Freire, P. *Pedagogy of the heart.* New York: Continuum, 2006.

Freire, P. *Pedagogy of the oppressed.* New York: Herder and Herder, 1970.

Freire, P. *Pedagogy of the oppressed.* Translated by Myra Bergman. New York: Continuum, 1993.

Freire, P., and D. Macedo. *Literacy: Reading the word and the world.* Critical Studies in Education Series. West Hadley, MA: Bergin and Garvey, 1987.

Frerichs, R., ed. *The many roles of cooperating teachers: An orientation program for new cooperating teachers* (ERIC Document Reproduction Service No. ED440929), 1997.

Frey, L. L., and G. Roysircar. "Effects of acculturation and worldview for White American, South American, South Asian, and South East Asian students." *International Journal for the Advancement of Counseling* 26, no. 3 (2004): 229–248.

Fromkin, V., and R. Rodman. *An introduction to language.* Fort Worth, TX: Harcourt Brace College Publishers, 1998.

Frost, D., J. Durrant, M. Head, and G. Holden. *Teacher-led school improvement.* London: RoutledgeFalmer, 2000.

Fullmer, D. W., and H. W. Bernard. *Counseling: Content and process.* Chicago: Science Research Associates, 1964.

Fuss, D. *Inside/out: Lesbian theories, gay theories.* New York: Routledge, 1991.

Gabbard, D. A., ed. *Knowledge and power in the global economy.* Mahwah, NJ: Lawrence Erlbaum, 2000.

Gadamer, H.-G. *Truth and method.* 2d rev. ed. New York: Continuum, 2004.

Gadotti, M. *Pedagogy of praxis: A dialectical philosophy of education.* Teacher empowerment and school reform series. Albany: State University of New York Press, 1996.

Galbraith, J. K. *The culture of contentment.* Boston: Houghton Mifflin, 1992.

Gall, M. D., J. P. Gall, and W. R. Borg. *Educational research: An introduction.* 8th ed. Boston: Pearson Education, 2007.

Gallagher, S. *Hermeneutics and education.* Albany: State University of New York Press, 1992.

Garcia, R. *Teaching for diversity.* Bloomington, IN: Phi Delta Kappa Educational Foundation, 1998.

Gardner, H. *Frames of mind.* New York: Basic Books, 1993.

Garfield, J., and I. Gal. "Teaching and assessing statistical reasoning." In *Developing mathematical reasoning in grades K-12,* edited by L. Stiff, 207–219. Reston, VA: National Council Teachers of Mathematics, 1999.

Garner, R. "Metacognition and executive control." In *Metacognition and reading comprehension,* by R. Garner, 123–152. Norwood, NJ: Ablex Publishing, 1987.

Garnett, K., and J. Fleischner. "Mathematical disabilities." *Pediatric Annals* 16, no. 2 (1987): 159–176.

Gay & Lesbian Alliance against Defamation. http://www.glaad.org.

Gay, G. *Culturally responsive teaching: Theory, research, and practice.* New York: Teachers College Press, 2000.

Gay, G., and T. Howard. "Multicultural teacher education for the 21st century." *Teacher Educator* 36, no. 1 (2000): 1–16.

Gay, Lesbian, and Straight Education Network (GSLEN). http://www.glsen.org.

Gee, J. P. "What is literacy?" *Journal of Education* 170, no. 3 (1989): 162–181.

Geertz, C. *The interpretation of cultures.* New York: Basic Books, 1973.

Geertz, C. *Thick description: Toward an interpretive theory of culture.* New York: Basic Books, 1973.

Geertz, C. *Works and lives: The anthropologist as author.* Stanford, CA: Stanford University Press, 1988.

Gelso, C. J., and B. R. Fretz. *Counseling psychology.* Fort Worth, TX: Harcourt, Brace, & Jovanovich, 1992.

Gender Spectrum. "Gender spectrum family." http://www.genderspectrum.org/.

Gere, A. R., J. Buehler, C. Dallavis, and V. S. Haviland. "A visibility project: Learning to see how preservice teachers take up culturally responsive pedagogy." *American Educational Research Journal* 46, no. 3 (2009): 816–52.

Gilligan, C. *In a different voice: Psychological theory and women's development.* Cambridge, MA: Harvard University Press, 1982.

Giroux, H. A. "Border pedagogy in the age of postmodernism." *Journal of Education* 170, no. 3 (1988): 162–181.

Giroux, H. A. *Pedagogy and the politics of hope: Theory, culture, and schooling.* Boulder, CO: Westview Press, 1997.

Giroux, H. A. "Schooling as a form of cultural politics." In *Critical pedagogy, the state, and cultural struggle,* edited by H. A. Giroux and P. McClaren, 125–151. Albany: State University of New York Press, 1989.

Giroux, H. A. *Schooling for democracy: Critical pedagogy in the modern age.* London: Routledge, 1989.

Giroux, H. A. *Theory and resistance in education: A pedagogy of opposition.* South Hadley, MA: Bergin and Garvey, 1983.

Giroux, H. A., and P. L. McClaren. "Introduction: Schooling, cultural politics, and the struggle for democracy." In *Critical pedagogy, the state, and cultural struggle,* edited by H. A. Giroux and P. McClaren, xi–xxxv. Albany: State University of New York Press, 1989.

Giroux, H. A., and R. Simon. "Popular culture and critical pedagogy: Everyday life as a basis for curriculum knowledge." In *Critical pedagogy, the state, and cultural struggle,* edited by H. A. Giroux and P. McClaren, 236–252. Albany: State University of New York Press, 1989.

Gladding, S. T. *Counseling: A comprehensive profession.* Columbus, OH: Merrill–Prentice Hall, 2000.

Gladding, S. T. *The counseling dictionary: Concise definitions of frequently used terms.* Columbus, OH: Merrill–Prentice Hall, 2001.

Gladding, S. T. *Group work: A counseling specialty.* 3d ed. Upper Saddle River, NJ: Prentice Hall, 1999.

Gleason, J. B., ed. *The development of language.* 4th ed. Boston: Allyn & Bacon, 1997.

Gleason, J. B., and N. Ratner. *Psycholinguistics.* Fort Worth, TX: Harcourt Brace College Publishers, 1998.

Glesne, C. *Becoming qualitative researchers: An introduction.* 2d ed. White Plains, NY: Longman, 1999.

Goal setting tutorial. "Why you should set goals." http://www.topachievement.com/tutorial/why.html.

Going, A. J. "The South and the Blair education bill." *The Mississippi Valley Historical Review* 44, no. 2 (1957): 267–290.

Goldenberg, I., and H. Goldenberg. *Family therapy: An overview.* 4th ed. Pacific Grove, CA: Brooks/Cole, 1996.

Goleman, D. *Emotional intelligence.* New York: Bantam Books, 1995.

Gollnick, D., and P. Chinn. *Multicultural education in a pluralistic society.* 5th ed. Columbus, OH: Merrill, 1998.

Good, C. V. *Dictionary of education: Prepared under the auspices of Phi Delta Kappa.* 2d ed. New York: McGraw-Hill, 1959.

Good, C. V. *Dictionary of education: Prepared under the auspices of Phi Delta Kappa.* 3d ed. New York: McGraw-Hill, 1973.

Goodlad, J. I., R. Soder, and K. A. Sirotnik, eds. *Places where teachers are taught.* San Francisco: Jossey-Bass, 1990.

Goodson, I. F., and A. L. Cole. "Exploring the teacher's professional knowledge: Constructing identity and community." *Teacher Education Quarterly* 21, no. 1 (1994): 85–105.

Goodwin, A. L., and C. Oyler. "Teacher educators as gatekeepers: Deciding who is ready to teach." In *The handbook of research on teacher education: Enduring questions in changing contexts.* 3d ed., edited by M. Cochran-Smith, S. Feiman-Nemser, and D. J. McIntyre, 468–492. New York: Routledge, 2008.

Goodyear, R. K., and J. W. Lichtenberg. "A scientist-practitioner perspective on test interpretation." In *Scientist-practitioner perspectives on test interpretation,* edited by J. W. Lichtenberg and R. K. Goodyear, 1–14. Boston: Allyn & Bacon, 2000.

Gordon, H. *The history and growth of vocational education.* Needham Heights, MA: Allyn & Bacon, 1999.

Gorski, P. C. "What we're teaching teachers: An analysis of multicultural teacher education coursework syllabi." *Teaching and Teacher Education* 25, no. 2 (2009): 309–318.

Gove, R. B. *Webster's third, new international dictionary.* Springfield, MA: G. & C. Merriam Co., 1971.

Grant, C., ed. *Educating for diversity: An anthology of multicultural voices.* Boston: Allyn & Bacon, 1995.

Grant, C., and G. Ladson-Billings, eds. *Dictionary of multicultural education.* Phoenix, AZ: Oryx, 1997.

Gray, K. *The role of career and technical education in American high schools: A student centered analysis.* Washington, DC: Office of Vocational and Adult Education, 2002. http://www.ed.gov/offices/OVAE/HS/gray.doc.

Gray, K., and E. Herr. *Workforce education: The basics.* Boston: Allyn & Bacon, 1998.

Graybill, E., and C. Morillas. *School climate for lesbian, gay, bisexual, and transgender youth: An overview of the literature.* Atlanta: Georgia State University Center for School Safety, School Climate, and Classroom Management, 2009. http://education.gsu.edu/schoolsafety/docs/graybill_whitepaper.pdf.

Green, C. R., H. Flowe-Valencia, L. Rosenblum, and A. R. Tait. "The role of childhood and adulthood abuse among women presenting for chronic pain management." *Clinical Journal of Pain* 17 (2001): 359–364.

Greenburg, C. L. *A circle of trust: Remembering SNCC.* New Brunswick, NJ: Rutgers University Press, 1998.

Greenhaus, J. H., and G. A. Callanan. "Employee career indecision." *Journal of Vocational Behavior* 41 (1992): 251–258.

Gregory, R. L., ed. *Oxford companion to the mind.* New York: Oxford University Press, 1987.

Greytak, E., J. Kosciw, and E. Diaz. *Harsh realities: The experiences of transgender youth in our nation's schools.* New York: Gay, Lesbian, and Straight Education Network, 2009. http://www.glsen.org/binary-data/GLSEN_ATTACHMENTS/file/000/001/1375–1.pdf.

Grossman, H. *Teaching in a diverse society.* Boston: Allyn & Bacon, 1995.

Grossman, M. *The ABC-CLIO companion to the Civil Rights Movement.* Santa Barbara, CA: ABC-CLIO, 1993.

Grouws, D. A., ed. *Handbook of research on mathematics teaching and learning: A project of the National Council of Teachers of Mathematics.* New York: Macmillan, 1992.

Grubb, W. N. *Edging toward effectiveness: Examining postsecondary occupational education.* Washington, DC: U.S. Department of Education, 1999. http://www.ed.gov/offices/OUS/PES/NAVE/GrubbI.html.

Grubb, W. N. *Honored but invisible: An inside look at teaching in community colleges.* New York: Routledge, 1999.

Grubb, W. N. *Working in the middle: Strengthening education and training for the mid-skilled labor force.* San Francisco: Jossey-Bass, 1996.

Grubb, W. N., N. Badway, D. Bell, D. D. Bragg, and M. Russman. *Workforce, economic and community development: The changing landscape of the entrepreneurial community college.* Mission Viejo, CA: League for Innovation in the Community College, 1997.

Grubb, W. N., N. Badway, D. Bell, and E. Kraskouskas. *Community college innovations in workforce preparation: Curriculum integration and tech prep.* Mission Viejo, CA: A joint publication of the League for Innovation in the Community College, National Center for Research in Vocational Education, and National Council for Occupational Education, 1996.

Guba, E. G., and Y. S. Lincoln. *Effective evaluation*. San Francisco: Jossey-Bass, 1981.

Guba, E. G., and Y. S. Lincoln. *Fourth generation evaluation*. Newbury Park, CA: Sage, 1989.

Guilford, J. P. *The nature of human intelligence*. New York: McGraw-Hill, 1967.

Guillaume, A. M., and H. K. Yopp. "Professional portfolios for student teachers." *Teacher Education Quarterly* 22, no. 1 (1995): 93–101.

Guinee, K. "The little searcher that could: Middle-school students' search string construction during web-based research." PhD diss., Harvard University, 2007.

Guskey, T. R. *Evaluating professional development*. Thousand Oaks, CA: Corwin Press, 2000.

Gutek, G. L. *American education 1945–2000: A history and commentary*. Prospect Heights, IL: Waveland Press, 2000.

Gutek, G. L. *Pestalozzi and education*. New York: Random House, 1968.

Guthrie, J. W., ed. *The Encyclopedia of education*. 2d ed. New York: Macmillan, 2003.

Guy, T. C. "Alain Locke and the AAAE Movement: Cultural pluralism and Negro adult education." *Adult Education Quarterly* 46, no. 4 (1996): 209–223.

Haberman, M. "The pedagogy of poverty versus good teaching." *Phi Delta Kappan* 73, no. 4 (1991): 290–294.

Habermas, J. *Communication and the evolution of society*. Boston: Beacon Press, 1979.

Habermas, J. *The theory of communicative action*. Boston: Beacon Press, 1984.

Habermas, J. *The theory of communicative action*. Cambridge: Polity Press, 1986–1989.

Hagestad, G. O. "A gray zone? Meeting between sociology and gerontology." *Contemporary Sociology* 28, no. 5 (1999): 514–517.

Hallahan, D. P., and J. M. Kauffman. *Exceptional learners: Introduction to special education*. Needham Heights, MA: Allyn & Bacon, 2000.

Hallman, P. J. *Field-based teacher education: Restructuring Texas teacher education*. Austin: Texas State Board for Educator Certification (ERIC Document Reproduction Service No. ED42066), 1998.

Hambleton, R. K., and R. Jones. "Comparison of classical test theory and item response theory and their applications to test development." *ITEMS: The Instructional Topics in Educational Measurement Series*, Module 16 (1993): 181–189.

Hamesse, J., ed. *Manuels, programmes de cours et techniques d'enseignement dans les universités médiévales: Actes du Colloque international de Louvain-la-Neuve (9–11 Septembre 1993)*. Louvain-la-Neuve: Institut d'Études Médiévales de l'Université Catholique de Louvain, 1994.

Hamilton, N. *Zealotry and academic freedom: A legal and historical perspective*. New Brunswick, NJ: Transaction Publishers, 1995.

Hamilton, S. F., and K. Hurrelmann. "The school-to-career transition in Germany and the United States." *Teachers College Record* 96, no. 2 (1994): 329–344.

Hammerness, K., L. Darling-Hammond, P. Grossman, F. Rust, and L. Shulman. "The design of teacher education programs." In *Preparing teachers for a changing world: What teachers should learn and be able to do*, edited by L. Darling-Hammond and J. Bransford, 390–441. San Francisco: Jossey-Bass, 2005.

Hammersley, M., and P. Atkinson. *Ethnography: Principles in practice*. 2d ed. New York: Routledge, 1995.

Hanson, W. E., K. T. Curry, and D. L. Bandalos. "Reliability generalization of Working Alliance Inventory scale scores." *Educational and Psychological Measurement* 62 (2002): 659–673.

Harcourt School Publishers. *Harcourt multimedia math glossary*. http://www.harcourtschool.com/glossary/math/index.html.

Harel, G., and J. Confrey. eds. *The development of multiplicative reasoning in the learning of mathematics.* Albany: State University of New York Press, 1994.

Hargreaves, A. *Changing teachers, changing times: Teacher's work and culture in the postmodern age.* New York: Teachers College Press, 1994.

Hargreaves, A. "Contrived collegiality: The micropolitics of teacher collaboration." In *The politics of life in schools: Power, conflict, and cooperation,* edited by J. Blase, chap. 3. Newbury Park, CA: Sage, 1991.

Harms, T., D. Cryer, and R. M. Clifford. *Infant/toddler environment rating scale.* New York: Teachers College Press, 1990.

Harper, C. A. *A century of public teacher education.* Washington, DC: American Association of Teachers Colleges, 1939.

Harreé, R., and R. Lamb, eds. *The dictionary of developmental and educational psychology.* Cambridge, MA: MIT Press, 1986.

Harreé, R., and R. Lamb. *The encyclopedic dictionary of psychology.* Cambridge, MA: MIT Press, 1983.

Harris, E. W. "Segregation, desegregation, resegregation: Lessons learned about equality in our schools." http://filebox.vt.edu/chre/elps/EPI/SYMPOSIUM/HARRIS.htm.

Harris, M. *Theories of culture in postmodern times.* Walnut Creek, CA: AltaMira Press, 1999.

Harris, T. L., and R. E. Hodges. *A dictionary of reading and related terms.* Newark, DE: International Reading Association, 1981.

Harris, T. L., and R. E. Hodges. *The literacy dictionary: The vocabulary of reading and writing.* Newark, DE: International Reading Association, 1995.

Harrison, M., and S. Gilbert. *Schoolhouse decisions of the United States Supreme Court.* San Diego, CA: Excellent Books, 1997.

Hart, Juliet E. "Strategies for culturally and linguistically diverse students with special needs." *Preventing School Failure* 53, no. 3 (2009): 197–206.

Hartmann, R.R.K., and F. C. Stork. *Dictionary of language and linguistics.* London: Applied Science Publishers Ltd., 1972.

Harvard Graduate School of Education. "Usable knowledge: Connecting research and practice for leaders in education." http://www.uknow.gse.harvard.edu.

Harvill, L. M. "Standard error of measurement." *ITEMS: The Instructional Topics in Educational Measurement Series,* Module 9 (1991): 253–262.

Hatton, N., and D. Smith. "Reflection in teacher education: Towards definition and implementation." *Teaching and Teacher Education* 11, no. 1 (1994): 33–49.

Hawke, L. M., and M. F. Hawke. "Professionalism: Differences in perception between teacher educators and pre-service teachers, 2000." http://www.atee.org/htm/abstracts/cshawke.html.

Hawkins, D. "I, thou, and it." In *The informed vision: Essays on learning and human nature,* by D. Hawkins, 51–64. New York: Algora, 2002.

Hayes, M. "Assessment of a field-based teacher education program: Implications for practice." *Education* 122, no. 4 (2002): 700–705.

Haywood, K., and N. Getchell. *Life span motor development.* Champaign, IL: Human Kinetics, 2001.

Hazewinkel, M., ed. *Encyclopaedia of mathematics.* Norwell, MA: Kluwer Academic Publishers, 1993.

Headland, T. N., K. L. Pike, and M. Harris. *Emics and etics: The insider/outsider debate.* Newbury Park, CA: Sage, 1990.

Heafford, M. R. *Pestalozzi: His thought and its relevance today.* London: Methuen, 1967.

Heater, D. "Area Studies." In *The international encyclopedia of education: Research and studies,* edited by T. Husen and T. N. Postlethwaite, 308–309. Oxford: Pergamon Press, 1985.

Hellison, D. R. *Teaching responsibility through physical activity.* Champaign, IL: Human Kinetics, 2003.

Henry, W. P., H. H. Strupp, T. E. Schacht, and L. Gaston. "Psychodynamic approaches." In *Handbook of psychotherapy and behavior change,* 4th ed., edited by A. E. Bergin and S. L. Garfield, 467–508. New York: Wiley & Sons, 1994.

Heppner, P. P., J. M. Casas, J. Carter, and G. L. Stone. "The maturation of counseling psychology: Multifaceted perspectives, 1978–1998." In *Handbook of counseling psychology,* 3d ed., edited by S. D. Brown and R. W. Lent, 3–49. New York: Wiley & Sons, 2000.

Herbst, J. *And sadly teach: Teacher education and professionalization in American culture.* Madison: University of Wisconsin Press, 1989.

Herek, G. M. "The context of anti-gay violence: Notes on cultural and psychological heterosexism." *Journal of Interpersonal Violence* 5, no. 3 (1990): 316–333.

Herek, G. M. "Sexual prejudice and gender: Do heterosexuals' attitudes toward lesbians and gay men differ?" *Journal of Social Issues* 56, no. 2 (2000): 251–266.

Hershey, A.M., M. K. Silverberg, T. Owens, and L. K. Hulsey. *Focus for the future: The final report of the national tech prep evaluation.* Princeton, NJ: Mathematica Policy Research, 1998.

Herskovits, M. J. *Cultural relativism: Perspectives in cultural pluralism.* New York: Vintage Books, 1973.

Hilbert, R. A. "Competency-based teacher education versus the real world." *Urban Education* 16, no. 4 (1982): 379–398.

Hill, A. C. "Black education in the seventies: A lesson from the past." In *The black seventies,* edited by Floyd Barbour, 51–67. Boston: Porter Sargent Press, 1970.

Hill, C. E., and K. M. O'Brien. *Helping skills: Facilitating exploration, insight, and action.* Washington, DC: APA Books, 1999.

Hirsch, E. D., J. Kett, and J. Trefil. *Cultural literacy: What every American needs to know.* Boston: Houghton Mifflin, 1987.

Hirst, P. H. "The theory-practice relationship in teacher training." In *Partnership in initial teacher training,* edited by M. B. Booth, V. J. Furlong, and M. Wilkin, chap. 6. London: Cassell, 1990.

Hodges, R. E., ed. "What is literacy? Selected definitions and essays from *The literacy dictionary: The vocabulary of reading and writing.*" Newark, DE: International Reading Association (ERIC Document Reproduction Service No. ED437646), 1999.

Hofstadter, R. *Academic freedom in the age of the college.* New Brunswick, NJ: Transaction Publishers, 1996.

Holland, D., W. Lachicotte, D. Skinner, and W. C. Cain. *Identity and agency in cultural worlds.* Cambridge, MA: Harvard University Press, 1998.

Holland, D., and N. Quinn, eds. *Cultural models in language and thought.* Cambridge: Cambridge University Press, 1987.

Holmes Group. *Tomorrow's schools: Principles for the design of professional development schools.* East Lansing, MI: Holmes Group, 1990.

hooks, b. *Teaching to transgress: Education as the practice of freedom.* New York: Routledge, 1994.

Hopke, W. E., ed. *Encyclopedia of careers and vocational guidance.* 8th ed. Chicago: J. G. Ferguson, 1990.

Horton-Ikard, R., M. Munoz, S. Thomas-Tate, and Y. Keller-Bell. "Establishing a pedagogical framework for the multicultural course in communication sciences and disorders." *American Journal of Speech-Language Pathology* 18, no. 2 (2009): 192–206.

Houston, J. E. *Thesaurus of ERIC descriptors.* 13th ed. Phoenix, AZ: Oryx Press, 1995.

Howe, N., and W. Strauss. *Millennials go to college: Strategies for a new generation on campus.* Washington, DC: American Association of Collegiate Registrars and Admissions Officers, 2003.

Hoy, W., and C. Miskel. *Educational administration.* 4th ed. New York: McGraw-Hill, 1991.

Hoy, W., and C. Miskel. *Educational administration: Theory, research, and practice.* 6th ed. Boston: McGraw-Hill, 2001.

Hoyle, E., and J. Megany, eds. *The professional development of teachers.* London: Kogan, 1980.

Hudson, L. M., D. A. Bergin, and C. F. Chryst. "Enhancing culturally responsive pedagogy: Problems and possibilities." *Teacher Education Quarterly* 20, no. 3 (1993): 5–17.

Hudson, P. *History by numbers: An introduction to quantitative approaches.* London: Arnold; copublished in the United States by Oxford University Press (New York), 2000.

Hughes, F. P. *Children, play and development.* Needham Heights, MA: Allyn & Bacon, 1999.

Hughes, J., L. Dubsky, and P. Staniszewski. *Understanding educational planning: An illustrated guide for school districts.* Danbury, CT: Connolly-Cormack Publishers, 1997.

Human Rights Campaign: Working For Lesbian, Gay, Bisexual and Transgender Equal Rights. "Glossary of terms." http://www.hrc.org/issues/3336.htm.

Hunter, D. A. "The rhetorical challenge of Afrocentricity." *Western Journal of Black Studies* 7, no. 4 (1984): 239–243.

Hurst, C. G. *Passport to freedom: Education, humanism & Malcolm X.* Hamden, CT: Linnet Books, 1972.

Husen, T., and T. N. Postlethwaite, eds. *The international encyclopedia of education.* New York: Pergamon, 1985.

Husen, T., and T. N. Postlethwaite, eds. *The international encyclopedia of education.* 2d ed. New York: Pergamon, 1994.

Illinois Task Force on Academic and Occupational Integration. *Blurring the lines: Integrating academic and occupational instruction at the community college.* Springfield: Illinois Community College Board, 1997.

Imber, M., and T. Van Geel. *Education law.* 2d ed. Mahwah, NJ: Lawrence Erlbaum, 2000.

Imel, S. "One-stop career centers." *ERIC Digest No. 208.* Columbus, OH: ERIC Clearinghouse on Adult Career and Vocational Education (ERIC Document Reproduction Service No. ED434244), 1999.

"In the family: LGBT terms and vocabulary." *Youth in motion, frameline.* http://frameline.org/youthinmotion/index.html.

Indiana Center for Postsecondary Research. "About the National Survey of Student Engagement." http://nsse.iub.edu/html/about.cfm.

Indiana Center for Postsecondary Research. "National Survey of Student Engagement benchmarks of effective educational practice." http://nsse.iub.edu/pdf/nsse_benchmarks.pdf.

Innovation in Digital & Electronic Art (IDEA). IDEA Glossary of Internet Terms. "Cyberspace." http://www.idea.org.uk/online_training/course/gloss.htm.

Institute for Personality and Ability Testing. *Measuring intelligence with the Culture Fair Tests* (Manual for scales 2 and 3). Champaign, IL: The Institute for Personality and Ability Testing, 1959.

International Data Group (IDG) and CIO. "Customer relationship management (CRM) definition and solutions." http://www.cio.com/article/40295/CRM_Definition_and_Solutions.

Interoperability Clearinghouse Glossary of Terms. "Best practice." http://www.ichnet.org/glossary.htm.

Intersex Society of North America. http://www.isna.org/faq/what_is_intersex.

Ivey, A. E., N. B. Gluckstern, and M. B. Ivey. *Basic attending skills*. 3d ed. North Amherst, MA: Microtraining Associates, 1993.

Ivey, A. E., N. B. Gluckstern, and M. B. Ivey. *Basic influencing skills*. North Amherst, MA: Microtraining Associates, 1997.

Ivey, A. E., and M. B. Ivey. *Intentional interviewing and counseling: Facilitating client development in a multicultural society*. 4th ed. New York: Brooks/Cole, 1999.

Ivey, A. E., M. B. Ivey, and L. Simek-Morgan. *Counseling and psychotherapy: A multicultural approach*. 4th ed. Boston: Allyn & Bacon, 1997.

Jacobs, H. *Weatherman*. Berkeley, CA: Ramparts Press, 1970.

James, G. *Mathematics dictionary*. 3d ed. Princeton, NJ: Van Nostrand, 1968.

James, J., and R. C. James, eds. *Mathematics dictionary*. 3d ed. New York: Van Nostrand Reinhold Co, 1968.

James Madison University. 1996–97 *Graduate Catalog*. http://www.jmu.edu/gradschool/catalog/96/O-eduH.html.

Janoff-Bulman, R. "Characterological versus behavioral self-blame: Inquiries into depression and rape." *Journal of Personality and Social Psychology* 37 (1979): 1798–1809.

Jarolimek, J. *Social studies in elementary education*. 8th ed. New York: Macmillan, 1990.

Jarvis, P. *International dictionary of adult and continuing education*. London: Routledge, 1990.

Jarvis, P. *International dictionary of adult and continuing education*. Rev. ed. London: Kogan Page, 1999.

Jochems, W., J. van Merrienboer, and R. Koper. *Integrated e-learning: Implications for pedagogy, technology and organization*. New York: Routledge Falmer, 2003.

Johns, H. *Personal development in counsellor training*. New York: Cassell, 1996.

Johnson, A. G. *The Blackwell dictionary of sociology: A user's guide to sociological language*. Cambridge, MA: Blackwell, 1995.

Johnson, D. "Nonverbal learning disabilities." *Pediatric Annals* 16, no. 2 (1987): 133–141.

Johnson, D. H. "The cultivation of children's bodies toward intricate thinking and sensitive behavior." In *Education and hope in troubled times: Visions of change for our children's world*, edited by H. S. Shapiro, 157–167. New York: Routledge, 2009.

Johnson, D. W., and R. T. Johnson. "Social skills for successful group work." *Educational Leadership* 47 (1990): 29–33.

Johnson, D. W., R. T. Johnson, and E. J. Holubec. *Cooperation in the classroom*. New Brighton, MN: Interaction Book Co., 1984.

Johnson, J. R., and A. S. McIntosh. "Toward a cultural perspective and understanding of the disability and deaf experience in special and multicultural education." *Remedial and Special Education* 30, no. 2 (2009): 67–83.

Johnson, J. W. *Historic U.S. Court Cases 1690–1990: An encyclopedia*. New York: Garland, 1992.

Johnson, K., and H. Johnson. *Encyclopedic dictionary of applied linguistics: A handbook for language teaching*. Oxford: Blackwell Publishers, 1998.

Jones, T. J. *Negro education: A study of the private and higher schools for colored people in the United States: Prepared in cooperation with the Phelps-Stokes Fund*. Washington, DC: U.S. Government Printing Office, 1917.

Jorgenson, L. P. *The state and the non-public school, 1825–1925*. Columbia: University of Missouri Press, 1987.

Just the facts about sexual orientation & youth: A primer for principals, educators and school personnel. http://www.apa.org/pi/lgbc/publications/justthefacts.html.

Kamil, M. L., P. B. Mosenthal, P. D. Pearson, and R. Barr. *Handbook of reading research*. Vol. 3. Mahwah, NJ: Lawrence Erlbaum, 2000.

Kammen, C., and N. Prendergast. *Encyclopedia of local history*. Walnut Creek, CA: Alta-Mira Press, 2000.

Kantor, Harvey, and Robert Lowe. "Terms of inclusion: Unity and diversity in public education." *Educational Theory* 57, no. 3 (2007): 369–388.

Kaplan, H., and B. Sadock. *Comprehensive textbook of psychiatry*. 4th ed. Baltimore, MD: Williams & Wilkins, 1985.

Karagueuzian, D. *Blow it up!* Boston: Gambit Incorporated, 1971.

Karenga, M. *Introduction to black studies*. 2d ed. Los Angeles: University of Sankore Press, 1993.

Karush, W. *Webster's new world dictionary of mathematics*. New York: Prentice Hall, 1989.

Katterle, Z. B., and R. E. Pike. *A compilation of laws and proposals relating to federal aid to education*. Pullman: State College of Washington, 1949.

Katz, L. G., and S. C. Chard. *Engaging children's minds: The project approach*. Norwood, NJ: Ablex, 1989.

Katz, M. B. "Chicago school reform as history." *Teacher's College Record* 94, no. 1 (1992): 56–72.

Kazan, T. S. "Dancing bodies in the classroom: Moving toward an embodied pedagogy." *Pedagogy* 5, no. 3 (2005): 379–408.

Kazdin, A. E., ed. *Encyclopedia of psychology*. New York: Oxford University Press, 2000.

Kegan, R., and L. L. Lahey. *How the way we talk can change the way we work*. San Francisco: Jossey-Bass, 2001.

Kegan, R., and L. L. Lahey. *Immunity to change: How to overcome it and unlock the potential in yourself and your organization*. Boston: Harvard Business Press, 2009.

Kelly, A. E., and R. A. Lesh. *Handbook of research design in mathematics and science education*. Mahwah, NJ: Lawrence Erlbaum, 2000.

Kennedy, D. *Academic duty*. Cambridge, MA: Harvard University Press, 1997.

Kennedy, M. "Inexact sciences: Professional education and the development of expertise." *Review of Research in Education* 14 (1987): 133–167.

Kenwright, Kathy. "Clickers in the classroom." *TechTrends: Linking Research and Practice to Improve Learning* 53, no. 1 (2009): 74–77.

Kerr, B. A., and S. L. Ghrist-Priebe. "Intervention for multipotentiality: Effects of a career counseling laboratory for gifted high school students." *Journal of Counseling & Development* 66 (1988): 366–369.

Killion, J., and C. Harrison. *Taking the lead: New roles for teachers and school-based coaches*. Oxford, OH: National Staff Development Council, 2006.

Kilpatrick, W. H. "The project method." *Teachers College Record* 19, no. 4 (1918): 319–335.

Kirst, M. W. "Equity for children: Linking education and children's services." *Educational Policy* 8, no. 4 (1994): 583–590.

Klauke, Amy. "Magnet schools." *ERIC Digest Series Number EA 26.* Eugene, OR: ERIC Clearinghouse on Educational Management (ERIC Document Reproduction Service No. ED293225), 1988. http://www.ed.gov/databases/ERIC_Digests/ed293225.html.

Kleinman, D. L. *Politics on the endless frontier: Postwar research policy in the United States.* Durham, NC: Duke University Press, 1995.

Kliebard, H. M. *Schooled to work: Vocationalism and the American curriculum, 1876–1946.* New York: Teachers College Press, 1999.

Kliebard, H. M. *The struggle for the American curriculum, 1893–1958.* New York: Routledge, 1995.

Knezevich, S. J. *Administration of public education.* 3d ed. New York: Harper & Row, 1975.

Knowles, M. S. *The modern practice of adult education: From pedagogy to andragogy.* Englewood Cliffs, NJ: Adult Education, 1980.

Koretz, D. "Using student assessments for educational accountability." In *Improving America's schools: The role of incentives,* edited by E. A. Hanushek and D. W. Jorgenson, 171–196. Washington DC: National Academy Press, 1996.

Koros, A. C., and H. A. Silvergate. *The shadow university: The betrayal of liberty on America's campuses.* New York: The Free Press, 1998.

Kosciw, J., and E. Diaz. *The 2005 national school climate survey: The experiences of lesbian, gay, bisexual, and transgender youth in our nation's schools.* New York: Gay, Lesbian, and Straight Education Network, 2006.

Kramarae, C., and P. Treichler. *A feminist dictionary.* Boston: Pandora Press, 1985.

Kuh, G. D., and S. Hu. "Unraveling the complexity of the increase in college grades from the mid-1980s to the mid-1990s." *Educational Evaluation and Policy Analysis* 21, no. 3 (1999): 297–320.

Kuhn, T. S. *The structure of scientific revolutions.* 3d ed. Chicago: University of Chicago Press, 1996.

Kumashiro, K. *Troubling education: Queer activism and antioppressive pedagogy.* New York: RoutledgeFalmer, 2002.

Kuper, A., and J. Kuper. *The social science encyclopedia.* 2d ed. New York: Routledge, 1996.

Ladson-Billings, G. *The dreamkeepers: Successful teachers of African-American children.* San Francisco: Jossey-Bass, 1994.

The land-grant tradition. Washington, DC: National Association of State Universities and Land-Grant Colleges, 1995.

Lather, P. "Issues of validity in openly ideological research: Between a rock and a soft place." *Interchange* 17 (1986): 63–84.

Laughlin, H. *The ego and its defenses.* 2d ed. New York: Jason Aronson, 1979.

Lavin, D. E. *Changing the odds: Open admissions and the life chances of the disadvantaged.* New Haven, CT: Yale University Press, 1996.

Lavin, D. E., R. D. Alba, and R. A. Silberstein. *Right versus privilege: The open-admissions experiment at City University of New York.* New York: Free Press, 1981.

Lawrence, M., A. O'Donnell, and G. J. Pollrand. "Assessments in science: The development and evaluation of a video assessment in physics." *Educational Assessment* 2, no. 4 (1995): 275–293.

Lawton, D., and P. Gordon. *Dictionary of education.* 2d ed. London: Hodder & Stoughton, 1996.

Learnthat. "Synchronous discussion." http://www.learnthat.com/define/view.asp?id=270.

Lee, S. J. "Behind the model-minority stereotype: Voices of high- and low-achieving Asian American students." *Anthropology and Education Quarterly* 25, no. 4 (1994): 413–429.

Legal Information Institute. http://www2.law.cornell.edu.

Leinhardt, G. "Getting to know: Tracing students' mathematical knowledge from intuition to competence." *Educational Psychologist* 23, no. 2 (1988): 119–144.

Leistyna, P., A. Woodrum, and S. A. Shernblom, eds. *Breaking free: The transformative power of critical pedagogy.* Harvard Educational Review, Reprint Series no. 27. Cambridge, MA: Harvard Educational Review, 1996.

Lemert, C. *Sociology after the crisis.* Boulder, CO: Westview Press, 1995.

Lemieux, A. "Gerontagogy beyond words: A reality." *Educational Gerontology* 26, no. 5 (2000): 475–479.

Leopold, A. *A Sand County almanac, and sketches here and there.* New York: Oxford University Press, 1949.

Lesser, L. K., and A. Gelnaw. *Making room in the circle: Lesbian, gay, bisexual, and transgender families in early childhood settings.* San Rafael, CA: Parent Services Project, 2005.

Lessinger, L. M. *Every kid a winner: Accountability in education.* New York: Simon and Schuster, 1970.

Lett, J. *The human enterprise: A critical introduction to anthropological theory.* Boulder, CO: Westview Press, 1987.

Levesque, K., D. Lauen, P. Teitelbaum, M. Alt, S. Librera, and MPR Associates, Inc. *Vocational education in the United States: Toward the year 2000.* Washington, DC: U.S. Department of Education, Office of Educational Research and Improvement, 2000.

Levinas, E. *Totality and infinity: An essay on exteriority.* Pittsburgh, PA: Duquesne University Press, 1969.

Levy, L., and K. L. Karst, eds. *Encyclopedia of the American constitution.* Vol. 5. New York: Macmillan, 2000.

Lewin, K. "The problem of changing food habits." *Bulletin of the National Research Council* 108 (1943): 35–65.

Lewis, T. "From manual training to technology education: The continuing struggle to establish a school subject in the USA." *Journal of Curriculum Studies* 27, no. 6 (1995): 621–645.

Li, Q. "New bottle but old wine: A research of cyberbullying in schools." *Computers in Human Behavior* 23, no. 4 (2007): 1777–1791.

Lickona, T., and R. M. Hanson. *Character education: Restoring respect and responsibility in our schools* [videocassette]. Port Chester, NY: National Professional Resources, 1996.

Lim, C.-I., K. L. Maxwell, H. Able-Boone, and C. R. Zimmer. "Cultural and linguistic diversity in early childhood teacher preparation: The impact of contextual characteristics on coursework and practica." *Early Childhood Research Quarterly* 24, no. 1 (2009): 64–76.

Lim, S. K. *Cultural materialism.* http://www.indiana.edu/wanthro/mater.htm.

Lincoln, Y., and E. Guba. *Naturalistic inquiry.* Beverly Hills, CA: Sage, 1985.

Lindamood-Bell Learning Processes. http://www.lindamoodbell.com.

Lindsey, R. B., K. N. Robins, D. B. Lindsey, and R. D. Terrell. "Cultural proficiency: Changing the conversation." *Leadership* (March–April 2009): 5–12. http://www.acsa.org/FunctionalMenuCategories/AboutACSA/CommitteesGroups/EAD-for-Success/Cultural-proficiency.aspx.

Littrell, J. J. *From school to work.* South Holland, IL: Goodheart-Willcox Co., 1991.

Locke, A.L.E., and L. Harris. *The philosophy of Alain Locke: Harlem renaissance and beyond.* Philadelphia: Temple University Press, 1989.

Lovell, J. T., and K. Wiles. *Supervision for better schools.* 5th ed. Englewood Cliffs, NJ: Prentice Hall, 1983.

Lowery, C. D., and J. F. Marszalek, eds. *Encyclopedia of African-American civil rights.* Westport, CT: Greenwood Press, 1992.

Lowie, R. *History of ethnological theory.* New York: Farrar and Rinehart, 1937.

Luker, R. E., ed. *Historical dictionary of the civil rights movement.* Lanham, MD: Scarecrow Press, 1997.

Lum, L. "Handling 'helicopter parents.'" *Diverse: Issues in Higher Education* 23, no. 20 (2006): 40–42.

Lunenburg, F., and A. Ornstein. *Educational administration.* 2d ed. Belmont, CA: Wadsworth, 1996.

Lynch, C. A. "Institutional repositories: Essential infrastructure for scholarship in the digital age." *ARL: A Bimonthly Report,* no. 226 (February 2003): 1–7. http://www.arl.org/resources/pubs/br/br226/br226ir.shtml.

Lynch, R. "New directions for high school career and technical education in the 21st century." *Information Series No. 384.* Columbus, OH: ERIC Clearinghouse on Adult, Career and Technical Education, The Ohio State University (ERIC Document Reproduction Service No. ED444037), 2000.

Macgillivray, I. K. *Gay-straight alliances: A handbook for students, educators, and parents.* New York: Harrington Park Press, 2007.

MacWhinney, B., and C. Snow. *The CHILDES project: Tools for analyzing talk.* Hillsdale, NJ: Lawrence Erlbaum, 1995.

"Magic and the supernatural in the Ancient World." http://www.tulane.edu/spaeth/magic98/examq/examq.jan20–22.html.

Magolda Baxter, M. B. *Knowing and reasoning in college: Gender-related patterns in students' intellectual development.* San Francisco: Jossey-Bass, 1992.

Maher, F. "Toward a richer theory of feminist pedagogy: A comparison of 'liberation' and 'gender' models for teaching and learning." *Journal of Education* 169, no. 3 (1987): 91–100.

Mahrer, A. R. "Existential-humanistic psychotherapy and the religious person." In *Religion and the clinical practice of psychology,* edited by E. P. Shafranske. Washington, DC: American Psychological Association, 1996.

Malaguzzi, L., S. Spaggiari, and C. Rinaldi. *The hundred languages of children.* Reggio Emilia, Italy: Department of Education, 1987.

Manos, M. A. "Helicopter parents: Empathetic or pathetic?" *Phi Kappa Phi Forum* 89, no. 3 (2009): 21.

Mark, A. E., and P. D. Boruff-Jones. "Information literacy and student engagement: What the national survey of student engagement reveals about your campus." *College & Research Libraries* 64, no. 6 (2003): 480–493.

Marsick, V., and J. Mezirow. "New work on transformative learning" *Teachers College Record* [online]. 2002, ID no. 10876. http://www.tcrecord.org.

Martin, G. C., and M. F. Seay. "Programming the community education concept." In *Community education: A developing concept,* edited by M. F. Seay and Associates, 189–204. Midland, MI: Pendell, 1974.

Martin, R. J. "Multicultural social reconstructionist education: Design for diversity in teacher education." *Teacher Education Quarterly* 21, no. 3 (1994): 77–89.

Martorella, P. *Teaching social studies in middle and secondary schools.* Englewood Cliffs, NJ: Merrill, 1996.

Math Central. 2001. "Mathematics glossary—middle years." http://mathcentral.uregina.ca/RR/glossary/middle/index.html.

Mathematical Concepts, Inc. 2001. "Math spoken here! An arithmetic and algebraic dictionary." http://www.mathnstuff.com/math/spoken/here/1words/words.htm.

MathVIDS. Video Instructional Development Source. http://www.coedu.usf.edu/main/departments/sped/mathvids/index.html.

Matsuda, M. J., C. R. Lawrence III, R. Delgado, and K. Crenshaw. *Words that wound: Critical race theory, assaultive speech, and the First Amendment.* Boulder, CO: Westview Press, 1993.

Matthew Shepard Foundation. *Our story.* http://www.matthewshepard.org/site/PageServer?pagename=Our_Story_Main_Page.

Mautner, T., ed. *The dictionary of philosophy.* Cambridge, MA: Blackwell Publishers, 1996.

May, W. T., and N. L. Zimpher. "An examination of three theoretical perspectives on supervision: Perceptions of pre-service field supervision." *Journal of Curriculum and Supervision* 1, no. 2 (1986): 83–99.

Mayer, R. E. *Multimedia learning.* New York: Cambridge University Press, 2001.

McAdam, D. *Political process and the development of black insurgency, 1930–1970.* Chicago: University of Chicago Press, 1985.

McAdam, D. "Recruitment to high-risk activism: The case of Freedom Summer." *American Journal of Sociology* 92 (1986): 64–90.

McAlindon, H. R. *Enhancing quality through innovation.* Emeryville, CA: Parlay International, 1993.

McBrien, J. L., and R. S. Brandt. *The language of learning: A guide to education terms.* Alexandria, VA: Association for Supervision and Curriculum Development, 1997.

McCarthy, C. *The Wisconsin idea.* New York: Macmillan, 1912.

McCarthy, T. *Ideals and illusions.* Cambridge, MA: MIT Press, 1991.

McClenaghan, W. A., and F. A. Magruder. *Magruder's American government.* 75th ed. Needham, MA: Prentice Hall, 1992.

McDonald, J., N. Mohr, A. Dichter, and E. McDonald. *The power of protocols: An educator's guide to better practice.* 2d ed. New York: Teachers College Press, 2007.

McGee, C. A. "Intellectual leadership and the influence of African American scholars on multicultural education." *Education Policy* 9, no. 3 (1995): 260–280.

McGrath, E. J. "Area studies." *Journal of Higher Education* 22, no. 5 (1951): 236–242, 283–284.

McKernan, J. "Varieties of curriculum action research: Constraints and typologies in American, British and Irish projects." *Journal of Curriculum Studies* 25, no. 5 (1993): 445–457.

McLaren, P. *Life in schools: An introduction to critical pedagogy in the foundations of education.* 5th ed. New York: Pearson/Allyn and Bacon, 2007.

McLaren, P. L. "On ideology and education: Critical pedagogy and the cultural politics of resistance." In *Critical pedagogy, the state, and cultural struggle,* edited by H. A. Giroux and P. McLaren, 174–204. Albany: State University of New York Press, 1989.

McLaughlin, T. H., and J. M. Halstead. "Education in character and virtue." In *Education in morality,* edited by J. M. Halstead and T. H. McLaughlin, 132–164. London: Routledge, 1999.

McLean, M., D. B. Bailey, and M. Wolery. *Assessing infants and preschoolers with special needs.* Columbus, OH: Prentice Hall, 1996.

McMillan, C.J.B. Review of *Approaches to teaching,* 2d ed., by G. D. Fenstermacher and J. F. Soltis. *Educational Studies* 24, no. 2 (1992): 142–148.

McMillan, D. W., and D. M. Chavis. "Sense of community: A definition and theory." *Journal of Community Psychology* 14 (1986): 6–23.

McNair, R. E. "Working in the mathematical frame: Maximizing the potential to learn from students' mathematics classroom discussions." *Educational Studies in Mathematics* 42, no. 2 (2000): 197–209.

McRobbie, J. "Using portfolios to assess student performance." *Knowledge Brief,* No. 9. San Francisco: WestEd, 1992.

McRobbie, J., J. D. Finn, and P. Harman. "Class size reduction: Lessons learned from experience." *Policy Brief* no. 23. [WestEd]. (August 1998). ED423600. http://www.eric.ed.gov/PDFS/ED423600.pdf.

MegaMath. "Graphs and graph theory." http://wwwc3.lanl.gov/mega-math/gloss/graph/gr.html.

Menand, L. *The future of academic freedom.* Chicago: University of Chicago Press, 1996.

Merrell, K. W., B. A. Gueldner, S. W. Ross, and D. M. Isava. "How effective are school bullying intervention programs? A meta-analysis of intervention research." *School Psychology Quarterly* 23, no. 1 (2008): 26–42.

Merriam, S. B. *Qualitative research and case study applications in education.* San Francisco: Jossey-Bass, 1998.

Merriam, S. B., ed. *An update on adult learning theory.* New Directions for Adult and Continuing Education series No. 57. San Francisco: Jossey-Bass, 1993.

Merriam, S. B., and R. S. Caffarella. *Learning in adulthood: A comprehensive guide.* 2d ed. San Francisco: Jossey-Bass, 1999.

Merriam, S. B., and P. M. Cunningham, eds. *Handbook of adult and continuing education.* San Francisco: Jossey-Bass, 1989.

Merriam-Webster online. http://Merriam-Webster.com.

Merriam-Webster's collegiate dictionary. 10th ed. Springfield, MA: Merriam-Webster, 1993.

Metzler, M. W. *Instructional models for physical education.* 2d ed. Scottsdale, AZ: Holcomb Hathaway, 2005.

Meyer, E. "A feminist reframing of bullying and harassment: Transforming schools through critical pedagogy." *McGill Journal of Education* 43, no. 1 (2008): 33–48.

Mezirow, J. *Transformative dimensions of adult learning.* San Francisco: Jossey-Bass, 1991.

Mezirow, J. D., and Associates. *Fostering critical reflection in adulthood.* San Francisco: Jossey-Bass, 1990.

Mezirow, J. D., and Associates. *Learning as transformation.* San Francisco: Jossey-Bass, 2000.

Mickelson, R. A. "Minorities and education in plural societies." *Anthropology and Education Quarterly* 24, no. 3 (1993): 269–276.

Microsoft Encarta. http://encarta.msn.com.

Mid Atlantic Equity Consortium. http://www.maec.org.

Miller, G. "General education and distance education: Two channels in the mainstream." *Journal of General Education* 50, no. 4 (2001): 314–322.

Miller, G. *Wordnet 1.6.* Cambridge, MA: MIT Press, 1998.

Miller, J. "Domination and subordination." In *Race, class and gender in the United States,* 2d ed., edited by P. S. Rothenberg, 108–116. New York: St. Martin's Press, 1992.

Miller, L. P., and L. A. Tanners. "Diversity and the new immigrants." *Teachers College Record* 96, no. 4 (1995): 671–680.

Miller, M. D., and A. E. Seraphine. "Can test scores remain authentic when teaching to the test?" *Educational Assessment* 1, no. 2 (1993): 119–129.

Miller, M. T., J. W. Murry Jr., and B. Kang. "Sabbatical leave programs as form of faculty development." *Academic Leadership* 4, no. 1 (2007): 1.

Miller, R. "Education after the empire." In *Education and hope in troubled times: Bold visions of change for our children's world,* edited by H. Svi Shapiro, 121–133. New York: Routledge, 2009.

Miller, W. R., and S. Rollnick. *Motivational interviewing: Preparing people to change addictive behavior.* New York: Guilford, 1991.

Minnich, E. K. *Transforming knowledge.* 2d ed. Philadelphia: Temple University Press, 2005.

Mississippi Department of Human Services. "What is a vulnerable adult?" http://www.mdhs.state.ms.us/fcs_aps.html#vulnerable.

Mitchell, B. M., and R. E. Salsbury, eds. *Encyclopedia of multicultural education.* Westport, CT: Greenwood Press, 1999.

Mitchell, W. A. "Federal aid for primary and secondary education." PhD diss., Princeton University, 1948.

Moll, R. *The public Ivys: A guide to America's best state colleges and universities.* New York: Viking, 1985.

Molnar, A. *School commercialism: From democratic ideal to market commodity.* New York: Routledge, 2005.

Montague, W. E., and F. G. Knirk. "Findings matrix: What works in adult training." *International Journal of Educational Research* 19, no. 4 (1993): 345–430.

Montalto, N. *History of the intercultural educational movement, 1924–1941.* New York: Garland, 1982.

The Montessori Foundation. http://www.montessori.org.

Montessori, M. *The Montessori method.* New York: Frederick A. Stokes Company, 1912.

Moodley, K. *Beyond multicultural education: International perspectives.* Calgary, Alberta: Detselig Enterprises, 1992.

Moore, D. "Toward a theory of work-based learning." *Institute for Education and the Economy Brief,* no. 23 (1999).

Moore, K. D., S. Hopkins, and R. Tullis. "NCATE standards: Restructuring teacher education." *Teacher Education Quarterly* 21, no. 2 (1994): 27–36.

Morris, C., ed. *Academic Press dictionary of science and technology.* San Diego: Academic Press, 1992.

Morris, S. C., and F. S. Ludovina. "Responding to undocumented children in the schools." *ERIC Digest.* Charleston, WV: ERIC Clearinghouse on Rural Education and Small Schools (ERIC Document Reproduction Service No. ED433172), 1999.

Morris, W., ed. *The American heritage dictionary.* 2d college ed. Boston: Houghton Mifflin, 1982.

Morris, W., ed. *The American heritage dictionary of the English language.* New York: American Heritage, 1970.

Morris, W., ed. *The American heritage dictionary of the English language.* Boston: Houghton Mifflin, 1981.

Morrison, G. S. *Early childhood education today.* Upper Saddle River, NJ: Prentice Hall, 1998.

Morrison, T. *Playing in the dark: Whiteness and the literary imagination.* Cambridge, MA: Harvard University Press, 1992.

Morse, J., and P. Field. *Qualitative research methods for health professionals.* 2d ed. Thousand Oaks, CA: Sage, 1995.

Mosquin, T., and J. S. Rowe. "A manifesto for Earth." *Biodiversity* 5, no. 1 (2004): 3–9. http://www.ecospherics.net/pages/EarthManifesto.html.

Motteram, G., and G. Forrester. "Becoming an online distance learner: What can be learned from students' experiences of induction to distance programmes?" *Distance Education* 26, no. 3 (2005): 281–298.

Mueller, S. *Upgrading and repairing PC's.* 12th ed. Indianapolis, IN: Que, 2000.

Muller, P. C. *The community teacher: A new framework for effective urban teaching.* New York: Teachers College Press, 2001.

Murphy, K. R., and C. O. Davidshofer. *Psychological testing: Principles and applications.* 4th ed. Englewood Cliffs, NJ: Prentice Hall, 1998.

Nabakov, P., ed. *Native American testimony: A chronicle of Indian-White relations from prophecy to the present, 1492–1992.* New York: Penguin, 1992.

Naglieri, J. A., and J. P. Das. "The PASS cognitive processing theory." In *Handbook on testing,* edited by R. F. Dillon, 138–163. Westport, CT: Greenwood, 1997.

National Academic Advising Association (NACADA). "Concept of academic advising." http://www.nacada.ksu.edu/Clearinghouse/AdvisingIssues/Concept-advising-introduction.htm.

National Association for Sport and Physical Education. *Moving into the future: National physical education standards: A guide to content and assessment.* St. Louis: Mosby, 1995.

National Association of Cognitive Behavioral Therapists Online Headquarters. http://www.nacbt.org/.

National Association of Independent Schools. http://www.nais.org.

National Board for Professional Teaching Standards. http://www.nbpts.org.

National Board for Professional Teaching Standards. "National Board certification for teacher leaders." http://www.nbpts.org/products_and_services/national_board_certifica1.

National Board for Professional Teaching Standards. *Take one! transforms a school into a professional learning community.* Arlington, VA: National Board for Professional Teaching Standards, 2009.

National Center for Learning Disabilities. http://www.ncld.org/.

National Clearinghouse on Child Abuse and Neglect. 2002. "Child abuse and neglect state statutes elements. What is child maltreatment?" http://www.calib.com/nccanch/pubs/factsheets/childmal.cfm.

National Clearinghouse on Child Abuse and Neglect. "Defining child maltreatment." http://www.calib.com/nccanch/pubs/usermanuals/basic/section2.cfm.

National Commission on Teaching and America's Future. http://www.nctaf.org/.

National Council for Accreditation of Teacher Education (NCATE). http://www.ncate.org.

National Council for Accreditation of Teacher Education. "About NCATE." http://www.ncate.org/public/aboutNCATE.asp.

National Council for Accreditation of Teacher Education. "NCATE at 50: Continuous growth, renewal, and reform." http://www.ncate.org/documents/15YearsofGrowth.pdf.

National Council for the Social Studies (NCSS). *Expectations of excellence: Curriculum standards for the social studies,* Bulletin 89. Washington, DC: National Council for the Social Studies, 1994.

National Council of Teachers of Mathematics. *Principals and standards for school mathematics.* Reston, VA: National Council of Teachers of Mathematics, 2000.

National Education Association. Issues and Action. "The truth about tenure in higher education." http://www.nea.org/he/tenure.html.

National Education Association. Issues and Action. "Vouchers." http://www.nea.org/home/16378.htm.

National Education Association. Issues and Action. "Welcome to the National Education Association." http://www.nea.org.

National Institute for Literacy. "Work readiness credentials." http://www.nifl.gov/lincs/discussions/workplace/07work_ready.html.

National Institute of Health. *Measuring and improving costs, cost-effectiveness, and cost-benefit.* Publication no. 99–4518, August 1999. http://www.nida.nih.gov/IMPCOST/IMPCOSTIndex.html.

National Institute on Alcohol Abuse and Alcoholism. http://www.niaaa.nih.gov/.

National School Reform Faculty (NSRF). "National school reform faculty: Harmony Education Center." http://www.nsrfharmony.org.

National Staff Development Council (NSDC). http://www.nsdc.org.

National Work Readiness Council. "National work readiness credential." http://www.workreadiness.com.

Neilsen, W. A., ed. *Webster's new international dictionary of the English language.* 2d ed. unabridged. Springfield, MA: G. & C. Merriam Company, 1934.

Nelson, R. O., and D. H. Barlow. "Behavioral assessment: Basic strategies and initial procedures." In *Behavioral assessment of adult disorders,* edited by D. H. Barlow, 13–43. New York: Guilford Press, 1981.

Newmann, F. M., T. A. Bertocci, and R. M. Landsness. "History's role in civic education: The precondition for political intelligence." In *Educating the democratic mind,* edited by W. C. Parker, 241–262. Albany: State University of New York Press, 1996.

Nicodemi, O., M. A. Sutherland, and G. W. Towsley. *An introduction to abstract algebra with notes to the future teacher.* Upper Saddle River, NJ: Pearson Education, 2007.

Nieto, S. *Affirming diversity: The sociopolitical context of multicultural education.* 3d ed. New York: Longman, 2000.

Nieto, S. *The light in their eyes: Creating multicultural learning communities.* New York: Teachers College Press, 1999.

Nietz, J. *Old text books.* Pittsburgh, PA: University of Pittsburgh Press, 1961.

Ninio, A., and C. Snow. *Pragmatic development.* Boulder, CO: Westview Press, 1996.

Niss, M. "Assessment in geometry." In *Perspectives on the teaching of geometry for the 21st century,* edited by C. Mammana and V. Villani, 263–274. Boston: Kluwer, 1998.

Niss, M. "Dimensions of geometry and assessment." In *Perspectives on the teaching of geometry for the 21st century,* edited by C. Mammana and V. Villani, 263–274. Boston: Kluwer, 1998.

No Child Left Behind. http://www.nclb.gov/.

Noddings, N. *Caring, a feminine approach to ethics and moral education.* Berkeley: University of California Press, 1984.

Noddings, N. "For all its children." *Educational Theory* 43, no. 1 (1993): 15–22.

Noffke, S. E. "The work and workplace of teachers in action research." *Teaching and Teacher Education* 8, no. 1 (1992): 15–29.

Noguera, P. "Latino youth: Immigration, education and the future." *In Motion Magazine,* March 5, 2006. http://www.inmotionmagazine.com/er/pn_lyief.html.

Nord, W. A. *Religion and American education: Rethinking a national dilemma.* Chapel Hill: University of North Carolina Press, 1995.

North Central Regional Educational Laboratory (NCREL). "NCREL's policy briefs: Decentralization: Why, how, and toward what ends?" 1993. http://www.ncrel.org/sdrs/areas/issues/envrnmnt/go/93–1site.htm.

North Central Regional Educational Laboratory (NCREL). *Pathways to school improvement.* http://www.ncrel.org.

Norton, A. *The QPB dictionary of ideas.* New York: Quality Paperback Book Club, 1996.

Nussbaum, M. C. *Cultivating humanity: A classical defense of reform in liberal education.* Cambridge, MA: Harvard University Press, 1997.

Odden, A. R. *Critical issue: Transferring decision-making to local schools: Site-based management.* North Central Regional Educational Laboratory, 1995. http://www.ncrel.org/sdrs/areas/issues/envrnmnt/go./go100.htm.

ODLIS: Online dictionary of library and information science. http://lu.com/odlis/.

Office of Research, Office of Educational Research and Improvement (OERI), U.S. Department of Education. Education Consumer Guide. "Mentoring." http://www.ed.gov/pubs/OR/ConsumerGuides/mentor.html.

Ogbu, J. "The individual in collective adaptation: A framework for focusing on academic underperformance and dropping out among involuntary minorities." In *Dropouts from school: Issues, dilemmas, and solutions,* edited by L. Weis, E. Farrar, and H. Petrie, 181–204. Albany: State University of New York Press, 1989.

Ogbu, J. "Variability in minority school performance: A problem in search of an explanation." *Anthropology and Education Quarterly* 18, no. 4 (1987): 312–334.

Ogle, D. M. "K-W-L: A teaching model that develops active reading of expository text." *Reading Teacher* 39 (1986): 564–570.

O'Grady, W., and M. Dobrovolsky. *Contemporary linguistic analysis: An introduction.* Toronto: Copp Clark, 1996.

O'Grady, W., M. Dobrovolsky, and M. Aronoff. *Contemporary linguistics: An introduction.* 2d ed. New York: St. Martin's Press, 1993.

Oliver, D. W., and J. P. Shaver. "Using a jurisprudential framework in the teaching of public issues." In *Educating the democratic mind,* edited by W. C. Parker, 145–170. Albany: State University of New York Press, 1996.

Olson, D. H., and C. D. Claiborn. "Interpretation and arousal in the counseling influence process." *Journal of Counseling Psychology* 37 (1990): 131–137.

Olson, L. "Tugging at tradition." *Education Week* 18 (1999): 25.

Oppenheim, Charles. "Electronic scholarly publishing and open access." *Journal of Information Science* 34, no. 4 (2008): 577–590.

Organisation for Economic Co-operation and Development (OECD). *OECD Glossary of Statistical Terms.* "Discussion Forum." http://stats.oecd.org/glossary/detail.asp?ID=6715.

Ormrod, J. *Human learning.* 3d ed. Upper Saddle River, NJ: Merrill, 1999.

Orr, M., and D. Bragg. "Policy directions for K-14 education: Looking to the future." In *Educational policy in the 21st Century,* vol. 2, *Community colleges: Policy in the future context,* edited by B. Townsend and S. Twombly, 101–127. Westport, CT: Ablex, 2001.

Osin, L., P. Nesher, and J. Ram. "Do the rich become richer and the poor poorer? A longitudinal analysis of pupil achievement and progress in elementary schools using computer-assisted instruction." *International Journal of Educational Research* 21, no. 1 (1994): 53–64.

Ovando, C., and V. Collier. *Bilingual and ESL classrooms: Teaching in multicultural contexts.* 2d ed. Boston: McGraw-Hill, 1998.

Overton, W. "Developmental psychology: Philosophy, concepts, and methodology." In *Theoretical models of human development,* edited by R. Lerner, chap. 3. Vol. 1 of *Handbook of child psychology,* edited by W. Damon. New York: John Wiley & Sons, 1998.

Owens, R. G. *Organizational behavior in education*. Boston: Allyn & Bacon, 1995.

Packard, T. "TQM and organizational change and development." In *Total Quality Management in the social services: Theory and practice,* edited by B. Gummer and P. McCallion, 209–228. Albany, NY: Professional Development Program of Rockefeller College, 1995.

Page, G., and J. Thomas. *International dictionary of education*. London: Kogan Page, 1997.

Paige, R., N. S. Rees, M. J. Petrilli, and P. Gore. *Alternative routes to teacher education*. Washington, DC: U.S. Department of Education, 2004. http://www2.ed.gov/admins/tchrqual/recruit/altroutes/report.pdf.

Parents, Families and Friends of Lesbians and Gays. "PFLAG's history." http://community.pflag.org/Page.aspx?pid=267.

Paris, S., M. Y. Lipson, and K. K. Wixson. "Becoming a strategic reader." In *Theoretical models and processes of reading,* 4th ed., edited by R. B. Ruddell, M. R. Ruddell, and H. Singer, chap. 37. Newark, DE: International Reading Association, 1994.

Parker, J. G., and S. R. Asher. "Peer relations and later personal adjustment: Are low-accepted children at risk?" *Psychological Bulletin* 102 (1987): 357–389.

Parker, S., ed. *McGraw-Hill dictionary of mathematics*. New York: McGraw-Hill, 1997.

Parker, S., ed. *McGraw-Hill dictionary of scientific and technical terms*. 5th ed. New York: McGraw-Hill, 1994.

Parker, W. *Social studies in elementary education.*11th ed. Upper Saddle River, NJ: Merrill, 2001.

Parnell, D. *The neglected majority*. Washington, DC: American Association of Community Colleges, 1985.

Parsons, C. J., and S. J. Hughes. *Written communication for business students*. 2d ed. London: Edward Arnold, 1975.

Parsons, J. J., and D. Oja. *Computer concepts*. 4th ed. Cambridge, MA: Course Technology, 2000.

Pascoe, C. J. *Dude, you're a fag: Masculinity and sexuality in high school*. Berkeley: University of California Press, 2007.

Patton, M. Q. *Qualitative research and evaluation methods*. 2d ed. Newbury Park, CA: Sage, 1990.

Pearson, A. T. "The competency concept." *Educational Studies* 11, no. 1 (1980): 145–152.

Pedersen, P. B. "Culture-centered ethical guidelines for counselors." In *Handbook of multicultural counseling,* edited by J. G. Ponterotto, J. M. Casas, L. A. Suzuki, and C. M. Alexander, 33–49. Thousand Oaks, CA: Sage, 1995.

"Pell grants at a glance." *Chronicle of Higher Education* 37, no. 33 (1991): A22.

Pennsylvania Department of Education. *Teacher certification system*. https://www.tcs.ed.state.pa.us/.

Pentony, D., R. Smith, and R. Axen. *Unfinished rebellions*. San Francisco: Jossey-Bass, 1971.

Pepitone, J. S. *Future training*. Dallas, TX: AddVantage Learning Press, 1995.

Perkins, D., E. Jay, and S. Tishman. "New conceptions of thinking: From ontology to education." *Educational Psychologist* 28, no. 1 (1993): 67–85.

Perkinson, H. J. *Teachers without goals/students without purposes*. New York: McGraw-Hill, 1993.

Petersen, A. C., N. Leffert, and K. Hurrelmann. "Adolescence and schooling in Germany and the United States: A comparison of peer socialization to adulthood." *Teachers College Record* 94, no. 3 (1993): 611–628.

Peterson, E. A., ed. *Freedom road: Adult education of African Americans*. Melbourne, FL: Krieger, 1996.

Peterson, K. D., N. Benson, A. Driscoll, R. Narode, D. Sherman, and C. Tama. "Preservice teacher education using flexible, thematic cohorts." *Teacher Education Quarterly* 22, no. 2 (1995): 29–42.

Petrocelli, J. V. "Processes and stages of change: Counseling with the transtheoretical model of change." *Journal of Counseling & Development* 80 (2002): 22–30.

Pfaffenberger, Bryan. *Webster's new world dictionary of computer terms*. New York: Que, 1999.

Phelps-Stokes Fund. "Celebrating our 90th year." http://www.psfdc.org/.

Philips, S. U. "Colonial and postcolonial circumstances in the education of Pacific peoples." *Anthropology and Education Quarterly* 23, no. 1 (1992): 73–78.

Phillippe, K., and M. Valiga. *Faces of the future: A portrait of American community college students*. Washington, DC: American Association of Community Colleges, 2000.

Pickett, J. P. *The American Heritage dictionary of the English language*. 4th ed. Boston: Houghton Mifflin, 2000.

Pickreign, J. *Sequential nature of geometric thought*. 2001. http://www.ric.edu/jpick/mathed_topics/geometry/geometry.html.

Piper, M. K., and R. W. Houston. "The search for teacher competence: CBTE and MCT." *Journal of Teacher Education* 31, no. 5 (1980): 37–40.

Planned Parenthood. "Sexual orientation and gender." http://www.plannedparenthood.org/health-topics/sexual-orientation-gender-4329.htm.

Platt, P. "Grapho-linguistics: Children's drawings in relation to reading and writing skills." *The Reading Teacher* 31, no. 3 (1977): 262–268.

Polya, G. *How to solve it: A new aspect of mathematical method*. 2d ed. Princeton, NJ: Princeton University Press, 1973.

Portes, A. *The new second generation*. New York: Russell Sage Foundation, 1996.

Poster, C. D., S. Blandford, and J. M. Welton. *Restructuring: The key to effective school management*. New York: Routledge, 1999.

Potter, R. E. *Tuition fees and pauper schools* (ERIC Document Reproduction Service No. ED133011), 1975.

Powell, A. B., and M. Frankenstein, eds. *Ethnomathematics: Challenging eurocentrism in mathematics education*. Albany: State University of New York Press, 1997.

Powell, A. G., E. Farrar, and D. K. Cohen. *Shopping mall high school: Winners and losers in the educational marketplace*. Boston: Houghton Mifflin, 1985.

Powers, M. K. "Area studies." *Journal of Higher Education* 26, no. 2 (1955): 82–89, 113.

The Prentice-Hall encyclopedia of mathematics. Englewood Cliffs, N.J.: Prentice-Hall, 1982.

Principles and standards for school mathematics. Reston, VA: National Council of Teachers of Mathematics, 2000.

Prochaska, J. O., and J. C. Norcross. *Systems of psychotherapy: A transtheoretical analysis*. 3d ed. Pacific Grove, CA: Brooks/Cole, 1994.

Program for the Study of Women and Gender: Queer Studies. Smith College. http://www.smith.edu/swg/queerstudies.html.

Project Approach in Early Childhood and Elementary Education. http://www.project-approach.com/definition.htm.

Project Management Enterprises, Inc. *Adult literacy thesaurus: Alphabetical format*. Bethesda, MD: Project Management Enterprises, 1997.

Prosser, D. "Institutional repositories and open access: The future of scholarly communication." *Information Services & Use* 23, no. 2/3 (2003): 167–170.

"Provisions of the Arizona Career Ladder Law, Article 1.1: Career Ladder and other performance incentive programs, S.B. 1521–1990 (Chapter 319)." http://www.ade.az.gov/asd/CareerLadder/Provisions_of_CL_Law_and_Code.pdf.

The Public Sector Network News, Fall 1994: 11–12. "TQM—The most-asked questions." http://deming.eng.clemson.edu/pub/ tqmbbs/prin-pract/questns.txt.

Pugach, M. C., and C. L. Wesson. "Teachers' and students' views of team teaching of general education and learning-disabled students in two fifth-grade classes." *Elementary School Journal* 95, no. 3 (1995): 279–295.

Purves, A. C., ed. *Encyclopedia of English studies and language arts,* vol. 1. New York: Scholastic, 1994.

Purves, A. C. "Setting standards in the language arts and literature classroom and the implications for portfolio assessment." *Educational Assessment* 1, no. 3 (1993): 175–199.

Queer Theory.com. "Academic programs in lesbian, gay, bisexual, transgender and queer studies." http://www.queertheory.com/academics/syllabi/lgbt_programs.htm.

Quigley, B. A. *Rethinking literacy education: The critical need for practice-based change.* San Francisco: Jossey-Bass, 1997.

Radin, P. *The method and theory of ethnology: An essay in criticism.* New York: Basic Books, 1965.

Rainer, R. K., and E. Turban. *Introduction to information systems: Supporting and transforming business.* 2d ed. New York: John Wiley & Sons, 2008.

Random House Webster's college dictionary. New York: Random House, 1991.

"Reader-Response Criticism." http://www.cnr.edu/home/bmcmanus/readercrit.html.

Reber, A. S. *Penguin dictionary of psychology.* New York: Penguin Books, 1985.

Reber, A. S. *Penguin dictionary of psychology.* 2d ed. New York: Penguin Books, 1995.

Reese, W. J. *The origins of the American high school.* New Haven, CT: Yale University Press, 1955.

Reichstetter, R. "Defining a professional learning community: A literature review." *E&R Report* No. 06.05 (2006). http://www.wcpss.net/evaluation-research/reports/2006/0605plc_lit_review.pdf.

Reid, W. A. "Curriculum, community, and liberal education: A response to the Practical 4." *Curriculum Inquiry* 14, no. 1 (1984): 103–111.

Reis, Beth. *Eleven overlapping complex aspects of sexuality.* Seattle: Safe Schools Coalition, 2004. http://www.safeschoolscoalition.org/ElevenAspectsofSexuality.pdf.

Responsible Education About Life (REAL) Act. Washington, DC: Advocates for Youth, 2009. http://www.advocatesforyouth.org/storage/advfy/documents/fsreal.pdf.

Reutter, E. E. *The law of public education.* 3d ed. Mineola, NY: The Foundation Press, 1985.

Reynolds, A. L. "Challenges and strategies for teaching multicultural counseling courses." In *Handbook of multicultural counseling,* edited by J. G. Ponterotto, J. M. Casas, L. A. Suzuki, and C. M. Alexander, 312–330. Thousand Oaks, CA: Sage, 1995.

Reynolds, C. R., and E. Fletcher-Janzen, eds. *Encyclopedia of special education: A reference for the education of children, adolescents, and adults with disabilities and other exceptional individuals.* 3d ed. Hoboken, NJ: Wiley, 2007.

Rhodes, F. *The creation of the future: The role of the American university.* Ithaca, NY: Cornell University Press, 2001.

Richards, H. V., A. F. Brown, and T. B. Forde. *Addressing diversity in schools: Culturally responsive pedagogy.* (Practitioner brief of the National Center for Culturally Responsive Educational Systems). Tempe, AZ: NCREST, 2006.

Richards, J. C., J. Platt, and H. Platt. *Longman dictionary of language teaching & applied linguistics.* Harlow, UK: Longman, 1992.

Rickard, C. E., and M. A. Harding. "Strategic planning: A defined vision to facilitate institutional change." *College and University* 5, no. 3 (2000): 3–6.

Rieber, R. W., and A. S. Carton, eds. *The collected works of L. S. Vygotsky,* vol. 1, *Problems of general psychology.* New York: Plenum Press, 1987.

Riggs, R. O., and others. "Sexual harassment in higher education from conflict to community." *ERIC Digest.* Washington, DC: ERIC Clearinghouse on Higher Education (ERIC Documentation Reproduction Service No. ED 364124), 1993.

Rink, J. E. *Designing the physical education curriculum: Promoting active lifestyles.* New York: McGraw Hill, 2009.

Rink, J. E. *Teaching physical education for learning.* Boston: McGraw-Hill, 2002.

Rink, J. E. *Teaching physical education for learning.* 6thed. New York: McGraw Hill, 2010.

Rist, R. C. "Race, policy, and schooling." *Society* 12, no. 1 (1974): 59–63.

Roames, R. L. "A history of the development of standards for accrediting teacher education." *Action in Teacher Education* 9, no. 3 (1987): 91–101.

Robertson, I. *Society: A brief introduction.* New York: Worth Publishing, 1989.

Robinson, K. H. "Reinforcing hegemonic masculinities through sexual harassment: Issues of identity, power and popularity in secondary schools." *Gender and Education* 17, no. 1 (2005): 19–37.

Robinson, V. "Dialogue needs a point and purpose." *Educational Theory* 45, no. 2 (1995): 235–249.

Roget's 21st century thesaurus. Nashville, TN: T. Nelson, 1992.

Roopnarine, J. L., and J. E. Johnson, eds. *Approaches to early childhood education.* Upper Saddle River, N.J.: Prentice Hall, 2000.

Rosales, F. A. *Chicano! The history of the Mexican-American Civil Rights Movement.* 2d rev. ed. Houston, TX: Arte Publico Press, 1997.

Ross, E. W. *The social studies curriculum: Purposes, problems, and possibilities.* Albany: State University of New York Press, 1997.

Ross, J., and E. Regan. "Sharing professional experience: Its impact on professional development." *Teaching and Teacher Education* 9, no. 1 (1993): 91–106.

Rossman, G., and S. Rallis. *Learning in the field: An introduction to qualitative research.* Thousand Oaks, CA: Sage, 1998.

Roth, R. "Standards for certification, licensure, and accreditation." In *Handbook of research on teacher education,* edited by J. P. Sikula, T. J. Buttery, and E. Guyton, 242–278. New York: Macmillan Library Reference, 1996.

Roth, W., and G. M. Bowen. "Knowing and interacting: A study of culture, practices, and resources in a grade 8 open-inquiry science classroom guided by a cognitive apprenticeship metaphor." *Cognition and Instruction* 13, no. 1 (1995): 73–128.

Rothenberg, P. *Race, class, & gender in the United States.* 2d ed. New York: St. Martin's Press, 1992.

Roughgarden, J. *Evolution's rainbow: Diversity, gender and sexuality.* Berkeley: University of California Press, 2004.

Rourke, B., and K. Tsatsanis. "Syndrome of nonverbal learning disabilities: Psycholinguistic assets and deficits." *Topics in Language Disorders* 16, no. 2 (1996): 30–44.

Ruder, R. "Leadership styles of restructuring." *Schools in the Middle* 8, no. 7 (1999): 6–8.

Rugg, H., and L. Krueger. *Man and his changing society.* Boston: Ginn, 1936–1938.

Ruth, S., ed. *Issues in feminism.* 3d ed. Mountain View, CA: Mayfield, 1995.

Ryle, G. *The concept of mind.* London: Hutchinson and Co., 1949.

Ryndak, D. L., L. Jackson, and F. Billingsley. "Defining school inclusion for students with moderate to severe disabilities: What do experts say?" *Exceptionality* 8, no. 2 (2000): 101–116.

Saeman, H., and J. Thomas, eds. "It's a new world where 'multiculturalism' speaks volumes." *The National Psychologist* 10 (2000). http://nationalpsychologist.com/articles/art_v10n3_3.htm.

Said, E. *Orientalism*. New York: Pantheon Books, 1978.

Sale, K. *SDS*. New York: Random House, 1973.

Salzman, Jack, ed. *Encyclopedia of African-American culture and history*. New York: Macmillan Library Reference, 1995.

"The San Francisco College state strike." http://www.library.sfsu.edu/strike/.

Sapon-Shevin, M. "To touch and be touched: The missing discourse of bodies in education." In *Education and hope in troubled times: Bold visions of change for our children's world*, edited by H. Svi Shapiro, 168–183. New York: Routledge, 2009.

Sarason, S. B. *Psychological sense of community: Prospects for a community psychology*. San Francisco: Jossey-Bass, 1974.

The Saskatchewan Teacher's Federation. "Research and issues in education." http://www.stf.sk.ca/.

Sattler, J. M. *Assessment of children*. Rev. and updated 3d ed. San Diego, CA: Jerome M. Sattler, 1992.

Schank, R. C. "Goal based scenarios: A radical look at education." *Journal of the Learning Sciences* 3, no. 4 (1993/1994): 429–453.

Schank, R. C., A. Fano, B. Bell, and M. Jona. "The design of goal-based scenarios." *Journal of the Learning Sciences* 3, no. 4 (1993/1994): 305–345.

Schickedanz, J. A. *More than the ABCs: The early stages of reading and writing*. Washington, DC: National Association for the Education of Young Children, 1986.

Schön, D. A. *The reflective practitioner: How professionals think in action*. New York: Basic Books, 1983.

Schubert, W. H. *Curriculum: Perspective, paradigm, and possibility*. New York: Macmillan, 1986.

Schwab, J. J. "Education and the state: Learning community." In *The great ideas today*, edited by R. M. Hutchins and M. J. Adler, 234–271. Chicago: Encyclopedia Britannica, 1976.

Schwandt, T. A. *Dictionary of qualitative inquiry*. 2d ed. Thousand Oaks, CA: Sage, 2001.

Schwandt, T. A. *Qualitative inquiry: A dictionary of terms*. Thousand Oaks, CA: Sage, 1997.

ScienceDaily. "Mathematical model." http://www.sciencedaily.com/articles/m/mathematical_model.htm.

Science Policy Research Division, Congressional Research Service, Library of Congress. 1975. *The National Science Foundation and precollege science education: 1950–1975*. Report prepared for the Subcommittee on Science, Research, and Technology of the Committee on Science and Technology, U.S. House of Representatives. 94th Cong., 2d sess., 1976.

Scott, M., A. Scherman, and H. Phillips. "Helping individuals with dyslexia succeed in adulthood: Emerging keys for effective parenting, education, and development of positive self concept." *Journal of Instructional Psychology* 19, no. 3 (1992): 197–204.

Sears, J. T., ed. *Youth, education, and sexualities: An international encyclopedia*. Westport, CT: Greenwood, 2005.

Seay, M. F. "The community education concept—A definition." In *Community education: A developing concept,* edited by M. F. Seay and Associates, 3–15. Midland, MI: Pendell, 1974.

Seigfried, C. *Pragmatism and feminism: Reweaving the social fabric*. Chicago: University of Chicago Press, 1996.

Seligman, M., and M. Csikszentmihalyi. "Positive psychology: An introduction." *American Psychologist* 55 (2000): 5–14.

Seller, M. S. *Women educators in the United States, 1820–1993: A bio-bibliographical sourcebook*. Westport, CT: Greenwood Press, 1994.

Semmes, C. E. *Cultural hegemony and African American development*. Westport, CT: Praeger, 1992.

Serow, R. C. "Education and the service ethic." *Educational Foundations* 5, no. 4 (1991): 69–86.

Sexuality Information and Education Council of the United States. http://www.siecus.org.

Shafritz, J. M., R. P. Koeppe, and E. W. Soper, eds. *The Facts on File dictionary of education*. New York: Facts on File Publications, 1988.

Shapiro, S. B. "The body: The site of common humanity." In *Body Movements: Pedagogy, politics, and social change*, edited by H. S. Shapiro and S. B. Shapiro, 337–352. Cresskill, NJ: Hampton Press, 2002.

Shapiro, S. B., and H. S. Shapiro. "Silent voices, bodies of knowledge: Towards a critical pedagogy of the body." In *Body movements: Pedagogy, politics and social change*, edited by H. S. Shapiro and S. B. Shapiro, 25–44. Cresskill, NJ: Hampton Press, 2002.

Shaughnessy, J. M. "Research on statistics learning and reasoning." In *Second handbook of research on mathematics teaching and learning*, edited by F. Lester, 957–1009. Reston, VA: National Council of Teachers of Mathematics, 2007.

Sherman Swing, E. "Humanism in multicultureland: A comparative looking glass." *Educational Foundations* 9, no. 1 (1995): 73–94.

Shkedi, A., and G. Horenczyk. "The role of teacher ideology in the teaching of culturally valued texts." *Teaching and Teacher Education* 11, no. 2 (1995): 107–117.

Shor, I. *Empowering education: Critical teaching for social change*. Chicago: University of Chicago Press, 1992.

Shreeves, S. L., and M. H. Cragin. "Introduction: Institutional repositories: Current state and future." *Library Trends* 57, no. 2 (2008): 89–97.

Shulman, L. S. "Knowledge and teaching: Foundations of the new reform." *Harvard Educational Review* 57, no. 1 (1987): 1–22.

Shulman, L. S. "Pedagogies of uncertainty." *Liberal Education* 91, no. 2 (2005): 18–25.

Shulman, L. S. "Those who understand: Knowledge growth in teaching." *Educational Researcher* 15, no. 2 (1986): 4–14.

Shulman, L. S., C. M. Golde, A. C. Bueschel, and K. J. Garabedian. "Reclaiming education's doctorates: A critique and a proposal." *Educational Researcher* 35, no. 3 (2006): 25–32.

Siedentop, D. *Introduction to physical education, fitness, and sport*. Mountain View, CA: Mayfield, 1992.

Siedentop, D., P. A. Hastie, and H. van der Mars. *Complete guide to sport education*. Champaign, IL: Human Kinetics, 2004.

Siedentop, D., and D. Tannehill. *Developing teaching skills in physical education*. Mountain View, CA: Mayfield, 2000.

Siegelman, C. K. *Life-span human development*. Pacific Grove, CA: Brooks/Cole, 1999.

Simon, M. A. "Prospective elementary teachers' knowledge of division." *Journal of Research in Mathematics Education* 24, no. 3 (1993): 233–254.

Simpson, J. A., and E.S.C. Weiner. *The Oxford English dictionary*. 2d ed. New York: Oxford University Press, 1989.

Skemp, R. R. "Relational understanding and instrumental understanding." *Mathematics Teaching* 77 (December 1976): 20–26.

Skemp, R. R. "Relational understanding and instrumental understanding." *Arithmetic Teacher* 26, no. 3 (1978): 9–15.

Skinner, B. F. *The behavior of organisms: An experimental analysis.* New York: Appleton-Century, 1938.

Sleeter, C., ed. *Empowerment through multicultural education.* Albany: State University of New York Press, 1991.

Sleeter, C. E., and C. A. Grant. *Making choices for multicultural education: Five approaches to race, class, and gender.* Columbus, OH: Merrill, 1988.

Sleeter, C. E., and C. A. Grant. *Making choices for multicultural education: Five approaches to race, class, and gender.* 3d ed. New York: Wiley, 1999.

SmartBiz. http://www.smartbiz.com/sbs/arts/exe92.htm.

Smith, C. L., E. G. Payne, and G. M. Thornton. *Standards and guidelines for work-based learning programs in Georgia.* Atlanta: Georgia Department of Education, 2001.

Smith, D. D. *Introduction to special education: Teaching in an age of opportunity.* Needham Heights, MA: Allyn & Bacon, 2001.

Smith, R., D. Pentony, and R. Axen. *By any means necessary.* San Francisco: Jossey-Bass, 1970.

"SNCC 1960–1966: Six years of the Student Nonviolent Coordinating Committee." http://www.ibiblio.org/sncc/.

Snow, C. E., M. S. Burns, and P. Griffin, eds. *Preventing reading difficulties in young children.* Washington, DC: National Academy Press, 1998.

Socialstudies.com. http://www.socialstudies.org.

"Some cultural forces driving literary modernism." http://www.brocku.ca/english/courses/2F55/forces.html.

Southwest Educational Development Library (SEDL). "Advancing research and improving education." http://www.sedl.org.

Spafford, C. S., A. J. Pesche, and G. S. Grosser. *The cyclopedic education dictionary.* Albany, NY: Delmar Publishers, 1998.

Sparks, D. "A paradigm shift in staff development." *Journal of Staff Development* 15, no. 4 (1994): 26-29.

Spradley, J., and D. McCurdy. *Conformity and conflict: Readings in cultural anthropology.* 8th ed. Boston: Little, Brown, 1997.

Spring, J. *The American school, 1642–2000.* 5th ed. New York: McGraw-Hill, 2001.

Spring, J. *Deculturalization and the struggle for equality: A brief history of the education of the dominated cultures in the U.S.* Boston: McGraw-Hill, 2004.

Squires, D. A. *Aligning and balancing the standards-based curriculum.* Thousand Oaks, CA: Corwin Press, 2005.

Stablein, J. E., D. S. Willey, and C. W. Thompson. "An evaluation of the Davis-Eells (Culture-Fair) Test using Spanish and Anglo-American children." *Journal of Educational Sociology* 35, no. 2 (1961): 73–78.

Stanley, W. B. "Social reconstructionism for today's social education." *Social Education* 45, no. 5 (1985): 384–389.

State University of New York at Buffalo, 1993. "MED 604 course description." http://www.buffalostate.edu//Grad/med604.html.

Steady, F. C. *The black woman cross-culturally.* Rochester, NY: Schenkman Books, 1990.

Stedman, T. L. *Stedman's medical dictionary.* 26th ed. Baltimore, MD: Williams & Wilkins, 1995.

Steffe, L., and T. Kieren. "Radical constructivism and mathematics education." *Journal for Research in Mathematics Education* 25, no. 6 (1994): 711–733.

Steffe, L., and P. W. Thompson. "Teaching experiment methodology: Underlying principles and essential elements." In *Research design in mathematics and science education*, edited by R. Lesh and A. E. Kelly, 267–307. Hillsdale, NJ: Erlbaum, 2000.

Steffe, L., E. von Glasersfeld, J. Richards, and P. Cobb. *Children's counting types: Philosophy, theory and application.* New York: Praeger Scientific, 1983.

Stephen Downes, Stephen's Web. "Beyond management: Personal learning environment." http://www.downes.ca/presentation/225.

Stooper, E. *The Student Nonviolent Coordinating Committee: The growth of radicalism in a civil rights organization.* Brooklyn, NY: Carson, 1989.

Strong, S., and C. D. Claiborn. *Change through interaction: Social psychological processes of counseling and psychotherapy.* New York: Wiley, 1982.

Sullivan, N. *A critical introduction to queer theory.* New York: New York University Press, 2003.

Suttle, B. B. Review of *The rehabilitation of virtue: Foundations of moral education*, by R. T. Sandin. *Educational Studies* 25, no. 1 (1994): 39–42.

Sykes, G. "Teacher education and the predicament of reform." *Against mediocrity: The humanities in America's high schools*, edited by C. E. Finn, D. Ravitch, and R. T. Fancher, 172–194. New York: Holmes and Meier, 1984.

Szasz, M. C. *Education and the American Indian: The road to self-determination since 1928.* Albuquerque: University of New Mexico Press, 1999.

Tabachnich, B. R., and K. Zeichner, eds. *Issues and practices in inquiry-oriented teacher education.* London: Falmer Press, 1991.

Tabachnich, B. R., and K. Zeichner. "Preparing teachers for cultural diversity." *Journal of Education for Teaching: International Research and Pedagogy* 19 (1993): 4–5, 113–124.

Taylor, E. "The theory and practice of transformative learning: A critical review." *Information Series No. 374.* Columbus, OH: ERIC Clearinghouse on Adult, Career, and Vocational Education, Ohio State University (ERIC Document Reproduction Service No. ED423422), 1998.

Taylor, J. M., C. Gilligan, and A. M. Sullivan. *Between voice and silence.* Cambridge, MA: Harvard University Press, 1995.

Teach for America. "About us." http://www.teachforamerica.org/about/index.htm.

The teacher as change agent. M.A. Degree in Curriculum Instruction: SDSU Chula Vista Elementary School District. http://edweb.sdsu.edu/STE/grad/mathprog.html.

Teachers of English to Speakers of Other Languages (TESOL). http://www.tesol.org.

Teachers Support Network. "TeacherTools and advice: F.A.Q.'s attaining your teaching certificate." http://www.teacherssupportnetwork.com/corporate/TeacherTools AdviceArticle.do?id=16.

TechTerms.com. "Blog." *The Tech Terms computer dictionary.* http://www.techterms.com/definition/blog.

TechTerms.com. "Wiki." *The Tech Terms computer dictionary.* http://www.techterms.com/definition/wiki.

"Tenure." In *The concise Columbia electronic encyclopedia.* 3d ed. New York: Columbia University Press, 1994. http://www.encyclopedia.com/searchpool.asp?target@ DOCTITLE%20tenure.

Tiedt, P., and I. Tiedt. *Multicultural teaching: A handbook of activities, information, and resources.* 5th ed. Boston: Allyn & Bacon, 1999.

Title IX Education Amendments of 1972. http://www.dol.gov/dol/oasam/public/regs/statutes/titleix.htm.

Tom, A. *Redesigning teacher education.* Albany: State University of New York Press, 1997.

Tom, A. "Stirring the embers: Reconsidering the structure of teacher education programs." In *Changing times in teacher education,* edited by M. F. Wideen and P. P. Grimmett, chap. 9. London: Falmer Press, 1995.

Tomorrow's teachers: A report of the Holmes Group. East Lansing, MI: Holmes Group, 1986. (ERIC Document Reproduction Service No. ED270454). http://www.eric.ed.gov/PDFS/ED270454.pdf.

Tönnies, F. *Gemeinschaft und Gesellschaft: Abhandlung des Communismus und des Socialismus als empirischer Culturformen.* Leipzig, Germany: Fues, 1887.

Townley, A. "Introduction: Conflict resolution, diversity, and social justice." *Education and Urban Society* 27, no. 1 (1994): 5–10.

TransactiveOnline.org. "The words we use." http://www.transactiveonline.org/documents/words_we_use.htm.

TransYouth Family Allies: Understanding Through Education. http://www.imatyfa.org/.

Traweek, D., and V. W. Berninger. "Comparisons of beginning literacy programs: Alternative paths to the same learning outcome." *Learning Disability Quarterly* 20, no. 2 (1997): 160–168.

Triola, M. *Elementary statistics.* 11th ed. Boston: Addison-Wesley, 2010.

Trueba, H. T. "Race and ethnicity: The role of universities in healing multicultural America." *Educational Theory* 43, no. 1 (1993): 41–54.

Tuijnman, A. C., ed. *International encyclopedia of adult education and training.* Oxford: Elsevier Science, 1996.

Turnbull, A. P., and H. R. Turnbull. *Families, professionals and exceptionality: A special partnership.* Columbus, OH: Merrill–Prentice Hall, 1997.

Turner, R. H. "Sponsored and contest mobility and the school system." *American Sociological Review* 25 (1960): 855–867.

Tyack, D. B. "Constructing difference: Historical reflections on schooling and social diversity." *Teachers College Record* 95, no. 1 (1993): 8–34.

Uchiyama, K., and J. Radin. "Curriculum mapping in higher education: A vehicle for collaboration." *Innovative Higher Education* 33, no. 4 (2009): 271–280.

Udelhofen, S. *Keys to curriculum mapping: Strategies and tools to make it work.* Thousand Oaks, CA: Corwin Press: 2005.

Unger, H. G. *Encyclopedia of American education.* New York: Facts on File, 1996.

Unger, H. G. *Encyclopedia of American education.* 2d ed. New York: Facts on File, 2001.

UNICEF. "UNICEF in action." http://www.unicef.org/uwwide.

"UNICEF." In *The concise Columbia electronic encyclopedia.* 3d ed. New York: Columbia University Press, 1994. http://www.encyclopedia.com/html/I/IX1-U1N1I1C1E1F1.asp.

United Nations Educational, Scientific and Cultural Organization. "About Unesco." http://www.unesco.org/general/eng/about/index.html.

The universal encyclopedia of mathematics. New York: Simon and Schuster, 1964.

University of Northern Iowa, College of Education. http://www.uni.edu/coe/.

University of Rhode Island, School of Education. *Student teacher handbook for middle level education.* http://www.soe.uri.edu/forms/mid_handbook/.

University of Southern Maine Center for Sexualities and Gender Diversity. http://usm.maine.edu/glbtqa/index.htm.

Urdang, L. *The Random House college dictionary.* New York: Random House, 1973.

U.S. Department of Education. Elementary & Secondary Education, Title IX, General Provisions. Sec. 9101 Definitions. "Scientifically based research." http://www.ed.gov/policy/elsec/leg/esea02/pg107.html.

U.S. Department of Education. "Federal Pell Grant Program." http://www.ed.gov/programs/fpg/index.html.

U.S. Department of Education. "FERPA: Frequently asked questions." http://www.ed.gov/policy/gen/guid/fpco/faq.html.

U.S. Department of Education. "Funding your education: Student financial assistance programs." http://www.ed.gov/prog_info/SFA/FYE/FYE02/indexfye.html.

Use of school choice. Washington, DC: U.S. Department of Education, Office of Educational Research and Improvement, National Center for Education Statistics, 1995.

Vacca, R. T., and J. L. Vacca. *Content area reading: Literacy and learning across the curriculum.* 6th ed. New York: Longman, 1999.

Valli, L., and P. Rennert-Ariev. "New standards and assessments? Curriculum transformation in teacher education." *Journal of Curriculum Studies* 34, no. 2 (2000): 201–225.

Van Hiele, P. "Developing geometric thinking through activities that begin with play." *Teaching Children Mathematics* 5, no. 6 (1999): 310–316.

Veenman, S., Y. Leenders, P. Meyer, and M. Sanders. *Evaluation of a pre-service programme based on direct instruction* (ERIC Document Reproduction Service No. ED353248), 1992.

Verharen, C. C. "A core curriculum at historically black colleges and universities: An immodest proposal." *Journal of Negro Education* 62, no. 2 (1993): 190–203.

Vocational Education Act of 1963, *U.S. Code,* vol. 77, sec. 403 (1963).

Vojtek, R., and R. Vojtek. "Action plan goes to the heart." *Journal of Staff Development* 19, no. 3 (1998): 61–63.

Vygotsky, L. S. *Mind in society: The development of higher psychological processes.* Cambridge, MA: Harvard University Press, 1978.

Wagner, T. *The global achievement gap: Why even the best schools don't teach the new survival skills our children need—and what we can do about it.* New York: Basic Books, 2008.

Walter, J. L. *Becoming solution-focused in brief therapy.* New York: Brunner/Mazel, 1992.

Walters, A. S., and D. M. Hayes. "Teaching about sexuality: Balancing contradictory social messages with professional standards." *American Journal of Sexuality Education* 2, no. 2 (2007): 27–49.

Warford, L., and W. J. Flynn. "New game, new rules: The workforce development challenge." *Leadership Abstract* 13, no. 2 (2000): 1–4.

Warren, K. J. *Ecofeminism: Women, culture, nature.* Bloomington: Indiana University Press, 1997.

Warren, K. J. *Ecological feminist philosophies.* Bloomington: Indiana University Press, 1996.

Washington, J. *A journey into the philosophy of Alain Locke.* Westport, CT: Greenwood Press, 1994.

Washington State Department of Social and Health Services. *Adult protective services.* http://www.aasa.dshs.wa.gov/Programs/aps.htm.

Watson-Gegeo, K. A. *Communicative routines in Kwara'ae children's language socialization: Final report to the National Science Foundation.* Washington, DC: National Science Foundation, 1986.

Webster's II new college dictionary. Boston: Houghton Mifflin, 1995.

Webster's ninth new collegiate dictionary. 9th ed. Springfield, MA: Merriam-Webster, 1989.

Weiner, B. "Ability versus effort revisited: The moral determinants of achievement evaluation and achievement as a moral system." *Educational Psychologist* 29, no. 3 (1994): 163–172.

Weiner, L. *Preparing teachers for a new educational paradigm: Lessons from the 1960's.* San Francisco: American Educational Research Association (ERIC Document Reproduction Service No. ED349289), 1992.

Weinstein, C. S., S. Tomlinson-Clarke, and M. Curran. "Toward a conception of culturally responsive classroom management." *Journal of Teacher Education* 55, no. 1 (2004): 25–38.

Weis, L. "Identity formation and the processes of 'othering': Unraveling sexual threads." *Educational Foundations* 9, no. 1 (1995): 17–33.

Weiten, W. *Psychology: Themes and variations.* 4th ed. New York: Brooks/Cole, 1998.

Welter, R., ed. *American writings on popular education: The nineteenth century.* Indianapolis, IN: Bobbs-Merrill, 1971.

Wentzel, K. R. "The academic lives of neglected, rejected, popular, and controversial children." *Child Development* 66, no. 3 (1995): 754–763.

West, B., E. N. Griesbach, J. D. Taylor, and L. T. Taylor. *The Prentice-Hall encyclopedia of mathematics.* Englewood Cliffs, NJ: Prentice Hall, 1982.

West Virginia University: College of Human Resources Education. "Clinical experiences." http://www.wvu.edu/hre/teacher-ed/clinical.htm.

Wexler, P. "Curriculum in the closed society." In *Critical pedagogy, the state, and cultural struggle,* edited by H. A. Giroux and P. McClaren, 92–104. Albany: State University of New York Press, 1989.

Wheatley, G. H. "Constructivist perspectives on mathematics and science learning." *Science Education* 75, no. 1 (1992): 9–21.

Whitehead, A. N. *The aims of education and other essays.* New York: Macmillan, 1929.

Whitson, J. A., and W. B. Stanley. "'Re-minding' education for democracy." In *Educating the democratic mind,* edited by W. C. Parker, 309–336. Albany: State University of New York Press, 1996.

Wieruszowski, H. *The medieval university: Masters, students, learning.* Princeton, NJ: D. Van Nostrand, 1966.

Wild, C. J., and M. Pfannkuch. "Statistical thinking in empirical inquiry." *International Statistical Review* 67, no. 3 (1999): 223–248.

Wilhelm, R. W. "Columbus's legacy, conquest or invasion? An analysis of counterhegemonic potential in Guatemalan teacher practice and curriculum." *Anthropology and Education Quarterly* 25, no. 2 (1994): 173–195.

William, J. D., and G. C. Snipper. *Literacy and bilingualism.* New York: Longman, 1990.

William T. Grant Foundation Commission on Work, Family, and Citizenship. *The forgotten half: Non-college youth in America: An interim report on the school-to-work transition.* Washington, DC: William T. Grant Foundation Commission on Work, Family and Citizenship, 1988.

Williams, R. L. *The collective black mind: An Afro-centric theory of black personality.* St. Louis, MO: Williams & Associates, 1981.

Williams, R. L. *Essentials of total quality management.* New York: American Management Association, 1994.

Willis, P. E. *Learning to labor: How working class kids get working class jobs.* New York: Columbia University Press, 1981.

Willis, P. E. *Learning to labour: How working class kids get working class jobs*. Farnborough, UK: Saxon House, 1977.

Wilson, R. A. "Integrating outdoor/environmental education into the special education curriculum." *Intervention in School & Clinic* 29, no. 3 (1994): 156–159.

Winch, C., and J. Gingell. *Key concepts in the philosophy of education*. London: Routledge, 1999.

Wingfield, E., L. Freeman, and J. Ramsey. *Science teaching self-efficacy of first year elementary teachers trained in a site-based program* (ERIC Document Reproduction Service No. ED439956), 2000.

Witte, J. F. "Wisconsin ideas: The continuing role of the university in the state and beyond." *New Directions for Higher Education* 112 (2000): 7–16.

Women's Therapy Center. "Issues of interest: Feminist therapy: A working definition." http://www.libertynet.org/wtc/issuesof.htm.

Wong, H. K. "New teacher induction: The foundation for comprehensive, coherent, and sustained professional development." In *Teacher mentoring and induction: The state of the art and beyond*, edited by H. Portner, 41–58. Thousand Oaks, CA: Corwin Press, 2005.

Wood, D., J. C. Bruner, and G. Ross. "The role of tutoring in problem solving." *Journal of Child Psychology and Psychiatry* 17 (1976): 89–100.

Wood, F. H., and J. E. Killian. "Job-embedded learning makes the difference in school improvement." *Journal of Staff Development* 19, no. 2 (1998): 52–54.

Woodson, C. G. *The education of the Negro prior to 1861: A history of the education of the colored people of the United States from the beginning of slavery to the Civil War*. Brooklyn, NY: A & B Books Publishers, [1919] 1996.

Woodson, C. G. *The mis-education of the Negro*. Africa World Press ed. Washington, DC: Africa World Press, [1933] 1990.

Woodward, C. V. *Origins of the New South, 1877–1913*. Baton Rouge: Louisiana State University Press, 1971.

Woolard, K. A. "Language variation and cultural hegemony: Toward an integration of sociolinguistic and social theory." *American Ethnologist* 12, no. 4 (1985): 738–748.

The World Bank Group. http://www.world bank.com.

World Health Organization. "Strategy for integrating gender perspectives into the work of the World Health Organization." http://www.searo.who.int/LinkFiles/Gender_Women_and_Health_Strategy_GWH.pdf.

Wortham, S. C. *Assessment in early childhood education*. 3d ed. Upper Saddle River, NJ: Prentice Hall, 2001.

Wrenn, C. G. "The culturally encapsulated counselor." *Harvard Educational Review* 32 (1962): 444–449.

Wynne, E., and K. Ryan. *Reclaiming our schools: Teaching character, academics, and discipline*. 2d ed. Upper Saddle River, NJ: Merrill, 1997.

Xu, J. "Using multimedia vocabulary annotations in L2 reading and listening activities." *CALICO Journal* 27, no. 2 (2010): 311–327.

Yalom, I. D. *The theory and practice of group psychotherapy*. 4th ed. New York: Basic Books, 1995.

Yanagimoto, T. "Teaching modeling as an alternative approach to school mathematics." *Teaching Mathematics and Its Applications* 24, no. 1 (2005): 1–13.

Yen, W. M. "Scaling performance assessments: Strategies for managing local item dependence." *Journal of Educational Measurement* 30, no. 3 (1993): 187–213.

York-Barr, J., and K. Duke. "What do we know about teacher leadership? Findings from two decades of scholarship." *Review of Educational Research* 74, no. 3 (2004): 255–316.

Young, T. W. *Public alternative education: Options and choice for today's schools.* New York: Teachers College Press, 1990.

Zeichner, K. M. "Traditions of practice in U.S. preservice teacher education programs." *Teaching and Teacher Education 9,* no. 1 (1993): 1–13.

Zeleny, J. "Obama signs hate crimes bill." The Caucus Blog. *New York Times,* October 28, 2009. http://thecaucus.blogs.nytimes.com/2009/10/28/obama-signs-hate-crimes-bill/.

Zevin, J. *Social studies for the twenty-first century.* New York: Longman, 1992.

Zimmerman, B. J., and D. H. Schunk. *Self-regulated learning and academic achievement: Theory, research and practice.* New York: Springer-Verlag, 1989.

Zinn, H. "Schools in context: The Mississippi idea." *The Nation.* November 23, 1964, 371–375.

Zinn, H. *SNCC: The new abolitionists.* Boston: Beacon Press, 1965.

Zinnbauer, B. J., K. I. Pargament, B. Cole, M. S. Rye, E. M. Butter, T. G. Belavich, K. M. Hipp, A. B. Scott, and J. L. Kadar. "Religion and spirituality: Unfuzzying the fuzzy." *Journal for the Scientific Study of Religion 36* (1997): 549–564.

Zirkel, P. A., and S. Nalbone Richardson. *A digest of Supreme Court decisions affecting education.* Bloomington, IN: Phi Delta Kappa, 1998.

Zirkel, P. A., S. Nalbone Richardson, and S. S. Goldberg. *A digest of Supreme Court decisions affecting education.* Bloomington, IN: Phi Delta Kappa, 1995.

Zisman, P., and V. Wilson. "Table hopping in the cafeteria: An exploration of 'racial' integration in early adolescent social groups." *Anthropology and Education Quarterly 23* (1992): 3.

Contributors, First Edition

Individuals named in boldface type directly under the subject area are the contributing editors for that topic.

A list of contributor initials used throughout the Dictionary can be found at the end of this section.

ADULT AND ALTERNATIVE EDUCATION

John P. Comings
Senior Research Associate, Lecturer on Education, Director, NCSALL, Harvard Graduate School of Education

Lisa Soricone, *Harvard Graduate School of Education*

ART EDUCATION

Jessica Hoffmann Davis
Director of the Arts in Education Program; The Patricia Bauman and John Lundrum Bryant Senior Lecturer in Arts in Education, Harvard Graduate School of Education

K. Page Boyer, *Harvard Business School*
Karin B. Cooper, *Harvard Graduate School of Education*
Kim Frumin, *Harvard Graduate School of Education*
Lama Jarudi, *Harvard Graduate School of Education*
Tyler Kemp-Benedict, *Harvard Graduate School of Education*
Yujie Julia Li, *Harvard Graduate School of Education*
Jane B. Lindamood, *Harvard Graduate School of Education*
Katie McCarthy, *Harvard Graduate School of Education*
Ethan Mintz, *Harvard Graduate School of Education*
Anne Proctor, *Harvard Graduate School of Education*
Laura Wayth, *Harvard Graduate School of Education*

CAREER AND VOCATIONAL EDUCATION

James E. Bartlett
Visiting Assistant Professor, Department of Human Resource Education, University of Illinois at Urbana Champaign

Debra D. Bragg
Professor and Director, Office of Community College Research and Leadership, University of Illinois at Urbana-Champaign

Jeffrey A. Cantor, *Norwalk Community College*
Susan Faulkner, *Educational Consultant*
Howard R. D. Gordon, *Marshall University*
Kenneth Gray, *Pennsylvania State University*
Chadwick Higgens, *Louisiana State University*
Sandra Kerka, *Ohio State University*
Jennifer Morales, *Ascot Avenue Elementary School, Los Angeles*
Susan Sears, *Ohio State University*

CONTINUING EDUCATION AND PROFESSIONAL DEVELOPMENT

Clifford Baden
Harvard Graduate School of Education

Joan M. Burke, *University of Georgia*
Jannette Gutierrez, *University of Georgia*
JuSung Jun, *University of Georgia*
Amelia Maness, *University of Georgia*
Catherine Monaghan, *University of Georgia*
Mary Kathryn Robinson, *University of Georgia*
Janice Saturday, *University of Georgia*
Diane Vreeland, *University of Georgia*

COUNSELING AND GUIDANCE

William E. Hanson
Assistant Professor, Department of Educational Psychology, University of Nebraska-Lincoln

Felito Aldarondo, *Purdue University*
Kate A. Barrett, *University of Nebraska-Lincoln*
Jennifer Bruning Brown, *Stanford University*
Laura Burlingame-Lee, *Colorado State University*
Patricia Cerda, *University of Nebraska-Lincoln*
Kathleen Condon, *University of Northern Colorado*
Susan C. M. Crane, *University of Northern Colorado*
Kyle T. Curry, *University of Nebraska-Lincoln*
Suzanne Cutler, *University of Nebraska-Lincoln*
Don Daughtry, *University of North Dakota*
Mary E. Dawes, *Arizona State University*
Maria de la Luz Perez, *University of Wisconsin-Madison*

Brett Deacon, *Minneapolis VA Medical Center*
Melissa Ferguson, *University of Louisville*
Lisa L. Frey, *University of Oklahoma*
Christine A. Gibbon, *University of Nebraska-Lincoln*
Michael G. Gottfried, *Valparaiso University*
J. Irene Harris, *Texas Tech University*
Tania Israel, *University of California-Santa Barbara*
Brian D. Johnson, *University of Northern Colorado*
Robin E. Macdonald, *University of Wisconsin-Madison*
Melissa C. Magreta, *University of Wisconsin-Madison*
Elissa M. McElrath, *University of Oklahoma*
Laura-Renee Mendoza, *University of Wisconsin-Madison*
Brad M. Merker, *University of Nebraska-Lincoln*
Asa M. Miura, *University of Wisconsin-Madison*
Allison Olson, *University of Wisconsin-Madison*
Douglas H. Olson, *Minneapolis VA Medical Center*
Carey A. Pawlowski, *University of Nebraska-Lincoln*
Kelly S. Petska, *University of Nebraska-Lincoln*
Robert N. Portnoy, *University of Nebraska-Lincoln*
Michael J. Scheel, *University of Nebraska-Lincoln*
Jenjee Sengkhammee, *University of Wisconsin-Madison*
Meredith K. Taylor, *Virginia Commonwealth University*
Tammi Vacha-Haase, *Colorado State University*
Angela Byars Winston, *University of Wisconsin-Madison*
A. Yang, *University of Wisconsin-Madison*

EARLY CHILDHOOD EDUCATION

Yash Bhagwanji
Assistant Professor, Department of Teaching and Learning, College of Education and Human Development, University of Louisville

Donna Bell, *National Center for Family Literacy*
Jeffrey Berg, *University of Louisville*
Todd Brown, *University of Louisville*
Melissa Carpenter, *University of Louisville*
Cybil Cheek, *University of Louisville*
Kristina Christensen, *University of Louisville*
Mark Condon, *University of Louisville*
Amanda Davis, *University of Louisville*
Elizabeth Everett, *University of Louisville*
Melissa Ferguson, *University of Louisville*
Jill Jacobi-Vessels, *University of Louisville*
Rich Luekenga, *University of Louisville*
Kelly McPerson-Shuff, *University of Louisville*
Victoria Molfese, *University of Louisville*
Jamie Morgenstern, *University of Louisville*
Jessica Neamon, *University of Louisville*
Elizabeth Rightmyer, *University of Louisville*

J. Lea Smith, *University of Louisville*
Ximena P. Suarez-Sousa, *University of Louisville*
Shona Terrell, *University of Louisville*
Anna Twyman, *University of Louisville*
Phoebe Williamson, *University of Louisville*

EDUCATION HISTORY

Victoria-Maria MacDonald
Associate Professor, Department of Educational Leadership and Policy Studies, Florida State University

Scott Walter
Interim Assistant Director for Public Service and Outreach Librarian, Washington State University

Alex J. Angulo, *Harvard Graduate School of Education*
Mark Bay, *Cumberland College*
Scott Beck, *University of Georgia*
Jayne Beilke, *Ball State University*
Mary S. Black, *University of Texas at Austin*
Brent Blanton, *University of Southern California*
Ronald Butchart, *University of Georgia*
Timothy Reese Cain, *University of Michigan*
Janell Carter, *Wilkens University*
Melissa Cast, *University of Nebraska-Omaha*
Nadine Cohen, *University of Georgia*
Jackie Cossentino, *University of Maryland*
Stephanie Davis-Kahl, *University of California-Irvine*
Laura Dewhirst, *Florida State University*
Linda Eisenmann, *University of Massachusetts, Boston*
Anne Fields, *Ohio State University*
Wanda Gill, *United States Department of Education*
Adam Golub, *University of Texas at Austin*
Lisa Gonzalez, *Christian College*
Millie Gore, *Midwestern State University, Kansas*
Jan Price Greenough, *University of California-Berkeley*
Cheryl Grossman, *Ohio State University*
Laurel Haycock, *University of Minnesota*
Rita Herron, *Florida State University*
Elaine Gass Hirsch, *Lewis & Clark College*
Andrea Howard, *Florida State University*
Karen L. Janke, *Indiana University*
Christine King, *Purdue University*
Kevin Kosar, *New York University*
Lee LaFleur, *Cornell University*
Jeneen LaSee-Willemssen, *The Conserve School*
Keith Leitich, *Seattle, WA*
Marlow Matherne, *Florida State University*

Douglas Mikutel, *Florida State University*
Jenna Montgomery, *Florida State University*
Patricia Moran, *Florida State University*
Laurie Mullen, *Ball State University*
Sharon K. Naylor, *Illinois State University*
CM! Palacio, *Florida State University*
Connie Phelps, *University of New Orleans*
Beth Rapps, *Independent Scholar*
Stephanie Robinson, *Ball State University*
Denise Rosenblatt, *National Library of Education*
John Rudolph, *University of Wisconsin-Madison*
Shennika Rutledge, *Florida State University*
Kimberly Schlussel, *Arlington, Virginia, Public Schools*
Gregory Spano, *University of New Orleans*
Eileen Tamura, *University of Hawaii*
Natalia Taylor, *Georgia State University*
Kim Tolley, *Independent Scholar*
Aleta Underwood, *Florida State University*
Jennie Ver Steeg, *Northern Illinois University*
Helga Visscher, *University of Alabama*
Heather Voke, *Association for Supervision and Curriculum Development*
Linda Weber, *University of Southern California*
M. Keith Whitescarver, *College of William and Mary*
Andrea Williams, *Midwestern State University, Kansas*
Christine Woyshner, *Temple University*
William Wraga, *University of Georgia*

EDUCATIONAL ADMINISTRATION, MANAGEMENT, AND POLICY

Robert O. Slater
Professor, Department of Educational Administration, Texas A&M University

Carolina Leal, *Texas A&M University*
Marilyn Martin, *Texas A&M University*
Billy Duane McFadden, *Texas A&M University*
Troy Mooney, *Texas A&M University*
Teresa Parish, *Texas A&M University*
Jerri B. Roemer, *Texas A&M University*
Betty Sanders, *Texas A&M University*
Jill K. Steward-Trier, *Texas A&M University*
Kathy Stewart, *Texas A&M University*
Lee Yeager, *Texas A&M University*

EDUCATIONAL PHILOSOPHY

John Covaleskie
Professor of Education, Northern Michigan University

Jan Bengtsson, *Göteborg University*
Donald Bloomenfeld-Jones, *Arizona State University*

Deron R. Boyles, *Georgia State University*
Nicholas C. Burbules, *University of Illinois at Urbana-Champaign*
Eva Maria Cadavid, *University of Rochester*
Stephen Clinton, *The Orlando Institute*
Paul S. Collins, *University of Rochester*
Randall Curren, *University of Rochester*
Peggy Ruth Geren, *Augusta State University*
Ignacio Gotz, *New School of Hofstra University*
Thomas F. Green, *Syracuse University*
Maughn Gregory, *Montclair State University*
Ian Harris, *University of Wisconsin-Milwaukee*
Felicity Haynes, *University of Western Australia*
Robert D. Heslep, *University of Georgia*
Ken Howe, *University of Colorado*
José A. Ibáñez-Martín, *University Complutense of Madrid*
Patrick Keeney, *Okanagan University College*
Laura Kerr, *Stanford University*
Rodman King, *University of Rochester*
Natasha Levinson, *Kent State University*
David Levy, *University of Rochester*
William Losito, *University of Dayton*
Michael B. Mathias, *Union College*
Alven Nieman, *Notre Dame University*
Jana Noel, *California State University, Sacramento*
Suzanne Rice, *University of Kansas*
Emily Robertson, *Syracuse University*
Marjorie Hodges Shaw, *Cornell University*
Barbara Thayer-Bacon, *Bowling Green State University*
Roben Torosyan, *Pace University*
Gabriel Uzquiano, *University of Rochester*
Susan Verducci, *Stanford University*
Gregory R. Wheeler, *University of Rochester*
Kevin Williams, *Dublin City University*

EDUCATIONAL RESEARCH: QUALITATIVE

Richard Schmertzing
Associate Professor of Educational Leadership, Department of Educational Leadership, Valdosta State University

Jeffrey David Ehrenreich, *University of New Orleans*
Janice Janz, *Tulane University*
Bradley A. U. Levinson, *Indiana University*
Joseph A. Maxwell, *George Mason University*
A. Lorraine Schmertzing, *Valdosta State University*
Marydee A. Spillett, *University of New Orleans*
Shana Walton, *Tulane University*
Barbara Wand, *Tulane University*

EDUCATIONAL TECHNOLOGY AND MEDIA

Kathleen Guinee
Harvard Graduate School of Education

Ann Crawford, *Trinity College*
Heping Hao, *State University of New York at Albany*
L. Jon Hobbs, *State University of New York at Albany*
Ilona E. Holland, *Harvard Graduate School of Education*
Elias Holman, *Harvard Graduate School of Education*
Trudilyne Leone Lord, *Harvard Graduate School of Education*
Pamela L. Whitehouse, *Harvard Graduate School of Education*
Zheng Yan, *State University of New York at Albany*

ELEMENTARY EDUCATION

Bonnie Betts Armbruster
Professor, Department of Curriculum and Instruction, University of Illinois at Urbana-Champaign

GENERAL EDUCATION

John W. Collins III
Librarian, Monroe C. Gutman Library, Harvard Graduate School of Education

Nancy Patricia O'Brien
Head, Education & Social Science Library, University of Illinois at Urbana-Champaign

Preston B. Cline, *Harvard Graduate School of Education*
Thomas Hehir, *Harvard Graduate School of Education*
Stephanie L. Standerfer, *University of Virginia*
Jeffrey M. Wright, *Harvard Graduate School of Education*
Tim Wright, *Stevens Point Area Public Schools, Stevens Point, Wisconsin*

HIGHER EDUCATION

Cameron Fincher
Regents Professor of Higher Education and Psychology, Institute of Higher Education, University of Georgia

Paul S. Baker, *Hampden-Sydney College*
Randall V. Bass, *Valdosta State University*
Jenny W. Best, *University of Georgia*
John M. Casey, *University of Georgia*
James Eck, *Rollins College*
Elizabeth Farokhi, *Georgia State University*
Catherine Finnegan, *University of Georgia*
John Fleischmann, *Georgia State University*
Susan H. Frost, *Emory University*
Marc Galvin, *University of Georgia School of Law*
Timothy Letzring, *University of Mississippi*

Claire Major, *University of Alabama*
Doug Mann, *University of Georgia*
Tom Redmon, *Southern Association of Independent Schools*
Randy L. Swing, *Brevard College*

LANGUAGE ARTS AND READING

Julie Marie Wood
Lecturer on Education, Human Development and Psychology, Harvard Graduate School of Education

Zoe Agnew, *Harvard Graduate School of Education*
Marianne Castano, *Harvard Graduate School of Education*
Mary Helen Immordino-Yang, *Harvard Graduate School of Education*
Jane Katz, *Harvard Graduate School of Education*
Hyun-Jung Kim, *Harvard Graduate School of Education*
Mark Langager, *Harvard Graduate School of Education*
Stefka Masinova-Todd, *Harvard Graduate School of Education*
Jill Korey O'Sullivan, *Harvard Graduate School of Education*
Yuuko Uchikoshi, *Harvard Graduate School of Education*
Amy Warren, *Harvard Graduate School of Education*

MATHEMATICS EDUCATION

Anne Reynolds
Associate Professor, Department of Instructional Leadership and Academic Curriculum (ILAC), Mathematics Education, University of Oklahoma

Keith V. Adolphson, *University of Oklahoma*
William Arbuckle, *University of Oklahoma*
Donald B. Cagle, *University of Oklahoma*
Darlinda Cassell, *University of Oklahoma*
S. Megan Che, *University of Oklahoma*
Cathy DeVaughan, *Southwestern Oklahoma State University*
Vicki Darlene Flournoy, *University of Oklahoma*
Karen Hemmerling, *University of Oklahoma*
Jaime Keel, *University of Oklahoma*
Ron Koehn, *Southwestern Oklahoma State University*
Gabriel Matney, *University of Oklahoma*
Stacy Reeder, *University of Oklahoma*
Kerri Richardson, *University of Oklahoma*
Paula Schornick, *Oklahoma Baptist University*
Sandra Davis Trowell, *Valdosta State University*
Elaine Young, *University of Oklahoma*

MEASUREMENT, EVALUATION, AND ASSESSMENT

Frederick G. Davidson
Associate Professor, Division of English as an International Language (DEIL), University of Illinois at Urbana-Champaign

Teresa Chen, *California State University at Long Beach*
Yeonsuk Cho, *University of Illinois at Urbana-Champaign*
Silva Dushku, *University of Illinois at Urbana-Champaign*
Kate Hahn, *University of Illinois at Urbana-Champaign*
Ashley Lanting, *Indiana University*
Brian Lynch, *Portland State University, Oregon*
Serena Pyo, *Woosong University, Taejeon, Korea*
Sara Cushing Weigle, *Georgia State University*

MULTICULTURAL AND MULTILINGUAL EDUCATION

J.Q. Adams
Professor, Multicultural Education, Educational and Interdisciplinary Studies, Western Illinois University

Gloria Delaney-Barmann, *Western Illinois University*
Sharon R. Stevens, *Western Illinois University*
Janice R. Welsch, *Western Illinois University*

PHYSICAL EDUCATION

Robert E. Frederick
Professor, Movement Arts, Health Promotion, and Leisure Studies, School of Education and Allied Studies, Bridgewater State College

RURAL EDUCATION

Lawrence E. Rogers
Associate Professor of Teacher Education, College of Education and Counseling, South Dakota State University

SECONDARY EDUCATION

Corey R. Lock
Professor, Department of Middle, Secondary and K12 Education, University of North Carolina-Charlotte

George A. Churukian
Professor Emeritus, Illinois Wesleyan University

James F. Burnham, *University of North Carolina-Charlotte*
Patricia J. Gibson, *University of North Carolina-Charlotte*
Darlene Guerrero, *Charlotte, North Carolina*
Debra S. Morris, *West Lincoln High School, Lincolnton, North Carolina*
Janice T. Ritter, *University of North Carolina-Charlotte*

SOCIAL STUDIES EDUCATION

Mary S. Black
Assistant Professor, Department of Curriculum and Instruction, College of Education, University of Texas at Austin

Irma Garcia Bakenhaus, *University of Texas at Austin*
Chara Haeussler Bohan, *Baylor University*
James J. Carpenter, *University of Texas at Austin*
Jamel K. Donnor, *University of Texas at Austin*
Cynthia Duda DuBois, *University of Texas at Austin*
Marilyn Eisenwine, *University of Texas at Austin*
Connie Elam, *University of Texas at Austin*
Kristi Fragnoli, *State University of New York at Cortland*
Melaney Kay Gillaspie, *Old Dominion University*
Judith A. Hakes, *University of Texas at Austin*
Chris Leahey, *University of Texas at Austin*
Karon Nicol LeCompte, *University of Texas at Austin*
Patricia D. Martin, *University of Texas at Austin*
H. Richard Milner, *University of Texas at Austin*
Frances E. Monteverde, *University of Texas at Austin*
J. Wesley Null, *University of Texas at Austin*
Jo Beth Oestreich, *University of Texas at Austin*
Karen Riley, *University of Texas at Austin*
E. Wayne Ross, *University of Louisville*
Kathleen Scott, *University of Texas at Austin*
Jared Stallones, *University of Texas at Austin*
Barbara S. Stern, *University of Texas at Austin*
Donna Love Vliet, *University of Texas at Austin*
Erik Wilson, *University of Texas at Austin*
Sandra E. Wolf, *University of Texas at Austin*

SOCIOLOGY OF EDUCATION

Hal F. Smith
Assistant Professor, School of Education, City College of New York

SPECIAL EDUCATION

Suzanne Ripley
Vice President and Director (NICHCY), National Information Center for Children and Youth with Disabilities, Washington, DC

Jessica C. Penchos, *Harvard Graduate School of Education*

TEACHER EDUCATION

Renee T. Clift
Professor, Department of Curriculum and Instruction, University of Illinois at Urbana-Champaign

Jeehae Ahn, *University of Illinois at Urbana-Champaign*
Russell Binkley, *University of Illinois at Urbana-Champaign*
Brenda L. Bowen, *University of Illinois at Urbana-Champaign*
Patricia Brady, *University of Illinois at Urbana-Champaign*
Cari L. Klecka, *University of Illinois at Urbana-Champaign*
Betty Liebovich, *University of Illinois at Urbana-Champaign*

Contributors, Second Edition

Individuals named in boldface type directly under the subject area are the contributing editors for that topic.

A list of contributor initials used throughout the Dictionary can be found at the end of this section.

ADULT AND CONTINUING EDUCATION

John P. Comings
Board President, Institute for Training and Development

Christine Smith, *University of Massachusetts, Amherst*

ART EDUCATION

Jessica Hoffmann Davis
Founder, Former Director, Arts in Education Program, Harvard Graduate School of Education

CAREER AND TECHNICAL EDUCATION

Steven Aragon
Associate Professor, Human Resource Education, University of Illinois at Urbana-Champaign

Elaine Adams, *University of Georgia*
James E. Bartlett, *North Carolina State University*
Neil A. Knobloch, *Purdue University*
Richard Zinser, *Western Michigan University*

CONTINUING EDUCATION AND PROFESSIONAL DEVELOPMENT

Joseph P. Zolner
Lecturer on Education, Senior Director of Higher Education Programs, Harvard Graduate School of Education

Mitalene Fletcher, *Harvard Graduate School of Education*
Stephen Hyde, *Harvard Graduate School of Education*
Larissa Noake, *Harvard Graduate School of Education*

EDUCATIONAL ADMINISTRATION, MANAGEMENT, AND POLICY

Rosemary Papa
Professor, Educational Leadership, Northern Arizona University

Charles M. Achilles, *Northern Arizona University*
Karyn Blair, *Northern Arizona University*
Ric S. Brown, *Northern Arizona University*
Lynette Cook-Francis, *University of Arizona*
Mary Dereshiwsky, *Northern Arizona University*
Roxanna Solley *Dewey, Tempe, Arizona*
James Louis Driscoll, *Mesa, Arizona*
Gary L. Emanuel, *Northern Arizona University*
Fenwick W. English, *University of North Carolina, Chapel Hill*
Maureen Kelly Flores, *University of Arizona*
Patricia G. Gibson, *Northern Arizona University*
Daniel Kain, *Northern Arizona University*
David J. Loutzenheiser, *Chandler, Arizona*
Lynnette Michalski, *Northern Arizona University*
Michelle Poppen, *Tucson, Arizona*
Lani Simmons, Tucson, Arizona
Stephen D. Sorden, *Northern Arizona University*
Matthew Davis Strom, *Chandler, Arizona*
Damon Twist, *Phoenix, Arizona*
Kasey Urquidez, *University of Arizona*

EDUCATIONAL PHILOSOPHY

Sean Blenkinsop
Assistant Professor of Education, Simon Fraser University

David P. Burns, *Simon Fraser University*
Neil Carter, *Christchurch Steiner School*
Trent Davis, *York University*
David Diener, *Indiana University*
Veronica K. Hotton, *Simon Fraser University*
Arun Karumanchiri, *Ontario Institute for Studies in Education, University of Toronto*
Jodi MacQuarrie, *Simon Fraser University*
Clayton Maitlan, *School District No. 42, Maple Ridge, British Columbia, Canada*

Diana Nicholson, *University of Victoria*
Trevor Norris, *Ontario Institute for Studies in Education, University of Toronto*
Bruce Novack, *Truman College*
Charles Scott, *Simon Fraser University*
Timothy Waddington, *Simon Fraser University*

EDUCATIONAL PSYCHOLOGY, COUNSELING, AND GUIDANCE

Thomas Steuart Watson
Professor, Educational Psychology, Department of Educational Psychology, Miami University

EDUCATIONAL TECHNOLOGY AND MEDIA

Kathleen Guinee
Senior Lecturer, Northeastern University

Alex Brosowsky, *Northeastern University*
Kellie M. Doty, *Harvard University*
Weimiao Fan, *State University of New York at Albany*
Janet Gronneberg, *Center for Applied Special Technology*
Heping Hao, *Harvard Business School Publishing*
L. Jon Hobbs, *Evaluation and Training Institute*
Lai Lei Lou, *University at Albany, State University of New York*
Shawn Mahoney, *Harvard Graduate School of Education*
Laurie Poklop, *Educational Technology Center, Northeastern University*
Allison Ruda, *Northeastern University Online*
Yuriko Sasaki, *State University of New York at Albany*
Dan Schoenfeld, *State University of New York at Albany*

GENERAL EDUCATION

John W. Collins III
Librarian, Member of the Faculty, Monroe C. Gutman Library, Harvard Graduate School of Education

Nancy Patricia O'Brien
Professor and Head, Education and Social Science Library, University of Illinois at Urbana-Champaign

Eileen Berger, *Harvard Graduate School of Education*
Jennifer Bryan, *Harvard Graduate School of Education*
Preston B. Cline, *University of Pennsylvania*
Ann S. Flentje, *Harvard Graduate School of Education*
Benjamin Gallup, *Massachusetts Institute of Technology*
Neil Lipsitz, *College of the Holy Cross*
Alicia Safier, *Harvard Graduate School of Education*
Nancy Safier, *Harborlight Montessori School*
Mark Shelton, *Harvard Graduate School of Education*

HIGHER EDUCATION

Sharon K. Naylor
Professor, Illinois State University

Jean B. MacDonald, *Illinois State University*
Pam Werre, *Minnesota State University Moorhead*

LANGUAGE ARTS AND READING

Julie Marie Wood
Harvard Graduate School of Education

Jennifer DeBara Crandell, *Harvard Graduate School of Education*
Rachel Currie-Rubin, *Harvard Graduate School of Education*
Christina L. Dobbs, *Harvard Graduate School of Education*
Margaret Mary Dubeck, *Harvard Graduate School of Education*
Jessica Scott, *Harvard Graduate School of Education*

MATHEMATICS EDUCATION

Anne Reynolds
Associate Professor, Kent State University

Michelle L. Frederick, *Ravenna City Schools*
Jenna Marie Gordon, *Kent State University*
Ronda L. Kirsch, *Kent State University*
Sister Mary Theresa Sharp, S.N.D., *Kent State University*
Peggy M. Slavik, *Baldwin-Wallace College*
LeAnn Diana Zanni, *Kent State University*

MEASUREMENT, EVALUATION, AND ASSESSMENT

Yeonsuk Cho
Associate Research Scientist, Center for Validity Research, Educational Testing Service

Minjeong Jeon, *University of California, Berkeley*
Hye Joo Lee, *Georgia Institute of Technology*
Guangming Ling, *Educational Testing Service*
Jonathan Schmidgall, *University of California, Los Angeles*
Rick Tannenbaum, *Educational Testing Service*
Jing Xu, *Iowa State University*

MULTICULTURAL AND MULTILINGUAL EDUCATION

Annie C. Paprocki
Assistant Professor, Education and Social Science Library, University of Illinois at Urbana-Champaign

NEUROSCIENCE IN EDUCATION

Jennifer Thomson
Assistant Professor of Education, Harvard Graduate School of Education

Samantha Daley, *Harvard Graduate School of Education*
Matthias Faeth, *Harvard Graduate School of Education*
Derrick Hull, *Harvard Graduate School of Education*
Priya Kalra, *Harvard Graduate School of Education*
Jamie O'Keeffe, *Harvard Graduate School of Education*
Nancy Schoolcraft, *Harvard Graduate School of Education*
Meghan Taevs, *Harvard Graduate School of Education*

PHYSICAL EDUCATION

Karen Richardson
Associate Professor, Physical Education and Health Department, Bridgewater State College

RURAL EDUCATION

Lawrence E. Rogers
Professor of Teacher Education, South Dakota State University

SECONDARY EDUCATION

Leila E. Villaverde
Associate Professor, Educational Leadership and Cultural Foundations, University of North Carolina at Greensboro

Whitney Paige Akers, *University of North Carolina at Greensboro*
Brian Dwight Ammons, *University of North Carolina at Greensboro*
Sabrina Boyer, *University of North Carolina at Greensboro*
Erin Brownlee Dell, *University of North Carolina at Greensboro*
Ty-Ron M. O. Douglas, *University of North Carolina at Greensboro*
Sarah Margaret Heying, *University of North Carolina at Greensboro*
Dara Nix-Stevenson, *University of North Carolina at Greensboro*
Adrienne Sansom, *University of North Carolina at Greensboro*

SOCIAL STUDIES EDUCATION

Nancy Gallavan
Associate Dean, College of Education, University of Central Arkansas

TEACHER EDUCATION

Dorene Ross
Professor, College of Education, University of Florida

Alyson Adams, *University of Florida*
Elizabeth Bondy, *University of Florida*

Nancy Dana, *University of Florida*
Stephanie Dodman, *University of Florida*
Elyse Hambacher, *University of Florida*
Desirae Krell, *University of Florida*
Dianne Murphey, *University of Florida*
Colleen Packer, *University of Florida*
Marissa Stukey, *University of Florida*
Katie Tricarico, *University of Florida*

Contributors by Initials

aa	Alyson Adams*		ay	A. Yang
ab	Angela Byars Winston		baul	Bradley A. U. Levinson
ab1	Alex Brosowsky*		baw	Barbara Wand
ac	Ann Crawford		bba	Bonnie Betts Armbruster
acp	Annie C. Paprocki*		bd	Brett Deacon
ad	Amanda Davis		bda	Brian Dwight Ammons*
af	Anne Fields		bdj	Brian D. Johnson
ag	Adam Golub		bgr	Beth Rapps
ah	Andrea Howard		bhg	Benjamin Gallup*
ahs	Alicia Safier*		bjl	Betty Liebovich
aja	Alex J. Angulo		bkl	Brian Lynch
ak	Arun Karumanchiri*		blb	Brenda L. Bowen
al	Ashley Lanting		bmm	Brad M. Merker
alm	Amelia Maness		bn	Bruce Novack*
als	A. Lorraine Schmertzing		bs	Betty Sanders
alw	Andrea Williams		bsb	Brent Blanton
amm	Asa M. Miura		bss	Barbara S. Stern
amr	Anne Reynolds**		bt-b	Barbara Thayer-Bacon
an	Alven Nieman		cag	Christine A. Gibbon
ao	Allison Olson		cap	Carey A. Pawlowski
ap	Anne Proctor		cas	Christine Smith*
ar	Allison Ruda*		caw	Christine Woyshner
as	Adrienne Sansom*		cb	Chara Haeussler Bohan
asf	Ann S. Flentje*		cd	Cynthia Duda DuBois
at	Anna Twyman		ce	Connie Elam
aw	Amy Warren		cf	Cameron Fincher

cf1	Catherine Finnegan	ea	Elaine Adams*
ch	Chadwick Higgens	eb	Elizabeth Bondy*
chb	Clifford Baden	ebd	Erin Brownlee Dell*
chm	Catherine Monaghan	ec	Eva Maria Cadavid
cjb	Jeffrey Berg	ecb	Eileen Berger*
ck	Christine King	ecr	Elizabeth Rightmyer
ckc	Cybil Cheek	ee	Elizabeth Everett
cl	Carolina Leal	ef	Elizabeth Farokhi
cld	Christina L. Dobbs*	egh	Elaine Gass Hirsch
clk	Cari L. Klecka	eh	Elias Holman
clp	Connie Phelps	eh1	Elyse Hambacher*
cm!	CM! Palacio	eht	Eileen Tamura
cm1	Claire Major	em	Ethan Mintz
cm2	Clayton Maitlan*	emm	Elissa M. McElrath
cma	Charles M. Achilles*	er	Emily Robertson
cmdv	Cathy DeVaughan	ew	Erik Wilson
cp	Colleen Packer*	ewr	E. Wayne Ross
crl	Chris Leahey	ey	Elaine Young
crl1	Corey R. Lock	fa	Felito Aldarondo
crsg	Cheryl Grossman	fd	Frederick G. Davidson
cs	Charles Scott*	fem	Frances E. Monteverde
db	Debra D. Bragg	fh	Felicity Haynes
db1	Donna Bell	fwe	Fenwick W. English*
dbc	Donald B. Cagle	gac	George A. Churukian
db-j	Donald Bloomenfeld-Jones	gd-b	Gloria Delaney-Barmann
dc	Darlinda Cassell	gl	Guangming Ling*
dd	Don Daughtry	gle	Gary L. Emanuel*
dd1	David Diener*	grw	Gregory R. Wheeler
ddr	Dorene Ross*	gs	Gregory Spano
dek	Desirae Krell*	gtm	Gabriel Matney
dg	Darlene Guerrero	gu	Gabriel Uzquiano
dh	Derrick Hull*	hbv	Helga Visscher
dho	Douglas H. Olson	hfs	Hal F. Smith
djl	David J. Loutzenheiser*	hg	Howard R. D. Gordon
djr	Denise Rosenblatt	hh	Heping Hao**
dl	David Levy	h-jk	Hyun-Jung Kim
dlk	Daniel Kain*	hl	Hye Joo Lee*
dlt	Damon Twist*	hrm	H. Richard Milner
dm	Billy Duane McFadden	hv	Heather Voke
dm1	Doug Mann	ieh	Ilona E. Holland
dm2	Dianne Murphey*	ig	Ignacio Gotz
dmv	Diane Vreeland	igb	Irma Garcia Bakenhaus
dn	Diana Nicholson*	ih	Ian Harris
dns	Dara Nix-Stevenson*	ja	Jeehae Ahn
dpb	David P. Burns*	jac	Jeffrey A. Cantor
drb	Deron R. Boyles	jah	Judith A. Hakes
ds	Dan Schoenfeld*	jam	Joseph A. Maxwell
dsm	Debra S. Morris	jas	Jessica Scott*
dv	Donna Love Vliet	jb	James E. Bartlett**
dwm	Douglas Mikutel	jb1	Jan Bengtsson

jb2	Jennifer Bryan*	js2	Jonathan Schmidgall*
jbb	Jennifer Bruning Brown	jsj	JuSung Jun
jbl	Jane B. Lindamood	jt	Jill K. Steward-Trier
jbm	Jean B. MacDonald*	jt1	Jennifer Thomson*
jbo	Jo Beth Oestreich	jtr	Janice T. Ritter
jc	John Covaleskie	jv	Jennie Ver Steeg
jc1	Janell Carter	jw	Jeffrey M. Wright
jc2	Jackie Cossentino	jwb	Jenny W. Best
jcp	Jessica C. Penchos	jwc	John W. Collins III**
jd	Jessica Hoffmann Davis**	jwg	Jannette Gutierrez
jdc	Jennifer DeBara Crandell*	jwn	J. Wesley Null
jde	Jeffrey David Ehrenreich	jx	Jing Xu*
jdk	Jaime Keel	jz	Joseph P. Zolner*
je	James Eck	kab	Kate A. Barrett
jf	John Fleischmann	kbc	Karin B. Cooper
jfb	James F. Burnham	kc	Kathleen Condon
jg	Jan Price Greenough	kd	Kellie M. Doty*
jg1	Janet Gronneberg*	kdc	Kristina Christensen
jh	L. Jon Hobbs**	kf	Kim Frumin
jih	J. Irene Harris	kf1	Kristi Fragnoli
ji-m	José A. Ibáñez-Martin	kg	Kenneth Gray
jjc	James J. Carpenter	kg1	Kathleen Guinee**
jk	Jill Korey O'Sullivan	kgh	Karen Hemmerling
jkd	Jamel K. Donnor	kh	Ken Howe
jld	James Louis Driscoll*	kh1	Kate Hahn
jlj	Jill Jacobi-Vessels	kku	Kasey Urquidez*
jlr	John Rudolph	kl	Keith Leitich
jls	J. Lea Smith	klb	Karyn Blair*
jlw	Jeneen LaSee-Willemssen	klj	Karen L. Janke
jm	Jennifer Morales	km	Katie McCarthy
jm1	Jodi MacQuarrie*	kms	Kelly McPerson-Shuff
jmb	Joan M. Burke	kmt	Katie Tricarico*
jmc	John M. Casey	knl	Karon Nicol LeCompte
jmg	Jenna Marie Gordon*	kpb	K. Page Boyer
jmo	Jamie Morgenstern	kpr	Karen Richardson*
jmw	Julie Marie Wood**	kr	Kerri Richardson
jn	Jana Noel	kr1	Karen Riley
jne	Jessica Neamon	krk	Kevin Kosar
jok	Jamie O'Keeffe*	ks	Kathy Stewart
jpc	John P. Comings**	ks1	Kathleen Scott
jqa	J. Q. Adams	ks2	Kimberly Schlussel
jr	Jerri B. Roemer	ksp	Kelly S. Petska
jrb	Jayne Beilke	kt	Kim Tolley
jrj	Janice Janz	ktc	Kyle T. Curry
jrk	Jane Katz	kva	Keith V. Adolphson
jrm	Jenna Montgomery	kw	Kevin Williams
jrs	Jared Stallones	las	Lisa Soricone
jrw	Janice R. Welsch	lbl	Laura Burlingame-Lee
js	Janice Saturday	lcf	Lynette Cook-Francis*
js1	Jenjee Sengkhammee	lcw	Linda Weber

ld	Laura Dewhirst		mlp	Maria de la Luz Perez
ldz	LeAnn Diana Zanni*		mlp1	Michelle Poppen*
le	Linda Eisenmann		mm	Marilyn Martin
lev	Leila E. Villaverde*		mm1	Marlow Matherne
lg	Lisa Gonzalez		mmd	Margaret Mary Dubeck*
lh	Laurel Haycock		mrs	Marissa Stukey*
lj	Lama Jarudi		ms	Mark Shelton*
ljl	Lee LaFleur		msb	Mary S. Black
ljm	Laurie Mullen		mt	Meghan Taevs*
lkk	Laura Kerr		nb	Nicholas C. Burbules
llf	Lisa L. Frey		nc	Nadine Cohen
lll	Lai Lei Lou*		nc1	Neil Carter*
lmm	Lynnette Michalski*		nfd	Nancy Dana*
lms	Lani Simmons*		nk	Neil A. Knobloch*
ln	Larissa Noake*		nl	Natasha Levinson
lp	Laurie Poklop*		nl1	Neil Lipsitz*
lr	Lawrence E. Rogers**		npg	Nancy Gallavan*
lrm	Laura-Renee Mendoza		npo	Nancy Patricia O'Brien**
lw	Laura Wayth		nrs	Nancy Safier*
ly	Lee Yeager		ns	Nancy Schoolcraft*
mas	Marydee A. Spillett		nt	Natalia Taylor
mb	Mark Bay		pbc	Preston B. Cline**
mbm	Michael B. Mathias		pdm	Patricia D. Martin
mc	Marianne Castano		peb	Patricia Brady
mc1	Mark Condon		pgg	Patricia G. Gibson*
mc2	Melissa Carpenter		pjg	Patricia J. Gibson
mc3	Melissa Cast		pjm	Patricia Moran
mcm	Melissa C. Magreta		pk	Patrick Keeney
mds	Matthew Davis Strom*		pk1	Priya Kalra*
med	Mary E. Dawes		plw	Pamela L. Whitehouse
mf	Melissa Ferguson		pmts	Peggy M. Slavik*
mf1	Mitalene Fletcher*		prg	Peggy Ruth Geren
mf2	Matthias Faeth*		ps	Paula Schornick
mg	Maughn Gregory		psb	Paul S. Baker
mg1	Millie Gore		psc	Paul S. Collins
mg2	Marc Galvin		pw	Phoebe Williamson
mgg	Michael G. Gottfried		pw1	Pam Werre*
mhi-y	Mary Helen Immordino-Yang		rb	Ronald Butchart
mhs	Marjorie Hodges Shaw		rbp	Rosemary Papa*
mid	Mary Dereshiwsky*		rc	Randall Curren
mj	Minjeong Jeon*		rcr	Rachel Currie-Rubin*
mje	Marilyn Eisenwine		rdh	Robert D. Heslep
mjs	Michael J. Scheel		rdk	Ron Koehn
mkg	Melaney Kay Gillaspie		reb	Russell Binkley
mkr	Mary Kathryn Robinson		rem	Robin E. Macdonald
mkrf	Maureen Kelly Flores*		rf	Robert E. Frederick
mkt	Meredith K. Taylor		rih	Rita Herron
mkw	M. Keith Whitescarver		rjt	Rick Tannenbaum*
ml	Mark Langager		rk	Rodman King
mlf	Michelle L. Frederick*		rl	Rich Luekenga

rlk	Ronda L. Kirsch*		srs	Sharon R. Stevens
rls	Randy L. Swing		ss	Susan Sears
rnp	Robert N. Portnoy		st	Shona Terrell
ros	Robert O. Slater		sv	Susan Verducci
rsb	Ric S. Brown*		sw	Scott Walter
rsd	Roxanna Solley Dewey*		sw1	Shana Walton
rt	Roben Torosyan		tb	Todd Brown
rtc	Renee T. Clift		tc	Teresa Chen
rvb	Randall V. Bass		td	Trent Davis*
rws	Richard Schmertzing		tfg	Thomas F. Green
rz	Richard Zinser*		th	Thomas Hehir
sa	Steven Aragon*		ti	Tania Israel
salb	Scott Beck		tkb	Tyler Kemp-Benedict
sb	Sabrina Boyer*		tl	Timothy Letzring
sb1	Sean Blenkinsop*		tll	Trudilyne Leone Lord
sc	Stephen Clinton		tm	Troy Mooney
sc1	Suzanne Cutler		tmod	Ty-Ron M. O. Douglas*
scmc	Susan C. M. Crane		tn	Trevor Norris*
scw	Sara Cushing Weigle		tp	Teresa Parish
sd	Silva Dushku		tr	Tom Redmon
sd1	Samantha Daley*		trc	Timothy Reese Cain
sdc	Sherry D. Ceperich		tsw	Thomas Steuart Watson*
sds	Stephen D. Sorden*		tvh	Tammi Vacha-Haase
sdt	Sandra Davis Trowell		tw	Tim Wright
sew	Sandra E. Wolf		tw1	Timothy Waddington*
sf	Susan Faulkner		vdf	Vicki Darlene Flournoy
sh	Stephen Hyde*		vkh	Veronica K. Hotton*
shf	Susan H. Frost		vm	Victoria Molfese
sk	Sandra Kerka		vmm	Victoria-Maria MacDonald
sld	Stephanie Dodman*		weh	William E. Hanson
slr	Stacy Reeder		wf	Weimiao Fan*
sls	Stephanie L. Standerfer		wg	Wanda Gill
sm	Shawn Mahoney*		wgw	William Wraga
smc	S. Megan Che		wja	William Arbuckle
smh	Sarah Margaret Heying*		wl	William Losito
smt	Stefka Masinova-Todd		wpa	Whitney Paige Akers*
smts	Sister Mary Theresa Sharp, S.N.D.*		xss	Ximena P. Suarez-Sousa
sn	Sharon K. Naylor**		yb	Yash Bhagwanji
snr	Stephanie Robinson		yc	Yeonsuk Cho**
sp	Serena Pyo		yjl	Yujie Julia Li
sr	Suzanne Ripley		ys	Yuriko Sasaki*
sr1	Suzanne Rice		yu	Yuuko Uchikoshi
sr2	Shennika Rutledge		za	Zoe Agnew
srd	Stephanie Davis-Kahl		zy	Zheng Yan

About the Editors

JOHN W. COLLINS III is librarian at the Monroe C. Gutman Library and a member of the faculty at the Harvard Graduate School of Education. Dr. Collins received the Distinguished Education and Behavioral Sciences Librarian Award from the Association of College & Research Libraries in 2008. He is coeditor of *Digital Reference Service in the New Millennium: Planning, Management, and Evaluation* and coauthor of "Proposal for the Creation of a Subdiscipline: Education Informatics," a feature article in *Teachers College Record* (October 2010).

NANCY PATRICIA O'BRIEN is head of the Education and Social Science Library at the University of Illinois at Urbana-Champaign. She is the author of *Education: A Guide to Reference and Information Sources* and coeditor of the *Directory of Test Collections in Academic, Professional and Research Collections*. She is the 1997 recipient of the Distinguished Education and Behavioral Sciences Librarian Award from the Association of College & Research Libraries.